M000316483

INDIAN BUDDHISM

INDIAN BUDDHISM

A. K. WARDER

MOTILAL BANARSIDASS PUBLISHERS
PVT. LTD. • DELHI

First Edition: Delhi, 1970
Second Revised Edition: Delhi, 1980
Reprinted: Delhi, 1991

©MOTILAL BANARSIDASS PUBLISHERS PVT. LTD.
ALL RIGHTS RESERVED

ISBN : 81-208-0818-5

Also available at:
MOTILAL BANARSIDASS
41 U.A., Bungalow Road, Jawahar Nagar, Delhi 110 007
120 Royapettah High Road, Mylapore, Madras 600 004
16 St. Mark's Road, Bangalore 560 001
Ashok Rajpath, Patna 800 004
Chowk, Varanasi 221 001

PRINTED IN INDIA
BY JAINENDRA PRAKASH JAIN AT SHRI JAINENDRA PRESS, A-45 NARAINA INDUSTRIAL AREA, PHASE I, NEW DELHI 110 028 AND PUBLISHED BY NARENDRA PRAKASH JAIN FOR MOTILAL BANARSIDASS PUBLISHERS PVT. LTD., BUNGALOW ROAD, JAWAHAR NAGAR, DELHI 110 007

To

NARGEZ

PREFACE TO THE SECOND EDITION

The Second Edition is revised in the light of Buddhist research since 1965, when the First was completed. The largest revision is the section on Diṅnāga, the Sanskrit materials collected by Kitagawa (1965) and Hattori (1968, etc.) making it possible to offer a fairly comprehensive account of his philosophy based on his own words. It is a heavy loss to these sparsely cultivated studies that Hidenori Kitagawa did not live to complete the English translation of *Pramāṇasamuccaya* II-IV, and VI, with additional Sanskrit fragments, which he began when the author invited him to Toronto as Visiting Professor in 1972.

The question of the school to which Diṅnāga belonged has proved strangely intractable. His influence was so great that his work was appropriated by practically all schools of philosophy, Buddhist and non-Buddhist, adapted or interpreted to harmonise with their views. The Sthaviravāda on the one hand and the Vijñānavāda on the other seem to accept his epistemological doctrines, studying his works, or more often those of his successor Dharmakīrti and others, in their own schools. Professors Hattori and Kitagawa, among others, have assumed, following certain Chinese traditions, that Diṅnāga was a Vijñānavādin, though this appears to lead to insuperable difficulties of interpretation. In the First Edition we followed Stcherbatsky in taking Diṅnāga as a follower of Asaṅga who retreated from idealism to realism and effectively established a new school of Buddhism, which we called the Pramāṇa School The thesis of Frauwallner on the two Vasubandhus was accepted and it was naturally assumed that Diṅnāga was a pupil of the earlier one, Asaṅga's brother, though Frauwallner himself was vague and afterwards inconsistent about this. Frauwallner's chronological arrangement of Diṅnāga's works and perception of his philosophical evolution from idealism to realism was likewise followed. Doubts about the 'object' of the *Ālambanaparīkṣā*, however, threw this whole evolution in question and seemed to confirm the statements of Vācaspatimiśra and others that Diṅnāga, as well as Dharmakīrti, was a Sautrāntika. This would make it likely that he was a pupil of the Vasubandhu who wrote the *Abhidharmakośabhāṣya*. The author's student, A. S. Moriya, has made a thorough study of this problem, in a PhD thesis on Dharmakīrti, and concluded that both he and Diṅnāga were Sautrāntikas. This conclusion has been adopted in this Second Edition, and the appropriate revisions made, the most essential evidence being noted.

The question of 'objects', a word which has been used to translate so many Sanskrit and Pali terms and which was the starting point for our clarification of Diṅnāga's views, had led to further investigations even before the First Edition was published, a note being added in the Index (p. 599) to the effect that *ālambana* meant only the internal object in consciousness. This note made in 1968 when indexing from the page proofs was subsequently expanded into the paper 'Objects' published in 1975. The results of these studies have been incorporated in the present Edition, translating *ālambana* as 'support' and so on.

Related to all the above discussions is the question of 'perception' (variously used by writers in English) and 'sensation' and of a more precise understanding of the ancient Buddhist doctrine of the five 'groups' (*skandhas*). It seems closer to translate *pratyakṣa*, knowledge or cognition through the senses, as 'sensation', reserving 'perception' for the ancient term *saṃjñā*, the mental registering of a sense experience which later is taken to include identifying it through some concept. In the scheme of the groups, sensation or sense experience, the five senses, is included in 'matter' (*rūpa*). It therefore seems inappropriate to translate *vedanā* as 'sensation' as hitherto. Being the reaction of happiness, unhappiness, elation, depression or equanimity, according to the schools, to an experience, *vedanā* seems to come fairly close to 'emotion' and is so translated in this Edition. Perhaps it was originally as vague in reference as the English word 'feeling', or as broad as experience in general, but by using 'emotion' we may hope to indicate the direction in which the term was becoming specialised in more systematic analysis and to separate it from the physical experience of the senses.

The fundamental concept of *dharma* has been further studied by the author and the results published in the essay 'Dharmas and Data' (1971). The conclusion there that a *dharma* is most nearly equivalent to a 'principle', rather than to an 'element' or a 'sense datum' or simply a 'phenomenon', has been embodied in the present Edition. The paper 'The Concept of a Concept' (1971) entails no revision but is rather an appendix on the question of there being two levels of discourse in the Buddha's words, the everyday and the philosophical, especially as worked out in the Sthaviravāda School (cf. pp. 150-2 below). Related to it is the paper 'Is Nāgārjuna a Mahāyānist?' (1973), reflecting more precise translations of that philosopher's critiques given in the textbook *Outline of Indian Philosophy* (University of Toronto 1967, Motilal Banarsidass 1971; which also contained a first revision of our study of Diṅnāga in the light of the work being done by Kitagawa and Hattori). This progress in understanding the author of the *Mūlamadhyamakakārikā* has led to some revisions below (especially on p. 379).

The brief account of Harivarman's **Tattvasiddhiśāstra* (pp. 419-21) has been rewritten in the light of a PhD thesis by another of the author's students, Professor S. Katsura (1974). Similarly some revisions on p. 357 result from the research thesis of Professor N. Schuster (1976) and the early development of the Mahāyāna might now have been set out in much more detail in the light of that work on the *Ugraparipṛcchā* and other texts in the *Mahāratnakūṭa*. It has been a pleasure and an encouragement to have such students, working on some of the most important but difficult problems of Buddhism. To those already mentioned must be added, besides Professor Priestley who gave much help to the First Edition and whose translation of the five philosophical works of Nāgārjuna is impatiently awaited, Professor F. Watanabe (1976) and Mr. K. Fujimoto, who, before his lamentable disappearance from Toronto during the attempt of fanatics to destroy the PhD programme in Buddhism in 1977, had made a complete English translation of the *Madhyamakāvatāra* and *Bhāṣya* of Candrakīrti, traditionally the standard introduction to Madhyamaka.

After the fragments of Diṅnāga, the most important accession to the primary sources has been the Sanskrit text of the *Abhidharmakośabhāṣya*, edited by P. Pradhan. The field has been enriched by the printing of numerous Sanskrit and Pali texts hitherto not available and in some cases unknown, which as they reached us found their way into the Bibliography and occasionally supplied a reference in the text. It should hardly be necessary to repeat here that this book is based entirely on the primary sources, not on secondary sources. A few secondary sources which were found useful as preliminary guides, verified or corrected later through the primary sources, have been included in the Bibliography, for example the works of Stcherbatsky, but no attempt has been made to review the mass of modern writings on Buddhism. Translations, however, have generally been included as of interest to readers.

It has been hard to get all the Index references correct, and so we have to advise the reader that a few references, and cross-references in the text itself, are one page out.

What is Buddhism ? The Buddha was a philosopher whose doctrine approximated that set out in our chapters 4 to 6. This is not the 'Theravāda' (Sthaviravāda) of the Pali 'Canon', though the latter happens to be the most important source now available for reconstructing it. Theravāda will be found in its proper place in chapter 9. Our chapters 3 to 6 present the ground which is common to all known schools of Buddhism. They interpreted this and all of them added new doctrines to it, with varying degrees of justification. The doctrine of chapter 4, the thirty-seven principles 'on the side of enlightenment', be it noted, includes the eightfold way, which includes the four truths, which include conditioned origination, the origination of principles from causes, the fundamental insight which is the subject of our chapter 5. Thus chapter 4 presents the practice, chapter 5 the theory, of the Buddha; in general terms meditation, or concentration (*samādhi*), and understanding (*prajñā*). Chapter 6 then presents that other great branch of the practice taught by the Buddha, namely its application to society and by laymen, the lay 'disciples' being as much part of the original Buddhist 'community' as the monks and nuns and an essential connection appearing between the happiness of society and the happiness even of the individual who has 'gone forth' to homelessness.

Of the schools which preserved the philosophy of the Buddha, the Sthaviravāda (Theravāda), Bahuśrutīya and Sautrāntika, among those known to us, appear the most faithful to his ideas. Where these three agree, as they usually do, we can say that we have authentic Buddhist tradition. Everything else is part of the history of philosophy and of religion, interesting in its own right and often derivable, with more or less distortion, from some aspect of the original teaching. Even the strange concept of the *dharmakāya* in Mahāyāna, a metaphysical 'absolute', can be argued for on the basis of the uniformity of nature as propounded in the *Saṃyukta* (see p. 117 below), though the Buddha could not have accepted the hypostatisation of this empirically discovered principle into an eternal entity. The least authentic growth in any Buddhist school is anything in the nature of a claim to authority, as on the part of teachers, in place of the original appeal to experience, to verifiability.

The essential practice of meditation has proved more constant than the critical, empiricist and ethical philosophy which interested only a few people and has often been overlaid with fanciful speculations attractive to the majority. Theravāda, Zen and Lamaism, for all their superficial differences, share common ground in the practice of meditation, which is the ground of original Buddhism and qualifies them to take the name of followers of the Buddha.

The study of the purely literary aspects of the Buddhist tradition, touched on in chapters 8 and 9, has been further developed in a separate work, *Indian Kāvya Literature*, where the works of Aśvaghoṣa, Śūra, Candragomin, Dharmakīrti as poet, the songs of Saraha and Kāṇha, Śivasvāmin's epic and so on will be found discussed in the context of Indian literature and criticism.

A.K. Warder
1980

CONTENTS

PREFACE

A glance at a few of the countless modern books dealing with 'Buddhism' will soon convince the inquirer that Buddhism is all things to all men. Such a conclusion, though nebulous and not very informative, might even be upheld as now valid. Whether Buddhism has always been so nebulous is much more disputable. There are seemingly authoritative books which, taken collectively, make widely divergent and sometimes totally opposed claims about the original teaching of the Buddha, and it is at least clear that by the second century A.D. there were schools of Buddhism in India which differed very greatly though they all claimed to teach the actual doctrine of the Buddha. In this situation modern writers, especially scholars, have taken sides in the ancient controversy or, in the name of that extreme caution which some suppose to be the hall mark of the sound academic, have claimed that we do not know what the Buddha taught and cannot now find out.

When so much has been written and is yet so inconclusive it seems vain to offer a solution to the problem of what Buddhism was originally, and in an earlier work[1] the present writer had practically renounced any such purpose and recommended sticking directly to the ancient texts in their original languages. However, people still demand an answer to this question and at the same time it appears tantalisingly possible to discover the answer. This book, then, is an attempt to give an answer and more especially to demonstrate its correctness by applying acceptable methods of deduction to the available evidence. The discussion of methodology with which we are thus obliged to burden this volume is as far as possible confined to the Introduction, though it has affected the presentation that follows as well and perhaps made this look more like a marshalling of evidence than a survey of the subject. The reader who is in

1. *Introduction to Pali* page xi.

a hurry to look at the doctrines and willing provisionally to take the solution of problems of authenticity on trust may skip most of the Introduction.

The book is planned in the form of a historical survey of Buddhism as it developed and spread in the land of its origin. The main object is to present the doctrines and elucidate them : the historical background is merely sketched in as part of the elucidation, as situations to which Buddhist thinkers were responding and as a framework in which successive ideas may be placed in order (this order is illuminating: when we know who a man's immediate predecessors were we are better able to see what he is getting at). The most extensive historical sketch occurs at the beginning, with a view to presenting India as it had been before the time of the Buddha and leading up to the setting in which Buddhism originated.

The author is deeply indebted to Professor J. W. de Jong and Mr. C. D. C. Priestley for verifying the numerous references to Chinese versions of the *Tripiṭaka* texts and assisting in comparing their readings for the most essential terms with the Indian sources. Acknowledgements are also due to Mr. A. Yuyama for information on the discussions of Japanese scholars about the schools to which the Chinese versions of the *Āgamas* belong and to Professor H. V. Guenther for information on some of the Tibetan sources.

A. K. Warder
1965

INTRODUCTION

The Sources of our Knowledge of Buddhism—Methodology—The Tripiṭaka—The Mātṛkā—The Schools—The Internal Chronology of the Tripiṭaka—Buddhism Contrasted with Rival Teachings—Interpretation

The Sources of our Knowledge of Buddhism

The materials at our disposal consist firstly and mainly of a large body of ancient texts, though they are unhappily only a small fraction of the great literature of which they once formed a part. Most of the ancient literature of Buddhism and of India generally was obliterated by the Muslims when they swept through Western, Central and Southern Asia with the sword and especially with fire, the greatest disaster being their conquest of the homeland of Buddhism at the beginning of the thirteenth century A.D. All the great Buddhist libraries of India were sought out and incinerated, so that of Indian Buddhist texts in their original languages we have at our disposal only (a) the 'canon' of one of the many ancient schools, preserved intact in Ceylon, Burma, Cambodia and Siam, (b) an incomplete canon as recognised in the latest phase of Indian Buddhism, together with a selection of ancillary works, preserved in Nepal, and (c) a few scattered texts in Indian languages preserved elsewhere, for instance in Tibet, in Japan, in certain Jaina libraries in Western India or buried in vaults in Central Asia. We have also large collections of translations into non-Indian languages, primarily Chinese and Tibetan. These are more complete than the original collections now extant, and represent a greater number of ancient schools of Buddhism, but they are still rather limited as being selections only from the original corpus of texts and as representing primarily only those later schools of Buddhism which became permanently established in East Asia.

Along with these ancient texts we possess a larger body of medieval and modern texts purporting to expound their doctrines, either as direct commentaries or as independent expositions. They are written in many different languages. Of those written in India we have only a part, whether in the original or in translations, and moreover we are worse off in respect of these ancillary works than we are in respect of the ancient canonical texts. The schools which have flourished down to modern times outside India, on the other hand, have produced and preserved comprehensive libraries of ancillary works, moreover they have kept alive oral traditions of interpretation handed on from teacher to student. The living traditions of the meaning of what is written have been the basis of all modern understanding of Buddhist doctrines. From the diverse living schools we have to trace back a way towards the correct understanding of the meaning of the earliest texts as intended by their authors.

Our other important materials are the archaeological sources relating to the history of Buddhism : ancient monuments or their ruins, pagodas and temples, monasteries and universities, sculptures and paintings, which to some extent reflect the doctrines of their times. Above all the excavations of ancient sites with contemporary documentation in the form of inscriptions have served as checks on chronology

Methodology

Do the ancient texts available to us contain any of the actual teaching of the Buddha ? Many of them purport to do so, but there is a certain amount of conflict among them in matters of doctrine, and in any case we are not prepared to accept them at their face value without checking their authenticity.

According to the unanimous traditions of all the schools of Buddhism, after the death, or rather the *parinirvāṇa*, of the Buddha his words so far as remembered by his followers were collectively rehearsed. Each dialogue or lecture remembered was endorsed as an accurate account by those who had been present at the event, and the whole body of texts thus established and arranged was thenceforward handed on by oral tradition. After some centuries the texts were written down and preserved by manuscript as well as oral tradition. This body of texts came to be called the *Tripiṭaka*, meaning the three traditions of handing down the teaching—since the texts were grouped in three sections. Are we in possession of this *Tripiṭaka* as recognised by the early Buddhists, if possible before they split up into schools ?

The Tripiṭaka

In fact we have several *Tripiṭakas*. From Ceylon and South East Asia we have the recension of the Sthaviravāda school, called *Tipiṭaka* in its own, Pali, language. From China we have a vast *Tripiṭaka* in Chinese, consisting primarily of translations of Indian texts. We have a similar *Tripiṭaka* from Tibet in the Tibetan language, of which there is also a Mongolian translation. In fact the Chinese and Tibetan *Tripiṭakas* have a complex history in several differing and gradually growing recensions, though we need not complicate the present discussion with further details. In either case the translators and compilers believed in the existence of *The Tripiṭaka* in India, the texts of which were gradually being collected from India, translated and incorporated in the local recension—a task which remained unfinished even after many centuries of effort.

This incompleteness was not entirely the fault of the Chinese or the Tibetans, or the Indian scholars who helped make the translations. Even as they worked, the Indian Buddhists were producing new texts which purported to be authentic, or at least which later on were taken as authentic words of the Buddha. Moreover older texts sometimes had additions made to them, so that eventually new translations seemed called for : in a number of cases we have several successive translations of what is supposed to be the same text, of gradually increasing length. Indian Buddhism was still growing and changing, and new schools found room in their recensions of the *Tripiṭaka* for texts giving authority to their new ideas. There was no centralised control to prevent this, on the contrary the organisation of Buddhism was always polycentric, in fact democratic : each local group was autonomous.

In this situation we need not despair. The Buddhists in India and elsewhere recorded their history and we have a number of ancient and medieval texts extant to guide us.[1] They are unanimous that after the original collective rehearsal of the *Tripiṭaka* the Buddhists remained united for about a century but later disagreed irreconcilably and gradually split up into separate schools. There are supposed to have been eighteen of these early schools by about the first century B.C., each with

1. See Bibliography C. Buddhist Histories.

its own recension of the *Tripiṭaka.* Of the recensions of these schools we now possess only one complete, but we have substantial sections of half a dozen others.[1] In addition we have various references to the content of these 'canons'. For example the philosopher Nāgārjuna (second century A.D.) quotes a text and his commentator Candrakīrti (c. A.D. 600) informs us that it was to be found in the canons of all the schools.[2]

Though all our sources agree on the eighteen schools having a *Tripiṭaka* in varying recensions, some of our sources maintain the authenticity of certain other texts not found in the canons of these schools. These texts are those held genuine by the later school, not one of the eighteen, which arrogated to itself the title of Mahāyāna, 'Great Vehicle'. According to the Mahāyāna historians these texts were admittedly unknown to the early schools of Buddhists. However, they had all been promulgated by the Buddha. His followers on earth, the *śrāvakas* ('pupils'), had not been sufficiently advanced to understand them, and hence were not given them to remember, but they were taught to various supernatural beings and then preserved in such places as the Dragon World (under the earth) or among the gods. Early in the second century A.D. (i.e. some time after the reign of the emperor Kaniṣka) numerous teachers appeared in India who were capable of interpreting these special texts, which accordingly were brought out from their hiding places and made known on earth.[3]

With the best will in the world we cannot accept this or similar accounts as historical facts. Even if we admit the possibility of a secret transmission of doctrine and texts it is a curious aspersion on the powers of the Buddha that he failed to do what others were able to accomplish 600 years later. To clinch the matter we have the fact that linguistically and stylistically the Mahāyāna texts belong to a later stratum of Indian literature than the *Tripiṭaka* known to the early schools. Everything about early Buddhism, and even the Mahāyāna itself (with the exception of the Mantrayāna), suggests that it was a teaching not meant to be kept secret but intended to be published to all the world, to spread enlightenment, and we are on safe ground

1. See Bibliography A.
2. *Mūlamadhyamakakārikās* with Candrakīrti's *Prasannapadā*, ed. by La Vallée Poussin, St Petersburg 1903-13, p. 269 (on XV. 7).
3. e.g. Tāranātha, Schiefner's translation, 61 ff.

only with those texts the authenticity of which is admitted by all schools of Buddhism (including the Mahāyāna, who admit the authenticity of the early canons as well as their own texts), not with texts accepted only by certain schools. Mahāyāna Buddhism will be examined in its proper historical context below. We shall find that it in fact developed gradually out of one, or a group, of the eighteen early schools, and that originally it took its stand not primarily on any new texts but on its own interpretations of the universally recognised *Tripiṭaka*. In our own study of the doctrines of that *Tripiṭaka* we may certainly give due weight to those interpretations along with others.

When we examine the *Tripiṭakas* of the eighteen schools, so far as they are extant, we find an agreement which is substantial, though not complete. Even the most conservative of the early schools seem to have added new texts to their collections. However, there is a central body of *sūtras* (dialogues), in four groups, which is so similar in all known versions that we must accept these as so many recensions of the same original texts. These make up the greater part of the *Sūtra Piṭaka*, one of the three sections or traditions which make up the *Tripiṭaka*. Since it is the *sūtras* which are recognised as the primary source for the doctrine of Buddhism, we shall proceed below to take the text which might be critically edited by comparing their different recensions as the basis of our exposition of the doctrine as it evidently existed before the schisms which divided the schools. It may be noted here that whatever textual discrepancies are found hardly affect the doctrine.[1]

It is of course important to ascertain which schools the available recensions belong to, so that by taking the history of their schisms as a 'stemma' of the textual tradition we can see to what point in the latter an 'archetype' established by collation may be assigned. The Pali recension is that of the Sthaviravāda school. The fragmentary texts now available in Sanskrit are generally agreed to be, except for certain very brief fragments, of the Sarvāstivāda (or its later offshoot the Mūlasarvāstivāda). In Chinese we now have complete translations of each of the four groups (*āgamas*), an incomplete translation of one of them and numerous versions of individual *sūtras*. They do not belong

1. cf. Lamotte : *Histoire du bouddhisme indien*, Vol. I, p. 171.

to a single school. Unfortunately the Chinese tradition is vague about their affiliations and it has proved difficult to establish their schools. A number of Japanese scholars have worked on the problem and for the most part we depend on their findings for such conclusions as we can offer here.[1]

The affiliation of the Chinese version of the *Dīrgha* (T 1) seems to be a matter of conjecture. The usual conjecture is that it belongs to the Dharmaguptaka school.

The version of the *Madhyama* (T 26) seems to be agreed to belong to the Sarvāstivāda, since it agrees closely with the extant fragments of the Sanskrit version, which have been ascribed to that school.

The complete translation of the *Saṃyukta* (T 99) belongs to the Sarvāstivāda, as is now established by its exact agreement with the fragments of the Sanskrit *Saṃyukta* (published by Tripāṭhī). The incomplete version (T 100) is ascribed by Chinese tradition to the Kāśyapīya school (there seems to be no strong reason to doubt this, though some of the Japanese writers have declared it 'uncertain').

There has been a great deal of controversy about the *Ekottara* (T 125), variously attributed to the Dharmaguptakas (e.g. Matsumoto) or to the Mahāsaṃghikas (Akanuma, but then he qualifies this as more precisely the Prajñaptivāda offshoot of that school) or left uncertain. The arguments for assigning it to the Mahāsaṃghika do not seem very strong : on the contrary the text contradicts certain doctrines of that school (e.g. it holds, like the Sthaviravāda, Dharmaguptaka and Mahīśāsaka, that *arhants* cannot relapse and there are serious discrepancies between it and the Mahāsaṃghika *Vinaya*, which is extant in Chinese). To assign it to a sub-school such as the Prajñaptivāda does not evade all the difficulties. In fact it seems very likely that this *Ekottara* is a Dharmaguptaka text, since it shows agreement with known Dharmaguptaka views which appear characteristic of the school so far as our knowledge extends. Thus this *Ekottara* states that there are 250 Prātimokṣa rules for monks, a figure which among the *Vinayas* now available agrees only with that of the Dharmaguptakas (the '*Caturvarga Vinaya*'). Again the *stūpa* (pagoda) features prominently in both texts.

1. Akanuma, Matsumoto, Hirakawa, Tatsuyama. See Bibliography I.

(There have certainly been Mahāyānist interpolations in this *Ekottara*, as is universally agreed.)

The Chinese *Āgamas* thus seem to include recensions of the Sarvāstivāda, Dharmaguptaka and Kāśyapīya. By collating them with the Sthaviravāda recension we may thus reach an archetype which existed before the schisms which brought these schools into being. The Sarvāstivāda seceded from the Sthaviravāda probably during the reign of Aśoka Maurya (3rd century B.C.) and the Kāśyapīya (or Haimavata) and Dharmaguptaka became separate schools probably early in the 2nd century B.C. (on these schisms see below, Chapters Eight and Nine).

Among the numerous Chinese versions of separate *sūtras* it is very likely that other schools are represented but much harder to find out which they are. For the present work they have rarely been used. One which has been used is An Shih Kao's version of the *Mahānidāna Sūtra*, which proved very close to the Sthaviravāda. We do not know which school this version belongs to, whilst the fact that An Shih Kao worked as early as the 2nd century A.D. increases his value.

For the *Vinaya Piṭaka* the position is more favourable than for the *Sūtra* since we have (in Chinese) the Mahāsaṃghika recension. This when collated with the Sthaviravāda will carry us back to the first schism among the Buddhists (in the 4th century B.C.), beyond which only an actual document of earlier date would take us. Since the *Vinaya* is concerned with discipline and only incidentally with doctrine it will not take us very far in reconstructing the latter. The collation of the *Vinayas* shows that the Mahāsaṃghika version agrees fairly closely with the Sthaviravāda. It is remarkable that for the Prātimokṣa rules the Sthaviravāda recension is closer to the Mahāsaṃghika than it is to any other recension extant, though the others are of schools which seceded from the Sthaviravāda and might be expected to agree with it. Unhappily we seem to have no Mahāsaṃghika *Āgama* : the close agreement of the *Vinayas* of the two schools which bear the names of those which came into existence as a result of the first schism suggests that both have remained conservative, as compared with their offshoots, and that a Mahāsaṃghika *Āgama*, if ever one came to light, would agree more closely with the Sthaviravāda than the latter does with its offshoots the Sarvāstivāda, Dharmaguptaka, etc. Though the probability is strong that the Sthaviravāda versions of the four main groups of *sūtras* are more archaic than the Sarvāstivāda *Āgamas* (which are longer and can be shown to include a number of late additions), in the absence of actual Mahāsaṃghika texts to confirm this we here treat the Sarvāstivāda recension as of equal weight to the Sthaviravāda.

The Mātṛkā

The third section or tradition of the *Tripiṭaka* is the *Abhidharma*, which term meant originally 'concerning the doctrine' and afterwards was used for a systematic study of the doctrine. It is in this section of the *Tripiṭaka* that there is the greatest discrepancy between the versions of the various schools. In fact it is clear that the *Abhidharma* texts were the last to be elaborated in their final form. They represent the systematic work of the schools to abstract from the corpus of separate dialogues which had been remembered and handed down a comprehensive, unified body of doctrine. In preparing their systematic books the schools began to apply the special theories on which they disagreed, and some of the *Abhidharma* books actually contain arguments refuting the theories of opposed schools. However, there is still a great measure of common material shared by the schools, material which appears largely to have been extracted from the dialogues and arranged by topics.

Most of the accounts of the original collective rehearsal of the *Tripiṭaka* state that the *Abhidharma* section was included, implying that the *Abhidharma* texts as current in the various schools were supposed to have been elaborated already at that rehearsal. Some accounts on the other hand say instead that what they call the *Mātṛkā* was rehearsed. *Mātṛkā* means a 'matrix' or a list of topics, a set of notes giving just the headings of a body of doctrine. Many of the *Abhidharma* texts extant give such *Mātṛkās* either initially, like a table of contents, or at the beginning of individual chapters. It seems very probable that in the earliest period this third section of the *Tripiṭaka* consisted simply of some set of *Mātṛkā* headings, possibly propounded by the Buddha himself when giving systematic instruction to his followers, and that this was only later fully elaborated into *Abhidharma* expositions. From the available *Abhidharma* texts it is possible to suggest which were the most original *Mātṛkā* headings, but it is uncertain how many of all the known headings might have been included in the earliest list, or before the schools began to divide.

The question of the *Mātṛkā* has been studied by the present writer in an introductory essay to the edition of the Pali manual of *Abhidharma* called *Mohavicchedani*, which purports to be a commentary on the *Mātṛkā*.[1] It is there suggested that a set of seven headings found in all the sources was original, and may have constituted the whole *Mātṛkā* at first. What is perhaps most remarkable about this set is that it appears also in a very prominent position in one of the dialogues, the *Mahāparinirvāṇa Sūtra*, which describes the last months of the Buddha's existence on earth. There,[2] shortly before the end, the Buddha convenes his followers and gives them a summary of the principles which he has discovered, and which they should study and put into practice so that the 'best life', i.e. the Buddhist Way, should endure long for the benefit and happiness of many people. The summary which follows is precisely this set of seven headings. Here then we have another indication, common to all the schools so far as the relevant texts have survived, as to what the original essential doctrines were.

The Schools

We have mentioned the early schools of Buddhism, supposed to have been eighteen in number, and that they agree substantially on a central body of texts representing the teaching of the Buddha. We noted also that every school possessed additional texts of its own, that there were greater discrepancies and even mutual polemics in their *Abhidharmas*, and that it was these disagreements which caused them to separate. What did they disagree about ? Do their disagreements affect the fundamental doctrines and make it uncertain what these were ?

From the mutual polemics between the schools, and from a number of histories of the schisms, we find that the major grounds of disagreement were the following :

1. P.T.S., London, 1961, xix ff, esp. p. xxi.
2. Sthaviravāda version in Pali : D II 120, Sarvāstivāda in Sanskrit: MPS (Waldschmidt) p. 224. Chinese versions in T 1 No. 2, etc.

Can an *arhant* (one who has attained peace of mind, freedom from all attachments) relapse again into worldly entanglements?

Besides the mental principles which are morally good and bad, is there a third class which are morally indifferent?

Is the 'person' (*pudgala*), an expression sometimes used by the Buddha in the dialogues, a real entity which, moreover, transmigrates from one living body to a new one, or is this just a conventional expression of everyday language, to be replaced by strict analysis into the real principles of existence in philosophical discourse?

If not the 'person', then do the groups (*skandha*) of principles transmigrate?

Is progress in understanding the truth gradual or does insight come all at once?

Do all natural principles, whether past, present or future, 'exist'?

Are Buddhas supernatural (or transcendental)?

Are all the dialogues direct (definitive) statements, or are some indirect statements requiring special interpretation?

Are all forces (*saṃskāra*) momentary?

Can good conduct grow unconsciously?

There is little here to affect the main doctrines, or even the great mass of detailed working out in the dialogues. The schools seem to have been agreed on the wording of what the Buddha had said. The disputes concern subsidiary matters on which the texts were not explicit or where there was a possibility of varying interpretations.

We shall follow the history of the rise of the schools in detail in the appropriate chapter. The results of comparing their answers to the above questions and attempting by a sort of textual criticism of the eighteen (or more) traditions to establish the original opinion suggest that the earliest Buddhists thought that:

An *arhant* can relapse.

The 'person' is not a real entity.

The natural principles do not always 'exist'.

All forces are momentary.

The groups of principles do not transmigrate.

They probably held that progress is usually gradual. As to the remaining grounds, where the apparently unanimous view of the Mahāsaṃghika and the schools which derived from it is opposed to the view of the Sthaviravāda and its offshoots the balance is even. Here the Mahāsaṃghika have the advantage, since we know very little of the differences of opinion between its branches which might have shown us that some of these agreed with the Sthaviravāda group and so presumably held the more original opinion. We are therefore uncertain whether it was at first held that there were morally indifferent mental principles (it probably was), or whether all the dialogues are direct statements,[1] or whether good conduct can grow unconsciously. On the question of the transcendental nature of the Buddha, though all the Mahāsaṃghika group probably affirmed this in some form they appear to have disagreed on the details. Thus one among them actually seceded from the group on this ground, calling itself the 'Transcendental School' (Lokottaravāda), presumably in opposition to the others who may have held the view only in a much less extreme form. It is further clear that among the Mahāsaṃghika group the transcendentalist ideas continued to grow in influence until they gave birth to the 'Great Vehicle'. All this suggests that such ideas were an innovation on the part of this group, about which they were uncertain at first but which gradually gathered momentum.

In the light of this discussion we are able to say that no school represents what appears to have been the original set of views, with the possible, but improbable, exception of the Mahāsaṃghika. As mentioned above, we get a false impression of unanimity among the latter group of schools simply because we lack information on their internal debates. Whether such an 'original set of views' on these particular points was consciously held by the earliest Buddhists is very doubtful. Many of the problems may simply not have been raised before the period of the schisms.

The Internal Chronology of the Tripiṭaka

Given the *Tripiṭaka* as established by the consensus of opinion of the early schools, can we go further and distinguish within it texts which are earlier and later? This might enable us to say that, although the *Tripiṭaka* we could establish represented the

1. Probably not, since the Mahāsaṃghikas mostly reject it.

texts recognised by all Buddhists not earlier than a hundred and thirty-seven years after the *parinirvāṇa* (the probable date of the first schism), the doctrine had, or had not, undergone some development during that period. Some progress has been made towards clarifying the stratification of the Sthaviravāda *Tripiṭaka* in Pali, this being the only recension intact in an Indian language.

Most attempts to outline the history of this collection of texts have been based on largely subjective impressions as to what was early and are of little use to us. There is, however, one objective technique of textual analysis which can be applied to parts of the *Tripiṭaka*: the study of metre. In a previous piece of research[1] the present writer has traced the history of versification through the period of composition of the Sthaviravāda Canon and shown that the verse texts in the latter are not all the work of a short period but appear to have been composed over several centuries (the research of course covers the whole Canon, including texts added after the schisms). The metres in use changed considerably during that period, hence it seemed possible to arrange the verse texts in successive strata. In the Conclusion of that work some brief observations were made indicating what we might discover of the development of the doctrine from that arrangement. The results ascertainable by this method can be applied here. The prose texts, which are more extensive and much more important, cannot easily be correlated with these verse strata and have not yet been subjected to any such rhythmical analysis, though possibly they could be. Even from the verse texts alone, however, we can secure some important data on the history of Buddhist doctrine.

Buddhism Contrasted with Rival Teachings

How did Buddhism stand in opposition to Brahmanism ('Hinduism'), the Lokāyata (Naturalism, Materialism), the Agnostics, Ājīvakism, Jainism and other schools of thought at the time of its origin ? The contrast between these schools of thought may show what doctrines were characteristic and essential in Buddhism. An attempt to define original Buddhism

1. *Pali Metre.*

in this way has been published as an article.[1] In the heyday of extreme scepticism as to whether we knew anything at all of what the Buddha taught this exercise was useful; it still helps to emphasise some of the important features of his doctrine.

Interpretation

If the early Buddhists themselves came to disagree on their doctrine, though very little on the readings of their texts, our interpretation of the latter will be difficult and must surely remain inconclusive on some points. The methods so far discussed can give us the texts, in Pali or Sanskrit, but we cannot translate them into English for the purposes of this book without interpreting them. In the *Introduction to Pali* referred to in the Preface a selection of Pali texts is given in the original language and the object is to enable the reader to find his own way in interpreting them. Even there particular lines of interpretation are suggested through the vocabularies which had to be given. In the Preface to that book certain methods of interpretation are recommended, which were applied in the making of the vocabularies. The argument of that Preface need not be repeated here, but the methods can be summarised.

The meanings of terms have to be determined by judging the contexts in which they occur. Here it may be possible to work from more obvious everyday contexts to the abstract philosophical statements.

The basis for our understanding of meanings must be the exegesis of the Buddhist schools, whose pupils we now are. We can check their interpretations by seeing whether the schools agree among themselves, and then go back to the *Tripiṭaka* contexts and see how they work out in the system of what was believed to be the Buddha's language when taken by itself.

We assume here that the differences of dialect known to have existed between the texts of the early schools of Buddhism do not affect the interpretation of at least their philosophical statements : it was just a matter of transposition of terms into a slightly different phonetic system. In the *Introduction to Pali* we

1. 'On the Relationships between Early Buddhism and other contemporary Systems,' BSOAS, 1956, 43-63.

were limited to the Pali dialect and to the traditional interpretations (at least as basis) of the Sthaviravāda school which used it. Here we attempt to interpret the dialect of the Buddha (though we do not know which particular dialect he used) according to the consensus of opinion of all the schools. We adopt the convention of giving the terms usually in their Sanskrit form, since the latter dialect became standardised in India as the language of philosophical discussion and learning generally, though only long after the time of the Buddha. This convention simplifies our presentation by keeping all the terminology, early and late, in one phonetic system.

CHAPTER ONE

INDIAN CIVILISATION BEFORE THE BUDDHA

The Indus Civilisation—The Aryans—Brahmanism—Vyāsa

The Indus Civilisation

Civilisation appears in India, according to the archaeological evidence, about 3000 B.C., in other words about 2500 years before the Buddha and about as remote in time from him as he is from the present day. It was at first a 'Bronze Age' civilisation, roughly comparable with the civilisation which appeared at the same time in Mesopotamia, or with the rather later Shang civilisation in China. Its main centres, according to our present knowledge, were two great cities, one in the Panjab and one in Sindh, whose sites are marked by and named after the modern villages of Harappā and Mohenjo Dāro. Since these lie near the Indus (Sanskrit Sindhu) and one of its tributaries, and the harnessing of the waters of that great river system evidently formed the basis of the civilisation, it is appropriate to name it after the river. However, it has already been established that the Indus civilisation spread Eastwards into the Ganges valley and South-East at least across Gujarat. It therefore covered a wider area than the contemporary civilisations of Mesopotamia or Egypt, whilst the standardisation of technology throughout that area suggests political unification: a far flung empire.

Archaeological findings tell us a good deal about this technological development and something of the economic system. We can see something of the art of the Indus empire and infer a little about its religion, much less about its political system. Inscriptions have been found—many hundreds of them—but unfortunately they have not yet been satisfactorily deciphered. Thus we are not certain who these people were : whether they were akin to any known people and spoke a language similar to any we know, or whether they were linguistically isolated, like the Sumerians who founded the Mesopotamian civilisation, and without later descendants continuing their language. In a general cultural sense we can certainly say they were Indians, and that the later inhabitants of India have been their heirs in this sense, whether or not any of them have inherited their language. It is fairly certain at least that the Indus people were not Aryans (all the archaeological evidence is against bringing any Aryan people from Central Asia to India so early): the most likely hypothesis is that they were Dravidians, akin to, or even the ancestors of, the modern Tamils and other peoples of South India.

In religion the Indus people appear to have had a cult of a Great God some of whose characteristics suggest that he was the prototype of the modern Śiva (who has always been especially popular among the Tamils): on the one hand he seems to symbolise creation and fertility, on the other he may appear in the rôle of an ascetic, or a *yogin* developing his supernatural powers. A remarkable relief shows him surrounded by various animals, suggesting for him the epithet *paśupati* ('lord of animals') which is properly Śiva's. The cult was associated with temples, which again is especially characteristic of the cult of Śiva in later times.

There is also evidence for the great Goddess as in the Śaiva tradition, though it would perhaps be difficult to point to any specific feature here linking these two manifestations of such a widespread religious phenomenon.

A Sacred Tree appears and reminds us of the Tree of Śiva—the Himālayan *devadāru* (deodar)—and the sacred trees in modern Śaiva temples, as well as of the Buddhist Tree of Enlightenment. There were sacred as well as mythological animals and monsters, and the sculptor's art which depicts them has the same realism and vitality as that of the early Buddhist period (Mauryan, etc.), suggesting the same Indian tradition.

The Aryans

According to the archaeological evidence Aryan people entered India at about the time of the collapse of the Indus civilisation (about 1600 B.C.). In fact they were probably barbarian invaders who conquered the Indus people and destroyed their cities. These Aryans spoke an early form of Sanskrit, called 'Vedic' after the earliest extant Indian texts (the *Veda*) which can at present be read. The earliest of these Vedic texts of the

Aryans were perhaps composed two or three centuries after the conquest. This conquest is vaguely remembered in the *Veda*: the god Indra destroyed the citadels of the enemy (which presumably were the cities and smaller settlements of the Indus people), he released the cattle (because the Aryans were still nomadic herdsmen, and no doubt disapproved of cattle being shut in in fields by the settled villagers) and he released the rivers (which had been dammed and channelled for irrigation purposes by the settled agriculturalists). Their tradition then was that they had restored the natural freedom of the universe.

Civilisation thus suffered a temporary eclipse at the hands of these barbarian nomads. Very soon, however, the barbarians began to follow the ways of the people they had conquered: they settled permanently in villages and eventually in cities, they kept their cattle in fields (though perhaps Indian cattle have ever since enjoyed a freedom of movement not paralleled elsewhere) and they harnessed the rivers for irrigation. When it came to the interpretation of the ancient texts it proved possible to forget the historical background and supply instead a mythological meaning connecting Indra with the monsoon.

The *Veda* mentions besides Indra some of the human leaders of the Aryans and their achievements, but its historical allusions are scattered. There were other texts which were actual histories, and these are referred to in the later parts of the *Veda* (from about the 9th century B.C. onwards), but in the forms in which they have come down to us these histories, the *Purāṇas*, are many centuries later than the Vedic period. In these late versions, much revised and enlarged and probably reworked chronologically according to artificial schemes, we can gain some idea of the traditions current in India before the Buddha's time about the origin of civilisation and the numerous dynasties of kings, together with some of the priests, poets and philosophers of ancient times. It is not yet clear how far, if at all, this history incorporates traditions of the Indus people. The Aryan conquest is not recorded in any recognisable form and all the dynasties are supposed to have ruled within the territory of ancient India (which included modern Afghanistan) from the outset. The period of civilisation recorded is sufficient, even after making the maximum allowance for inflation, to cover the Indus age as well as the Aryans in India. The only major distinction of races which appears is that between the Solar and Lunar dynasties of kings, which might seem to be significant although the two are related: the Solar Dynasty was founded by Manu, son of the Sun (God), the Lunar by Purūravas, grandson of the Moon (God) and son of Manu's daughter. Since some of the Lunar kings are mentioned in the earliest Vedic texts, whilst the Solar kings apparently are not, we might conjecture that the Solar kings were the Indus emperors, whose traditions were later combined with those of the Aryans to produce a synthetic history. At present this is pure conjecture and it seems futile to dwell on it.

For the period from the Aryan conquest to about the 13th century B.C. we can trace several lines of Lunar kings, lines which equally well can be explained as tribes of the Aryan people and not dynasties of their rulers. They were frequently at war among themselves as well as with other peoples. In about the 13th century B.C. Saṃvaraṇa, ruler of the Paurava line of Lunar kings, after first losing his kingdom to another branch of the line recovered it through the help of a brahman and then established an empire over all other kings. His son Kuru and his descendants maintained this imperial claim for many centuries, and for significant periods were able to give it reality at least for a large part of Northern India. This Lunar, or Paurava, Empire was the scene of the consolidation of the 'Brahmanical' civilisation of India : the way of life, the religion and much else that has since been looked back upon as the classical model by orthodox Indian thought.

During the period of the Paurava Empire the ancient Vedic texts were collected, many more were composed, and older and newer texts were formed into a Canon of scriptures collectively called the *Veda* (some of its constituents are also called '*Vedas*' individually). In actual fact there was not a single Canon, but several recensions belonging to as many schools of priests, much as the *Tripiṭaka* among the early Buddhists later, but that is of little importance for our present discussion. The word *Veda* means 'knowledge'. The Canon is therefore the collected learning of the brahmans, or priests. It consists of poetry, songs, ritual and philosophy.

During the 9th century B.C., approximately, when the Paurava Empire was at the height of its power, there lived a group of priests, poets and other creative thinkers who are credited with the composition of a number of texts, some literary and others technical, which attained virtually the status of scriptures without actually being included in the Vedic Canon. Other compositions of the same group, and statements attributed to them, were included in the Canon, being presumably regarded as inspired in a different way, but it is in the non-canonical texts that their views found the fullest scope. The extant versions of these texts outside the *Veda* are of varying degrees of authenticity, not having been preserved as carefully as the *Veda*, but even where they are not authentic they are important as showing how that classical age was looked back upon in later times.

Through these extant versions purporting to be their work we can see an attempt by the thinkers of about the 9th century B.C. to stabilise what they considered best and right in the traditions which had come down to them. They considered their own age to be decadent and to fall far short of the moral standards of antiquity. Though it was not a propitious time for good government or a virtuous life, it was still possible, and most desirable, for heroes and good men to uphold the ancient religion and to perform their social duties. On all this we may add the comment that according to the archaeological evidence the period c. 1000-800 B.C. was the beginning of the Iron Age in India, likely therefore to be a period of great change, uncertainty and increasing bloodiness of warfare—this last development being in fact most deeply imprinted in the epic and historical tradition of India.

From the *Veda* effectively codified under the Pauravas, and from the compositions attributed to this group of thinkers of about the 9th century B.C., orthodox and conservative thought in India has since derived its religion, its ritual, its philosophy, its heroic epic, its ancient historical traditions, its laws, its geometry, its astronomy and its linguistic science. All this constitutes what is generally known as 'Brahmanism', as a civilisation, a way of life, a religion and much else. In a sense this formative period of Brahmanism was a 'heroic period', that of the most famous heroes celebrated in the epic. The epic is supposed to have been composed in this period, but was long handed down by oral tradition, which continually inflated it.

This process of elaboration and reinterpretation was afterwards continued by later poets in separate works on epic themes, and especially by dramatists who represented epic heroes on the stage and so popularised the Brahmanical traditions whilst adapting them to their own times.

Brahmanism

It would be out of place in this book to elaborate much on Brahmanism (more accurately 'Vedism' or *Vaidika*, from *Veda*, the proper Indian term, less accurately 'Hinduism', a foreign word which means little more than 'Indianism'), and our treatment must be an impressionistic sketch by way of background.

The word *brahman* meant in the early Vedic period a sacred text, with an underlying sense of 'great' or 'excellent'. Later, in the time of the Pauravas, *brahman* was personified as the Supreme Being or God *brahman* (Masculine, Nominative *brahmā*), the original Being out of whom the universe evolved. Sometimes this *brahman* is instead conceived more abstractly and philosophically as the impersonal absolute, with neuter gender, but nevertheless as having life (since the life of the whole universe emanated from it and is sustained by it). From *brahman* is derived *brāhmaṇa*, meaning a priest in possession of the sacred texts, or later a priest of God, which we anglicise as 'brahman' (or 'brahmin') and from which European writers have coined the derivative 'Brahmanism'.

Anciently the Vedic religion of the Aryans had consisted primarily in the worship of gods, and the poetry and songs preserved in the *Veda* and forming its oldest component are mostly hymns of praise and supplication. The gods were derived from the ancient Indo-European pantheon and represent on the one hand social abstractions and on the other natural phenomena. In the period of the Paurava codification, however, we are confronted with an entirely different religion, despite the continuing use of the old hymns. Offerings to the gods had long formed a part of the ancient religion, but these now became its centre, its essence. The ritual to which they had given rise became the 'science' of obtaining all good things and the gods fell into place as the servants of the ritual, necessary merely to receive the offerings. The desired good results of the ritual action were to come about not through any favour of the gods but directly as the mysterious effects of the action itself, success depending on the precision with which this had been performed. Henceforth the really important and operative part of the *Veda* was the ritual part, interpreted as a set of injunctions governing correct performance.

The loss of practically all their independent significance by the gods had left the field of theology, cosmology and cosmogony open to new speculation, more sophisticated, more abstract, more systematic. It was here that the notion of the absolute or supreme being developed, the great *brahman.* Here also cosmogony gave birth to philosophy as a reasoned explanation of the origin and development of the universe. The earliest speculations of this kind appear already in some of the Vedic poetry and again entwined with explanations of the ritual in the ritual texts, but the latest part of the *Veda* consists of texts primarily devoted to this early philosophy (the *Upaniṣads*, or rather the five earliest among them, which alone are strictly canonical *Veda* and preserve the ideas of the Paurava period : *Chāndogya*, *Bṛhadāraṇyaka*, *Aitareya*, *Kauṣitaki* and *Taittiriya*).

The poetry of the Aryans was antagonistic to the more original inhabitants of India and their civilisation, but by the Paurava period this old antagonism and even the fact of the conquest appears to have been practically forgotten. A considerable amount of intermixture of the conquering and conquered peoples had evidently taken place, indeed it has even been suggested[1] that the brahmans, the hereditary priesthood among the presumed conquerors, were for the most part descended from the priests of non-Aryan peoples, probably of the Indus civilisation, who had managed to insinuate themselves into this favoured position in a spirit of compromise and in virtue of their superior education and intellectual skills. It is true that the brahman genealogies are doubtful and in part unaryan looking, but unlikely that the more original Indians had succeeded in assimilating their conquerors to such a great extent in so early a period. There are few, though there certainly are some, ideas in the Vedic Canon which came into the

1. By Pargiter : *Ancient Indian Historical Tradition*, Chapter XXVI.

traditions of the Aryans from outside instead of developing within. Perhaps a significant element in the ritual, or in philosophical speculation, came from the Indus people, but there is little or no evidence to decide such questions. In Paurava texts outside the Vedic Canon, however, there is much that is generally thought to be of non-Aryan origin. It is clear (and is not affected by the problems of the chronology of the epic and the histories, ascribed to Paurava authors but much later in their extant forms) that there was a gradual synthesis of the Aryan and the more originally Indian traditions. This trend is characteristic for the history of Indian thought, which usually developed not by exclusion but by assimilation. The doctrines of alien traditions were not rejected but were suitably explained, so that they fitted into some grand scheme. At the same time they might be modified and reformed to produce an overall harmony.

The most prominent non-Aryan elements in the Brahmanism of the epic and the histories (*purāṇas*) are the mythologies of the great Gods Viṣṇu (Vāsudeva) and Śiva and of the great Goddess Devī. These three were probably quite separate in origin, belonging to three different peoples in India. The Goddess as now known is often associated with either Viṣṇu or Śiva as a subordinate partner or consort, but these may be early syntheses. The mythology of Viṣṇu by itself seems to suggest a synthesis between several separate gods, who came to be regarded as manifestations of the same supreme being. As eventually incorporated into the histories these various conceptions of the godhead were brought into relation with *brahman* or Brahmā in various ways, depending on which one of the four was held to be the really ultimate godhead and which subordinate manifestations. Their appearance in books of history was due to the fact that the latter began with narratives of the creation and evolution of the universe, therefore with theology.

Another probably non-Aryan element in the histories is the accounts of the origin and progress of civilisation, including the election by the people of the first king and lawgiver (to ensure the maintenance of principle in social relationships), and the legend of king Pṛthu, who levelled the Earth, developed agriculture and trade, and built cities and villages.

Among doctrines probably non-Aryan is that of reincarnation or transmigration of the soul, which is barely mentioned in the latest part of the *Veda* but taken practically for granted in the non-Vedic Brahmanical tradition. This was very likely originally connected with—it certainly fits well with—the way in which the evolution of the universe and the scale of time are conceived in the histories. The universe evolves, or revolves, through enormous cyclic periods of hundreds or thousands of millions of years, at the ends of which it is dissolved into its constituent elements, including the souls, and then re-evolved either by natural processes or by the action of God. There were very great differences of doctrine here between various schools of thought within the Brahmanical tradition, particularly on the question whether originally, before the above cyclic periods, the souls and other atomic elements had not existed but had been created out of the supreme being or out of nothing. Very important, it would seem, for all religious and philosophical ideas in India is the vastness of the time scale assumed, which in fact agrees well with that established for the universe by modern astronomy and contrasts most strongly with the traditions of Western religions (the Babylonians had certain similar ideas, on a more limited scale). The Indian ideas of time were in fact quite early related to astronomical observations, particularly of the movements of the planets. The latter appear at first to be erratic, but on further observation and study may be seen to follow repeating patterns. Combine the movements of all the planets into an overall repeating pattern and you will find, depending on the precision of your observations and calculations, an exceedingly long cycle of time marked out in the heavens. The Indians assumed that at the beginning of some cyclic period all the planets should have been in one place, or on the same starting line (longitude), and their attempts to determine the date of this grand conjunction many millions of years ago seemed to confirm the practically inconceivable age attributed to the universe by speculative thought.[1]

1. There is plenty of evidence for enormous time scales in pre-Buddhist India. On the conjunctions of planets see e.g. Burgess' translation of the *Sūryasiddhānta*, 15 ff. and 328 of the Calcutta reprint, 1935, and Needham, *Science and Civilisation in China III*, 119 f., 202 (I-Hsing, a Buddhist monk), cf. also Colebrooke, *Miscellaneous Essays*, vol. II, 329 ff. and 426, London, 1873. See p. 40 below for the Ājīvaka tradition.

Lastly we might mention that the legal traditions and many of the social customs formulated in the earliest law books give the impression of not being Aryan in origin. Thus the conventional four stages of life (*āśramas*) later regarded as part of the foundations of orthodox society (studentship—married life—retirement—renunciation) are not mentioned in the *Veda*. The last of these stages and the growing practice of renouncing the world at any age reminds us of the evidence for there being ascetics in the ancient Indus society rather than of anything in the Aryan tradition.

The conception of liberation from transmigration would seem to go not simply with transmigration itself but with the vastness of the time scale recognised in Indian thought. It is almost certainly not Aryan in origin, the Aryan tradition having been of a future life in some sphere of existence not altogether different from the Earth (one such sphere was the Moon) and developing into the conception of a desirable heaven attainable by means of ritual action. Speculation about liberation of the soul, on the other hand, tried to conceive of some state entirely transcending the empirical universe, such as union with the supreme being. It appears in a vague form only in the very latest parts of the *Veda*, and is still not very prominent even in the early non-Vedic Brahmanical tradition. The attainment of heaven remained the dominant idea.

Vyāsa

According to later tradition[1] the *Veda* was 'arranged' in the Paurava period (as we noted above) by a poet named Vyāsa, who would be one of the group of thinkers of about the 9th century B.C. which we have referred to. This name in fact means in Sanskrit 'The Arranger' and can be only a title conferred on the poet. He is referred to also by a more personal name, Kṛṣṇa Dvaipāyana, but even this indicates his obscure origin, since Dvaipāyana is not a family name derived from his father but was coined from his having been born on an island. In fact he was illegitimate and his ancestry mixed, though in part brahman. His mother was a fisher girl who operated a ferry boat, his great grandfather was Vasiṣṭha, one of the major

1. The *Purāṇas*, see Pargiter op. cit. p. 318.

Vedic poets. Vyāsa is certainly a legendary figure, perhaps altogether mythical, yet he represents the effective founding of Brahmanism as it has since prevailed. He was the sage who knew the ancient traditions better than anyone else, systematised them and handed them down to posterity in a definitive form. It is significant that he does not appear to be mentioned in any text certainly authentic for the Paurava period, though a number of other teachers and sages are. For example the later texts of the *Veda* itself name the grammarian Śākalya, who certainly had a hand in arranging the oldest of the Vedic texts, Śaunaka who composed ancillary works on phonetics and compiled indexes of the *Veda*, the ritualist Kauśītaki and the philosophers Śāṇḍilya, Uddālaka and Yājñavalkya. Their views are given, sometimes at considerable length. According to the tradition Vyāsa was their senior contemporary or predecessor, why then is he not mentioned? Perhaps he is no more than an amalgam of the sages and teachers of the period, created by a later age to represent the establishment of Brahmanism as an attempted restoration of what was supposed to have been the ancient way of life as it was before the decadence of the Iron Age.

Vyāsa's supposed date corresponds to about 900 B.C. The *Veda* has been preserved in its poetical sections practically as it was in that period, whilst the prose books of ritual and philosophy were added at about that time and some of them later. Besides arranging the *Veda* Vyāsa is credited with a vast amount of more original work. He is supposed to have composed the epic (the great *Mahābhārata*) and some histories (*purāṇas*). If the *Veda* records the ancient ways which should be restored, the epic exemplifies the decadence of the Iron Age which had just begun, in its narrative of a disastrous civil war among the Pauravas. Vyāsa would be the contemporary of the heroes of the epic, a witness of some of its action and even a participant. The versions of the epic and the histories which have come down to us, however, are very much later than the Paurava period. They show us that period not as it was but as it was believed to have been after their fluid tradition had absorbed much that did not originally belong to it.

Chapter Two

INDIA IN THE TIME OF THE BUDDHA

Social and Political Crisis—The Philosophical Tradition—The Śramaṇas—The Śramaṇas and Society—The Main Śramaṇa Schools other than the Buddhists

Social and Political Crisis

After the great emperor Janamejaya (probably 9th century B.C.), during whose reign the Paurava Empire seems to have reached its maximum prosperity and power and to have been adorned by several of the most creative thinkers who contributed to the formation of Brahmanism, there was a gradual decline. The decisive turn seems to have been in the 8th century B.C., in the reign of Nicakṣu, when the Paurava capital, Hastināpura on the upper Ganges, was devastated by a flood. He transferred the capital to Kauśāmbī on the Yamunā. After this event the creative period of Brahmanism appears to have come to an end: lines of teachers are recorded and there was clearly some revision of Vedic texts and more of the epic and histories, but original composition seems to have been confined to the subsidiary studies, ritual, law, linguistics, astronomy and geometry. These studies were important for the history of science but of no direct consequence for Brahmanism as a religion or philosophy or guiding ideology. Moreover even among them there is hardly any work extant which might belong to the century and a half after Nicakṣu; the great period in these special studies begins later.

After the moving of the capital the empire broke up, the local rulers and states which had been under Paurava hegemony asserting their independence. By the time of the Buddha (500 B.C.) sixteen major states were counted in northern India, among which one of the smaller and weaker was that of the Pauravas. There were numerous minor states. The major states (and the minor) had many different types of government; in particular some were monarchies, others republics. Thus the India of the Buddha was a very different place from the India of Vyāsa. The states were frequently at war, and several of them sought universal hegemony. However, it was not the most orthodox states or the most legitimate dynasties which were the most successful in these struggles. On the contrary the Pauravas faded away in a haze of nostalgia and romance, and the real struggle was between the Vṛji Republic, the most powerful republican state, and the kingdom of Magadha.

Magadha appears to have been the least orthodox of the monarchies. It was situated on the periphery of the region of Brahmanical influence and its kings developed a highly autocratic and centralised system of government not provided for in Brahmanism. Brahmanism prescribes the duties of kings rather than their powers and provides a variety of checks on their actions. In fact, the *Veda* does not necessarily require monarchical government, even though later the Brahmanical tradition increasingly favoured it. Indeed we probably ought rather to say that under the trend towards monarchy of later times it was those Vedic schools which had been associated with the famous Paurava monarchy, not others which might have flourished under republican governments, which were favoured and have survived. The earlier Vedic texts think rather in terms of assemblies and various apparently autonomous groups in society, and of the persuasive power of speech, than of autocratic and centralised rule. The later Vedic texts, the majority of which—as now extant—show that they were composed under the Paurava Empire, are aware of republican governments in the outlying regions surrounding the central Paurava (or 'Kuru-Pañcāla') kingdom.[1]

This struggle in the Buddha's time was a contest in economic power, political craft and administrative efficiency, in which the Brahmanical tradition had little to offer either to the rulers or to the people. Both its rituals and its philosophy seemed irrelevant. The question was no longer one of establishing a harmonious empire, with an emperor ruling justly according to the traditional usages of Vedic society, treating his people and vassal rulers affectionately, if sometimes firmly, and restrained and guided by the code of duties prescribed by the *Veda* and interpreted by the brahmans. In that traditional society an

1. e.g. *Aitareya Brāhmaṇa*, viii 14 (Keith's translation is not correct).

individual could pursue his life in reasonable peace and freedom, seeking and to a fair extent obtaining the good things of this world, and if he conformed to *dharma* (the Brahmanical concept of duty and justice) he had been respected for it and found it conducive to his well being. But in the 6th century B.C. economic progress—the exploitation of natural resources and the development of industry and above all trade—had let loose quite new forces in society: instead of wealth being measured primarily in kind (especially in cattle) a money economy had developed. Unprecedented wealth followed its own laws of circulation, and the states tried to control it by legislation. The new class of merchants tended to become wealthier than kings, and the latter reacted to this with more arbitrary rule and confiscations on flimsy pretexts: they opposed political force to economic force. The rulers of North India experimented with various new forms of government, but the general trend was towards centralisation of power in the hands of a monarch. In this society most people found their freedom seriously and increasingly restricted, their property and their lives insecure, the future uncertain and probably worse than the past.

There was much discussion of real or imaginary past golden ages and of just emperors who had made the world harmonious and happy, but the model offered by the Brahmanical tradition failed to make any headway. Good men found themselves without a place and without any freedom in the increasingly centralised society ruled by money and force. For a time hopes seem to have centred on the Vṛji Republic, which was based on old traditions of social harmony and respect for the individual, but in the struggle for survival against Magadha it became clear to men such as the Buddha that its position was precarious, that it was only a matter of time before the greater wealth of Magadha overwhelmed it. Moreover the basis of its defence was a pure conservatism of adhering to the ways of old and resisting the corrupting power of the new society of Magadha (exercised through bribery and sowing dissension). The Republic seemed to have no power of development which might enable it to oppose to autocracy a more economically viable form of society. The Buddha admired the Republic's ancient customs, its democratic government, its respect for wise men, but he did not see in it a political solution to the problem of human happiness. He and other philosophers of the time looked elsewhere for a solution, not primarily in society but in the first place away from it. In effect they contracted out of society in order to preserve their freedom; they abandoned the quest for wealth and power and sought peace of mind and spiritual experiences. Only from an independent vantage point could they hope—as they certainly did hope—to exercise any influence on the society they had left, to infuse into it better ideals than money and violence.

The Philosophical Tradition

In the preceding chapter the philosophical texts of the *Veda* have been mentioned, but nothing has been said about their nature and methods, apart from the original relation to cosmogony and the later conception of an absolute *brahman*. In the later, conservative, Brahmanical tradition whatever had been received into the Vedic Canon was treated as revealed dogma (and anything else was lost). Careful reading of some of the texts on the other hand reveals a substantial amount of not merely original, but critical thought in the *Veda*. These evident criticisms of the Vedic tradition were explained away and harmonised with the overall dogmatic system by the later Brahmanical schools, but their methods seem not to have been lost on later critics who remained outside these schools: the Buddha himself is recorded[1] to have held that the original brahmans were good men and the *Veda* (originally) true doctrine but that both had become corrupt and needed to be completely reformed (for example; one should become a brahman by virtue, not by heredity; the brahmans had become mere repeaters of texts, not creative thinkers or 'meditators', since the *Veda* had been compiled). What might the Buddha and his contemporaries have learned from early Vedic philosophy?

In the earliest Vedic poetry the universe has its basis in the activities of the gods. Its laws are the laws of certain gods, the universe itself was created, or more precisely 'built' (like a house) by the gods.[2] It is in the development of cosmogonic

1. e.g. D. III 94, I 104 (see p. 273 of the commentary on this for corruption of the texts).

2. e.g. RVS ii 15.2 f, i 159, iv 56, vi 17.7, iii 55.19 f, x 149, x 81, x 72, etc.

speculations from this mythology that we can most easily trace the growth of philosophy. There is a quest for some more rationalistic explanation of the evolution of the universe, ending in the *Upaniṣads* with an explanation which dispenses with supernatural gods or a God and explains the universe out of itself. It is itself a living being, even a divinity, but it develops according to natural processes which can be understood by scientific observations and experiments. Accompanying this quest, or rather preceding it and stimulating it, we find expressions of doubt concerning the gods and the mythology. Do the gods exist? If they do, at least the stories about them traditionally told are untrue. What existed at first? Can anyone know this? Can even the highest Deity know this? Certainly the gods do not know, since at first they did not exist.[1]

Of the main steps in this line of development we may note first the poem RVS X 129 (date probably between 1200 and 1000 B.C.). Here it is suggested that at first there was neither being nor non-being, but somehow the One, a living being, came into existence, embracing everything in itself, through the influence of heat (apparently its own heat). From desire arose mind. Then a measuring line (a significant idea) was stretched horizontally across, dividing what existed into male and female principles. At this point the speculation breaks off, but it is asked: Who really knows? Not the gods! Only He who surveys the universe from the highest heaven perhaps knows, or perhaps He too does not know.

At the end of the development we may look at the doctrine of Uddālaka as recorded in the *Upaniṣads*.[2] (Uddālaka lived in the time of Janamejaya, probably 9th century B.C.) He first rejects a traditional (Vedic) account of evolution to the effect that originally there was nothing, non-being. If that were so, he asks, how could being have come out of it? So at first there was being. Uddālaka also rejected ritualistic explanations of phenomena: that a certain thing is so because a certain ritual is performed in a certain way.[3] The original being, according to him, is that which underlies everything in

1. e.g. RVS ii 12.5, viii 100.3, ŚBr 11.1.6. 9-10, RVS x 129.
2. *Chāndogya U.* vi.
3. ŚBr 11.4.1 shows the traditional views upheld against him.

the universe. It is in everything, though it is too fine to be visible. By natural processes it became many beings: first it produced heat, out of this, which also was alive like the original being, came water and out of the latter came 'food' (*anna*), which seems by extension to include all solid matter. These three living elements, called also 'divinities', then gave rise to everything in the universe, including man and ultimately mind. Thus there is no supernatural, external, agency but only 'being' itself, the original matter of the universe, out of which everything comes and back into which everything goes at death.

So far the explanation is rational enough, but much more important is the way Uddālaka justifies his explanations. He appeals at each step to actual observations of phenomena and sometimes to experiments which demonstrate that things are as he suggests. In looking for the sequence of evolution he proceeds by tracing things back to their causes by actual investigation. He proves the dependence of mind on food by the experiment of fasting. By way of methodology he distinguishes real substances from mere modifications different only in name. Despite nominal differences we can generalise about a whole range of phenomena which in fact have a common substance.

There are implied in this development the ideas and methods of science. We do not know what science except the natural science of Uddālaka himself. First the spirit of doubt and enquiry, of not accepting traditional, mythopoeic or ritualistic, explanations. Then classification and scientific generalisation. Above all observations and experiments, by which causes can be found out and inductions arrived at. The law of the gods gives way to natural law, a concept which becomes all powerful later, when Buddhism and other extra-Vedic philosophies develop.

The Śramaṇas

The Buddha belonged to a new movement in philosophy which grew up under the social conditions described in the first section of this chapter. The brahmans were, or had become, a hereditary priesthood, and the earlier philosophers and poets whose work is known to us, being preserved in the Brahmanical literature, were either brahmans or men who became brahmanised, at least posthumously, by being accepted into the ranks of the orthodox. The new movement on the other hand was led by men who were not brahmans, but came from all ranks of society, and who instead of joining the Brahmanical schools set up independent schools. Some brahmans also joined these schools, but they thereby left the Brahmanical tradition and were assimilated into the new movement, which was essentially a classless one.

The philosophers of the new schools were called *śramaṇas*. They were men who had contracted out of ordinary society and become wanderers, living either by gleaning what they could in the woods and fields or by begging. Their aim was to discover the truth and attain happiness, or at least peace of mind. Having abandoned all social commitments they were free to spend their time thinking, trying out ascetic practices, studying nature, and of course teaching. They set up schools and trained pupils to remember and disseminate their teachings, and they also lectured in the villages and cities, even before kings if invited. The contents of this public lecturing were extremely diverse, but they tended to be ethical, to instruct people how to live, and the food or even fees they received could be regarded as a justifiable return for the teaching they dispensed.

The *śramaṇas* rejected the *Veda*, and the authority of the brahmans, who claimed to be in possession of revealed truths not knowable by any ordinary human means. They ridiculed the complicated rituals, and tried to show the absurdity of the *Veda*, as a canon of ultimate truths, by pointing out contradictions in it and drawing attention to some passages which seemed either rather futile or highly unethical, or even completely nonsensical, if supposed to be pronouncements having absolute authority (since a great part of the *Veda* consists of ancient poetry and legends, this was not very difficult). The *śramaṇas* went further than this and declared that the entire Brahmanical system was fraudulent: a conspiracy against the public by the brahmans for the purpose of enriching themselves by charging exorbitant fees for the performance of bogus rites and the giving of futile advice.[1]

1. The Buddhists have preserved some typical verses to this effect in the *Tripiṭaka* (Pali J VI 206-14). The views of the Lokāyata School are reported for example in the first chapter of SDS.

In place of this authoritarian tradition the *śramaṇas* sought to find satisfactory explanations of the universe and of life by genuine investigations and by reasoning. They believed they could ascertain natural laws by their own efforts, without benefit of authority from the ancients or of supernatural guidance, and that these laws would be absolutely valid and must be accepted because anyone who cared to undertake a proper investigation could verify them.[1] In brief, their outlook was that of scientists investigating the nature of the universe, though they were guided by the practical aim of applying the knowledge they gained in the quest for happiness.

Like Uddālaka before them, the *śramaṇas* were evidently closely in touch with, and even partly responsible for, the considerable progress made in the natural sciences in their period. They were particularly interested in astronomy and mathematics and some of them were connected with medicine.[2] Their doctrines usually included some kind of description of the universe: of the elements out of which it is constructed, their classification, the way the universe evolves and the position of living beings in it. Again, their conception of the universe was that it was a natural phenomenon, evolving of itself according to ascertainable natural laws : it was not subject to the control of gods or a God and had not been created by such supernatural powers. If there were gods, as some of them admitted might be the case, these were natural beings on a level with men and animals, inhabiting a different region but just as subject to natural laws as men : they were not immortal, but lived and died as men did.[3]

It is noteworthy that most of the *śramaṇas* believed in transmigration in some form : either of a 'soul' or of a stream of consciousness from a dying body to a newly conceived one. We have noted above that by this period the Vedic or Brahmanical schools also had accepted this idea and incorporated it into their tradition. Many people at this time seem to have

1. In Buddhism see e.g. the Pali references under *ehipassika*, 'verifiable', in PTC vol. I, p. 436. For the Lokāyata only knowledge verifiable by the senses was admissible.

2. See e.g. the references in REBCS, p. 51.

3. The *Tripiṭaka* contains satirical dialogues on the gods and particularly on Brahmā, e.g. Pali *Kevaddha* (D No. 11) = Chinese version of *Dīrgha* No. 24 in T 1.

believed that they could remember their past lives. The acceptance of transmigration perhaps reflects the refusal to accept the apparently arbitrary experiences of happiness and unhappiness of men within a single life : a belief in some kind of natural law of compensation at work in the universe ensuring eventual justice. At the same time most of the philosophers of this period regarded life in the universe as on the whole unhappy, concluding that their aim should be, not to be reborn in it in better circumstances, which anyway would be temporary, but not to be reborn at all. At this point the subject becomes difficult : what could it mean, not to be reborn in the universe ? Would one's soul or consciousness go somewhere else, go into a dormant state, or cease to exist altogether ?

Out of the *śramaṇa* movement of the 6th century B.C. a large number of separate schools of philosophy developed. From the many more or less scientific, more or less speculative, systems propounded at least five major organised schools were successful enough to become strongly established and play dominant parts in the history of philosophy in India (and sometimes outside) for at least the next two thousand years. They soon split up into sub-schools and all of them modified their doctrines in the course of time, but despite the later appearance of a few entirely new schools it was those which had originated in the period of the Buddha which thenceforth gave a general direction to Indian philosophy and provided a framework for its discussions. The brahmans of course reacted by developing philosophical systems of their own, meeting the new ideas with adaptations of their doctrines.

In the long run, though apparently not at first, by far the most successful and important of the *śramaṇa* schools was that founded by the Buddha. At first the Buddha was just one of very many wandering teachers in the Vṛji Republic, Magadha and other countries of northern India about 500 B.C. He collected a fair number of followers, though not as many as some of his rivals, and he promulgated a doctrine which has all the main characteristics of the *śramaṇa* movement, which on the surface at least is just a typical *śramaṇa* doctrine. He rejected all authority except experience : the student should experiment for himself and see that the teaching is true, not accept it because the Buddha says so. The universe is subject to natural laws only, by studying which one can attain freedom and happiness. The most important laws are laws of causation, moral as well as physical. Transmigration is provided for in that consciousness continues from life to life in accordance with the laws of moral causation. The aim is to end this transmigration and attain final peace. The most essential and characteristic part of the teaching is a scheme of training and study to attain this aim.[1] The Buddha here assumes that the aim of all living beings is the attainment of happiness and his teaching is presented as a way of achieving this aim, either absolutely and finally in liberation from transmigration, final peace, or relatively in an improvement of circumstances for those not yet ready to renounce the world. Moral conduct thus follows from the desire for happiness when the laws of moral causation are correctly understood, it is not a duty, as the brahmans maintained. As a background to his doctrine the Buddha enumerated and classified the constituent elements [2] of the universe. In the scheme of training the most important part is not moral conduct, which though essential is only a preliminary, but meditation, in which the truths about the nature of the universe and one's own being are contemplated and the consciousness becomes gradually abstracted and detached.

The Śramaṇas and Society

Such was the reaction of philosophers of the 6th century B.C. to the problems of life in that period. They rejected the values of ordinary society, with the very important exception that they agreed, with most people, that happiness was the aim. Naturally their conceptions of happiness and how actually to attain it diverged widely from ordinary ideas. They lived as far as possible outside ordinary society, seeking truth and happiness, and most of them decided that real happiness consisted in peace of mind. Some of them returned to society as teachers, trying to persuade people that the usual ways of seeking happiness through wealth and power would not work and would in fact lead to more unhappiness. The trend of society, many of them sought to point out, was to produce

1. This is a sketch of the Buddha's teaching, to be justified later.
2. The 'principles', his most original hypothesis.

more and more unhappiness, to get steadily worse. Hence there was a need to counter this process within society (as well as outside it), to produce more happiness by applying the truths which the philosophers had discovered, this happiness being again primarily peace of mind.

As well as teaching this reform in society, in the form of moral teachings, these *śramaṇas* sought pupils who would leave society and follow them in their wanderings. Some of them established regular communities (*saṃgha*) outside ordinary society, outside the jurisdiction of governments but having their own codes of discipline. These communities of 'monks' and 'nuns'—as we may very approximately term them in English—were at first groups of wanderers in the forests. Later they developed organised settlements, sometimes on the outskirts of towns and supported in a regular manner by sympathetic laymen and even by governments. The Buddhist communities have an elaborate constitution based in part on that of the Vṛji Republic. The groups of Buddhist monks are independent of one another and there is no supreme head. The monks meet regularly in council and decide issues by majority vote, differences between groups being settled in the same way by convening a general congress and debating and voting on the issues. Representatives and other officers of the groups are elected by their members.[1] Thus the Buddhist communities formed a separate society of their own, as did certain other *śramaṇa* communities. The relations between these communities and governments were complicated and sometimes difficult, especially as the governments of states in and after the Buddha's time were organising society in an increasingly centralised manner. A *śramaṇa* community of any size and influence in the country would clearly be a disruptive element in a centralised state, especially if its constitution was republican and democratic and the state was a monarchy.

The kingdom of Magadha, in fact, gradually extended its power over almost the whole of India and thus became capable of exerting considerable control over the *śramaṇa* communities. The effect of this on the history of Buddhism must be studied

1. The constitution of the Buddhist communities was codified in their *Vinaya* books, one of the three sections of the *Tripiṭaka*, and will be considered in more detail below (Ch. 3 ff).

below. Here we may note that it is of the utmost importance for understanding the history of India and of Indian religion and philosophy that the political unification realised by Magadha did not last. Non-unification, non-centralisation, means freedom from any single controlling authority. It makes possible intellectual freedom. It enables philosophers to be independent of governments, because if they find one government uncongenial they need not remain on its territory but can emigrate. On the other hand there were certain disadvantages for Indian philosophy in the lack of political stability which non-unification entailed and especially in the fact that the various states in India were much weaker in the face of foreign invasions than a united empire would have been. Foreign invasions were at times absolutely disastrous for the intellectual life of India and particularly for Buddhism.

The Main Śramaṇa Schools other than the Buddhists

The ultimate origins of the *śramaṇa* movement are obscure and we can trace its history only from the time of the organisation of permanent communities during the lifetime of the Buddha (B.C. 566 to 486). There are traditions about more ancient teachers, often in very remote periods, but so far it has not been possible to establish the historicity of any of them. For the most part such traditions appear to be attempts by various schools to assert the antiquity and absolute truth of their doctrines by attributing them to legendary teachers of the past who, if they discovered the truth, must be presumed to have discovered the same truth as more recent teachers of the school. The ascetic practices, or even merely the renunciation of society, of the *śramaṇas*, have led to speculation that their tradition goes right back to the presumed ascetics of the Indus Civilisation, or on the other hand to the Shamanism of Central Asia and presumably of the early Aryans. This would hardly affect our understanding of the schools of the Buddha's time as new, as reacting to new developments in history by producing new doctrines. If the life of wandering in the forests was old, most of the philosophies of the 6th century B.C. were new, taking account of the advances of science and of the social and political changes in Magadha, Vṛji and other countries. It is especially noteworthy that our sources indicate that the establishment of organised communities of *śramaṇas* as opposed to individual wanderers was an innovation at the beginning of the 5th century B.C.[1] This organisation may have been a response to the centralising policies of the states of the time.

The main organised schools of *śramaṇas* in the time of the Buddha were, besides the Buddhists, the Ājīvaka, Lokāyata, Jaina and Agnostic (Ajñāna) schools.

The name Ājīvaka originated from the *ājiva*, the way of life, of the wandering *śramaṇas*. It was taken by a large school or community founded by a group of prominent teachers in Kośala (West of Vṛji) in B.C. 489. The leader of this school was Gośāla (died B.C. 488), who had propounded its central doctrine, that of fatalism, and was afterwards revered as a silent sage. The Ājīvakas believed in transmigration on a grand scale, each individual soul passing automatically into final peace after having experienced every possible kind of life in turn (lastly that of an Ājīvaka wanderer). This series of incarnations of the soul was supposed to take nearly thirty million million million, multiplied by the number of grains of sand in the bed of the river Ganges, years. The school developed an elaborate system of divination and prognostication by the interpretation of dreams and other omens. Ājīvakas were sometimes employed by kings to make predictions, but the original function of this knowledge of the future and its inescapable experiences was presumably to induce a spirit of resignation and peace of mind. The possibility of making a correct prediction was the best evidence for all events being determined in advance by Fate (*Niyati*).

In harmony with this determinism was the doctrine of 'inaction' (*akriyā*) originally propounded by another Ājīvaka teacher, Pūraṇa (died c. B.C. 503). All the supposed actions of men, 'good' or 'bad', are no actions at all, produce no effect or influence on the future (hence the school rejects moral causation). From another teacher, Kakuda (in Pali Pakudha), the Ājīvakas took their doctrine of the constituent elements of the universe, which were uncreated, uncuttable, sterile, immovable and rigid. These undergo no alteration or transformation and do not interact. Any supposed action passes

1. See REBCS 47 ff.

ineffectively between their atoms. There are seven of these elements (or 'substances', *kāya*) : earth, water, heat, air, happiness, unhappiness and soul (or 'life', *jīva*).[1]

The Lokāyata, the name of which probably meant originally 'natural science' or 'naturalism' (investigation of nature), was a materialist school. As opposed to the Ājīvakas they asserted complete freedom, absolute free will, as the natural way of life and were also known as the Do-as-you-like school (*yadṛcchāvāda*). Everything happens through the spontaneous actions of nature (*svabhāva* i.e. the own-nature, of each phenomenon). The school agreed with the Ājīvakas in rejecting moral causation, but for opposite reasons : all acts and experiences are spontaneous, not determined by anything; moreover there is no soul and no transmigration which could make the working out of moral causation possible. The aim of living beings is happiness, but for this school the highest happiness attainable is that of the pleasures of the senses (*kāma*). The pleasure of human relationships is also particularly mentioned. Unlike the Buddhists and probably most philosophers of the time, the Lokāyata school held that there is more happiness than unhappiness in life, what is needed being discrimination and the recognition (and acceptance) that happiness is by nature transient, permanence being boring and disgusting and contrast essential for enjoyment, whilst overcoming difficulties leads to increased pleasure.

According to this school the universe is constituted out of four elements : earth, water, heat and air. All phenomena consist of combinations of these four, and consciousness is such a compound, or rather a property of the elements combined in a particular way as a living body.

The most prominent Lokāyata teacher of the Buddha's time was Ajita, but he was not regarded in later times as the founder of the school. It is a legendary Bṛhaspati who was later regarded as the founder of the school and the composer of its basic text or *sūtra*.[2]

---

1. For the Ājīvakas see HDA.
2. Unfortunately there is as yet no serious full scale study of the Lokāyata published, D. Chattopadhyaya's being perverse in rejecting most of the evidence though containing much of interest. See REBCS 52-57 and *Outline of Indian Philosophy*, pp. 33-40, 124-28.

The Jainas appear to have originated by secession from the Ājīvakas under their leader Mahāvīra, the Jina. They maintained a doctrine of a transmigrating eternal soul, like that of the Ājīvakas, which could attain perfect happiness through the cessation of transmigration in a kind of supreme heaven. Unlike the Ājīvakas they asserted free will, which had to be strenuously exercised to bring about ultimate bliss. The Jainas taught moral causation, and insisted that the balance resulting from bad actions in the past had to be exhausted by severe asceticism, indeed self-torture, before the soul could free itself from incarnation.

The Jainas have been the most scrupulous of all Indian schools in their devotion to the ethical principle of not taking life, of a life of complete harmlessness. Equally they have often been the champions of toleration, and their philosophy was well suited to form a basis for this in that it included the doctrine of 'non-extremism' (*anekānta*), that there are many standpoints from which an object may be contemplated, all existing things being infinitely complex so that apparently contradictory predicates may be asserted of them. Thus an object considered as its elements is eternal, but as a modification of them it is not eternal.[1]

The Agnostics maintained that no conclusive knowledge about any of the matters debated by the philosophers is possible. For purposes of argument they developed a technique of systematic evasion, but generally they appear to have deprecated argument as leading to bad tempers and loss of peace of mind. Instead they seem to have advocated friendship. They pointed out that the various speculative doctrines, especially about the nature of the soul, were mutually contradictory. Such speculation could only be confusing and harmful or lead to harmful actions (such as disputes) and ultimately remorse and consequent obstruction (to peace of mind) and should therefore be avoided. In the time of the Buddha the teacher Sañjayin was well known as the leader of this school.[2]

1. On Jainism see DJ.
2. REBCS 53. In the *Tripiṭaka* : Pali D I 58 f and 24 ff. Other references in HDA 21 ff.

CHAPTER THREE

THE LIFE OF THE BUDDHA

Chronology and Birth — Renunciation and Englightenment — Teaching and Organising — The Last Months and the Parinirvāṇa

Chronology and Birth

The life of the Buddha is part of the background to his teaching. The early *Tripiṭaka* did not contain any comprehensive account of the teacher's life, although the circumstantial details of setting of its dialogues give it incidentally something of the form and atmosphere of a biographical or historical record. The *Sūtra* section is a record of numerous episodes in the life of the Buddha ('Bhagavant', 'Master') and of the Buddha's discourses on various occasions. The *Vinaya* section is a record of the foundation of the Buddhist community by the Buddha after his enlightenment and of its gradual development (especially in regard to organisation and discipline) under his supervision.[1] Only the *Mātṛkā* or *Abhidharma* gives no indication of the times, places or persons present when its doctrines were promulgated and is a bare statement of the doctrines themselves (we may ignore here as later fabrications the statements of the commentaries on the circumstances of utterance of the third section). The *Sūtra* and *Vinaya* texts thus contribute some episodes of biographical interest. Though some of these are assigned to the period immediately after the enlightenment and others to that leading up to the *parinirvāṇa*, there is for the most part no continuity, no indication when in the intervening period other episodes belong. In short it is the doctrine which is the centre of interest throughout and which for the most part determines the arrangement, not the teacher.

In a very few early texts the Buddha is represented as telling his followers something of his life before the enlightenment and of that decisive event itself (some narrate episodes from his previous lives, which we may leave for a later chapter).

In this chapter we review from these scattered notices the

1. It is in fact a legal code.

available record, in its most ancient and authentic form, of the Buddha's life. That life was evidently inessential for the doctrine of early Buddhism and did not interest the compilers of the *Tripiṭaka*, who were content to record as carefully as they could the words of their teacher, the words which were their 'master' once the Buddha was no more. Later, however, interest in the remarkable personality who had discovered their doctrine and founded their community grew among the Buddhists. More comprehensive narratives were then elaborated out of the available texts and fluid tradition. The edifying legend which resulted will find its proper place in another chapter (Ch. 9).

There has been a long controversy over the precise date of the *parinirvāṇa*. Two studies along different lines, by Bareau[1] and Eggermont,[2] appear to the present writer to establish the date 486 B.C. as practically certain, and it is adopted here as a basis for all our chronology. In one of the early texts authenticated by several schools of Buddhists[3] the Buddha states that he was twenty-nine years of age when he 'left the world', and that that event happened more than fifty years ago. This was said immediately before the *parinirvāṇa*, perhaps on the very last day itself. The age attained by the Buddha is thus given as more than 79 years, and the later tradition gives him a full eighty at the moment of *parinirvāṇa*. There is some reason to doubt this figure of eighty, as a very early interpolation, since it makes it difficult to reconcile the Buddhist and Brahmanical traditions about the life of King Bimbisāra of Magadha, the Buddha's contemporary. It could perhaps be reduced by up to twenty years to produce a more authentic figure, but the research required to settle the point will be very complex and must be left to future specialists in chronology. The matter is not of crucial importance for us : it affects the birth, renunciation and enlightenment of the Buddha but not any of the other dates given in this book. We therefore adopt 566 B.C. as a provisional date for the birth and 537 B.C. for the renunciation of the Buddha. Later tradition, but

1. See JA 1953, 27 ff.

2. *The Chronology of the Reign of Asoka Moriya*, Leiden, 1956, particularly pp. 138 and 143.

3. D II 151, Waldschmidt MPS 376 f.

apparently no very early text, places the enlightenment six years after the renunciation, hence our provisional date for the enlightenment is 531 B.C.

The Buddha, or rather the *bodhisattva*, 'being for (future) enlightenment' but not yet *buddha*, 'enlightened', was born in the Śākya Republic, which was the city state of Kapilavastu, a very small state just inside the modern state boundary of Nepal against the Indian frontier. In an old text[1] of the Sthavira school, but probably not part of the earliest *Tripiṭaka*, the future Buddha tells King Bimbisāra, at their first meeting, that he is from Kośala, implying that the Śākyas were then subject to that other powerful kingdom of northern India, but internally their constitution was republican.[2] The future Buddha was born in an aristocratic (warrior) and wealthy family. He tells a wanderer in one of the early texts[3] that he spent his youth in luxury, enjoying the pleasures of the senses and having three palaces or halls (*prāsāda*), one for each of the three main seasons (the Rains, Winter and Summer). This, we may note, was the conventional luxury for a wealthy person of the time, whether a warrior or a merchant.

Renunciation and Enlightenment

In the same text[4] the Buddha continues: 'Enjoying myself with superhuman music in the Rainy Hall during the four months of the Rains I did not descend from the terrace of the Hall. After some time, having known in their true nature the origination, extinction, enjoyment and disadvantage of, and liberation from, pleasures, I gave up the desire for pleasure, rejected the lust for pleasure and lived without thirst (desire), with my thoughts calmed internally. I saw other beings not free from passion for pleasures, eaten up with desire for pleasure, burning with lust for pleasure, indulging in pleasures. I did not long for them, did not take pleasure in them. Now what was the cause ? That delight, Māgandiya (the wanderer's name), (which is) apart from pleasures, apart from bad principles, which even stands completely

1. Sn 422.
2. See D I 87 ff.
3. M I 504=T 26 (Chinese *Madhyama*) No. 117.
4. Translated from the Sthaviravāda Pali version.

surpassing divine happiness, enjoying that delight I did not long for inferior ones, did not take pleasure in them.'

In another early text[1] the Buddha carries his story further, talking to his followers : 'I myself, monks, before the enlightenment, being only an unenlightened being for (future) enlightenment, having myself the principle of birth (i.e. being one who was born as a living being) I looked for just the principle of birth, having myself the principle of aging I looked for just the principle of aging, having myself the principle of getting ill... (the text continues with dying, grief and defilement, the principles of which were sought, and goes on) ... Suppose I, having myself the principle of birth, having discovered the disadvantage in the principle of birth, were to look for the not born, unsurpassed, safe from the yoke (i.e. the influence of pleasure, etc.), extinction (*nirvāṇa*,—of existence or here specifically of birth)? (the text continues with the not aging, unsurpassed, etc., extinction of aging, the not getting ill, not dying, not grieving and undefiled extinctions of the other principles mentioned, then goes on) ... After some time, monks, being only young, a boy, black-haired, endowed with good youth, in the first period of life, although my parents were unwilling and weeping, with tears on their faces, I went forth from home to homelessness, shaving off my hair and beard and dressing in brown clothes (i.e. the rags worn by wanderers).

'Having gone forth searching for what is good, looking for the unsurpassed, excellent state of calm, I approached Ārāḍa Kālāma...' Ārāḍa was a *śramaṇa*, and the future Buddha asked to live the 'best life', i.e. a celibate life, according to Ārāḍa's doctrine and discipline. The *śramaṇa* agreed and the future Buddha studied his doctrine, not taking it merely on trust but ascertaining and experiencing its truth for himself. The doctrine led through a series of meditation exercises up to the 'sphere of nothingness', i.e. being conscious of nothing at all, in a state of deep abstraction. The Buddha remarks here that the 'trust' (or 'confidence'), 'energy', 'self-possession', 'concentration' and 'understanding' were not Ārāḍa's alone but his also, he acquired these—elsewhere called 'faculties' and 'strengths'—himself, not merely relying on the accomplishments

1. M I 163 ff=T 26 No. 204. Translated from the Pali version.

of his teacher. He soon acquired whatever Ārāḍa had to teach, and the latter was so impressed that he suggested sharing the leadership of his group of wanderers with him. The future Buddha, however, was not satisfied with this doctrine and withdrew: 'This doctrine does not lead to indifference, dispassion, cessation, calm, insight, enlightenment or liberation (extinction, *nirvāṇa*), but only to transmigration to the sphere of nothingness (conceived as a high plane of existence of consciousness)...'

The future Buddha then went to another *śramaṇa* teacher, Udraka Rāmaputra, with very similar results except that Udraka's doctrine led a stage further, up to the 'sphere of neither perception nor non-perception', an even higher plane to which consciousness might transmigrate. Again he was not satisfied and withdrew.

Then: 'Monks, searching for what is good, looking for the unsurpassed, excellent state of calm, proceeding on my journey into Magadha in due course I approached the military town of Uruvilvā. There I saw a delightful place: a lovely grove of the forest where the river flowed clear, delightful with good beaches, and a cowherds' village within reach. I thought it was delightful... and adequate for 'exertion' (i.e. the *śramaṇa* type of training and meditation)...'

Before continuing with the account of this text we may refer to another early one[1] where the Buddha reminisces about his life in the forest immediately before the enlightenment, and which also describes that event. 'It is hard to be adequate for those remote abodes, the woods and hills of the forest. Solitude is hard. It is hard to enjoy being alone. It is as if the woods steal the mind of a monk who does not concentrate.' He continues that *śramaṇas* or brahmans who are not pure in their physical actions, speech and minds are in fact summoning fear and fearful things, both of which are bad. (The Sthaviravāda commentary explains 'fearful things' as meaning that if they had injured someone the offended person might follow them with murderous intent.) Being pure, however, the future Buddha felt secure in the forest. The text continues with many

1. M I 17 ff=T 125 (Chinese *Ekottara*) k. 23, 665b-6; cf. T 26 k. 25 p. 589 c.

details concerning the character necessary for a wanderer in the forest if he is to succeed in achieving concentration as a basis for meditation. All these form part of the Buddhist teaching and need not be discussed here, where we are concerned with whatever can be gathered of a biographical nature.

Meditating at night—a practice which the future Buddha says he took up at this time—can be still more hair-raising and terrifying: animals come, a peacock breaks a twig, the wind rustles fallen leaves. He resolved to dispel the fears which beset him at that time: if he was walking up and down when fears arose he continued to walk until he had dispelled them, or if he was standing still, or sitting down, he again remained in the same position until he had dispelled the fears. Then he 'initiated energy, undeterred, attended to self-possession, not distracted, calmed his body, not excited, and concentrated his thoughts, focused on one point.' Gradually abstracting his mind from all attachments he then entered successively on four stages of meditation (*dhyāna*), attaining a state of perfect equanimity, free from any unhappiness or happiness. In the same night, his thoughts thus concentrated, he exerted himself and acquired three 'sciences' or 'knowledges' (*vidyā*) during the first, middle and last watches of the night respectively: he recollected his former lives, he understood the transmigration of beings according to their actions, bad conduct leading to misery and good conduct to a good destiny, finally he discovered the 'Four Truths', the basic doctrine of Buddhism, which is the knowledge of how the 'influences' (*āsrava*) can be exhausted. These influences (passion, desire for existence and ignorance) keep one in transmigration, to know that they are exhausted in one is to know that one will not be reborn, that one is freed, and this knowledge the Buddha had that night. At the same time the Four Truths formed the essentials of the content of his enlightenment, and having discovered them he was henceforth known as the Buddha (though this is not actually stated in the present text). He understood in their true nature (1) unhappiness, (2) its origination, (3) its cessation and (4) the way leading to this cessation.

This other text thus appears to describe the final 'exertion' (*pradhāna*), whereby the Buddha became enlightened, in one way, whilst the text we were looking at before, having brought the future Buddha to the 'delightful place' near Uruvilvā, goes on[1] in its own way to describe the enlightenment: 'Having the principle of birth, having discovered the disadvantage in the principle of birth, looking for the not born, unsurpassed, safe from the yoke, extinction (of birth), I acquired the not born, unsurpassed, safe from the yoke, extinction (*nirvāṇa*)...' (Likewise he acquired the extinction of aging, illness, dying, grief and defilement). 'Knowledge arose in me, and insight: my freedom is certain, this is my last birth, now there is no rebirth.' The stress here is on 'extinction' (*nirvāṇa*) rather than enlightenment, but the text continues:

'Then I thought:[2] I have acquired this doctrine which is profound, difficult to see, difficult to understand, true, excellent, beyond the scope of deduction, subtle, discoverable by a wise man (only). But this creation takes delight in a home, is delighted by a home, welcomes a home. For a creation which thus delights in, is delighted by and welcomes a home this matter is difficult to see, namely causal connection (or perhaps better 'conditionality'—*idaṃpratyayatā*, literally 'this-conditionality', being conditioned by a specific thing), conditioned origination (*pratītyasamutpāda*). This matter also is difficult to see, namely the calming (*śamatha*) of all forces (*saṃskāra*: this conception will be discussed in detail later), the rejecting of all attachments, the exhausting of desires, dispassion, cessation, extinction. If I were to teach the doctrine and others did not grasp it, that would be weariness and trouble for me.'

These texts indicate that the enlightenment consisted from one point of view in acquiring the three 'sciences', which included the understanding of transmigration and the Four Truths concerning the mechanism of transmigration and how to end the influences which bind one to it. From another point of view it was the acquisition of extinction (of birth, etc.), *nirvāṇa* for the Buddha. Then again, looking more deeply into the enlightenment, into the doctrine which it discovered, the content of the sciences, it is described as a theory of conditionality, of origination, and of calming, of cessation. Origination and

1. Translated from MI 167 ff.
2. This paragraph is not in the Chinese version.

cessation are in fact the second and third of the Four Truths: the theory of conditioned origination is the expansion of the second truth, how unhappiness, etc., originates; cessation follows as the corollary that if the conditions are removed their result does not originate, which is the third truth.

Teaching and Organising

The texts we were following last continue[1] with accounts of the Buddha's decision to teach. At this decisive moment, when the likelihood of his doctrine not being acceptable to others made the Buddha hesitate to teach, it is said in the Sthaviravāda version that Brahmā became aware of the situation and alarmed that the world would 'perish' because the doctrine was not taught. It appears strange that the God of Brahmanism should be brought in to guide the Buddha. The intention must have been to place the Buddha above Brahmā by making the latter appear in the role of a suppliant. As in other texts where Brahmā appears, the aim may have been satirical, making the supposed creator and master of the world afraid that his creation would perish unless the Buddha saved it.

Brahmā comes down from his heaven and appears before the Buddha, saluting him reverently, and assures him that there will be some who can grasp the doctrine. He complains that an impure doctrine has appeared in Magadha, which does not lead to not dying (*amṛta*), and consequently asks the Buddha to teach. Then the Buddha, on account of his compassion for beings (a significant *motif*), surveys the world with his Buddha's insight and sees the varying qualities and faculties of beings, some of whom may be able to understand the doctrine.

Considering to whom he might first teach his doctrine, the Buddha thinks of Ārāḍa and Udraka, but is told by deities (or spirits, *devatā*) that both have recently died. He then thinks of five companions of his in his wanderings and ascetic practices before the enlightenment. He finds by his insight that they are near Vārāṇasī (Benares) and resolves to go there. On the way he meets an Ājīvaka named Upaka, who remarks on his happy, contented appearance and asks whose doctrine he follows. The Buddha replies that he has no teacher, that he

1. M I 168 ff=T 26 k. 56, 777-78.

is freed, the influences being exhausted in him, that he is enlightened. The Ājīvaka is sceptical, saying 'It may be so', shaking his head and going away by a different road (this can also be interpreted as by a wrong road: the ambiguity is no doubt deliberate, the reaction of the Ājīvaka symbolising that of all those who were not ready to understand the new doctrine).

The Buddha finds his former companions in a park (now called Sārnāth) near Vārāṇasī. They first resolve to treat him without respect because he had given up the severe ascetic practices he was formerly following with them and relapsed into a life they regard as worldly. This refers to the tradition of the extreme asceticism tried out by the future Buddha, which he eventually gave up as useless, attaining enlightenment whilst living moderately and taking a reasonable amount of food. The tradition does not occur in the texts we have so far followed, except by implication here, though it is found in many later ones.

On the Buddha's approach, however, the five former companions receive him with respect in spite of themselves and become his pupils. He tells them how (as described above) having the principle of birth and discovered its disadvantage he has acquired extinction. Knowledge then arose in them, and insight: our freedom is certain, this is our last birth, now there is no rebirth.

From this point we follow some other texts in order to obtain a consensus of opinion among the schools as to how the doctrine was first elaborated. We are now concerned not with events narrated by the Buddha and afterwards remembered by his followers but with the events of his career as a teacher as directly remembered by them and recorded in the *Tripiṭaka*. The Sthaviravāda recension of the latter contains in its *Sūtra* section[1] a record of the 'starting of the wheel of the doctrine'. A similar account is given in the *Vinaya* section[2] of the same recension, where it is embedded in a continuous narrative of the events after the enlightenment. Corresponding parts of the *Vinaya* according to three other schools (Sarvāstivāda, Mahīśāsaka and Dharmaguptaka), their recensions being extant

1. S V 420 ff. Sanskrit fragments *Turfan* 581.
2. Vin I 10 f.

in Chinese translations,[1] give very similar accounts of this whole narrative. These schools all belong to the Sthaviravāda group. For the other great group of early schools, the Mahāsaṃghika, we have to turn to a much later text which was included in the *Vinaya* of one of its schools, the *Mahāvastu* of the Lokottaravāda, which is available in its original language. Though it is presumably much later than the original *Vinaya* of the Mahāsaṃghikas (which is extant in Chinese and which does not contain this narrative) it helps to show that the narrative was widely accepted among the early schools (the *Sūtra* section of the Mahāsaṃghika recensions of the *Tripiṭaka* is not available to us). We now follow the Sthaviravāda *Sūtra*.

'There (in the park near Vārāṇasī) the Master ('Bhagavant', i.e. the Buddha) addressed the group of five monks: These two extremes, monks, ought not to be pursued by one who has gone forth (from home, from 'the world'). Which two? That which is among passions, practising the enjoyment of passions, inferior, vulgar, common, barbarian, not connected with welfare; and that which is devoted to weariness of oneself, unhappy, barbarian, not connected with welfare. Monks, not going to either of these extremes the intermediate way, illuminated by the thus-gone (*tathāgata*, i.e. the Buddha), making insight, making knowledge, leads to calm, to insight, to enlightenment, to extinction (*nirvāṇa*). And which, monks, is that intermediate way illuminated by the thus-gone...? It is just the excellent way having eight factors, as follows: right theory, right intention, right speech, right action, right livelihood, right exercise, right self-possession, right concentration.'

The avoidance of the two extremes, of 'wearying' oneself (i.e. asceticism) as well as of passions, is obviously appropriate as a reply to the criticism of his companions that the Buddha had relapsed. The eightfold way which is intermediate between these extremes is the fourth truth, the way leading to cessation, which has been mentioned above. The texts next go on to elaborate the Four Truths themselves: this we can leave until we come to study the doctrine.

From this point until the last days of the Buddha we have to rely on the *Vinaya* section of the *Tripiṭaka*. The recensions mentioned above give a continuous narrative of the organisation

1. T 1435, T 1421 and T 1428 respectively.

of the communities of Buddhist monks, and of some other events, for a short period after the starting of the wheel of the doctrine. They then change to an arrangement by topics of the organisation and discipline, instead of a chronological arrangement. The *Mahāvastu* has parallel accounts of several of the early events, but does not concern itself with organisation or discipline to any extent. The arrangement by topics of these matters is supplied for the Mahāsaṃghika school by the *Skandhaka* book of their *Vinaya*, which is generally similar to the Sthaviravāda *Khandhaka* books apart from the absence of the opening narrative part of the latter.

The Sthaviravāda and Lokottaravāda accounts[1] (which we follow as belonging to the most distantly related among those available; the other schools whose accounts are available support them) agree that afterwards the Buddha addressed his five followers again with a much more difficult discourse. It concerned the doctrine of *anātman*, 'non-self', also translatable 'non-soul' (since the brahmans, at least, often use *ātman* in the latter sense), and the analysis of experience into five groups or categories (*skandha*): matter, emotion, perception, forces (energy), consciousness. Each of the groups is said to be *anātman*, non-self, because one cannot control it, saying 'Let it be thus...' We shall discuss this doctrine in a later chapter.

The accounts next give a dialogue between the Buddha and the monks: 'What do you think, monks, is matter permanent or impermanent? —Impermanent, sir. —But if it is impermanent is it unhappiness or happiness?[2] —Unhappiness, sir. —But if it is impermanent, unhappiness, having the principle of change, is it proper to envisage it as This is mine, I am this, This is my self (*ātman*)? —It certainly is not, sir. —In this case, therefore, monks, whatever is matter, whether past, future or present, internal or external, gross or subtle, inferior or superior, far away or in one's presence, all matter should be seen in its true nature with right understanding as This is not mine, I am not this, This is not my self.' The dialogue continues with the other groups, from emotion to consciousness,

1. Vin I 13 ff and *Mahāvastu* III 335 ff. Also S III 66 ff.

2. We follow the Sthaviravāda version; the Lokottaravāda gives the same words but inserts some other passages among them by way of comment.

substituted for matter, the replies being the same. The Buddha concludes that the good pupil, who learns from what he hears, seeing thus will be indifferent to matter, emotion, perception, forces and consciousness, being indifferent he will become dispassionate, through dispassion he will become free, he will have knowledge that he is freed in what is freed. He will understand that birth is exhausted, the best life has been properly lived, the business has been done, afterwards there will be no more of this world. The five monks all became freed after this dialogue.

From here the continuous accounts (the *Mahāvastu* is not continuous and not in chronological sequence and does not have most of the episodes which follow) describe the recruiting of more monks to the Buddhist community by the Buddha. Many young men of the merchant class in Vārāṇasī leave 'the world' to follow the Buddha. The parents and wife of one of these become lay disciples, thus establishing another branch of the community: those in the world who by giving alms to the monks become a regular source of support for them. When he has sixty monks the Buddha sends them out in all directions to teach.

After this the organisation of the community becomes more complicated. In the first place the Buddha delegates to his monks the right to admit recruits to the community. After this it becomes necessary from time to time to impose restrictions on entry: the candidates must have certain qualifications. It became important to avoid clashes with secular authority and law, as well as to prevent people joining for entirely wrong motives. For example a story is told (on a much later occasion, after the Buddha has gone to Magadha) that King Bimbisāra ordered his generals to march out to quell some trouble on the borders. Some of the soldiers decide that it is a bad thing to fight, desert the army and join the Buddhist community. It is of course a serious crime by secular law to aid and abet desertion, and the King lodges a complaint, whereupon the Buddha promulgates a rule that those in the royal service may not be admitted to the community. It is also found necessary to make rules against admitting persons suffering from certain diseases and deformities. Slaves may not be admitted unless first released from slavery, otherwise again there will be trouble with the secular law. Thieves, debtors and murderers are excluded when they seek to evade the consequences of their actions by 'leaving the world'. As a rule anyone under the age of twenty is not to be admitted.

After the events in Vārāṇasī the Buddha returned to Uruvilvā in Magadha. Here the *Vinaya* in its different recensions (confirmed by the *Mahāvastu*) narrates a strange event when the Buddha meets three ascetics with matted hair (*jaṭilas*), all of the Kāśyapa clan and each having numerous followers. The Buddha asks to stay the night in Uruvilvā Kāśyapa's fire temple (the ascetic is apparently an orthodox brahman maintaining a sacred fire). The ascetic objects on the ground that there is a dangerous dragon (*nāga*) there. The Buddha is not afraid of dragons and insists, the ascetic giving way. The dragon tries to overcome the Buddha by breathing forth fire and smoke, but the Buddha is too powerful for him and subdues him. Convinced of the marvellous power of the Buddha the three Kāśyapas and their followers join the Buddha's community.

The Buddha next goes on to Rājagṛha, the capital of Magadha, invited by King Bimbisāra. The King is pleased with the Buddha's teaching and becomes a lay disciple. According to the Sthaviravāda *Vinaya* he then presents a park for the use of the Buddhist community.

Next follows (confirmed by the *Mahāvastu*) the story of how the Buddha gained his two best followers, Śāriputra and Maudgalyāyana.[1] A wanderer named Sañjayin, whom the *Mahāvastu* (but not the texts of the other schools) identifies with the leader of the Agnostics, was staying in Rājagṛha with some of his followers. Among the latter were Śāriputra and Maudgalyāyana, who were great friends. Śāriputra met one of the Buddhist monks, was most impressed by his calm and pleasant bearing, and asked him who his teacher was and what his doctrine. The monk says that he has not learned much of the doctrine but can state the meaning (*artha*) of it very briefly. Śāriputra was brilliant of intellect and did not need any elaborate explanations, a hint of the doctrine would be enough to give him insight into it. So he asked for just the

1. Vin I 39 ff., *Mahāvastu* III 56 ff.

meaning without elaboration. The monk tells him the Master teaches the origination of principles from causes.

This is enough to give Śāriputra insight into the doctrine. He at once tells Maudgalyāyana and they decide to go to the Buddha. They first tell Sañjayin, who refuses to go with them, but all the other followers of Sañjayin go. The Buddha welcomes the two friends to his community and says they will be his best pupils.

The Sthaviravāda and other *Vinayas* after this narrate further elaborations of the organisation of the community. Teachers (*upādhyāyas*) are instituted within the community to guide new monks in manners and decorum. More rules on admission are formulated, most of which were noticed above. It is in connection with these that a visit by the Buddha to Kapilavastu, the city of his birth, is narrated. The *Mahāvastu* describes[1] this visit at far greater length. Among its many episodes it confirms the only one noticed by the Sthaviravāda *Vinaya*, the going forth from the world of the Buddha's son Rāhula.

In the early texts we have examined there is no mention of the Buddha having had a son, but later accounts make much of this and of his marriage while he was living a luxurious and aristocratic life before the renunciation. The Sthaviravāda *Vinaya* says[2] simply that the Buddha went from Rājagṛha to Kapilavastu and there visited the house of his father, Śuddhodana the Śākya. Rāhula's mother then said to Rāhula: 'Rāhula, this is your father. Go and ask for your inheritance'. Rāhula does so. The Buddha turns to Śāriputra and tells him to let Rāhula go forth as a novice in the community.

At this point Śuddhodana asks for a boon from the Buddha. When the future Buddha left home Śuddhodana was very unhappy, likewise when his other son Nanda (the Buddha's half-brother) left (he too is elsewhere recorded to have joined the community of monks) and now Rāhula is leaving he is exceedingly unhappy (the Commentary notes that the family line will be cut off, this is what Śuddhodana is thinking). Affection for one's son cuts into the skin, the flesh, even into the

1. III 90 ff. (the episode of Rāhula at 142 f.).
2. Vin I 82.

marrow of one's bones. He therefore asks that the community should not admit a son without the consent of his father and mother. The Buddha agrees to this and adds it to the rules.

Rules of training for the novices are next laid down, and punishment for their infringement. The punishment consists merely of putting certain places temporarily out of bounds for an offender, except in case of a very serious offence, for which he can be expelled from the community. Monks also could be expelled if it was found that they had been admitted without proper qualifications or for wrong motives. After giving many instances of irregular procedures the Sthaviravāda *Vinaya* has the Buddha lay down the full formal procedure (*karman*, 'action') for entrance (*upasampadā*) into the community (this is the second and final stage of joining, the first being the 'going forth' from the world).

At various places rules governing formal procedures by the Buddhist community are worked out. It becomes clear that this community consists simply of any number of small groups in different localities. If these number twenty or more monks they are fully autonomous and can perform any 'action', if they are smaller than that there are some actions which they cannot legally perform. These communities were defined by demarcating boundaries within which certain individuals were normally resident, and which were narrow enough to permit the whole of each community to meet in one place regularly without difficulty. To be legally valid, any action taken by a community must be approved when it is complete: all members must be present except in very exceptional circumstances, such as illness, when an opinion or vote could be conveyed by proxy. The business of these meetings was made effective in the form of resolutions, which had to be approved unanimously to be valid. It is laid down that every endeavour should be made, by argument and compromise and conciliation of dissident opinions, to attain this unanimity. Failure in this would threaten the community with a schism, which was regarded as extremely dangerous. No higher authority than the separate communities was set up, other than the Buddha himself as long as he lived and the doctrine and discipline as promulgated by him. It was the doctrine which the Buddha intended to be the sole authority: even the discipline he thought should be subject to modification by the community if they thought fit after his *parinirvāṇa* (by the entire community in this case, probably), though in the event this right was not taken advantage of by his followers.

It was in connection with the organisation of the separate communities that King Bimbisāra is recorded to have suggested that the Buddhist monks should observe the ceremony of *poṣadha*, a kind of sabbath day, or rather night, traditionally observed by communities of *śramaṇas*. On the eighth, fourteenth and fifteenth nights of each lunar half month each community would assemble for discussions on the doctrine (the assembly thus took place at the full Moon and at weekly intervals thereafter).

Whereas the events up to the visit to Kapilavastu appear to have taken place within the first year after the enlightenment, the institution of the *poṣadha* seems to have been approved by the Buddha somewhat later. It is stated that some time after the *poṣadha* was instituted the Buddha proposed that the monks should recite their rules of training at the ceremony. Now in that book of the *Vinaya* where these rules are collected and laid down there is an introductory narrative[1] in which Śāriputra asks the Buddha to formulate a code of discipline so that the best life may last long (the occasion was during a shortage of food, when the possibility of Buddhism being brought to an end, as by starvation of the monks, was discussed: Śāriputra thought that the monks should be restrained from offensive behaviour by listing a code of offences, and that the result would be that the community would long enjoy the support of the laity, even in difficult times). The Buddha, however, decides to wait for offences actually to occur before attempting to formulate a code. In the event, the first offence noticed by the Buddha occurs in Vaiśālī (capital of Vṛji), and according to the code of the Lokottaravāda school[2] it happened in the fifth year of the teaching (after the enlightenment). Thereafter other offences took place in the fifth and sixth years and later, and were gradually added to the code.

1. In the Sthaviravāda version Vin III 3 ff.

2. *The Prātimokṣa-Sūtra of the Māhāsaṅghikas* (—Lokottaravādins), edited by Pachow and Mishra, Allahabad, 1956, p. 5 of the text. But *Sāratthadīpanī* (I p. 401) gives year 12 for the first minor offence and 20 for the first major one (cf. Vin A I p. 213).

If we follow this chronology the proposal to recite the code could not have been made until at least the fifth year of the teaching. The *poṣadha* ceremony itself may not long have preceded the institution of the recital. The code of offences to be avoided by the monks is called the 'liberation' (*prātimokṣa*). Either before or at each ceremonial recitation any monk who had committed any offence listed was required to confess it. The object of this was that the monks would both be restrained from committing offences and relieved from remorse after committing an offence by undergoing the appropriate punishment. The four most serious offences entailed expulsion from the community. The remainder were punished by the disgrace of a period of probation, or temporary suspension from full membership of the community, or simply of public confession. There was no question of any kind of physical punishment. Once the 'liberation' had been recited and any offences dealt with, a community could consider itself 'pure' and fit to transact other business.

There seems to be no chronological arrangement in the accounts of the laying down of further rules of organisation and discipline in the *Vinaya*. It was probably fairly early that the rule of residence in one place for the Rains was made. Travel was difficult in that season, and, what was more to the point, travellers were liable to damage crops when roads were impassable. The various Buddhist communities were therefore required to remain stationary during the Rains, each monk remaining for at least three months (a Sthaviravāda commentary notes that the exact prescription of the period was made twenty years after the enlightenment[1]). This period of residence for monks who previously had wandered at large at least within the limits of the territory of their community (and they might freely wander elsewhere as well) led naturally to the use of buildings. The trend was for dwellings for whole communities to be built together, eventually, therefore for permanent 'monasteries' to be established. How far this went during the lifetime of the Buddha is not known, but the *Vinaya* records very detailed rules governing the types of buildings allowable, their furniture and equipment and proper behaviour in them.

1. AA II 97.

The main groups of rules remaining concern the dress of the monks and their food and medicine.

At the end of these topics of organisation an important event is narrated which presumably took place later in the Buddha's teaching career. This is the institution of a community of nuns. It was at Vaiśālī[1] that the Buddha agreed to this, reluctantly we are told, at the request of his aunt Mahāprajāpatī, who became the leader of the women's community. The Buddha apparently feared that this community was liable to bring ill repute on his whole organisation and result in a premature end to Buddhism. In the hope of offsetting this danger he promulgated additional rules to restrict the nuns and made them strictly subordinate to the monks.

Before we leave the *Vinaya* it is worth noting the evidence it provides as to the character of the Buddha. The promulgation of rules of discipline is clearly not the primary concern of the teacher, who is shown reluctant to formulate rules and willing to have the less important ones abolished.[2] He is always most ready to take extenuating circumstances into consideration, particularly illness, including mental illness. It is the doctrine and the 'excellent way having eight factors' which the Buddha is concerned with, and restraint and discipline ought to follow automatically from the latter without separate prescription. In fact the motive for formulating disciplinary rules is very frequently said to be public opinion, of the laity whether Buddhist or non-Buddhist: the outward conduct of the community should be such as to inspire confidence and respect, even though it may concern trivial matters such as dress which have no bearing on the practice of the way. In some cases, of course, rules have to be promulgated to check the behaviour of those who have no real vocation for the 'best life', who may have joined the community for wrong or confused motives.

Two episodes in the *Vinaya* delineate very clearly the attitude of the Buddha, his fundamental tolerance and compassion, which are found everywhere in his teaching and are here exemplified in practice. In the first[3] a general named

1. Śrāvastī, Lokottaravāda (Roth p. 6).
2. This willingness is recorded in a *Sūtra* text, D II 154.
3. Vin I 232 ff, especially p. 235.

Siṃha, of Vṛji, a lavish patron of the Jainas, hears the Buddha praised when the latter visits Vaiśālī and decides to go himself to see him. Siṃha is so pleased with the Buddha that he asks to be accepted by him as a lay disciple. In accepting him, the Buddha urges him not to withdraw the regular alms which he has long been giving to the Jainas.

The second episode[1] concerns a monk suffering from dysentery. The Buddha wandering round a dwelling-place of the community with his most faithful attendant Ānanda (his cousin) sees the sick monk lying helpless in his own excrement. He approaches and asks him: 'What is your illness, monk ?'. The monk says: 'I have a disorder of the stomach, Master'. 'Then have you an attendant, monk ?' 'No, Master'. 'Now why do the monks not attend to you ?' 'I do nothing for the monks, sir, therefore the monks do not attend to me.' Then the Master addressed the venerable Ānanda: 'Go Ānanda, bring water, we will bathe this monk.' 'Yes, sir.' Having assented to the Master the venerable Ānanda brought water. The master poured water and Ānanda washed him thoroughly, then the master seized the monk by the head and the venerable Ānanda took him by the feet and they lifted him up and put him on a bed. Then the Master because of this, in this connection, had the community of monks assemble and questioned the monks: 'Monks, is there in such and such a dwelling a monk who is ill ?' 'There is, Master.' 'What is the illness of that monk, monks ?' 'That venerable one is ill with a disorder of the stomach, sir.' 'Now has that monk an attendant, monks ?' 'No, master.' 'Now why do the monks not attend to him ?' 'That monk, sir, does nothing for the monks, therefore the monks do not attend to him.' 'Monks, you have no mother, no father, who might attend to you. If you do not attend to one another then who will attend to you ? Monks, he who would attend on me, he should attend to one who is ill.'

Despite his care in organising the community the Buddha was faced with very serious internal trouble in it towards the end of his career. From later Buddhist histories we learn that King Bimbisāra of Magadha was succeeded by his son Ajātaśatru

1. Vin I 301 f.

eight years before the *parinirvāṇa*, which would be 494 B.C. A little before this Devadatta, a cousin of the Buddha who had joined his community, conceived the ambition of becoming the leader of the monks himself. The story is told in the *Vinaya*[1] in connection with the legislation to prevent schisms and partly in the *Mahāvastu* (which, however, has little but embellishments to the main story) and in some Sarvāstivāda texts.[2]

Devadatta suggests to the Buddha that as he is now old he should retire and let Devadatta lead the community.[3] The Buddha refuses. Devadatta is a friend of Prince Ajātaśatru, and, annoyed by the Buddha's refusal and especially by the latter's having the community warned against him, he confides in the Prince and solicits his sympathy. He suggests that the Prince is in a similar position, waiting to become king. Suppose the Prince were to kill the King and Devadatta were to kill the Buddha, then they could be king and *buddha* themselves. Ajātaśatru agrees and attempts to assassinate his father. He is foiled by the ministers, but Bimbisāra, on learning from his son that he wants the kingdom, abdicates and Ajātaśatru becomes king. Devadatta then asks him to have the Buddha killed. Ajātaśatru sends assassins but they fail. In the Buddha's presence they become his lay disciples instead. Devadatta then tries himself to kill the Buddha by rolling a stone down a mountainside onto him. The Buddha escapes with an injury to his foot. When all violent attempts fail Devadatta makes a schism in the community by proposing stricter discipline: the monks should live only in the forest and not come to the villages, they should wear only rags and not accept gifts of robes, nor should they accept invitations to meals but only alms in their begging bowls, they should live in the open and not in dwellings, they should be vegetarians (the Buddha allowed whatever food was given, provided animals were not specially killed to provide alms food). The Buddha rules that any monk who wishes may follow these

1. Vin II 184 ff.

2. For references see Edgerton's *Dictionary*, p. 271; add the Mūlasarvāstivāda *Vinaya*, Gilgit MS., section edited by Gnoli and Venkatacharya.

3. Vin II 188.

suggestions, but refuses to make them obligatory. Devadatta thereupon makes a schism, being supported by some other monks.

There is a little later evidence that Devadatta had some success, and that his schismatic community survived for several centuries. If so it would appear that the accounts of his violence and involvement in political plots are exaggerated by the partisans of the Buddha who record them. Whatever the truth, Devadatta's ambitions caused a serious crisis in the Buddhist community. At one time according to the *Vinaya*[1] five hundred monks followed him, though Śāriputra is supposed to have brought them back again. Later accounts[2] make Devadatta die before the Buddha. As for Ajātaśatru, having gained his object he sought to consolidate his position and even to befriend the Buddha, as we read in the *Sūtra*.

The *Sūtra* section of the *Tripiṭaka* contains innumerable scattered episodes in the teaching of the Buddha, from which we can take only a few significant points here. In many of the texts, especially the shorter ones, the Buddha is speaking to his monks, but in a considerable number, particularly among the longer texts, he meets brahmans, other *śramaṇas*, kings and nobles and men and women of many different professions in the cities (most of the dialogues take place in, or on the outskirts of, the great cities of the Ganges plain, especially Śrāvastī the capital of Kośala, then the biggest Ganges kingdom). To those living 'in the world' and not expected yet to renounce it the Buddha recommends social virtues and good friendship, as promoting the happiness of those practising them as well as of those with whom they live and work. Humour abounds in his discourse, for example when he narrates stories to illustrate the degeneration of society resulting from the attempts of kings to prevent crime[3], in the irony with which he discusses the practices and beliefs of the brahmans,[4] or when he describes the pompous humbug of 'God' (Brahmā), who pretends to be all-powerful and omniscient and claims to have created

1. Vin II 199.
2. See DPPN I, p. 1110, for references.
3. D No. 26=T 1 No. 6, p. 167 below.
4. D Nos. 3, 4, 5, 13, 25 (an ascetic not necessarily a brahman) and 27=T 1 Nos. 20, 22, 23, 26, 8 and 5. cf. pp. 162, 177 below.

the universe, but is chiefly concerned to avoid having his ignorance exposed in public.[1]

The all-pervading element in the character of the Buddha as illustrated in the dialogues, however, is his calm, his peaceful, unsentimental quest for truth, his self-possessed exemplification of the intermediate way he teaches, his unpretentious but rigorous questioning of those he meets, in order to elucidate the truth from them, in preference to lecturing to them. It is almost superfluous to say that the whole approach is intellectual, not emotional. However, the element of compassion must not be overlooked, though not dominant it would seem to be essential. It is presented as the motive for all the Buddha's teaching and organising, it inspires the moral teaching although the latter is also intellectually grounded: compassion and concern for the welfare of all living beings is frequently spoken of. A certain form of meditation is often spoken of by the Buddha, and recommended for laymen and monks (used to get rid of the 'obstacles') alike, consisting in pervading the four directions successively with thought charged with 'loving kindness' (or 'benevolence', *maitrā*), with compassion, with sympathetic joy (i.e. joy at the well-being of others, of those who are fortunate) and with equanimity. Through considering all beings as like oneself (*sarvātmatā*, i.e. putting oneself in the place of others) one should make the thought, thus charged, sublime and immeasurable so that it pervades the whole universe.[2]

It is most characteristic of the Buddha that he always adapts his talk to the person he is conversing with. His courtesy in argument results from this: it is certainly not his way to denounce the opinions and practices of another to his face and challenge him to justify them. His method rather is to seem to adopt the other's point of view and then by question and answer to improve on it until a position compatible with his own has been arrived at. Thus he leads his partner in discussion towards the truth as he has discovered it, but so that the partner seems

1. D No. 11, also No. 1 (pp. 17 ff.) =T No. 24, also No. 21, p. 154 below.

2. For references see PTC under *appamāṇa*, contexts *cetasā vipulena mahaggatena appamāṇena*. Chinese e.g. T 99 section 27 No. 32.

himself to continue his own quest, in whatever form it had taken, and to arrive at higher truths than he had previously been aware of, or more convincing moral ideas. The method is well illustrated by the numerous discussions with brahmans, for example all but one of the dialogues referred to above to exemplify irony (the odd one is a similar dialogue with an ascetic, who may or may not be a brahman). Among them will be found expressed several times the Buddha's criticism of the system of hereditary social classes (the so called 'castes'), especially of the hereditary priesthood of the brahmans themselves: in these dialogues brahmans are shown as led on to admit that the real brahman is he who is a brahman by character, not by birth.

Among the latest of the dialogues is presumably that in which the Buddha is visited by King Ajātaśatru, the latter having consolidated his position after his father's abdication (the unhappy Bimbisāra was imprisoned and then left to starve, according to the Sthaviravāda commentary on this dialogue).[1]

One full Moon night (the traditional time for meditation and philosophical discussion in ancient India, as well as certain religious ceremonies, and the chief *poṣadha* night of the Buddhists, as noticed above) the King feels exaltation as he sits on the flat roof of his palace with his ministers. He proposes to visit some brahman or *śramaṇa* who may set his thoughts at peace, and invites suggestions. Some of the ministers suggest in turn three Ājīvaka teachers and one each of the Lokāyata, Agnostic and Jaina schools. The King greets all these proposals with silence. Then a doctor named Jīvaka suggests the Buddha (Jīvaka's story is told at some length in the *Vinaya*; he gave medical treatment to the monks and supported them by gifts). Ajātaśatru agrees and sets out in state, riding an elephant and with a large escort, for Jīvaka's mango wood (near Rājagṛha), where the Buddha is staying with a large community of monks.

As they approach in the dark the King becomes apprehensive of a trap, thinking presumably of his past support for Devadatta. The mango wood is perfectly still: although there should be several hundred monks there not a cough can be

1. D No. 2=T I No. 27. Commentary DA 132 ff. MSV Gilgit III part 4, 213 ff. and in the part Professoir Tucc is publishing.

heard. Jīvaka reassures him by pointing out that lamps are burning in the pavilion. The King dismounts from his elephant and goes on into the pavilion. Jīvaka points out the Master sitting against the central column, facing East with the community of monks in front of him. Ajātaśatru stands to one side after approaching the Buddha and contemplates the perfect silence of the community, like a perfectly clear lake, and expresses the wish that Prince Udāyibhadra might acquire the same calm as the community (the Prince is his son and heir and Ajātaśatru evidently fears he might have inherited his own impatience to become king). According to the commentary the King does not express this aloud, but the Buddha divines his thoughts. The Master remarks somewhat cryptically to the King that the latter has followed his affections (meaning, the commentary says, that seeing the community he has followed his affection, just as water flows downhill). The King says that Prince Udāyibhadra is dear to him, and repeats his wish. Then he salutes the Master and the community and sits down.

Ajātaśatru asks leave to put a question for the Buddha to explain. The question is that whereas the various secular professions produce visible results, making their practitioners happy and pleased, as well as their families and friends, moreover making possible donations to brahmans and *śramaṇas*, which should be conducive to attaining heaven, what is the visible result of being a *śramaṇa*, if any ? The Buddha asks if he has tried this question on others, and what replies he got, and the King tells him the replies of the six teachers of various schools his ministers had mentioned at the beginning of this dialogue, all of whom he had visited before. All the replies are presented as irrelevant to the question: the teachers had propounded some of their special doctrines, their theories and in the case of the Jaina his practice, but no result is mentioned except that the Ājīvakas say it doesn't matter what you do, you will experience happiness and unhappiness according to fate, and actually nothing can happen to the seven elements, whilst the Lokāyata philosopher is made to say only that we all die anyway and that is the end for fools and wise men alike. The Agnostic for obvious reasons evades the question and says he wouldn't give an answer even if he had one.

The Buddha then offers his reply. First, suppose a slave of the King were able to join a *śramaṇa* community, having thought 'I am a man, the same as the King, why shouldn't I be free ?', wouldn't it be a visible result if afterwards the King greeted him with respect as a free man ? The King agrees. He agrees also that a peasant householder, paying taxes and increasing the treasury, would be more contented and more respected if he became a wanderer. The Buddha then describes how such a recruit might be trained under a *buddha*, in self-possession, contentment, compassion and so on, and would feel free and happy as he meditated. The King agrees that this too is a visible result, and afterwards the Buddha works up through various kinds of meditation to the acquisition of the 'sciences', including the Four Truths and knowledge that the influences have been exhausted, that one is freed from transmigration. The King agrees that all these are visible results, each better than the last.

Pleased with the reply, Ajātaśatru asks to become a lay Buddhist, adding that he had been a fool, acted badly in taking his just father's life for the sake of sovereignty. Would the Master accept his confession for the sake of restraint in future ? The Buddha says that since the King sees it as a transgression and confesses it truthfully he can accept it.

The King then takes his leave. The Buddha remarks to the monks that the King was wounded and afflicted: if he did not have such a crime on his conscience he would have understood the doctrine.

The Last Months and the Parinirvāṇa

The final episodes of the Buddha's life are narrated at some length in the *Mahāparinirvāṇa Sūtra* of the *Sūtra* section of the *Tripiṭaka*. This is available to us in several recensions.[1] Here we shall follow the Sthaviravāda, as the best preserved, omitting anything not confirmed by other versions. The main episodes are translated, with a minimum of comment and continuity.

1. D No. 16=T 1 No. 2, other Chinese versions are T 5 (diverges from the Pali), T 6 and T 7 (both closer); MPS (Waldschmidt) is the Sarvāstivāda version in Sanskrit (parallel texts from the *Vinaya* of that school in its Tibetan and Chinese versions are also given).

The text begins with the Buddha staying in Rājagṛha. At that time King Ajātaśatru was planning to attack Vṛji. Before doing so he sent his minister Varṣākāra to the Buddha, to present his compliments and good wishes, inform the Master of the proposed invasion and report any comments he might make, since what he said would not be untrue. Varṣākāra carries out this extraordinary mission to the champion of non-violence, finding him (sitting) with Ānanda standing behind fanning him. The Master turns to Ānanda :

'Have you heard, Ānanda, whether the Vṛjis have frequent assemblies, are devoted to the Assembly ? —I have heard so... sir. —As long as the Vṛjis have frequent assemblies, are devoted to the Assembly, increase can be expected for them, not decline. Have you heard, Ānanda, whether the Vṛjis assemble in unanimity, rise in unanimity, carry out the Vṛji business in unanimity ? —I have... —As long...increase can be expected for them, not decline. Have you heard whether the Vṛjis do not authorise what has not been authorised, do not abolish what has been authorised, proceed conforming to the Vṛji principles as authorised in ancient tradition ? —I have ... —Have you heard whether the Vṛjis entertain, give respect to, revere, honour those among them who are elders and consider them worth listening to ? I have... —Have you heard whether the Vṛjis do not drag away the women and girls of the tribes and force them to live with them ? —I have heard that they do not... —Have you heard whether the Vṛjis entertain, give respect to, revere, honour the shrines of the Vṛjis, at home and elsewhere, and do not rescind the just tithe given before, made before ? —I have... —Have you heard whether as regards the 'worthy ones' (*arhant*, used by the Buddhists for the 'perfected one' who has acquired enlightenment, attained extinction, in the *Tripiṭaka* usually synonymous with *samyaksaṃbuddha*, 'perfectly enlightened', i.e. a title of the Buddha ; here apparently used in a wider sense or an older sense which is wider) of the Vṛjis the true safety and shelter and protection is properly arranged, that worthy ones may come to the country in future and those already there may live comfortably in the country ? —I have...'

The Buddha tells Varṣākāra that he himself had taught the Vṛjis these seven principles leading to prosperity when in

Vaiśālī and that as long as they remain increase and not decline can be expected for the Vṛjis. The minister remarks that even one of these principles should accomplish this, not to speak of all seven. The Vṛjis are invincible in war, as far as King Ajātaśatru is concerned, except through propaganda, through making them divided and opposed to each other. He then takes his leave.

Soon afterwards the Buddha has all the monks in the vicinity assembled in the audience hall and lectures them on seven principles leading to prosperity for monks. These are based on those for the Vṛjis: frequent assemblies, unanimity in business, conformity to the training as it has been authorised, respect for the elders of the community and listening to them, not getting under the control of desires which lead to rebirth, preference for living in the forest and attention to their personal self-possession with the thought that congenial fellows in the best life may come and that those who have come already may live in comfort. The text continues with several more groups of seven principles, which however are specific to the Buddhist community, such as the seven factors of enlightenment (we shall meet these again below).

Some time after this the Buddha, with a large community of monks, leaves Rājagṛha and makes his way gradually towards the North and West, in fact towards the Vṛji Republic (the texts note a number of stages on the way). He in due course reaches the Ganges at the village of Pāṭaligrāmaka. Here he has a number of lay disciples, householders, who come to see him. To them he gives a different kind of lecture, on the question of virtue or good conduct,[1] as follows.

'Householders, there are these five disadvantages of bad character, of failure in virtue.[1] Which five ? The first disadvantage is that one of bad character, who has failed in virtue, incurs a great confiscation of property through negligence of his affairs ...The second is that a bad report of the fame (i.e. a report of the ill fame) is disseminated of one of bad character who has failed in virtue...The third is that whatever assembly he approaches, whether of warriors, priests (brahmans), house-

1. The Sarvāstivāda version speaks instead of 'care', 'non-negligence', but otherwise the points are practically the same.

holders or *śramaṇas*, one of bad character, who has failed in virtue, approaches diffident and shamefaced...The fourth is that one of bad character, who has failed in virtue, dies bewildered...The fifth is that after death, after the body splits up,one of bad character who has failed in virtue is reborn in misery, an evil destiny, ruin, purgatory. These are the five disadvantages of bad character, of failure in virtue.

'Householders, there are these five advantages in being virtuous, of success in virtue. Which five ? The first advantage is that one who is virtuous, who has succeeded in virtue, through care of his affairs acquires a great mass of property... The second is that a good report of his fame is disseminated... The third is that whatever assembly he approaches, whether of warriors, priests, householders or philosophers, he approaches confident, not shamefaced...The fourth is that he dies not bewildered...The fifth is that after death, after the body splits up, one who is virtuous, who has succeeded in virtue, is reborn in a good destiny, in a heaven world. These are the five advantages in being virtuous, of success in virtue.'

'Then the Master instructed, exhorted, excited and delighted the Pāṭaligrāmaka lay disciples for much of the night with doctrinal talk, and then dismissed them.' He spent the night in the local rest house at the invitation of the lay disciples of the village.

At that time the minister Varṣākāra (with another minister according to the Sthaviravāda version) was in Pāṭaligrāmaka 'building a city to repel the Vṛjis'. Evidently Ajātaśatru is on the defensive, convinced of the strength of the Vṛjis. Pāṭaligrāmaka was on the frontier, formed here by the River Ganges, in an important strategic position on the direct route between Rājagṛha and Vaiśālī and protected on one flank by a major tributary of the Ganges. Hence the decision to build a fortress there, in fact to build a walled city as a bastion and doubtless as a base for future operations across the river. In fact the village, renamed Pāṭaliputra, rapidly became a great city and a later king of Magadha transferred his capital there. When the rulers of Magadha extended their empire over almost the whole of India Pāṭaliputra became for a time the greatest metropolis India has ever seen. The Buddhists of the first century after the *parinirvāṇa* may perhaps be suspected of slightly embroidering this part of the narrative to connect their Master with the new and prosperous capital.

The text says that the various sites on the land where the city is to be built are occupied by deities or spirits (*devatā*), some superior, some intermediate, some inferior. There is some confusion between the versions, but it appears that the Buddha is able to see these deities occupying the sites and tells Ānanda that people of corresponding superior, intermediate and inferior rank will live in houses on these sites. He says it is as if the minister was taking counsel with the gods in building the city. He predicts that Pāṭaliputra (using the new name) will be the chief city and centre of commerce in the country of the Aryans and as far as trade extends, adding that there will be three dangers for it : from fire, from water (floods) and from internal dissensions.

The Buddha meets Varṣākāra again, and the minister invites him, with the community, to a meal the next day. The food is excellent. According to the Sarvāstivāda version the minister expresses the wish that through this alms to the community the deities of the city may long prosper and be happy : the gift is dedicated in their name. In the Sthaviravāda version also the Buddha expresses his appreciation in verses: in whatever place a wise man arranges his dwelling and feeds the virtuous, if he dedicates gifts to the gods (*devatās*) they, being honoured, will honour him; they will have compassion on him, like a mother on her own son, and a man when the gods (*devas*) have compassion will always see good fortune.

When the Buddha leaves, the minister follows him, with the idea that the place where he leaves the site will be named the Gautama Gate (Gautama being the Buddha's clan name) and the landing place from which he crosses the Ganges will be named the Gautama Ferry. The Buddha leaves (according to the Sarvāstivāda version by the West gate) and the gate by which he leaves is named accordingly. The versions differ about the details at the river crossing, but agree that the Buddha uses supernatural power so that he is not seen to cross the river at all. He vanishes on this side and rises up on the other side. The Sarvāstivāda version nevertheless says that that crossing place was named Gautama Ferry, whilst the Sthaviravāda version, which is more ancient, says only that the

Gautama Gate was named. The latter seems more to the point and helps to make the whole scene symbolic of the Buddha's attainment of the 'other side' of transmigration, i.e. extinction (*nirvāṇa*), by the power of meditation. Here again we seem to see the text embellished and made more than a simple narrative. The Buddha is again made to recite a verse suited to the occasion : 'People make a causeway over the pools or bind together a raft, when they would cross the flood, the lake; wise men have (already) crossed over.' The meaning seems to be that while people struggle in the flood of transmigration the wise have renounced desire and attained extinction.

The Buddha then continues on his way through Vṛji. At various places on the way, in both Magadha and Vṛji, he gives discourses to the monks: the versions differ as to where each discourse was given, but in the course of the text mention the same places and the same talks. The latter include talk on the Four Truths and a lecture which is simply summarised under the headings: virtue, concentration, understanding; concentration penetrated with virtue has great results, great benefit; understanding penetrated with concentration has great results, great benefit (this clause not in Sarvāstivāda version); thought penetrated with understanding becomes perfectly free from the influences (Sarvāstivāda substitutes 'from passion, aversion and delusion'; Sthaviravāda adds 'to wit the influences of passion, desire for existence, opinion and ignorance'). At Nādikā the Buddha tells Ānanda that a disciple should have 'confidence founded in understanding' of the Buddha, the doctrine and the community.

In due course the Buddha reaches Vaiśālī, the Vṛji capital. Here he has many disciples, including the celebrated geisha Āmrapālī. At this period she was wealthy and of a respectable age, since she was famous already in the time of Bimbisāra and before Jīvaka (Bimbisāra's and then Ajātaśatru's court physician) was born, if we are to believe his story in the *Vinaya*. According to Sthaviravāda tradition she afterwards became a Buddhist nun, and a poem then composed by her is preserved in their *Tripiṭaka*. She hears that the Master has arrived in Vaiśālī and is staying in her mango wood, and drives out in a carriage to see him. He 'instructs, exhorts, excites and delights her with doctrinal talk', as is usual with lay disciples, then she invites him with the community to a meal the following day (cf. pp. 238-9 below).

The Licchavis (one of the tribes who confederated to form the Vṛji Republic, and the most important one, the founders of Vaiśālī itself) of Vaiśālī also heard of the Buddha's arrival and drove out to see him in their four divisions (clans ?), the blue, yellow, red and white (with chariots, clothes, weapons, ornaments, etc., of their own colours). When they appeared in the distance the Buddha said to the monks: those of you who have never seen the Thirty Three Gods (the gods of the *Veda*), look at the assembly of Licchavis, if you look at the Licchavi assembly you can visualise the assembly of the Thirty Three! On arrival the Licchavis receive the usual instruction but are disappointed when they seek to invite the Buddha, having been forestalled by Āmrapāli. They snapped their fingers: alas, we are defeated by the mango girl, alas, we are deceived by the mango girl!

The next day Āmrapāli herself serves the Buddha and the community. According to the Sthaviravāda text she then presents the mango park to the community, whilst the Sarvāstivāda text contents itself with praising her gift of the meal. The Buddha afterwards goes on to a village near Vaiśālī. There he tells the monks to prepare for the Rains, staying at different places all round Vaiśālī in groups of friends, himself staying in the village. According to the Sarvāstivāda version this scattering was a response to a severe famine which had occurred, but the Sthaviravāda tradition knows nothing of this, its commentary merely remarking that the village where the Buddha stayed could neither accommodate nor feed so many monks.

During the Rains the Buddha had a severe illness, with violent pains which seemed likely to be fatal. He accepted them with self-possession, thinking that it was not proper to attain extinction (final *nirvāṇa*) without addressing his followers, without taking leave of the community of monks. He then checked his illness with energy and it abated. When he had recovered he sat outside the dwelling. Ānanda expressed his concern: my body was as if drunk, I lost my bearings, I could not remember the doctrine, because of the Master's illness, nevertheless it would be some reassurance for me if I knew the Master would not attain extinction until he had promulgated something about the community of monks. The Buddha replied:

'What does the community of monks expect of me, Ānanda ? I have taught the doctrine without omission, without excluding anything. As to this, Ānanda, the thus-gone one (Buddha) does not have a 'teacher's fist' with reference to the doctrine (i.e. he does not keep anything back). If anyone should think that he should watch over the community of monks or that the community of monks should refer to him, then let him promulgate something about the community of monks. The thus-gone does not think that he should watch over the community of monks or that the community of monks should refer to him. Why should the thus-gone promulgate something about the community of monks ? Ānanda, I am now aged, old, an elder, my time has gone, I have arrived at the period of my life, which is eighty years. Just as an old cart is made to go by tying it together with bands, so I think the thus-gone's body is made to go by tying it together with bands. Ānanda, on an occasion when the thus-gone by withdrawing his attention from all signs, by the cessation of some emotions, enters into the signless concentration of thought and stays in it, on that occasion the thus-gone's body is made comfortable.

'Therefore Ānanda in this case you should live with yourselves as islands, with yourselves as refuges, with no one else as refuge; with the doctrine as an island, with the doctrine as a refuge, with no one else as refuge. And how, Ānanda, does a monk live with himself as an island, with himself as a refuge, with no one else as a refuge, with the doctrine as an island, with the doctrine as a refuge, with no one else as a refuge ? In this connection, Ānanda, a monk lives with reference to the body (or to substances generally) observing the body, energetic, conscious, self-possessed, having eliminated desire and aversion for the world; with reference to emotions observing emotions, energetic, conscious, self-possessed, having eliminated desire and aversion for the world; with reference to thought observing thought, energetic, conscious, self-possessed, having eliminated desire and aversion for the world; with reference to principles observing principles, energetic, conscious, self-possessed, having eliminated desire and aversion for the world. Thus a monk lives with himself as an island...with no one else as a refuge. Ānanda, those who live now, or will live after me, with themselves as islands, with themselves as refuges, with no one else as refuge; with the doctrine as an island, with the doctrine as a refuge, with no one else as refuge; they will be the highest of all my monks, whoever like the training.'

'Then the Master (the text continues) dressing in the morning and taking his bowl and (outer) robe entered Vaiśālī for alms. Having gone through Vaiśālī for alms, after his meal when he had returned from the alms collecting he addressed the venerable Ānanda : 'Ānanda, take the seat (i.e. the cloth which was spread for the Buddha to sit on), we will go to the Cāpāla Shrine for the siesta.' 'Yes, sir' the venerable Ānanda assented to the Master, took the seat and followed behind the Master. Then the Master went to the Cāpāla Shrine and sat down on the prepared seat. The venerable Ānanda saluted the Master and sat down at one side. The Master said to the venerable Ānanda as he sat at one side: 'Vaiśālī is delightful, Ānanda, ...the Cāpāla Shrine is delightful (he mentions other places in Vaiśālī or Vṛji as delightful also, mostly, perhaps all, shrines which were sacred trees).'

On this occasion, the text goes on, the Buddha spoke of the four 'bases of power' (which will be considered below) and hinted that if he applied these forces he could live longer, could go on even for an aeon. Ānanda however misses the hint and the opportunity (for which he is severely blamed by the community afterwards), and when Death (personified as Māra, the god of death and passion—which are equivalent in Buddhist doctrine) approaches him the Buddha agrees to enter final extinction, since he has completed his teaching. He tells Death he will enter final extinction three months from now. When he finally decides to get rid of his life forces there is an earthquake. An earthquake is supposed to be a portent of some unusual event, and this episode, though seemingly an embellishment of the simple narrative, is evidently ancient, since it occurs in the various versions of the text. The followers of the Buddha could not record the *parinirvāṇa* without mentioning an appropriate portent and having the Master comment on it. Ānanda asks why the Earth has quaked and the Buddha tells him the causes of earthquakes, leading up to this one. He says that the Earth quakes when a 'being for enlightenment' (*bodhisattva*) descends into his mother's womb and agáin when he is born. It quakes when a thus-gone attains enlightenment, when he starts the wheel of the doctrine, when he decides to get rid of his life forces and when he finally attains extinction.

Now Ānanda realises that he might have asked the Buddha to live longer when the possibility was hinted at, and begs him to live on for the happiness of mankind, but it is too late, the decision has been made. After this the text somewhat inconsistently makes the Buddha speak of impermanence as if he could not defy this natural law. It seems probable that the episode of the possibility of his living longer, the visit from Death, and Ānanda's supposed fault, together with the discussion of portents relating to a Buddha's life, was not originally part of the text, though it was inserted in it very early. We are already in the presence of the legend of the Buddha, rather than his life, which will develop from this embryo phase into the tremendous cosmic drama which inspired so much art in later centuries.

The Buddha then tells Ānanda to convene the monks in the audience hall (the Sarvāstivāda version places this at Cāpāla Shrine, but the Sthaviravāda has it in the famous Hall of the House with a Gable, in the Great Wood near Vaiśālī; this was a pillared hall with a private room for the Buddha above, the 'gable' being a high ridged and overhanging barrel-vaulted roof such as was characteristic of ancient India). The Buddha sits down on the seat prepared for him and addresses the monks.

'Monks, the principles which I have discovered and taught should be well learned by you, and practised, developed and cultivated, so that this best life should be enduring and last long for the benefit and happiness of many people, for compassion for the world, for the welfare, benefit and happiness of men and gods. And which are those principles...? They are as follows:

Four bases of self-possession,

Four right exertions,[1]

1. T 6 and T 7 clearly understood *pradhāna* here, agreeing with the Pali; the other Chinese versions understood *prahāṇa*, 'abandoning'.

Four bases of power,[1]
Five faculties,
Five strengths,
Seven factors of enlightenment,
The excellent eightfold way.'

We shall consider this summary of the Buddha's teaching in the next chapter. After giving it the Buddha leaves Vaiśālī for the last time and continues on his way from village to village. He speaks from time to time of virtue, concentration, understanding and freedom, but when he reaches the city of Bhoganagaraka he gives some apparently new instructions. It is the *Sūtra* and *Vinaya* which should be taken as the authority for what he has taught. Suppose a monk should claim to have heard something from the Master, or from a community, or from learned elder monks, it should be checked with the *Sūtra* and reviewed against the *Vinaya*. If it agrees with the *Sūtra* or the *Vinaya* it can be accepted as properly remembered, if not it is not the words of the Buddha and should be rejected.

The Buddha next goes on to Pāpā, capital of the small Southern Malla Republic, which was in the foothills of the Himālaya North-West of Vṛji. There he is met by the lay disciple Cunda, a smith, and invited with the monks to a meal. According to the Sthaviravāda version the Buddha becomes very ill after this, but the Sarvāstivāda text does not mention it. Immediately afterwards the Buddha continues on his way towards the city of Kuśinagarī, which is about three miles further on. Here his journey will end. Kuśinagarī was the capital of another small republican city state, that of the Northern Mallas, the two Mallas being separated by a river. On the way he meets Putkasa, a Malla minister who has been a lay disciple of Ārāḍa, the Buddha's first *śramaṇa* teacher. Putkasa is impressed by the Buddha's imperturbable concentration, believes it to be superior to Ārāḍa's and transfers his allegiance to the Buddha. He presents a pair of golden coloured robes to the Buddha, who wears them, but Ānanda thinks the Buddha's skin looks brighter. Later the Buddha thinks of Cunda, who is likely to feel regret that the Buddha should attain extinction after eating the meal given by him.

1. T 1 (p. 16 col. 3) and T 6 insert the 4 meditations after this.

He asks Ānanda to dispel this regret by telling Cunda that to have given the last meal before the *parinirvāṇa* is as good as to have given the last meal before the enlightenment.

After crossing the River Hiraṇyavatī the Buddha reaches the Upavartana Wood near Kuśinagarī (it was a wood of the tall *śāla* trees, *Shorea robusta*). Here Ānanda makes a bed between two trees, with the head to the North. The Buddha lies down on his right side, with one foot resting on the other, self-possessed and conscious. The monks gather round. The Master tells Ānanda not to grieve, and speaks of impermanence: it is impossible that what is born, synthesised, has the principle of decay, should not decay; everything dear and pleasing has the principle of varying, separating, changing. In the last watch of the night his *parinirvāṇa* will take place. He gives instructions that afterwards his body should be cremated. When an emperor dies his ashes are collected in an urn and a monument (*stūpa*, 'pagoda') is erected over it: the same should be done for a Buddha. The Buddha also tells Ānanda there are four places which are beautiful and inspiring for those trusting in him: the places where the thus-gone was born, where he attained enlightenment, where he started the wheel of the doctrine and where he attained final extinction (this text gave authority for pilgrimages to these places, which have been popular ever since).

Ānanda is sent to invite the Mallas of Kuśinagarī to see the Buddha before his final extinction. A wanderer named Subhadra was there and heard of this. He thought perhaps the Buddha could remove his doubt, went to the wood and asked Ānanda to let him speak to the Master. At first Ānanda refuses, thinking the Buddha should not be harassed with questions at this time. However, the Buddha overhears this discussion and asks Ānanda to let Subhadra see him. After greeting him Subhadra explains that there are many philosophers who lead and teach communities and are well thought of by many people, instancing some of the Ājīvakas and Ajita, Sañjayin and the leader of the Jainas. Have they all, or some of them, made discoveries with their assertions, or not? The Master tells him not to trouble about such things, but that in any doctrine and discipline in which the excellent eightfold way is found true *śramaṇas* will be found at various stages on the way to extinction, where it is not found they will not be found. In his doctrine it is found, and here there are true *śramaṇas*. The assertions of others are empty. Subhadra becomes the Buddha's last personal disciple and soon attained extinction. The text continues as follows.

'Then the Master addressed Ānanda: It might be that you would think, Ānanda, that the teaching has lost its teacher, our teacher does not exist. It should not be seen thus. The doctrine and discipline which I have taught and declared will be the teacher after me.

'Now at present the monks speak to each other using the expression 'sir !', they should not speak thus afterwards. A junior monk should be addressed by an elder monk by his name or clan or as 'sir !', an elder monk should be addressed by a junior monk as 'sir !', (*bhadanta*, a more polite expression) or as 'venerable'.[1]

'If it wishes, Ānanda, after me the community may abolish the more minor rules of training.

'The monk Chanda, Ānanda, should undergo the *brahma* punishment.—Which is the *brahma* punishment, sir? —Chanda, Ānanda, may say what he likes, but he should not be spoken to, admonished or instructed by the monks.

'Then the Master addressed the monks : It may be, monks, that some monk has doubt or perplexity about the Buddha, the doctrine, the community, the way or the practice. Ask, monks. Don't have regret afterwards, because your teacher was in your presence and you could not question the Master in his presence. When he had spoken thus those monks were silent. The Master addressed the monks a second and a third time...could not question the Master in his presence. For the third time those monks were silent. Then the Master addressed the monks: It may be, monks, that you do not ask out of respect for the teacher. So let a friend inform a friend. When he had spoken thus those monks were silent.

'Then the venerable Ānanda said this to the Master: It is surprising, sir, it is wonderful, sir. I am so confident in this community of monks, that there isn't one monk who has doubt

---

1. *āyasmant*, a term used also by Buddhist lay disciples in addressing one another.

or perplexity about the Buddha, the doctrine, the community, the way or the practice. —From confidence you speak, Ānanda. The thus-gone has actual knowledge that in this community of monks there isn't one monk who has doubt or perplexity about the Buddha, the doctrine, the community, the way or the practice. For of these five hundred monks, Ānanda, the last monk is 'in the stream', has the principle of non-ruin, is certain, is depending on complete enlightenment.

'Then the Master addressed the monks: Well, now monks I am addressing you. The forces have the nature of cessation. (You should succeed, through care.[1])

'This was the last speech of the thus-gone. Then the Master attained the first meditation. Coming out from the first he attained the second meditation. Coming out from the second he attained the third meditation. Coming out from the third he attained the fourth meditation. Coming out from that he attained the sphere of the infinity of space. Coming out from the attainment of the sphere of the infinity of space he attained the sphere of the infinity of consciousness. Coming out from that he attained the sphere of nothingness. Coming out from that he attained the sphere of neither perception nor non-perception. Coming out from that he attained the cessation of perception and emotion.[2]

'Then the venerable Ānanda said to the venerable Aniruddha: Aniruddha, is the Master extinct ? —Ānanda, the Master is not extinct, he has attained the cessation of perception and emotion. Then the Master came out from the attainment of the cessation of perception and emotion and attained the sphere of neither perception nor non-perception... (and continued through the attainments and meditations as before in reverse order down to the first meditation...) Coming out from the first meditation he attained the second meditation. Coming out from the second meditation he attained the third meditation. Coming out from the third meditation he attained the fourth meditation. Coming out from the fourth meditation the Master immediately attained extinction.'

1. Not in the Sarvāstivāda (Sanskrit) version. The Chinese versions vary, T 1 having a more elaborate exhortation to be careful.

2. Interpreted according to S IV 217 and A IV 409, cf. *AKBhāṣya* p. 72.

CHAPTER FOUR

THE DOCTRINE OF THE BUDDHA

The Buddha's Summary of his Principles Promulgated at Vaiśālī—Self-possession—Exertion—Power—The Faculties—The Strengths—Enlightenment—The Way—Practice and Truth

The Buddha's Summary of his Principles Promulgated at Vaiśālī

In following the final episodes of the Buddha's life according to the *Mahāparinirvāṇa Sūtra* we found that when in Vaiśālī on his way to Kuśinagarī he convened the monks and laid down what appears to be a summary of his teachings. This seems to have been a response to Ānanda's expression of concern that the Buddha might attain final extinction without 'promulgating something about the community.' The Buddha has explained that the doctrine should be the 'refuge' for the monks, and later he says it will be the teacher after he has gone. There is nothing else to 'promulgate'.

The Vaiśālī summary appears to have been common to all schools of Buddhism. Apart from the versions of the *Mahāparinirvāṇa Sūtra,* which give it such prominence, we find the same list of seven topics, from the four bases of self-possession to the excellent eightfold way, in many other texts of all known schools. The Mahāyāna schools are no exception; for example in the Madhyamaka theory of interpretation of the Perfection of Understanding *Sūtras* as teaching the way or practice of Buddhism, codified in the *Abhisamayālaṅkāra*, these seven topics, called here (and in many other texts) the thirty seven principles on the side of enlightenment, are an essential part of the omniscience of the Buddha, are the characteristics of enlightenment of the Buddha, of *bodhisattvas* and *śrāvakas*.[1] In the Vijñānavāda theory they are detailed in what is perhaps the most fundamental theoretical text of the school, the *Madhyāntavibhaṅga*, in its fourth chapter, most of which is devoted to them.

1. *Abhisamayālaṅkāra* topic (*artha*) 31. See p. 411 below.

That these topics constituted the basic doctrines of Buddhism as originally propounded by the Buddha seems to be confirmed by the history of the third section of the *Tripiṭaka*, the *Mātṛkā* or *Abhidharma*. As we noted in the Introduction above, discussing the *Mātṛkā*, the latter appears to have consisted at first of just these seven topics. Very likely the summary of the doctrine given by the Buddha at Vaiśālī gave rise to the idea of a *mātṛkā* and in due course to the various elaborations of it as *Abhidharma*.

It will not have been forgotten that in the description of the enlightenment and of the early teaching of the Buddha the Four Truths are prominent, and they are probably the most frequently occurring points made in the discourses of the Buddha. The texts which elaborate the seven topics in fact bring them in as presupposed by them, so a discussion of the topics will lead on to the Truths as well. The theory of causation, often discussed by the Buddha and also part of the enlightenment, is really an expansion of the Second Truth. Impermanence, stressed in the earliest and latest teaching of the Buddha, is part of the theory of causation. The avoidance of extremes, strictly held to though variously interpreted by all schools of Buddhism, constituted the first teaching given by the Buddha to the five monks. The intermediate way avoiding the extremes is nothing but the eightfold way, the seventh topic.

Thus all the prominent doctrines of the teaching as given by the *Tripiṭaka* and handed down as a heritage by all the schools of Buddhism form an interlocking whole which will be covered by discussing the seven topics promulgated at Vaiśālī. We are not yet concerned with what the schools made of this teaching later.

The summary given at Vaiśālī is a bare list. In order to know what these principles were in detail we have to look at other texts, taking our usual precaution to see that the statements we follow are common Buddhism and not the interpretations of a single school only. Some of the topics are given in more detail elsewhere in the *Mahāparinirvāṇa Sūtra*. For others and for fuller discussions we have to go to other texts of the *Sūtra* section of the *Tripiṭaka*. The four bases of self-possession have been touched on in our extracts from the *Mahāparinirvāṇa Sūtra* (p. 74 above), in connection with oneself and the doctrine as 'refuge'. The four bases of power were mentioned shortly afterwards, at the Cāpāla Shrine. The seven factors of enlightenment are listed as one of the groups of seven principles mentioned by the Buddha when lecturing the monks in Rājagṛha after the discussion about the Vṛjis near the beginning of the *Mahāparinivāṇa Sūtra*. The eightfold way is mentioned several times in this *Sūtra* (as one of the Four Truths and by itself when talking to Subhadra) but is not further elaborated. The *Sūtra* section of the *Tripiṭaka* contains a separate *sūtra* of some length on the four bases of self-possession, which deals very elaborately with the topic and touches on some of the others in connection with it (the way, the seven factors of enlightenment, also the Four Truths), as well as a collection of short *sūtras* on the same topic.[1] There are similar collections of short *sūtras* on the other topics in the summary.[2] We may now take up the seven topics in turn and see what the *Tripiṭaka* says about them.

Self-possession

The *sūtra* on self-possession, the *Smṛtyupasthāna Sūtra*, begins as follows.[3] 'Thus I have heard. Once the Master was living in Kuru. In Kuru there is a town named Kalmāṣadamya. The Master addressed the monks there: "O monks!" "Sir!" the monks assented to the Master. The Master said this: "Monks, this way is a single way for the purification of beings, for passing beyond grief and lamentation, for the extinction of unhappiness and depression, for the acquisition of method, for the experience of extinction; namely the four bases (*upasthāna*)[4] of self-possession (*smṛti*).[5] Which are the four? In this connection, monks, a monk lives with reference to the body (or 'substance',

1. Sthaviravāda D No. 22 almost identical with M No. 10=Chinese *Madhyama* T 26 No. 98. S V 141ff.=Chinese *Saṃyukta* (T 99) section 24.

2. S V 1ff.=T 99 sections 28, 27, 26, no collections on the others but scattered *sūtras* in sections 31, etc. (see below).

3. Following the Sthaviravāda version M No. 10=D No. 22 (except that the D version has an additional section on the Truths and the way).

4. Sometimes written and interpreted as *prasthāna*, but without variation in meaning. Cf next page, footnote.

5. The Chinese adds : to eliminate the 'obstacles' one should practise these and the factors of enlightenment.

kāya) observing the body, energetic (*ātāpin*), conscious (deliberate, *saṃprajāna*), self-possessed (*smṛtimant*), having eliminated desire (*abhidhyā*) and aversion (*daurmanasya*) for the world; with reference to emotions (*vedanā*) observing emotions, energetic, conscious, self-possessed, having eliminated desire and aversion for the world; with reference to thought (*citta*) observing thought, energetic, conscious, self-possessed, having eliminated desire and aversion for the world; with reference to principles (*dharma*) observing principles, energetic, conscious, self-possessed, having eliminated desire and aversion for the world.

"And how, monks, does a monk live with reference to the body observing the body? (In this connection, monks, a monk goes to the forest or to the foot of a tree or to an empty house. He sits down cross-legged, holding his body erect and setting[1] self-possession in front of him).[2] He breathes in, just self-possessed. He breathes out, just self-possessed. Breathing in long he understands that he breathes in long, or breathing out long he understands that he breathes out long. Breathing in short he understands that he breathes in short, or breathing out short he understands that he breathes out short. He trains thinking 'I breathe in experiencing my whole body'. He trains thinking 'I breathe out experiencing my whole body.' He trains thinking 'I breathe in making calm the forces of my body.' He trains thinking 'I breathe out making calm the forces of my body.'

("Monks, as a skilful turner or a turner's apprentice understands that he turns long when he turns long or understands that he turns short when he turns short, just so a monk understands that he breathes long...he trains...). Thus he lives observing the body with reference to the internal body (i.e. his own body), or he lives observing the body with reference to an external body (or substance), (or he lives observing the body with reference to both internal and external bodies. Or he lives observing the nature of origination with reference to the body, or observing the nature of cessation with reference to the body, or observing the nature of origination and cessation with

1. *upa-sthā* (whence *upasthāna*), 'attend to', 'set up', 'rest on'.
2. Bracketed portions not in the Chinese.

reference to the body.) Or his self-possession has been set up[1] thinking 'the body exists' (until it is sufficient for[2] knowledge, sufficient for mindfulness.[3] He lives unattached and is not attached to anything in the world.) Thus monks a monk lives with reference to the body observing the body." '

The *Sūtra* continues by saying that a monk should train in the same way when he is walking, standing, sitting or lying down. In whatever position his body is held he understands it is just so. Likewise whether he is going out or returning, looking, carrying anything, stretching out or drawing in, eating, chewing, tasting, sleeping, waking, speaking or performing any other bodily function. He should also consider the various elements and organic substances out of which the body is constituted, and reflect on what must happen to it after death, its gradual decomposition and reduction to a few scattered bones. In this way he bears in mind the 'cessation' of the body and cultivates non-attachment.

This is the first basis of self-possession: the observation of the body. The second basis has reference to emotions. The *Sūtra* continues: 'In this connection, monks, a monk feeling a pleasant emotion understands that he is feeling a pleasant emotion, feeling an unpleasant emotion understands that he is feeling an unpleasant emotion, feeling an emotion which is neither pleasant nor unpleasant understands that he is feeling an emotion which is neither pleasant nor unpleasant. Or feeling a sensual pleasant emotion...or a non-sensual pleasant emotion...' The text goes on with a sensual unpleasant emotion and the other possible combinations. The section concludes as does each part of that on the first basis: 'Thus he lives observing emotions with reference to internal emotions...to external emotions... (to both. Or he lives observing the nature of origination with reference to emotions, or observing the nature of cessation with reference to emotions, or observing the nature of origination and cessation with reference to emotions.) Or his self-possession has been set up thinking 'emotions exist' (until it is sufficient for knowledge, sufficient for mindfulness).

1. *pratyupasthita*.
2. —*mātra*, 'measuring'. Bracketed portions not in Chinese.
3. *pratismṛti*, practically synonymous with *smṛti*.

He lives unattached and is not attached to anything in the world.'

The third basis, having reference to thought, begins: 'In this connection a monk understands passionate thought as passionate thought.' It continues with thought without passion, with or without aversion, with or without delusion, limited or diffuse, sublime (elevated) or not, surpassed or unsurpassed, concentrated or not concentrated, freed or not freed. The conclusion is the same as before, leading up to non-attachment.

The fourth basis begins: 'And how, monks, does a monk live with reference to principles observing principles ? In this connection, monks, a monk lives with reference to principles, observing principles with reference to the five obstacles (*nivaraṇa*). How...? In this connection, monks, a monk when internal will to pleasure (*kāmacchandas*) exists understands that he has internal will to pleasure, or when internal will to pleasure does not exist understands that he does not have internal will to pleasure. Also he understands how will to pleasure which had not occurred has its occurrence, how will to pleasure which had occurred has its abandoning, and how abandoned will to pleasure does not have its occurrence in future.' The text continues in the same way for the other four obstacles (to freedom from mental attachment to the world), which are malevolence (*vyāpāda*), stupidity (*styānamiddha*), vanity (*auddhatyakaukṛtya*, defined in commentaries as concern about the opinion of others) and uncertainty (*vicikitsā*). This part concludes as usual with non-attachment.

This first part was probably the most important and essential training in observing principles, but the Sthaviravāda version continues with many further groups of principles.[1] First we have the five 'attachment groups' (*upādānaskandhas*): the monk observes matter (*rūpa*), emotion (*vedanā*), perception (*saṃjñā*), forces (*saṃskāras*) and consciousness (*vijñāna*) and their origination and extinction. (These five groups, we see elsewhere, where intended as embracing all the principles which occur in the universe—with the exception of 'extinction',

1. The Pali and Chinese agree again on the factors of enlightenment. Thus the original text simply opposed these good principles to the obstacles, cf. p. 94.

nirvāṇa, if that is counted as one — and therefore all worldly experience; it is these which form the basis of all possible attachment to the world.)

Likewise the monk may observe principles with reference to the six pairs of 'spheres' (*āyatana*), internal and external: sight (the sense of) and sights or visible objects, hearing and sounds, smell and scents, taste and tastes, body (touch) and tangibles, mind and principles (as mental objects). In this case the monk should understand the 'connection' (or 'union', *saṃyojana*) which occurs conditioned by each pair, how a connection which had not occurred (before) occurs, how a connection which has occurred is abandoned, and how an abandoned connection does not have its occurrence in future. Again the text leads up to non-attachment. By 'connection' in this context is understood the entanglement of the senses in their objects and the resulting mental principles which hinder progress on the way.

Next the monk may observe principles with reference to the seven factors of enlightenment. These constitute a separate topic and will be considered below, but it is most important to see how they fit in at this point in the monk's training as described in the *Smṛtyupasthāna Sūtra*. Having acquired a degree of self-possession and non-attachment he now aims more positively for enlightenment. The first factor of enlightenment is self-possession itself, considered as an attainment, so at this turning point the monk has to see that this has been consolidated before going on to the other factors. At first here the monk should understand whether he has the internal self-possession factor of enlightenment, then the occurrence of it if it has not occurred and the perfection (*pàripūri*, also written *pāripūri*) for 'development' (*bhāvanā*) of it when it has occurred. After giving the other factors of enlightenment the text as usual leads up to non-attachment.

Finally[1] the monk should observe principles with reference to the Four Truths: 'In this connection, monks, a monk understands in its true nature (*yathābhūtam*) "this is unhappiness"; he understands in its true nature "this is the origination of unhappiness"; he understands in its true nature "this is

1 Not in Chinese, nor in M.

the cessation of unhappiness"; he understands in its true nature "this is the way leading to the cessation of unhappiness".' The usual conclusion follows.

Thus the *Sūtra* leads up to the factors and content of enlightenment. It ends by saying that those who develop these four bases of self-possession will attain either insight (*ājñā*) in this present life (i.e. become an *arhant*, one who has attained freedom — commentary) or not coming again into existence in this world (*anāgāmitā*) even if attachment remains during this life. Even in as little as a week of this development such a result can be attained. The Master ends as he began by saying that this way is a single way for the purification of beings, for passing beyond grief and lamentation, for the extinction of unhappiness and depression, for the acquisition of method, for the experience of extinction, namely the four bases of self-possession.

The collection of short *sūtras* on the same topic in the *Saṃyukta* adds little of significance to this detailed exposition. The five obstacles constitute what is bad, the four bases of self-possession what is good (*kuśala*). A monk should regard these four as his proper place or range, where he will be safe from Death. Self-possession should be pursued for one's own safety and for that of others, for one protects another by protecting oneself and one protects oneself by protecting another.

Exertion

In the training in self-possession there have been several references to the question of the occurrence of principles which had not occurred before, the abandoning of principles which had occurred, the not occurring in future of something abandoned (e.g. an obstacle, a bad principle), and the perfection for development of something which has occurred (a factor of enlightenment, which is good). All this is the subject matter of the four right (*samyak*) exertions (*pradhāna*). These are set out in a formula which occurs at various places in the *Tripiṭaka*.[1] It runs:

1. Sthaviravāda e.g. M III 251 f, S V 244, D II 312 f ; Chinese versions in T 26 No. 31 and T 99 section 31, No. 19 ; Sarvāstivāda in their *Mahāparinirvāṇa Sūtra*, MPS (Waldschmidt) p. 174.

'In this connection a monk produces (*jan* causative) will (*chandas*), exercises (*vi-ā-yam*), initiates (*ā-rabh*) energy (*vīrya*), applies (*pra-grah*) and exerts (*pra-dhā*) thought (*citta*) for the non-occurrence (*anutpāda*) of evil (*pāpaka*), bad (*akuśala*) principles (*dharmas*) which have not occurred. (Secondly) He produces will, exercises, initiates energy, applies and exerts thought for the abandoning (*prahāṇa*) of evil, bad principles which have occurred. (Thirdly) He produces will, exercises, initiates energy, applies and exerts thought for the occurrence (*utpāda*) of good (*kuśala*) principles which have not occurred. (Fourthly) He produces will, exercises, initiates energy, applies and exerts thought for the persistence (*sthiti*), the not forgetting (*asaṃpramoṣa*), the being more (*bhūyobhāvatā*), prevalence (*vaipulya*), (development—*bhāvanā*, not in the Sarvāstivāda version,) perfection (*paripūraṇa*) of good principles which have occurred.'

Power

In the discussion with Ānanda at the Cāpāla Shrine (p.75 above) the Buddha is supposed to have hinted that by applying certain 'forces' (*saṃskāras*) he could live longer. These forces are the four bases (*pāda*) of power (*ṛddhi*). They are set out in a brief formula which occurs at several places in the *Tripiṭaka*[1]. It goes as follows: 'A monk develops the basis of power which is endowed with the forces of exertion for concentration of will (*chandas*). He develops the basis of power which is endowed with the forces of exertion for concentration of thought (*citta*). He develops the basis of power which is endowed with the forces of exertion for concentration of energy (*vīrya*). He develops the basis of power which is endowed with the forces of exertion for concentration of investigation (*mīmāṃsā*).' Little more is said about these, but they usually occur in the context of the four right exertions and were interpreted at least by the Sthaviravāda School as indicating the motive forces which enable a monk to carry those out.[2] It will be noticed that three of the four distinguishing features of these

1. Sthaviravāda version : D III 221 f., cf. Chinese version of *Saṃgīti Sūtra* (T 1 No. 9); Sarvāstivāda version in Sanskrit p. 94.
2. e.g. S V 268 f.

bases, will, thought and energy, are mentioned in the formula for the exertions. Perhaps the point which should be stressed in the bases of power, however, is that they are concerned with concentration (*samādhi*).

The Faculties

A considerable number of 'faculties' (*indriya*) are mentioned at different places in the *Tripiṭaka*, but the Buddhist traditions are unanimous that the five intended in the summary of doctrine we are now considering are confidence (*śraddhā*), energy (*vīrya*), self-possession (*smṛti*), concentration (*samādhi*) and understanding (*prajñā*).[1] The collection of short *sūtras* on this topic in the *Saṃyukta* supplies the following elucidations. Confidence means that one should have confidence in the enlightenment of the thus-gone. Energy corresponds to initiating energy and abandoning bad principles and acquiring good ones. Self-possession is said to include a good memory for what was done or said long ago as well as the four bases of self-possession described above. Concentration means withdrawing one's thought from distractions, concentrating it and attaining the four meditations. Understanding means understanding origination and cessation and the Four Truths.

Confidence is further connected with getting 'in the stream', i.e. being convinced that the doctrine is sound and setting out on the way. This has four factors, elsewhere stated to be the Buddha, the doctrine, the community and virtue (so one must have confidence in all these).[2] Energy is to be seen as the four right exertions. Understanding is indicated to be basic in that the other four do not endure without it.

By the perfection of these five faculties one becomes an *arhant*, freed from the influences. Having them in a lesser degree one attains intermediate stages on the way.

The three topics considered previously, self-possession, exertion and power, appear to form an orderly whole, a system of training leading up towards enlightenment and two necessary factors ancillary to it. The faculties, however, do not obviously follow on at this point. They partly overlap the

1. Sthaviravāda S V 193 ff=Chinese *Saṃyukta* T 99 section 26 (starting with No. 2). Sanskrit p. 153 of *Saṃgīti*.

2. See pp. 196 (footnote) and 198 below.

earlier topics and partly introduce new ideas which we may naturally seek to relate to the system. It seems clear, in fact, that the arrangement of the seven topics is a numerical order so far as the number of items in each topic varies: four, five, seven, eight. The present topic comes at this point because it has five items. Only within the three topics having four items the sequence was a more natural one.

The evidence of the texts just scanned suggests that confidence should come at the beginning if we consider the whole summary as indicating the way of the Buddha. Before setting out to verify the truth of enlightenment one must be convinced that—to put it as vaguely and generally as possible—there may be something in it, so this is the initial entry 'into the stream'.

A 'faculty' such as confidence is reckoned in these texts as a mental faculty in the same sense (using the same word *indriya* for it) that sight, hearing, smell, taste and touch are physical 'faculties'.

Whilst confidence makes the initial step possible, energy is the faculty which makes possible exertion for further progress. The use of the faculty of self-possession has been described at length above.

Concentration has so far occurred as a central factor in the bases of power, each of which operates through this faculty. Here, however, a new and most important subject is introduced: the practice of meditation (*dhyāna*). It seems that the exercise known as the four meditations was not specifically Buddhist, but had been taught earlier by such *śramaṇas* as Ārāḍa and Udraka, from whom the future Buddha learned them. This might account for their not being separately listed as a topic in the Buddha's summary of his doctrines, but being taken as generally known and as included under other topics, though essential. Nevertheless the four meditations are frequently described in the *Tripiṭaka*, the formula for them being as follows.[1]

'Becoming separated from pleasures (*kāma*), becoming separated from bad (*akuśala*) principles, a monk enters and

---

1. Sthaviravāda D I 73 ff., M I 21 f., S V 318 (Commentary e.g. DhsA 164 ff.), corresponding to Chinese versions in T 1 No. 27, T 125 k. 23 666, T 99 section 29 No. 18. Sarvāstivāda Lal 343f. Lokottaravāda *Mahāvastu* I 228.

remains in the first meditation, in which there is reasoning (*vitarka*) and reflection (*vicāra*), which is born of separation (*viveka*), which has joy (*prīti*) and happiness (*sukha*). Through the calming of reasoning and reflection he enters and remains in the second meditation, which internally is serenity (*saṃprasāda*) and singleness (*ekotibhāva* — a synonym for concentration) of thought (*cetas*), is without reasoning and reflection, is born of concentration (*samādhi*), has joy and happiness.[1] Through dispassion from joy he enters and remains in the third meditation, remaining detached (*upekṣaka*, 'equanimous'), self-possessed (*smṛtimant*) and conscious (deliberate, *saṃprajāna*), experiencing happiness in his body (in his mental being, according to the Sthaviravāda interpretation), the (meditation) which the Aryans (*ārya*, translatable as the 'excellent ones' or 'noble ones') describe as detached, self-possessed, remaining happy. By abandoning both happiness and unhappiness, by the extinction of his former elation (*saumanasya*) and depression (*daurmanasya*), he enters and remains in the fourth meditation, which is without unhappiness and without happiness and is the purity (*pariśuddha*) of equanimity (*upekṣā*) and self-possession.'

The significance of this exercise is suggested by the Buddha's own use of it mentioned in the previous chapter : on the night of his enlightenment when he used it to concentrate his thoughts before acquiring the three 'sciences' (including the Four Truths) ; again immediately before attaining extinction in the *parinirvāṇa*.

Concentration will be mentioned again under each of the remaining topics, along with this meditation exercise. We shall therefore return to the subject later, particularly when describing the way.

Understanding is evidently a faculty which must be active at all stages of training or of the way. The other faculties 'do not endure' without it, hence their effective operation presupposes it. At the end of the way we find the understanding of origination and cessation and of the Four Truths, the content of enlightenment. When we read about the way we shall see understanding placed at the beginning of it, but if we consider the present topic as part of the training for enlightenment it

1. The Sarvāstivāda and Lokottaravāda versions make 'through serenity and singleness of thought' instead part of the process of entering.

will seem natural that understanding follows concentration. Here the five faculties evidently dominate the training in turn, in the order stated.

The first factor of the way is knowledge of the Four Truths, as a science to be studied and understood; enlightenment means the actual realisation of these for oneself. We may leave the Truths themselves, and the subject of origination and cessation, in other words causation, until we come to the way.

The function of understanding can be further illustrated by referring back to the brief discourses of the Buddha mentioned in the account of his last wanderings before the *parinirvāṇa*, which we can quote from the last chapter : a disciple should have 'confidence founded in understanding' of the Buddha, the doctrine and the community; 'understanding penetrated with concentration has great results, great benefit, thought penetrated with understanding becomes perfectly free from the influences.' (p. 72 above.)

The Strengths

Among the 'strengths' (*bala*) mentioned in the *Tripiṭaka* the five intended here, according to the testimony of the Buddhist traditions, are confidence, energy, self-possession, concentration and understanding.[1] Thus they appear the same as the five faculties but called 'strengths' instead. The explanations of the schools agree that the difference is simply one of degree : when a faculty is unshakable it becomes a 'strength.'[2] The *Tripiṭaka* does not authorise us to say more than this, in fact it does not authorise us to say as much unless we read into the simple meanings of the words 'faculty' and 'strength' this particular distinction. There appears to be no text which does more than merely enumerate the strengths.

---

1. Sthaviravāda S V 249, A I 39, 42f., III 9ff.; Chinese *Saṃyukta* T 99 section 26 Nos. 36, 38 substitutes 'self-respect' and 'fear of blame' for self-possession and concentration, but this (Sarvāstivāda) school recognised the usual five *Saṃgīti* p. 153 ; cf. work quoted in next note, IV 283ff., and the *Vṛtti* to the *Abhidharmadīpa*, 359 and 361.

2. Sthaviravāda DhsA 124 ; Sarvāstivāda tradition see tne *Abhidharmakośa* translated by La Vallée Poussin, Vol. IV p. 286.

Enlightenment

The seven factors (*aṅga*) of enlightenment (*saṃbodhi* or simply *bodhi*) are self-possession, discrimination of principles (*dharma-vicaya*), energy, joy (*prīti*), tranquillity (*prasrabdhi*), concentration and equanimity (*upekṣā*).[1] The collection of *sūtras* on this topic in the *Saṃyukta* provides the following elucidations. The 'food' for the occurrence of all of them and for their development and perfection when they have occurred is methodical (*yoniśas*) attention (*manasikāra*). 'When a monk[2] thus remaining secluded recollects and reasons about the doctrine (which he has heard) he initiates the self-possession factor of enlightenment. Then he develops the self-possession factor of enlightenment. The self-possession factor of enlightenment, being developed by the monk, attains perfection. Remaining thus self-possessed he discriminates, reflects on and investigates that doctrine with understanding. When thus...with understanding, then he initiates the discrimination of principles factor of enlightenment... (as he develops this to perfection)...with understanding, he initiates energy, undeterred. At that time he initiates the energy factor of enlightenment...non-sensual joy occurs in one who has initiated energy...then he has initiated the joy factor of enlightenment...of one who has joy in his mind the body and the thought become tranquil...then he has initiated the tranquillity factor of enlightenment...one whose body is tranquil is happy, one who is happy concentrates his thought...then he initiates the concentration factor of enlightenment...with his thought concentrated he becomes thoroughly equanimous... then he has initiated the equanimity factor of enlightenment.'

Śāriputra says that he spends the different parts of the day in whichever factor of enlightenment he wishes. By developing the seven factors a monk becomes free from the influences. By initiating them he gets rid of stupidity and vanity, as well as freeing his thought. Then the factors of enlightenment are contrasted with all five 'obstacles' : it is a question of methodical attention to and then developing and making prevail one or the other group (S V 71f., 84f.).

1. D II 79, III 251 f., 282, S V 63 ff.; Chinese T I Nos. 2, 9, 10, T 99 section 27 ; MPS (Waldschmidt) p. 288. Sanskrit fragments of *Bodhyaṅga-saṃyukta Turfan* 533.

2. Translated from S V 67ff. Not traced in the Chinese.

The 'foods' for the occurrence and making more of the obstacles are as follows : the food of the will to pleasure is the sign (*nimitta*) of lustre (or 'beauty', *śubha*), the food of malevolence is the sign of repulsion (*pratigha*, or 'resistance'), the food of stupidity is discontent, laziness, languor, surfeit after meals and feebleness of thought, the food of vanity is lack of calm, the food of uncertainty is any principle about which there is uncertainty. By unmethodical attention to each of these foods the corresponding obstacles occur and increase (S V 103).

The foods for the occurrence and making more of the factors of enlightenment are as follows : the food of the self-possession factor is any principle with respect to which there is self-possession, the food of the discrimination of principles factor is principles which are either good or bad, either blameworthy or blameless, either inferior or superior, the contrast of black and white, the food of the energy factor is the element of initiating, the element of going out, the element of courage, the food of the joy factor is any principle with respect to which there is joy, the food of the tranquillity factor is tranquillity of body and tranquillity of thought, the food of the concentration factor is the sign of calming (*śamatha*), the sign of being undisturbed, the food of the equanimity factor is any principle with respect to which there is equanimity. By methodical attention to these the factors of enlightenment occur and are brought to perfection (S V 104 f.).

As opposed to all these one can have no food, fasting (*anāhāra*), for each principle. In this case we have methodical attention to starving the obstacles, whilst the factors of enlightenment are starved simply by unmethodical attention to their proper foods. In the case of the obstacles one starves the will to pleasure by methodical attention to the sign of foulness (or 'ugliness', *aśubha*), malevolence by the freeing (*vimukti*) of thought (*cetas*) by benevolence (or 'loving kindness', *maitrā*), stupidity by the elements of initiating, going out and courage, vanity by calming thought, uncertainty by methodical attention to principles which are either good or bad, either blameworthy or blameless, either inferior or superior, or have the contrast of black and white (S V 105 f).

There is also the question of the right or wrong occasions for developing the various factors. When thought is feeble it is not the occasion for tranquillity, concentration or equanimity. On the other hand discrimination of principles, energy and joy can then be used to arouse thought. Then when thought is elated the position is reversed: one should use tranquillity, concentration and equanimity, not the other three. Self-possession, however, is always useful (S V 112 ff).

In order to get rid of the obstacles an exercise is recommended which has been mentioned in the previous chapter, that of pervading the four directions successively with thought charged with benevolence, compassion, sympathetic joy and equanimity, everywhere, through considering all beings as like oneself, making thought, charged with benevolence, etc., large, sublime, immeasurable, without hatred, non-violent, so that it pervades the whole universe. This explains the 'freeing of thought by benevolence' referred to above, adding to it 'freeing of thought by compassion (*karuṇā*)'; 'freeing of thought by sympathetic joy (*muditā*)' and 'freeing of thought by equanimity.' A monk should develop the self-possession factor charged with benevolence, and with the other principles (compassion, etc.), likewise the other factors of enlightenment. Then if he wishes he will be able to remain having perception of what is distasteful in what is not distasteful, or of what is not distasteful in what is distasteful. Or if he wishes he can have perception of what is distasteful in both or of what is not distasteful in both. Or he can avoid both the distasteful and not distasteful and remain equanimous (detached), self-possessed and conscious (S V 115ff).

If he has the factor of enlightenment charged with benevolence he can then enter into the 'lustrous' or 'beautiful' (*śubha*) freedom (*vimokṣa*). 'The freeing of thought by benevolence' has 'beauty' as its highest excellence. If the factor is instead charged with compassion he can transcend all material perception, all perception of resistance, all attention to variety of perceptions and enter into the sphere of the infinity of space. This is the highest excellence of the 'freeing of thought by compassion.' If the factor is charged with sympathetic joy he can transcend the sphere of the infinity of space and enter into the sphere of the infinity of consciousness, which is the highest excellence of the 'freeing of thought by sympathetic joy'. If the factor of enlightenment is charged with equanimity he can transcend the sphere of the infinity of conciousness and enter into the sphere of nothingness, which is the highest excellence of the 'freeing of thought by equanimity' (S V 119 ff).

As to the question of what is distasteful in what is not distasteful, this may probably be explained by the later recommendation of such exercises as the perception of a skeleton. Though this text does not say why this is recommended, except as conducive to insight and freedom, we know from other sources that the object is to oppose this kind of perception to that of beauty in the body.

Since it has been expressly stated that the different factors of enlightenment may be used on various occasions, even on any occasion, there would seem to be no question of an orderly progress here from self-possession to equanimity. Nevertheless the order of enumeration of the factors is constant and our study of the foregoing topics suggests that self-possession comes at an early stage, with concentration leading up to equanimity coming later. One of the texts scanned above also gives the factors in series as leading on from one to the next. There would then be a basic order, with variations possible as desired. It seems further to be implied that one who has already attained freedom from the influences and is an *arhant* (as was Śāriputra), may continue to practise these exercises, to spend his time in the various factors. Considering the factors from this point of view we are studying a stage of the way close to enlightenment, or even at the end after its attainment, rather than the earlier stages of exertion indicated by the preceding topics. Apart from this presumed difference of viewpoint or application some of the factors have been dealt with at length under other topics, and others mentioned. Self-possession being an independent topic has been sufficiently discussed above. Energy likewise has been expounded in some detail. Concentration appears in various contexts and has been particularly treated as a faculty. We can add here from the enumeration of 'foods' of the factors the association of concentration with the term 'calming', which becomes a key concept in many later discussions of the way among the Buddhist schools.

In the expression 'discrimination of principles' we meet once more the term *dharma* in its meaning of 'principle'.

We have met it especially in the fourth basis of self-possession, where the 'principles' observed included the five obstacles, the attachment groups, the spheres (the six senses and their respective objects) and the seven factors of enlightement. Under 'exertion' we saw that some principles at least were classifiable as 'good' or 'bad'. The five faculties being faculties in the same sense as the senses may be presumed to be principles just as these are (certainly they were so taken in the schools of Buddhism). Other things mentioned above which the schools have generally considered to be principles include 'reasoning', 'reflection', 'happiness', 'unhappiness', 'elation' and 'depression' (in connection with meditation, joy and equanimity are certainly principles, being factors of enlightenment), also the five strengths, 'attention', 'calming', 'benevolence', 'compassion' and 'sympathetic joy'. There are many others (for example the eight factors of the way and the four elements earth, water, heat and air, which latter are divisions of 'matter', the first attachment group). What is a 'principle' ? What is the significance, if any, of the fact that the Sanskrit word *dharma* has come to have two distinct meanings, 'principle' and 'doctrine', which are even liable to confusion in some contexts (including the present 'discrimination of principles') and have been the subject of a certain amount of mystification by some modern writers on Buddhism ?

The basic or more original meaning of *dharma* appears to have been 'nature', what truly exists, true reality, what actually is in the universe. An enumeration of *dharmas* (plural) will then be a list of what there is in the universe, the entities of which it is composed, it may reduce to its real elements as opposed to less real combinations of them or superficial appearances. In this book we use 'principles' for *dharma* in the sense of these entities, understanding 'natural principles', many of them 'natural elements' as irreducible principles out of which the universe and all experience is constructed. On the other hand a philosophy which claims to give a true account of the universe or of the human predicament in it is a doctrine of nature, of nature as it really is, a natural doctrine, a true doctrine. In this sense we might even render the Buddha's *dharma*=doctrine as his 'truth'. However, the term *dharma* in this sense of doctrine was applied to all current doctrines, including all those of opponents which were held to be false by the speaker using the term. Consequently we cannot well use 'truth' here and must prefer a neutral term such as 'doctrine' corresponding to the faded or differentiated meaning. Faced with this 'polysemia' of *dharma*, then, we proceed in this book as if we were dealing simply with a pair of homonyms in the original language, and translate accordingly (we hope rightly in each context).[1] For the time being we are not concerned with other differentiations of meaning of the word *dharma*.

The factor 'discrimination of principles' has been exemplified above as methodical attention to principles, discriminating them as 'good' or 'bad' and the like. It has been said also that this discriminating is done 'with understanding', presumably the faculty of understanding. In fact this factor appears to be a synonym for understanding, and was so taken by the schools.

Joy has been mentioned under the faculty of concentration. In the four meditations it is one of the principles present in the first and second, but transcended in entering the third, where it is replaced by equanimity. The texts on the factor of enlightenment speak more precisely of 'non-sensual' joy and say that it may exist with respect to any principle. Clearly it means, as a factor of enlightenment, joy with respect to the principles encountered in the training, zest (as it has sometimes been translated) for the earlier meditation exercises, for exertion. To make progress towards enlightenment it is necessary to be pleased with the means being used, having detached oneself from worldly pleasures.

This mental joy produces tranquillity both of the body and of thought, and tranquillity facilitates concentration. In describing how he meditated before attaining enlightenment, the Buddha in one of the passages translated above mentioned that he initiated energy, attended to self-possession, calmed his body and concentrated his thoughts. Here 'calmed' is from the same verb as the noun 'tranquillity'. These contexts should

1. In the West we owe our understanding of the meaning of the term *dharma* to the work of Rosenberg and Stcherbatsky. The latter's CC is a good introduction to the subject, but the original work of Rosenberg is well worth reading. He studied the subject in Japan. See now 'Dharmas and Data', where we have traced the sense from 'maintaining' to 'principle'.

exemplify the meaning of tranquillity as a factor of enlightenment.

The remaining factor is equanimity. The four meditations lead up to this as their consummation, and in the course of them it supersedes joy. In the series of factors of enlightenment it again appears as the consummation. Like joy, its 'food' is simply any principle with respect to which it exists. All the discussions we meet, and those we shall meet when we investigate the way, indicate that this represents the highest and final phase of the training. Concentration leads up to equanimity. In a state of equanimity with respect to all principles one can see the truth, attain enlightenment. This is how one becomes enlightened. One must become completely detached (equanimous) in order to see the true nature of principles, to understand the Four Truths in their true nature. This is the essential function of equanimity as a factor of enlightenment. Yet there is more to equanimity than even this: it is the highest of the 'immeasurable' principles for the exercise of pervading the universe with thought charged with it. This serves among other things to get rid of the 'obstacles'. When one charges the factors of enlightenment with equanimity one can enter the sphere of nothingness and attain 'freeing of thought by equanimity'.

The Way

The way (*mārga*, also *pratipad*, the 'practice', which is used as a synonym), which is eightfold or more literally has eight factors (*aṅga*), is often called 'excellent' (*ārya*). The term *ārya* here is particularly difficult to translate, though the difficulty does not (or should not) affect the actual doctrine. Its original meaning is the Aryan people, a meaning which it still retained in and long after the Buddha's time (the proper name for northern India being Āryāvarta, the 'sphere of the Aryans'). Evidently by the Buddha's time it had developed a group of secondary meanings: a 'noble' or 'honourable' person or 'gentleman' (which is used in polite address) and anything 'excellent' or 'good' or 'proper' or 'best'. Undoubtedly it originally expressed that prejudice in favour of itself which every people and every nation seems to have, and it is remarkable that the Buddhists, and presumably the Buddha himself, should have been driven to use it. However, it did not impede appreciably the later spread of Buddhism among the 'barbarians': the schools interpreted the term as meaning simply 'excellent' and forgot its origin.

Like the factors of enlightenment, the factors of the way do not necessarily, it seems, have to be practised in the order in which they are enumerated. On the contrary they are to be developed more or less simultaneously. As on previous occasions we can probably assume that the various factors were intended to be dominant at different stages, but not to the exclusion of the others. The eight factors are: right (*samyak*) theory (*dṛṣṭi*), right intention (*saṃkalpa*), right speech (*vāc*), right action (*karmānta*), right livelihood (*ājīva*), right exercise (*vyāyāma*), right self-possession and right concentration.[1]

The *Madhyama sūtra* (the *Satyavibhaṅga Sūtra*) on the Four Truths mentioned in our list of sources gives the following elucidations. Right theory is knowledge (*jñāna*) of the Four Truths. Right intention means renunciation (*naiṣkramya*), non-violence (*avyāpāda*) and harmlessness (*avihiṃsā*). Right speech means abstaining from falsehood, malicious speech, harsh speech, frivolity and nonsense. Right action (or work) means abstaining from taking life, from taking what is not given and from misconduct in pleasures. Right livelihood means making one's living rightly. Right exercise means the four right exertions (as in the topic set out above). Right self-possession is the four bases of this as described already and right concentration is the four meditations as given under concentration as a faculty above.

The same *sūtra* gives some elucidation of the Four Truths which we can conveniently take up under this topic. There will be little to add about exercise, self-possession or concentration. The remaining factors concern virtue (*śīla*), a subject frequently spoken of by the Buddha (for example the regular lecture mentioned in the last chapter, on virtue, concentration and understanding, and any number of detailed discussions in the *Tripiṭaka*) but which has not been treated under the preceding six topics. The *Saṃyukta* collection adds very little.

1. *Sūtra* and *Vinaya* references above in narrating the first teaching of the Buddha. More details in M No. 141=Chinese *Madhyama* No. 31 ; S V 1 ff partly in Chinese *Saṃyukta* section 28.

The Four Truths are, as stated already in describing the enlightenment, (1) unhappiness, (2) its origination, (3) its cessation and (4) the way leading to this cessation. Since the way, our present topic, is also the fourth truth, the discussion leads round in a circle: the first factor of the way is knowledge of the Four Truths, the fourth truth is the way. This makes it clear that the truths are basic: they are the first factor of the way, the way is the last truth. This 'science' of Buddhism begins with the knowledge of unhappiness and leads via self-possession and concentration to enlightenment. But enlightenment also is 'discovery', or at least 'understanding in their true nature', of the truths. The difference evidently is that when one has the Buddha or his doctrine as teacher one begins by being informed of the truths as something to be known. Whether one immediately understands them fully depends on one's individual experience. The way is intended to prepare the trainee for this full understanding, which may come only long afterwards, after much exercise in detachment and self-possession, much meditation and exercise of the understanding faculty. What was first picked up as a piece of information will not be fully understood until the trainee sees its truth himself, through his own experience. He must not just believe it, he must verify it. There is a text which occurs in many places in the *Tripiṭaka*[1] which explains what is meant by confidence (the faculty) in the Buddha, the doctrine and the community (cf. the discussion of confidence as a faculty above). The formula for the doctrine is : 'The doctrine has been well told by the Master; it is visible (*sāṃdṛṣṭika*), timeless (*akālika*), verifiable (*aihipaśyika*), fruitful (*aupanayika*), to be experienced (found, known, discovered : *vedayitavya*) individually (personally : *pratyātmam*) by discerning persons (*vijñu*)'. One may first have mere confidence in this doctrine, but one is not enlightened until this has been superseded by first hand experience of its truth, by understanding applied to one's own past and present observations.

The *Satyavibhaṅga Sūtra* elucidates the Four Truths as follows. (1) Birth is unhappiness (*duḥkha*), so is old age, dying, grief, lamentation, pain, depression, misery, not getting what one

1. Sthaviravāda references under *ehipassiko* PTC I p. 436. *Mahāvastu* III 200, *Śikṣāsamuccaya* 323.

wants. Briefly the five attachment groups constitute unhappiness. These items are further explained, but they are probably sufficiently self-evident already. 'Birth' is rebirth. (2) The origination (*samudaya*) of unhappiness is desire (*tṛṣṇā*) leading to rebirth. This is desire which is charged with pleasure and passion, pleased with whatever it encounters, it is desire for pleasure, desire for existence, desire for non-existence (for annihilation according to the Sthaviravāda commentary). (3) The cessation (*nirodha*) of unhappiness is the absolute cessation in dispassion of, the abandoning of, rejection of, freeing from, not clinging to, that same desire. (4) The practice is the way having eight factors, as set out above.

The unhappiness, therefore, which one has to verify in one's own experience, to understand in its true nature, is whatever is unsatisfactory in life; ultimately it is all principles (these being comprised in the five groups of attachment). The desire for any object of attachment produces unhappiness in the form of that object. Why is this? The answer has been given in the preceding chapter in one of the Buddha's first discourses, that on 'non-soul'. Each of the five groups is non-soul, or not one's own, because one cannot control it (if one cannot control it one must be dissatisfied, unhappy). Each group is impermanent, keeps changing, and this again means unhappiness (even good things are soon lost). Finding this 'not one's own-ness', this impermanence, in the groups one should become indifferent to them and attain dispassion.

On origination there are many *sūtras* explaining in detail how desire leads to rebirth, how the whole process of transmigration carries on according to the Buddhist understanding of it. This is the theory of causation, of conditions, which will be studied in the following chapter. In connection with it we may take up some important incidental questions, including that of precisely what is meant by 'non-soul'.

Cessation means breaking the causal sequence : remove the cause (e.g. desire) and the effect (e.g. unhappiness) will cease to appear. The third truth is therefore the possibility of extinction (*nirvāṇa*).

This knowledge constitutes the theory of the way, the first of its eight factors. Opposed to it, as the *Saṃyukta* points out in the first of its *sūtras* on the way, is ignorance (*avidyā*), which produces wrong (*mithyā*) theory, wrong intention, wrong speech: eight wrong factors opposite to the right ones of the way. We have now to consider right intention, speech, action and livelihood, and so complete our account of the Buddha's 'principles for the welfare, benefit and happiness of men.'

The second factor, right intention, is classed in another *sūtra* of the *Madhyama*[1] under 'understanding', along with right theory. This *sūtra* classifies all the factors of the way under the three heads of virtue, concentration and understanding (in that order, not in the usual order of the statements of the way). The intention of renunciation is clearly part of the 'understanding' which is essential to the practice of the way. At the same time the intention of non-violence and harmlessness would seem to take us into the field of virtue. This factor might then be considered as transitional between understanding and virtue. Everything is interconnected in the doctrines of the Buddha. They form a consistent and organic whole, so that the complete understanding of any part includes the understanding of the whole, of all the other parts. As to the order of presentation, virtue—concentration—understanding, it is that of the standard lecture given by the Buddha from time to time on his wanderings, as summarised in the *Mahāparinirvāṇa Sūtra*. Either one starts simply by observing the virtues recommended by the Buddha, for example in his discourses to lay disciples, and later takes up concentration and meditation leading up to understanding, or one begins by learning the theory, with understanding, which indicates the advantages of virtue and the necessity of it as a prerequisite for concentration, and then proceeds to train in concentration.

The three remaining factors of the way belong unambiguously to the class of virtue. In one's speech and actions one should be truthful and harmless. One should gain one's livelihood harmlessly, presumably avoiding even indirect injury to others as 'right action' means avoiding direct injury. This affects the life of a monk as well as of a layman, since the monk also though living by begging may be frequently in contact with the laity, teaching them as well as begging from them, and this

1. M I No. 44 (p. 301)=Chinese T 26 No. 210.

opens opportunities for seeking favour by improper practices. We shall consider the teaching for the layman, for the worldly society, in a later chapter. For the monk virtue is a straightforward, if not an easy, matter. The standard which forms the basis of his moral philosophy is simply non-attachment. Non-attachment to the principles of the world means avoiding the obstacles to freedom from mental attachment to the world (the *nīvaraṇas*), primarily desire and aversion, or the 'will to pleasure' and 'malevolence'. This moral standard covers all possible details of avoiding bad conduct.

Having studied the factors of enlightenment, however, we shall not forget that virtue for the Buddhist monk is a positive as well as a negative matter. In order to overcome the obstacles he should use three very positive moral forces : benevolence, compassion and sympathetic joy. He should seek to pervade the whole universe with these forces in his meditation, and it was surely his function also to seek to pervade society with these three through his teaching. Underlying these is a second moral standard : considering all beings as like oneself (*sarvātmatā*). One would like others to treat oneself with benevolence and compassion and to be joyful at any good fortune one may enjoy. This is a social standard, as non-attachment is not, though the two combine under the aegis of the factors of enlightenment in opposition to the obstacles, to the bad principles which muts be overcome.

Our sources have one more important point to add under the heading of the way. The *Saṃyukta* collection has a dialogue[1] in which Ānanda remarks to the Buddha that half of the 'best life' is good friendship (*kalyāṇamitratā*), good companionship (*kalyāṇa-sahāyatā*), contact with the good (*kalyāṇasaṃparka*). The Buddha objects : 'Not so Ānanda! No ! It is the whole of the best life, good friendship, good companionship, contact with the good! A monk who is a good friend, a good companion, in contact with the good may be expected to develop this excellent eightfold way and cultivate it...' It is the guidance and inspiration of a good companion on the way which above all helps a monk progress, as the first Buddhist monks were inspired by the best of all 'good friends', the Buddha himself.

1. A Sanskrit version is available from the Sarvāstivāda tradition in the *Avadānaśataka* (Vol. I p. 240).

Practice and Truth

The principles thus set out evidently form a programme of practical training, having in mind certain aims, namely happiness, knowledge, enlightenment. We might try to summarise the whole programme as follows, though there is no *Tripiṭaka* authority for this and the impression grows on the student that all the factors are to be cultivated together rather than serially, forming as it were a fugue in which a dozen different subjects combine in a tremendous crescendo leading up to enlightenment. A student who has a certain amount of confidence in the doctrine equips himself with the theory of the Four Truths. Having right intention and some understanding he conforms to virtue and practices discrimination of principles. He concentrates his will, thought, energy and investigations and so increases his self-possession and goes on to practice concentration, developing joy in this practice and tranquillity of body and thought, so that his meditations bring him to equanimity. Then his understanding can exercise its full potentiality and he should be able to attain enlightenment, to verify in his own experience, understand in their true nature, the Four Truths.

Though this is a way of training, it presupposes theory, the theory of the Four Truths, and a knowledge of certain observed facts about the nature of the universe, of life. As confidence is replaced by understanding the observation of facts gains in importance : for example the facts of causes or conditions in life, the principles or natural constituents of the universe through which the way leads. These facts, the truth about causation, the nature, that is the principles, of the universe, are discussed in other texts of the *Tripiṭaka*, which we may consider in the next chapter.

CHAPTER FIVE

CAUSATION

Conditioned Origination—The Four 'Foods'—Is there a Soul?—Consciousness—Impermanence—Freedom—Experience—Knowledge of Objective Facts—Did the Buddha Claim Omniscience?—Two Levels of Statement—The Gods

Conditioned Origination

In the description of the enlightenment the Buddha is said to have reflected that a certain matter would be 'difficult to see', namely specific conditionality (*idaṃpratyayatā*) or 'conditioned origination.' This evidently refers to the essence of the doctrine and particularly of the Four Truths, the conditioned origination of unhappiness. That the Buddha's doctrine is essentially a doctrine about conditions and causes is suggested by many other texts in the *Tripiṭaka.* For example in the account of how Śāriputra became a follower of the Buddha, summarised in Chapter Three, all that was necessary to give Śāriputra insight into the doctrine was to tell him that 'the Master teaches the origination of principles from causes'. Given unhappiness and the wish to eliminate it, the essence of the Buddha's teaching is that this wish can be realised because unhappiness depends on causes: remove the causes and unhappiness will cease. What the causes are is then evidently the basis of knowing what action to take to eliminate unhappiness, what way to follow.

The origination of unhappiness is the second truth. So far we have learned that it is that kind of desire which leads to rebirth which is the origination of unhappiness. That kind of desire, further, is 'charged with pleasure and passion', 'pleased with whatever it encounters', and is desire for pleasure, existence or non-existence (pp. 102f. above). Many *sūtras* explain the relationship between this desire and unhappiness in detail.[1] The longest and fullest of these is the *Mahānidāna*

1. D No. 15=T 1 No. 13 (also T 14 by An Shih-kao, T 26 No. 97 and T 52, a shorter version by Shih-hu) ; S II 2ff.=T 99 sections 12, 14, 15= Sarvāstivāda *Nidāna Saṃyukta* ed. Tripāṭhi. Sanskrit fragments of the *Mahānidāna Sūtra Turfan* 581, 865, 868.

Sūtra, the Great Sūtra on *nidāna* ('cause', 'source', 'origin'). We may follow the Sthaviravāda version, checking with the Chinese translations (of which there are several). This version locates the *Sūtra* at Kalmāṣadamya, like the Great Sūtra on self-possession. The text is in the form of a dialogue between the Buddha and Ānanda. After the opening, Ānanda says to the Master: 'It is surprising, sir, it is wonderful, sir, how profound this conditioned origination (*pratītyasamutpāda*) is and how profound is its illumination. Yet it seems to me as if very simple.'

The Buddha replies: 'Say not so, Ānanda, say not so. This conditioned origination is profound and its illumination is profound. Through lack of understanding, lack of comprehension, of this doctrine, this creation does not escape transmigration (*saṃsāra*), which is misery, an evil destiny, ruin, as if it had become tangled in a loom, with its threads twisted and knotted, or were (a rope) of rushes and straw..

'If asked whether old age and dying exist through a specific condition (*idaṃpratyayāt*, 'through this-condition'), one should say that they do so exist. If asked through what condition old age and dying exist one should say that old age and dying exist through the condition of birth.' The Buddha continues that birth exists through the condition of 'existence' (*bhava*), existence through the condition of attachment (*upādāna*), attachment through the condition of desire (*tṛṣṇā*).—Thus we seem to have bridged the gap from unhappiness (typified by old age and dying) to desire, but we should not jump to any conclusion before we have looked at the further explanation of this 'desire'.—The Buddha continues that desire exists through the condition of emotion (*vedanā*), emotion through the condition of contact (stimulus) (*sparśa*)[2], contact through the condition of a sentient body (*nāmarūpa*), a sentient body through the condition of consciousness (*vijñāna*), and consciousness through the condition of a sentient body. He then summarises this sequence, from a sentient body to

2. T 26 and Shih-hu insert the condition 'six spheres' at this point. See below p. 114f.

consciousness, from consciousness to a sentient body, from a sentient body to contact, and so on down to old age and dying, adding further that from old age and dying originate grief, lamentation, pain, depression and misery. Thus we have the origination of this entire mass of unhappiness.

The Buddha now adds some further elucidations. In what way is it to be ascertained that old age and dying exist through the condition of birth? If there were no birth at all, in any way, of anything or anywhere (examples of different kinds of sentient beings are added), in the complete absence of birth, through the cessation of birth, would old age and dying be discerned ? No. Therefore, in this case, precisely this is the cause (*hetu*), the source (*nidāna*), the origination (*samudaya*), the condition (*pratyaya*) of old age and dying, namely birth.

If there were no existence of any description, as sensual existence, imponderable existence or immaterial existence ('imponderable' refers to the existence of the higher gods, 'immaterial' to the higher spheres in which consciousness can exist in meditation, those of the infinity of space, infinity of consciousness, nothingness and neither perception nor non-perception), there would likewise be no birth.[1]

If there were no attachment of any description, as attachment to pleasure, attachment to opinion, attachment to virtue and vows or attachment to the theory that there is a soul (*ātman*), there would in the same way be no existence.[2]

Again, if there were no desire, to wit desire for sights, sounds, scents, tastes, tangibles or principles (as mental objects) there would be no attachment.[2]

If there were no emotion at all, emotion produced by contact of the sight, hearing, smell, taste, touch or mind, there would similarly be no desire.[3]

At this point, before we come on to the elucidation of contact, the sentient body and consciousness, there is a digression or excursus on the question of desire, which brings in a further sequence of conditions and leads to the description of

---

1. This sentence is not in the Chinese versions.
2. Not in the Chinese. But *AKBhāṣya* see p. 307 on attachment.
3. T. 26 has instead happy, unhappy and neither.

desire as desire for pleasure, existence or non-existence, which we had met before. It will perhaps make the exposition clearer, however, if we complete the original sequence first.

If there were no contact at all, contact of the sight, hearing, smell, taste, touch or mind, there would be no emotion.

The elucidation of the term 'sentient body' requires first the study of the question of its composition, as a compound of matter (*rūpa*) plus sentience (*nāma*). By whatever features (*ākāra*, 'peculiarity'), characteristics (*liṅga*), signs (*nimitta*) or summarised descriptions (*uddeśa*) there is a concept (*prajñapti*, 'making known', see on this the article 'The Concept of a Concept') of the body of sentience (*nāmakāya*), in the absence of these features, characteristics, signs and summarised descriptions, there would be no contact (union) of the designation (*adhivacana*) with the body of matter (*rūpakāya*). By whatever features, characteristics, signs and summarised descriptions there is a concept of the body of matter, in the absence of these there would be no contact of resistance (*pratigha*) in (of, with) the body of sentience. In the absence of those features, characteristics, signs and summarised descriptions by which there is a concept of both the body of sentience and the body of matter there would be neither contact of the designation nor contact of resistance. In the absence of those features, characteristics, signs and summarised descriptions by which there is a concept of a sentient body there would, therefore, be no contact [Q.E.D.].

If consciousness did not descend into the mother's womb there would be no formation ('coagulation', *sam-murcch*) of a sentient body in the mother's womb.[1] Or if, after descending into the womb consciousness were to pass away, the sentient body would not be produced for this world. Or if the consciousness of a boy or girl were cut off while still young there would be no increase, growth or consolidation of the sentient body.

On the other hand if consciousness did not obtain a resting place in a sentient body there would be no production of the origination of birth, old age, dying and pain in future. Consequently a sentient body is the cause, source, origination, condition of consciousness.

1. Cf. *AKVyākhyā* p. 669.

This part of the argument concludes: 'To this extent, Ānanda, one may be born, grow old, die, pass away, be reborn (transmigrate), to this extent there is a way for designation (*adhivacana*), a way for language, a way for concepts (*prajñapti*), to this extent there is scope for understanding, to this extent the cycle (of the universe) revolves for the discernment of 'this world' (*itthatva*), namely (to the extent that there is) the sentient body with consciousness.'

Let us now return to the excursus in connection with desire. This begins: 'Desire conditioned by emotion, searching (*paryeṣanā*) conditioned by desire, gain (*lābha*) conditioned by searching, decision (*viniścaya*) conditioned by gain, will (*chandas*) and passion (*rāga*) conditioned by decision, coveting (*adhyavasāna*) conditioned by will and passion, possessing (*parigraha*) conditioned by coveting, selfishness (*mātsarya*) conditioned by possessing, guarding (*ārakṣa*) conditioned by selfishness: in the affair of guarding many evil, bad principles are produced, resorting to force, resorting to the sword, quarrelling, strife, disputes, insults, malice and falsehood. These are then traced back again : in the complete absence of guarding there would be no resorting to force and the other bad principles, in the complete absence of selfishness there would be no guarding, in the complete absence of possessing there would be no selfishness, and so on down to in the complete absence of searching there would be no gain, in the complete absence of desire, to wit desire for pleasure, desire for existence, desire for non-existence, there would be no searching.[1] The excursus concludes: 'Thus, Ānanda, these two principles (according to the Sthaviravāda commentary desire as the basis of the cycle of transmigration, and conventional desire, presumably desire as condition for attachment and as condition for searching respectively) by being a pair (similar) come together as one through emotion.'

The main sequence here, from old age and dying having birth as condition (or from grief, etc., having old age and dying as condition) to contact having a sentient body as condition and the reciprocal conditionality of a sentient body and cons-

1. An Shih-kao has the first two kinds of desire, the other Chinese versions omit all three (Taisho Vol. I p. 243a, lines 19-20). cf. *AKBhāṣya* p. 286.

ciousness, is clearly a description of the process of transmigration (or rebirth). Certainly it was so understood by all the schools of Buddhism. The unhappiness met with in life, typified by growing old and dying, has birth (i.e. rebirth) as its indispensable condition, and this in turn depends on (previous) existence. It was the desire which operated in the preceding life which served as condition for attachment and this as condition for (continuing) existence, the last as condition for rebirth, i.e. the birth into the present life. As to the basis of that desire, the conditions for it in turn, this was ultimately the sentient body with consciousness of that life, serving as a basis through the contact of its six senses (the five senses plus the mind) and emotion, the immediate condition for desire. The other sequence from desire is secondary and is generally ignored in later discussions. It evidently shows desire as the basis not of transmigration but of immediate bad results in the same life: the use of force, malice, falsehood, etc.

The various elucidations of the terms in the sequence raise some further points of interest. Attachment to pleasure is simple enough as a condition for continuing existence, but attachment to opinions or to virtue and vows is less obvious. Presumably the wish to continue performing the duties and rituals of 'virtue' and 'vows' is a sufficient condition (the commentarial explanation relates these to the Brahmanical religion and to asceticism). Any kind of false opinion leads to wrong actions, or at least to absence of right actions, and consequently to continued existence and transmigration. The belief that one has a soul is simply one of these false opinions, but it is often stressed in the Buddha's teaching as one particularly hard to eradicate, particularly dear to living beings, and held by most other schools of thought. In fact this particular belief is even in modern times so strong that some scholars working in the field of Buddhist studies have been unable, or most unwilling, to believe that the Buddha rejected it (since they found his teaching otherwise congenial, or else because they could not believe that any successful religion could have rejected it). As a good deal of uncertainty has been spread by these scholars it will be worth while later in this chapter to review some of the *Tripiṭaka* texts bearing on the question of a 'soul'. At the same time it will be desirable to collect information on the process of transmigration, on what, if anything, transmigrates, since it is sometimes supposed that there could be no transmigration without a permanent entity, a soul, to transmigrate. For the time being we can point out that the present text, referring to 'attachment to the theory that there is a soul' as a condition to be eliminated, sufficiently demonstrates that the Buddha rejected this theory.

The discussion on the sentient body is a difficult one, especially as it brings in a number of technical terms of philosophy whose meanings we are not absolutely certain of for the Buddha's period. The drift of the argument seems to be that the 'body of matter' is inert and has nothing like 'designation' or description inherent in it, no ideas attached to it. On the other hand the 'body of sentience' has no resistance (presumably physical resistance) in it. Contact (stimulus) presupposes both resistance and designation (identification, contact with something), therefore a sentient (or living) body. It is of course sense-contact which is in question, not mere physical collision. Perhaps 'stimulus' would be a better equivalent. An inert body of matter would not register a contact. An immaterial body of sentience would not have any contact to register: an object would pass straight through it without producing any resistance, any stimulus.

Before we continue with the *Mahānidāna Sūtra*, which now develops some other topics, it will be useful to add here some gleanings on the sequence of conditioned origination from the *Saṃyukta*. First a general formula for attending (*manasi-kṛ*; *prati-ava-īkṣ* in the Sarvāstivāda text) methodically (*yoniśas*) to conditioned origination is mentioned.[1] It gives the general form of a statement of a condition: 'This being, this is. From the occurrence (*utpāda*) of this, this occurs. (This not being, this is not. From the cessation (*nirodha*) of this, this ceases.[2])' (Of course the alternate 'thises' refer to two different principles).

The most striking feature in the *Nidāna Saṃyukta* discussions is the addition of three more members to the main sequence.

1. S II 65, T 99 section 12 No 13. Tripāṭhi 145, also 147, 157, 170 for what follows.

2. Not in the Sarvāstivāda versions (either Sanskrit or Chinese).

Usually where the latter occurs we find next to 'emotion exists through the condition of contact' a new condition: 'Contact exists through the condition of the six spheres (*āyatana*)'. This is followed by 'the six spheres exist through the condition of a sentient body' and then 'a sentient body exists through the condition of consciousness' as before. This new condition in fact is little but an elucidation of 'contact'. The six spheres are the senses, the five senses and the mind as sixth, just as we read in the *Mahānidāna Sūtra* that if there were no contact at all, contact of the sight, hearing, smell, taste, touch or mind, there would be no emotion. It may be suggested that this new link shows a later development of the theory and that the *Saṃyukta* discussions are later than those of the *Dīrgha*. However, it would seem hard to prove this, and still harder to discover whether the development, if such it was, took place during the Buddha's lifetime or was worked out afterwards. If the latter was the case we can at least point out that the new condition (and the two others which follow below) is found in the teaching of all schools of Buddhism, and that it therefore presumably belongs to the earliest period, before the schisms.

More important are the other two new conditions. After 'a sentient body exists through the condition of consciousness' we find instead of 'consciousness exists through the condition of a sentient body' the new 'consciousness exists through the condition of the forces (*saṃskāras*, plural)'. Finally we have 'the forces exist through the condition of ignorance (*avidyā*)'. By way of elucidation of the two new conditions the *Saṃyukta* tells us;[1] 'There are these three forces: the force of the body (i.e. physical force), the force of speech, the force of thought.' Ignorance is lack of knowledge of the Four Truths. We know from the last chapter that ignorance produces wrong theory, wrong intention, wrong speech (p.104 above) and is the opposite of right theory, the first factor of the way. The 'forces' now under discussion are all those actions, or probably more strictly wrong actions, which lead to continuing transmigration, to rebirth. The word might also be translated by 'preparations'.

It seems clear, and this is how these two conditions were interpreted by all schools of Buddhism, that by taking the

1. S II p. 4, T 99 section 12 No. 16, Tripāṭhi 158 f.

sequence beyond consciousness and the sentient body the *Saṃyukta* has simply carried the process back again to a previous life. The only condition for the existence of consciousness and a sentient body, besides each acting as condition for the other, as stated in the *Dīrgha*, is previous existence, a previous life, of consciousness and a sentient body, in which a living being performed certain actions, exercised its 'forces'. These forces operating in the previous existence produce rebirth, produce consciousness and a sentient body in another existence, another life. There is one *sūtra* in the *Saṃyukta* which suggests how 'forces' and ignorance were added to the sequence successively, since it gives the sequence with forces but omitting ignorance. It says[1]: 'Following it (the eightfold way) I (the Buddha) discovered old age and dying and their origination, cessation and the practice leading to that cessation. Following it I discovered birth...existence...consciousness and its origination, etc. Following it I discovered the forces and their origination, cessation and the practice leading to that cessation.' The text ends there adding merely that the Buddha has described this way, the best life, to his followers. Ignorance is not mentioned, and knowledge is only implied in the discovery of the sequence. The possibility of connecting ignorance with the sequence as an ultimate condition would easily suggest itself at this point, however, and perhaps by tracing how the sequence was worked out in this way we can understand it better.

The *Saṃyukta* text quoted for the elucidation of the terms 'forces' and 'ignorance' adds elucidations of 'sentience', 'matter' and 'consciousness' not given in the *Mahānidāna Sūtra*. 'Sentience' means emotion (*vedanā*), perception (*saṃjñā*), volition (*cetanā*), contact (*sparśa*, i.e. 'stimulus') and attention (*manasikāra*).[2] 'Matter' means the four elements (*mahābhūta*, 'great existents'; the four are earth, water, heat and air) and matter which exists in dependence on (*upādāya*) the four elements (this is explained in the schools as meaning the five senses and matter as their five kinds of object, together with certain other physical facts which we need not consider here). The

1. S II p. 106, T 99 section 12 No. 5. Tripāṭhi 97 f. (but with all 12 conditions). See also the text referred to p. 117 below.

2. The Chinese has instead the 4 groups other than matter.

sentient body is sentience plus matter. 'Consciousness' means the six 'bodies of consciousness (*vijñānakāyas*)', namely consciousness of sight, consciousness of hearing, consciousness of smell, consciousness of taste, consciousness of touch, consciousness of mind.

These elucidations are clear and useful. The dependence of consciousness on a material substrate, on a sentient body, is emphasised here by stating that consciousness is comprehended in consciousness of the six senses. The description of sentience is very interesting.

The *sūtra* we referred to above as suggesting how 'forces' and 'ignorance' came to be added to the sequence has some further points bearing on the sequence as given in the *Dīrgha*. There is an elucidation of the reciprocal conditionality of a sentient body and consciousness which is not given in the *Mahānidāna Sūtra*, though it does occur in another *Dīrgha* text, the *Mahāvadāna Sūtra*.[1] In the latter text the Buddha recounts at length the early life and enlightenment of a previous Buddha. This text in fact seems to have formed the basis of the later legend of the Buddha, of 'our' Buddha, on the assumption that all Buddhas lead very similar lives. The legend we can consider in another chapter, what interests us now being that the *Mahāvadāna Sūtra* leads up to conditioned origination as the content of a Buddha's enlightenment, with one or two new points. First, a future Buddha is made to seek enlightenment because he is dissatisfied with his experience in the world. He meets an old, afflicted man, a sick man and a funeral procession, and says 'Fie upon birth, in as much as old age, disease and death will be discerned in one who has been born.' This adds disease to the unhappiness for which birth is a condition. Seeking later the condition for birth this Buddha becomes enlightened when through methodical attention he has insight (*abhisamaya*), having understood: existence being, birth is. From the condition of existence, birth is. The text runs through the sequence up to the reciprocal conditionality of a sentient body and consciousness in the same way. The *Saṃyukta* contains the same expression 'through methodical attention he has insight,

1. D No. 14=T 1 No. 1=Sarvāstivāda *Mahāvadāna* (Waldschmidt).

having understood...', and both texts likewise have the following statement:

'This consciousness turns back again from the sentient body. It does not go further. To this extent one may be born, grow old, die, pass away, be reborn, namely (to the extent that) consciousness exists though the condition of a sentient body, a sentient body through the condition of consciousness, the six spheres through the condition of a sentient body (this *Dirgha Sūtra* as well as the *Saṃyukta* text has the six spheres condition, but not forces and ignorance)....'

This elucidation is merely another way of saying that there can be no consciousness without a sentient body as a basis for it. The fact that the same *Saṃyukta* text afterwards adds the forces as a condition for consciousness, as we saw earlier, does not affect this provided that we understand the relation of the forces to consciousness according to the usual interpretation.

Another *Saṃyukta* text[1] gives the sequence without ignorance as a series of grounds (*vastu*) of knowledge (*jñāna*). In fact there are four grounds for each member of the sequence: knowledge of the condition itself, of its origination, of its cessation and of the practice leading to its cessation, this last being the eightfold way. The Sthaviravāda text adds for each member of the sequence, each condition, that this knowledge, when a pupil has it, is his 'knowledge about the principle (*dharma*)'. When he has seen, ascertained, attained 'timelessly' (producing immediate results or known to be true regardless of time ?), plumbed this principle he draws a scheme (*naya*, 'plan') with reference to the past and the future. Whatever *śramaṇas* or brahmans have discovered the forces (or whatever the principle, the condition, is), their origination, etc., in the past, or will discover the forces, etc., in the future, all of them have discovered or will discover them to be just as I discover them to be now. This is his 'knowledge about the inference (*anvaya*)'. This text emphasises that the laws of nature, as we may call them, discovered by the Buddha (and checked by his pupil) are always true. The inference follows that whoever, whenever, discovers them must find them to be the same.

1. S II 56 ff., T 99 section 14 No. 15.

The Four 'Foods'

Several of the *Saṃyukta* texts on conditioned origination bring in another kind of causal relation, that of four kinds of 'food' (*āhāra*). There is also a *Dīrgha* text[1] which says: 'All beings (*sattvas*) persist through food; all beings persist through the forces.' Only the first kind of food is food in the literal sense of what creatures eat. The second is 'contact' (*sparśa*, 'stimulus'). The third is volition of the mind. The fourth is consciousness. Through these beings persist and are enabled to be produced (to be reborn). The source, the origination, of these four foods, however, is desire. From this we are led through the sequence desire, emotion and the rest down to ignorance.[2]

Another text[3] elucidates the four foods. Ordinary food is connected with the passions of the five senses. Contact (stimulus) is connected with emotion. Volition of the mind is volition, wishing, aspiring for something (e.g. to be out of extreme danger and pain). It is connected with desire. Consciousness-food is described as experience through the sentient body, the latter being specially connected with consciousness. When ordinary food is fully understood (*parijñāta*) passion is fully understood. When contact is fully understood emotion is fully understood. When volition of the mind is fully understood the three desires (presumably for pleasure, existence or non-existence) are fully understood. When consciousness-food is fully understood the sentient body is fully understood.

Further,[4] if there is passion, pleasure, desire for ordinary food, then consciousness finds a resting place and grows there. Then there is descent of a sentient body (into the womb), and as a result increase of the forces (*saṃskāras*). Where there is increase of the forces there will be production of rebirth (*punarbhava*) and so of future birth, old age, dying, grief and all kinds of unhappiness. It is exactly the same if there are passion,

1. D III 211 (in T 1 No. 9).
2. S II 11 f., T 99 section 15 No. 9.
3. S II 99 f., T 99 section 15 No. 11.
4. S II 101, T 99 section 15 No. 12. The latter combines: 'If there is passion for these four foods then consciousness...'

pleasure, desire for the other three kinds of food: consciousness will find a resting place and grow, with the same results.

Is there a Soul?

'Who eats the consciousness-food ?' asked one of the monks[1] when the Buddha had spoken of 'beings' persisting and being reborn through the four foods. 'Not a sound question (*kalya*, 'sound', 'proper')', replied the Master, 'I do not say 'eats'... If you were to ask "of what" is the consciousness-food that would be a sound question. The consciousness-food is the condition for the future production of rebirth.'

In the same way the Buddha explains that it is not sound to ask who touches, who desires, and so on. One may ask, however, through what condition there is touch (contact, stimulus) or desire.

Another question asked[2] is (only in the Sthaviravāda version) 'Of whom is there old age and dying ?' Again the question is unsound, wrongly formulated. If you say that old age and dying is one thing but that this old age and dying is 'of' another thing (or person) both expressions have the same meaning, only the wording of the expressions is different. It is the same as in the case of the two (false) opinions: (1) the life-principle (*jīva*: one conception of the 'soul') is the same thing as the body (*śarīra*), (2) the life-principle is one thing and the body is another thing. With either of these opinions one cannot lead the best life. Not going to either of these extremes (*anta*) the thus-gone teaches the doctrine intermediately (by the mean, *madhyena*). It is the same if the question refers to birth or any of the other conditions. This conception of a mean between two extremes brings us to the essence of the Buddha's understanding of the nature of the universe. We met the same formulation of avoiding extremes and going by the mean in the first teaching of the Buddha to the five monks. There, however, the extremes are real, being indulgence and asceticism, and the mean is the way to attain calm. Here the extremes are non-existent, are false opinions (though attachment to them still leads to wrong action and continued transmigration,

1. S II 13, T 99 section 15 No. 10. cf. MPPŚ (Lamotte) p. 32.
2. S II 60 ff.

as opposed to the 'best life', i.e. the way, which is the mean in the former sense). The universe is not like that. It is in fact more complex, and the theory of conditioned origination is the true explanation, the true description, of the life-process which the soul theories were designed to explain. There will be more to say on this question later, and we shall find Buddhist philosophers returning to it again and again as the central point of their doctrine as we trace the history of Buddhism in India.

In another text[1] a brahman asks whether he who acts is the same as he who experiences (the result), or whether one acts and another experiences. The Buddha replies (in the Sarvāstivāda version that this is undetermined) that these are two extremes (the Sarvāstivāda specifies the eternalist and the annihilationist), which he avoids, teaching a doctrine intermediately, in fact teaching the sequence of conditioned origination.

Similarly a monk asks Śāriputra[2] whether each condition in the sequence is made by oneself, made by another, made by both oneself and another, or lastly being without self-making or other-making (but spontaneously (*adhītya*, causelessly) originated). He is told that none of these four alternatives is correct, but that each member of the sequence exists through the condition of the next member. This method of stating four alternatives, all rejected as false, is a standard method of argument in later Buddhist philosophy. Here the alternatives are simply rejected; later the actual refutations are filled in, showing that each position is untenable, that the opponent is in a 'tetralemma' (*catuṣkoṭi*). It is noteworthy that this text like the *Mahānidāna* takes the sequence only as far as consciousness and the sentient body.

There are other variants on this theme in the *Saṃyukta*. This body is not yours, nor is it another's. It should be seen as an old action (*karman*) 'synthesised' ('accumulated', *abhisaṃskṛta*), willed (*abhisañcetita*), experienced.[3] The Buddha is asked[4] whether unhappiness is made by oneself, by another,

1. S II 75f., T 99 section 12 No. 18. Tripāṭhī 165-7.
2. S II 112ff., T 99 section 12 No. 6. Tripāṭhī 107ff.
3. S II 64f., T 99 section 12 No 13. Tripāṭhī 144f. (with slight variation).
4. S II 19f., T 99 section 12 No. 20. Tripāṭhī 172 ff.

by both, or by neither, being spontaneous (or without a cause), and when he rejects all these he is asked whether then unhappiness does not exist, or finally whether he does not know or see unhappiness.

In this last text the Buddha gives some explanation of why he rejects the alternatives.[1] To say that he who acts is the same as he who experiences, that unhappiness is made by oneself, is to arrive at eternalism (*śāśvatatva*, that there is an eternal self or soul). To say that one acts and another experiences, that unhappiness is made by another, is to arrive at annihilationism (*uccheda*, that there is a self, but it is annihilated at death). The true explanation, as before, is the sequence of conditions. Yet another text[2] reaffirms : happiness and unhappiness are originated through conditions.

At this point we may return to the *Mahānidāna Sūtra*, which after discussing the sentient body and consciousness goes on to the question of a self or soul.[3] The term used in the discussion is *ātman*. This word is basically a reflexive pronoun meaning 'himself', 'herself', 'oneself', 'myself', 'yourself', etc., according to the context. In the genitive case it may mean 'my own', 'your own', 'his own', etc. It was also used, however, to refer to a conception of an essential self in a person, in fact of a 'soul'. Some (but not all) Brahmanical speculation in the *Upaniṣads* uses the word *ātman* in this latter sense. Clearly the word cannot be satisfactorily translated into English, since the English word 'self' did not develop such a meaning. It seems best to use 'soul' where the word is used in that sense, as a noun, and 'himself', etc., where it is the pronoun. In Brahmanical theories of a soul *ātman* remained the most usual term (the Jainas preferred *jiva*).

The Buddha now reviews some of the theories of a soul (*ātman*). It has been considered as material or immaterial, as limited in size or infinite. Some think it exists (only) in the present life (these are the annihilationists, says the commentary), others that it continues to exist in future (lives or existences :

1. A Sanskrit version of this is found at Tripāṭhī 166 (cf. T 99 section 12 No. 18).

2. S II 38, T 99 section 14 No. 1.

3. T 1 No. 13 omits this and the remainder of the *Sūtra*. We follow it in T 14, T 26 No. 97 and T 52, as well as the Pali.

the eternalists), or that even if it is not originally of a nature to exist in future ('immortal', as one would say in English), it can be made so (*upa-klp*, 'prepared'). Now how do they envisage (*sam-anu-dṛś*, perhaps 'observe', i.e. think they make actual observation of it, not merely conceive it) a soul? Some envisage (or observe) it as emotion (*vedanā*) : my soul is emotion, others as not emotion, as 'not experiencing.'

Now in the case that the soul is supposed to be emotion it should be stated whether it is happy, unhappy or neither (in a state of equanimity), since emotions are of these three kinds. These three cannot exist simultaneously on the same occasion (the soul can be only one at a time). Moreover it is a fact that all these emotions are impermanent (*anitya*), synthesised (*saṃskṛta*, 'activated', cf. *saṃskāra*, 'force'), originated through conditions, having the principle of becoming exhausted (disappearing), having the principle of cessation, etc. In that case one would have to say when experiencing e.g. a happy emotion 'this is my soul', but when that emotion ceases one would have to say 'my soul has ceased to exist !' Thus this conception of a soul supposed to be observed (envisaged) in the visible world leads to the conclusion that it is impermanent, a mixture of happiness and unhappiness (i.e. a compound, not an ultimate entity), having the principle of production and cessation, which is not satisfactory. (It may be noted here that this critique bears on the Brahmanical doctrine, afterwards maintained by the Vedānta school, that the soul is pure joy or happiness.)

On the other hand if the soul is envisaged as not emotion, not experiencing, one would ask : where experience is completely non-existent, would there be the thought 'I am'? Surely not, so that the other alternative also is unsatisfactory. Even if the soul is described, not as being emotion, but as having emotions, then if the emotions absolutely ceased would there be the thought 'I am this' ?

The Buddha then continues : 'Since, Ānanda, a monk (i. e. one whose understanding is sound) does not envisage a soul as emotion, nor a soul having no experience, nor a soul as having emotions and of the principle of having emotions, he is not attached to anything in the world. Not being attached he does not long for (desire) anything, and so he individually (personally, with reference to himself : *pratyātmam*) attains extinction.

He understands that birth is exhausted, the best life has been properly lived, the business has been done, afterwards there will be no more of this world.

'If anyone should say, Ānanda, with reference to a monk whose thoughts are thus freed: "The thus-gone exists after death" is his opinion, that would be unsound. If instead: "The thus-gone does not exist after death", that would be unsound. If instead : "The thus-gone both exists and does not exist after death," that would be unsound. If instead : "The thus-gone neither exists nor does not exist after death", that would be unsound. Why ? As far as there is designation, as far as there is a way for designation; as far as there is language, as far as there is a way for language; as far as there is concept, as far as there is a way for concepts; as far as there is understanding, as far as there is scope for understanding; as far as there is the cycle (of the universe), as far as the cycle revolves; having ascertained (*abhi-jñā*) that, a monk is freed. If anyone should say: "A monk having ascertained that and being freed does not know, does not see", that is his opinion, it would be unsound.'

There are several points to discuss here. In the first place in regard to the various conceptions of the soul the Buddha's position would appear to be that any conception giving the soul certain properties, such as emotion or happiness, is redundant, since the properties themselves are principles synthesised, impermanent, originated through conditions, but nevertheless adequate to account for the observed facts. No permanent, eternal, soul can possibly be demonstrated to exist through the changing principles of the universe. Thus a soul as a substrate bearing changing principles is redundant; a soul having the same nature as these principles is not only redundant but cannot be eternal. Finally a soul not having any identifiable properties (as e.g. emotion) is as nothing, could not be the basis of the idea of a self, a subject, of the thought 'I am'.

In connection with this point, illustrated by the suggestion that the soul is or has emotion, we may refer to another *sūtra*[1], where the Buddha notes a wider range of theories of a soul. He there says: 'Those *śramaṇas* and brahmans who in many

1. S III 46f., T 99 section 2 No. 13 (Vol. II p. 11b, 1ff.).

ways envisage a soul all do so by envisaging the five attachment groups or one of them. Which five? In this connection, monks, an uneducated ordinary person...envisages matter as a soul, or a soul as possessing matter, or matter in a soul, or a soul in matter. Or he envisages emotion, perception, the forces, or consciousness as a soul, possessed by a soul, in a soul, or a soul in them. Envisaging[1] this he gets the thought "I am"..Being ignorant he thinks this, or "I am this", or "I shall be", or "I shall not be", or "I shall be material", or "I shall be immaterial", or "I shall be having perception (*saṃjñin*)", or "I shall be without perception", or "I shall have neither perception nor non-perception"...But one who is educated abandons ignorance and gets knowledge (science)...and does not have any of these thoughts. With this may be compared also the *Vinaya* text translated in Chapter Three (p. 53 above). It seems clear enough that the Buddha rejects any conception of a soul or essential self.

To show further the actual arguments advanced by the Buddha against the soul theories we may add a translation of part of the dialogue between him and the wanderer Proṣṭhapāda in the *Dīrgha*.[2] The discussion here is about meditation and how one reaches the 'summit of perception.' Then Proṣṭhapāda raises the question of a soul: 'Is perception the soul of a man, sir, or is perception one thing, soul another?' The Buddha : 'What now, Proṣṭhapāda, do you assume a soul?' 'I assume a gross soul, sir, material, made of the four elements, feeding on solid food.' Yet if your soul were gross, Proṣṭhapāda, material, made of the four elements, feeding on solid food, in that case for you perception would be one thing, soul another. Then on this assumption you have to ascertain how perception can be one thing, soul another. Just let this gross...soul be, Proṣṭhapāda, for then a man's perceptions occur as one thing but cease as another thing...' Then Proṣṭhapāda proposes to assume a 'mental soul' with perfect faculties, complete in its faculties. The Buddha's objection remains the same : perceptions would then occur as one thing but cease as another. Lastly Proṣṭha-

1. The following only in the Sthaviravāda version.

2. D No. 9=T 1 No. 28. The Chinese (Vol. I p 110c), however, omits part of the argument, particularly the phrase 'perception (etc.) would be one thing, soul another' each time it occurs.

pāda proposes an immaterial soul, 'consisting of perception.' The objection is still the same. The force of the objection appears to be that on any of these theories perception occurs as a faculty of the soul, or as the soul itself, but must cease as simple perception (since the soul does not cease but continues). Alternatively the meaning is, and our translation should read : '...you have to ascertain how perception can be one thing, soul another... for then a man's perceptions occur as another thing (than soul) and cease as another thing (than soul)', since the soul exists before and after the occurrence and cessation of the perception. These different interpretations do not affect the essential argument : if the soul is permanent or continuing it cannot explain transient principles such as perception, nor can these be used to prove its existence. The Sthaviravāda Sub-commentary (*Ṭikā*) *Līnatthappakāsinī* explains that the soul itself would be without perception and unconscious (*acetana*). The argument will be further elaborated and clarified by later Buddhist philosophers.

Another point here is the question about the thus-gone (often a title of the Buddha himself, here of a monk who is freed) after death (or after final extinction). Does he exist, not exist, or both, or neither? This is in form the tetralemma of which we met an instance earlier (whether a condition is made by oneself, another, both, or neither). The interpretation of the Buddhist schools of this tetralemma is that 'thus-gone' here means simply the 'being' (*sattva*) assumed to be under discussion. As there is no continuing being, which would be tantamount to a soul, the alternatives do not apply, as in the case of a condition supposed to be made by oneself, etc., which in fact occurs through the next member of the sequence. There is no being, or 'thus-gone', which exists, or is destroyed at death, etc. There is only the sequence of conditions, the cycle of the universe so conditioned.[1]

On the subject of tetralemmas we should note another set of four alternatives in the *Saṃyukta* text just quoted: is the supposed soul matter (for example), or does it possess matter,

1. S IV 384 (T 99 section 5 No. 4) says that the thus-gone truly, really, does not exist (*upa-labh,* passive) in the visible world (*dṛṣṭa dharma*) (*upalabh* may, especially later, mean 'be perceived', but still in the sense that 'not perceived' implies definitely not there at all).

or is it in matter, or is matter in it? The first two possibilities are covered by the discussion on whether the soul is emotion, or has emotions, in the *Mahānidāna Sūtra*, given above. The other two possibilities are clearly no better than the second, implying that the soul is different from matter (or from emotion, etc.), and therefore cannot be proved to exist through properties of the latter. This method of examining a theory was used by later Buddhist philosophers and developed further. In effect it reduces to a dilemma: is the soul the same as matter or different from it, equivalent to the question mentioned near the beginning of this section: is the life-principle (*jīva*, or soul) the same thing as the body or is the life-principle one thing and the body another. For the Buddha these alternatives are unreal, non-existent. What exists is conditioned origination. There are no permanent entities at all, whether a soul as 'life-principle', 'being' or 'self', or matter, emotion, perception, forces or consciousness. The soul does not exist at all as a separate entity; matter, etc., are impermanent.

To conclude this section on the question of a soul we may return to the *Saṃyukta*. In one *sūtra* there[1] the Buddha says to the monks: An uneducated ordinary person may become indifferent, dispassionate, freed, with respect to this body consisting of the four elements, because it can be seen to grow and decay...But as to what is called 'thought', 'mind', 'consciousness', an uneducated ordinary person is not able to become indifferent, dispassionate, freed in that connection. Why? Because for a long time this has been coveted, possessed, held on to: 'This is mine', 'I am this', 'This is myself (soul, *ātman*)' ...it would be better if he accepted the body consisting of the four elements as himself (his soul), but not thought...The body endures for a number of years, but thought, mind, consciousness, changes all the time. ('When it arises it is one thing, when it ceases it is another.')

Consciousness

We have seen that consciousness cannot exist apart from a sentient body, that it is simply consciousness of the senses or of 'mind', that it 'feeds' on experience through the sentient

1. S II 94f., T 99 section 12 No. 7. Tripāṭhi 115 ff.

body (which can be fully understood by fully understanding consciousness), that 'consciousness-food', which evidently is merely consciousness itself, is the condition for the future production of rebirth, and that being impermanent, transient, it is anything but an eternal soul. After rejecting the theories of a soul the *Mahānidāna Sūtra* returns to the subject of consciousness.

'There are these seven stations (*sthiti*) of consciousness, Ānanda, and two spheres. Which seven? The first is those beings which have a diversity of bodies and a diversity of perceptions, as human beings, some gods and some unhappy spirits (the latter means beings reborn as animals, demons, ghosts or in purgatory according to the Sthaviravāda explanation). The second is those beings which have a diversity of bodies but a unity (similarity) of perception, as the gods of Brahmā's retinue ('having bodies like Brahmā's') produced by the first (meditation—commentary). The third is those beings which have unity of body but a diversity of perceptions, as the gods of the world of radiance. The fourth is those beings which have unity of body and unity of perception, as the gods of the lustrous (or 'beautiful') world (who according to the commentary enjoy the highest, unalloyed happiness, the sole defect of which is that it is temporary, not eternal). The fifth is those beings which have by completely transcending perceptions of matter, by the extinction of perceptions of 'resistance' (*pratigha*) and by being without attention to diversity of perceptions gone to the sphere of infinity of space, thinking 'Space is infinite'. The sixth is those beings which have completely transcended the sphere of infinity of space and gone to the sphere of infinity of consciousness, thinking 'Consciousness is infinite'. The seventh is those beings which have completely transcended the sphere of infinity of consciousness and gone to the sphere of nothingness, thinking 'Nothing exists'. (All these stations can be attained in meditation, the last three it seems only by meditation, having no proper inhabitants or 'gods'. We are intended to note that the range of consciousness of a human being in meditation goes far beyond the spheres of the gods, all of whom, Brahmā included, occupy a low position in the universe little better than that of human beings and in certain respects worse.)

'(The two spheres, which are beyond consciousness but still part of the cycle of the universe, are) The sphere of beings having no perception and secondly the sphere of neither perception nor non-perception.

'One should understand each of these nine...its origination, its cessation, its enjoyment ('taste'), its disadvantage and its liberation (i.e. liberation from it). However, it would not be sound to be pleased with any of them...Having known ('ascertained') them and their origination, etc., in their true nature a monk has become free (*vimukta*) through non-attachment (*anupādā,* adverbial, 'being without attachment'). Such a monk, Ānanda, is called freed by understanding.'

By way of comment on this passage we may refer again to the *Saṃyukta*[1]. 'That which one wills, determines, tends to do (*anu-śi,* have a latent tendency for, resulting from past experience), is a support (*ālambana*) for a station(ing) of consciousness. When there is a support, there is a resting place (*pratiṣṭhā*) of consciousness ('A support being, a resting place of consciousness is'). When consciousness has rested there and grown, there is production of rebirth in future... (and the resulting unhappiness...)'. Even if only the tendency remains it will serve as a support, with the same result, but if one neither wills nor determines nor tends to do anything there will not be a support for a station of consciousness, there will be no resting place and consequently no future production of rebirth and unhappiness.

In this way the process of transmigration continues. Transient though consciousness is, it will continue to serve as a condition for more consciousness as long as there is any tendency to do, much more so any actual volition. Before it ceases it will have produced a support, a station or resting place, for a further impulse of consciousness, a different consciousness, and so on indefinitely, through life after life (serving as condition for the production of successive sentient bodies), until the tendency ends.

Impermanence

There have been several references above to the impermanence of principles. In one of the first dialogues with the five monks when he begins his teaching the Buddha asks whether

1. S II 65f., T 99 section 14 No. 19. See 'Objects'.

matter and the other groups are permanent or impermanent, and it is agreed that all are impermanent (p. 53 above). In this chapter it has been emphasised that consciousness is more impermanent than matter. In a Sthaviravāda *Saṃyukta* text[1] it is said that each member of the sequence of conditions is impermanent (*anitya*), synthesised (*saṃskṛta*), originated through conditions, having the principle of becoming exhausted (*kṣayadharma*), having the principle of cessation...

Since the five groups comprise all principles that exist, it seems clear that all principles are impermanent. There is an interesting text in the *Saṃyukta*, the *Kātyāyanāvavāda Sūtra*,[2] which bears on this question and links it to that of the nature of the universe as corresponding to a mean position between extreme views which have been put forward by other philosophers (see pp. 119 ff and 125 f. above).

Kātyāyana asks the Master about right theory. The Buddha explains : 'The majority of people have depended on the pair it-is-ness (*astitā*, existence-ism) and it-is-not-ness (*nāstitā*, non-existence-ism, nihilism). One who sees the origination of the universe in its true nature, through right understanding, is unaware of is-not-ness (nihilism, non-existence of principles) with reference to the universe. One who sees the cessation of the universe in its true nature, through right understanding, is unaware of is-ness (existence of principles) with reference to the universe. The majority of people have been bound by means ('by a basis', *upadhi*, in the Sanskrit), by attachments (and by involvements). Now, he who does not plan for (*upaiti*), get attached to (*upādatte*), fix his attention on (*adhitiṣṭhati*), means and attachments, on fixing the attention of (*adhiṣṭhāna*) thought (*cetasas*), on the tendency (*anuśaya*) to involvements (*abhiniveśa*), thinking "I have a soul",—he does not doubt, he is not uncertain, that only unhappiness occurs when there is (any) occurring (Sthaviravāda commentary : i.e. that only the five attachment groups occur, that no being or soul occurs), that only unhappiness ceases when there is (any) ceasing. In this case he really has knowledge, he does not have

1. S II 26.
2. S II 17, T 99 section 12 No. 19. Tripāṭhī 167 ff. The Madhyamaka philosopher Nāgārjuna takes his stand on this text (MK XV 7) and his commentator Candrakīrti (fl. end of 6th century A.D.) informs us that it occurs in the recensions of the *Tripiṭaka* of all the schools of Buddhism.

it through the condition of another's (he has direct personal perception of it—commentary). To this extent, Kātyāyana, there is right theory.

'That all exists (*sarvam asti*) is one extreme, Kātyāyana. That all does not exist (*sarvaṃ nāsti*) is the second extreme.[1] Not going to either of these extremes the thus-gone teaches the doctrine by the mean (by the intermediate way—Sanskrit version): the forces exist through the condition of ignorance, consciousness exists through the condition of the forces, etc.; thus we have the origination of this entire mass of unhappiness. But through the absolute cessation in dispassion of ignorance we have the cessation of the forces, through the cessation of the forces the cessation of consciousness, etc.; thus we have the cessation of this entire mass of unhappiness.'

This text is a difficult one, but when taken in the light of the various aspects of the doctrine as set out in the texts already considered its meaning seems clear. There are no permanent or eternal principles in the world, or even principles which having come into existence remain in existence. On the other hand there is not a total absence of principles, or even the total destruction of all principles one after another without leaving a trace of their ever having existed. The real nature of the universe is that it consists of temporary principles, which cease to exist, but not without serving as conditions for further temporary principles, not without continuity. As opposed to this continuity of transient parts we have the alternative extremes of the continuity of a permanent entity, 'is-ness', and transient principles disappearing without any continuity, 'is-not-ness'. It is the shifting mass of transient principles which constitutes unhappiness, and that is all that there is, all that occurs. There is just unhappiness itself, and no unhappy beings or souls. The avoidance of the tendency to involvement, of possessiveness implied by the idea of having a soul, hints at the freedom to which right understanding leads through not being pleased with any of the stations of consciousness, or spheres, and not willing any more supports which could provide such stations.

---

1. These two sentences are missing in the Sarvāstivāda version (as read here the first contradicts the view of that school). Candrakīrti reads them without *sarvam*, i.e. 'That it exists..' or simply 'Exists..'

Freedom

Having thus outlined the stations of consciousness, freedom through non-attachment and freedom through understanding, the next, and last, part of the *Mahānidāna Sūtra* further elaborates the subject of freedom.

'There are these eight freedoms (*vimokṣa*), Ānanda. Which eight ? The first is that being (oneself) material (or at the material level of consciousness) one sees material objects (this is the simple contemplation of some material object in order to compose the mind). The second is that having internally perception of the immaterial one sees, externally, material objects. The third is when one has become intent on only the thought "It is lustrous (or 'beautiful', *śubha*)".[1] The fourth is when by completely transcending perceptions of matter, by the extinction of perceptions of resistance and by being without attention to diversity of perceptions one enters and remains in the sphere of infinity of space, thinking "Space is infinite." The fifth is when having completely transcended the sphere of infinity of space one enters and remains in the sphere of infinity of consciousness, thinking "Consciousness is infinite". The sixth is when having completely transcended the sphere of infinity of consciousness one enters and remains in the sphere of nothingness, thinking "Nothing exists". The seventh is when having completely transcended the sphere of nothingness one enters and remains in the sphere of neither perception nor non-perception. The eighth is when having completely transcended the sphere of neither perception nor non-perception one enters and remains in the cessation of perception and emotion. These, Ānanda, are the eight freedoms.

'Since, Ānanda, a (trained) monk attains these eight freedoms in the normal order, also in reverse order and in both orders alternately, and attains and comes out from them wherever he wishes, whichever he wishes and as long as he wishes, and enters and remains in them after himself having ascertained and experienced uninfluenced freedom of thought (*cetas*), freedom

---

1. This may be explained through the 'freeing of thought by benevolence' (p. 96 above). cf. Ps II 39.

through understanding, even in the visible world, through the exhaustion of the influences, he is called a monk who is freed from both aspects (from his body of matter and from his body of sentience—Sthaviravāda commentary). There is no other freedom from both aspects which is higher than or superior to this freedom from both aspects.

The *Saṃyukta* texts add a few more points to the account of freedom given here and in various passages quoted earlier. The statement that if its condition is absent a principle does not exist is variously elaborated. We have met more than once the expression 'absolute (*aśeṣa*) cessation in dispassion', among others, for the rejection of a condition, for getting free from it. An addition to the descriptions given so far is found in a *Saṃyukta* text[1] which speaks of a monk who through indifference, through dispassion, through cessation, has become free through non-attachment. It adds that it would be proper to say of him that he had attained extinction (*nirvāṇa*) in the visible world (*dṛṣṭa-dharma*). In another Sthaviravāda text[2] it is asked through what sort of freedom (*vimokṣa*) one understands that birth is exhausted and that afterwards there will be no more of this world, and answered that it is through freedom internally (*adhyātmam*), through the exhaustion of all attachment, so that there will be no flowing in of the influences.

From the last part of the *Mahānidāna Sūtra* and from the discussion of the factors of enlightenment in the preceding chapter we see that a monk could attain enlightenment and extinction in this world, in this life, and then spend his time in the freedoms, or in the various factors of enlightenment. He continues to live in the world, but is completely without attachment to anything.

Experience

The *Saṃyukta* texts on conditioned origination further emphasise the point that all this theory, and the attainment of freedom, are to be directly experienced by the monk. This of course has been discussed in the previous chapter, particularly under right theory as factor of the way : the truths are to be understood

1. S II 18, T 99 section 15 No. 1.
2. S II 53f.

in their true nature, to be in effect actually discovered for himself by each person following the way. He has before merely heard of the truths; now he really knows them by verifying them for himself. From the point of view of the present chapter we have found that a monk must ascertain for himself the facts set out under the heading of conditioned origination, then he can be said to know them and see them.

A monk should thoroughly investigate (*pari-man* desiderative) the (many kinds of) unhappiness in the world, and how they are conditioned or caused, likewise how they may cease. In the same way he should thoroughly investigate all the other members of the sequence of conditioned origination.[1] In the light of the knowledge he thus gains he should become not attached to anything in the world, not synthesising (*abhi-sam-kṛ*, i. e. not synthesising new conditions for himself), not willing (*abhi-sam-cit* causative=use one's volition). As a result of this he desires nothing and so he personally (individually) attains extinction and knows that afterwards there will be no more of this world.

More emphatic is the text[2] which says that apart from (without) confidence (i. e. in what someone has said) or liking or tradition (*anuśrava*) or reflection on peculiarities (*ākāra*, as reasons, i. e. presumably simply reasoning) or approving after considering (*nidhyānakṣānti*) one's (mere) opinion a monk has personal knowledge of the conditions and of extinction, which is cessation of existence.

Various attainments are mentioned from time to time in the *Tripiṭaka* as accomplishments of the Buddha, of monks, or of other *śramaṇas*. In essence they all seem to arise from different meditation exercises, including the claims of mysterious psychic powers such as the ability to project one's thought anywhere in the material world, and even to project a mind-made body visible to other people. A *Saṃyukta* text,[3] however, dismisses all such attainments, including even those corresponding, it seems, to two of the 'three sciences' acquired by the Buddha at his enlightenment (recollection of his former lives and understanding,

1. S II 81f., T 99 section 12 No. 10. Tripāṭhi 127 ff
2. S II 115 ff., T 99 section 14 No. 9. See further OIP p. 49.
3. S II 121 ff., T 99 section 14 No. 5.

direct knowledge, of the transmigration of beings according to their actions), with the single exception of becoming freed by understanding (*prajñāvimukta*). This is explained as meaning that first there is knowledge of the stations (*sthiti*) of principles and afterwards knowledge with reference to extinction. (All principles, like consciousness, which of course is one of them, have their 'stations', i. e. their places in sequences of conditions.) It is further elucidated by discussion of the five groups and their impermanence, etc., and of the sequence of conditioned origination. Another text[1] defines knowledge of the stations of principles directly in relation to conditioned origination, in that the absence of its condition results in the non-existence of a principle, and this knowledge of principles as having the principle of exhaustion, cessation, etc., is knowledge of their stations.

Knowledge of Objective Facts

The monk must experience the true nature of the universe for himself in order to attain freedom : it is not enough just to take even the Buddha's statements on trust, just to learn the doctrine. From this position made clear above it is but a short step to another *Saṃyukta* text on conditioned origination,[2] which states that each principle in the sequence is the condition for the next whether there are occurrences of thus-gones (i.e. enlightened ones, Buddhas, to teach conditioned origination) or not. 'This element (*dhātu*, the Sthaviravāda commentary says this refers to the particular condition, the nature — *svabhāva* — of the condition, under discussion, such as birth as the condition for old age and dying) is established (*sthita*), there is a station for principles (*dharmasthititā*, the fact of there being a station, or stations, for principles), there is a regularity of principles (*dharmaniyāmatā*), there is specific conditionality (*idaṃpratyayatā*). This a thus-gone attains enlightenment about...and teaches...opens, analyses, makes easily understood; and you should see it.' Again '(e. g) The forces exist through the condition of ignorance: thus, monks, that which in this connection is truth (*tathatā*, 'thus-ness' — Pali

1. S II 60, T 99 section 14 No. 16.
2. S II 25 ff., T 99 section 12 No. 14. Tripāṭhi 148 f.

and *Mahāvyutpatti* 1709, variants are *satyatā* and *yathatathā*), not untruth (*avitathatā*), not otherwise (*ananyathatā*), specific conditionality, is called conditioned origination (*pratītyasamutpāda*).' We may mention finally a text[1] in this collection where the Buddha praises Śāriputra for having well penetrated (comprehended) the 'element of principles (*dharmadhātu*).' Here we translate the term *dhātu* as 'element' as above, this being the nearest equivalent, but the original term means an element in the sense of something having an ultimate nature, an ultimate reality. The *dharmadhātu* here is therefore the reality of principles, the real nature of principles, and the Sthaviravāda commentary[2] explains it as their conditioned nature, their nature of being evolved through a particular condition.

The nature of the universe, therefore, about which the Buddha teaches his doctrine, is taken in the *Tripiṭaka* as something objectively real. It is there to be discovered by anyone who can discover it, and whoever discovers it must make the same discovery, namely of facts of causality or conditionality. These facts of conditionality, these natural laws, moreover, are universal and apparently immutable, though everything that exists is impermanent, constantly changing. They are so whether Buddhas appear in the universe or not, and, as we saw earlier in this chapter (p. 117), the Buddha believed that whenever *śramaṇas* or brahmans discovered the conditions they must find them to be the same.

Did the Buddha Claim Omniscience ?

Most schools of Buddhism have held that the Buddha was omniscient, that he literally was aware of everything that had ever taken place, was at present happening, or would happen in the future. Since other *śramaṇas* had made this claim, or had it made for them, it was perhaps natural that Buddhists should wish to set their teacher at least as high as anyone had suggested it was possible to get. However, the *Tripiṭaka* preserves

1: S II 56, T 99 section 14 No. 3.

2. *Sārathappakāsinī*, ed. Piyatissa, Colombo, 1927 (Hewavitarne Bequest Series), Part II p. 50.

express repudiations of such a claim by the Buddha. In one *sūtra*[1] *Ānanda* ridicules those who claimed omniscience as follows.

Suppose we have a teacher who knows everything, sees everything, 'admits' to having complete(without remainder, absolute) knowledge and vision, in that whatever he is doing, whether awake or asleep, his knowledge and vision is constantly and continually 'set up'. He goes to a house for alms (being a *śramaṇa*, begging for his food) but gets nothing and is instead bitten by a dog, or he gets chased by a fierce elephant or a bull. He asks people their names, and the way to the village or town. If you ask him how this could be, he replies that it had to happen, he was destined to be bitten, chased, etc. (this *sūtra* is in fact aimed principally at the Ājīvakas, who claimed omniscience for their sages, particularly for Gośāla). Ānanda remarks that a discerning person will not be impressed by such a teacher, will not be encouraged to follow his version of the 'best life'.

Ānanda then describes his own teacher, the thus-gone, the Buddha who has himself ascertained, observed and made known this universe, etc. What he teaches is the way leading to acquisition of the 'three sciences', recollection of his former existences, understanding of the transmigration of 'beings' according to their actions, knowledge of the exhaustion of the influences. These are the content of the Buddha's enlightenment, as we saw in Chapter Three.

In another *sūtra*[2] the Jaina leader (Mahāvīra, in the *Tripiṭaka* known as Jñātaputra), who also claims omniscience, is described as answering irrelevantly, changing the subject and getting annoyed and angry when asked questions about the origin of things.

The *Madhyama* also contains a *sūtra*[3] in which there is a discussion as to whether the Buddha regards omniscience as impossible, where he is given as saying that it is impossible that one should know and see everything 'at once'. Here omniscience as such is not repudiated, but the Sthaviravāda recension of the *Madhyama* preserves a *sūtra*[4] which is quite

1. Sthaviravāda version M No. 76.
2. M No. 79, T 26 No. 208.
3. M No. 90, T 26 No. 212.
4. M No. 71.

categorical. To quote the Buddha as claiming to know and see everything, to have complete knowledge and vision, is to misrepresent him, to slander him with a falsehood. What then does he claim? Simply that he has the 'three sciences'. This *sūtra* has not been traced in any other recension of the *Tripiṭaka* and would be excluded from consideration by our general rule. It cannot be said, however, that the denial of the omniscience of the Buddha was a doctrine peculiar to the Sthaviravâda school, for that school has on the contrary strongly urged that he was omniscient, even in texts included in its *Tripiṭaka* and peculiar to it.[1] Instead we ought probably to admit this *sūtra* as an authentic part of the earliest *Tripiṭaka*, but likely to have been suppressed by most Buddhists of later times as offensive to their traditions of the greatness of their teacher. The repudiation of omniscience and the statement that being a Buddha means having discovered, ascertained, the three sciences, would seem to harmonise much better with the doctrine as we have found it so far, and with the description of the enlightenment we have found in the earliest texts, than a claim to know and see all things.

In this connection there has been among modern students of Buddhism a certain amount of discussion about the Buddha's doctrine of a mean, rejecting various extremes. In a number of texts in the *Tripiṭaka* the Buddha simply sets aside certain questions, gives no direct answer, and offers instead his own doctrine. Some moderns have rushed in to say that either the Buddha knew the 'answers' to the questions, but thought it well to withhold them from his followers, or he simply did not know the 'answers.'

These questions have been covered in part in our study of 'causation', but some still remain. We saw when discussing impermanence (pp. 128 ff. above) that the following questions had been raised, and variously answered by different schools of thought. Does the universe 'exist'? Does it 'not exist'? (Or does all exist, or not exist?) Here the solution most obviously was that the Buddha could not answer 'yes' or 'no' to either alterna-

1. e.g. Ps I 131 ff.

tive, not because he did not know which was correct, or withheld the answer, but because according to his 'science' it would be false to say categorically that the universe, or everything in it (all principles), existed or that it did not exist. These answers, for him, or for India in his day, meant that the universe, or more accurately its constituents, was either permanent, that its principles were eternal entities; or alternatively that it, or they, did not effectively exist since they vanished without trace. He rejected both extremes as false, and because such questions, formulated in this way, were misleading: to ask whether a principle exists, implying as answer either that it does or that it does not, sidetracks the enquiry from the proper line of advance 'by the mean' into the study of conditioned origination. Principles do not categorically exist, they are impermanent, or in a sense (impermanently) they exist and in a sense they do not exist (having ceased to exist).

In that discussion we referred back to some other similar questions. Does the thus-gone exist after death ? Or not ? Or both exist and not exist ? Or neither ? Again the correct interpretation of this appears to be that such an enquiry is misleading. There is no being, such as a thus-gone, who could either exist or cease to exist. There is only the sequence of conditions, which may occur or cease according to the laws discovered by the Buddha. It is the same when the questions are about the supposed relation of a soul, or life-principle, to matter, to a body. There is no soul... Of whom is there old age and dying ? Another unsound question. Is it the same person who does an action and (later) experiences its result ? Or is it a different person ? These also are two extremes. There is no 'person'. In a sense the former agent and the later patient might be regarded as one individual, but the continuity is only that of a sequence of impermanent mental and other events, hence it will be better not to hypostatise the sequence as an entity, as if there were something that had not changed. Is a given condition made by oneself, or by another, or by both or neither (without a cause) ? All four alternatives are incorrect. The condition exists through its own condition (the preceding member of the sequence.)

Having looked at these examples we are in a position to

examine other groups of questions to which the Buddha had
no categorical answer. In the dialogue with Proṣṭhapāda[1]
quoted above the discussion goes on from the question of a
soul to that of the universe. Proṣṭhapāda asks: 'Is the universe
eternal (*śāśvata*)? Is only this true, the alternative false?'
The Buddha replies: 'It is undetermined (*avyākṛta*) by me
whether the universe is eternal.' Proṣṭhapāda then asks: 'But
then, sir, is the universe non-eternal?' The Buddha again
replies that this is undetermined by him. Proṣṭhapāda further
asks whether the universe is finite or infinite, whether the
life-principle is the same as the body or different from it,
whether the thus-gone exists after death or not or both or neither.
The Buddha gives similar replies. Proṣṭhapāda continues:
'Why, sir, is it undetermined by the Master?' The Buddha
says: 'Proṣṭhapāda, this is not connected with welfare, not
connected with the doctrine, is not the beginning of the best
life, does not lead to indifference, dispassion, cessation, calm,
insight, enlightenment, extinction. Therefore I have not
determined it.' —'But what, sir, has been determined by the
Master?' —'I have determined: This is unhappiness; this
is the origination of unhappiness; this is the cessation of unhappiness; this is the way going to. the cessation of unhappiness.'

Thus the Buddha rejects ten extreme views as irrelevant to
the business in hand, which requires instead the study of the
Four Truths. Since Proṣṭhapāda has just been represented
as unable to understand the problem of perception and the
'soul', it is perhaps not surprising that the Buddha should not
here go into the other questions (for which he has been taxed
with ignorance). As we have seen, he had a very definite and
comprehensible position in regard to at least the questions
about an alleged 'soul', life-principle, being, thus-gone (as a
being, an entity), and the like. This accounts for six of Proṣṭhapāda's questions. We are left with the problem of the
universe. The question whether the universe is infinite or
finite in space and time appears to be still open at the time
of writing, and one wonders whether it will ever be capable
of solution. Kant thought not, and set up the finiteness and

---

1. D No. 9, T 1 No. 28.

infinity of the universe in time and space as a pair of 'antinomies' of pure reason. Either view, he thought (and demonstrated), could be 'proved' by argument, consequently the reason itself is in need of more critical investigation. Was the Buddha, who seems to have been prepared to solve the other three antinomies of Kant,[1] unable to solve this one or unwilling to study it ? Did he simply admit that this lay beyond our knowledge?

As a provisional solution we may note that the Sthaviravāda commentary says that Proṣṭhapāda asked these questions about the universe 'in connection with' the soul, the subject of his former problem. In other words, wishing to discuss whether the soul, in which he believed, but which the Buddha rejected, was eternal and infinite, he brought up the question of whether the universe has such a nature. We might provisionally conclude from this that a 'universe' (*loka*, or 'world', the Upaniṣadic *brahman*?) as an entity having permanence, or ceasing (whether in time or in space), was to the Buddha as much a fiction as a soul, a permanent 'being', or a being lasting some time and then suddenly cut off at death. Is the proper answer: there is no universe, continuing in space or time, nor is there a total destruction of the universe, without trace? Does the question simply reduce to that of 'it-is-ness' versus 'it-is-not-ness'? If so, the full solution is: there is no continuing (infinite) or totally destroyed (finite) universe, there is no such entity, there is only the sequence of conditioned origination.

There are however other *sūtras* bearing on this problem. In one a wanderer of the Vatsa clan asks the Buddha[2] the same ten questions as Proṣṭhapāda, to each of which the Master replies 'I am not of that opinion (*dṛṣṭi*).' At the end the Vatsa asks the Buddha what disadvantage he sees in these opinions, that he avoids them completely. He is told that they are all wildernesses, 'connections' (*saṃyojana*, the term is practically

1. Every composite substance in the world consists of parts...no composite thing consists of parts, no simple substance exists : the Buddha would presumably have accepted the former view ; causality according to the laws of nature, plus a causality of freedom, he would surely have accepted ; that there exists any 'absolutely necessary being' he denied.

2. M No. 72, T 99 section 34 No. 24.

synonymous with others such as influences, attachments, obstacles, etc., meaning a connection with some such bad principle as passion, aversion, (false) opinion, and the like), having unhappiness, remorse, misery and lust and not leading to indifference, dispassion, etc., enlightenment, extinction. This is the disadvantage. The thus-gone does not hold any opinion at all. Instead he has actually seen matter, emotion, perception, forces and consciousness and their origination and cessation. Thus by the exhaustion, cessation, etc., of all tendencies to the conceit of an ego or a 'mine' (soul, possession) he is freed, without attachment.

The Vatsa then asks where a monk whose thoughts are thus freed is reborn (or transmigrates, *upa-pad*). He is told 'is reborn' does not apply (*upa-i*) to him. Nor does 'is not reborn', nor both these, nor neither. He becomes 'unknowing', bewildered, whatever confidence he had in the Buddha disappears. The Buddha uses the simile of a fire to make the attainment of extinction clear. Just as a fire is kept alight through the condition of attachment to firewood and grass and is extinguished in the absence of this, so a thus-gone who might be 'declared' (described, conceived, identified) through his matter, emotion, perception, forces or consciousness cannot be said to be reborn, or not, or both, or neither, in the absence of these. Just as one could not say of the fire where it had been 'reborn', so one could not say of the thus-gone (after death) where he had been reborn. (The term 'extinguished' used of the fire is the same as that used for a person who has attained extinction, though in this passage it is not applied to the thus-gone.) Probably this argument is to be understood in the light of our earlier discussions on the problem of the thus-gone. It is interesting but does not apparently clarify the antinomies about the universe in space and time.

For a further discussion of these we have to go to a celebrated *sūtra* in the *Dirgha*, the *Brahmajāla*.[1] Here we find the Buddha rejecting not merely ten but a scheme of sixty two opinions (*dṛṣṭis*) all said to be held by some brahmans and *śramaṇas*. Of these, eighteen are theories about the past or

1. D No. 1, T 1 No. 21, Tibetan Weller, *Asia Major* 1933.

the origin of the universe or of a soul (held by the *pūrvāntakalpakas*, 'arrangers (imaginers) of the former end'), forty four are theories about the future or final end of a soul (held by the *aparāntakalpakas*, 'arrangers of the after end'). It is said that all those who theorise about either the origin or the end do so in one or other of these sixty two ways. Of the eighteen grounds (*vastus*) of the former group four are those of the eternalists (*śāśvatavāda*), four those of some-things-eternalists (*ekatyaśāśvatika*;—and some not eternal), four more those that the universe is finite, infinite, both, or neither, four more those of evasive agnostics, the last two those of the spontaneously-originated-ists (*adhītyasamutpannikas*, some recensions seem[1] to have read here *ahetusamutpattikas*, 'causeless-originationists'; the meaning is the same). Of the latter group of forty four grounds thirty two assume survival of a soul after death (sixteen that it has perception, eight that it has no perception, eight that it neither has nor has not perception), seven are views of annihilationists (*ucchedavāda*;—of a soul at death) and five those of 'extinction' in the visible world (*dṛṣṭadharmanirvāṇavāda*).

We notice in reading this *sūtra* that the 'universe' and the 'soul' are treated very much on the same level, in the same manner. It is the assumption of the existence of either or both these which leads to the assumption of one of the opinions. Is it then the assumption of a 'universe', not the assumption of its infinity, etc., which is the basic mistake, as in the case of the 'soul'? Given a permanent, enduring universe it might, seemingly it must, be eternal or else be destroyed, extend to infinity in all or some dimensions or not so extend. Given only sequences of conditions in which there is nothing permanent, no permanent being, no *brahman*, the problem does not arise, or at least not in such a crude and futile form. The main purpose of the *sūtra* is to describe how people think up the sixty two opinions, not to discuss the opinions themselves (again this implies their futility as false deductions from premises already false, and the futility of talking about them). A few extracts will perhaps make the Buddha's attitude clear.

1. Yaśomitra, *Abhidharmakośavyākhyā* (ed. Wogihara) p. 449 ; from the Sarvāstivāda version ?

The first three kinds of eternalist are those who to varying degrees have acquired the science of recollecting their former lives. Since they have this knowledge of their former existence for a long period of time they conclude from it that they, i.e. their souls (*ātman*, or selves) and the universe have always existed, are eternal, 'sterile', 'immovable as peaks', 'remaining firm as pillars', that beings transmigrate eternally. The fourth kind are described as logicians and metaphysicians who have deduced by logic (*tarka*) or concluded from their metaphysical investigations (*mimāṃsā*) that the soul and the universe are eternal (Chinese omits 'by logic').

The first case of the some-things-eternal opinion arises as follows in the course of the evolution of the universe: 'There is an occasion, monks, when at some time or other, after a long time, this universe (*loka*) dissolves (*sam-vṛt*, or 'involves'). When the universe is dissolved the majority of beings are dissolved in the world of radiance (*ābhāsvara*, one of the worlds of imponderable matter, inhabited by gods). They remain there for a very long time, made of mind, feeding on joy, self-luminous, living in the sky and staying beautiful.

'There is an occasion, monks, when at some time or other, after a long time, this universe evolves (*vi-vṛt*). When the universe is evolving the *brahma*-mansion appears, empty. Then a certain being, because his (previous) life is exhausted, or because his merit is exhausted, passes away from his world-of-radiance body and is reborn in the empty *brahma*-mansion. He remains there for a very long time, made of mind, feeding on joy, self-luminous, living in the sky and staying beautiful.

'Being alone there for a long time he feels uneasiness, loneliness and longing: "If only other beings would come to this world!" Then some other beings, because their lives are exhausted, or because their merit is exhausted, pass away from their world-of-radiance bodies and are reborn in the *brahma*-mansion in association with that being. They too remain there for a very long time, made of mind, feeding on joy, self-luminous, living in the sky and staying beautiful.

'In this connection, monks, that being who has been reborn first thinks he is God (Brahmā): "I am God, Great God, the Overlord, Unconquered, Seeing-universally, Wielding-power, Lord (*Īśvara*), Maker, Creator, Best, Ordainer, Master,

Father of beings who have been and will be. These beings have been created by me. Why? Formerly I thought: "If only other beings would come to this world!" As soon as I formed this aspiration in my mind these beings came to this world." Those beings who had been reborn afterwards thought: "This gentleman must be God, Great God, the Overlord, Unconquered, Seeing-universally, Wielding-power, Lord, Maker, Creator, Best, Ordainer, Master, Father of beings who have been and will be. We have been created by this gentleman, by God. Why? We saw him here reborn first, whilst we have been reborn afterwards."

'In this connection, monks, the being who has been reborn first is longer lived, more handsome and superior; whilst those who have been reborn afterwards are shorter lived, less handsome and inferior. Now it is the case, monks, that a being passes away from that body and comes to this world (our world of human beings), and when he has come to this world he goes forth from home to homelessness (i.e. becomes a *śramaṇa*, or a brahman seer). When he has gone forth from home to homelessness, in consequence of his ascetic energy, exertion, practice, diligence and right attention he attains a concentration of thought of such a sort that in his concentrated thought he recollects that former life, but he recollects nothing beyond (before) that. He says: "That gentleman, God, Great God, the Overlord, Unconquered, Seeing-universally, Wielding-power, Lord, Maker, Creator, Best, Ordainer, Master, Father of beings who have been and will be, by whom we were created; he is permanent, fixed, eternal, not having the principle of change; he will remain there eternally, whilst we who were created by God, we are impermanent, unstable, non-eternal, short-lived, having the principle of passing away and coming here."'

This is the first kind of some-things-eternalist (whose genesis we have quoted at length partly because we shall have occasion to refer to it later). The second and third kinds are also theologians, but in their last existences, which is all they can recollect when they have become ascetics like their colleague above, they belonged to two different classes of gods. The second theologian had been a god of the class Debauched by Frivolity. As a result of excessive frivolity, laughter and love-making they lost their self-possession and passed away. The theologian thought there were two classes of gods, those Debauched by Frivolity and those who were not. The latter retained their self-possession by avoiding excess and are eternal, remain gods eternally. The former, like himself, are non-eternal and have come to this (human) world. The third theologian had been a god of the class Debauched in Mind. These gods thought about one another excessively, so that their thoughts became debauched and their bodies and thoughts tired, and they passed away. This theologian too thought there were two classes of gods, those Debauched in Mind, like himself, and those who were not. Again the latter, who did not think about each other too much, avoided getting debauched and tired and were eternal as gods. The former were non-eternal and had come to this world.

The fourth kind of some-things-eternalist is a logician or metaphysician. His argument is : 'That which is called sight, hearing, smell, taste and touch (body)', that self (*ātman*) is impermanent, unstable, non-eternal, having the principle of change. That which is called thought or mind or consciousness, however, that self (*ātman*) is permanent, fixed, eternal, does not have the principle of change and remains there eternally.'

Thus in each of the four cases some things are eternal and some are not.

Those who hold that the universe is finite, infinite or both are again ascetics, who attain three different types of concentration of thought. The first in his concentration of thought has a perception of the finite with reference to the universe; the second has similarly a perception of the infinite. They conclude accordingly that the universe is finite or infinite. The third has a perception of the finite in the vertical dimension but a perception of the infinite horizontally, and concludes that the universe is both finite and infinite.

He who holds that the universe is neither finite nor infinite is a logician or metaphysician who is simply said to assert, following his own (unstated) deductions, that the theses of his three colleagues are all false.

The first three kinds of agnostic do not understand what is good and what is bad in their true nature, consequently they think that to attempt to explain what is good or bad would arouse will, passion, anger and aversion. These in turn would cause falsehood, that would cause remorse, and that would be an obstacle (to the best life). They differ only in that the first is deterred by fear of and disgust at falsehood, the second by fear of attachment and the third by fear of examination (being argued with). All three resort to perpetual evasion: 'I do not say yes, I do not say it is true, I do not say it is otherwise, I do not say it is not, I do not say it is not not.'

The fourth agnostic is 'dull and extremely stupid.' He is quoted as saying: 'If you ask me whether another world exists, if I thought it did exist I would explain that to you. I do not say yes. I do not say it is true. I do not say it is otherwise. I do not say it is not. I do not say it is not not. If you ask me whether another world does not exist .. both..neither.. whether beings transmigrate ... do not ... both ... neither ... whether good and bad actions have any fruit and result ... do not ... both ... neither ... whether a thus-gone exists after death ... does not ... both .. neither ... I do not say it is not not.'

The first of the two kinds of spontaneous-originationists has in a former existence been a being having no perception (a kind of god). These gods pass away as soon as any perception occurs in them. If one of them, reborn in this world and become an ascetic, acquires the concentration of thought in which he can recollect his former existence, it seems to him that he originated spontaneously with that first perception which ended it. He concludes his soul originated spontaneously, and that the universe likewise originated spontaneously. Why? 'Formerly I was not. After not being I have now been changed to beingness.' The second spontaneous-originationist arrives at the same conclusion through logic and metaphysics.

Such are the eighteen grounds of the 'arrangers (imaginers) of the former end.' The forty four grounds of those who look to the future, the 'arrangers of the after end,' are dealt with more briefly, so that they can be summarised here without detaining us too long. They cannot, of course, be accounted for by partial memories of the past and for the most part they are merely stated as speculative grounds without any explanation.

The sixteen survivalists who hope to have perception (*saṃjñin*) after death differ as to the nature of the surviving soul (*ātman*). It could be material, immaterial, both, or neither. It could be finite (in space), infinite, both, or neither. It could have unity of perception or diversity of perceptions. Its perception could be restricted or immeasurable. It could be completely happy, or unhappy, or both, or neither.

The eight who assume no perception in a surviving soul differ similarly as to its nature but are naturally restricted to grounds corresponding to the first eight above. Those who assume it neither has nor has not perception hold the same eight alternative opinions as to its nature.

The first annihilationist assumes that there is a soul, a material soul made of the four elements and produced by the mother and father. When the body breaks up this soul is annihilated (*ud-chid*), perishes utterly, is not after death. To this extent this soul is rightly and utterly annihilated. In this way he declares the annihilation (*uccheda*), destruction, non-existence of an existing being (*sattva*).

The second annihilationist agrees with him that this soul exists, but does not accept that it is 'to this extent rightly and utterly annihilated.' According to him there is another soul (also called *ātman*) which is divine (*divya*) but material, having sensual scope, eating solid food. This soul is annihilated when the body breaks up, perishes utterly, is not after death, is rightly and utterly annihilated to this extent. The difference between these two annihilationists is rather obscure and the Sthaviravāda commentary for once offers no help. From the known views of two different schools of the later Lokāyatas, the Dhūrtas ('Rogues') and the Suśikṣitas ('Cultivated'), who maintained respectively that there is no such entity as the soul and that there is a temporary reality resulting from the combination of the four elements as long as the body lives, we can perhaps get some light. The difference would appear to be over whether there is any sense in which there is a 'soul' distinct from the four elements and having its own peculiar properties different from theirs. The first view would be that consciousness is simply a property of the four elements combined and so are any other properties ascribed to a soul; the 'soul', if we so call it (the first annihilationist does, the 'Rogues' did not), is no more than these properties of the elements combined, which disappear when they are separated at death. The second view would be (there may be such properties but) there is actually a distinct entity which arises from the elements in combination as a living body, which is consciousness, though being dependent on the elements it is annihilated when these separate. We should perhaps allow for a slight garbling of the two theories in an opponent's version of them, which could be explained here as necessitated in order to bring the first theory literally under the heading 'annihilationism', which the Buddhists applied to the Lokāyata: in strict Lokāyata terms there would be no 'annihilation', since there was no soul to be annihilated (and the elements were not annihilated, they were held to be permanent atoms, combining and separating).

The remaining five annihilationists all agree with the first that his 'soul' exists, but not that it is 'to this extent rightly and utterly annihilated' (there is something else to be annihilated before the annihilation is 'right' and 'utter', is complete). Like the second annihilationist they assume another soul, but instead of being sensual and feeding on solid food it is respectively made of mind (is a mental soul), or able to go to the sphere of infinity of space, or to the sphere of infinity of consciousness, or to the sphere of nothingness, or to the sphere of neither perception nor non-perception. As with the second annihilationist, this other soul is in each case annihilated when the body breaks up, and this is the right and utter annihilation.

Finally we have the five grounds of those who maintain extinction in the visible world. According to the first the soul (*ātman*) enjoys itself, being presented with, provided with, the five strands of pleasure (i.e. the pleasures of the five senses). To this extent it has attained the highest extinction (*nirvāṇa*) in the visible world.

The second objects that pleasures are impermanent, 'unhappy', having the principle of change, so that grief, lamentation, pain, depression and misery result from them. Consequently when the soul separates itself from pleasure and enters the first meditation (as described in the previous chapter under the faculty of concentration), then it has attained the highest extinction in the visible world.

The other three grounds are that it is the attainment of the second, third and fourth meditations respectively which constitute the highest extinction in the visible world.

The thus-gone understands all these sixty two 'cases of opinion', but not holding on to them he has personally found 'extinguishing' (*nirvṛti*)...and is freed.

These extracts would seem to confirm that the notions of 'soul' and 'universe' are very closely associated, belong to the same realm of ideas, from the standpoint of the Buddha. If we are right in concluding that for the Buddha there was no such entity as the 'universe', then we must infer that for him the question of its being finite or infinite in space and time is meaningless instead of being beyond our knowledge. There remains, however, the sequence of conditioned origination, or more generally transmigration (*saṃsāra*), and this the Buddha is recorded to have said quite categorically is beginningless (*anavarāgra*; the exegesis of all schools generally takes this to mean endless as well, but there is a sense in which *nirvāṇa* is the end of it, for a particular person, although transmigration as a whole is presumably endless). There is section of the *Saṃyukta*[1] on this point. Its refrain is: 'This transmigration is beginningless, the former point (*koṭi*, i e. the point of origin) is not discerned. Beings (*sattvas*) pass on and circulate (transmigrate), having the obstacle of ignorance and the 'connection' of desire.' This is illustrated by a number of similes, some very striking, such as that the tears shed by the monks he is addressing, during their long transmigrating, joined to what is not pleasing, separated from what is pleasing, are more than the water in the four oceans.

Having clarified our terminology, then, and from the Buddha's point of view distinguished transmigration, as the mass of beginningless sequences of conditions and the proper subject of his scientific investigations, from a metaphysical 'universe', we find him accepting the infinity of transmigration as his answer to the first antinomy. We should misrepresent him, however, if we failed to insist that his position here is not a metaphysical

1. S II 178 ff. (section 15), T 99 section 34 and the end of 33. (34 : All beings are beginningless, transmigration circulates for a long time, the former point of unhappiness is not known ; 33 : All beings are in beginningless transmigration, deluded by ignorance, bound by desire, and circulate for a long time, the former point...). Quoted by Nāgārjuna, see 'Is Nāgārjuna a Mahāyānist ?' p. 80 ; Sanskrit fragments of *Anavatāgra* (sic) *Turfan* 167.

one such as would correspond properly to the infinity of the universe 'proved' by the pure reason. It would surely be more accurate to describe his attitude in our own language as 'scientific', based on empirical investigation and concluding that transmigration is infinite, at least as regards its beginning, in the absence of any evidence of an ultimate origin.

Two Levels of Statement

Since the Buddha sometimes speaks in terms of 'beings' being 'reborn' (and of the 'universe' evolving), as if accepting the opinion that there is some kind of permanent soul, which he elsewhere rejects, there might appear to be some obscurity or inconsistency in his doctrine. The unanimous answer of the Buddhist schools to this difficulty is that two types of statement have to be distinguished in the *Tripiṭaka*. Sometimes the Buddha used conventional everyday terms, such as 'being', 'person', adopting the popular viewpoint as if some unchanging entity went on from life to life. At other times he speaks of a sequence of conditions with no permanent entity among them, of desire existing through a condition but no one who 'desires'. It is this latter type of statement which is directly connected to his exposition of 'truths', and which moreover he himself regarded as a matter 'difficult to see'. Unless we attribute to him or to the compilers of the *Tripiṭaka* an incredible ineptitude, entirely at variance with the subtlety and precision of most of the discourses ascribed to him, we must follow this interpretation according to two levels of statement, in popular terms and in terms of strict truth. We are in fact obliged by our method of enquiry to follow the unanimous teaching of the schools of Buddhism, and finally and decisively the *Tripiṭaka* itself in the earliest form in which we can now restore it explicitly recognises that there are two levels of statement.

The interpretation of the schools distinguishes everyday language as literally 'concealing' (*saṃvṛti*) from philosophical language as 'ultimate' (*paramārtha*). To interpret any text in the *Tripiṭaka* we have first to settle whether it is of the latter kind, which they called 'having its meaning drawn out' (*nitārtha*), i. e. to be taken as it stands, as an explicit and definitive statement, or of the former kind, which they called 'having its meaning requiring to be drawn out' (*neyārtha*), i.e.

which requires to be restated to relate it to the philosophical
standpoint of ultimate truth.

In the *Tripiṭaka* the *Dīrgha* group's *Saṅgīti Sūtra*[1] speaks of
four 'knowledges' (*jñāna*), one of which is in the Sthaviravāda
version 'concealing' knowledge (the Chinese has apparently
'common knowledge') and another knowledge with reference
to the doctrine (in both versions). The other two are knowledge
about the inference (Chinese : of the 'not known'), i.e. that the
truth is always true (see p. 117 above), and knowledge about
other people's thoughts. Here the first might be contrasted, as
'concealing', with all the other three as of the direct type and
the distinction of the schools is at least suggested. More explicit
is a text in the Sthaviravāda *Ekottara* group[2] which says: 'These
two slander the thus-gone. Which two? He who elucidates a
dialogue whose meaning requires to be drawn out (*neyārtha*)
as one whose meaning is drawn out (*nītārtha*) ; and he who
elucidates a dialogue whose meaning is drawn out as one whose
meaning requires to be drawn out.'

This can only be understood as implying the rule of interpretation observed by the schools. Since the same terms are found
in a Sarvāstivāda *Sūtra* (see previous footnote) as well as a
Sthaviravāda the rule appears to be fairly ancient, at least, and
a search of the Chinese *Āgamas* might bring to light some parallels. The *Saṅgīti Sūtra* has only one of the terms later standard
but seems to confirm the same distinction, even if it is complicated by two further types of 'knowledge'.

Even if the rule of interpretation was not overtly formulated
by the Buddha himself, the fact that it is recorded in at least
two recensions of the *Tripiṭaka* (possibly a third, if we admit
the *Saṅgīti* reference) and that it was followed by all known
schools suggests that it had been clearly formulated within
about a century after the *parinirvāṇa*. To the Buddha the distinction probably seemed so obvious as to be taken for granted.
We shall find that in later centuries some of the schools disagreed

---

1. D No. 33 (III 226—cf. 277), T 1 No. 9 (p. 51a, 18). The Sarvāstivāda
Sanskrit version (p. 100) agrees with the Sthaviravāda. For 'common
knowledge' see Soothill, *Dictionary of Chinese Buddhist Terms*, p. 385. The
Pali *saṃmuti* if from *man* may suggest 'conventional' as original meaning.

2. A I 60. A presumably Sarvāstivādin *sūtra* quoted in the AK *Bhāṣya*
(p. 136) and Yaśomitra (p. 174) also uses the terms *nīta* and *neya*.

as to precisely which texts were to be assigned to each level of statement. The new schools of the Mahāyāna, in particular, circulating new texts with new doctrines, sought to discredit the more authentic parts of the *Tripiṭaka* as mere everyday 'concealing' discourses whose meaning required to be drawn out; only their special texts were set out in definitive philosophical terms (yet they disagreed among themselves later).

The Gods

The texts we have read so far make it abundantly clear that in the universe, or in transmigration (or out of it), as described by the Buddha there is no room for any kind of divine intervention. Its evolution is natural evolution according to laws of causation, natural laws. It has not been created by God, and if God (Brahmā), so called, thinks He is God and has created living beings He is in reality only an ordinary person suffering from a delusion. The gods are subject to the laws of nature which govern the rebirth and passing away of living beings, just as men are. Their privileges are only relative: they enjoy a higher standard of living than men do and live in a rather rarified atmosphere where there is nothing coarse, no solid food, no solid bodies; they are very handsome and live long, but eventually they die and are reborn elsewhere according to their actions, good or bad. They appear to have no power over men or in worlds outside their own. Any properly trained monk, moreover, can in his meditation enjoy not only the rarified atmosphere of the gods but still more rarified atmospheres inaccessible even to them.

However, the Buddha appears to admit the gods and God to his scheme of the universe, whereas the Lokāyata on the other hand rejected the lot as fictions of the brahmans. What is their place, according to him? What is their nature, besides what has been indicated above? Perhaps they 'exist' only at the everyday level along with the other conventions of polite conversation? Let us accompany a Buddhist monk on a tour of the heavens.[1]

Once upon a time in this very community of monks this

---

1. D No. 11 (I 215, ff.), T 1 No. 24.

reflection occurred in the thought of a certain monk: "Where do these four elements absolutely cease, to wit the earth element, the water element, the heat element and the air element ?" Then that monk attained such a concentration that in his concentrated thought the way leading to the gods appeared. Then he approached the gods of the (realm of the) Four Kings (the lowest heaven, the Kings preside over the four quarters) and asked them where the four elements absolutely ceased...The gods said: "Monk, we do not know where the four elements absolutely cease. There are, however, the Four Kings, more excellent than us, superior to us; they may know..." ' Then the monk approached the Four Kings and asked them the same question... They too admitted their ignorance and suggested trying the more excellent, superior Thirty Three gods (the traditional Vedic gods, who inhabit a loftier sphere than the gods of the quarters). These refer him to their king, Śakra (also called Indra, see Chapter One, *The Aryans*). He is equally ignorant and sends the monk on to the still higher sphere of the Yāma gods, they to their king Suyāma, he to the higher Tuṣita gods, they to their king Saṃtuṣita, he to the Nirmāṇarati gods, they to Sunirmita, he to the Paranirmitavaśavartin gods and they to their king Vaśavartin ('Wielding Power').

Though this text does not mention it, we have now, according to Buddhist tradition, reached the highest sphere of 'sensual existence' (see p. 109 above) or of the first station of consciousness (see p. 127 above). Vaśavartin, however, knows no more about the elements than his inferiors and can only refer the monk to the sphere of 'imponderable existence', the second station of consciousness, to the Brahma-bodied gods (whose bodies consist of imponderable matter). The monk accordingly attained such a concentration that in his concentrated thought the way leading to Brahmā appeared (by this the text in fact indicates the transition from the sensual to the imponderable sphere; the first meditation is supposed to 'produce' this sphere or station of consciousness). He approaches the Brahma-bodied gods with his question, but they too admit their ignorance. They tell him: "There is God (Brahmā), Great God, the Overlord, etc. (the usual titles follow, as before) ...He is superior to us; He may know..."

The monk asks where this Great God is at present. They say: "We do not know where God is, which way He is, whereabouts He is. Nevertheless, monk, when portents are seen: light is produced and radiance appears, then God will appear. This is the portent which happens before an appearance of God, that light is produced and radiance appears."

'Soon Great God appeared. Then the monk approached him and asked: "Where, sir, do these four elements absolutely cease, to wit the earth element, the water element, the heat element and the air element ?" When this was said Great God said to the monk: "I, monk, am God, Great God, the Over-lord, Unconquered, Seeing-universally, Wielding-power, Lord, Maker, Creator, Best, Ordainer, Master, Father of beings who have been and will be." The monk asked God again: "Sir, I am not asking you whether you are God, Great God, etc., but where the four elements absolutely cease..." But Great God repeated the same answer...and the monk asked a third time...Then Great God took the monk by the arm and led him away to one side, and said to him: "In this connection, monk, the Brahma-bodied gods know that there is nothing which God has not seen, nothing which God has not known, nothing which God has not experienced. Therefore I do not explain in their presence. Monk, I do not know where the four elements absolutely cease..." ' God then sends the monk down to Earth to the Buddha, who tells him that the four elements cease absolutely only through the cessation of consciousness (i.e. they cease for one who attains *nirvāṇa*).

Of course the moral of this story is to set the Buddha above any gods or God and enlightenment above their limited knowledge, but taken in conjunction with the history of the first some-things-eternalist which we read in the *Brahmajāla Sūtra* it has the further interest of showing God at a later stage of His downward career. He began, it seems, by being genuinely deluded as to His position, but the illusion of His creativity, omnipotence and omniscience could not have lasted for long and now He is depicted as a conscious fraud. He gained ascendancy over the other Brahma-bodied gods merely because He happened to be born first in this particular evolution of the universe, not because of any special virtue: on the contrary it is suggested that He was the first to pass away from the higher world of radiance because His stock of merit was exhausted first.

No more need be said about the Buddha's attitude to God (Brahmā). He is in no way different from any other 'being' (even at the conventional, 'concealing' level) but like them represents a sequence of conditions. He happens to occupy an exalted station by the accident of birth, in spite of lack of merit. The religion of Brahmanism, which maintains that God is eternal, is founded on the original error of the Brahma-bodied gods and has been propagated in the world of men by some of them when reborn as brahman seers.

It would be possible to suggest that the theology of the Buddha was intended as wholly fictitious, as anti-theistic, edifying stories like these about God. Two points may be made here. Firstly the theology seems to reproduce quite accurately the popular or Brahmanical theology and mythology of the Buddha's day (which would be appropriate procedure in edifying fiction). Secondly the arrangement of the gods in certain spheres fits them into the universe of meditation of the Buddhist way which must be taken seriously as at the level of philosophical truth. The proper conclusion would seem to be that the Buddha conceded a certain reality to the Brahmanical or popular conceptions, as if accepting that they were based on genuine recollections of previous existences as gods, but absolutely rejected the idea that the gods differed essentially from men in having creative or controlling powers in the universe. They may exist, but they are as subject to the laws of nature as men are. Ascetics and monks may attain their worlds in meditation, may converse with them, but they are powerless to help men, even by teaching them, and any worship or cult directed towards them is futile. As to knowledge, men are superior: it is in the world of men that Buddhas attain enlightenment. The standards of good conduct, which we reviewed briefly at the end of our discussion on the Way in the last chapter, have nothing to do with theology: they derive from the study of conditioned origination, i.e. of the nature of the universe, of transmigration, and from the study of society (on which we shall have more to say later).

As to the religion of ritual and the sacrifice, which was such an important aspect of Brahmanism, we shall see that it was categorically opposed by the Buddha as detrimental to the well-being of society.

There is one more 'god' who demands our attention, Death (Māra), who in Chapter Three persuaded the Buddha to enter final extinction. In his other aspect as Passion he will become prominent in the Buddha legend as 'attacking' the future Buddha in the hope of preventing his enlightenment. In this case we seem to have, at least originally, in the time of the Buddha himself, a pure personification of death, later linked as re-death and rebirth with passion and desire. Māra represents the laws of conditioned origination in transmigration, in sensual existence, and does not seem to have been a Brahmanical or popular god. Some later Buddhist commentators,[1] however, found a place for him in the sphere of the Paranirmitavaśavartin gods, i.e. in a commanding position dominating sensual existence, as a kind of rebel infesting the borders of the realm of Vaśavartin. Others[2] were more inclined to banish him to the underworld as a devil.

We may conclude this chapter by referring to another *sūtra* where the gods are discussed.[3] The Buddha meets King Prasenajit of Kośala, who amongst other things asks him whether the gods exist. The Buddha asks him why he asks this question. The King asks whether the gods come to this world or not. The Buddha replies that they do if they are malevolent (*savyāvadhya*, or 'violent'), not if they are non-violent. The King similarly asks whether God (Brahmā) exists and whether He comes to this world. The reply is exactly the same. The Sthaviravāda commentary explains that by 'come to this world' is meant being reborn here. The gods, then, and God, are reborn on Earth if their thoughts are corrupted by malevolence or violence. Evidently it is one of the laws of causation that malevolence leads to rebirth in an inferior sphere.

---

1. Sthaviravāda : MA I 33 f.
2. Sarvāstivāda : *Abhidharmakośa* trs. LVP, references under Māra in the Index.
3. M No. 90 (II 130 ff.), T 26 No. 212.

Chapter Six

BUDDHISM AND SOCIETY

The Buddha and the World—Evolution and the Nature of Society—The Ideal Society—Good Government—Class and the Priesthood—Tha Buddha's Teaching to the Laity—The Lay Disciple

The Buddha and the World

The Buddha and his followers had 'gone forth' from the worldly society as wanderers and formed their own community in which to live the 'best life' and attain peace of mind, *nirvāṇa.* The movement thus started, however, was much more than this, more than the provision of an escape route for those who wished to contract out of transmigration. It was suggested in Chapter Two that *śramaṇas* such as the Buddha hoped from their vantage point outside society to exercise some influence inside it. In the intervening chapters we have met the Buddha and other *śramaṇas* discussing the problems of life with kings, ministers, soldiers, merchants, artisans and people of various professions, and unspecified 'householders'. In their wanderings among the villages of India they were constantly in touch with the ordinary peasants or farmers, begging food from them, holding private conversations and giving public lectures. It is more remarkable, perhaps, to notice that the Buddha is recorded to have spent so much of his time in the cities, or at least on their outskirts. His activities and organisation appear to have centred on the capitals of Magadha, Vṛji, Kośala and other countries, not on forest or mountain retreats. There is a general underlying assumption that beyond the immediate aim of individual peace of mind, or more probably in essential connection with it, lies the objective of the happiness of the whole of human society and the still higher objective of the happiness of all living beings. The standard of considering all beings as like oneself applies to the monk as well as to the layman, and he is to use the forces of benevolence, compassion and sympathetic joy, which derive from this, in his meditation, in order to overcome the 'obstacles' of the will to pleasure, of malevolence, stupidity, vanity and uncertainty. Clearly it was the Buddha's intention to propagate such ideals in society generally, as an answer to the evils of the age, and not to restrict them to a private circle. We should remember also that besides the two branches of the monks and the nuns two other branches of the total Buddhist community were formally established[1] by the Buddha: the lay men and lay women (*upāsakas* and *upāsikās*) who had taken 'refuge' (*śaraṇa*) in the Buddha, the Doctrine and the Community, just as a monk or nun had gone forth to follow the Buddha.

The purpose of this chapter is to review the Buddha's teaching about society and to laymen.

Evolution and the Nature of Society

The *Brahmajāla Sūtra* which we studied in the preceding chapter describes briefly the 'involution' and 'evolution' of the universe and the appearance during the latter phase of the sphere of the *brahma*-mansion, of the gods elsewhere called Brahma-bodied. Another *sūtra* in the *Dīrgha*[2] refers to the same involution and evolution, with the majority of beings in the world of radiance (which, it appears, is not affected by the cycles of the more material universe), but continues to describe how beings come to 'this world' from the world of radiance and how human society evolves. It does not concern itself with the gods, and its avowed object is to account for the appearance in society of class distinctions, and especially of the hereditary priesthood of the brahmans, whose claims it was one of the primary objects of the Buddha to debunk.

'When the universe is evolving the majority of beings pass away from their world-of-radiance bodies and come to this world. They remain for a very long time made of mind, feeding on joy, self-luminous, living in the sky and staying beautiful. At that time, Vāsiṣṭhas (the Buddha is speaking to two novices, brahmans by birth), there is just one mass of water, obscurity, the darkness of obscurity (i.e. this world). The Sun and Moon

1. See p. 54 above.
2. D No. 27 (III 84 ff.), T 1 No. 5. Also AK III 98 and *Bhāṣya*,= *Mahāvastu* I 338 ff., Rockhill 1 ff.—MSV (SOR) I 7 ff.

are not discerned, nor the constellations of stars, nor day and night, nor the month and the fortnight, nor the year and the seasons, nor male and female. Beings are classified simply as 'beings'.

'Then at some time or other, after a long time, an 'enjoyment solid (literally 'earth', in the sense of the element)' became spread out over the water for those beings. Just like the skin ('film') on hot milk as it cools, so it appeared. It had colour, scent and taste. Its colour was like that of ghee or butter. Its taste was like that of pure, sweet, wild honey.

'Then a certain being, being wanton (*lola*, or 'restless'), thought "Sir! What can this be?" and tasted the enjoyment earth with a finger. As it tasted the enjoyment earth with its finger it was pleased, and desire (*tṛṣṇā*) arose within it. Other beings following the idea (*dṛṣṭi*, 'opinion') of that being tasted the enjoyment earth with their fingers. As they tasted it they were pleased and desire arose within them. Then those beings fell upon it, breaking it in pieces with their hands in order to eat it. Because of this their self-luminosity disappeared.

'When self-luminosity disappeared the Sun and Moon appeared, the constellations of stars appeared and day and night were discerned. As the months and fortnights were discerned, so were the year and the seasons. To this extent, Vāsiṣṭhas, this universe is evolved again.'

These beings continued for a long time feeding on the 'enjoyment earth', and as they did so 'roughness' appeared in their bodies. Colour and 'discolouration' were also discerned, so that some were beautiful and some ugly. The beautiful ones despised the ugly, and in consequence of this pride and arrogance the enjoyment earth disappeared. Afterwards a fungus appeared on the ground, like a mushroom, which had a similar delightful taste to the enjoyment earth, and beings fed for a long time on that. As they did so their bodies became still rougher and more various in colour (beauty), and the beautiful ones became more proud and arrogant until the fungus disappeared. Then a creeper appeared, with the same delicious taste. The same process continued and it too disappeared.

'Then, Vāsiṣṭhas, when the creeper disappeared, a rice plant appeared for those beings, which ripened without cultivation, was without any husk or coating on its grains, was sweet scented and produced rice. If this was collected in the evening for the evening meal, it had grown again and was ripe in the morning. If it was collected in the morning for the morning meal, it had grown again and was ripe in the evening. No reaping was discerned. Then those beings fed on the rice which ripened without cultivation...their bodies became still rougher and more coloured and discoloured, and the characteristic of the female appeared in woman, and of the male in man. And a woman thought about a man excessively, and a man about a woman. Thinking about each other excessively, passion occurred in them and lust arose within their bodies. Through the condition of lust they indulged in the principle (*dharma*) of sex. When other beings saw them indulging in the principle of sex, some threw mud, some threw ash, some threw cow dung, crying: "Perish ! Dirty !" "How could a being do that sort of thing to a being?" Now at present, too, in some countries, when a bride is led out some people throw mud, some ash, some cow dung. So they follow ancient tradition, a primeval expression, but they do not grasp its meaning.

'What was agreed to be bad (*adharma*, bad principle, unlawful) at that time, Vāsiṣṭhas, is at present agreed to be good (*dharma*, principle, lawful; in these expressions *dharma* may have its legal sense, which we have not met before in this survey, except implicitly when referring to the 'laws' of the Brahmanical tradition in Chapter One). At that time those who indulged in the principle of sex were not allowed to enter a village or town for a month or two months.

'Since those beings indulged excessively in (that) bad principle, they went into houses to do it secretly. Then a certain being, being lazy, thought: "Sir ! Why should I be troubled with collecting rice in the evening for the evening meal and in the morning for the morning meal ? Supposing I were to collect rice once only for the evening and morning meals ?" Then that being collected rice once only for the evening and morning meals. Then another being approached him and said: "Come, sir, let us go to collect rice." "Enough, sir, I have collected rice once only for the evening and morning meals." Then, Vāsiṣṭhas, the other being, following that being's idea, collected rice once only for two days, thinking that would be good.'

This idea spread, and they collected enough rice for up to a week at a time, but: 'Because those beings made a store of rice and relied on it for eating, a coating and a husk enveloped the rice grain, when it was plucked it did not grow again, reaping was discovered and the rice stood in clusters (i.e. presumably was grown in fields).' The beings then assembled and lamented their gradual decadence from bodies of mind feeding on joy to their present state: 'Bad principles have appeared among the beings.' But they decided to divide the rice plants and establish boundaries (in other words they invented private property).

'Then a certain being, being wanton, guarding his own share, took another share, which was not given to him, and ate it. So they seized him and said: "Sir, you do badly, in as much as you take another share not given to you, guarding your own, and eat it. Do not do that sort of thing again." ' He agreed, but did it again a second and a third time. He was seized and rebuked again, then some hit him with their hands, some pelted him with clods, some beat him with sticks. Since then taking what was not given, blame, false speech and resorting to force (or to punishment) have been known ('discerned').

The beings assembled again, discussed these bad principles that had been discerned among them, and proposed: 'Supposing we were to elect one being, who would become indignant with us when it was right to be indignant, would blame when it was right to blame, would banish when it was right to banish? We will grant him a share of rice.'

'Then those beings, Vāsiṣṭhas, approached that being among them who was most handsome, most beautiful, most lovely, most superior, and said to him: "Come, sir. Be indignant when it is right to be indignant, blame when it is right to blame, banish when it is right to banish. We will grant you a share of rice."' He agreed, and started to perform these duties and to receive the share of rice. 'Because he was elected by the people, Vāsiṣṭhas, he was called the Great Elect. Thus the first expression applied to him was derived. Because he was the lord of the fields (or lands) he was called Warrior (the words 'warrior' and 'field' sound similar in the original language: this is not historical but only fanciful) ...Because he delighted others with principle (*dharma*) he was called King ('king' could be derived from the verb 'to delight') ...'

In this way the 'circle' or class of warriors, the aristocracy, is said to have originated, but the Buddha adds that it is good principle or justice (*dharma*) which is the best thing among the people, both in the visible world and with reference to a future state.

Next the Buddha accounts for the origin of the priesthood, the brahmans. 'Among those beings some thought that bad principles had appeared among the beings, in that taking what was not given, blame, false speech, resorting to force and banishment will be discerned. Suppose they were to keep off bad, evil principles ?' They did so and consequently the name brahman (*brāhmaṇa*) was first derived for them (in the vernacular languages of the Buddha's day the name might look as if it could be derived from the verb 'keep off'; this again is pure fancy). These brahmans went to the forest and lived in leaf huts, meditating. They did not prepare or cook their own food but went morning and evening to a village or town to seek it. On account of their meditating they received as a second name that of 'meditators'. Some, however, were unable to meditate, so they spent their time making books. As they did not meditate they were called 'non-meditators' (= 'teachers', this is a pun in the original language). At that time they were agreed to be inferior, but now they are considered the best. (The books they made are of course the books of the Vedic Canon.)

A third class of the beings took to various kinds of business and formed the mercantile and productive class (the *vaiśyas*, supposed to be connected with *viśva*, 'all', i.e. all kinds of business, all trades, and in this case the derivation is etymologically respectable).

Those beings who remained became hunters, the lowest occupation of all, and were called *śūdras* (which in the vernacular rhymes with 'hunter' and with 'minor', i.e. low, but the historical origin of this class seems to have been that they were conquered peoples reduced to the position of helots which they really for the most part occupied in the Buddha's day;

all inferior groups, together with forest and mountain tribes living by hunting, were lumped in by Brahmanical theory as the fourth and lowest class).

Thus all four classes came from the same common origin and the distinction was at first purely occupational (and the brahmans lived a praiseworthy life of meditation and simplicity, retired from the world, very like the life of the wandering *śramaṇas* of the Buddha's day). Lastly those of any of the four classes who were dissatisfied with the life of their class became *śramaṇas*, going forth from home to homelessness.

Finally bad conduct, bodily, verbal or mental, leads to a bad destiny, good conduct to a good destiny, regardless of whether the agent belongs to one class or another. Mixed conduct leads to a mixed destiny, a mixture of happiness and unhappiness. By restraint and by developing the seven principles 'siding with' enlightenment (presumably the seven 'factors of enlightenment') anyone, regardless of class origin, can attain *nirvāṇa*.

This text is one of many in the *Tripiṭaka* directed against the claims of the brahmans to be of different origin from the rest of humanity, born from the mouth of Brahmā, having a hereditary prerogative to teach, guide and spiritually govern the rest of society. It should be noted that the Buddha's opposition is not total: rather he seeks to conciliate and win over the brahmans of his day to his new way of thinking. He flatters them that their class was formed originally from good motives and had good traditions. It is only more recently that it has become degenerate and its way of life harmful, in that the sacrifices of their ritual are harmful as well as futile, are a travesty of the original sacrifice (we shall discuss this below), their Vedic Canon is now corrupt and perverted, though originally it may have contained sound moral injunctions, and the advice and guidance they give to others, claiming supernatural authority, is often misleading and harmful. It is an essential part of the Buddha's aim to substitute purely moral standards for all hereditary privilege, to assert the equality of all beings before the laws of nature, their equal freedom to shape their destinies within the conditions and causality of the universe as discovered by him. The brahmans are now ignorant of the truths of the universe, but they can learn them (as many did, becoming followers of the Buddha) and then join in spreading them and in exemplifying and teaching good conduct. Originally a man was not a brahman by birth, but by a high standard of conduct, and this state of affairs should be restored in society.

Before considering any more texts concerned with the brahmans and class, however, we have others to look at which discuss social evolution further. So far we have seen what amounts to a Buddhist version of the traditions of the *Purāṇas* (cf. Chapter One), with the evolution of the universe out of darkness, the origin of mankind, the first king (later Buddhist commentators identify the Great Elect with Manu, the founder of the Solar Dynasty). It was probably intended to look like a corrected version, acceptable as such to those accustomed to the *Purāṇas* (which may have been less theistic then than they are today), or even believed to be a successful restoration of the true facts from garbled Brahmanical tradition in the light of 'modern scientific' investigations (i.e. the doctrines reported in the preceding chapter). There is no primeval One Being, i.e. Brahmā or *brahman*, which somehow wishes to become many and becomes the universe : in the natural process of evolution Brahmā is one among many 'beings', or sequences of conditions, and his idea that his wishing for company resulted in creation is an absurd error. Mankind means other but similar beings, not inferior or different in kind except to the extent that their conduct may vary. All men are born equal, and born equal to the gods, to 'God' Himself. What they become depends on their own conduct. The Brahmanical myths about the origins of the different races and classes of men are nonsense. The first king was not of divine origin, in any sense in which all men are not divine; he did not rule as of right but was elected. We have noted in Chapter One that the *Purāṇas* themselves preserve legends of an original anarchy in society ended by the election of the first king : here at least the Buddha could find some suggestion among the conflicting tangles of ancient tradition that what he believed to have been the true facts had once been recorded and only later were submerged in mythology.

Buddhist sources take little interest in the dynasties of kings supposed to have followed after the Great Elect. The *Tripiṭaka* shows interest in the theory of government, in basic principles which might be illustrated from history, but not in detailed records of the past. The *Mahāparinirvāṇa Sūtra*, which tells us the last events in the life of the Buddha, shows the Buddha discussing the principles of republican government, so important for the Buddhist community, bearing moreover on current affairs. Other *sūtras* discuss the deeds of great kings or emperors (*cakravartins*) of the past.

A *Dīrgha sūtra*[1] gives an account of the reigns of three successive emperors who attempted to rule justly, presumably in the tradition of the Great Elect, but eventually failed, whereupon society plunged headlong down the path of degeneration, or more precisely of violence, which has brought it to its present perilous state. The reign of the first,[2] which lasted for thousands of years (for human life was much longer when social degeneration had not gone very far), was illustrated by the presence in the sky of a 'wheel gem', perhaps a comet, or a nova, which circled like the Sun and Moon. The emperor knew, it seems, that this celestial phenomenon marked his reign of principle, and after some thousands of years he posted a man to keep it under observation and report if it retired or fell from its place (the Sthaviravāda commentary explains that he did this by setting up a kind of astronomical instrument at the gateway of the citadel). When told that this had happened he knew his reign had come to end and he must abdicate, become a homeless wanderer and seek celestial pleasures instead of human ones.

He installed his eldest son as ruler and went forth as a homeless seer (*ṛṣi*). A week later the 'wheel gem' disappeared. The new ruler was disturbed at this and went to consult his father. The royal seer told him that the celestial 'wheel gem' was not part of his paternal inheritance. If he conducts himself according to the Aryan (or 'excellent') imperial conduct (or 'government') it is possible that the wheel gem may appear. Asked what this conduct is, he says that, depending on principle (*dharma*), respecting and honouring principle, under the banner of principle, etc., his son should organise safety, shelter and protection among the people, for warriors who had submitted, for brahmans, householders, townspeople, country folk, *śramaṇas*, beasts and birds. No unjust action should start in his realm. If anyone in

1. D No. 26. T 1 No. 6.
2. Dṛḍhanemi; in Mithilā, MSV, SOR I p. 20.

the realm should be poor, money should be granted to them. He should regularly approach those *śramaṇas* and brahmans in the realm who had abstained from excess and negligence, who were established in tolerance and gentleness, who tamed, calmed and extinguished themselves, and ask advice from them : what is good, what bad, what is to be reproached, what irreproachable, what is to be indulged in (or 'pursued'), what not? By my doing what, would there long be hardship and unhappiness, or on the other hand by my doing what, would there long be benefit and happiness? Listening to them he should avoid the bad and conduct himself conforming to the good.

He acted accordingly, and the wheel gem appeared; he knew he was a (true) emperor. The wheel gem moves round to the four quarters and the emperor follows it with his army. Everywhere the hostile kings submit and ask for instruction. He tells them living beings should not be killed, what was not given should not be taken, misconduct in pleasures should not be carried on, falsehood should not be spoken, intoxicants should not be drunk, you should rule (collect taxes) in moderation (literally 'according as it has been ruled/collected').

After some thousands of years the wheel gem retires, falls from its place, and he in turn knows his reign is ending. He installs his eldest son and goes forth to homelessness. The wheel gem disappears, but this time the son does not go to the royal sage to ask him about the Aryan imperial conduct. Instead he governs according to his own opinions (*mata*) and the countries do not afterwards flourish as they did before. The privy councillors, councillors, ministers of the treasury, soldiers, gate keepers and learned men assemble and complain. They inform the king that they, and others like them in the realm, remember the Aryan imperial conduct and can explain it to him. He agrees and holds consultation in assembly with them, and organises safety, shelter and protection.

The king fails, however, to grant money to the poor. As a result poverty becomes widespread. Then a man takes what was not given, commits what is called 'theft'. He is seized and taken before the king. The king asks him whether it is true that he has committed theft and he admits it. When asked why he says he could not make a living. The king grants him money and tells him to make a living with it, look after his parents and family, undertake business and set up uplifting donations to *śramaṇas* and brahmans, which would lead to heaven, result in happiness. The man agrees.

Others hear that the king rewards thieves and proceed to imitate this man. Eventually the king reflects that if he grants money to whoever takes what was not given, to thieves, in that way this stealing will increase. He decides to take preventive measures, and orders the next thief to be executed, with duc ceremony.

This does not have the effect intended. In future thieves carry sharp swords and murder their victims. They band together and raid villages and towns, even cities, and commit robbery on the roads. Thus because the king did not grant money to the poor poverty became widespread, followed by stealing, violence, murder and false speech (explained later). As a result of the prevalence of falsehood human life became shorter.

At this point the origin of false speech is explained. A man who committed theft was taken before the king to be tried and sentenced. He denies stealing, speaks a conscious falsehood. Later, malice originates in people denouncing others for theft.

As the process of degeneration continues, human beings lose their beauty as well as having their lives shortened. They are not all equally ugly, however, and the result of that is that some of them misconduct themselves with others' wives. Thus 'misconduct in pleasures' becomes widespread.

From this point on various other principles become widespread and life gets shorter and shorter as a result. Details of the origin of the principles are not given, but the principles are, in order of occurrence : harsh speech, nonsensical chatter, coveting, malevolence, wrong theories, unlawful passion (incestuous), inordinate desire (greed), unnatural (homosexual) conduct, unfilial conduct towards mother or father, disrespect towards *śramaṇas*, brahmans and elders. By the time all these have become widespread human life is reduced to two hundred and fifty years and will decrease further to one hundred years. We have now presumably reached the Buddha's own day, when the maximum was supposed to be a hundred years.

The *Sūtra* continues with a prediction about the future, which is optimistic, although the Buddha believed that things would have to get very bad indeed before men came to their senses (two and a half millennia later history has surely endorsed this conclusion). Life will be reduced to ten years (sexual maturity at five). Only the most insipid food will be available. Good conduct will disappear completely, even the word 'good' (or perhaps more accurately 'the idea of the good' —neuter) will not exist among men, let alone any one who does a good action. Those who are unfilial and disrespectful (as above) will be honoured and praised, just as at present those who are filial and respectful are honoured and praised. No family relationships will be recognised and men will live like goats, dogs, etc.

Human beings at that time will bear sharp hostility, malevolence, angry and murderous thoughts towards one another, such as a hunter bears towards beasts. They will hold 'sword interval' weeks when they look upon one another as beasts and go around with sharp swords taking each others' lives.

Then some of them will think: 'Let us not take...let no one take my life...suppose we withdraw to a thicket, or rugged mountains, and live, eating fruit and roots.' They will do so for the 'sword interval' weeks, coming out and embracing one another afterwards, assembling singing and encouraging each other: 'It's wonderful, sir, you are alive !' In this way a good-principle is rediscovered among men: abstention from taking life. As a result they find their lives increase and their appearance improves, so they look for more good principles. Gradually they will rediscover all the good principles opposed to the bad principles which had become widespread before. The whole process of degeneration will be reversed until 'this Rose Apple Continent' (i. e. India, the Southern Continent of the land-mass of Eurasia) will be powerful and prosperous, with a vast population ('like purgatory', the Buddha remarks ambiguously, thinking probably of his preference for seclusion). Vārāṇasī will be the capital, but it will then be called Ketumatī. An emperor named Śaṃkha ('Conch') will rule there and the wheel gem will appear again. Śaṃkha will conquer the whole Earth without force, without the sword, by principle (*dharma*).

To complete the well-being of mankind the next Buddha, Maitreya, will then occur in the world, will teach the doctrine and show the 'best life' (and will have many more followers than the present Buddha). At its conclusion the *Sūtra* summarises the doctrine, including self-possession, meditation and the exercise of pervading the whole universe with thought charged with benevolence, compassion, sympathetic joy and equanimity.

The Ideal Society

The texts in the preceding section show us the Buddha's idea of the perfect ancient society before degeneration took place, which is also of interest as the happy society of the future, restored after the abolition of war and violence. The conception of evolution is characteristically Buddhist in that the loss of the original innocence took place through the operation of the causal laws concerning attachment, desire and so on. Someone became 'wanton' (*lola*) and tasted the Earth, as a result feeling (sensual) desire (*tṛṣṇā*). Of all this we have had a detailed account in the last chapter. Here what interests us is the nature of the society of happy beings, beautiful, radiant, feeding on joy. Even when beings had become more like human beings, living on the Earth and enjoying delicious plants growing on it, there was for a long time no essential social change.

The most important feature of this society was that it was classless. The object of the first discourse is to show that the claims of the brahmans are baseless and to maintain that all beings are equal before the moral law (good conduct will lead to a good destiny, etc.). There was no priesthood, also there was no aristocracy and no king. As a kind of government there was simply the assembly of all the people, which eventually established private property and thereby ensured the doom of the ancient society. There was no work, but only food gathering at need, for each meal. The food plants were abundant and prolific, so that all needs were easily satisfied and the question of private property could not arise. Equally there was no basis for any violence or use of force, just as in the absence of property there could be no theft. It would seem also that there was no religion, since there were no priests. Moreover in the absence of immorality there would seem to have been no ideas of good conduct until at the end of this period sex and property originated. If there were no *śramaṇas* there was presumably no philosophy. Only in the happy society of the future, which will be happy not because it is innocent but because of moral progress, there will certainly be a code of ethics and finally a new Buddha will restart the doctrine of Buddhism (it appears to be implied that in the lowest phase of degeneration when any idea of 'good' disappears Buddhism must disappear too along with any other philosophies or religions which teach about the good; the regeneration will apparently take place without benefit of any systematic teaching, through the discovery in practice of the essential social principle of non-violence).

If a happy society is to be restored, then, with or without Buddhism, the following are the moral principles which must prevail. (1) The primary principle, the first which must be established and from which the others would seem to follow or derive, is 'abstention from taking life.' In a time when 'sword intervals' (= wars ?) are frequent, social regeneration will be begun by people who withdraw from society, boycott the fighting. This will increase the expectation of life, and it seems to be assumed that its advantages will be so self-evident at that time that the majority will come to follow the principle. Before that time, in the phase of degeneration, its advantages will apparently not be self-evident to very many people. A little warfare is not enough: only a massive general slaughter can produce the requisite impression. With this principle it is natural to group its more general statements found in these texts: non-violence and non-malevolence. In addition those who withdrew from war lived on fruit and roots, i. e. were vegetarians. (2) Property is represented as an evil, as a basic evil from which many other evils flowed, but it seems that under present conditions (lack of abundance of food) it is a necessary evil. Consequently it must be respected and the second principle is 'abstention from taking what was not given.' Another expression for this in our texts is non-coveting. (3) The family and marriage, though also unknown in the happy society of the past, have also to be respected. 'Abstention from misconduct in pleasures', which is equivalent to abstention from adultery in contexts like these, is the main principle.

Filial respect, which is stressed in the second text, could be regarded as associated with this principle, or as a separate principle. 'Respect for the eldest' probably means conceding precedence to an elder or eldest brother. (4) The last of the main principles is truth: 'abstention from false speech'. With this are associated avoiding all kinds of harmful speech: malicious, harsh, etc. A few other principles are mentioned occasionally, are presumably good but not basic: the bad principles prevalent in the phase af degeneration included wrong theories and disrespect towards *śramaṇas* and brahmans (these might be included with false speech). Finally the emperor when instructing his vassals included not drinking intoxicants among his precepts (the reason for this, we find in other texts, is that in a state of intoxication people are liable to perpetrate bad actions). Moderation in taxation belongs rather to the principles of government.

Good Government

Before we review the principles of good government from the texts so far considered we may add a further text from the *Dirgha*[1] which discusses the duties of a king. The Buddha is here talking to a brahman about the requisites of the 'sacrifice', requisites which bear on the question of the rôle of the brahmans in society and may be considered later, but he illustrates his views with the following story.

'Once upon a time, brahman, there was a king named Great Realm. He was rich, had great wealth, great property, much gold and silver, many resources for pleasure, much money and grain, full treasuries and storehouses. Then the following idea occurred in the mind of King Great Realm when he was alone and secluded: "I have acquired abundant human property. I have conquered and exploit a large circle of the Earth. Suppose I were to perform a great sacrifice which would be for my benefit and happiness for a long time?" (He is of course thinking of a future, non-human, life; of the Brahmanical doctrine that one can attain heaven by perform-

2. D No. 5, T, No. 23.

ing particular sacrifices.) Then, brahman, King Great Realm addressed the brahman who was his chaplain... (told him of his idea, and that he wished to perform a great sacrifice, and added:) "Advise me, sir, what would be for my benefit and happiness for a long time."

'When he had said this the chaplain said to King Great Realm: "The country of His Majesty the King is full of oppression and subversion. We see bandits attacking villages, towns and cities and committing robbery on the roads. If His Majesty the King collected the tithe when the country is full of oppression and subversion, that would be doing what should not be done. It might be that Your Majesty would think the revolt (literally the 'standard') of the brigands could be suppressed by means of executions, imprisonment, confiscations, threats or banishment. However, this revolt of the brigands will not be suppressed perfectly in that way. Those who survive the killings will afterwards harass the King's country. However, depending on the following policy this revolt of the brigands will be suppressed perfectly: Now, let His Majesty the King grant seed and fodder to those in his country who take up agriculture and cattle breeding. Let His Majesty grant capital to those in his country who undertake commerce. Let His Majesty dispense wages and food to those in his country who undertake the royal service. Those people, being intent on their own work, will not harass the King's country and at the same time there will be a great accumulation for the King (we have to understand that 'moderate' taxation will continue on the incomes of the people). Through the country remaining secure and without oppression or subversion I think men will live with open houses, glad and rejoicing, making their children dance."' Great Realm is said to have agreed and to have implemented this policy with complete success.

We can now summarise the principles of good government, not forgetting those of republican government recommended by the Buddha in connection with the Vṛjis. These principles could easily be extended by considering the government of the Buddhist community, which was organised as a republic (see Chapter Three) and offers elaborate procedures for the functioning of local democratic units of administration, but it will be enough here to state the principles directly formulated for secular governments.

It may be asked whether the Buddha favoured republican or monarchical government. Since he formed his own community in imitation of the former, refused to appoint a 'successor', even denying for himself the prerogative of leadership in any sense of exclusive guardianship, we must conclude he preferred a republic. However, he seems to have accepted monarchy also, perhaps as a necessary evil in a degenerate period of history, in that he was ready to discuss how to make it a success. He perhaps thought democracy could not function effectively in an age of violence, that republican governments like the Vṛjis were not likely to withstand the forces of more strongly centralised powers, or the corrupting influence of money, so that the irresistible strength of an autocrat would be needed to maintain order and some degree of justice. In this case he would be concerned to give his advice that the autocrat should be benevolent, which would redound to his own good as well as the people's, and should be so far democratic as to heed the recommendations of the assemblies of his subjects.

The Buddha's recommendations for republican government were that the Assembly should be held frequently and should aim at unanimity in its proceedings, that the republic should conform to the principles authorised in ancient tradition, that elders should be honoured and listened to, that women and girls should be protected, that shrines and tithes to support them should be respected, and that 'worthy ones' (*arhants*) should find shelter in the republic to encourage them to live there. On conformity to tradition we might observe that, since the society of the past, before degeneration had gone so far, was happier, better governed, more moral than that of the present, it would be well to follow its laws. Presumably this conservatism would not apply in a period of regeneration, unless the principles of the remote ancient society before degeneration were those to be conformed to. The significance of the 'shrines' (*caitya*) is not clear. Later they were assimilated to the monuments or pagodas (*stūpa*) of the Buddha and sometimes of Buddhist monks.

The recommendations recorded for monarchies are rather different in character. There is no question of unanimity, but the policy of conciliation recommended to King Great Realm is intended to produce a similar harmony. The regular consultations with *śramaṇas* and brahmans of good conduct advised by the royal seer to his son are the nearest equivalent to the frequent meetings of the assembly. For conformity to ancient principles we have what seems to be the primary duty of a king, for which the first king was elected, namely the upholding of principle. For the honouring of elders and seeking of their advice, and possibly for the encouragement of 'worthy ones' (who would be *śramaṇas,* possibly brahmans) to settle in the country, we have again the seeking of advice from abstemious and diligent *śramaṇas* and brahmans, who were tolerant, gentle and calm. Like Great Realm's chaplain, they would explain what is good and what bad, what should be done and how to produce benefit and happiness. As to protection, instead of the specific mention of women, and worthy ones, we find the organising of safety, shelter and protection for the whole of society, and even for beasts and birds. There is nothing in these texts about shrines.

There are, further, several additional pieces of advice for kings. In upholding principle, wrongdoers are to be rebuked and if necessary banished: such at least were the instructions given to the first king. This, taken in conjunction with the teaching of all these texts, and particularly with the policy of conciliating a rebellious society, suggests that punishments should be as mild as possible. In fact this is an obvious corollary of the Buddha's whole doctrine and attitude, and reminds us of the methods of discipline prescribed for the communities of monks and nuns. For his own support the king is to receive a share of the produce of the country, that is, he imposes taxes, which are recommended to be moderate. This last recommendation is given to his vassals (local rulers, kings of the several countries) by an emperor who commends to them also the four main moral or social principles we have already discussed (non-violence, non-coveting, abstention from misconduct in pleasures, truthfulness), and not drinking intoxicants. This implies that it is the duty of a ruler to teach his subjects these principles of good conduct. The emperor who gave this advice is supposed to have conquered the whole Earth without the use of force. The future emperor Śaṃkha will do the same: he wlll 'conquer by principle (*dharma*)', without the sword. The idea is that all mankind will wish to live under a just government and will freely and readily submit to it.

There are in addition recommendations of an economic character which are of the utmost importance and interest. Though they are primarily economic, in fact the well-being of society depends on this sound economic basis, according to the Buddhist system. It is economic prosperity and expansion which conciliates the subjects of Great Realm, is the only effective means of ending their revolt, and at the same time enriches the king himself, since his investment in his country brings a return (through taxation) and his wealth in fact accumulates. The pacification and economic well-being of society are moreover essential for the success of Buddhism itself, for its communities and their 'best life' to flourish and spread, for its doctrines to be studied. The Buddha did not expect his doctrine to survive the ultimate decadence and all engulfing violence of the phase of degeneration of civilisation which was to follow his own time: on the contrary it would need another Buddha, when not only peace but also prosperity was restored, to start the doctrine again, to re-establish the best life, i.e. the Buddhist communities. It is self evident that if the Buddhist communities depend primarily on alms given by laymen and village and town dwellers at large, the monks going round every morning with their bowls to collect food, the society must be fairly prosperous to support them. But it is also clear from the Buddha's theory of history, as we have reviewed it, that it is people who are in a reasonably prosperous state, in a favourable phase of the evolution of society, who can be expected to reflect on the realities of happiness and unhappiness, to find that even the much sought pleasures of a prosperous life (or a life of luxury such as the Buddha reported he had led himself before the renunciation) are still forms of unhappiness in the ultimate analysis, and to give up the worldly life and lead the 'best life' as Buddhist monks or nuns.

It is the duty of a king, then, to prevent poverty—the

root of so many evils, as we have been shown—by grants to the poor. This principle of the ancient emperors, which maintained both prosperity and morality until one of them failed to continue it, is elucidated by the advice to Great Realm. Three productive (economically) classes of society are envisaged. The peasantry or farmers are to be supplied with seed to expand their agriculture and with fodder if they take up cattle breeding. Traders are to be supplied with capital to undertake their operations. The third class probably (to judge from Indian society as described in the *Tripiṭaka*) included a great variety of wage earners working in the royal service, not merely officials, soldiers and the like. It was usual in that period for various industries, such as mining, the metal industries and the textile industry, to be organised directly by the government (the *Arthaśāstra*, c. 300 B. C., recommends a state monopoly in several industries, especially mining). Some industries were carried on by merchants, more by guilds of craftsmen, but the Buddha's advice to kings to dispense wages and food to those in the royal service certainly means that the basic industries of the country are to be expanded by the ruler increasing his labour force. Other industries would be expanded by part of the capital grants to merchants, as well as indirectly encouraged by successful trade.

The implementation of this economic policy is said to have brought security (so that people left their doors open) and rejoicing.

Class and the Priesthood

In the texts we have read in this chapter we have found several discussions on class and arguments against any special position and privileges for the brahmans. Some of the essential points of the Buddha's teaching on this were summarised above (pp. 163f.). Classes were originally occupational, not hereditary, and ought to be so again (they would then cease to be classes in the Brahmanical sense). Any person could become a *śramaṇa*, regardless of his class origin : on this there is another *sūtra*[1] which insists on the point that persons of any of the four classes could attain enlightenment and *nirvāṇa*, if they are intelligent. Equally

1. M No. 90 (II 128), T 26 No: 212.

people of any class are reborn according to their actions, without discrimination on grounds of class.[1] Another text[2] observes that hereditary privilege is at present so far unreal that in practice who is master and who is servant depends on wealth (this observation, however, is not ascribed to the Buddha himself, but to one of the monks after his final extinction).

The Buddha's views on service are given in another sūtra.[3] A brahman once explained to him that the brahmans declare that there are four kinds of service : of a brahman, of a warrior, of one of the agricultural-mercantile class (*vaiśya*) or of a helot (*śūdra*). The distinction is that a person of any of the four classes may serve a brahman, a warrior may be served by another warrior or by either of the lower classes, a *vaiśya* may be served by a *vaiśya* or by a helot, a helot may be served only by another helot. (Thus there is a hierarchy from the brahman down to the helot.) When the Buddha asks whether all people concede this preeminence to the brahmans, the brahman admits they do not. The Buddha then objects that the brahmans are acting as people who thrust disagreeable food on others and then make them pay for it. At the same time he does not hold that everyone should be served (by anyone) or that no one should be served. If the service will cause the person served to be better (morally), he may be served, if it will make him worse he should not be served. This applies to all regardless of class. Whether a person is a better person or a worse person does not depend on high birth, nor on superior colour (? —*varṇa*, which also means 'beauty' and 'class', so here the last may well be intended), nor on superior property. If one of high birth, etc., takes life, steals or commits other bad actions his high birth will not make him 'better'. If he abstains from such actions his high birth will not make him 'worse'.

The brahman continues that there are four kinds of wealth, according to the brahmans, four kinds of wealth proper to the four classes : alms for brahmans, bow and quiver for warriors,

1. For another *sūtra* emphasising this see M No. 93, T 26 No. 151.
2. M No. 84, T 99 (*Saṃyukta*) section 20 No. 12.
3. M No. 96, T 26 No. 150.

agriculture and cattle breeding for *vaiśyas*, the sickle and the carrying-pole for helots. It is improper for any of them to despise their proper wealth, as it is (especially) improper for a watchman to steal. Again the Buddha asks whether all people concede this, and makes the same objection when told not. The difference of class by birth tells us merely a person's origin, it means no more than the difference between several fires as 'wood fire', 'grass fire', etc. A person may leave home for the homeless life from a brahman, warrior, *vaiśya* or helot family and be successful in following the doctrine and discipline of the thus-gone. Cannot persons of all four origins develop thoughts of benevolence, without hatred, without malevolence? The brahman admits that this is so.

In a discussion with some brahmans[1] the Buddha is told that they declare there are five characteristics which distinguish the brahman class. A brahman should be (1) well-born (he should be able to trace back his brahman ancestors for seven generations on both his father's and his mother's sides), (2) a teacher (of the Three *Vedas*, the ancillary lexicons, books on ritual, grammar, etc., and the historical traditions), (3) handsome, of the *brahma*-colour, etc., (4) virtuous and (5) wise (in the performance of the ritual). The Buddha asks one of them whether the list can be reduced, and it is agreed (by this one, at least) that colour is unimportant and could be left out, that the *Veda* and birth could be left out, but virtue and wisdom are essential (from the Brahmanical point of view, perhaps, a brahman need not teach but must be able to perform the rituals). The Buddha then goes on to redefine these essentials, virtue and wisdom, on Buddhist principles. Virtue should be following the moral principles of Buddhism. For wisdom in the ritual he substitutes Buddhist 'understanding', and explains it as the four meditations and the 'three sciences' of the enlightenment (the three sciences are of course to be substituted for the three 'knowledges', *vedas*, of Brahmanism).

We have seen already that the theology of the brahmans was incorrect, and should be replaced by the science of causation. As to the ritual, the sacrifice, the Buddha recommended to

1. D No. 4, T 1 No. 22.

kings the substitution of economic investment, as in the story of Great Realm. However, the story continues that when Great Realm had carried out this policy, ended the revolt, brought about great prosperity and accumulated his own treasure he still wished to perform a great sacrifice of the traditional kind. Under his chaplain's guidance this became a great festival for the whole population. It was paid for entirely by the king, without levying the tithe or accepting contributions from his subjects. No animals were sacrificed, even plants were not cut down for sacrificial purposes; only butter, sesame oil, curds, honey and the like were used as offerings. No violence was used on slaves, labourers, etc., in the preparations: all the work was on a voluntary basis and what was not done voluntarily was not done at all. This, the Buddha adds, was an inferior kind of sacrifice, which might satisfy those anxious to perform a Brahmanical sacrifice, though it was reformed to exclude violence. A far superior sacrifice is to establish perpetual donations to those who have 'gone forth', and are virtuous, a still better one is to build a dwelling for the community (of monks), still better are becoming a lay Buddhist, following the Buddhist moral principles (as a layman), becoming a monk and attaining *nirvāṇa*.

In the Buddha's time, to judge from his remarks in another *Dirgha sūtra*,[1] the brahmans, or some of them, lived a luxurious life, were well dressed, well fed, had many servants, lived in mansions, and so on. This he thought was in striking contrast with the ancient brahman seers who had composed the *Veda* (cf. also the original brahmans in the account of social evolution above). Now, brahmans lived like aristocrats, in fact some of them were endowed with lands out of the royal domains by kings, as fiefs (there is one such in the present *sūtra*, another in that last referred to, another in that on Great Realm, and yet others). The ancient brahmans may have been genuine seers, but the modern ones cannot become seers merely by learning the verses and prayers of the *Veda* (the *mantras*) the ancients had composed.

The main point on the brahmans is, however, that they were

1. D No. 3, T 1 No. 20. Sanskrit fragments *Turfan* 495, 885, 978.

no different in nature from other people. Their claim to 'purity' (*śuddhi*) is nonsense,[1] as is their claim to be the 'white' (*śukla*) colour whilst the other classes are 'black' (*kṛṣṇa*). According to the Buddha all four classes are equally 'pure', and what matters is their conduct. Although the Buddha thus rejected their special claims and sought to reform their entire ideology, he wished to do so by conciliating the brahmans, by restoring them, according to his version of history, to their original condition. In effect his idea was to assimilate the brahmans to the *śramaṇas*: to establish that anyone could become a brahman by adopting a simple life of meditation and virtuous, tolerant and gentle conduct. The name 'brahman' would be retained and other terms such as 'sacrifice' might continue to be used, but they should have reformed meanings consonant with Buddhist principles. In future 'brahman' and '*śramaṇa*' should be synonymous, and all those who joined this class of people, devoted to high moral aims and the quest for enlightenment and *nirvāṇa*, should follow the 'best life' (*brahma*-life) as described by the Buddha.

It is almost superfluous to add that the Buddha did not have in mind here any administrative measures or other methods except that people would be persuaded by their own experience and observations that his discoveries were true and his recommendations good. Ii emperors were to expand their realms only by principle and without the use of force, then the great debate as to what doctrines were true would proceed under conditions of the most perfect intellectual freedom. There is plenty of evidence for the Buddha's tolerant attitude in practice in these dialogues with brahmans, more in similar discussions with *śramaṇas* or lay followers of other schools, such as the Jainas.[2]

The Buddha's Teaching to the Laity

Having considered the Buddha's views about socety and his recommendations to governments we may now ask what teaching he offered to the laity, the ordinary people who were

1. M No. 93, T 26 No. 151.

2. M No. 56, T 26 No. 133 (a Jaina layman persuaded to follow the Buddha should not discontinue his donations to the Jaina monks); M No. 101, T 26 No. 19 ; M No. 35, T 99 section 5 No. 8.

unlikely to leave the worldly society, to 'go forth', and to those who became his lay followers, Buddhist laymen (*upāsakas*) and laywomen disciples (*upāsikās*).

The *Dīrgha* contains a *sūtra*[1] in which the Buddha admonishes a layman following the morning ritual of the Brahmanical religion. When staying near Rājagṛha the Master once when entering the city for alms saw a householder hailing (worshipping) the six directions (the four quarters and up and down), his hair and clothes wet (after the ritual bathing). The Buddha asked him why he did this, and was told that his father had enjoined the ritual on him as his dying wish. The Buddha then says that, in the 'discipline' (*vinaya*) of the Aryans (i.e. the excellent ones, as understood by the Buddha) this is not the way in which the six directions should be worshipped.

The Aryan pupil (*śrāvaka*, here the Buddhist layman ; the term is sometimes applied to monks, but the Buddha appears normally to have used it for lay disciples in training and to have referred to the monk in training as *bhikṣu*, 'monk') should regard his parents, teachers (*ācārya*), wife and children, friends, servants (slaves and wage labourers), *śramaṇas* and brahmans, as respectively the six directions (East, South, West, North, Down, Up.) In order to prepare himself for these six relationships he should observe the following (discipline), which will also lead him to 'victory' in both worlds (this life and the next), and to rebirth in heaven after death. First he must give up the four kinds of defilement in action. Secondly he must not do a bad action through any of four circumstances (*sthānas*). Thirdly he must not indulge in the six openings to loss of property. Thus he should be without fourteen evils. The Buddha now explains all this in detail.

The four kinds of defilement in action are infringements of the four main moral or social principles we found in the Buddha's recommendations for society: not taking life, or what was not given, abstention from misconduct in pleasures, truthfulness.

The four circumstances through which a bad action may be done are taking a wrong course through (1) 'will' (*chandas*,

1. D No. 31, T 1 No. 16 (also T 26 No. 135 and other Chinese versions).

i.e. through one's wish or desire; the word is possibly here an abbreviation for *kāmacchandas*, the will to pleasure), (2) aversion (or 'anger',—*doṣa* in 'Buddhist' Sanskrit, equivalent to 'Classical' *dveṣa*), (3) delusion (*moha*—the opposite of understanding) or (4) fear (*bhaya*).

The *sūtra* goes into the six openings to loss of property in more detail. The first is the habit ('practice', *anuyoga*) of taking various kinds of intoxicating (alcoholic) drink as a circumstance for negligence (*pramāda*). There are six disadvantages in this: visible (i. e. direct, immediate) loss (literally 'confiscation', but it may not here mean a fine) of money, increase of quarrelling, liability to illness, production of ill fame, indecent exposure and weakening of the understanding. (In other words there may be negligence in any of these ways, the first resulting in direct loss and the others indirectly in loss of property; the first may mean simply reckless expenditure).

The second opening is frequenting the streets at inappropriate times. This also has six disadvantages: one is oneself unprotected and unsafe, so are one's wife and children, so is one's property, one may be suspected in some criminal case, untrue reports grow, one meets unhappiness in many (unforeseeable) forms.

The third opening is addiction to assemblies (*abhi-car* means acting wrongly, being possessed by, misconducting oneself, hence *abhicaraṇa*, 'addiction'; the festival assemblies *samājas* themselves need not be harmful). This also is said to have six disadvantages, perhaps merely for the sake of symmetry. They are merely that one is (constantly) asking where is there dancing, singing, instrumental music, epic recitations, clapping (as rhythmic amusement), drumming (of a particular kind, *kumbhatūṇa*, perhaps the single big drum played by many people together which is still found in Ceylon). The Sthaviravāda commentary explains here that one goes off to whichever village or town has an assembly the next day, spending the whole day preparing clothes, scents, garlands, etc., for the trip; the assembly may last several days, so that one's work is seriously interrupted. In other words there is no moral objection to the assemblies themselves here, for laymen (whereas it is considered inappropriate for a monk or nun to attend them), but overfrequent excursions will lead to financial loss.

The fourth opening is the practice of gambling, as circumstance for negligence. Its six disadvantages are, that in winning one generates hatred, when losing one regrets one's lost wealth, there is the actual loss of money, one's words are not heeded in assemblies, one is despised by one's friends and advisers, one is not desired for marriage on the ground that a gambler is not adequate to support a wife.

The fifth opening is association with bad friends. Its six disadvantages are six kinds of bad friend : gamblers, wantons, drunkards, dishonest men, deceivers (the distinction between these and the last is not clear), violent men. Afterwards the Buddha expands on the subject of bad friends, enemies posing as friends, and divides them in four classes : the one who takes everything, the one who only talks, the flatterer, the fellow waster. The first of these is an enemy posing as a friend through four circumstances : he takes everything, he wants much for little, he does what should be done only from fear, he pursues only wealth (for himself). Likewise the one who only talks about the hospitality (he would have given you, says he had had prepared for you—commentary) in the past, his future hospitality, he favours you with (kind but) meaningless talk, and when something ought to be done at the present moment he explains that he has just met with a disaster. Likewise the flatterer approves evil, disapproves of good, speaks praise in one's presence, speaks dispraise in one's absence. Lastly the fellow waster is a companion in drinking, in frequenting the streets at inappropriate times, in addiction to assemblies, in gambling. Contrasted with these bad friends, enemies in disguise, are the true friends, whom we may consider later.

The sixth and last opening to loss of property is the habit of laziness. Its six 'disadvantages' are six excuses for not doing any work, so that one exhausts the property one has and does not get any more. One says : It is too cold. It is too hot. It is too late. It is too early. I am too hungry. I am too full.

These fourteen evils are further paraphrased in verses, perhaps to make them easier to remember. The importance here attached to wealth, apparently as the indispensable basis for all good conduct, is most remarkable, and deserves to be stressed, along with the recommendations we have read concerning economic development and the consequent well being of society, in order to refute the view often expressed that Buddhism is concerned only with renunciation, is only for ascetics, is wholly unworldly and irrelevant to social problems, and so on, a view equally false whether intended as praise or dispraise of its subject. Summarising this discipline, we find it covers (1) the principles of ethics, which have been elucidated in other *sūtras* and are entirely social principles; (2) the circumstances of bad conduct, which are largely similar to the main 'bad principles' which obstruct the way to enlightenment and *nirvāṇa* (primarily desire and aversion, and delusion; fear was spoken of in a different connection above : solitude in the forest in the narratives about the enlightenment of the Buddha), and which are on the other hand individual ethical principles (though here applied to the lay or worldly life they seem more directly inspired by the way to *nirvāṇa* and the training of a monk, and might be seen as a possible preparation for the way of non-attachment) ; (3) the maxims of prudent worldly conduct leading to (individual and family) prosperity, which are maxims of wealth (*artha*), not of principle (not of *dharma* in the sense of justice, virtue, ethics).

Coming now to the six kinds of human relationship to be substituted for the directions, there are five circumstances through which each group of persons is to be set up as a 'direction'.

Thinking that he was supported by them a son should support his parents, should do things which ought to be done by them, should establish the family (as regards wealth — commentary), should engage in the family heritage (keep up its tradition), should grant donations for his parents (on their behalf — Sthaviravāda commentary) after their deaths.

As an apprentice one should 'set up' one's teachers by rising (on seeing them coming), by attending on them (i. e. visiting them, seeking audience), by listening to them attentively, by serving them, by learning the trade thoroughly.

One's wife should be 'set up' by respect, by avoiding disrespect, by faithfulness, by handing over authority, by giving her adornments.

Friends should be 'set up' by gifts, affectionate speech, helpfulness, treating them like oneself (sharing their happiness and unhappiness) and not going back on one's words.

Slaves and servants should be 'set up' by arranging the work according to their ability, by granting food and wages, by attending to them in illness, by sharing special enjoyments with them, by releasing them (from work) on time.

Śramaṇas and brahmans should be 'set up' by benevolent actions, speech and thoughts, by keeping one's house open to them, by providing for their physical needs.

The six groups should reciprocate by exercising their compassion (*anu-kamp*), and again there are five circumstances for each relationship, except the last.

Parents should keep one away from evil, introduce one to good, have one trained to a trade, unite one with a proper wife and hand over the inheritance in time.

Teachers should discipline one well, teach one thoroughly, pass on the whole trade, give (good) references to their friends and colleagues, ensure one's security (a secure livelihood through the trade) wherever one goes.

A wife should arrange the work (of the household) well, treat the servants well, be faithful, look after the income, be skilful and diligent in everything that ought to be done.

Friends should save one from being negligent, save the property of one who is negligent, be a refuge to one who is afraid, not abandon one in misfortune, cherish the other's children.

Slaves and servants should rise before the master (*arya*), go to bed after him, take only what he gives them, do their work well, spread his fame and praise.

Śramaṇas and brahmans are distinguished by reciprocating in six circumstances instead of only five. They should keep one away from evil, introduce one to good, be compassionate towards one with their minds benevolent (literally 'good', *kalyāṇa*), let one hear what one had not heard, clarify what one has heard, describe the way to heaven.

Balancing the four principles underlying the well being of society in the most general way, which are negative in formulation although positive recommendations are implied by them, we find in this system of relationships a detailed and specific positive code of social behavour. It is surely worthy of remark that there is nothing here of any relationship to the government or the king (since these admonitions were delivered in Magadha, moreover in the capital). We are remote trom the atmosphere of, say, a feudalistic society with its loyalties and obligations. In fact the outlook] seems to be the democratic life of a city state or republic such as the Śākyas or Vṛjis, or even of the more perfect society supposed to have existed before the election of the first king (before the institution of government?). In this scheme the government is presumably to be concerned only with the upholding of the four general principles, i.e. the administration of justice, in return for being supported by taxes.

To complete our review of this *sūtra* for the individual in the lay or worldly society we have to consider the four classes of real or good friends (*suhṛd*) whom the Buddha opposes to the 'enemies posing as friends' described above. The four are the friend who is a helper, the one who shares the same happiness and unhappiness, the one who tells you what is for your welfare, and the one who is compassionate. Each is a good friend through four circumstances. The helper saves one from being negligent, saves the property of one who is negligent, is a refuge to one who is afraid (so far like the friend above reciprocating the relationship of friendship), on an occasion when there is business to be done he grants one double the outlay asked for. The one who shares the same happiness and unhappiness lets you into his secrets, keeps your secrets, does not abandon you in misfortune (cf. above), sacrifices even his life for the sake of his friend. The one who tells you what is for your welfare (like a *śramaṇa* or brahman) keeps you away from evil, introduces you to good, lets you hear what you had not heard, describes the way to heaven. The compassionate friend is not pleased through your bad fortune, but is pleased through your good fortune, checks others from speaking dispraise of you, praises those who speak praise of you. As in the other parts of this *sūtra* this text is partly paraphrased, with appropriate similes, in verses.

As good friendship is said by the Buddha to be the whole of the 'best life' of the monks (p. 105 above) so here friendship receives the greatest stress in the life of the householder. Especially in the maxims of friendship we notice the working out of the basic social standard of considering all beings as like oneself ('all-self-ness') inherent in all the Buddha's social teaching (cf. p. 105 above).

The Lay Disciple

At the conclusion of the admonitions to a layman which we have just read, we are told the householder asked to be a lay disciple (*upāsaka*) of the Buddha. He says that he goes to the Master (Bhagavant, i.e. the Buddha) as a refuge (*śaraṇa*), likewise to the Doctrine and to the Community of Monks as refuges. Going to these three 'refuges' constitutes formally becoming a lay disciple in Buddhism. The foregoing admonitions are of course wholly applicable to the lay disciple, but they are equally applicable to any layman, to society at large. For the actual Buddhist lay disciple there is a further systematic course of instruction (*ānupūrvi kathā*),[1] which, however, could be regarded as abstracted from these admonitions. In the Sthaviravāda version the summary of this runs: discourses on donation (*dāna*), virtue (*śīla*) and heaven (*svarga*); the disadvantage, meanness and defilement of pleasures; the benefit in renunciation. The Mahāsaṃghika version substitutes 'merit' and 'the result of merit' for the last two items. The essentials, however, are donation, which means primarily giving alms to monks (equivalent to providing for the physical needs of *śramaṇas*), virtue, which means primarily observing the four main social principles (not taking life, etc.) and heaven. As to heaven, we saw above (pp. 69f) that the way to it is virtue or good conduct. It is implied, therefore, that besides the natural laws of the sequence of conditioned origination, whereby, as we saw, desire (for the pleasures of the senses) leads to continued involvement in transmigration and (in the *Saṃyukta*, at least) the forces, that is actions, lead to rebirth, there are further laws according to which various kinds of action lead to particular kinds of rebirth. Although the monk who aims direct for *nirvāṇa* is not concerned, perhaps, with any kind of rebirth, and such details find no place in the theory of his training, the layman who is not ready for this supreme aim is very much concerned with rebirth and is assumed to wish to go to one or other of the heavens of the gods. There are two *sūtras* in the *Madhyama*[2] which tell us a little about this doctrine of

1. D I 110, M I 379 (in *sūtra* already referred to above : D 3, M 56), *Mahāvastu* III 257 with variant ending.

2. M Nos. 135 and 136, T 26 Nos. 170 and 171. A Sanskrit version of the first in Hoernle, *Manuscript Remains of Buddhist Literature found in Eastern Turkestan*.

precise retribution. It is a doctrine on which the authentic *Tripiṭaka* has very little to say, and which perhaps had not been elaborated in more than a very general way by the Buddha himself, but which the schools of Buddhism later worked out in much detail, seeking no doubt to make their teaching to laymen more forceful by the inclusion of circumstantial particulars of the destinies attending every kind of action.

In the first of these *sūtras* the Buddha is asked why men are seen to live in such a variety of circumstances, inferior and superior, short lived and long lived, suffering much or little illness, having little or great wealth, having understanding or poor understanding, and so on, His answer is that all this depends on action (*karman*), it is action which divides beings in this way. Asked to elaborate this he says that if, for instance, a man or woman takes life, say as a hunter, he or she will be reborn in misery, an evil destiny, ruin, purgatory. Or, failing that, if he or she is again born as a human being it will be as a short lived one. In the opposite case of one who abstains from taking life, is compassionate for the benefit of all living beings, the rebirth will be in heaven or, failing that, as a human being with long life.

One who harasses other beings with violence, short of actually taking life, will be reborn, if not in purgatory then as a human being suffering from much illness, and the reverse in the opposite case. Similarly anger and malevolence result in ugliness, the opposite in loveliness. Envy (*irṣyā*) leads to an inferior birth, lack of it to a superior one. Lack of generosity leads to poverty, generosity to wealth. Pride and arrogance leads to a socially low (despised) birth, the opposite to a high one. One who frequents *śramaṇas* and brahmans asking them about the good, the bad, etc., will be reborn with understanding, one who does not will have a poor understanding.

The next *sūtra* first clarifies the point whether actions of body, speech and mind are all equally significant, or whether only the latter are significant (the Buddha always stresses the mental part of action, the intention, in contrast particularly to the Jainas, and consequently was misrepresented as denying any significance to bodily or vocal actions). All are significant and may have happy, unhappy or neutral results, but only if they are voluntary (*sāṃcetanika*), i.e. accompanied by volition. It continues with an explanation that the working out of the results (*vipāka*) of actions may be very complicated, so that one who takes only a short view may be misled. It is even possible that one who has taken life may be reborn in heaven—because of some good action done before or after the bad one—or that one who has done a good action may go to purgatory. Some *śramaṇas* and brahmans, the Buddha says, have been misled by such cases into concluding that there is no such thing as good action, or a result of good conduct.

The precise mechanism of rebirth as result of past actions is hardly made clear in the *Tripiṭaka*. We may suppose that the Buddha believed that a bad action, such as harming another person, has an effect also on the person who does it. It may dispose him to have bad principles in the series of his thoughts, a continuing viciousness of nature. This viciousness may at death lead him to appropriate surroundings; it is also a form of strong attachment to the world, perhaps therefore disposing him towards the grossest spheres of existence as opposed to the lighter realms of the gods. A good action would have the opposite kind of effect on the person who does it, as it were an uplifting effect, conducive to detachment as well as less gross existence.

We can further illustrate the talk on heaven when teaching laymen from the following interesting *sūtra* in the *Madhyama*.[1] Śāriputra receives news that a brahman layman of Rājagṛha has become 'negligent' (*pramatta*, or 'careless') : he is using ('leaning on') the king to rob the brahman householders, and using the latter to rob the king. (An interesting sidelight on the kingdom of Magadha; it seems this brahman was a tax collector.) The *sūtra* notes that his former wife had been 'confident' (presumably a Buddhist having confidence in the Buddha, Doctrine, etc.), but she had died and his present wife was not.

Śāriputra goes to meet the brahman, as if by chance, passes the time of day with him and then enquires whether he is 'careful' ('diligent', *apramatta*). The brahman asks how he can

1. M No. 97, T 26 No. 27.

be when he has to support his parents, wife and children, slaves and labourers, do his duty to friends, relations, guests, departed spirits (his ancestors), the gods, and the king, besides looking after his own body. Śāriputra asks whether he thinks a man who had been unjust and dishonest (*viṣama*) but alleged his parents as the cause would be spared by the guardians of purgatory, likewise if he alleged any of the brahman's other excuses as the cause. The brahman agrees that such a man would be consigned to purgatory just the same, regardless of his excuses. Śāriputra concludes that it is better to be just and impartial (*sama*): there are other ways to support one's parents, etc., which are meritorious and do not require bad actions. The brahman expresses his appreciation of Śāriputra's discourse and goes off.

On a later occasion the brahman is very ill and thinks he is about to die. He sends a message for Śāriputra to come and see him, out of compassion. Śāriputra finds him in a bad way, and discusses future possibilities: which destiny would he prefer, purgatory, to be an animal, a human being, or any of the various classes of gods? The brahman is intent on the heaven of Brahmā (as are all brahmans, Śāriputra thinks). Śāriputra tells him the way to union with Brahmā is to practice the exercise of pervading the whole universe with thought immeasurable, without hatred, etc., and charged with benevolence, compassion, sympathetic joy and equanimity, considering all beings as like oneself (the exercise used by monks to get rid of the 'obstacles', as we saw above). The brahman asks Śāriputra to convey his respects to the Buddha, and the monk leaves. Soon afterwards the brahman dies, and the *sūtra* tells us he was in fact reborn in the world of Brahmā.

This seems rather easy for a dishonest tax collector; however, he would presumably meet the results of his injustice eventually, for heaven is far from being a final state. Or perhaps his change of heart had been so real and effective that he had balanced out his wickedness already, and his non-violent and benevolent meditation was powerful enough to overcome all trace of it.

As a further elucidation of the systematic instruction of lay disciples we may proceed to another *Madhyama sūtra*,[1] which

1. M No. 81, T 26 No. 63, *Mahāvastu* I 326ff.

is curious in that it is a story told by the Buddha about a former *buddha* named Kāśyapa. This *buddha* had an outstanding lay disciple who was a potter named Ghaṭīkāra. Ghaṭīkāra abstained from taking life, taking what was not given, misconduct in pleasures, false speech, and moreover from intoxicating drink as a circumstance for negligence. We may note here that these five principles of conduct, rather than the presumably more original and essential group of four, were generally taken by the later schools as indicating the essential minimum of virtue (*śīla*) required in order to be a lay Buddhist, and known as the 'five precepts' (*pañca śikṣāpadāni*) or 'five virtues' (*pañca śīlāni*). Ghaṭīkāra has the further virtue (required of monks, but not of laymen, for whom like all the other rules for monks it is optional, though of course good) that he does not use gold and silver, moreover as a potter he avoids harming animal life when collecting his clay from the earth. The different recensions of this text add further virtues, but agree only in these six. They also agree in praising his extraordinary generosity, particularly to the *buddha*.

As a further note on 'donation' (*dāna*) we may add from the conclusion of another *Madhyama sūtra*[1] that this might consist of feeding, clothing monks, and having dwellings (*vihāra*) built for them. Much more elaborate rules about this are contained in the *Vinaya*, with reference to what kinds af gift the communities of monks and nuns may accept, and were briefly touched on in Chapter Three.

Since the 'disadvantage of pleasures' was mentioned in at least the Sthaviravāda version of the systematic instruction its explanation may be added from a *Madhyama sūtra* on unhappiness.[2] For the sake of pleasures people work hard at various trades (to earn the requisite wealth), putting up with many kinds of discomfort such as cold, heat, flies, hunger, thirst, etc. If they nevertheless fail they grieve, lament, complain, etc. If they succeed in gaining wealth they are still unhappy and melancholy when they think of the possibility of losing it, through kings, thieves, fire, flood or heirs they dislike.

---

1. M No. 52, T 26 No. 217.
2. M No. 13 (M I 85ff), T 26 No. 99.

Then for the same pleasures people dispute with one another, fight, go to war, get killed and wounded. Or they commit burglary, robbery, adultery, etc., and if caught are violently punished. Finally as result of bad conduct for the sake of pleasures they are reborn in purgatory.

A fuller discourse to Buddhist lay disciples is given in the Sthaviravāda *Madhyama* by Ānanda to the Śākyas,[1] in the presence of the Buddha and with his approval. The Aryan pupil (*śrāvaka*), says Ānanda, is virtuous, guards his senses, knows the (proper) measure in his food, is watchful, is endowed with seven good principles and practices the four meditations. Explaining these points he is brief on virtue, inculcates detachment through guarding the senses, suggests food should be taken so that the body may endure and not for ostentation, etc., and under watchfulness indicates purifying the thoughts on all occasions and a habit similar to self-possession, though without using this term. Coming to the seven good principles, he states these as being confident, having self-respect, fearing blame, being learned, energetic, self-possessed and having understanding.

The first of these is having confidence in the enlightenment of the thus-gone: the Master is perfectly enlightened (this is actually part of a formula which occurs more fully elsewhere:[2] the Buddha has himself discovered and made known the nature of the universe, teaches the doctrine; the doctrine is visible, timeless, verifiable, fruitful, to be experienced individually by discerning persons; the community of pupils [sic: *śrāvakas*, so apparently not restricted to the monks but the entire community of Buddhists] has practised well, practised straight, practised the method, practised the proper course ...is worthy of gifts...).

Self-respect and the fear of blame check one from bad conduct. Being learned means remembering what one has heard of good doctrines relating to the best life and comprehending them. Being energetic corresponds to the principles

1. M No. 53.

2. See above p. 102 ; for the fullest form see references under *ujupaṭipanno* PTC I 373. Similar (but not identical, especially as concerns the 'community', which may be a later elaboration of the Sthaviravāda school) formulae in *Mahāvastu* III 200 and *Dharmasaṅgīti Sūtra* as quoted in the *Śikṣāsamuccaya*, 322 ff. c. f. D I 87.

of exertion (Chapter Four above), for abandoning bad principles and entering into good principles, also being firm in courage, etc.

Self-possession here is described in a cryptic sentence which has puzzled the commentators of the schools,[1] and might be read as: having constant self-possession and a good memory ... (following the Chinese interpretation; the Sthaviravāda substitute 'self-possession and wisdom', in Pali *satinepakka*, for 'constant self-possession').

Understanding means the understanding which penetrates origination and cessation and leads to the perfect exhaustion of unhappiness (i.e. understanding of the Four Truths and the Way).

These seven good principles have some resemblance to the 'faculties' (Chapter Four), moreover they are immediately followed here by the meditations, in other words the use of (the faculty of) concentration. Here then we have a course of training for the lay disciple, broadly corresponding to that for the monk. In fact the Aryan pupil who is all these things just set out, says Ānanda, is capable of being enlightened, of attaining the unsurpassed (i.e. *nirvāṇa*), which is safe from the yoke (of the influence of pleasure, etc.).

Ānanda concludes his discourse by elucidating this last point. The Aryan pupil capable of being enlightened, as a result of his purity of equanimity (attained through meditation) and self-possession recollects his former lives, understands the transmigration of beings according to their actions, enters into uninfluenced freedom of thought, freedom through understanding, even in the visible world, through the exhaustion of the influences, himself ascertaining and experiencing it, and remains in it. In this way he has both good conduct and science (*vidyā*), good conduct being his virtue and science his attainment of enlightenment.

A lay disciple is thus stated here to be capable of acquiring the 'three sciences' which constitute enlightenment and of attaining *nirvāṇa*. That a lay disciple (*upāsaka*) can attain *nirvāṇa*, or freedom, is also stated by the Buddha in the

1. Sthaviravāda MA III 30 (*kasmā...*), for the Chinese reading see Edgerton BHSD under *nipaka*.

Saṃyukta[1] and in the *Madhyama*,[2] but there was some discussion about this question. The Buddha appears often to have hesitated to teach laymen more than virtue, along with generosity and heaven. For example there is a *sūtra* in the *Madhyama*[3] in which a novice monk is asked by a prince in Rājagṛha what the doctrine is. After some hesitation he expounds the training of a monk, but the prince remarks that it is impossible that a monk could have the concentration of thought described. The novice tells the Buddha of this, but the Buddha asks how one could expect anything else: it is impossible that such a prince immersed in pleasures could learn about renunciation.

Evidently, then, teaching should not be indiscriminate but should be restricted to what the person spoken to could be expected to understand. Hence the stress on virtue and heaven when addressing laymen, even Buddhist laymen, despite the fact that all this is still a matter of involvement in the world, in transmigration, is only relatively good, as contrasted with evil and purgatory, is far from the supreme good of non-attachment and *nirvāṇa*. At best, the practice of this relative good was a preparation which brought the understanding of the supreme good nearer, so that a virtuous layman might eventually be ready to benefit from hearing the whole of the doctrine.

There is a remarkable *sūtra* in this connection in the *Madhyama*.[4] Of all the Buddha's lay disciples the wealthy householder Anāthapiṇḍada is one of the most famous. Early in the teaching career of the Buddha he bought a park near Śrāvastī, the capital of Kośala, from Prince Jeta and donated it to the community of monks.[5] He had a residence built in it for the use of the Buddha and gradually added many other buildings. The Buddha in fact seems to have spent more time here and in Śrāvastī than anywhere else: he is recorded to have spent most of his rainy seasons there, and far more *sūtras* give this as their place of origin than any other place. Anāthapiṇḍada thus provided the Buddha with his favourite residence

1. S V 410, T 99 section 41 No. 2.
2. M I 490 ff, T 99 (*Saṃyukta*) section 34 No. 26.
3. M No. 125, T 26 No. 198.
4. M No. 143, T 26 No. 28.
5. Vin II 154 ff., *Avadānaśataka* I 313, MSV III 134 ff.

and the main base of his organisation. The Buddha gave him the usual systematic instruction on generosity, virtue, heaven, etc., adding the Four Truths when he saw that the householder's thoughts were ready for this. But the *Madhyama sūtra* just mentioned tells us of the death of Anāthapiṇḍada many years later as follows.

In his last illness Anāthapiṇḍada sends a messenger to convey his respects to the Buddha, then resident at Jeta's Park, and to Śāriputra, asking the latter to have compassion and come and see him. Śāriputra goes, with Ānanda, and speaks to Anāthapiṇḍada of non-attachment to the senses (in order to gain relief from pain), of non-attachment to all contacts (stimuli), emotions, to the elements (*dhātus*), non-attachment to the five groups, even to the spheres of infinity of space, infinity of consciousness, nothingness or neither perception nor non-perception. He should not be attached to this world or have consciousness depending on it. Nor should he be attached to another world or have consciousness depending on it. He should, in short, train himself not to be attached to anything that could be seen, heard, sensed, cognised, sought or reflected on by the mind, to have no consciousness depending on any of these.

After hearing this Anāthapiṇḍada wept. He had attended on the Buddha so long, and on monks with well developed minds (i.e. advanced in the doctrine), but had never before heard a doctrinal discourse like this. Śāriputra explains that such discourses are not clear to those living in the world ('house-dwellers'), but only to those who have gone forth. Anāthapiṇḍada objects that such a discourse can be clear to those in the world, there are some who have 'little dust in their eyes', who are lost through not hearing the doctrine but will be able to grasp the doctrine.

Soon afterwards Anāthapiṇḍada died and was reborn as a Tuṣita god (which seems pretty poor, considering that a rapacious tax collector could reach the superior world of Brahmā; however, we have learned that the working out of actions is very complicated, and may presume also that Anāthapiṇḍada still retained his attachment to sensual existence despite Śāriputra's admonitions). That night he appeared before the Buddha in the Park as a radiant divinity and uttered verses praising the Park which produced his joy, the doctrine and Śāriputra. The Buddha approved and so the god departed, satisfied.

This text does not make it clear whether the Buddha agreed to the request that lay disciples should hear all the doctrine. Presumably he adhered to his position of judging what his hearers could grasp. There is a *sūtra* in the *Saṃyukta*[1] in which a layman, the mayor of a village (of Nālandā, it appears) takes up the same point with the Buddha, asking whether he has compassion for the benefit of all living beings. If so, why does he teach the doctrine to some thoroughly but to others not so thoroughly? The Buddha replies with a simile of a peasant having fields of differing qualities, who would sow the best one first. In the same way the Buddha regards the monks and nuns as his best field and the lay disciples as the next best, and proceeds accordingly.

We find, then, that at different places in the *Tripiṭaka* lay disciples are differently taught: sometimes virtue and heaven, sometimes the Four Truths, sometimes the law of conditionality ('whatever has the principle of origination, all that has the principle of cessation'[2]), sometimes non-attachment. Their attainments are equally various. One lay disciple, the householder Citra, was so learned [one of the 'seven good principles', p. 192 above] that he taught the doctrine to monks.[3] In doing so he referred to the *Brahmajāla Sūtra* (see Chapter Five) and explained a variety of advanced doctrines.

In mentioning the varieties of the Buddha's teaching and reviewing the discourses on heaven, etc., of the present chapter we ought to recall the two levels of statement discussed above (pp. 150 ff.). Generally in this more 'popular' teaching people are encouraged to believe that they themselves will somehow continue and transmigrate, as if they were permanent beings. In elementary moral teaching the Buddha does not mention the essential impermanence, the discontinuity,

1. S IV 314 ff., T 99 section 32 No.11. Elsewhere in the *Saṃyukta* (S V 407, T 99 section 37 No. 11) a lay Buddhist objects when the Buddha recommends regular study of profound *sūtras* that this is difficult for laymen, so he is recommended, besides the five precepts, to have confidence in the 'refuges' and virtue instead.

2. D I 110, end of T 1 No. 20.

3. S IV 281 ff., T 99 section 21, MSV III 21.

of the 'being' or 'person'; that there is a sequence, or a stream of consciousness stationed in sentient bodies, but no entity that endures, no real ego or soul. The unsophisticated were not expected to understand this new way of looking at experience, this critical philosophical analysis of the data. It was better, apparently, that they should believe in the crude picture of the universe generally current in the world, and not be confused by hearing the doctrine of impermanence and no soul which might lead them to assume the opposite extreme of annihilationism, that there is no sequence even, no continuity at all in existence and no working out of the moral results of actions.

One or two points of major significance remain in the teaching to lay Buddhists. Śāriputra taught a brahman, above, to attain the world of Brahmā by means of the exercises with 'immeasurable' thought (in the later schools known for short simply as the 'immeasurables' : i.e. the immeasurable thought charged successively with benevolence, compassion, sympathetic joy and equanimity as four immeasurables). Lest this should be thought to debase the exercise we may glance at a discussion[1] between an architect of Śrāvastī and four monks whom he invites to a meal with him. When they have eaten, the architect asks one of the monks, Aniruddha, about some admonitions given him before by monks. He has been recommended to develop the 'immeasurable (*apramāṇa*) freedom of thought' by some monks and the 'sublime (*mahadgata*, literally 'gone large', 'magnified') freedom of thought' by others. Are these the same or different ? He himself thinks they are the same, only the words are different. Aniruddha then explains that they are in fact different. The immeasurable freedom of thought is the exercise just mentioned (which we remember was used by monks to get rid of the obstacles to freedom from attachment, and find here recommended to a lay disciple for the same purpose of freedom). The sublime (magnified) freedom of thought is a different type of exercise consisting in concentration on a particular material object, such as the root of a tree, a field, and eventually the whole Earth, thinking 'it is sublime (or magnified)' and remaining pervading it, intent on it, with

1. M No. 127, T 26 No. 79.

that thought. This latter type of freedom of thought varies in sublimity (magnitude) according to the size of the object contemplated. It is meant to develop the thought, to enlarge it. (The former freedom is on the other hand immeasurable, though the word infinite is not actually applied to it.)

We have read of visits to dying laymen by monks, with appropriate discourses to prepare them for death, or rather for a good destiny. It is of interest to find that lay disciples too were expected to perform this important task, and that the Buddha instructed them in how to admonish (*ava-vad*) another lay disciple who is ill, afflicted, seriously ('excessively'—*bāḍha*) ill. He gives the following instructions to the Śākya lay disciple Mahānāman ('Nandin' in the Chinese), who asks how a lay disciple 'with understanding' should admonish another, also 'with understanding', under these circumstances.[1] (The Sthaviravāda commentary interprets 'with understanding' as meaning simply that he really is a Buddhist.)

First he should be reassured in four ways by speaking of confidence in the Buddha, the Doctrine, the Community (and virtue).[2] The formulae noted above are to be used. (For virtue there is a similar one which says it is liberating, etc., and leads to concentration.) Then he should be asked whether he is thinking of his parents or of his wife and childern. If he is, he should be told that he is subject to dying ('has the principle of dying') whether he thinks of them or not, and that it will be good to give up thinking of them. If he does this he can be asked whether he is thinking of (this can also be translated 'expecting', 'intending'—*apekṣā*) the five kinds of human pleasures of the senses (the implication is that he is seeking rebirth such as will provide enjoyment of them). If he is, he should be told that divine pleasures are superior, and that he should set his thoughts on the (various classes of) gods, successively, each being superior to the last. Having eventually set his thoughts on the world of Brahmā, he should be told finally that that is impermanent, unstable, included in (or involved in, *paryāpanna*) an existing body (*satkāya*), so that it would be good to bring his thought out of the world of

1. S V 408 ff., T 99 section 41 No. 2.
2. 'Virtue' is added only in the Sthaviravāda version.

Brahmā and imagine (or visualize, *upa-sam-hṛ*) it as in the cessation of an existing body (i. e. *nirvāṇa*). If he does this, the Buddha adds, there is no difference in freedom between him and a monk who frees his thought from the influences.

Little or nothing is said in the *Tripiṭaka* of any regular ceremonies to be observed by lay disciples. Thus there seems to be no record of any regular meeting and confession of offences against the discipline or virtue discussed in this chapter, such as the communities of monks and nuns held. On the other hand occasional confessions were certainly in order, for example that of Ajātaśatru (above, p. 67). The *Vinaya*,[1] incidentally, lists eight offences against the community of monks for which a lay disciple may be punished by the monks' refusing to accept alms from him (defaming a monk without foundation, etc.). If a layman so punished afterwards confesses his offence he may be rehabilitated by a vote of the community of monks concerned. As to regular ceremonies, however, it should not be overlooked that observing the *poṣadha*, or 'sabbath' night, is sometimes praised in laymen in the *Tripiṭaka* as one of the virtues,[2] and it seems almost to be taken for granted as a traditional ceremony. In later times it has certainly been observed by Buddhist laymen, who moreover may undertake to fulfil additional precepts, or fasts, for the occasion. The Sthaviravāda tradition records[3] that seven lay disciples (including Anāthapiṇḍada and Citra) had regular 'retinues' of lay disciples (five hundred each), implying an organisation of lay communities, but there is hardly any hint of such organisation in the *Tripiṭaka.*

To conclude this chapter it is worth noting a discussion between the Buddha and a brahman[4] concerning the relative merits of the household life and going forth as a wanderer (or monk). The brahmans favour (as they have always done) the household life as being most fruitful, this brahman says, and consider going forth less fruitful, what does the Buddha say? The reply is that one cannot be categorical (*ekāṃśa*, definite)

1. Vin II 124ff.
2. D III 145 (in No. 30=T 26 No. 59). The emperors in D No. 26 (T 1 No. 6) observe the wheel gem from the terraces of their palaces on the *poṣadha* night (D II 1 60).
3. SA III 291.
4. M No. 99, T 26 No. 152.

about this but must make distinctions (*vibhajya*, dividing, differentiating). One may be successful or fail in either way of life, for example in agriculture or commerce just as in going forth. However, after some discussion on the good principles recognised by brahmans (to which the Buddha adds compassion), it is agreed that they are found more frequently among those who have gone forth than among householders. Householders engaged in business do not constantly tell the truth, for example, whereas one who has gone forth may do so, being little concerned. However, the Buddha then concludes this discussion by saying that the purpose of such virtue in one who has gone forth is to produce that kind of joy in the good life which enables him to develop thought which is without hatred or malevolence (which is a preliminary to his further training).

Chapter Seven

COLLECTING THE TRIPIṬAKA

The First Rehearsal of the Tripiṭaka—The Empire of Magadha—The Vaiśālī Affair and the Assembly of 700 *Monks—The First Schism—The Abhidharma*

The First Rehearsal of the Tripiṭaka

After the Final Extinction (*parinirvāṇa*) of the Buddha, and the cremation of his body, the community of monks chose five hundred *arhants* ('worthy ones', 'perfected ones') to work together to compile the doctrine and the discipline, in order to prevent the true doctrine from being submerged in false doctrines. Each of the recensions of the *Vinaya* now available contains an appendix which narrates how one of the senior monks, Kāśyapa (usually distinguished from others of the name by the epithet *mahant*, 'great', thus Mahākāśyapa), presided over this assembly, which worked systematically through everything the Buddha was remembered to have said and produced an agreed canon of texts embodying it.[1] The versions differ over the details but agree in broad outline. The *arhants* met in Rājagṛha, since that great city could most easily support such a large assembly for several months: we notice once again how the organisation of the Buddhists centred on great cities; it was apparently not possible in any other way to convene a meeting large enough to be authoritative for the entire community, given its democratic constitution.

The 'doctrine' (*dharma*) was first recited by Ānanda, who being the Buddha's personal attendant had heard more than anyone else. Kāśyapa asked him about all the dialogues, etc., he remembered, and the assembly endorsed his versions as correct. The doctrine thus compiled became known as the *Sūtra Piṭaka*, the collection of *sūtras* (the term *piṭaka* probably signifies a 'tradition' of a group of texts).

1. See Lamotte HBI 136ff., with his note on the bibliography.

The discipline was similarly recited by Upāli, a specialist in that subject, and codified as the *Vinaya Piṭaka* (the contents of this have been incidentally reviewed in Chapter Three above).

On the third *piṭaka* which should make up the *Tripiṭaka* ('Three *Piṭakas*') there is disagreement. The Sthaviravāda and Mahāsaṃghika versions do not mention its recitation, and since the agreement of these two schools should establish the oldest available textual tradition it appears that originally there were only two *piṭakas*. However, even the Mahāsaṃghika account mentions the *Abhidharma* as among the texts handed down after the rehearsal. The Mahīśāsaka version makes no mention of a third *piṭaka*. The Sarvāstivāda and Dharmaguptaka *Vinayas* on the other hand have Ānanda reciting the *Abhidharma* as well as the *Sūtra*. The Kāśyapīya (=Haimavata) mentions the *Abhidharma Piṭaka* without saying who recited it. A later text of the Sarvāstivāda, School, the *Aśokāvadāna*, states that Kāśyapa recited the *Mātṛkā* or *Mātṛkā Piṭaka* (two versions of the text). The same tradition is found in the *Vinaya* of the Mūla Sarvāstivāda School, a late offshoot of the Sarvāstivāda which thoroughly revised and enlarged its *Tripiṭaka*. Whether a *Mātṛkā* or *Abhidharma* was actually recited at the First Rehearsal or not, all the early schools were equipped with a third, *Abhidharma*, *Piṭaka*, as we shall see when we come to discuss them.

According to the consensus of the schools the *Sūtra Piṭaka* was arranged in five *āgamas*, 'traditions' (the usual term, but the Sthaviravādins more often call them *nikāyas*, 'collections'). The order also is generally agreed (Sthaviravāda and Mahāsaṃghika, also Mahīśāsaka) to be as follows: (1) *Dirgha Āgama* ('Long Tradition', about 30 of the longest *sūtras*); (2) *Madhyama Āgama* ('Intermediate Tradition', about 150 *sūtras* of intermediate length; the short *sūtras*, the number of which ran into thousands, were classified in two ways as) (3) *Saṃyukta Āgama* ('Connected Tradition', *sūtras* classified by topic, for example the *sūtras* on conditioned origination which we studied in chapter Five); (4) *Ekottara Āgama* ('One Up Tradition', *sūtras* on enumerated items classified according to the numbers of the items in sections of ones, twos, threes...up to elevens); (5) *Kṣudraka Āgama* (outside the first four *āgamas* there remained a number of texts regarded by all the schools as of inferior importance, either because they were compositions of followers of the Buddha and not the words of the Master himself, or because they were of doubtful authenticity, these were collected in this 'Minor Tradition').

This order of the five 'traditions' happens also to be the order of their authenticity, probably because it was easier to insert short texts among a large number or to get a composition of doubtful origin admitted to the already doubtful Minor Tradition of a school. This is soon ascertained by comparing the various available recensions as we have in the preceding chapters. It has been suggested that some schools did not have a Minor Tradition at all, though they still had some of the minor texts, incorporated in their *Vinayas*, hence the 'Four Āgamas' are sometimes spoken of as representing the *Sūtra*.

The most noticeable feature of the Minor Tradition is that its texts are for the most part in verse, as opposed to the prevailing prose of the rest of the *Tripiṭaka*. In other words, whatever else may be said about their authenticity, they are poetic compositions which may stimulate interest in the doctrine but are as remote as possible from being systematic expositions of it. We have naturally ignored them in investigating the teaching of the Buddha, but they are of much interest in themselves, as literature, and in connection with the popularisation of Buddhism in the centuries following the *parinirvāṇa*, when in fact many of them were composed.

The original nucleus of the *Kṣudraka* common to all the schools may have contained the following parts : (1) *Khaḍgaviṣāṇagāthā* ('Rhinoceros Strophes', a poem by a sage living alone in the forest, usually explained as by a *pratyekabuddha*, an 'isolated *buddha*' or 'private *buddha*,' meaning one who has attained enlightenment on his own in the forest, without being taught by a *buddha*, and who also does not venture to teach anyone else after his enlightenment); (2) *Munigāthā* ('Recluse Strophes' on the same theme as the preceding poem); (3) *Śailagāthā* ('Śaila's Strophes', a dialogue in verse between the Buddha and a brahman named Śaila); (4) *Arthavargiyāṇi Sūtrāṇi* ('The *Sūtras* of the Welfare Group', but the title given here may be a 'wrong Sanskritisation' of the original Prakrit title, the Sthaviravāda Pali version reading *Aṭṭhaka* —and being interpreted as *Aṣṭaka*, which would mean '...of the Groups of Eights'—sixteen short poems on the doctrine, ethical or moral in content); (5) *Pārāyaṇa* ('The Way Across', sixteen brief verse dialogues between the Buddha and brahmans on the doctrine, mostly consisting of a bare question and answer); (6) *Sthaviragāthā* ('Strophes of the Elder Monks', autobiographical lyrics); (7) *Sthavirīgāthā* ('Strophes of the Elder Nuns', similar to the last); (8) *Ityukta* ('It was Said Thus', a collection of short discourses in prose with verses which purport to be by the Buddha; the Sthaviravāda commentary on them states that they were remembered by a slave girl in Kauśāmbī who became a lay disciple and used to listen to the Buddha teaching the monks, and were circulated by her in the Paurava capital until they came to the knowledge of the monks in time for the First Rehearsal—the monks having apparently forgotten their lessons).

Three other parts of the collection seem at least in origin to have been nothing but anthologies from the *Tripiṭaka* of (9) *Udānas* ('Exalted Utterances', we have had an example of such a verse above, p. 71), (10) *Dharmapadas* ('Verses on the Doctrine') and (11) *Jātakas* (stories of previous lives of the Buddha, for example the brahman who was Great Realm's chaplain in the story told above, pp. 171 f., is said to have been the Buddha in a former life, consequently the story is a *jātaka*; however the *Jātaka* available as a separate work consists almost entirely of verses, some of these being mere memorial verses as a device to recall a story). The latest part, if it was part (see p. 206), of this nucleus would be the (12) *Avadānas* (stories of monks and nuns, mostly of their previous lives).[1]

The First Rehearsal is recorded to have taken place during the rainy season of the first year after the *parinirvāṇa*, the latter event being the era from which the Buddhists have reckoned their chronology. It does not now appear to be possible to determine the exact extent and contents of the *Tripiṭaka* thus collected, in fact as we have seen it may at first have consisted of only two *piṭakas*, not three, namely the Doctrine and the

1. On the (13) *Peṭakopadeśa* as a probable original *Kṣudraka* text see pp. 220, 223, 278, 316 below.

Discipline. It is clear that some texts were subsequently added, even before the schisms of the schools, for example the account of the First Rehearsal itself, an account of a second such rehearsal a century later and a number of *sūtras* which actually state that they narrate something which took place after the *parinirvāṇa* or which refer to events known to have taken place later. It is interesting that the account in the *Vinaya* records that at least one monk preferred to disregard the version of the Buddha's discourses collected at this rehearsal and remember his own, as he had received it from the Buddha. This was Purāṇa, who returned from the South after the Rehearsal. The elders invited him to possess himself of the collection rehearsed but he politely declined. If there were a number of monks in distant parts who missed the First Rehearsal it is likely enough that quite a number of discourses remembered by them and handed down to their pupils existed, which were missed at the Rehearsal though perfectly authentic. Under these conditions it would seem reasonable to incorporate such discourses in the *Tripiṭaka* later, despite the risk of accepting unauthentic texts. The *Mahāparinirvāṇa Sūtra*, as we read above (p. 77), makes the Buddha himself lay down a rule to cover just this situation: if someone claims to be in possession of an authentic text not in the *Sūtra* or in the *Vinaya*—again two *piṭakas* only—it should be checked against the *Sūtra* and *Vinaya* and accepted only if it agrees with them. Such agreement or disagreement may have seemed obvious enough at first. Later it was far from obvious and depended on subtle interpretations; thus the schools came to accept many new texts, some of which surely contained new doctrines.

It appears that during the Buddha's lifetime and for some centuries afterwards nothing was written down: not because writing was not in use at the time but because it was not customary to use it for study and teaching. It was used in commerce and administration, in other words for ephemeral purposes; scholars and philosophers disdained it, for to them to study a text presupposed knowing it—by heart. To preserve a large corpus of texts meant simply the proper organisation of the available manpower. Few monks at any period seem to have known the whole *Tripiṭaka*. The original division of the *Sūtras* into several *āgamas*, 'traditions', seems primarily to have reflected what monks could reasonably be expected to learn during their training. Thus in Ceylon, at least, in the Sthaviravāda School, it is recorded[1] that the monks were organised in groups specialising in each of the *āgamas* or the *Vinaya* or the *Abhidharma*, handing these texts down to their pupils and so maintaining the tradition. In fact even ten years after his full 'entrance' into the community a monk was expected to know, besides part of the *Vinaya* discipline obligatory for all, only a part, usually about a third, of his *āgama*, and these basic texts are pointed out in the commentary on the *Vinaya*. A monk belonging to the *Dīrgha* tradition, for example, should know ten of its long *sūtras*, including the *Mahāparinirvāṇa*, the *Mahānidāna* and the *Mahāsmṛtyupasthāna* which we have studied in earlier chapters. He was then regarded as competent to teach. Among the Sthaviravādins there were even slight differences of opinion on certain matters between the several traditions of the *sūtras*. Thus the *Dīrgha* tradition did not admit the *Avadānas* to have been a text authenticated by recital at the First Rehearsal, whereas the *Madhyama* tradition did: they thus differed as to the extent of the *Tripitaka*.

If there were a standard *Tripiṭaka* as established at the First Rehearsal one might expect its texts to be fixed in their actual wording, and therefore in their language. This, however, does not appear to have been the case. The followers of the Buddha were drawn even during his lifetime from many different countries and spoke, if not completely different languages, at least different dialects. It has been shown[2] that the early Buddhists observed the principle of adopting the local languages wherever they taught. Probably they owe much of their success in spreading the Doctrine and establishing it in many countries to this. The Buddha himself is recorded to have enjoined his followers to remember his doctrine in their own languages, not in his language, nor in the archaic but respectable cadences of the Vedic scriptures of the brahmans. The recensions of the *Tripiṭaka* preserved in different countries of India therefore differed in dialect or language from the earliest times, and we

---

1. In the commentaries of the school. See Adikāram's *Early History of Buddhism in Ceylon*, 24 ff.

2. By Lin Li-Kouang : *L'aide-mémoire de la vraie loi*, 216 ff.

cannot speak of any 'original' language of the Buddhist canon, nor, as it happens, have we any definite information as to what language the Buddha himself spoke.[1] At the most, we can say that the recension in the language of Magadha may have enjoyed some preeminence for the first few centuries, since 'Māgadhisms' have been detected even in non-Māgadhī Buddhist texts. This may have reflected the political supremacy of Magadha.

The Empire of Magadha

During the Buddha's lifetime Magadha was merely one of numerous rival states. The Buddha taught in it and is recorded to have met its two successive kings who were his contemporaries. It is probable that these meetings are historical, for Indian kings at all times have generally been amused to meet philosophers, whatever may have been their policies. Nevertheless the attitude of the kings to the Doctrine seems ambiguous: at best they may have thought some of the Buddha's ideas politically opportune rather than absolutely desirable. In fact the Buddha spent relatively little time in Magadha, teaching in at least half a dozen other states. It is most unlikely that the Buddha sought any special relationship with the kings of Magadha. Any suggestion of such a relationship may be suspected of having the needs of a later situation in the political history of India in view. Buddhism thus spread at first for the most part outside the frontiers of Magadha. It reached the majority of the countries of India before the Magadhan supremacy, and it did so as a strictly non-political and non-worldly organisation. However, in a century and a half the spread of Buddhism was overtaken by the expansion of Magadha, so that for a time hardly a single community of monks could be found outside the frontiers of the empire. A special relationship did develop then, as we shall see in the next chapter.

In B. C. 483, three years after the *parinirvāṇa*, King Ajātaśatru of Magadha conquered the Vṛji Republic (his minister Varṣākāra, whom we met in Chapter Three, having succeeded in spreading internal dissension in the Vṛji state and the Magadhans having also developed improved chariots and new

1. Presumably the dialect of Kośala, p. 45 above.

war engines for hurling missiles) and thus started his country decisively on its imperial career.[1] The conquest of Kośala soon followed. It was the next king, Ajātaśatru's son Udāyibhadra, who made Pāṭaliputra (see p. 70 above) the capital. By about 410 B. C. there was a revolt of the 'citizens' (*nāgaras*) against this Haryaṅka Dynasty. They deposed the tyrannical king and elected the minister Śiśunāga to rule, who founded a new dynasty. This Śiśunāga was himself of aristocratic Vṛji (more specifically of Licchavi, one of the clans confederated in the Republic) ancestry, his father being a 'warrior' (*rājan*) and his mother a geisha,[2] and his dynasty is variously known as the Licchavi Dynasty or the Śaiśunāga Dynasty. We might perhaps speak of a 'revenge' of the Vṛjis at this time, though it was far from leading to the reestablishment of the Republic. It does, however, seem to have resulted in a period of restored prosperity for Vaiśālī, the former capital of the Republic. About 410 B. C. Śiśunāga conquered the powerful kingdom of Avanti, in western India (capital Ujjayinī), and so consolidated an empire 'from the Western to the Eastern Oceans' across northern India. It seems to have been his predecessor Darśaka (the last of the Haryaṅka Dynasty) who had finally absorbed the Paurava kingdom round Kauśāmbī (then known as the Vatsa kingdom, the name of the country round Kauśāmbī) by taking the Pauravas under his protection.[3] The kings of Avanti had been equally trying to bring the Paurava kingdom under their protection, and were probably Magadha's most serious rival for the empire of India. Thus the old quarrel was ended by Śiśunāga, who finally settled who was to inherit the Empire of the Pauravas.

If we suspect a closer relationship of the Buddhist community with the Vṛji Republic than with the kingdom of Magadha, given the Buddha's approval of the Vṛji constitution, we certainly find evidence of patronage of the community by the Licchavi Dynasty, particularly by Śiśunāga's son and successor Aśoka the Black (Kālāśoka).

1. See among other sources DA 522.
2. *Vaṃsatthappakāsinī* I 155 f.
3. See Bhāsa's play *Svapnavāsavadatta*, though its synchronisms of kings are difficult to reconcile with those of the *Tripiṭaka*.

The Vaiśālī Affair and the Assembly of 700 Monks

During the reign of Aśoka the Black, one hundred years (or a hundred and ten in some versions) after the *parinirvāṇa* (B.C. 386 or 376), the monks living in Vaiśālī had relaxed certain rules of the discipline. In particular they collected gold and silver and money from the lay disciples. A monk arriving from elsewhere protested against this infringement of the discipline, and thus set in motion an interesting series of legal proceedings among the Buddhist communities, which were recorded in the *Vinaya*.[1] The extant recensions of the *Vinaya* agree on the main point, that the Vaiśālī community was out of order, and thus indicate that the Buddhists at this time remained united and overcame the threat of a schism. Perhaps the most important part of the affair is that it shows with greater clarity than any other ancient doçument how the democratic organisation of the early communities worked, in particular what happened if there was disagreement between independent communities, not within one legally constituted community; how the Buddhist community as a whole, which had no single head or central authority, could settle such a case.

All the versions of the *Vinaya* agree that the chief ground disputed was the question of cash donations to the monks. The Mahāsaṃghika version mentions only this, but the Sthaviravāda account and all the others available (which are of schools related to the Sthaviravāda rather than to the Mahāsaṃghika) add nine seemingly minute grounds. It is uncertain whether the Mahāsaṃghikas have suppressed these as trivial, or because they themselves later relaxed on them, or whether they were instead added afterwards by the Sthaviravādins. Five of the grounds concern food and drink, one seats, two the procedure for meetings of communities, one whether one should conduct oneself in conformity with one's teachers' conduct (regardless of the *Vinaya* code). In fact the Mahāsaṃghika version is very brief in its account of the entire proceedings, and there is reason to suspect that it is a tradition handed down by monks sympathetic to the Vaiśālī community, who were unable to ignore the episode completely but wished to pass over it as lightly and discreetly as possible. The position of the Mahāsaṃghikas

1. See Lamotte HBI loc. cit. and 143 ff.

will be discussed further later in this chapter; the point here is that it is worth mentioning details not found in their account, but present in other intact *Vinaya* accounts, and to suggest that there are grounds for holding that the balance of probabilities is against their version of this affair being more authentic than that of the Sthavira group of schools.

In protesting against donations of money the monk visiting Vaiśālī, whose name was Yaśas, urged the lay disciples not to make such contributions. Later the Vaiśālī monks offered him his 'share' of the contributions collected, which he refused. Indignant at his behaviour, the Vaiśālī community then carried out an 'action of reconciliation' (*pratisaṃharaṇīyakarman*) against him, a legal act which required that he confess his offence of abusing and defaming the lay disciples (by objecting to their contributions) to the said lay disciples and ask them to forgive him. Since they were apparently perfectly within their legal rights in carrying out this action Yaśas submitted to their decision and acted accordingly, taking another monk with him as witness (as was legally correct). However, he repeated to the lay disciples a discourse of the Buddha which enumerated various faults of *śramaṇas* and brahmans, which included accepting gold and silver. Thus he convinced them that his position was correct and that the Vaiśālī monks were neither *śramaṇas* nor Buddhists.

The witness duly reported the event to the community. They then charged him with another offence, that of revealing confidential business of the community (i.e. the discussion whether money contributions were permitted by their discipline) to outsiders without their permission. They assembled, and by way of punishment carried out an 'action of suspension' (*utkṣepaṇīyakarman*, temporary suspension of membership of the community) against him. This was the standard punishment for such offences as not seeing an offence, not making amends for one or not giving up wrong opinions.[1]

Yaśas immediately left Vaiśālī and went to seek support among the communities of the West. The versions disagree on the precise details of his movements but agree that he found support in Kauśāmbī and Mathurā (the latter a rising city further up

1. See I. B. Horner BD III 28 footnote

the Yamunā) and also in Avanti. Great trouble was taken to seek out elder monks whose opinions were likely to be respected and to enlist their support for the strict observance of the *Vinaya* discipline, but it is clear that there was no central or individual authority to whom an appeal could be made to lay down the law or decide the issue.

The Western monks saw that it would be futile to carry out any legal action merely in one of their own communities. There would be nothing to prevent the Vaiśālī monks from adhering to their position and continuing to produce legislation in favour of it. Also it would not be sufficient for just one of their communities to take any kind of action, such as going to Vaiśālī to oppose the offending community. It was necessary, especially against such a strong community as that of Vaiśālī, to convene, if not all the Buddhist communities of India, at least an impressive representation from them. To this end messengers were sent out in all directions and the monks were asked to assemble in Vaiśālī. The Vaiśālī monks likewise, when they heard what was happening, attempted to enlist support from elsewhere. Altogether seven hundred monks gathered in Vaiśālī. They then assembled as a community (legally they would now constitute the community of monks resident within the boundaries of Vaiśālī, but 'morally'—perhaps legally also—they might be held to represent Buddhism as a whole; their number is carefully recorded in all the accounts and was obviously thought to carry great weight), wishing to decide the affair.

The debate went on endlessly (the Sthaviravāda version says that there was not a single speech of which the meaning was clear, but is alone in this not very flattering exaggeration of the disorderly proceedings of the seven hundred : a filibuster is perhaps implied). One of the most senior monks, who was respected by the Vaiśālī monks as well as those from the West, then proposed that a committee (**udvāhikā*) be appointed to investigate the matter, with equal representation from both sides: four monks chosen by the Easterners (i.e. the Vaiśālī party) and four by the Westerners. This referring of a matter to a committee is standard practice, according to the *Vinaya*, when a debate becomes endless and 'there is no speech of which the meaning is clear'—hence the expression of the Sthaviravādins above is merely a stock phrase.[1] The proposal is agreed unanimously, a committee is elected and withdraws to deliberate quietly. The elders representing the Western party on the committee are able to convince the others by reference to the *Vinaya* that the ten grounds maintained by the Vaiśālī monks are contrary to the discipline, and finally they report unanimously in that sense. The committee presents its report very carefully, ground by ground and referring to the appropriate *Vinaya* rules for each, so that it is impossible for anyone in the assembly to controvert its findings. The monks are convinced and the community accepts that the ten grounds are contrary to the discipline. At this conclusion of the affair, the accounts agree that the *Vinaya* was rehearsed again, as at the First Rehearsal, by the seven hundred monks. The Dharmaguptaka version states that the Doctrine (i.e. the *Sūtra*) was rehearsed as well, and several later accounts maintain that this was a 'second' rehearsal of the *Tripiṭaka*, reaffirming or settling the extent of its texts. Among these later accounts, the Sthaviravāda commentary notes[2] that Aśoka the Black was of the party of the Vaiśālī monks. The *Mahāvaṃsa* adds[3] further that his sister persuaded him to transfer his support to the orthodox party, and that the assembly was held under his patronage. This royal interest is not impossible, but may be suspected of being a mere reflection of later relationships between kings and the Buddhist community. The Mahāsaṃghika recension of the *Vinaya*, which we noted above deals very briefly with the Vaiśālī affair, lays greatest stress on the rehearsal of the *Vinaya*.

The First Schism

According to the calculations of Eggermont,[4] Aśoka the Black (also known as Kākavarṇa, 'Crow-colour', and apparently in some records as Nandivardhana[5] or Nandin[6]) reigned from

1. Sthaviravāda Vin II 95 ff. Qualifications of a committee member also at A V 71 f.
2. *Samantapāsādikā* I 33.
3. IV 31 ff.
4. *The Chronology of the Reign of Asoka Moriya* pp. 161-163.
5. Eggermont op. cit. p. 154.
6. Tāranātha (Schiefner) p. 41.

B.C. 396 to 360. One source states that his death was violent,[1] and in any case it appears there was a revolt and his sons were put under the protection of its leader, Mahāpadma Nanda, who made himself king and thus founded the Nanda Dynsty. Mahāpadma further extended the Empire of Magadha, mainly, it would seem, towards the South.[2] According to the *Purāṇas* this ruler of low (*śūdra*, helot) origin exterminated the ancient noble families of warriors (*kṣatriyas*), and all the sources agree that he amassed incredible wealth. We may suppose a highly centralising tendency in his policy, the abolition of local autonomies which may well have remained under the Śaiśunāgas, whether of the Vṛjis and other republics which had submitted, or of princes of conquered dynasties who may still have ruled as vassals in their ancestral domains.

It was during his reign, it would seem, that the first schism in the Buddhist communities occurred. The exact date has been much discussed, since the various schools differ in their chronologies.[3] The *Vinayas* do not continue their historical records beyond the Vaiśālī Assembly, so we have to turn to a variety of historical records, accounts of the opinions of the schools and incidental information in commentaries. One history which preserves some ancient and authentic records, the *Dipavaṃsa* of the Sthaviravāda school, states that after the Vaiśālī affair the monks of Vṛji were not reconciled to the decision of the assembly and held a new 'rehearsal', which they called the 'Great Rehearsal' (*Mahāsaṃgīti*), at which they altered the *Tripiṭaka* to suit their own views and added new texts. Thus a schismatic school arose. Professor Lamotte has suggested[2] that later the Sthaviravāda school departed from this account and dated the first schism later, but in fact the *Mahāvaṃsa*, to which he refers, still gives its account of the schismatic schools immediately after the Vaiśālī affair, whilst the *Nikāyasaṃgraha* in its account of the supposed Pāṭaliputra Assembly of B.C. 250 presupposes the existence of seventeen schismatic schools by that date. However, it would seem

1 Bāṇa, *Harṣacarita*, noted by Lamotte HBI 105; cf. Majumdar : *Classical Accounts of India* pp. 129 and 172 (Mahāpadma would be the barber).

2. K. A. Nilakanta : *A History of South India*, OUP 1958, 79ff.

3. Lamotte HBI 312 ff.

unlikely, indeed impossible, that the 'Great Rehearsal' was held immediately after the Vaiśālī settlement. It is this Great Rehearsal which is supposed to be the origination of the Mahāsaṃghika school, yet the *Vinaya* of that school, as we have seen, agrees with the opinion of the orthodox party in condemning the Vaiśālī monks. Thus the communities remained united for some time after the Vaiśālī affair, all concerned, it appears, accepting the decision arrived at, and if any dissident feeling remained it awaited—as has been suggested in the Introduction above after reviewing the disputes between the schools (p. 12)—the arising of questions which did not seem to be directly answered by anything in the *Tripiṭaka*.

The most probable date is thus some time after Vaiśālī and some time before the period of Aśoka Maurya, and there is in fact an account of the First Schism which gives just such a date, namely the tradition of the Saṃmitīya school recorded by Bhavya (Bhāvaviveka) and the Tibetan historians (probably following him).[1] This account places the event in B.C. 349, 'during the reigns of Nanda and Mahāpadma'. If this is not simply a mistake for Mahāpadma Nanda we must suppose that 'Nanda' here represents one of Aśoka the Black's sons still nominally reigning under Mahāpadma's protection (or Mahāpadma's own son Dhanananda). On this occasion a monk, about whose name there are disagreements in the various accounts of the schism, put forward five grounds, of which four concern the question of the nature of an *arhant* (perfected one, worthy one) and none have any direct bearing on the discipline. An assembly took place at Pāṭaliputra—some accounts say with the support of the king, or the two kings, or even under their arbitration—and the majority, it would appear, voted in favour of these grounds. This majority constituted itself into the Mahāsaṃgha, the 'Great Community', or Mahāsaṃghikas. The minority which rejected the grounds, and which apparently included a number of the most senior monks ('elders', *sthaviras*), refused to submit to this decision and constituted themselves into the School of the Elders, the Sthaviravāda. There is a good deal of evidence that the Sthaviravāda

1. See Lamotte HBI 308 and 315 and the references there given. This account seems the most trustworthy and independent.

was very strong in the Western countries of north India, in the same communities which formerly rallied round Yaśas, and rather less evidence that the Mahāsaṃgha represented to some extent the Eastern party.[1] If this is so it might explain the relative weakness of the Sthaviravāda at Pāṭaliputra, which is in the East, and their being outvoted there. At the same time, though there does seem to have been a tendency to geographical distribution of the schools these groupings are not clear cut: most of the schools maintained some representation in the old regions of the Buddha's activities in the East, and particularly at the imperial capital, Pāṭaliputra, whilst the Mahāsaṃgha was represented at scattered places in the West and the far North-West. Moreover, the divided schools do not seem to have been estranged by unbuddhistic feelings of bitterness and hostility, for all that they denounce each other's propositions in their theoretical works; on the contrary monks of different schools are found later to live side by side in the same dwellings (*vihāras*) in apparent harmony, and wandering monks were not troubled by questions about their affiliation to a school when seeking lodgings among distant communities.[2]

As to the founder of the Mahāsaṃgha, the Saṃmitīya tradition calls him Bhadra, who enunciated the five grounds 'which afterwards were adopted by Nāga and Sāramati'. Other sources,[3] however, call him Mahādeva and say that his grounds were adopted by the assemblies of the Nāgas (plural), of the Easterners (variant: 'Borderers') and of the Bahuśrutas (the Learned—afterwards the name of a school of the Mahāsaṃgha). Evidently Bhadra equals Mahādeva, whose grounds were accepted by certain schools (assemblies, rather than persons), which would be the Mahāsaṃgha and/or some of its later offshoots. Some confusion may have arisen because there is another celebrated Mahādeva among the Mahāsaṃgha schools, who later produced further schisms within them. As to the other names, they are all restored from Tibetan or

1. The primary discussion of this geographical distribution is in Przyluski: *La légende de l' empereur Aç̧oka*, Paris, 1923, but there has been some criticism of his conclusions. We may leave details until we come to the individual schools. Lamotte HBI 578 ff.

2. Lamotte HBI 573.

3. Lamotte HBI 302 ff. from Vasumitra, etc.

Chinese translations and are conjectural. It would probably be better to read Nāgara ('of the cities') for Nāga, understanding the communities of certain cities (in Magadha and Vṛji ?) as opposed to the 'Borderers'.

The five grounds are (1) that an *arhant* can be seduced by another person, (2) that an *arhant* may be ignorant of some matters, (3) that an *arhant* may be in doubt, (4) that an *arhant* may receive information from (be instructed by) another person, (5) that one may enter the Way as the result of spoken words.

The explanation of the first ground is that an *arhant* may have erotic dreams due to visitations by goddesses. The next three grounds are really different aspects of a single point, which is the same question which we discussed in Chapter Five: did the Buddha claim omniscience ? If *arhants* (of whom the Buddha was of course one) were completely omniscient they would not have to ask the way when travelling, and so on, would have no doubt whether they actually were *arhants*. Bhadra (Mahādeva) thus maintained that they were not omniscient in this sense, although they were freed. The last ground perhaps means that one can enter the Buddhist way merely through words, rather than through one's experience. It might even refer to ritualistic formulae used to 'induce' the way, as opposed to meditation.

The whole trend here is evidently to make the state of being an *arhant* more easily attainable than Bhadra's opponents believed. At the same time it is clear that these opponents were alleged to be setting a higher standard for the *arhant* than the *Tripiṭaka*, according to our reading of it in Chapter Five, warrants. The Buddha himself, we were there led to believe, did not claim complete omniscience such as would enable him to know the name of every person he met without being told and to find his way anywhere in the world with no guide. Enlightenment to him did not mean this kind of magical performance, but the understanding of certain truths and consequent mental freedom.

It is, as we saw, the canon of the Sthaviravādins themselves which contains the most categorical repudiation of the kind of omniscience a magician or conjuror might pretend to,[1]

1. M No. 71.

and in fact in their critique of the five grounds[1] they do not seem to have gone so far as their opponents suggest. They were, however, uncompromising on the first ground: a real *arhant* was of such a nature that he was beyond any influence at all, moreover the attainment of this state was definitive and final. On the other hand in dealing with the second and third grounds[2] they carefully limit the question to knowledge of the truths of Buddhism, the three sciences, etc., and set aside as irrelevant to knowledge, in the sense of progress on the Buddhist way, the 'knowledge' of names, geography, species of plants and the like.[3] They maintain the same distinction on the fourth ground:[4] an *arhant* may be informed of people's names and so on by another person, but cannot be instructed in the Buddhist doctrine and way, which he understands perfectly. It is clear that Bhadra and the Mahāsaṃgha went further and admitted other limitations of an *arhant's* knowledge, even in regard to the truths and the way of Buddhism, but our sources do not seem to give us information on how far they went. Perhaps both parties exaggerated each other's positions in order to make them obviously contrary to the *Tripiṭaka*. On the fifth ground the Sthaviravādins suggest[5] that their opponents held that the use of speech was necessary to entering into the meditations, which would clearly be contrary to the *Tripiṭaka*, or to entering on the way, which is less clearly so but which they interpret as meaning that by uttering the correct speech one enters the way regardless of one's actions, such as murder.

We seem led to the conclusion that the two parties were less far apart than at first sight they appear to be, except on the first ground. The Sthaviravāda were categorical that an *arhant* was by nature beyond the reach of any possible seduction; the Mahāsaṃgha allowed an *arhant* to be seduced in a dream. Between these opinions no compromise could be found, despite all the Buddha's injunctions (in the *Vinaya*) on the reconciliation of dissident views. The majority of the assembly held that an involuntary happening was no indication of whether

1. Kvu I 163 ff.
2. Kvu I 173 ff.
3. Kvu I 179 f.
4. Kvu I 187 ff.
5. Kvu I 195 ff., also 203 f.

one was an *arhant* or not, and thereby no doubt made it possible for more persons to be recognised as *arhants*. The minority, which included, apparently, most of the elders, refused to countenance such a weakness, such an evident attachment to the world.

No compromise having been reached, the two parties separated and became two schools of Buddhism. Afterwards they gradually came to disagree on several more grounds, partly through working out the implications of their positions. In particular the nature of the Buddha was reconsidered. In the *Tripiṭaka* he is not apparently distinguished from any other *arhant*, except that he had the exceptional genius necessary to discover the truths unaided whilst the others were helped by his guidance. The Sthaviravāda remained closer to this conception, though gradually they attributed a higher status to the Buddha, eventually complete 'omniscience' (*sarvajñatā*),[1] especially in their more popular propaganda. The Mahāsaṃgha, on the other hand, having relaxed or at least not made more stringent the conditions for an *arhant*, found it desirable to make a clear distinction in the case of the Buddha: he was a being of quite a different nature, far above other human beings or perhaps not really a human being at all. They thus began that transformation of the Buddha, and his doctrine, which led step by step to the Mahāyāna, from the humanism of the original *Tripiṭaka* to the supernaturalism of most of the Mahāyāna *sūtras*.

The first schism was followed by several others within each of the two schools it produced. A more comprehensive summary of the eventual doctrinal positions of each school can conveniently be given after these later schisms have been traced.

The Abhidharma

It is doubtful, as we saw above, whether any *Abhidharma* texts such as we find current in the schools were recited at the First Rehearsal. Perhaps nothing more than a *Mātṛkā* then existed, the extent of which it is very difficult to determine. By comparing the available *Abhidharma* texts, however, we are led to the conclusion that already within the first two centuries after

1. Ps I 131 ff.

the *parinirvāṇa*, and in great part before the First Schism, a substantial development had taken place. It is true that among the available texts of the schools there is not a single work which can be shown to be common even to two schools, let alone to all. Perhaps if we had a Mahāsaṃghika text (apart from the very late *Tattvasiddhiśāstra* of the Bahuśrutika school) our picture would be different, but since we find even two branches of the Sthaviravāda (the Sthaviravāda proper and the Sarvāstivāda) differing widely in their texts it is not probable (though not absolutely impossible) that the Mahāsaṃghika *Abhidharma* agreed closely with either of them. That both these Sthaviravādin schools count seven treatises as constituting their *Abhidharmas* seems to be mere coincidence, unless we suppose that the united Sthaviravāda already had seven treatises, which the schismatic Sarvāstivāda rejected and replaced by new works. However, if no texts agree as closely as the *Vinayas* or the *Sūtras* of the schools, there are some major agreements in the matter of the texts from which we can infer the nature of the earliest *Abhidharma* tradition. The *Saṃgītiparyāya* of the Sarvāstivādins is a special case, being simply a recension of the *Saṃgīti Sūtra* of the *Dīrgha* with commentary added.

What is an *Abhidharma* text? A *mātṛkā* is a set of headings serving as notes on the doctrine. Thus in Chapter Four we took a *mātṛkā* from Chapter Three and elaborated it. An *abhidharma* is such an elaboration (most *Abhidharma* texts propose such a *mātṛkā* at the beginning and then proceed to elaborate it), but as a rule it is rather more than that, more than a selection of appropriate *Sūtra* texts supplying the required details. An *abhidharma* analyses the materials it collects from the *Sūtra*, poses questions and answers them, works out a systematic treatise. In a sense then it explains the *Sūtra*, but naturally it tends to go beyond this in systematising the doctrine. Most, perhaps all, schools of Buddhism agree that this work of systematisation began already during the lifetime of the Buddha. The Master himself, apparently, did not undertake it beyond sometimes proposing *mātṛkās*, but continued giving discourses on aspects of the doctrine in his day to day teaching activity and producing dialogues of very varied kinds in discussion with the very various people he met. It is certain of his leading monks, above all Śāriputra, who were charged with 'research' or elaboration on *abhidharma* lines.[1] In the *Saṃgītisūtra* and in the Sarvāstivāda *Saṃgītiparyāya*, in fact, it is Śāriputra who expounds a systematic treatise to the monks in the presence of the Buddha, the latter merely approving it at the end. Other traditions associate an elder named Kātyāyana with this type of work. The *Ekottara Āgama*[2] has the Buddha praise him for being the best at analysing in detail what has been stated briefly. According to the Prajñaptivāda school of the Mahāsaṃgha[3] he composed a treatise which in particular discriminated between the two levels of statement (see pp. 150ff.) in the *sūtras*, the 'ultimate' and the 'concealing'. It appears that a version, probably apocryphal, of this treatise was handed down in that school. The Sthaviravāda has a text on interpretation ascribed to Kātyāyana, the *Peṭaka-upadesa*. The Mahīśāsakas also had a *Peṭaka* (*Ps Gaṇṭhipada* p. 106). The *Vinayas* of the Dharmaguptakas and Kāśyapīyas state that an *Upadeśa* was recited at the First Rehearsal, in the *Kṣudraka*.[4]

The *Saṃgītiparyāya* may be taken as the most primitive *Abhidharma* text now available. In fact it is an enormous *mātṛkā*, lists of principles mentioned in the *sūtras* grouped somewhat arbitrarily in ones, twos, threes, etc. up to elevens. Altogether there are more than two hundred headings, each containing from one to eleven 'principles'. Most of them are explained by quoting the *Sūtra*, i.e. by the '*sūtra*-analysis' or 'without questions' (*apraśnaka*) method. As the *Tattvasiddhi* presupposes a very similar *mātṛkā* it appears that the Bahuśrutīyas had a similar *Abhidharma* text.

The *mātṛkā* which we studied in Chapter Four served as the kernel of a very different type of text, which was *abhidharma* in the full sense of discussion on the doctrine (*dharma*). The *Vibhaṅga* of the Sthaviravāda, the *Dharmaskandha* of the Sarvāstivāda, the *Śāriputrābhidharmaśāstra* (which seems to belong to the Dharmaguptakas, known from the Dharmaguptaka *Vinaya* to have had an *Abhidharma* in four sections, as this is—Przyluski and Lamotte have gone astray in reading

1. Lamotte HBI p. 209 notes the agreement of the Vātsiputrīya tradition with the Sthaviravāda.
2. Sthaviravāda recension A I 23.
3. Lamotte HBI p. 208.
4. HBI p 276; Przyluski, *Concile* p. 179.

the *Vinaya* reference as giving five sections[1]) are three texts of different schools which are nevertheless akin, though very far from identical, or even recensions of one archetype, and appear to have grown out of this kernel. In each of them a dozen or more other headings were added to the presumed original seven, so that the five groups (*skandhas*), the spheres (*āyatanas*) of the senses and the elements (*dhātus*—of which there are various sets) on the one hand and the Four Truths and the sequence of conditions (*pratyayas*) on the other were covered, thus making the treatise more comprehensive (the four meditations and other topics were also supplied). There is evidence that several other schools had similar texts, for the *Śāriputrābhidharmaśāstra* is a work in four sections[2] called Sapraśnaka ('with questions'), Apraśnaka ('without questions'), Saṃyukta-saṃgraha ('conjoined and inclusion', i.e. principles occurring together and inclusion in classes as two basic kinds of relation between principles) and Nidāna ('source', causation), and somewhat similar sections have been noted by Lamotte[3] in the *Abhidharmas* as described in other schools. The Kāśyapīya (Haimavata) in particular had Sapraśnaka, Apraśnaka, Saṃgraha ('inclusion'), Saṃyoga ('conjunction') and Sthāna ('place', 'case', 'circumstance', a word which also came to mean 'cause', 'basis'), which seems to be the same four sections arranged as five. The Dharmaguptas had four sections with partly different names, which may yet have been similar in content.

---

1. Lin, *Aide-mémoire*, p. 45, suggested the Mahīśāsakas, whilst the Mahāsaṃgha also is a possibility. That the school is doubtful reflects partly our unfortunate ignorance of the Mahāsaṃgha and partly the great antiquity of this text, which does not make clear any position in regard to the main controversies of the schools (further study may shed a little more light : thus the text recognises nine unsynthesised principles). One might possibly infer the Mahāsaṃgha *mātṛkā* from certain lists in the *Prajñāpāramitā*, since this appears to derive from the Caitika/Śaila school of Mahāsaṃgha. For example the 10,000 recension (Konow, 10 ff.) lists the groups, spheres, elements, Truths, conditions, self-possession, exertion, (etc. up to) the way, three entrances to freedom (emptiness, the signless and the uncommitted—see below Chapter Nine, p. 313, for the Sthaviravāda equivalent), meditation, the immeasurables (see p. 197 above), etc. See now 'The Ghosts of Nirvāṇa'.
2. Lamotte HBI pp. 208 f.
3. HBI p. 198.

Of these four or five sections it is the first two only which parallel the *Vibhaṅga* and *Dharmaskandha* and elaborate the score or so of headings we have just referred to. The Sthaviravāda and Sarvāstivāda had separate treatises on the subjects of the remaining sections: the *Dhātukathā* and *Dhātukāya* on classification and conjunction of principles; the *Paṭṭhāna* and part of the *Vijñānakāya* on conditions ('cause', etc.). Both these latter works, however, are relatively late, and we might suggest that the elaborations on the conditions in the *Vibhaṅga* and *Dharmaskandha* were sufficient parallel, but for the fact that the *Śāriputrābhidharmaśāstra* (perhaps the oldest *Abhidharma* extant) has some elaboration going beyond those texts (33 **hetus* including 10**pratyayas*, **sarvatraga*, etc.).[1] The *Paṭṭhāna* operates with twenty-four kinds of *pratyaya* (the Sarvāstivādins were satisfied with only four, though they added six kinds of cause, *hetu*). The *Tattvasiddhi* of Harivarman, representing the Bahuśrutīya, whilst presupposing a text very similar to the *Vibhaṅga*, *Dharmaskandha* and *Sapraśnaka-Apraśnaka*, including the topic of the 'persons' *pudgalas*, rejects inclusion and conjunction (see the Thesis of the author's student, Professor S. Katsura, 1974, p. 77, which at last has fully clarified this important work, the only *abhidharma* treatise known of any of the Mahāsaṃgha schools). According to the Sthaviravāda *Kathāvatthu* Commentary (p. 94) other schools rejected inclusion and conjunction, such as the Rājagirikas and Siddhārthikas, both of which belong to the Mahāsaṃgha group (see p. 290 below). It is not clear whether the Mahāsaṃgha group as a whole rejected this part of the *Abhidharma* and whether it was an innovation of the Sthaviravāda and its offshoots.

From this evidence we may conclude that the earliest form of *Abhidharma* we can reconstruct, and which was probably elaborated during the first two centuries after the *parinirvāṇa*, consisted of the following sections : (1) *Saṃgītiparyāya*; (2) *Apraśnaka* (of which the *Saṃgītiparyāya* may simply have constituted the first part) based on the *mātṛkā* of the practical doctrine, self-possession and other topics, explained by quotations

1. The twelve conditions in the sequence are expanded by taking old age, dying, grief, etc., and matter, sentience, as separate items; 'food' is another 'cause'.

from the *Sūtra*; (3) *Sapraśnaka* developed from the theoretical *mātṛkās* of the groups, sense-spheres, elements, Four Truths, etc., defined and then explained by the *abhidharma*-analysis which consists in the application to the principles concerned of certain dichotomies (contradictories) and trichotomies (contraries); (4) a study of conditions, perhaps called *Prasthāna*, dealing with the four conditions 'cause' (*hetu*), 'support' (*ālambana*), 'immediate' (*anantara*) and 'dominant' (*adhipati*) (the Sarvāstivāda, Harivarman and Nāgārjuna, p. 381 below, confirm that these were the original four conditions discussed here, the Sthaviravāda and *Śāriputrābhidharmaśāstra* also accept them, though they add many more conditions by subdividing the first). To these sections the Sthaviravāda group at least added the classification (inclusion) of principles into the groups, sense-spheres, elements, etc., and the conjunction of principles which can occur simultaneously (at the same point in a sequence). The *Peṭakopadeśa* on the interpretation of the *Sūtra* was probably originally part of the *Kṣudraka*, in other words an appendix to the *Sūtrapiṭaka*. However the Prajñaptivāda and possibly the Mahāsaṃgha group in general included it in their *Abhidharma*. As for the Sthaviravāda *Abhidhamma* extant in Pali, the school replaced the *Saṃgītiparyāya* by the *Dhammasaṃgaṇi* (pp. 302 ff. below). The *Apraśnaka* and *Sapraśnaka* were combined in the *Vibhaṅga* (as the Sarvāstivāda combined them in the *Dharmaskandha*), but the chapter on the 'persons' *pudgalas* was removed as dealing merely with concepts, not with ultimate reality, and kept as a separate book (the Sarvāstivāda appear to have suppressed the persons completely).

The *Apraśnaka* seems originally to have included self-possession, exertion, power, the way, meditation, the sequence of conditions in conditioned origination, miscellaneous 'knowledges' (*jñānas*), persons and perhaps actions and defilements and other topics. The *Sapraśnaka* included the groups, sense-spheres, elements, truths, faculties (which though from the practical doctrine consisted of a set of principles amenable to the *abhidharma*-analysis) and the factors of enlightenment. Both these sections consisted mainly of systematic restatements of the contents of the *Sūtra*, of collections of material on a given topic scattered throughout the *Sūtra Piṭaka*. Some further explanations were added and the aim set, and no doubt largely realised (it is completely realised in the extant Sthaviravāda *Abhidhamma*), was to produce a precise definition of every term in the system, assuming of course that the doctrine was a single consistent system. This included the identification of synonymous terms and sometimes the distinction of different meanings of the same word in different contexts. Under the *abhidharma*-analysis, the dichotomies or 'dyads' applied included thought and non-thought, a cause and not a cause, internal and external and many others. The trichotomies or 'triads' began with good, bad and indeterminate. This analysis clarified the position of every principle in the total system and its relation to all the others.

The study of conditions appears to carry the doctrine beyond what was taught by the Buddha, since there seems to have been no *sūtra* which enunciates these four, though the terms are used separately in different contexts. Whereas the conditions in conditioned origination are restricted to the question of transmigration, the origination of unhappiness, these four conditions are more general. The 'cause' was the most general of the four, covering such different cases as an action as condition for its result and a sense object as condition for the functioning of a sense organ. The 'support' as we have seen above is any condition for the occurrence of consciousness (p. 128). The 'immediate' is each moment in the stream of consciousness as condition for the next, the basic continuity of consciousness. The 'dominant' is a 'force' directing thought.

This activity of systematisation developed vigorously during the early centuries of Buddhism. As its implications were pursued further, disagreements sometimes arose and produced schisms among the Buddhists when they could not be resolved. The activity then continued with equal or greater vigour in the resulting schools, which consequently produced their independent *Abhidharma* treatises subsequently preserved in their separate traditions.

CHAPTER EIGHT

THE POPULARISATION OF BUDDHISM

Pagodas and Pilgrimages—Poetry and Story-telling—The Personality Schism—Aśoka: Buddhism to be Implemented—The 'All Exist' and other Schisms—Buddhist Poetry in the Time of Aśoka—The Results of the Great Experiment.

Pagodas and Pilgrimages

The Buddha was fond of shrines. When speaking of the hard life of a wanderer in the forest, such as his own life before the enlightenment (p. 47 above), he mentioned that on the *poṣadha* nights (see p. 58) of the wanderers it was his practice to frequent forest shrines and meditate there.[1] These places, it seems, were especially awe-inspiring and fearful. Most of them, probably, were sacred trees, which the local people in some remote settlement, or even wandering tribes of hunters, had for some reason selected as the abodes of spirits, gods and goddesses. It was probably customary for wandering *śramaṇas* to frequent these shrines: some of them very likely with the object of communicating with the spirits, but perhaps also because they too might receive offerings and respect from the local people, whom they might also teach on occasion. For the Buddha, however, the purpose of visiting shrines was meditation at night, when the local people would not disturb him and the only distraction might be animals coming to eat food offered to the spirit during the day and left under the sacred tree. At night this would be terrifying except to one who had attained great concentration and detachment, and so the future Buddha might have considered it a good exercise to practice self-possession and meditation under these conditions. By day on the other hand many of these shrines were 'delightful' places, as the Buddha remarked to Ānanda during his last visit to Vaiśālī (p. 75 above), at the Cāpāla Shrine, of that shrine and several others near the city.

1. M I 20 mentions this.

Perhaps the Buddha thought of instituting specifically Buddhist shrines, or of assimilating the existing shrines to the observance of the *poṣadha* (by laymen as well as monks) reformed into a specifically Buddhist ceremony. There is little more than a hint of this in the *Tripiṭaka* (p. 199 above), but in the *Mahāparinirvāṇa Sūtra* we have a rather different proposal put in the mouth of the Buddha (p. 78 above): after his cremation his ashes should be collected and a pagoda erected over them. The same text goes on to mention, besides this pagoda, three other places where those trusting in the Buddha might find inspiration: his birthplace, the place of his enlightenment and the place where he started the wheel of the doctrine. It is impossible to say whether the Buddha himself made these proposals, or whether the custom of visiting his tomb and other places connected with him grew up spontaneously after the *parinirvāṇa* and was afterwards authorised by the Buddhist communities by the addition of this passage to the *Sūtra*. The latter seems more credible, the former not quite in character with the Buddha as we have otherwise found him, but this is a purely subjective judgment.

The place of the enlightenment was a tree under which the Buddha sat in meditation on the night of the enlightenment. In fact this tree, or its successor, is still there, at the place now called Bodh Gayā, surrounded by throngs of pilgrims. It is a beautiful tree, though not now very large, its leaves a bright and translucent green. It is now flanked by a large temple (i.e. a 'shrine house'). The place where the wheel of the doctrine was started, in the park near Vārāṇasī, is marked by a pagoda, now a ruinous stump, surrounded by modern temples and *vihāras* (dwellings for monks). (The old monuments and buildings of the site, like those of Bodh Gayā and all the other Buddhist shrines, *vihāras* and the later universities of Northern India were razed to the ground by the Muslims after the Turkish conquest, the monks were massacred, libraries burned and Buddhism obliterated from the countries of its origin. Since the ending of Muslim rule Bodh Gayā has been restored and new *vihāras* and temples have been built at some of the other places.) The birthplace of the Buddha was also a park, and in fact a tree according to the tradition, against which his mother supported herself at the time of the event.

The Emperor Aśoka, whom we shall discuss later in this Chapter, has marked the site (now in Nepal and called Rummindeī from the ancient Lumbinī Park) by a stone column surmounted by a horse standing on an inverted lotus as the capital. (The horse has nothing to do with the birth, but probably symbolises the renunciation and legendary escape from Kapilavastu on horseback.) He erected a similar column in the Vārāṇasī park, but crowned with four lions standing appropriately on wheels and bearing a single larger wheel on their backs.

As for the pagoda to be erected over the Buddha's ashes, according to the *Mahāparinirvāṇa Sūtra* the surrounding states as well as the Northern Malla Republic laid claim to the ashes and a considerable quarrel arose. The claimants were pacified by a brahman who gave them a share each, thus eight shares were distributed and eight pagodas were built in different countries: Northern Malla, Southern Malla, Vṛji, Magadha (at Rājagṛha, for Ajātaśatru claimed his share), Śākya, Krauḍya, Bulaka and Viṣṇudvīpa. In addition the brahman made a pagoda in his own village over the urn in which he had collected the ashes and the (?) Mauryas, who arrived too late with their claim, made a pagoda over the charcoal embers of the Buddha's pyre (the Sarvāstivāda version calls these last *māṇavas*, 'young brahmans', but the Sthaviravāda text has them warriors, like all the other claimants except the Viṣṇudvīpa brahmans). Thus there were at first ten pagodas, of which eight were believed to contain actual physical relics of the Buddha. A festival was held at each of them, after which they continued to be honoured. These early 'pagodas' were probably nothing but hemispherical mounds, not unlike prehistoric tumuli, very different from the later constructions of brick and stone and the tall towers which gradually developed out of them and became the typical 'pagoda' shape now called to mind by that word. The Kuśinagarī pagoda thus had several rivals, and in fact the Krauḍya pagoda at Rāmagrāma was the most celebrated in legend, since it was believed to be guarded by dragons. Later, a shrine (temple) was built at the site of the *parinirvāṇa*.

Several other places connected with the life of the Buddha were gradually added to these centres of pilgrimage and adorned with suitable monuments. In addition, more remote cities and other places laid claim to similar fame, without benefit of authority in the *Tripiṭaka* until apocryphal texts could be manufactured to encourage the local enthusiasts, so that by the third century after the *parinirvāṇa* the wanderings of the Buddha seemed to have extended as far as the Hindu Kush to the North West and the Tamil country (Kāñcī) and Ceylon to the South. In this way the Buddha was as it were brought in person to inspire the people of many countries of the Indian continent. The monuments at the places of pilgrimage were decorated with reliefs depicting the popularly celebrated events in the life of the Buddha, many of which can still be admired either in their original places or in museums, and without doubt the pilgrims listened to the stories of the same episodes narrated by their guides. Perhaps they took away with them carved wooden souvenirs of their pilgrimage: a lotus from Kapilavastu, a tree from Bodh Gayā, a wheel from Vārāṇasī, a pagoda from Kuśinagarī, for as yet it was not the custom to represent the Buddha directly as a human figure. With these the pilgrims might set up their own household shrines on their return home.

Poetry and Story-telling

Let us now turn to the evidence of the literature paralleling this great movement to spread and popularise Buddhism. Here we may notice two distinct lines of development. Firstly the Buddhists participated in a new trend in poetry which originated in Magadha in about the same period as the Buddha and during the next three centuries or so created many new techniques of metrics and poetics.[1] Secondly in order to satisfy the popular demand for stories, legends and what is sometimes known as 'edification' many narratives were elaborated and appended to the *Kṣudraka Āgama*, or in some schools to the *Vinaya* (in the latter case the episodes from the life of the Buddha were greatly expanded and all kinds of stories and poetry inserted among them).

1. *Pali Metre* is a study of this new movement in metrics. Here we shall follow its conclusions as regards the chronology of this Sthaviravāda poetry, except that in the light of our comparative study of the literature of the Buddhist schools in this book we are now able to be less cautious in dating and place certain poems earlier. See also IKL Vol. II, Chapters XI and XII.

Some of the monks who followed the Buddha had been poets, or even actors, before they 'went forth', according to the Sthaviravâda tradition, and certainly their achievements are considerable, and professional, in the service of the doctrine. To the probably small kernel of verses by monks and nuns originally collected in the *Kṣudraka* more were gradually added through the centuries by poets of varying capacities. Probably the most famous poet among the followers of the Buddha was Vāgīśa, to whom the following verses (which belong to the earliest phase of Buddhist poetry and therefore are most likely to belong to the Buddha's lifetime) are ascribed. Vāgīśa had been a professional poet, and a specialist in improvised lyrics. Here is the first verse of an autobiographical poem:

> Intoxicated with poetry we wandered from village to village, from city to city,
> then I saw the Buddha who had gone beyond all principles.[1]

Here is a short poem on the Buddha:

> More than a thousand monks attend on the Well-gone
> as he teaches the clear doctrine, *nirvāṇa* which knows no fear from any source,
> They listen to the abundant doctrine taught by the Perfectly Enlightened One,
> — how glorious the Buddha is, facing the community of monks!
> O Master, your name is 'Dragon', best of sages,
> for like a great cloud you rain on your pupils.
> Leaving the afternoon rest from a wish to see the teacher,
> O great hero, your pupil Vāgīśa salutes your feet.[2]

On Śāriputra:

> Profound and wise, learned in the Way and the wrong way,
> Śāriputra of great understanding teaches the monks the doctrine;
> He teaches briefly, also speaks in detail,
> pours out his improvisation like the song of the myna bird;
> By his beautiful voice, soft and exciting,

1. Thag. 1253, also S I 196.
2. Thag. 1238-41, also S I 192-3.

the thoughts of the monks are elated and gladdened as they listen intently.[1]

Our translations are literal only, making no attempt to replace the poetic characteristics of the original. It can be seen, however, that Vāgīśa is applying the similes and some of the vocabulary of lyric poetry to his new subject. In another poem he likens the Buddha's words to cool rain which relieves us from the overpowering heat of summer (which makes clearer the comparison with a 'dragon' above; 'cool' implies leading to *nirvāṇa*, from the unhappiness of transmigration). Also the voice of the Buddha is compelling, like that of the wild goose.

The following poem is ascribed to Kāśyapa (apparently the president of the First Rehearsal), and is very much more poetic since he is describing the mountains. Though it is practically impossible to reproduce this in translation, we may note that the vocabulary of this piece is highly poetic: the ordinary everyday words for 'elephant', 'waters', 'clouds', 'peacocks', 'full of', 'places', etc., are avoided, and if they would be repeated synonyms are substituted (except in the refrain, which is an archaic touch):

Spread with garlands of *kareri* creeper, these are the places which delight the mind,
with the sounds of elephants delightfully resounding, these crags delight me.
Splendid with the colour of blue clouds, with cool clear waters,
covered with 'Indra's herdsmen' (ladybirds) these crags delight me.
Like ridges of blue clouds, like a fine barrel-vaulted house,
with the sounds of elephants delightfully resounding, these crags delight me.
Mountains whose surfaces, delightful, are rained on as the sages seek them out,
echoing the peacocks' cries these crags delight me.
Perfect when I wish to meditate, for exertion, self-possessed,
perfect for me, wishing for well-being, for a monk exerting himself,
Perfect when I wish to be comfortable, for a monk exerting himself,

1. Thag. 1231-3, also S I 190.

perfect for me, wishing to concentrate, for such a one exerting himself.
Clothed in *ummā* flowers, like the sky covered with clouds,
strewn with various flocks of birds these crags delight me.
Not full of worldly people, but sought out by herds of wild animals,
strewn with various flocks of birds these crags delight me.
With clear waters and broad rocks, full of yaks,
their pools covered with *sevāla* weed, these crags delight me.
I do not get such pleasure from the five kinds of musical instrument,
as when, with concentrated mind, I gain insight rightly into the doctrine.[1]

If not intended merely for circulation among the monks themselves, poetry such as this was aimed at an élite who might find a vocation for solitude, might join the community of monks, rather than at the masses. More popular, probably, were pieces in the epic style like this early poem on the future Buddha, on the renunciation:

I will sing the famous going-forth, how the man with insight went forth,
how, investigating, he made the going-forth splendid.
'Confined is this household life, a dusty sphere', he said,
'But going-forth is open' — seeing this he went forth.
And having gone forth he avoided bad actions,
abandoning bad speech he purified his way of life.

(the narrator plunges straight into an episode, famous later, of the future Buddha's meeting with King Bimbisāra of Magadha:)

The Buddha (but he is not yet the Buddha!) went to Rājagṛha, the Mountain Capital of Magadha,
to gather alms, he who was strewn with excellent marks;
Bimbisāra saw his from him palace,
and seeing him with those marks he spoke like this...

(the king comments on the noble appearance of the wanderer, and orders messengers to go and ask him where he is going; told he has gone to Mount Pāṇḍava, one of the five mountains flanking the Mountain Capital, after collecting alms, the king drives out in his chariot to see him, and after some polite talk to start the conversation continues:)

1. Thag. 1062-71.

'You are young, youthful, newly fledged,
handsome and tall like a well-born warrior
making the vanguard glorious, leading a troop of elephants!
—I'll give you lands, enjoy them!—Now tell me who you are'.
'In truth, O king, my country is on the slopes of the Himālaya,
endowed with wealth and energy, in Kośala,
My clan is the Solar one, by tribe I am a Śākya,
—from that tribe I have gone forth, not yearning for pleasures.
Having seen disadvantage in pleasures, security in renunciation,
I am going for exertion—it is this which excites my mind.'[1]

Another similar piece describes the 'exertion' to attain enlightenment, on the banks of the River Nairañjanā (near Uruvilvā and Bodh Gayā, but the latter is on rising ground some distance from the river). This scene develops into a dialogue with Death, who urges the future Buddha to give up the hard struggle, the asceticism and fasting, and make the most of his life—by all means doing good, but not exerting himself like this. The future Buddha rejects these words of temptation and hypocrisy, since the life recommended is only death postponed, and continues with his asceticism, with the drying up of his flesh and blood (likened to the nearby river, since it is the dry season), which makes his thought clearer and strengthens his self-possession, understanding and concentration. He repels the 'armies' of Death—passion, loneliness, hunger, thirst and others. The god goes off dejected—like a crow which mistook a stone for a piece of fat—letting his *viṇā* (lute) fall from under his arm in his depression.[2] This 'temptation by Death' just before the enlightenment became a most popular subject among the Buddhists, depicted through every medium of art and a typical episode in the legend of the Buddha which was gradually elaborated as a main part of the presentation of Buddhism to the masses.

Here is an autobiographical piece ascribed to the monk Sunīta:

---

1. Sn 405-9 and 420-4. cf. MSV, SOR I pp. 94-5.
2. Sn 425-49.

I was born in a low family, poor and starving,
my work was low — I was a sweeper
disgusting to men, despised, treated with contempt;
humbling my mind I would pay respect to many people.
Then I saw the Buddha leading the community of monks,
the great hero, entering the capital of Magadha.
I put down my carrying pole and approached to pay respect
— the highest of men waited, through compassion for me
— I saluted the teacher's feet, then waiting on the side
I asked the highest of all beings to let me go forth.

'Come, monk!' he said to me — that was my 'entrance' (to the community) (Sunīta follows the admonitions of the teacher and attains enlightenment and freedom, meditating at night, then :)

As the night ended and the sun rose,
Indra and Brahmā came and bowed to me with joined hands :
'Hail to thee, learned among men! Hail to thee, highest of men!
As the influences are exhausted in you, dear sir, you are indeed one worthy of gifts...'

In other words he is a true brahman, as good as any high class brahman by birth. He is also the superior of the gods, and God Himself, who come to pay their respects. At the end of the poem Sunīta tells us that the Buddha explained to him that the real brahman is one who lives the 'best life', with restraint and self-control.[1] Here then is another kind of popular expression of Buddhism : the levelling of class distinctions, or rather the substitution of merit for birth, the Buddha's complete lack of prejudice, and the idea that a monk may mix with the gods and even be their superior.

All the poems quoted so far seem to belong to the earliest phase represented in the extant Buddhist literature. The following is possibly as much as a century later, and may be dated to about 400 B.C. Here the ethical and social teaching of the Buddha is put into metrical form, and the poem is certainly for circulation in society, not merely for private recitation by monks :

1. Thag 620 ff.

One should act with skill in welfare, having understood the calmed state,
one should be capable, straight, very straight, using good words, soft, not arrogant;
And contented, easily satisfied, with little business and frugal habits,
calmed faculties, and wise, not proud or covetous among the people.
One should do nothing at all which is mean, which others, being discerning, would blame.
Let all beings be happy and secure, let all be happy!
Whatever living beings there are, timid or strong, without exception,
the tall or large, medium or small, minute or gross;
Those seen or unseen, living far away or nearby,
those born already and those yet seeking birth, let all beings be happy!
None should deceive another, or despise any, anywhere,
or, being angry, feeling repulsion, wish unhappiness for another.
As a mother would look after her only child, with her life,
even so should one develop one's thoughts, without limit, towards all beings.
Benevolent thoughts towards the whole world one should develop without limit,
above, below, all round, unconfined, without hatred, without rivalry;
Whether staying or going, sitting, lying down, one should be without stupidity,
one should resolve on this self-possession (through benevolence) — this, they say, is the best way of life.[1]

Amongst the more popular poetry of the Buddhists we find some pieces which appear to go outside the circle of strictly Buddhist ideas into the field of popular legends and stories. They may bear indirectly on Buddhist conceptions, or even show signs of assimilation and adaptation for didactic purposes. Going back for a moment to the earliest period we find these curious verses

1. Sn 143 ff. The last strophe is omitted, its metre indicating that it is a later addition.

in a *sūtra* of the *Dirgha* of the Sthaviravāda (No. 32), possessed also by the Sarvāstivādins[1] and the Chinese *Tripiṭaka*. They appear to belong to the same circle of ideas as the stories of the ideal society which we read in Chapter Six, but here this society is supposed to exist in an inaccessible part of the Earth at present, instead of the remote past or future :

In delightful Uttarakuru, near beautiful Mount Meru,[2]
men are born unselfish, without any possessions;
they sow no seed, draw no ploughs;
men enjoy rice growing wild, uncultivated.
The rice grains have no husk or coating, are clean and fragrant,
— they cook them in a gourd and then enjoy a meal ...
...There the trees are always in fruit, full of various flocks of birds,
resounding with peacocks and herons and soft cuckoos...[3]

The greatest collection of stories, at least in the Sthaviravāda *Tripiṭaka*, is the *Jātaka* section of the *Kṣudraka*. At present this collection contains about 550 stories, but these were brought together gradually round a much smaller kernel. This section of the *Kṣudraka* is in verse with the exception (which is mixed prose and verse) of only one story. For some stories, however, there is only one verse, whilst others are true epic pieces with up to nearly a thousand verses. Some, then, are complete epic narratives, whilst others merely assume the story instead of narrating it, are either memorial verses to recall it to a narrator who knows it and will retell it in his own words, or the 'highlights' of a story, such as the decisive exchanges in dialogue, serving in fact the same purpose. The stories were not written out in full by the Sthaviras for many centuries (when some of them seem to have been half forgotten), when they were given the form of a 'commentary' on the verses written (as we now have it in Pali) in Ceylon. A few *Jātaka* poems are as old as the earliest period, but the composition went on for several centuries. The following episode from one of the long epic pieces belongs to about 400 B.C., like the poem on benevolence above. The Buddha in one of his previous lives was a minister

1. *Āṭānāṭika Sūtra* (Hoffmann).
2. The central mountain of the Earth, i. e. the North Pole. Pali Neru.
3. D III 199 ff.

named Mahauṣadha, whose brilliance at court arouses deadly resentment from four other leading ministers. They insinuate to the king that he is a traitor, and suggest that he can be tested and found out by an apparently innocuous question about secrecy. If he says a secret should never be revealed to anyone at all, they suggest, he should not be trusted. The following dialogue ensues :

King : The five wise men have met — a question occurs to me, listen to it :
whether a blameworthy matter or a praiseworthy one, to whom may a secret be revealed ?

Senaka : Even you must reveal this, protector of the Earth, lord and endurer of burdens, tell us this;
reflecting on your will and pleasure, O king of men, the five wise men will speak.

King : A secret may be revealed to a wife, whether it is blameworthy or praiseworthy,
if she is virtuous, inaccessible to others, controlled by her husband's will, pleasing.

Senaka : A secret may be revealed to a friend, whether...
if he is a refuge to one in difficulty and afflicted, a resource, a support.

(The other three ministers who are party to the plot say respectively that a secret may be revealed to a virtuous brother, a good son and a loving mother, then :)

Mahauṣadha : The secrecy of a secret is good, the revealing of a secret is not praised,
a wise man should bear it whilst it has not borne fruit,
but when the matter is accomplished he may speak at pleasure.

(The king draws the intended conclusion and afterwards issues a secret order for Mahauṣadha to be executed, but this worries him when he thinks of the minister's former services, and he confides in the queen :)

Queen : Why are you perplexed, O king ? This that we hear is not the speech of the king of men !
thinking of what are you depressed ? O king I am not at fault (for asking).

King : 'The wise Mahauṣadha must be executed' : because

I have ordered the execution of the sage,
I am depressed thinking of it. O queen you are not at fault.

(Despite the secrecy of the order Mahauṣadha disappeared before he could be arrested. According to the 'commentary' — for these connecting links are mostly found only in the prose commentary, the actual verses giving the dialogues — he seizes control of the capital the next day and then faces the king. However, what follows does not confirm that he went as far as this, but only that he somehow secures another meeting with the king, with the other ministers present; we may suppose he emerges from hiding when given a guarantee of safety :)

King : You disappeared in the evening and now you come, hearing what was your mind apprehensive ?
Who said what to you, O wise one ? Now we shall hear those words, tell me that !

Mahauṣadha : 'The wise Mahauṣadha must be executed' :
if, O king, in the evening you discussed this confidentially,
privately told it to your wife, this secret, being revealed, was heard by me.

(The king sees the point and feels angry with the queen, but Mahauṣadha presses on with the following :)

The wicked deed of Senaka in the *śāla* wood, the low thing he did,
he told in private to a friend; this secret, being revealed, was heard by me.

(Senaka admits this and is arrested)

Your man Putkasa, O king, has a disease which makes him unfit for the royal service,
he told this in private to his brother...

(Arrest of Putkasa. Similarly the other two ministers are one unfit and the other in possession of a jewel which was missing; they had told their son or mother. Both are arrested, and Mahauṣadha concludes the proceedings by repeating his first verse about the secrecy of a secret being good...).[1]

1. *Jātaka* VI 379 ff.

It is hard to see what this had to do with Buddhist ethics, except to underline the fact that telling the whole truth is a virtue attainable only by *śramaṇas* who have 'left the world'. The point of the story, however, is really to glorify the Buddha in his past life for his wisdom. Its interest is also the dramatic presentation which it seems to imply, to need. Though there are no actual dramas in the *Tripiṭaka* (not counting late additions to the Tibetan *Tripiṭaka*, of course) there is evidence, as we shall see, that certain dramatic episodes in it, particularly in the *Saṃyukta*, were presented on the stage at festive assemblies. No doubt it was considered inappropriate for monks and nuns to go to the theatre, but this has led to misunderstanding and confusion among modern scholars. As we saw above (p. 182), assemblies do not seem to have been considered harmful for laymen, though 'addiction' to them could be. The point surely was the nature of the assemblies, and so the Buddhists gradually elaborated a repertoire of dramatic pieces as well as other types of literature, and we shall find in due course that they produced a range of full scale plays. A number of other dramatic dialogues, which unlike this one are Buddhist in content, may be dated in the same period and in the fourth century B.C.

Probably to the second half of the fourth century B.C. or later belongs a poem ascribed to the famous Āmrapāli (p. 72 above) after she became a nun, which teaches impermanence. Here are some verses from it:

Black like the colour of bees, and wavy was my hair,
through age it's like coarse hemp, truthful are these words, not false!
Smooth like a conch shell well polished, my throat was once lustrous,
through age it's ruined, destroyed, truthful are these words, not false!
Full and round, firm and high, my breasts were once lustrous,
in age which is like a drought[1] they hang dry, truthful are these words, not false!

1. Reading *iti*.

Like two elephant's trunks, my thighs were once lustrous,
through age they're like bamboo stems, truthful are these words, not false!
...Such was this body—shattered, the home of much suffering,
it's become like an old house with falling stucco, truthful are these words, not false![1]

The Personality Schism

Before we trace the literature and the popularisation of Buddhism further we must bring our history down to the third century after the *parinirvāṇa* and the third century B.C. The Emperor Dhanananda, son of Mahāpadma, was extremely unpopular on account of his oppressive and arbitrary rule. He insulted one of his ministers, Kauṭalya[2], who happened to be a man of genius and subtlety. Kauṭalya went 'underground' and laid plans with Candragupta, a prince connected with the royal family of Magadha and perhaps having as good a claim to the throne as Dhanananda. Eventually they succeeded in leading a revolt which ended the rule of Dhanananda, and in 317 B.C. Candragupta became emperor of Magadha and most of India. The dynasty descended from him is known as the Mauryas, this being presumably his family name, and some sources (Sthaviravāda) trace his descent from the Maurya Republic which took a share of the Buddha's ashes (p. 227 above). Either very early in his reign or even before his rebellion was carried to its successful conclusion Candragupta eliminated the Greek garrisons along the Indus and liberated that part of India from foreign rule. It was during the lifetime of the Buddha that the Persian emperors Kurash (Cyrus) and Dārāyavus (Darius) I conquered Gandhāra and Sindhu (Sindhu being the country of the lower Indus and Gandhāra including a section of the middle Indus with its tributary the Kubhā, modern Kābul, the latter country being the most ancient centre of the Vedic tradition—Uddālaka worked out his philosophy there). When Alexander overthrew

1. Thīg 252-70 (the Sthaviravāda version of the *Sthavirīgāthā*).

2. This is the correct spelling according to the manuscript evidence; it was used in the 'copy' of REBCS but altered by the editor before publication on the basis of 'popular etymology'.

the Persian Empire he laid claim to these territories of India and the allegiance of their Persian garrisons, and even tried to extend them further east, where he found (in Vāhīka, modern Panjāb) a mixture of small Indian republics and monarchies not unlike that of eastern India in the Buddha's time. The attempt proved abortive, but the weakening of some of these small states perhaps made it easier for Candragupta to incorporate them into the empire of Magadha. Even so some of the republics, particularly those not overwhelmed by Alexander (Yaudheya, Audumbara, Ārjunāyana, etc.) retained some degree of autonomy and continuity of their institutions, and became independent states again later. About 305-3 B.C. Seleucos Nikator as Alexander's successor reasserted his claims in India and marched to enforce them. He was decisively defeated by Candragupta and forced not only to surrender the disputed territories but also to surrender part of Iran (Aria, Arachosia, Gedrosia as well as the whole region up to the Hindu Kush). An alliance was then concluded between the Indians and the Greeks. Candragupta became the ruler of an empire twice as large as that of the Nandas, embracing almost the whole Indian world and with it probably all the communities of Buddhists.

It was during the reign of his son and successor Bindusāra (293-268 B.C.) that the Sthaviravāda underwent a further schism, and the Mahāsaṃgha likewise divided at an unknown date in about the same period. Two hundred years after the *parinirvāṇa*,[1] therefore in B.C. 286 if the date is precise, an elder named Vātsīputra appears to have prepared a new recension of the *Abhidharma* in nine sections (it is a matter of speculation what these were), which he claimed to have received from Śāriputra and Rāhula (and presumably intermediate teachers).[2] It was presumably in this, which seems to be irretrievably lost, that he formulated his special doctrine about the 'person' (*pudgala*): very likely one of the sections was devote entirely to this. The Sthaviravāda school divided over the question whether this concept, the 'person',

1. Bu-ston, Obermiller Vol. II p. 96; Bareau, *Les premiers conciles bouddhiques*, Paris, 1955, p. 116. HBI 308.
2. Lamotte HBI 209, 587.

should be reckoned as a real principle among those listed in the *Abhidharma* and at the ultimate (*paramārtha*) level of statement, or whether it is merely a word used in conventional language, like 'self' or 'soul', 'life-principle', 'being'. The Buddha uses the word in some of his discourses, as he uses 'being' in others: the question was whether he was just using everyday language in speaking to hearers who would not understand a philosophical statement, or whether he assumed any sort of reality apart from the groups, the senses and the various mental principles counted in the *Abhidharma.* Is 'person' no more than a kind of pronoun, a demonstrative like 'this' used when referring to a particular (philosophically speaking) collection of the elements or principles combined in a living body with consciousness ?

The orthodox Sthaviravādins thought that this was so, that this popular conception comes under the rubric in which the Buddha rejects such questions as 'who touches', 'who desires', 'who eats the consciousness-food', and so on (see pp. 118 ff. above). In their *Abhidharma*[1] they afterwards included an elaborate formal refutation of the proposition that the 'person' exists in the ultimate sense.

The followers of Vātsīputra, who came to be known as Vātsīputrīyas after him, accepted the 'person' as in some sense, at least, a reality. Like all Buddhists at all times they rejected the Brahmanical concept of an eternal soul. On the other hand they rejected the orthodox Sthaviravāda theory (which is also that of all schools of Buddhism other than the Vātsīputrīyas and their later offshoots) that a living being is nothing but the five groups with the senses. Between these two alternatives, however, they appear to have found it difficult to define what a 'person' could be, as a subject which continued and transmigrated. In fact they decided that it could not be said what it was, it was like the undetermined questions to which there was no categorical answer. Nothing could be predicated of the 'person'. They admitted, it appears,[2] that the person could not be regarded as different from the five groups (as another quite separate group), but held also that it was

1. Kvu 1 ff., very similar (but shorter) refutation in the Sarvāstivāda *Abhidharma*, *Vijñānakāya* Chapter II. See F. Watanabe, Thesis, 1976.
2. Lamotte HBI 673 f.

not the same as the groups.[1] No predicate could be applied to it, for example it could not be said that it was eternal or that it was non-eternal. Yet it could be cognised by the six kinds of consciousness (of the six senses), and it (alone) transmigrated from one body of the five groups to another.

At an unknown date, but within fifty years of this schism among the Sthaviravādins, the Mahāsaṃgha also split and produced two new schools (it appears that we should reckon the 'Mahāsaṃghikas' as a third continuing to exist alongside these as two offshoots—which would seem to imply two successive schisms, as in fact Paramārtha states: first the Ekavyavahārikas). At present scarcely any information about the history of the Mahāsaṃgha schools is available: all we possess is accounts of a few of their special doctrines alongside fuller general accounts of doctrines apparently held by all the Mahāsaṃgha schools collectively. The two schools which now appear were called the Ekavyavahārika and the Gokulika (there are variants for the latter: Kukkuṭika, Kukkulika, Kaukkuṭika, Kaurukullaka,[2] etc). The latter are believed to have been in some sense specialists in *abhidharma*, but the account of their doctrines in the Sthaviravāda tradition (*Kathāvattu* 208 ff and its commentary) says that they exaggerated a statement in the *Saṃyukta*[3] that the five groups are nothing but cinders (*kukkula* in Pali), as if it meant that there is no happiness whatever, of any kind, in the world, but only unrelieved unhappiness. Of the Ekavyavahārikas it is said by the very late authority Bhāvaviveka in his *Tarkajvālā* that they held that thought is by its nature pure and radiant, inaccessible to defilement. He also says they held that 'all principles are cognised in one moment' (in enlightenment, presumably ?). Other sources state that they held that all principles are mere names or concepts.[4]

1. Like fire (person) and fuel (groups), Harivarman; *AK Bhāṣya* p. 461.

2. Named after the monk Kurukulla ?—*Mañjuśrīmūlakalpa* p. 9.

3. S III 177. Paramārtha on the other hand says (Demiéville MCB I 42 f; 45ff.) that they held that the *Abhidharma* was the real teaching, whilst the *Sūtra* was adapted to circumstances. Also they practiced especially the faculty of energy (*vīrya*).

4. Kegon tradition (Takakusu, *Essentials of Buddhist Philosophy*, 118) and MCB I 45.

Aśoka : Buddhism to be Implemented

According to Jaina tradition Candragupta was a follower of their doctrine and at the end of his reign abdicated and became a Jaina monk. Bindusāra on the other hand, or at least his queen Dharmā, patronised the Ājīvakas,[1] who apparently were better qualified for the interpretation of omens than the brahmans (cf. p. 40 above). When the queen was pregnant one of them predicted that she would have a son (Aśoka) perfectly endowed and wealthy (? text corrupt) adding confidentially to the queen afterwards that he would be king also. In the event, and contrary to Bindusāra's wish that another of his sons (by a different queen) should succeed him, the ministers made Aśoka emperor in B.C. 268.[2] Prior to that he had served as 'prince' (*kumāra,* in effect governor) of the provinces of Gandhāra and of Avanti at different times (the system of provinces governed by princes is a characteristic part of Magadhan administration: in Aśoka's time there were at least four such provinces in addition to the metropolitan province of Magadha itself).

The Buddhist sources[3] indicate that Aśoka favoured the Ājīvakas after his consecration as Emperor, and in fact we shall see that he continued his donations to that sect through most, perhaps all, of his reign. The various Buddhist chronicles and legends (as time went on the narratives of old chronicles tended to be retold and embellished as edifying legends) suggest that at first Aśoka was a harsh and ruthless ruler, until he was convinced of his error by a Buddhist monk and become a lay Buddhist. His character was then transformed and he became a model emperor, 'Aśoka the Just'[4] (Dharmāśoka), as the tradition often calls him, distinguishing him from Aśoka the Black. It is the more 'embellished' legends which lay the most stress on this change, for obvious reasons of edification. What underlies the tradition is the real change of policy from one based probably on the amoral maxims of power worked out

1. *Vaṃsatthappakāsinī* I 189 ff.
2. *Divyāvadāna* 372 f., Przyluski : *Légende* pp, 234 f. (below we give the years B. C. which mainly overlap Aśoka's current regnal years).
3. Mostly gathered in Eggermont, *Chronology* and further reviewed by Lamotte, HBI 261 ff.
4. Or 'of Principle', cf. pp. 162, 165 above.

by Kauṭalya in his *Arthaśāstra* ('Science of Wealth', i.e. politics and economics) to the ethical social programme proposed by the Buddha.

We are in the fortunate position of being able to go back beyond the chronicles to Aśoka's own autobiographical record of his policies and struggles. Having decided to implement the principles of Buddhism in his vast empire he incorporated these principles in the imperial edicts issued from time to time to the provinces and districts. There was of course nothing new in the regular circulation of imperial commands through the Magadhan Empire, but in his determination to achieve the maximum publicity for the new policy, and to ensure that its implementation would continue long after his own time, Aśoka caused many of his edicts to be inscribed on stone columns and on rocks at all the principal centres of his realm. No doubt he used more ephemeral media as well, but to us he has bequeathed his ideas in lasting form, many of his inscriptions remaining in their original places or in museums.[1] About twenty of these edicts are preserved in multiple copies set up in different places. A dozen more inscriptions primarily of local interest are now known in single copies. Besides the three or four main Prakrit dialects used in different provinces of the Empire, Aśoka used Aramaic (for the Persian or Iranian speaking population accustomed to this official language of the Persian Empire) and Greek (for the Greek colonists in Arachosia, etc.).

In what seems to be the earliest of these inscriptions or edicts,[2] issued in B.C. 258, Aśoka tells us he had been a lay disciple (*upāsaka*) for more than two and a half years, consequently that he became one in B.C. 261, we may conclude, in the eighth year (current) of his reign. The Buddhist traditions, in fact, say that he met a Buddhist monk who convinced him so that he went to the refuges (the Buddha, the Doctrine and the Community), in other words became a lay Buddhist (they disagree over the name of the monk, since

1. The most convenient edition is Bloch's : *Les inscriptions d' Aśoka*, Paris, 1950, but this has to be supplemented by some inscriptions rediscovered since then : JA 1958 in particular; Lamotte, HBI 789 ff.

2. Bloch 145 ff inscribed at Brahmagiri, Rūpnāth and several other places, often called the 'Minor' Rock Edict.

more than one school of Buddhism claims the credit for this achievement). Soon afterwards, however (B.C. 261-0), Aśoka was engaged in a war of conquest against the country of Kaliṅga (the modern state of Orissa), on the East coast of India South of Magadha. It appears this country had formed part of the Magadhan Empire before but had regained its independence: Aśoka apparently was consolidating his empire at the beginning of his reign.

In an inscription of B.C. 256[1] Aśoka himself describes this war, which was the turning point in his life; a description of a victory by the conqueror himself which is perhaps without parallel: 'When Devānāmpriya Priyadarśin (the names or titles generally used by Aśoka in the edicts) had been consecrated (king) eight years, Kaliṅga was conquered by us. A hundred and fifty thousand living beings were carried off (presumably as slaves, etc.) from there. A hundred thousand were killed there. Many times that died (presumably from famine or disease caused by the war). After that, now that Kaliṅga is taken, Devānāmpriya ('Dear to the gods' —a royal title) is intensely concerned with principle (*dharma*, which may be assumed to have here a sense similar to the sense it has in connection with the 'just' emperors of the *Tripiṭaka*, pp. 162 ff. above, but which will be discussed below), loving principle and instructing in principle. Devānāmpriya is grieving over the conquest of Kaliṅga; for the conquering of an unconquered realm, where people are killed, or die, or are carried off, is a thought which is strongly felt, a heavy thought, in Devānāmpriya. Moreover Devānāmpriya has a heavier thought than that: the brahmans and *śramaṇas* and other sectarians (*pāṣaṇḍa*, followers of the various schools of religion or philosophy), or the householders among whom listening attentively to superiors, parents and elders is carried on, and right behaviour towards friends, acquaintances, companions, relatives, slaves and servants, and firm devotion (these are important virtues in Aśoka's system, see below)—some of them are harmed or killed or separated from those dear to them. Or if they themselves are fortunate, they are yet harmed in that—if they have any affection—their friends, acquaintances,

1. Bloch 125 ff., 'Rock Edict 13.'

companions or relatives meet with disaster. This likeness (*pratibhāga*) of all men (more idiomatically 'common humanity', presumably related to the Buddhist standard of considering all beings as like oneself) is a heavy thought in Devānāmpriya. And there is no country where these groups are not found, except among the Greeks, where there are no brahmans or *śramaṇas*, and nowhere is there a country where there are no men with confidence in one of the sects. However many people were killed, or died, or were carried off when Kaliṅga was taken, even one hundredth or one thousandth part of that would be a heavy thought in Devānāmpriya today.'

Thus Aśoka as a Buddhist of some conviction had at first continued the traditional imperial policy of Magadha, only to find his practice in inescapable conflict with his theory: his war multiplied the evils which Buddhism denounced, especially violence and taking life; moreover it damaged Buddhism itself, as well as other religions or philosophies (and Aśoka thought these were good too), by harming the *śramaṇas* (especially Buddhist monks) as well as lay disciples (the virtuous householders) in countries ravaged by war. His Buddhism was put to the test: was it sincere and practical, or just a diversion in leisure hours (as it had been for Ajātaśatru), or a crafty piece of state policy like religion according to Kauṭalya—useful in that it caused restraint and fear in others and therefore to be given lip service, only, by the king? He found he was sincere: whatever problems he faced as emperor, he believed Buddhism offered what was needed to solve them; overriding everything is his evident and deep conviction that non-violence is the primary principle of conduct, the greatest moral value. This was precisely the primary moral principle of Buddhism: 'abstention from taking life', realised in his individual experience and directly related by him to the 'likeness of all men', which is nothing but the underlying social standard of Buddhist ethics, considering all beings as like oneself. It seems very likely that he learned these principles from his Buddhist teachers; what is much more certain is that he ascertained the value, or the truth, of them in his own experience and restated them in his own words, for his own time.

Let us now follow Aśoka's career primarily through his own words, returning to the early inscription with which we began. He does not mention the war there, but he does say that a year before issuing the edict, and therefore in B.C. 259 and soon after the war, he had visited the Community (of Buddhist monks) and undertaken (Buddhism) strongly (*bāḍham prakrānta*). The result of that is, he continues, that gods have mixed with men in this Rose Apple Continent (India, see p. 168 above), which was not the case before. The meaning of this is not evident to us, since we have no information on the situation to which it refers. The most likely reference would appear to be to divine portents seen by men, indicating the presence of gods, such as the light and radiance said to precede an appearance of Brahmā (p. 154 above). Perhaps Aśoka was watching hopefully for the 'wheel gem' (p. 165) to appear in the sky, and he may have been encouraged by celestial phenomena, such as the appearance of a comet, a nova, or an exceptional display of meteors, to believe that his change of heart and of imperial policy had begun to make itself felt in the universe. That gods might appear to men was widely believed in India in this period, and we have seen an example of such an apparition accepted into the *Tripiṭaka* of at least one school of Buddhists, in Sunīta's poem (p. 233) in which Indra and Brahmā come to pay their respects to the newly enlightened monk. A number of parallels to this incident can be found among additions made to the Sthaviravāda *Tripiṭaka* probably in the Mauryan period itself, as we shall see later in this chapter. The popularisation of Buddhism which had such great successes in this period is shown by contemporary Buddhist literature to have made much use of 'edifying' stories bringing in gods, and it is not at all improbable that when Aśoka visited the Community he was treated to this aspect of popular Buddhism as well as to the more serious instruction appropriate for a Buddhist lay disciple. There is, it should be added here, no evidence that Aśoka ever concerned himself with the properly philosophical doctrines of Buddhism, such as conditioned origination and the real mechanism of transmigration, the question of a 'soul' and the attainment of *nirvāṇa*. If he did, he did not see fit to complicate his edicts to the people at large with them, and when we recall the Buddha's attitude to such an eminent lay disciple as Anāthapiṇḍada (pp. 194 ff. above) we may easily suppose either that the monks of Aśoka's time followed his example or that Aśoka himself did.

Aśoka's teaching, which follows in this inscription, is in fact similar to the Buddha's teaching to the laity. First he says that this (the undertaking of Buddhism) is not restricted to the great (or eminent—*mahātman*), but that the small (or lowly—*kṣudraka*) also could, by this undertaking, gain heaven (*svarga*). (We might almost suggest that the gods' mixing with men above means going to heaven, but there it clearly seems to be the other way round—the gods come to Earth.) Coming afterwards to the actual content of this 'undertaking' Aśoka enumerates: listening attentively to parents, to elders (*guru*, which includes teachers); compassion towards living beings; speaking the truth. These are the 'strands' (*guṇa*) of principle (*dharma*) which should be started (i.e. undertaken). Aśoka adds that apprentices should honour their teachers as they would relatives, this is an 'old principle'.

We note that of the four main moral principles laid down by the Buddha Aśoka concentrates on the first and the last: non-violence (or, positively, compassion) and truth. He has nothing to say about 'abstention from taking what was not given' or 'abstention from misconduct in pleasures'. The first of these he perhaps thought sufficiently covered by established law, or even by the first principle (i.e. not harming others). The second is partly covered, from different view-points, by respect for parents (hence for family life) and by concern for the happiness of others and self-control, both of which are advocated in other edicts. Aśoka amalgamates with the moral principles parts of the code of social behaviour, of the theory of human relationships, namely filial piety (honouring parents) and honouring teachers (he touches on other parts of this Buddhist code elsewhere).

The remaining part of this edict is concerned with its manner of promulgation and the method of carrying out of this royal 'command'. The edict is to be written on rocks and on stone columns. The local administrators (*rājūkas*: inspectors or commissioners) are to have it 'commanded' through their countries or districts by means of the drum (the usual way of making a royal proclamation).

In the same year of his reign Aśoka issued brief versions of a somewhat similar inscription in Greek and Aramaic, and special edicts for conquered Kaliṅga.

The Greek version[1] says that Aśoka has instructed men in rectitude (? *eu'sébeia*, which requires discussion) and made them more upright (?), and everything is prosperous in all the world. He abstains from taking life and has abolished hunting and fishing and encouraged self-control and obedience to parents and elders. In future, acting accordingly, (men) will be happier and better off (Lamotte, following Tucci, would like to understand this as 'happier in this world and the next,' conformably to other edicts issued later, but the evidence before us is rather that in the translation the edicts were handled very freely).

The Aramaic version[2] says that Aśoka has instructed men in truth (*?qšyṭ'*, probably to be vocalised as *qaššiṭā*), since when evil has diminished for all men and unhappiness (?) has disappeared : happiness (*šty*, corresponding to Avestan **šāti* ?) and peace (*r'm* corresponding to Avestan *rāman* ?) exist in the world. In food even, the king abstains from taking life and prohibits hunting and fishing. He has taught self-control and obedience to parents and elders. There are now no more hardships(?) for true men. Truth is of value to men and will continue to be so.

These versions are here freely paraphrased from those of Schlumberger, Carratelli (Lamotte HBI Addenda), Dupont-Sommer and Levi della Vida, the author not being competent in either Greek or Aramaic. It seems clear that the words here translated 'rectitude' and 'truth' were intended as equivalents for *dharma*, which we have preferred to render in these contexts as 'principle'. 'Truth' in the sense of 'uprightness', the ethical sense, is close enough, but the Greek word *eu'sébeia*, according to Liddell and Scotts' Dictionary, means rather 'reverence to gods and parents', 'loyalty', 'character for piety'. If we take it as an equivalent for 'principle' we apparently have to understand the archaic, even Vedic, and literal sense of 'maintaining', as rectitude or uprightness. The original *dharma* has many meanings, as we have seen, and differs as between Buddhism and Brahmanism. Perhaps Aśoka did not mind this ambiguity

---

1. *JA* 1958 pp. 2-3.
2. *JA* 1958 pp. 20-1.

and would not object to brahmans taking the term more or less in their own sense, provided it harmonised sufficiently with his ethical ideas. Dupont-Sommer has suggested that the Aramaic version is closer to the Indian original than is the Greek, and also that it has been adapted in terminology to the religious ideas of a Zoroastrian community. We may presume this is still more true of the Greek version, and avoid drawing rash conclusions from it to the meaning of Indian terms. It is worth noting that in later bilingual Indian and Greek inscriptions, mostly on coins, *dharma* is equated with *dikē*,[1] 'right' or 'justice'.

The Kaliṅga edicts[2] are addressed to Aśoka's high officials (*mahāmātra*, which often means minister) and magistrates (*vyāvahārikas*) there. They are responsible for many thousands of living beings and should seek to gain the affection (*praṇaya*) of the people, 'my children' (*prajā* : this may mean simply the people, the subjects, but elsewhere Aśoka clearly uses it in another equally common sense, 'children'). 'I wish them all benefit and happiness in this world and the next (*pāra*- 'beyond') world. We must be impartial (*madhya*) ; for example a man may be imprisoned and troubled, and then released, for no reason, and many others may be unhappy on account of this...One must not fall into spite (*irṣyā*, which more often means 'envy'), haste, cruelty, oppression, lack of attention, lassitude or weariness... One should think of getting free from debt (i.e. to the King) and thus gain two results : heaven and not being in my debt. This text (*lipi*) must be read aloud regularly...and put into practice by the magistrates (in one version; in the other 'high officials'). ...For this purpose I shall send out every five years a non-irascible inspector (reading *akṣaka* ? — but in the other version 'high official')...so know the purpose of this. Similarly the Prince at Ujjayinī (Avanti) will go out every three years, and he at Takṣaśilā (Gandhāra) ...'

The policy of conciliating a conquered country is clear, and the Emperor shows his seriousness and even anxiety by sending special inspectors and ordering the governors of other provinces (probably his sons) to check, evidently an

1. Examples given by Lamotte HBI pp. 421, 423.
2. Bloch, 136 ff.

extraordinary measure. The other Kaliṅga edict is similar. One version was at Tosalī, the provincial capital, and is consequently addressed to the 'Prince' there as well as the high officials. Again he says all men are his children and he wishes all benefit and happiness for them. Here he adds a reference to those outside his realm, the borderers, that they should be reassured that they will get only happiness, not unhappiness, from him and should therefore not be agitated on his account. (Apparently there were unconquered people, probably tribes in the 'Great Wilderness' (Mahākāntāra) of the mountainous and then inaccessible region between Kaliṅga and Avanti.) If possible he will 'tolerate' (or forgive, *kṣam*) them and they should understand this, practice principle and gain this world and the next...He is appointing agents (*yuktaka*) at different points for this...(Clearly there will be no further military expansion of the Empire, and Aśoka hopes this will be understood and the reason for it understood: he also seems to imply that he hopes to be able to tolerate the actions of the borderers but that there is a limit to this, beyond which he might have to resort to force. If they were uncivilised tribes in the forests and in the habit of raiding settlements or ambushing roads the position would be clear enough.)

In a later edict[1] Aśoka refers to another event of this same year (the tenth after his consecration, i.e. B.C. 259): In the past kings used to go out on journeys, (*yātrā*) for pleasure, for instance hunting and similar enjoyments. But Devānāmpriya Priyadarśin ten years after his consecration went out to the Enlightenment (Tree, i.e. he made a pilgrimage to Bodh Gayā). This is a journey for principle (*dharma*), on which there is the seeing of brahmans and *śramaṇas* and donations to them, seeing elders and assisting them with money, seeing the people of the country and instruction in principle and discussions about principle. There is greater pleasure by that means for King Devānāmpriya Priyadarśin, another 'share' (i.e. additional to the 'share' = taxes received by him from the people).

The later Buddhist histories refer to the same event, it

1. 'Rock Edict 8', Bloch 111 ff.

appears,[1] but in a legendary manner: Aśoka held a great festival after building numerous dwellings (*vihāras*) for the monks. Tāranātha actually mentions the visit to the Enlightenment Tree.

In the twelfth year (B.C. 257) we find another series of edicts issued:[2] (1) No votive offerings are to be made with living beings (i.e. animal sacrifice is prohibited). With some exceptions, assemblies (*samāja*) are bad (cf. p. 182 above). The killing of living beings for food has been restricted and will henceforth cease so far as the royal kitchen is concerned. (2) The King has everywhere established medical services for men and animals. Medicinal herbs have been distributed and planted everywhere for this purpose. Roots and fruits have been distributed and planted wherever they were lacking. Wells have been dug and trees planted along the roads for the enjoyment of men and animals. This has been done everywhere in the realm and among the borderers, including the Coḍas (Coḷas), Pāṇḍyas, Sātyaputras, Keraḍas (four countries of the extreme South of India: the states of Tamilnādu and Kerala with Southern Karṇāṭaka) as far as Tāmraparṇī (Ceylon) and the Greek King Aṃtiyoka (Antiochus II Theos of Syria) and his neighbours. (3) Everywhere in the realm my agents (*yukta*, officials), inspectors (*rājūka*) and district commissioners (*pradeṣṭṛ*) will go out on tour every five years with the 'instruction on principle' (*dharmānuśāsti*) and on other business. (What follows appears to be a summary of this 'instruction'.) Listening attentively to parents is good (*sādhu*), so is generosity to friends, acquaintances, relatives, brahmans and *śramaṇas*, also not taking life, little expenditure and little wealth. (4) For many centuries taking life has increased, and violence to living beings. So has lack of sympathy (*saṃpratipatti*—concurrence) for relatives and for brahmans and *śramaṇas*. Now the sound of drums is the sound of principle (*dharma*—and not of war). Now various divine sights (*rūpa*) are shown to men: mansions (*vimāna*, palaces of the gods), elephants, masses of fire, and others. This is because of the 'instruction in principle', which had not been known for

1. On this see Eggermont 90 ff.
2. Rock Edicts 1-4, Bloch 90 ff.

many centuries, of the King: not taking life, non-violence to living beings, sympathy for relatives, sympathy for brahmans and *śramaṇas*, listening attentively to parents, listening attentively to elders. This practice of principle will increase in these and other ways...moreover the sons, grandsons and great-grandsons of the King will increase it still further, until the universe involves ...instruction in principle is the best action...

This group of four edicts seems very closely related to the Buddhist texts we read in Chapter Six. There had been an ideal society in the past, which remained more or less intact until the emperors failed to maintain principle. It can be restored in the future until eventually the universe involves (and all beings go to the heaven of radiance). The main guiding principles there were non-violence, generosity (including grants to the poor in the *sūtra* on the emperors), learning what is good from *śramaṇas* and brahmans and finding out how to achieve benefit and happiness. Aśoka's remark about assemblies is no doubt to be understood in the light of the *sūtra* on 'discipline' for the layman: addiction to assemblies is harmful, but there are some assemblies which are good, probably because they illustrate principle or other good things. The performance of dramas was already a prominent feature of such public assemblies in India. The scanty evidence suggests that the drama grew out of dancing which represented myths and legends of the Brahmanical tradition, sometime before the 4th century B.C. (substantially earlier because we have a reference[1] from the time of the Nandas to text books on acting). Alongside the religious and heroic drama, comedies and satirical plays existed from an early period. Aśoka probably would not find much to his taste in the myths of the Brahmanical gods, or in the heroic episodes from the epic, or in comedy. On the other hand we have seen in this Chapter that by this period the Buddhists too were beginning to develop, if not yet drama proper at least dramatic dialogues apparently meant to be performed. The Buddhists substituted stories from the *Jātaka* for those of the epic, and adapted the mythical episodes, such as the wars between the gods and the demons, to illustrate

---

1. In Pāṇini's Grammar (IV. 3. 110), cf. IKL I pp. 18, 20, 123f., 133, II 110 ff.

Buddhist ethical ideas (as we shall see below); they also showed gods visiting the Buddha and popular episodes from the life of the Buddha. The allusion to 'good assemblies' therefore might well refer to these Buddhist performances of the period.

The 'divine sights' mentioned by Aśoka here are more difficult to explain. The most obvious possibility would be that this is another reference to divine portents seen by men in India as a response to the institution of principle by the emperor (but in so interpreting the earlier edict we were simply following a conjecture which seems probable). The present edict is more difficult because the whole text is obscurely constructed and can be read in different ways. We have no space here for discussion of textual problems, so it must suffice to say that the main alternative explanation is that the sights in question were not actual portents but shows put on by men, that Aśoka refers to processions or performances in which figures of the gods, or actors appearing as gods, were shown in their starry mansions, mounted on the celestial elephants (well known to Brahmanical mythology) and accompanied by heavenly fires (the element of fire and light prevails in the heavens).

To the same year (twelfth of the reign, B.C. 257) belong two short inscriptions[1] bestowing excavated dwellings and shrines (or temples) on the Ājīvaka Community (the excavation of dwellings, *vihāras*, and temples out of the solid rock of hillsides was regularly practised from this time on, particularly by the Buddhists; in fact little else survives from such an ancient period in India, structural buildings on the surface of the Earth having nearly all disappeared except for a few columns and the foundations which have in rare cases been identified; the reason for their popularity in India is immediately obvious to anyone who enters them: they remain delightfully cool and fresh on the hottest days). These Ājīvaka donations (another has been found from Aśoka's nineteenth year) continuing after the King had become a 'strong' Buddhist are important confirmation of his policy of toleration and support for all the 'sects'.

1. Bloch 156.

Probably to the same period belongs the inscription[1] at Bhābrā in the Matsya country (in North-East Rājasthān, corresponding roughly to the state of Jaipur). This is written in the form of a letter (there are similar letters in the *Tripiṭaka*, for example from Ajātaśatru to the Buddha, but conveyed orally by messengers) from Aśoka to the Community of Buddhist monks : 'King Priyadarśin of Magadha, having greeted the Community, says (may you be) having little illness and living comfortably (this is purely conventional, like 'best wishes'). Sirs! You know how great is my respect for and confidence in the Buddha, the Doctrine (*dharma*) and the Community (in other words that I am a Buddhist layman). Whatever has been said by the Master, the Buddha, all that is well said. Sirs ! It seems to me that in order that the True Doctrine (*saddharma*) may remain long I ought to say that these discourses on the Doctrine : *Vinayasamukkasse*, *Aliyavasāṇi*, *Anāgatabhayāni*, *Munigāthā*, *Moneyasūtte*, *Upatissapasine* and the *Lāghulovāde* concerning false speech, spoken by the Buddha, — I wish that many monks and nuns, likewise the laymen and laywomen, should hear frequently and consider these discourses on the Doctrine. I have had this written so that they may know my intention.'

As can be readily imagined, the naming of seven actual texts has led to repeated investigations by modern scholars in the attempt to identify them in the *Tripiṭaka*, with the usual contradictory conclusions which scholars are fond of arriving at, namely either that they are all to be found in the *Tripiṭaka* as known to us or that none of them can with any certainty be identified in it. Here, contrary to the usual method of this book, we give the actual words of Aśoka in Māgadhī, not in Sanskrit. It may be assumed that he was using a Māgadhī recension of the *Tripiṭaka*, still in the unadulterated Māgadhī, of which nothing appears to survive (the Sthaviravāda texts are in a Western dialect which seems to be Āvantī, the Sarvāstivāda texts are more or less in Sanskrit, the Lokottaravāda texts are in a partly Sanskritised Prakrit of uncertain dialect but central North Indian — Śaurasenī, or the dialect of Kośala ? — and not Māgadhī, there is one *Kṣudraka* text, possibly Dharmaguptaka, in Gāndhārī; at present no other *Tripiṭaka* texts seem to be available in Indian

1. Bloch 154 f.

languages, and the Chinese versions do not give us a very precise idea of the language of their originals or of the names of their constituent discourses). We know that even within the same school and dialect the same text may be referred to by different titles, still more so between different schools and dialects, hence the difficulty of identifying some of Aśoka's texts need cause no surprise. Some of them at least seem clear : the *Aliyavasāṇi* are the four *āryavaṃśas*,[1] that a monk should be contented with whatever he gets in the way of robes, food and resting place and should find pleasure in 'development' and abandoning. The *Anāgatabhayas*[2] are probably the five 'fears for the future' of monks in the forest, that they may meet with a premature death at the hands of men or animals, through accidents or bad food, etc., and thinking of this danger they should therefore be energetic to acquire and experience what they have not yet attained (i.e. in meditation, etc.). The *Munigāthā* is presumably the *Kṣudraka* text[3] listed in the last Chapter, the 'Recluse Strophes' in praise of the recluse who goes alone to find calm, annihilating the production of further existences, who is strong in understanding, virtue and concentration, finds pleasure in meditation and self-possession, is fearless as a lion, clean as a lotus and so on. The *Moneyasūtte* is probably a version of a very early Sthaviravāda poem,[4] now embedded in the later additions of a prologue and preliminary dialogue (easily distinguished by the difference of metre), on the same subject of 'recluseship' (*mauneya*), praising calm and detachment, considering others as like oneself and hence abstaining from violence, freedom from wishes, meditation in the forest, and the like. The *Lāghulovāde* specified to be about false speech must be the *sūtra* in the *Madhyama*[5] where the Buddha admonishes Rāhula (Māgadhī Lāghula) against 'conscious false speech.' The *Upatissapasine*, i.e. 'Question of Upatiṣya (=Śāriputra)' is a matter of guesswork because Śāriputra asks many questions in the *Tripiṭaka*. Lamotte

1 As at A II 27.ff.
2. E. g. at A III 100ff.
3. Sthaviravāda version at Sn verse 207 ff.
4. Sn 701 ff.
5. M No. 61, T 26 No. 14.

suggests[1] the so-called *Śāriputra Sūtra*, one of the *Arthavargīya Sūtras* in the *Kṣudraka*,[2] where Śāriputra asks about the life of the monk and is told by the Buddha that he should have no fears, should be energetic, should not steal or speak falsely, should cultivate benevolence, etc. Finally the *Vinayasamukkasse* may be either the 'exalted' *Vinaya* itself or, which comes to the same thing, a text 'exalting' the *Vinaya*, such as one in the Sthaviravāda *Ekottara*.[3] There are other possibilities for some of the texts mentioned, but these identifications seem probable. There is at least no question of having to look outside the *Tripiṭaka* as we now know it for Aśoka's selection, although he was using a version inaccessible to us.

Though he mentions lay disciples in his letter, the texts favoured by Aśoka all bear on the life of the monks (except in that that on false speech is of general application, though it too was an admonition to a monk—the Buddha's son Rāhula). They also, however, mention the ethical standards to which Aśoka was devoted. As elsewhere, Aśoka does not concern himself with the philosophy of Buddhism, except in this ethical and practical application of the standards of non attachment and of considering all beings as like oneself. It is the Way, not the theory, on which he concentrates, or rather on which he would have the monks, nuns and lay disciples concentrate. The Buddhist Community should perfect itself according to its standards and recommend itself to the laity in this way.

A further series of ten edicts was issued in B.C. 256.[4] Aśoka here shows himself pleased with his achievements so far and taking pride in them—as we shall see there were new developments in this year which show the Emperor optimistically realising his grand plan and having at least one major success in the international field. He begins: 'The good (*kalyāṇa*) is difficult; to initiate good is difficult. Now I have done much good. Now, my sons, grandsons and posterity, until the involution, continuing thus, will do good actions. But he who in this case lets even one point be abandoned will act badly, for bad is easy.'—We may think that here he is actually addressing his successors,

1. HBI p. 257.
2. Sn 955 ff.
3. A I 98 ff.
4. 'Rock Edicts 5-14', Bloch 101 ff.

urging them to continue the work he has initiated.—'In the past there were no "high officials (or ministers, *mahāmātra*) for principle (*dharma*)". They have been created by me thirteen years after my consecration. They are engaged with reference to all sects, for attention to principle and increase of principle, for the benefit and happiness of those connected with principle among the Greeks, Iranians, Gandhārans, Rāṣṭrikas (of the Sindhu region?), Pitinikas (of the country now called Gujarāt?) and other Westerners. And they are engaged among servants and masters (? reading as *bhaṭa* + *arya*), the brahmans and the wealthy, the poor, old people, for benefit and happiness, for the prevention of obstacles to those connected with principle. Also for the prevention of obstacles to the assisting of prisoners, for freeing them in certain circumstances...'

Thus a new high office has been created, a ministry of 'principle' in the special sense of Aśoka's system of ethics (distinct from the ordinary law). It is concerned with all sections of society, but particularly with the poor and otherwise needy. Its work concerns particularly the Western regions not long incorporated in Magadha and perhaps not yet reached to any appreciable extent by the Buddhist monks with their teaching (Gandhāra, probably Sindhu, the Greek and Iranian subjects of Arachosia, etc.).

In the second of these edicts Aśoka says that in the past there has sometimes been delay in actions for welfare, consequently he has now arranged that he can be reached at all times and in all places through persons stationed to inform him about the welfare of the people. If he gives orders for a donation or announcement orally, and the officials delay, or there is a dispute or 'intercession' (*nidhyāpti*) in the assembly (*pariṣat*), he should be informed immediately, everywhere, at all times. 'I have ordered this because I am never satisfied in undertakings and in the investigation of welfare, and because I consider that the benefit of all people is my business, and that can be done only in this way, and because there is no better action than the benefit of all the people. Whatever 'valour' (*parākrama*) I have is for getting free from debt to living beings In this world I make them happy and in the next may they gain heaven...'

Next Aśoka expresses the wish that all sects should live everywhere, for they all wish for self-control and purification of nature. People have varying wills and passions. They will do everything or only one point. For him who is not abundant in generosity or self-control or purification of nature or gratitude, firm devotion is always strong.— This is rather cryptic in the latter part, but the meaning of the first and the general idea seems clear : all sects are to be tolerated and encouraged to spread everywhere in the world, for all aim in some way for two essential points in self improvement. People vary greatly; perhaps, then, different sects' teachings suit them accordingly ? For the weakest of all, it seems, mere devotion (*bhakti*) is better than nothing, if it is 'firm'. The most interesting point, besides toleration (more fully discussed by Aśoka elsewhere), is that Aśoka wishes to spread all the sects, to encourage 'missionary' work. We shall see that he did this for Buddhism : we have no knowledge whether he also tried to spread Brahmanism, Ājīvakism and Jainism (the main sects he mentions in his edicts).

The next of the series is the one on the 'journey for principle' translated above (p. 251). Then Aśoka says : '...people perform varied benedictions (*maṅgala*), in illnesses, at weddings, on the birth of children, when going abroad, etc. In these cases women perform many and various benedictions which are trivial and futile. These benedictions have little result, but the benediction of principle has great result. It consists in right behaviour towards slaves and servants, honour towards elders, self-control (*saṃyama*) towards living beings, generosity to brahmans and *śramaṇas*, and other things of this sort. Then father, son, brother, husband, friend or acquaintance will say that this is good, this is the benediction which should be made— to the extent that his welfare (*artha*) is completed.' After this there are two alternative continuations in different inscriptions of this edict : (1) 'It is said that generosity is good, but there is no generosity or favour (*anugraha*) which is like the gift of principle or the favour of principle. One should be admonished by a friend, a true friend, a relative or a companion in every affair : this is what should be done, this is good. Through this one can attain heaven for oneself. And what is more worth doing than attaining heaven ?' (Again, as in the Buddha's 'systematic course of instruction' to lay disciples (see p. 187 above), the higher aim of non-attachment even to the next world, of *nirvāṇa* or freedom, is not mentioned. The edict is for the masses of the people : those who know of higher things do not need the emperor's instructions.) The other continuation is (2) 'When it is completed one will say: I will do this (benediction of principle) again, for other benedictions are doubtful. It may be that welfare will be produced (by the latter), but it may be not. In any case it is (in the latter) this-worldly, whereas the benediction of principle is timeless : if welfare is not produced in this world, infinite merit (*puṇya*) is generated in the next world; or if welfare is produced in this world then both are gained, welfare in this world and infinite merit in the next...' (One is reminded here of the 'unseen' result generated by the orthodox Brahmanical ritual, which bears fruit especially in heaven; the second continuation is in fact found in the North (North West) of India where Brahmanism had its original home, and Aśoka might deliberately have expressed himself in a manner which would seem familiar in Brahmanical circles.)

The next edict, the sixth of the series, reads : 'King Devānāmpriya Priyadarśin does not think that reputation or fame are of great significance, except that he wishes for the reputation and fame that now and in the future his people should listen attentively to principle and act in conformity to the conduct of principle...Whatever effort King Devānāmpriya Priyadarśin makes is all for the next world, so that there may be wholly 'non-danger' (*aparisrava*). Now this 'danger' is lack of merit. But this is difficult for small people or great people, except through the highest 'valour', renouncing everything, which is more difficult for the great.' Since in the Buddhist conception the 'next world', being the next life in transmigration, may be on this Earth as well as in heaven or purgatory, and likewise 'this world' is really just this (present) life, we shall probably be right in taking Aśoka's effort 'all for the next world' to refer to the future as a whole, embracing living beings reborn as men on Earth as well as the others. Alternatively he is just speaking of his personal hope for merit in his next world, to the exclusion of any desire for advantage in this present life, and then taking this as an example.

The seventh edict is little but a repetition of the first continuation of the fifth, connecting it with both the other continuation and the preceding part. It is worth looking at to see how Aśoka's wordings vary slightly and how he recombines his ideas : '...there is no generosity like the gift of principle, or the praise of principle, or the sharing of principle, or relationship in principle. In this connection it consists of : right behaviour towards slaves and servants, listening attentively to parents, generosity to friends, acquaintances, relatives, brahmans and *śramaṇas*, not harming living beings. It should be said by father, son, brother, husband, friend, acquaintance, relative, as far as neighbour : this is good, this should be done. Doing thus one gains this world and the next. There is infinite merit through this gift of principle'.

The eighth edict explains toleration towards all sects, continuing the thought of the third : 'King Devānāmpriya Priyadarśin honours all sects, those who have gone forth and householders (i.e. lay followers as well as *śramaṇas*; brahmans may be either). He honours them with generosity and with various honours. But Devānāmpriya does not think that generosity and honour is like (as good as) increase in value (in the essential part of a thing). Increase in value takes many forms, but the root of it is guarding one's speech, so that there may not be honour of one's own sect but blame of others without any connection (i.e. reason). When there is any connection it should always be done lightly. Others' sects should definitely be honoured in all connections : acting thus one increases one's own sect strongly and also helps others' sects. Acting otherwise one harms one's own sect and injures others' sects. For whoever honours his own sect or blames others' sects entirely (i.e. merely) through devotion to his own sect, thinking he will illuminate his own sect, acting thus he instead more strongly afflicts his own sect. Now only combination (*samavāya*, 'combination', 'union') is good, so that one may hear one another's doctrine (*dharma*) and listen attentively. Such is the wish of Devānāmpriya, so that all sects may be learned and may have good traditions (or good texts : *kalyāṇa āgama*). The sectarians in all places should say : Devānāmpriya does not think generosity and honour are like increase in value of all sects. Many are engaged in this matter : the high officials for principle...and other bodies. The result of this is increase of one's own sect and the illumination of principle.

The next edict is the one describing the conquest of Kaliṅga (p. 245 above). It has, however, an important continuation. First Aśoka recalls his policy, stated in the second 'Kaliṅga Edict' (p. 251 above), of tolerating, as far as possible, injuries inflicted by others : 'Whoever may cause injury, Devānāmpriya thinks he should be tolerated (or forgiven) if possible. Even the forest tribes in his realm Devānāmpriya conciliates and intercedes for. He tells them the origin (of his attitude) is remorse (evidently for the conquest of Kaliṅga), so that they (too) may be ashamed and may not kill. Devānāmpriya wishes non-injury for all beings, self-control, impartial conduct (*samacaryā*), tenderness. Devānāmpriya thinks this is the principal victory : the victory of principle. He has gained this here and over all the frontiers for six hundred leagues (roughly 2,700 miles, measured from the Western frontier this would easily cover the Greek states in Africa and Europe mentioned below), where are Antiochus (of Syria) the Greek king and beyond him four kings called Tulamaya (Ptolemy II of Egypt), Aṃtikini (Antigonus of Macedonia), Maga (Magas of Cyrene) and Alikasudara (Alexander of Epirus), and in the South Coḍa, Pāṇḍya, as far as Tāmraparṇī (Ceylon), as well as here in the King's realm among the Greeks and Iranians, Nābhakas and Nābhapaṃtis (not certainly identified, perhaps the people of Uḍḍiyāna and their neighbours, North of Gandhāra — valley of the River Suvastu), Bhojas and Pitinikas (of Southern Rājasthān and Gujarāt), Āndhras (of modern Āndhra, but probably extending further to the West) and Pāradas (there seems to have been a Pārada North of Uḍḍiyāna, but in the context of Āndhra an unknown Southern people may be referred to), everywhere they follow Devānāmpriya's instruction in principle. Where the ambassadors (*dūta*) of Devānāmpriya do not go, they too hearing of Devānāmpriya's conduct of principle, of the organisation of instruction in principle, act, or will act, in conformity to principle. What one gains by this is victory everywhere. Now everywhere victory has the taste of joy (*prīti*). This joy is obtained by the victory of principle. But this is a light joy. Devānāmpriya thinks a great result is only that which is connected with the next world. This victory of principle has been written for the purpose that my sons and grandsons should not think new victories are to be won. In their own (?) victory (in maintaining the Empire ?) only toleration and light punishment must please them, so that they should think only the victory of principle is a victory in this world and the next. Let all their pleasure be pleasure in principle, for this is for this world and for the next world as well.

The last edict of this series is merely a postscript saying that this writing on principle exists in brief, medium and detailed form; that not everything has been composed everywhere . . . Some matters which are 'sweetness' (*mādhurya*) are repeated so that people may practice them, also there may be mistakes in the writing (hence presumably people should compare different copies).

Taking up the most important 'victory of principle' edict we find in it Aśoka's clearest statement of his imperial policy. To follow the old policy, and that usual in the world at large, he ought to have set about the conquest of Syria and the other fragments of the former Persian Empire now under Greek rule. Given his resources and the commanding position already established by Candragupta in the West, as well as the divisions among the Greeks, this should not have been very difficult. The Greeks doubtless saw this and sought to maintain cordial relations, just as Aśoka was instructing his ambassadors to expound his 'principle' to them. Getting a seemingly favourable response Aśoka would attribute it to their understanding of his instruction in principle and rejoice in his 'victory of principle'. In actual fact the Greeks were pursuing their illusions of imperial glory by fighting amongst themselves, but Aśoka was either unaware of this or, more probably, expected them to learn gradually to do better.

Whatever the success of his ambassadors among the Greeks, the ambassadorial or other missions in the South had more permanent results. The most notable success was the 'victory of principle' in Ceylon. King Tiṣya of Ceylon welcomed Aśoka's son Mahendra, who had become a Buddhist monk, as ambassador, accepted the 'instruction' and became a Buddhist. This we learn from the Sthaviravāda histories preserved in Ceylon: in fact that school then became permanently established in the island, and has flourished there ever since (as it still does) with only momentary setbacks. The school there traces its tradition of texts and commentary on them from Mahendra himself. As Aśoka's son is held to have founded the community of monks in Ceylon, so a daughter of his is said to have established the community of nuns there. Many Sinhalese of aristocratic families (including the royal family) joined these communities and thus established them firmly among the local people. To seal the introduction of Buddhism, a cutting of the Enlightenment Tree was brought from Bodh Gayā and planted in Ceylon. King Tiṣya was reconsecrated as a Buddhist monarch; perhaps he also took the title Devānāmpriya at this time, which in the histories of Ceylon is the dynastic name of the long line of kings descended from Tiṣya.

Ceylon is the perfect, and the only known, example of a successful 'victory of principle'. In effect Ceylon became a close ally of Magadha, presents were exchanged and the ally adopted the ideology of the 'conqueror' completely, yet remained entirely independent politically. We do not know whether any king in South India (Coḍa, etc.) became a Buddhist, but it is certain that Buddhism became strongly established there too from Aśoka's time onwards.

The Sthaviravāda histories[1] record a systematic sending out of Buddhist missions to all parts of India, as well as Ceylon, at this time. They represent the whole operation as the work of their own school, just as they represent Aśoka himself as following their school. There may be some truth in this, but at least in view of Aśoka's professed support even of non-Buddhists and his general toleration we cannot follow the accounts of the school in making him become the exclusive patron of the Sthaviravāda. We notice, however, that the missions recorded refer to those regions in which the Sthaviravāda, as opposed to the Mahāsaṃgha (and the Vātsīputrīya), is known to have flourished. In each case, as in Ceylon too,

1. Summary in Lamotte HBI 320 ff.

the mission consisted of a group of five monks, that is to say a community competent to perform most actions, including the 'entrance' of new monks into the community provided they were outside the 'middle region' (of North India) where monks were numerous and a minimum of ten was required to perform the entrance.[1]

The histories describe the sending of missions to nine countries: Ceylon, Gandhāra (with Kaśmīra, Kashmere), the 'Greek people', Himavant (Himālaya, but apparently restricted to the upper Śatadru valley, which leads to the heart of the mountains), Aparāntaka (the West coastal region, in a restricted sense that of modern Mahārāṣṭra, in a broader sense including also Gujarāt and Sindhu), Mahiṣa (the central Narmadā valley), Mahārāṣṭra, Vanavāsa (the Nothern part of the state of Karṇāṭaka), Suvarṇabhūmi (Lower Burma, strictly the Mōn country).

It is noteworthy that Mahendra leading the Ceylon mission is stated to have set out from Vidiśā or from the Caityagiri ('Hill of the Shrine' now known as Sāñcī) a few miles from that city, capital of the Daśārṇa country between Avanti and Vatsa. This is in the heart of the region where the Sthaviravāda is known to have had its greatest strength in this period. He probably travelled via Kāñcī in the north of the Coḍa country, which later was a stronghold of the school. Although the histories do not mention this, it seems that Madhyama and Kāśyapa who led the mission to Himavant also started from Caityagiri, for inscriptions there record that their ashes were preserved in urns in one of the pagodas.

The mission to Gandhāra was led by Madhyāntika, known also to other schools of Buddhism, who preserve stories of how he established not only Buddhism but civilisation in Kaśmīra, till then a land of dragons. He is supposed in particular to have introduced the cultivation of the valuable saffron plant, source of prosperity to the valley. We may note that the Kashmiri historian Kalhaṇa records that Aśoka founded the old capital of Kaśmīra, Śrīnagarī, now ruins on the outskirts of modern Śrīnagara. Kaśmīra was long to be a stronghold of Buddhism.

1. Vin I 197, 319.

The 'Greek people' were probably those of the colonies within the Empire, particularly in Arachosia. Aparāntaka, Mahiṣa, Mahārāṣṭra and Vanavāsa form a continuous stretch of country down the Western side of India, carrying Buddhism beyond Avanti, which had perhaps been till this time the South-Western limit of the spread of the Doctrine. There is no other record of Buddhism spreading to Burma so early, though there is nothing impossible in this. It is curious, however, that Eastern India is not mentioned here, for a mission to Burma must have started from there (not yet from Ceylon!). The Burmese histories naturally accept this agreeable story of the antiquity of Buddhism in their country.

As to the East, it is likely that missions to Vaṃga (Bengal) and Kaliṅga (and afterwards Āndhra) were organised by the Mahāsaṃgha. It is strange that Coḍa finds no place, but it was always closely associated with Ceylon in its Buddhism.

Thus we see Buddhism spread over most of the Empire, and in the South well beyond it. Part of this expansion may have begun before Aśoka's reign, but such a grand strategy of missions is likely to have required the enthusiastic support of the emperor who dominated the whole continent of India to be successful. Whatever had been done before, we know from Aśoka's edicts that this support, especially for the popularising of Buddhism among the masses of the people, was richly bestowed on the Buddhist Community. At its origin Buddhism was international to the extent that the Buddha taught in at least half a dozen different countries and established a movement above political boundaries. Now that movement was momentarily enclosed in one Empire, with its allies to the South, but it was becoming more fully international in that it was established among non-Aryan peoples (Dravidians, Greeks, and probably others, if not yet the Mōns of Burma) in addition to every Aryan country, including distant Ceylon. According to Eggermont's rectified chronology[1] the mission to Ceylon arrived there in the twelfth year of Aśoka's reign (November, B.C. 257).

In this same period, according to the inscriptions and

1. *Chronology*, 99 ff.

the Buddhist histories, Aśoka was engaged in another method of spreading Buddhism: the erection of pagodas in all parts of his empire. An inscription[1] of the year 14 (255) finds him at Nigalisagar in Nepal, enlarging the pagoda of — not 'our' Buddha but the last but one before him (Konākamana), for by now the idea that the Buddha was one of a series was well established (see the *Mahāvadāna Sūtra* on some of them, p. 116 above). The year 20 (249) brought him on pilgrimage to Lumbinī Park, the birthplace of 'our' Buddha, Śākyamuni as Aśoka calls him in the inscription[2] there, where he announces a reduction in the tax paid by the village 'because the Master was born here'. According to the histories, however, which seem substantially confirmed by archaeology, he did far more than erect a stone column and double the size of Konākamana's pagoda. He opened up most of the original pagodas and took from them the relics of the Buddha. These he divided into 84,000 parts and built as many pagodas in order to distribute them all over his empire, to consecrate it, as it were, for Buddhism. According to the Sarvāstivāda tradition the monk Upagupta led Aśoka to all the most important places connected with the life, or legend, of the Buddha. The *Mañjuśrīmūlakalpa*[3] records the erecting of the stone columns to mark some of the sites. In this way Buddhism was made into something physically accessible to the entire population. At the same time there was a movement to reduce its teachings to stories and to artistic presentation in sculpture and painting, along with the symbols such as lotus, tree, wheel and pagoda representing the life of the Buddha.

According to the tradition[4] all Aśoka's pagodas were built simultaneously, and so that this could be done (and presumably so that they could all be inaugurated simultaneously) the monk Yaśas at the main *vihāra* in Pāṭaliputra, the capital, is said to have covered the Sun with his hand (as a signal). Eggermont takes this as a reference to the total solar eclipse visible in India on May 4th B.C. 249. The monks might in fact have predicted this eclipse and arranged for the completion of certain

1. Bloch 158.
2. Bloch 157.
3. Lamotte has translated the relevant passage, HBI 263 f.
4. *Aśokāvadāna*, Lamotte HBI 262, Eggermont, *Chronology*, 123.

important pagodas in time for it, after which the *poṣadha* night ceremonies (it being new moon) would follow at all the places.

In B.C. 243 a new series of edicts was issued and engraved on stone columns.[1] In this twenty sixth year of his reign one wonders whether any change in attitude will be reflected in the edicts, any development of thought reflecting Aśoka's experience so far in implementing his 'principle'. On the whole, however, these edicts reaffirm the earlier ideas with small adjustments of detail and perhaps here and there an added note of urgency or impatience, even anxiety about his administrative machinery.

'...This world and the next world are difficult to "concur in" (*sam-prati-pad*—harmonise with, or gain ?) except through the highest love of principle, the highest examining, the highest listening attentively, the highest fear, the highest energy (*utsāha*). But through my instruction with the intention of principle the love of principle has increased and will increase from day to day. My officers, high, low and intermediate, act in conformity and "concur" enough to exhort (or "make conform" ?) fickle persons (*capala*; this is a new note). Likewise the frontier high officials. This is the means (*vidhi*, or perhaps "injunction") : maintaining by principle, organising by principle, making happy by principle, protection by principle.

'...Principle is good. But what is principle ? It is little evil (or "influence", if *āsinava* is equivalent to *āsrava*), much good (*kalyāṇa*), compassion, generosity, truth, purity. The gift of insight also has been given by me in many ways. I have done various favours to bipeds and quadrupeds, birds and fish, up to saving their lives, and many other good things have been done by me...

'One will see only the good (in one's own actions) : I have done this good. One will not see the bad... —For this is difficult to look at. But this is to be seen thus: if it is irascibility, cruelty, anger, pride (conceit), envy (spite), then it is called "going to evil (or to the influences)"—let me not give way for this reason. It is to be seen strongly: this is for welfare in this world, or rather this is for welfare in the next world.

1. Bloch 161 ff.

'...My inspectors are responsible for hundreds of thousands of living beings among the people. I have given the inspectors authority to take action and to punish, so that they may continue their work encouraged and fearless, may bring and favour benefit and happiness to the people and the country. They will know what makes happy and unhappy, and with the agents (*yukta*) of principle (or perhaps simply those connected with principle as on p. 258, which may mean persons in official positions, locally, or even no more than those who are sympathetic to Aśoka's programme) will strongly (*vi-*) admonish the people and the country, so that they may gain this world and the next...It is to be wished that there should be impartiality (*samatā*) of practice (especially of legal procedure) and of punishment. So far this has been my practice: men in prison who are condemned to death have been given three days' grace; relatives will intercede (*ni-dhyā* causative) for their lives, or in the absence of these they will give donations for the next world or will fast...'

The fifth edict of this series gives a list of animals which are not to be killed (mostly wild animals not used for food: those which are so used have been the subject of earlier edicts urging abstention from animal food) and adds other laws protecting animal life from harm. The series concludes with a reaffirmation that the benefit and happiness of the world is Aśoka's concern, whether people are near or far he regards them as if they were his relatives, he has honoured all sects in various ways but he thinks the chief thing is to go to them himself.

We notice here that the general policy of non-violence does not exclude stern legal measures and the enforcement of law, with the use even of the death penalty. It is hard to say whether this was a new development in Aśoka's policy, following, perhaps, experiments in gentleness which failed to produce the desired results. Certainly we see that Aśoka was not as utopian and unrealistic as is sometimes supposed, but discriminated very carefully between his ultimate ideal, however impatient he was to attain it, and the practical situation which confronted him. Thus it has been thought that he was responsible for the decline of the Magadhan Empire which began within half a century of his death: that he had undermined its military power, having renounced war altogether, and left the frontiers open to the Greek barbarians, who speedily took advantage of the situation, whilst various provinces were seized by local adventurers. It has been suggested in an earlier publication[1] that, on the contrary, Aśoka's policy, his acceptance of Buddhism and attempt to apply it, was not the cause of an imperial crisis but rather the effect of the problems which confronted him. It is true that he himself expresses his horror at a slaughter in war which seems trivial by our modern standards, but at the same time he does not renounce what he calls 'victory'. Convinced that war is the wrong means, perhaps seeing further that war is not a means at all to any final and permanent victory over the whole known world (the recent history of Persia and Macedonia might have shown him this), he sought a better and more effective means to the same end, or at least to the modified end of a universal rule by principle, if not by a single emperor.

In the following year (242) is dated another series of general edicts[2] (but usually numbered merely as No. 7 of the preceding series), the last such series at present known, which, however, has so far been found on only one column, appended to the previous series. In the first of these Aśoka says that in the past kings had wished to increase principle but it had not increased. Wondering how he could make the increase of principle 'spring up' (*abhi-ud-nam*) he himself had thought of causing recitations of principle to be heard, and of various ways of disseminating instruction in principle. He had also created the columns of principle and the high officials for principle. In the second he says that he has had banyans planted along the roads to give shade to animals and men, and has had gardens of mangoes planted. He has had wells (or cisterns) dug at the half *krośas* (which would be at intervals of a little over half a mile) and resting places (?) made. Many wells (or more generally drinking places) have been constructed everywhere for the advantage (or profit) of animals and men. But the advantage of this is 'light', for former kings and himself have in various ways made the world happy with ways to

1. REBCS 46, footnote.
2. Bloch 168 ff.

happiness. He has done this rather so that they (people) shall follow the practice of principle (i.e., presumably, by giving material security he expects to provide a basis for principle in behaviour). In the third he refers again to the high officials for principle, who are engaged among all the sects, among their lay disciples as well as those who have gone forth. He has ordered them to be engaged with the Community (of the Buddhists), for its welfare, and with the brahmans, Ājīvakas and Jainas, and among various sects (here we see that Aśoka regards those four sects as the main ones, probably in that order of importance; in fact these are the only sects named in any of the inscriptions so far known). There are high officials for each sect. These and other officials are engaged in distributing his gifts and those of his queens and sons, who have been encouraged to give donations and follow the practice of principle so that the compassion, generosity, truthfulness, purity, tenderness and goodness (*sādhava*) of the people shall increase.

Next Aśoka says that whatever good things he has done, he has done that people, following the practice (following his example ?), will act in conformity to it and so make increase of : listening attentively to parents, listening attentively to elders, following the practice of seniors in age, sympathy for (or concurrence with) brahmans, *śramaṇas*, the poor, the unfortunate (or weak), down to slaves and servants. Finally, there are only two ways of increasing the principle of men: by regulations of principle or by intercession (or appeal, *nidhyāpti*; the idea is causing people to consider their behaviour). But in this connection regulations of principle are 'light', intercession is greater. He has made many regulations of principle, such as that such and such species are not to be killed, but it is through intercession (persuasion) that there is greater increase in principle of men, for harmlessness (*avihiṃsā*) towards beings, not taking the lives of living beings. He adds that he has done this so that his sons and descendants may follow the practice as long as the Sun and Moon exist... and that this writing of principle should be made where there are stone columns or stone tablets so that it may endure long.

The 'All Exist' and other Schisms

There is an undated edict[1] of a special kind which Eggermont suggests is later than the one we have just read (which otherwise would be the last now known, with the possible exception of an obscure undated inscription commemorating a donation by a 'second queen' not otherwise known). It concerns schisms in the Buddhist communities of monks and nuns. Aśoka expresses the wish that the Community remain in unanimity for a long time and lays down that any monk or nun who would split the Community should be made to dress in white clothes (the lay dress) and to live outside the dwelling (of the Community), in other words should be expelled. The high officials are to promulgate this in their districts, among the monks and nuns and also among the lay disciples.

Apparently the intention is that the secular authorities should force schismatics to live as laymen : clearly there was no power in the Buddhist communities themselves to prevent a schismatic group from going off, even if expelled by them, and continuing to live separately as a community of their own. This is evidently what happened at the several schisms which have been recorded. Aśoka's measure, however, would appear to be dangerous in that it might seem to give his officials (or himself) power to intervene between two parties in an internal dispute in the Community, and to decide which should be expelled if they could not be reconciled. In fact the Buddhist histories record interventions by Aśoka's ministers with disastrous results, of course through exceeding their instructions.

It is not known what Aśoka proposed to do about the fact that the Buddhists were already split into at least five schools. In view of his tolerance for a variety of sects outside Buddhism would he not tolerate schools within it ? Apparently his idea of 'increasing the value' of each sect included preventing internal dissension, and probably he thought he was carrying out the wishes of the Buddha himself in this, since there is much legislation in the *Vinaya* designed to prevent schisms. Can we discover which of the existing schools, if any, he preferred ? Among the schools it is the Sthaviravāda which claims the

1. Bloch 152 f. All three copies are mutilated near the beginning. A date could have been effaced.

closest association with the Emperor and records his direct intervention in the affairs of the Community, at first clumsily through a minister, later with the satisfactory result for the school of supporting them against groups holding false opinions, who were then expelled and made laymen. This affair, they say, was concluded by a 'third' rehearsal of the *Tripiṭaka.* The Sarvāstivāda school also claims a special association in that Upagupta, who led Aśoka on his great pilgrimage, was the leader of their school. Of other schools we seem to have no direct records, but only accounts perhaps partly derived from them in later Mahāyāna histories such as that of Tāranātha. These accounts do not record any schism or expulsion or rehearsal, but only that Aśoka instituted a quinquennial festival (*pañcavarṣa*) for the Community. There is considerable confusion in the records of the Sarvāstivāda and Mahāyāna writers, especially in that they have generally identified Aśoka the Just with Aśoka the Black when compiling accounts from earlier sources. The Sarvāstivādins have then recorded a schism with a decision by the Emperor against themselves, their expulsion and retirement to Kaśmīra, which afterwards with Gandhāra became their stronghold. This schism, however, would appear to be nothing but the First Schism when the majority of monks, with Nanda support, constituted themselves into the Mahāsaṃgha.[1] Thus all the events from the Vaiśālī Affair in the time of Aśoka the Black down to those of the reign of Aśoka the Just have been condensed into a single reign.

The most probable interpretation of the confused evidence is, as Bareau concluded, that Aśoka was closely associated with the Sthaviravāda school (not the Mahāsaṃgha schools or the Vātsīputrīya) and that it was this school which during his reign was threatened with a schism. This schism was that of the Sarvāstivāda, the All Exist School, which at this time seceded from the Sthaviravāda. As to the date of the schism, we may follow Eggermont in placing it not as given by the Sthaviravāda tradition (year 18 of Aśoka) but towards the end of the reign, probably in B. C. 237, which would also be the date of the schism edict. The Sthaviravāda tradition, we

1. We follow Bareau in all this, *Les premiers conciles.*

must note, does not record the affair as a schism, but simply as the expulsion of persons who were not Buddhists, followers of other sects who had joined the favoured Community. They were expelled not for reasons of discipline but for holding false (non-Buddhist) opinions about metaphysical questions. Now it is in fact the Sarvāstivāda school which has quite often been accused of holding a view indistinguishable from the Brahmanical Sāṃkhya philosophy (a form of 'eternalism'). If Aśoka carried out his threat of expulsion and reduction to the status of laymen against them then the Sthaviravāda would not record a schism within their community, although in fact the expelled monks evaded reduction to the laity by retiring to a remote part of the Empire and continuing their own community there. As they had themselves formed part of the united Sthaviravāda school favoured by Aśoka earlier in his reign they preserved a tradition that it was a monk of their own school, Upagupta, by whom the Emperor was guided in his good work of popularising Buddhism. The orthodox Sthaviravādins on the other hand have, according to Eggermont, invented an apocryphal 'third rehearsal', reaffirming their perfect orthodoxy and continuity, and at the same time backdated it to the time of the mission to Ceylon and made their school in the island stem directly from this orthodox rehearsal.

The peculiar doctrine of the Sarvāstivāda school, which gave it its name, is that all principles (all the elements or natural principles, *dharmas*, which by now had been carefully enumerated and classified in the *Abhidharma*) exist, and moreover this 'existence' embraces also the existence of past and future occurrences of the principles. Against this the orthodox Sthaviravāda maintained that as to past principles only those past actions which had not yet produced their results could be said in any sense to exist (being still in a sense effective), but even these could not be considered as existing themselves in the same way as present principles. No future principles could be said to exist. All those schools of Buddhism which make this distinction of principles in time into two categories, those which 'exist' and those which do not 'exist', are sometimes called *vibhajyavādins*, 'distinctionists', as opposed to the Sarvāstivādins (the Mahāsaṃgha and Vātsīputrīya schools were distinctionists, like the Sthaviravāda).

The critics of the Sarvāstivāda sometimes pointed out that if past principles continue to exist this implies eternalism, and is tantamount to the Sāṃkhya doctrine which by this time had been worked out among the brahmans, that the universe consists of eternal souls and eternal matter, all effects being pre-existent in their causes and all causes continuing to exist in their effects, so that the original, primeval matter existed eternally in all the modifications or effects arisen from it (this doctrine derived originally from the theories of Uddālaka, the original 'being' and everything evolved from it). It is perhaps remarkable that a doctrine of this kind should have led to a schism among the Buddhists: we can merely point out that this was the period of the elaboration of the *Abhidharma* as a comprehensive statement of the nature of the universe, of what exists as well as the causal processes which are the essence of Buddhist doctrine. Consequently a somewhat metaphysical disagreement could loom large in debates among the Buddhist communities at that time. The schools were now going beyond the doctrines as stated by the Buddha and raising points not clearly covered, even by implication, in his dialogues and discourses. The Mahāsaṃgha and Vātsīputrīyas experienced similar disagreements and resulting schisms in this period.

No evidence seems to be available indicating the precise dates of the schisms in other schools in the period after the 'personality schism' and the roughly contemporary schisms in the Mahāsaṃgha. After Vātsīputra had given his school the *Abhidharma* in nine sections, his followers set to work to develop this further by studying the *Sūtra*.[1] The result of these studies in *abhidharma*, however, was the production of no less than four new schools: dissatisfied with the *Abhidharma* in nine sections each of these added its own new texts to complete the statement of its doctrines.[2] The four new schools were called Dharmottarīya, Bhadrayāṇīya, Saṃmitīya and Ṣaṇṇāgarika. Little is known of them except for the Saṃmitīyas, whose special *abhidharma* text, the **Āśrayaprajñaptiśāstra*- (or **Saṃmitīyaśāstra*), happens to have been preserved in a Chinese translation.[3] No

1 Lamotte HB 587.
2. Lamotte HB 209.
3. Translated into English by K. Venkataramanan in *Viśvabhāratī Annals* Vol. V, 1953

other text of any of these schools, or of the Vātsīputrīya itself, appears to have survived. The special subject of the extant Saṃmitīya text is a particular explanation of the doctrine of the 'person' (as a 'concept based on the groups', i.e. not different from them). Very likely the corresponding special texts of its rival schools also dealt with this question, each in its own way. The traditional date for the schisms which produced these four schools is the middle part of the third century after the *parinirvāṇa*[1], which would cover approximately the reign of Aśoka. In later centuries the main centres of these schools seem to have been in Western Mahārāṣṭra, Gujarāt and Sindhu.

In roughly the same period the Mahāsaṃgha produced a new offshoot (from the Ekavyavahārikas ?), the Lokottaravāda, of whom at least four *Vinaya* texts have survived in Indian languages and been used in our earlier chapters, particularly for the life of the Buddha, as representing the Mahāsaṃgha tradition (*Mahāvastu*, *Prātimokṣasūtra*, etc.). The name of this school means 'transcendent' school, and refers to the nature of the Buddha as a being transcending the world.[2] In attaining *nirvāṇa* he would be agreed to be transcendent by all the schools, but the question at issue here was whether in some sense he was a special kind of being, a transcendent being, already before this, even before the renunciation, even at his birth. We do not know how far the Lokottaravāda school went along this line of speculation: the ultimate result of it was to lead to the transcendentalist views of the Mahāyāna on the nature of the Buddha. The chief contribution of the Lokottaravāda appears to have been their unorthodox *Vinaya* text, the *Mahāvastu*, as perhaps the first full scale attempt to collect all the traditions concerning the biography of the Buddha, including a good many *jātakas*, into one great book (even so it carries the story no further than the Buddha's visit to Kapilavastu and the going forth of Rāhula—see p. 56 above; evidently it was in fact an expansion of the original *Vinaya* narrative of the foundation of the Buddhist

1. Vasumitra, *Samayabhedoparacanacakra*.

2. Paramārtha (Demiéville *MCB* I 45) says that (opposing the Ekavyavahārikas) they held that only transcendent principles (which included the way) were real; worldly principles being mere concepts resulting from error (delusion), cf. Takakusu, *Essentials*, p. 118.

community). That this book has come down to us is due to the fact that it found favour among some of the Mahāyānists and was preserved in Nepal in Mahāyāna libraries. The text of the *Mahāvastu* as now extant may be the work of several centuries of gradual elaboration of doctrine. It states that even the body of the Buddha is not of this world, is transcendental (I 167f.), and his actions, though seemingly those usual among men, are done merely for the sake of convention, not through actual need. He, or rather in this case Buddhas, plural (I 168), never feel fatigue, though they conform to the practice of lying down, they wash their feet, though no dust can stick to them, and so on, everything about them is transcendental (I 159).

Some time after this 'transcendent schism' apparently in the Ekavyavahārika school, the Mahāsaṃghika's other offshoot the Gokulika (or Kukkuṭika or Kaurukullaka) school threw out two further branches, the Bahuśrutīya (probably first) and the Prajñaptivāda (which seceded from the Bahuśrutīya, according to Paramārtha). Both these seem to have arisen through the *abhidharma* type of discussions (in which the Gokulikas are believed to have specialised). The dates of their origin most probably fell towards the end of the third century B.C. The Bahuśrutīyas, whose name means 'learned', were founded by a monk named Yājñavalkya[1] and the Prajñaptivāda, the 'concept school' (on *prajñapti* cf. p. 110 above), by a certain Mahākātyāyana (but this latter may represent only a claim to derive from one of the Buddha's leading disciples, of that name, cf. pp. 219f., and therefore to teach the original doctrine of Buddhism). Like the Gokulikas, the Bahuśrutīyas hold[2] that all emotions are really unhappiness and all principles have the principle of falsity, only extinction is non-false and ultimately real. The five groups are real but are unhappiness, which also is ultimately real. But the groups

1. According to Paramārtha (Demiéville MCB I 48) Yājñavalkya was supposed to have been a personal pupil of the Buddha who had heard all his teaching but at the time of the *parinirvāṇa* was in deep meditation, from which he emerged two centuries later. Finding the old Mahāsaṃgha understood the *Tripiṭaka* only superficially he expounded its 'profound' meaning, thereby producing a schism. Agreeably to this legend the school of Yājñavalkya held as a special doctrine that life could be prolonged indefinitely by meditation (probably by the 'bases of power').

2. Harivarman's *Tattvasiddhi*, Thesis, Katsura, 1974.

are impermanent and perceiving this is knowledge of emptiness, their cessation is their non-soul-ness. The thought even of emptiness ceases in final extinction. The special doctrine of this school, according to Vasumitra, was that the Buddha had a 'transcendent' teaching, having the power to produce the way, indicated by the five words 'impermanence', 'unhappiness', 'emptiness', 'non-soul' and 'extinction'. The rest of his teaching was 'of the world'.

No Prajñaptivāda text seems now to be available. From the account of Vasumitra and the commentary of Paramārtha and Ki-tsang on it[1] we find they had a special *abhidharma śāstra* which explained the *Sūtra* by distinguishing various kinds of statement in it, and various statuses of object referred to. They applied the distinction of 'ultimate' (*paramārtha*) from 'concealing' (*saṃvṛti*) statements (see p. 150 above), i.e. of philosophical truth from everyday 'truth'. Their characteristic doctrine, on which, presumably, they seceded, was evidently the distinction of real (**tattva*) principles (*dharma*) referred to in the Buddha's teaching from mere 'concepts' (*prajñapti*), i. e. words which did not refer to ultimate realities (but presumably only to superficial appearances). Thus the twelve spheres (*āyatana*), i.e. the six senses and their six kinds of object, are not 'real' but 'conceptual' —likewise the 18 'elements', *dhātus*. On the other hand the five groups (*skandha*) are real, so is unhappiness. Apparently they set up as a separate category of statements in the *Sūtra* those about causation.

Buddhist Poetry in the Time of Aśoka

The Sthaviravāda *Tripiṭaka* preserves a poem[2] ascribed to one of Aśoka's brothers, Tiṣya, who became a monk. The metre seems to confirm this date. Here are some extracts:

...Alone and master of my welfare I'll quickly enter the delightful grove
which creates joy for ascetics and is frequented by wild elephants.
Having splashed my limbs in the cool mountain ravine

1. Vasumitra, *Samayabhedoparacanacakra*, translated by Bareau, *JA* 1954, 247f.; the commentary quoted by Lamotte HBI 208.

2. Thag 537 ff. cf. *Mahāvaṃsa* V. 154ff.

I'll walk about alone in the cool wood full of flowers...
I'll pierce through ignorance, sitting on the peak of a
mountain as the cool fragrant wind blows by...

More closely connected with the ideas of Aśoka himself is the poetry of the *Dharmapada*, included in the *Kṣudraka*. This is an anthology which drew on the more original parts of the *Sūtra* and added further verses to it. Most of it consists of single quatrains, sometimes a pair of them go together. These are probably of widely varying dates but the average metrical structure of the Sthaviravāda recension[1] indicates the early 3rd century B.C. as the average date. The important point about this anthology is its popular and non-technical character, expressing the social ideals of Buddhism and very much in harmony with the policy and 'practice' Aśoka was trying to implement. Here are a few quatrains :

Hatreds are never settled by hatred in this world,
by non-hatred they are settled — this is an eternal principle
(*dharma*). 5.
As one may make many garlands from a heap of flowers,
so in human life one should do much good. 53.
The scent of flowers doesn't go against the wind,
—not that of sandalwood nor *tagara* nor white jasmine,
—but the scent of the good goes against the wind,
the good man becomes known in all regions. 54.
Don't despise evil — 'It won't happen to me'—
a water jar is filled by tiny drops,
so a fool is gradually filled with evil. 121.
Who harms a harmless man,
a man pure and blameless,
the evil comes back to that fool
like fine dust thrown against the wind. 125.
Everyone dreads violence, life is dear to all :
comparing others with oneself do not kill or cause to kill. 130.
This ignorant man grows old like an ox:
his flesh increases but not his understanding ! 152.
Tolerance is the highest asceticism, and forbearance;

1. Dh. The verse numbers are given below.

the Buddhas say *nirvāṇa* is the highest (of all things):
he has not 'gone forth' who harms others,
he is not a *śramaṇa* who harasses another. 184.
Let us live very happy, not hating among the haters!
among hating men let us live not hating! 197.
Let us live very happy, who have no possessions,
let us feed on joy like the radiant gods! 200.
Conquering one generates hatred, the conquered remains in misery,
the calm one remains happy, having abandoned victory and defeat. 201.
Health is the highest gain, contentment the highest wealth,
trust the highest kinsman, *nirvāṇa* the highest happiness. 204.
Good men can be seen from afar like the Himālaya Mountain;
the bad cannot be seen even here like arrows shot in the night. 304.
As water on a lotus leaf, as a mustard seed on the point of a needle;
who does not cling to pleasures—him I call a brahman. 401.

The following significant verse which seems to belong to this period or later found a place in a *Jātaka* story (J V 483):

The sky extends far, far too spreads the earth,
the other side of the ocean they say is far,
yet farther than these they say, O king,
extends the influence of doctrines, whether true or false.

In this period can be dated probably the bulk of the dramatic dialogues in the *Saṃyukta* (according to the Sthaviravāda recension), which appear to present dramatically the contrast between Buddhist ideals and inferior ones. Perhaps these were for the good assemblies to which Aśoka alludes in one of his edicts (see pp. 252 ff. above). The first volume of the *Saṃyukta* contains about 300 pieces in mixed prose and verse and therefore assigned to the genre called *geya*, literally 'to be sung', by later commentators. Given the nature of these pieces 'sung' does not seem specially appropriate, so perhaps we should understand that these were meant 'to be performed', in a manner which would be appropriate (this is a conjecture[1], the tradition

1. But see now IKL I p. 156 and II p. 57.

does not seem to record such performances of these pieces and the commentary explains them without suggesting that they differ from other poetic texts). Nearly all these pieces are in dialogue form, especially with reference to their verses, which are uttered by different characters. In the majority of them a god utters a verse and the Buddha then caps it with a better one. About 60 of these pieces are much more dramatic in presentation: instead of the god quietly bowing to the superior ideal expressed by the Buddha an actual conflict is represented between the ideals of non-violence, forbearance and so on and the standards usually current in the world.

The wars between the gods and the demons were a popular theme of the old Brahmanical mythology. Some of the *Saṃyukta* pieces adapt these to Buddhist ends. For example in one of them[1] a battle takes place in which the gods are victorious and the king of the demons is captured and bound and brought before Śakra (Indra), the king of the gods. As he is dragged into Śakra's palace and then out again the demon shouts abusive words at the king of the gods (the actual words are not given in the text, this prose part of which merely summarises the action, but the commentary supplies examples : 'Thief ! Fool ! Ox! Donkey ! We'll win next time !'). Śakra remains silent in the face of this abuse, for which his charioteer Mātali upbraids him, and a verse dialogue takes place between these two:

M. Is it from fear, Śakra, or rather from weakness that you forbear,
hearing harsh words from Vemacitrin (the demon king)?

Ś. Not from fear nor from weakness do I tolerate Vemacitrin,
how could a discerning person like myself bandy words with a fool ?

M. Fools get angrier if no one stops them,
therefore a wise man should check a fool with violent punishment.

Ś. I think just this is the way to stop a fool:
that one who knows the other is enraged should be self-possessed and calm.

1. S I 221 f.

M. This forbearance seems to me a fault, O Vāsava (Śakra):
when a fool thinks: 'From fear he forbears with me',
the blockhead will bully you more, like a bull if you run away.

Ś. He may well think so, or not, 'From fear he forbears with me',
—there is no advantage greater than toleration, the highest of all good advantages;
Who indeed, being strong, forbears with one who is weak,
—that is called the highest toleration; the weak always forbear!
That strength is called weakness, whose strength is the strength of a fool;
there is no denier of strength which is guarded by truth.
The worse of the two, therefore, is he who counters anger with anger;
he who does not counter anger with anger wins a battle which is hard to win.
He brings about the advantage of both, his own and the other's,
who knows the other is enraged and yet is self-possessed and calm.
This is the healing of both, of oneself and the other;
people think: 'He is a fool'—if they know nothing of truth.

This is really rather out of character in the king of the gods, the old Aryan war god Indra, but in Buddhist texts he always appears as a good Buddhist: the Buddhists held that the brahmans misrepresented him in their *Veda*.

Another piece[1] is a variation on the Brahmanical myth of eclipses caused by a demon trying to swallow the Sun or Moon. In the original myth the attack is harmless because the demon had previously had his head cut off (though it remained immortal), so that the swallowed god immediately reappeared. In the Buddhist version the Sun God (or Moon God) instead appeals for help to the Buddha, in a verse. The Buddha then upbraids the demon (with a verse on compassion) who is unable to resist his words and releases his victim.

Even *nirvāṇa* can be shown dramatically[2]:

1. S I 50 f.
2. S I 133.

Death approaches the Buddhist nun Upacālā and asks her: 'Where do you wish to be reborn?' She replies: 'I do not wish to be reborn anywhere, sir.' Death utters this verse:

> 'There are the Thirty Three Gods, the Yāmas and the Tuṣitas,
> the Nirmāṇaratis and the Vaśavartins;
> let your mind aspire there, where you will experience pleasure.'

Upacālā:

> 'The Thirty Three Gods, the Yāmas and the Tuṣitas,
> the Nirmāṇaratis and the Vaśavartins,
> are bound by you with the fetters of pleasure and come again and again into Death's power.
> The whole universe is blazing, burning,
> the whole universe is flaming, shaking:
> The unshaken, immovable, not pursued by many people,
> where Death cannot go — my mind is devoted to that.'

Then Death, the evil one, was unhappy and depressed, thinking: 'The nun Upacālā knows me!' and he vanished.

The popular scene of the 'temptation' of the future Buddha by Death's daughters, Desire, Discontent and Passion, is also found in this collection.[1] They reproach him for being unfriendly, but he tells them his aim is to defeat 'the army of dear and sweet appearances' and attain welfare, peace of heart, understanding and true happiness.

The Results of the Great Experiment

There is evidence that Aśoka met with serious difficulties during the last years of his reign, apart from the schisms in the Buddhist communities. Here we have only the much later Buddhist histories to guide us, chiefly Sthaviravāda and Sarvāstivāda, and at the least they tend to exaggerate.[2] In B.C. 244, or possibly 240 (therefore either just before or just after the last two series of inscriptions), his chief queen Asaṃdhimitrā died.

1. S I 124ff.
2. See Eggermont's various discussions; Lamotte. HBI 269ff.

She had been a staunch friend, devoted to the Buddhist cause, and her loss was a disaster for the Emperor. In B.C. 240 (or 237 on the other system) he raised the ambitious and jealous Tiṣyarakṣā, who had gained influence over him by curing him of an illness, to the position of chief queen. Jealous of Aśoka's devotion to Buddhism she caused the Enlightenment Tree to be damaged three years later, though it was soon restored. She is said to have fallen in love with her stepson, Kuṇāla, the heir apparent, and then persecuted him when he rejected her, causing him to be blinded. This injury would disqualify him from ruling, thus had also the motive of removing him from the succession so that her own son could become emperor. However her scheme failed and was exposed, and it seems that during Aśoka's final illness it was Kuṇāla's son Saṃpadin (or Saṃprati) who was really in power. The main Buddhist source extant for the story of Kuṇāla, the *Divyāvadāna*, in fact says Saṃpadin became heir apparent and actually succeeded Aśoka when the latter died (in B.C. 232.)[1] Other sources, however, which include the Brahmanical histories, give various conflicting accounts of the succession, some saying that Kuṇāla in fact reigned for eight years, others that another grandson, Daśaratha, succeeded Aśoka. This latter actually records having reigned in an inscription in which he bestows excavated dwellings on the Ājīvakas. It is this final complication which suggests that the Empire was divided, Kuṇāla ruling in Gandhāra and the North West (with which he is especially connected in the literature) and Daśaratha in the East. Another possibility would be some kind of joint rule by the sons and grandsons of Aśoka.[2] In either case the later historians, particularly in the *purāṇas* (our main source for dynastic history after Aśoka), failed to understand the situation in the records before them and came to arbitrary and conflicting conclusions in the lists they eventually worked out.

Kuṇāla according to Buddhist sources suppressed a revolt in Gandhāra and later, apparently after Aśoka's death, fought a victorious war against the Greeks: it has been suggested against the Greek colonists of Bactria who revolted against the Seleucids

1. Divy 430, 433. Jaina tradition (Hemacandra: *Pariśiṣṭaparvan* IX 49-54) also makes Saṃpadin the successor of Aśoka.

2. A *kulasaṃgha*, Kauṭalya I. 17. 53.

of Syria, therefore as an ally of the latter. More doubtful tradition makes him responsible for the establishment of the Indian (Gandhāran) colony in Gaustana (Khotan, in Sinkiang), either directly, or indirectly by exiles who fled when he suppressed the revolt in Gandhāra.

If not immediately on Aśoka's death then at least eight years later Saṃpadin appears as ruler of the entire Empire. The *Divyāvadāna* says[1] that Aśoka's successor (as Saṃpadin was according to it) was not a Buddhist. In fact he was a Jaina and Jaina tradition[2] (which also makes him the direct successor of Aśoka) says that he built dwellings for the Jaina community 'even in non-Aryan countries', implying that he supported Jaina missions at least to South (Dravidian) India. In this way he was in some sense a continuator of his grandfather's work, but he may have restricted his support to one sect only. Certainly he did not please the Buddhists.

In B.C. 215 Saṃpadin was succeeded by Śāliśūka, who according to Brahmanical tradition[3] was an evil ruler opposed to *dharma* as understood by them though pretending to be *dhārmika*, 'just', and establishing what he called the 'victory of principle (*dharma*)'. Evidently he continued the policy of Aśoka, or claimed to do so, and very likely he was a Buddhist also. Unfortunately nothing more seems to be recorded of his reign (B.C. 215-202) except a somewhat obscure expedition of Antiochus III of Syria, who after suppressing the Bactrian colonists again (*c.* B.C. 206) crossed into India (i.e. the upper Kubhā valley, anciently called Kāpiśa) and 'renewed his friendship' with a certain Subhāgasena (probably Śāliśūka's governor or 'prince' in Gandhāra). This seems to imply that an Indian governor again assisted the Seleucid ally against rebels (supplying him with elephants), but it has been suggested that we should see here the beginning of Greek aggression against the unmilitary Empire of India, as also the rising movement of Brahmanical reaction against the impractical 'victory of principle' which left the frontiers insufficiently guarded.

Three more Mauryan emperors reigned after Śāliśūka, but only for short periods, of seven or eight years each, which

1. p. 418.
2. Lamotte HBI 284.
3. Lamotte HBI 284 f.

suggests their insecure position. The last of them, Bṛhadratha, was deposed in B.C. 180 by his commander in chief Puṣyamitra, who then ruled under the title of 'General' (*senāpati*). Puṣyamitra supported Brahmanism and revived the ancient rituals. Buddhist tradition speaks of a persecution of Buddhism by him, but it seems to be exaggerated. However, the victory of principle was ended.

The rebellious Bactrian Greeks succeeded in establishing their independence from Syria about B.C. 197. They fought with the Indians as well as the Seleucids and about the time of Puṣyamitra's revolt in India they invaded the North West and Gandhāra. Perhaps the revolt of the army in India was a result of its inability to stem this invasion, attributed to its great weakness under the Mauryan policy of principle. Puṣyamitra claims to have decisively defeated the Greeks, but they in fact consolidated their rule in Gandhāra during his reign. At the end of it (B.C. 151) they advanced further and conquered Vāhīka (the modern Panjāb). We now find the interesting phenomenon that whilst Puṣyamitra had restored Brahmanism as the ruling ideology of his Empire the Greeks came to adopt Buddhism. This confusing situation makes it extremely difficult for us to arrive at any simple generalisation concerning the result of Aśoka's great experiment. It is thought that Śāliśūka and his successors practically disarmed the Empire by applying Aśoka's policy (but it may not have been part of his policy at all to leave the frontiers insufficiently guarded) and so brought about the Bactrian invasion and the revolt of the General. Yet these Greek invaders, or some of them, supported Buddhism and 'principle' and seem to have facilitated the further spread of Buddhism into Bactria and beyond it to other parts of central Asia. One thing we can say: that Buddhism showed its truly international character. It could not serve as an Indian 'national' (if there can be such a thing) ideology to consolidate an Indian empire against non-Indians. It could serve only for an international empire uniting, not dividing, all mankind.

Yet there could be no 'Indian' ideology in a nationalistic sense. There was no Indian 'nation' unless we seek to restrict this to, at most, the Aryan speaking population—and even this was and is a series of countries with divergent languages.

It was this problem of cultural unification in India and even beyond which Buddhism met, and which even Brahmanism in this period sought to meet.[1] It may have been intended by rulers to serve as the basis of permanent political unification. It failed in this because it failed to set up any boundary between India and non-India, but the cultural unification itself brilliantly succeeded throughout the vast area of Indian civilisation. The diffusion of ideas through all the countries of that area became the permanent foundation of a common culture, infinitely complex and hard to define, which we now call 'Indian'. Political disunity and cultural unity accorded well with the outlook and needs of Buddhism : India became, at the cultural level, a kind of republic providing intellectual freedom for her philosophers and poets. As for *dharma*, variously understood by the orthodox Vedists (Mīmāṃsakas), or by the tradition of the *Rāmāyaṇa* (the ideal empire of Rāma) or that of the still developing Great Epic (Yudhiṣṭhira the 'just'), it remained the ideal of Brahmanism as of Buddhism. The name of Aśoka was not honoured by the brahmans but in many ways his ideals were, only they were ascribed to the idealised emperors of Brahmanical tradition, Yudhiṣṭhira and Rāma, who in the *Mahābhārata* and *Rāmāyaṇa* as they have come down to us stand respectively for the Buddhistic ideals of renunciation and compassion.

1. The *Mīmāṃsā Sūtra* of 'Jaimini' insists on the universality of Brahmanism. The injunctions of the *Veda* are of universal application and local customs have no authority. I 3.15 ff. with Śabara's commentary. Bādari held that all (including *śūdras*) could perform Vedic sacrifices (quoted by Jaimini VI. 1. 27).

Chapter Nine

THE EIGHTEEN SCHOOLS

The Schisms and Geography — The Sthaviravāda — Ceylon — The Commentaries — The Caitikas, Āndhra and the Sātavāhana Empire — The Lokottaravāda and Bahuśrutiya : The Legend of the Buddha and Aśvaghoṣa — The Sarvāstivāda, Proto-Sautrāntika and the Kuṣāṇa Empire — South East Asia — Art.

The Schisms and Geography

So far we have accounted for the existence of thirteen schools. Traditionally the eventual number, at least of the early schools (i.e. excluding the Mahāyāna schools), is eighteen. In fact since there are slight differences in the histories of them given in our various sources it is possible to raise the number to twenty-five or twenty six, although some of these were recognised to be additional to the eighteen and to have arisen later (the last of these schools was founded in the 4th century A.D.). To arrive at the number eighteen we have to draw the line at about 50 B.C. Three important schools broke away from the Sthaviravāda after Aśoka's time. Probably towards the end of the 3rd century B.C. the school generally known as the Mahīśāsakas seceded over some points in *abhidharma* (in which they agreed with the Sarvāstivāda : there are two kinds of 'cessation', space is not 'synthesised', *saṃskṛta* — or 'activated', cf. pp. 122 and 129 above); the name by which they are generally known seems to be a corruption of an original name indicating their origin in the Mahiṣa country (see p. 265 above). Somewhat later (*c.* B.C. 190 ?) the Sthaviras of the Himavant country (after which they are called Haimavatas) became an independent school often called the Kāśyapīyas after one of the original leaders of the mission to their country, Kāśyapa (p. 265). They represent another (but different) compromise between the Sthaviravāda and the Sarvāstivāda : the Sthaviravāda (and the Mahīśāsaka) adhere to the view that an *arhant* is beyond the reach of any seduction, cannot relapse, whereas the Sarvāstivāda and

Kāśyapīya adopt the Mahāsaṃgha opinion that his perfection is not so absolute. The third school seems to have seceded at about the same time; it is known as the Dharmaguptaka, after its founder Dharmagupta, and apparently originated in the Aparānta country. This school seems generally to agree closely with the Sthaviravāda (e.g. on the *arhant*), except that it had some leanings towards the Mahāsaṃgha : according to Vasumitra[1] it attached special importance to gifts 'to the Buddha' rather than to the Community and also to the honouring of pagodas, this latter point being confirmed by extant Dharmaguptaka texts.[2] This school made greater efforts than any other in spreading Buddhism outside India (to Iran, Central Asia and eventually China), with brilliant success; in this, besides the 'cult' of the pagoda it appears to have devised some other means of popularising Buddhism among the 'barbarians' who preferred the mysterious to the philosophical.[3] In the middle of the 1st century B.C. a section of the Mahāsaṃgha, led, according to Vasumitra, by a certain Mahādeva,[4] broke away (over a legalistic *Vinaya* point : 'entrance' to the community) in the Āndhra country and formed the Caitika school. This was soon rent by further schisms, producing the Apara Śaila and the Uttara (or Pūrva) Śaila schools. The Sthaviravādins record a large number of grounds maintained by these schools, but it is difficult to distinguish which of these were not shared with other branches of the Mahāsaṃgha (the Sthaviravāda tradition being handed down in South India and Ceylon was directly interested in the 'errors' of these close neighbours, tending at the same time to ignore the other Mahāsaṃgha schools apart from the general condemnation of their grounds enunciated at the time of the First Schism).[5] Thus we arrive at nineteen schools, unless we do not take the Caitika

---

1. See Bareau's translation, *JA* 1954 pp. 263 f. Vasumitra adds that most of their other grounds were similar to those of the Mahāsaṃgha, without, unfortunately, giving any more precise indication of them.
2. See Pa-chow, *A Comparative Study of the Prātimokṣa*, pp. 42 and 51 f.
3. Lamotte HBI 549.
4. See Lamotte HBI 309 f.
5. KvuA passim; the grounds have been collected for reference in *Points of Controversy*, xxff.

as remaining alongside its two offshoots but as simply split into them.[1]

To complete the roll of recorded schools we may briefly add here: (1) The Sthaviravāda underwent two schisms in Ceylon, producing the Abhayagirivāsins (or Dharmarucis after their founder) in B.C. 38 and the Jetavanīyas (or Sāgalīyas after their founder) *c.* 300 A.D., (2) the Caitikas in Āndhra during this period produced the Rājagirikas and the Siddhārthikas, and (3) the Sarvāstivādins in the North West produced the Saṃkrāntikas (a doubtful school which may be a mere corruption of the name of the next), the Sautrāntikas (a trend which began about 50 A.D. and was consolidated into a school probably early in the 2nd century A.D.) and the Mūlasarvāstivāda (still later, in the 3th or 4th century A.D.).

The schisms as they are recorded are based primarily on matters of doctrinal principle, though in certain cases rivalries of a more personal nature may have been involved, at least in bringing things to a head. At the same time from the Vaiśālī affair onwards there is a certain agreement between the geographical dispersion of Buddhism and its resolution into schools. The first serious differences to make themselves felt found the Buddhists tending to separate into a Western and an Eastern school, the great triangle of Kauśāmbī — Mathurā — Ujjayinī marking the West and Vaiśālī the centre of the East. At first it was still possible to prevent a schism, because it was still possible to hold a general assembly at which, apparently, all the local communities were satisfied that they were properly represented. Thirty-seven years later, when the First Schism occurred, this condition could perhaps no longer be satisfied. The Sthaviras were outvoted in the East, but may well have felt that if all the monks of their far flung establishments in the West had been counted they would have had the majority. There is evidence that most, perhaps all, of the schools were careful to maintain some representation at the imperial capital (Pāṭaliputra) and that some of them were at times widely scattered, but on the whole we find each school having its main strength in a particular region, even in a particular place. In

1. So Paramārtha seems to say (Demiéville MCB I 51) : 'Pūrva' could mean the 'Old' Caitika/Śaila school.

the period of the great missions, when the area covered by the communities of monks grew most rapidly, we notice the greatest number of schisms occurring, several of these in the newly established communities.

If Vātsīputra had anything to do with the Vatsa country (which is conjectural), and if he led the monks in that country in the 'personality schism' (which is still more conjectural), then the Sthaviravāda in this second schism divided again along the East—West axis, the Eastern point of the 'triangle' seceding. This is doubtful, but it is certain that when the school divided again it was the Northern point, Mathurā, which seceded and became, with the countries still further North (Gandhāra and Kaśmīra), the 'territory' of the Sarvāstivāda school. In a similar manner the Mahīśāsakas, Kāśyapīyas and Dharmaguptakas are found to break away respectively to the South of the Southern point (in Mahiṣa), North and North East of Mathurā (Himavant) and West of the Southern point (in Aparānta, but especially Gujarāt and Sindhu). The Kāśyapīyas in fact were a group of the Sthaviravāda cut off from the main Sthavira 'territory' in Avanti by the seceded Sarvāstivādins at Mathurā; for a long time they kept in touch with their original base near Vidiśā (Caityagiri, Sāñcī, where their inscriptions are found), and sometimes their opponents refer to them as simply Sthaviras, but they modified some of the Sthaviravāda views. The Sthaviravādins themselves spread rapidly South from Avanti into Mahārāṣṭra and Āndhra and down to the Coḷa country (Kāñcī), as well as Ceylon. For some time they maintained themselves in Avanti as well as in their new territories, but gradually they tended to regroup themselves in the South, the Great Vihāra (Mahāvihāra) in Anurādhapura, the capital of Ceylon, becoming the main centre of their tradition, Kāñcī a secondary centre and the Northern regions apparently relinquished to other schools. The Mahīśāsakas also established themselves in Ceylon and lived beside the Sthaviras in apparent harmony : eventually the Mahīśāsakas of Ceylon seem to have been quietly reabsorbed into the Sthaviravāda. The two new schools formed in Ceylon were the communities in two other *vihāras* at the capital (Abhayagiri and Jetavana), who broke away from the Great Vihāra.

In the movement North and West the Sarvāstivāda maintained establishments in Kośala (Śrāvastī) and Vārāṇasī as well as Mathurā (their main centre at first), but tended to concentrate in Gandhāra and Kaśmīra. The last two countries eventually became the centres of the new Mūlasarvāstivāda school. In a relatively late period we find the Sarvāstivādins in Central Asia and China. It was the Dharmaguptakas who were the first Buddhists to establish themselves in Central Asia. They appear to have carried out a vast circling movement along the trade routes from Aparānta North West into Iran and at the same time into Uḍḍiyāna (the Suvastu valley, North of Gandhāra, which became one of their main centres). After establishing themselves as far West as Parthia they followed the 'silk route', the East-West axis of Asia, Eastwards across Central Asia and on into China, where they effectively established Buddhism in the second and third centuries A.D. The Mahīśāsakas and Kāśyapīyas appear to have followed them across Asia to China. We have evidence of a North Western Mahīśāsaka establishment in Western Vāhīka (in the Salt Range) and of Kāśyapīya *vihāras* in Gandhāra. For the earlier period of Chinese Buddhism it was the Dharmaguptakas who constituted the main and most influential school, and even later their *Vinaya* remained the basis of the discipline there. Alongside it the other schools recognised as of importance (and whose texts were also studied) were the Mahīśāsakas, Kāśyapīyas, Sarvāstivādins and Mahāsaṃghikas (sometimes the Vātsīputrīyas are mentioned as a sixth school). The Mahāsaṃghika are found to have had at least one establishment in Kāpiśa, the Lokottaravāda one in Bactria and the Bahuśrutīya one in Gandhāra, but the main contact of the Mahāsaṃghikas with China was probably by sea from Tāmralipti at the mouth of the Ganges to the East coast of China.[1]

Among the schools which seceded from the Vātsīputrīyas the Dharmottarīyas are found in Aparānta in its restricted sense, on the coast of Mahārāṣṭra (at the great port of Śūrpāraka, the capital of the Aparānta country proper, and places nearby), and the Bhadrayāṇīyas on the edge of the Mahārāṣṭrian plateau

1. See Zürcher, *The Buddhist Conquest of China*, for the arrival of the Buddhists in China, simultaneously by land from the West and by sea from the East.

behind them (Nāsikā), but each had at least one *vihāra* in the other territory. Much more widespread and vigorous were the Saṃmitīyas, who spread across Avanti and Gujarāt to form their main centre in Sindhu, though they also maintained themselves in the East. The original Vātsīputrīyas seem to have remained in the East, settling in Kośala and Vārāṇasī and being (as were the Saṃmitīyas) one of the early schools which still flourished in the homeland of Buddhism in the time of the Pāla Empire (8th-12th centuries A.D.).[1]

The Mahāsaṃghikas remained in and around Pāṭaliputra as their main centre[2] but had establishments also in distant places such as Kāpiśa, Mathurā, Aparānta and Āndhra. The Ekavyavahārika are hardly known in later times and perhaps were reabsorbed into the Mahāsaṃghika. The Gokulika (Kaurukullaka) seem to have remained in the East, probably at Vārāṇasī. The extant Lokottaravāda texts declare they are works of the Lokottaravāda 'of the middle country', which means the central region of Northern India, but the school had a branch as far away as Bactria. The Bahuśrutīyas probably had their centre in Kośala, but were settled also in Gandhāra and Āndhra.[3] The Prajñaptivāda are not known to have spread outside the original Eastern territory of Buddhism. Of the Mahāsaṃgha the four schools: Mahāsaṃghika, Gokulika (Kaurukullaka), Lokottaravāda and Prajñaptivāda, continued to flourish in the East under the Pālas.[1] The Caitikas from their centre in Āndhra spread North West up the Godāvarī valley as far as Nāsikā and elsewhere on the edge of the plateau in that direction. Their four offshoots, the Apara Śaila, Uttara (Pūrva) Śaila, Rājagirika and Siddhārthaka seem all to have begun as the communities of particular *vihāras* around the Āndhra city of Dhānyakaṭaka, where the Caitikas originated.

Such is the rough outline[4] of the spread of the schools; it could be complicated by further details of their strengths in

1. Tāranātha p. 274.

2. Paramārtha (Demiéville MCB I 41, 43) restricts them at first to N. Aṅga ('Aṅga North of the Water (Ganges)'=Aṅgottarāpa), i.e. the country adjacent to Vṛji in the East (the NE corner of the modern state of Bihār), which perhaps was their primary centre.

3. Harivarman seems to have written near Pāṭaliputra.

4. Many of the details given here are taken from Lamotte's collection of data from the early inscriptions, HBI 578 ff.

various places, and more of their *vihāras*, noted by Chinese pilgrims in later centuries, but we need not go further into the mass of details. We leave aside the Buddhists in South East Asia, where the Sthaviravāda was in the long run the most successful school but far from being the only one to have flourished there. The Sthaviravāda continued also from time to time to establish new contacts and communities in Northern India, on the East coast in Kaliṅga and further North, on the West coast in Gujarāt, and in Magadha, especially at Bodh Gayā.

We have seen the main points of doctrine on which the schools disagreed, but we still have to make a brief survey of their special literature, which they added to their several recensions of the *Tripiṭaka*, in so far as it is accessible to us. In doing this we can add a few historical notes to continue the thread of the history of India (and now of Ceylon as well).

One further general point may be made first. According to the Tibetan historian Bu-ston,[1] either in the 1st century A.D. or earlier the *Tripiṭakas* of the 'Eighteen Schools' were written down, on account of the danger of faulty memorising. The memorising of texts continued long to be the main means of studying them, but the currency of written manuscripts seems to have encouraged whatever trends existed towards the study of texts as opposed to the practice of their teaching. Bu-ston's record is confirmed for the Sthaviravāda at least by their histories written in Ceylon, which state that their *Tripiṭaka* was written down in the 1st century B.C. The Tibetan writer adds, following earlier Indian sources (Vinītadeva, A.D. 700, and Padmākaraghoṣa), that four different languages were used: Paiśācī (of which Pali is evidently a dialect) by the Sthaviravāda group of schools, Prakrit by the Mahāsaṃgha, Apabhraṃśa by the Saṃmitīya (Vātsīputrīya) group and Sanskrit by the Sarvāstivāda. In fact this certainly represents only a later situation. More different dialects were certainly used in the different countries of India in early times, whilst Sanskrit, not being a vernacular language, was adopted only later and Apabhraṃśa is a form of vernacular which developed only by perhaps the 5th century A.D. One text survives in Gāndhārī, for example. We might consider this a mere provincial version, of

1. II 101.

course. Probably by the 7th century A.D. the main versions in use in the Buddhist centres of North India were in those four languages, but it is not certain that each of the eighteen or more schools had a recension in one of the four. The Sarvāstivāda had earlier used Prakrit but put their texts into standard literary Sanskrit during the early centuries A.D. The Saṃmitīya group must have put theirs into the then current vernacular of Northern and Western India only between the 5th and 7th centuries.

The Sthaviravāda

The Sthaviravāda as it spread through Western and Southern India and eventually to Ceylon remained very close in doctrine to the positions it took up in opposition to the Mahāsaṃgha at the First Schism. In other words the claim of the 'Mahāvihāravāsins' in Ceylon to be the original Sthaviravāda of the First Schism, as opposed to the Vātsīputrīyas, Sarvāstivādins and others can be upheld. Their characteristic doctrine originally was that of the incorruptible nature of the *arhant*; this they adhered to (as did the Mahīśāsaka and Dharmaguptaka), whereas the Vātsīputrīyas and Sarvāstivādins went over to the position of the Mahāsaṃgha. The Dharmaguptakas, we have seen, had leanings towards the Mahāsaṃgha on other grounds though not on this. The Mahīśāsaka are the closest rivals to be regarded as the original school, but they are generally supposed to represent a 'compromise' with the Sarvāstivāda, so that where they differ from the Sthaviravāda they are not preserving more original doctrines but borrowing from a different school (the doctrines in question are for the most part fairly recondite points of *abhidharma*; if anything they are less likely than the alternative Sthaviravāda points to represent a more original doctrine). Another characteristic doctrine found in the Sthaviravāda is that progress in understanding comes all at once, 'insight' (*abhisamaya*) does not come 'gradually' (successively—*anupūrva*).[1] Here again only the Mahīśāsakas shared their view,[2] all the other schools holding that insight was gradual (with the doubtful exception of the Ekavyavahārikas, who held that 'all

1. Kvu 212 ff. refutes the opposite view.
2. Vasumitra (Bareau JA 1954 p. 259).

principles are cognised in one moment', which could possibly be related; it is remarkable, however, that the Mahāyāna Dhyāna school in China have a similar view of 'sudden' progress in understanding).

Among the other grounds disputed between the schools (see pp. 12f. above) the Sthaviravāda hold that besides mental principles which are good and bad there is a third class which are morally indifferent (with the Sarvāstivāda and against the Mahāsaṃgha : the view entails that some actions have no moral result whereas the Mahāsaṃgha held that every action has a moral result[1]). The 'person' is not a real entity (against the Vātsīputrīyas, who seceded from them on this ground, as we saw above). Past and future principles (with the possible exception of past principles which have not yet produced their results — the school is not quite clear on this: the Mahīśāsakas reject the exception, the Kāśyapīyas accept it) do not exist (against the special doctrine of the Sarvāstivāda). Buddhas are not transcendental. Good conduct cannot grow unconsciously (with the Mahīśāsaka, against the Mahāsaṃgha[2]).

Of the eighteen or more recensions of the *Tripiṭaka* handed down in the schools the Sthaviravāda *Tripiṭaka*, now preserved in the Pali language (a West Indian language, apparently that of Avanti when the school had its main centre in that country), is certainly one of the most authentic, in the sense of preserving the discourses of the Buddha in their wording as recognised before the schisms. Unfortunately no other recension is intact, so that we cannot carry very far the comparisons which would show which one preserved the most original tradition (as we can for the disputed grounds[3] of doctrine, except that we would like more information about the differences within the Mahāsaṃgha to complete the enquiry). It is most significant that where the comparison can be made, and has been made,[4] a Sthaviravāda text agrees most closely with the corresponding Mahāsaṃghika text: the *Prātimokṣas* in the *Vinayas* of these two schools agree in being considerably shorter (having fewer rules) than any of the others extant (only the *Upālipariprcchā*

1. Kvu 464 ff.
2. Kvu 433 ff.
3. Above, pp. 11 ff.
4. By Dr. Pa-chow : *A Comparative Study of the Prātimokṣa*, p. 11.

Sūtra version is equally short — it is not established which school this belongs to). The Sarvāstivāda versions are the longest of all and have, therefore, the greatest number of unauthentic additions. The Mahīśāsaka version also is substantially longer. In other words the two most original schools have here preserved the most original texts and the schools which seceded from them have made substantial additions to these. On the other hand in the comparison of those *Vinaya* texts (admittedly additions to the actual discourses of the Buddha) which deal with the early history of the Community after the *parinirvāṇa* Przyluski and Hofinger have shown (in their studies on the First Rehearsal and on the Vaiśālī Affair) that the Mahīśāsaka recension is closest to the Sthaviravāda and the Mahāsaṃghika recension more remote (which is just what we should expect if these narratives were added close to the time of the First Schism or even after it and tend to show the early history of the Community as suggesting the integrity of the tradition of their respective schools).

If they preserved a very authentic body of original *Tripiṭaka* the Sthaviravāda certainly made substantial additions to this : these, however, took the form of new books rather than of insertions in the old ones, with the probable exception of some of the *Kṣudraka* texts which in all the schools seem to have grown gradually during a much longer period than the rest of the *Sūtra.* In fact it is likely that this 'Minor Tradition' was for a long time not regarded as strictly canonical (in the sense of words of the Buddha himself), was thus a supplement to the *Tripiṭaka* in which interesting or useful texts which had been produced from doubtful sources, or composed by monks and nuns recently, could be handed down. Even so where we can make a comparison we find the Sthaviravāda has the shortest recension of a text, consequently ceased to make additions to it earlier than other schools : the *Dharmapada* of their *Kṣudraka* contains 423 verses, the corresponding Sarvāstivāda text (called *Udānavarga*) has nearly 1,000 verses, the version in Gāndhārī which perhaps belonged to the Dharmaguptaka school (this is only a guess based on the fact that the text was found in Khotan and does not seem to be Sarvāstivādin : the Dharmaguptaka school were the pioneers of Buddhism in that country and the Sarvāstivādins become strong there in a later period, but other schools, for example the Kāśyapīyas, are likely to have been active there as well) has been estimated by its editor[1] to have contained, when intact, about 540 verses. The Sthaviravāda text called (in Pali) *Suttanipāta*, on the other hand, though having parallels in other schools for several of its constituent parts (namely the *Khaḍgaviṣāṇagāthā*, *Munigāthā*, *Śailagāthā*, *Arthavargiyāṇi Sūtrāṇi* and *Pārāyaṇa*), is not known to have had any corresponding text as a collection, so that many of the poems in it may have been composed in the school after the schisms.[2] Of possible additions to its *Kṣudraka* the (Pali) *Vimānapetavatthu* texts as well as the *Apadāna* proper correspond to the texts called *Avadāna* in other schools. Our metrical analysis dated the whole of these later than B.C. 200. The average date of their materials might be as much as a century later than this date. Slightly later still appears to be the Pali *Cariyāpiṭaka*, a small collection of *jātakas* without known parallel except the *Bodhisattvapiṭaka* of certain schools, which the Mahāyāna developed into a special collection of *sūtras* on their new ideal. A related narrative text is the Pali *Buddhavaṃsa*, which is perhaps to be dated in the 2nd century B.C. (it has not yet been fully analysed metrically). All these narrative texts belong to that phase of popularisation of Buddhism to which the convenient word 'edification' may be applied (cf. p. 228 above), and which seems to have been common to all the schools. That the Sthaviravādins had additional stories in their *Jātaka* is suggested by their own tradition,[3] which says that the Mahāsaṃgha 'rejected' part of 'the' *Jātaka* (since the school claimed that the whole of its own *Jātaka* was nothing but the original pre-schism text). Metrically, however, their *Jātaka* is substantially older on the average than the group of narrative texts we have just referred to : its average date seems to fall in the 4th century B.C., two centuries earlier, which of course does not exclude a wide range of dates on either side of this for a minority of its nearly 550 poems. Another substantial addition to the Sthaviravāda *Kṣudraka* is the Pali *Niddesa*, a collection of commentaries on some of the poems in the *Sutta*-

1. Brough : *The Gāndhārī Dharmapada*, London, 1962, 18 ff.
2. In *Pali Metre* it was concluded that at least one part of it (Sn 679-98) may have been as late as about B.C. 200; this in fact is an introductory narrative added to a more ancient poem.
3. *Dīpavaṃsa* V 37.

nipāta. There remains one other substantial addition, which will be discussed in connection with the *Abhidharma* texts, which it resembles (in Burma certain other texts are regarded as canonical which are not so accepted in Ceylon, they will be referred to below).

It is their *Abhidharma* which is the glory of the Sthaviravāda school. It consists of seven treatises in the *Abhidharma Piṭaka*, with which we can associate the Pali *Paṭisambhidāmagga* (or *-pakaraṇa*) included in the *Kṣudraka* of the *Sūtra* (on purely formal grounds : part of it contains a brief opening statement which makes it a discourse by the Buddha like the *sūtras*) and two texts which in the earlier history of the school and even today in Ceylon are not included in the *Tripiṭaka* at all (though they are in Burma, in the *Sūtra*), being ascribed to a monk (Mahākātyāyana, supposed to be the direct disciple of the Buddha and — significantly for the Sthaviravāda — the pioneer who established Buddhism in Avanti) : the Pali *Peṭakopadesa* and *Netti* (or *Nettippakaraṇa*). Of the latter two the second is little but a rewriting and rearrangement of the first, so that as regards content we are concerned practically with a single book. Of these (effectively) nine treatises the *Vibhaṅga* and the *Dhātukathā* have been discussed above (pp. 220ff.) in connection with the most original *Abhidharma* common to all the schools. What little in them may be innovations of treatment due to the studies of the school is more fully elaborated in the other treatises.

We have several times referred to the *Kathāvatthu* to elucidate the grounds on which the schools disagreed. This treatise is in fact a polemical one, consisting of the refutations in strict logical form of more than two hundred propositions maintained by the other schools of Buddhists. We should stress the point of the strict logical form : though in the *Sūtra* the general method of discussion is that of an empirical and rational enquiry all the emphasis there is on the empirical aspect, there are many arguments and debates with opponents but not, apparently, an overt awareness of what constitutes a valid proof. In the *Kathāvatthu*, on the other hand, we have the earliest known Indian philosophical work which proceeds on the basis of a set of established logical techniques : definition, distribution of terms, classification, relations between propositions as biconditionals or ponentials, quantification, the use of 'logical words' to give a standard formal presentation of all the arguments, and so on.[1] In fact the whole of the *Abhidharma Piṭaka* from its beginnings was a restatement of the doctrine of the Buddha in strictly formalised language, given however, as content, a large number of propositions from the *Sūtra* (of which the terms were then defined and classified) assumed to constitute a consistent system of philosophy. The distinction of two levels of statement is naturally fundamental to this restatement and with the exception of one book the whole of the Sthaviravāda *Abhidharma* may be taken as at the 'ultimate' or philosophical level, as completely objective and definitive and not taking account of the person to whom it might be addressed (as the Buddha was supposed to have done in many of the *sūtras*).

The Buddha himself had insisted on empirical verification of his statements. The internal consistency of his 'system' should be the result of congruence with objective fact and the universality of natural laws. In the *Abhidharma* on the other hand there is little concern with empirical reality (it would be incorrect to say no concern, for there are additions to the *Sūtra* system resulting from empirical observation). The aim of the study is to set forth the correct interpretation of the Buddha's statements in the *Sūtra* and to restate his 'system' with perfect accuracy. In the *Kathāvatthu* (and in similar works of other schools) we see further the study of logic applied to the question of the new propositions setting forth the grounds disputed between the schools. Most of the refutations in the *Kathāvatthu* turn on the question of consistency of new propositions with statements which all the schools agreed to be those of the Buddha. Since both sides as Buddhists accept the latter as true they try to prove that their own new propositions are consistent with them and that the new propositions of other schools contradict them. The Sthaviravādin debater (for the *Kathāvatthu* is cast in the form of public debates, not of private deductions) analyses the propositions of his opponents by substituting

1. A sample of the *Kathāvatthu* has been analysed to show its strictly formal character in the paper 'The Earliest Indian Logic', published in the *Trudi XXV Mejdunarodnogo Kongressa Vostokovedov*, Moscow, 1963, Vol IV pp. 56-68 (62-3 read 'ponential' passim and p. 63 under 'Type 11' read '[*b* is is ponential of *a* is]', p. 64 read q $\equiv$ p both times—biconditionals, p. 65 line 34 read 'by you by this assent', p. 66 read 'eye-sphere').

biconditionals, ponentials, etc., for them, or synonyms for their terms, or by bringing in a causal relation or the relation of membership of a class. He invariably finds two propositions which are so related (through these various relationships) that to be consistent one must either affirm them both or deny both, but his opponent has affirmed one and denied the other and is therefore refuted.

The *Kathāvatthu* is supposed to have been composed by an elder named (in Pali) Moggaliputta Tissa, a contemporary of Aśoka who instructed and guided the emperor, organised the missions (Mahendra who went to Ceylon was his own pupil) and led the Sthaviravādins at the All Exist schism. The work in fact begins with the refutation of the theory of a real 'person', and continues with the 'all exist', the propositions of the Mahāsaṃgha, and others. The nucleus of such a set of refutations of rejected grounds may have originated in the original Sthaviravāda school after the First Schism and have had further refutations added to it as more controversies occurred. The Sarvāstivāda share a basically similar refutation of the 'person' theory, for example, which could have been common property of the two schools before the 'All Exist' schism divided them. The additions to the *Kathāvatthu* undoubtedly continued long after that division, so that if Moggaliputta Tissa did in fact redact the refutations as they stood at the end of Aśoka's reign, his school later added many more to them.

Already in the earliest *Abhidharma Piṭaka* we can now reconstruct (see the end of Chapter Seven) one of the main objects of the discussions was to define all the terms in the system, pair off synonyms, classify all the principles under the several classes recognised, and exclude from consideration anything which was not accepted as a real, 'ultimate' principle (such as mere words, used in everyday language and therefore by the Buddha on occasion but not corresponding to any reality). The *Kathāvatthu* shows the techniques for this systematisation further advanced. Firstly there is the 'checking' (*saṃsyandana*) of any term presented for discussion against all the accepted terms of the system : how does it fit in ? Several subsidiary techniques are applied here, for example the checking by the 'tetrad scheme' (*catuṣkanaya*) : is the term identical (in fact if not in name) with another in the system, with which the check is being made, or is it part of that other, or is it different from that other, or is that other part of it ? (a controversial term would be thus checked against all the terms in the system). With this method we may compare that found in the *Saṃyukta* (p. 125f. above), where the supposed 'soul' is being in effect checked against the groups. Several other techniques are set out in the *Kathāvatthu* (they are reviewed in the paper mentioned in the preceding footnote).

It is one of these logical techniques which gave birth to another of the Sthaviravāda *Abhidharma* treatises, the *Yamaka*, which may therefore be described next. It is called literally 'clarification of expressions' (or 'number', *vacanaśodhana*) but refers in logic to checking whether a term is distributed in a proposition, i.e. whether all (*sarva*) instances of the term (principle) are covered by it or only some (*ekatya*) of them. The *Yamaka* is not a polemical work but a manual for the student of *abhidharma* (like the *Dhātukathā*)—for the advanced student who has already studied the 'system', but to become fully competent in it (and especially to be ready to take part in debates without being caught out by the use of words in varying senses, or figuratively, which an opponent might use to 'fault' his logic) requires exercise in the exact extension of the terms used. This book is perhaps the latest of those included in the *Abhidharma Piṭaka* of this school.

The only Sthaviravāda *Abhidharma* text which is not at the philosophical or ultimate level of statement is a short treatise on the concept of the 'person', the *Puggalapaññatti*, which in the standard order of the books immediately precedes the *Kathāvatthu* and therefore immediately precedes the refutation of the 'person' as a real, ultimate principle. This treatise collects most of the statements about 'persons' made in the *Sūtra*. In effect it defines 'them' as particular states or stages in the sequences of conditions, when there is a sentient body with consciousness, which give rise to the concept of a 'person'.[1]

The book which stands first in the standard order of books, the *Dhammasaṃgaṇi*, is infinitely more original and interesting

1. The *Śāriputrābhidharmaśāstra* includes a chapter on 'persons', which is generally similar to the *Puggalapaññatti* but somewhat fuller. Since Harivarman includes this topic (Katsura p. 74) it seems to be an original *Apraśnaka* text separated from the rest as not 'ultimate'.

than the collection of excerpts on the 'person', and shows the Sthaviravāda philosophers at work at the ultimate level, perfecting their system as a statement of what there is in the universe. The form of this work is extremely complex, since it is a combination of several different systems of terms which overlap one another to varying extents. The heart of it is the list of 'principles' (*dharmas*) recognised in the school, which had been collected from the *Sūtra* and classified. This enumeration of principles was supposed to cover everything which really exists, the 'elements' (another possible translation of *dharma*) of which the universe is constituted. In the *Dhammasaṃgaṇi* itself the enumeration is admittedly not complete, though the essentials are given, for 'others' are mentioned but not specified. Afterwards the school worked out all possible 'others' and produced a complete enumeration, which is given in their commentary on this text.

Collecting 'what there is' from the discourses of the Buddha the *Dhammasaṃgaṇi* has arrived at about two hundred principles, or rather two hundred names of principles which are real. However, there are many synonyms (since the Buddha had described the same principles in different terms in different contexts of discussion), so that this list reduces to well under one hundred when the synonyms are identified. It is convenient to review these principles under the headings of the five groups (*skandha*) into which they are classified (p. 86 above).

(1) matter (*rūpa*, i.e. physical principles)

earth	sight	visible object
water	hearing	sound
heat	smell	scent
air	taste	taste object
	touch	[tangible not distinct, reduces to earth, etc.]
femininity	gesture	lightness of matter
masculinity	speech	suppleness..
life (*jīvita*)	space	malleability..
		accumulation..
		extension..
		aging..
material-food		impermanence..

(the *Dhammasaṃgaṇi*—p. 177—defines 'earth' as the property of 'hardness', 'water' as 'cohesion' and 'air' as 'agitation', thus all these principles are of the nature of properties or qualities rather than substances; this may be regarded as in accordance with the idea of *dharma*, which seems originally to have been 'nature')

(2) emotion (*vedanā*)

happiness (or pleasantness, *sukha*)
elation (but the definition indicates that this reduces to 'happiness')
unhappiness (unpleasantness)
depression (again this reduces to unhappiness)
equanimity (*upekṣā*)

(3) perception (*saṃjñā*)

perception (itself, which is the only member of this group)

(4) forces (*saṃskāra*)

contact (stimulus)	concentration (of thought, and the 'faculty')
volition	energy (the faculty, and 'exercise')
reasoning	confidence
reflection	self-possession
joy	understanding (includes 'right theory')

(the right hand column here is basically the five faculties, but four of the factors of the way reduce to four of these, so do the five strengths, *bala*, reduce to these five; 'right intention' as factor of the way reduces to 'reasoning': from the moral point of view, however, energy — and exercise—may be either good or bad, there is a wrong way as well as a right way; concentration also may be good or bad, but confidence and self-possession are only good)
life (this principle is twofold, as matter and as force)
right speech (as factor of the way, and moral, not merely physical)
right action
right livelihood
wrong theory (wrong opinions)
wrong intention (reduces to reasoning)
self-respect (*hri*, a 'strength')

fear of blame (*apatrāpya*, also a 'strength', cf. p. 192)
lack of self-respect
lack of fear-of-blame
desire (in bad sense, 'greed' — *lobha*; various synonyms are listed)
aversion (malevolence, repulsion, etc., reduce to this)
delusion (wrong theory reduces to this)
non-desire
non-aversion (reduces to benevolence, its positive aspect)
non-delusion (reduces to understanding)
(the last six above are prominent in later theory as the basic 'roots' of action, three bad and three good)
vanity
uncertainty
tranquillity (of the sentient body, and of thought)
lightness (of the above)
suppleness...
malleability...
efficiency..
straightness...
being conscious (alert, deliberate, aware — *saṃprajanya*, reduces to understanding)
calming (*śamatha*, reduces to concentration)
insight (*vipaśyanā*, reduces to understanding)
intending to find out something unknown (a 'faculty')
the four influences (opinion is added to the original three, but it reduces to delusion, as does ignorance; passion reduces to desire, of which desire for existence is a form)
(there are numerous other 'forces', including the obstacles, the connections, the defilements, the attachments, and others, but all of them reduce to one or other of those given above, as do further synonyms for energy, concentration and understanding)

(5) consciousness (*vijñāna*)

thought (*citta*)
mind (a faculty or an element, *dhātu*, but it reduces to thought)
consciousness of sight (i.e. of the sense of sight)
consciousness of hearing
consciousness of smell
consciousness of taste

consciousness of touch
consciousness of mind (i.e. of the mind/thought of the previous moment)
(these last seven principles are all called 'elements', *dhātu*; they make up a set of eighteen such 'elements' with the five senses and the six objects of the senses and of mind, known to the original *Abhidharma* common to all the schools: the mental object, 'principles', *dharmas*, cuts across the classification into the groups, but excludes consciousness and those material principles which are objects of the other five senses)

(6) (unsynthesised element (*asaṃskṛta dhātu*, unactivated element)

extinction (*nirvāṇa*, which cannot be classified under the groups)

Apart from a supplement presumably added later (which adds further notes under the same headings) the matter of the *Dhammasaṃgoṇi* is set out under 164 headings. These headings are triads or dyads of classification into which the principles can be divided. It was found that when classifying principles (by dichotomy), if one took a simple class and its contradictory — for example those principles which function as causes and those which do not — one arrived at a 'dyad', a pair of classes into which all the given principles could be listed. On the other hand there are certain interesting classifications where one meets a pair of contrary classes (not simply a class and its contradictory) which in the nature of things admit of a third class between them, for example good, bad and indeterminate (*avyākṛta*, 'undetermined'). Of course, these can be reduced to pairs of contradictories (good and not good, etc.), but in a number of cases the Sthaviravādins found it more convenient to set up 'triads' of classes into which the principles could be classified. The properly *abhidharma* system thus elaborated contains one hundred dyads and twenty-two triads (into which principles can be exhaustively dichotomised or trichotomised). A further forty-two dyads were considered which were time honoured pairs from the *Sūtra* but were of a miscellaneous character (some of them not strict contradictories), relevant to some principles only and not accepted into the *abhidharma* system of the school.

By far the most important of these headings is the first

triad, that of good, bad and indeterminate. This is expanded to a very large treatise on its own by the introduction into it of further sub-classifications. The whole of it naturally falls into three parts: the lists of principles which are (1) good, (2) bad and (3) indeterminate. As a sub-classification, however, the school has introduced the distinction between those principles which occur in the sequence of thoughts and those which are 'matter' (occur in physical sequences), to which extinction (*nirvāṇa*) is appended as a separate 'element'. In the Buddhist system, or at least the Sthaviravāda system, only the principles of thought can be good or bad, so in effect it is simply the class of indeterminate principles which is subdivided into those of thought, of matter and extinction. Proceeding to the analysis of thought we find that the school has distinguished eighty-nine types of thought (*citta*) within this triad. These might be called 89 mental states (but they are not strictly states, they are active, they are 'occurrences') distinctive for the purposes of the system: the unreduced list of principles, minus of course the physical principles and extinction, is then checked against these 89 classes, which themselves fall into the three greater classes of good, bad and indeterminate.

It is impossible within the scope of this book to enter into all the details of this fascinating analysis of the stream of consciousness. The classes of thought cover the experience of living beings primarily with reference to the Buddhist way (or the lack of it) and with special attention to the various stages of meditation. Having listed and defined the principles which occur in different types of thought in the 'sensual' sphere we proceed to the 'imponderable' sphere of the four meditations and the 'immaterial' sphere which includes the infinity of space, the infinity of consciousness, nothingness and neither perception nor non-perception. Again the principles of the successive stages of the way are noted. The bad classes of thought are grouped according to their three bases: desire (passion, greed, bad desire), aversion (malevolence, anger, etc.) and delusion. Whether good or bad, thoughts may be the result of deliberate effort or direct responses without effort or reflection. Again they may be conjoined with opinion (theory, right or wrong) or without it. Good or bad, they may be charged with elation, or instead with equanimity. The two main sub-classes of indeterminate thoughts are those which are simple 'results' (*vipāka*) producing no further moral effects and those which are still 'acting' (*kriyā*) but whose acting is of no moral consequence.

As regards 'matter' the *Dhammasaṃgaṇi* distinguishes the four great elements (earth, water, heat and air) or 'great existents' as primary from all the others as secondary, as existing only in dependence on (*upādāya*) these four. It is worthy of special remark here that the Sthaviravāda classify space under matter and as one of the secondary varieties depending on the four great existents. Its definition, for them, is simply that it is the interstices between pieces of these four: it has no intrinsic nature of its own and it cannot be conceived except in relation to these. All the other schools of whom we have any record of their opinion on this subject, however, classify space under 'unsynthesised element', with extinction. For the Sthaviravāda extinction (*nirvāṇa*) is unique and utterly transcendent, whereas some of the other schools listed as many as nine principles under 'unsynthesised element'. This is one of the rare points where the Mahīśāsaka part company with the Sthaviravādins, as they too classify space as unsynthesised (in fact they have nine unsynthesised principles, as also do the Mahāsaṃghikas, or some of these, though the nine are only partly the same). Such a difference of opinion may seem exceedingly abstract and technical and without practical consequence, yet in fact it indicates a strikingly different view of the nature of the universe and of *nirvāṇa*.

Closely related to the *Dhammasaṃgaṇi* is the remaining and seventh of the *Abhidharma* treatises of the Sthaviravāda, the *Paṭṭhāna*. This immense work is a study of conditionality and so appears to have grown out of the last section of the 'original' *Abhidharma* which we tried to reconstruct above (p. 223). In the *Dhammasaṃgaṇi* it is noted that all the principles which occur in each of its classes (except extinction) are originated through conditions. The *Paṭṭhāna* then undertakes to give a full account of this conditioned origination. It does not, however, concern itself with the old sequence of conditions, which has been sufficiently discussed in the *Vibhaṅga*. Its subject is the nature of the conditional relation itself. The *Vibhaṅga* has anticipated this to a very small extent, but the *Paṭṭhāna* is exhaustive. It is not confined to the special case of the sequence of conditions in transmigration, but aims to give a general theory covering all kinds of conditional or causal relation.

The *Paṭṭhāna* is set out under the same headings of 22 triads and 100 dyads as the *Dhammasaṃgaṇi*, but with the complication that the headings are also combined with each other in various ways. The whole work consists of twenty four books in four sets of six each. The first set conforms to the formulation: '*a* occurs conditioned by *b* through the *x* condition', in which any of the items ('a good principle,' 'a bad principle', and so on) given under the headings may possibly be substituted for *a* and *b* and any kind of condition may be substituted for *x*. The second set substitutes the negative formulation: 'non-*a* occurs conditioned by non-*b* through the *x* condition.' The third set has: '*a* occurs conditioned by non-*b* through the *x* condition'. The fourth set has: 'non-*a* occurs conditioned by *b* through the *x* condition'. The six books in each set are (1) the triads alone, (2) the dyads alone, (3) the dyads combined with the triads (in that order), (4) the triads combined with the dyads, (5) the triads combined with the triads and (6) the dyads combined with the dyads. By feeding all the items into the available combinations within these basically simple structures of statement, substituting 24 different possible conditions (see below) in each case, and again the negations of these 24, substituting further six other formulations for 'conditioned by' in the above, one of the most amazing productions of the human mind has been elaborated. In it, all the permutations which might occur have been checked off if they can in fact occur in the universe according to the Buddhist analysis of the 'origination of principles from causes'. We have then a description not of what there is but of what happens: this is entirely in accordance with the Buddhist conception of the universe, that nothing 'is' (as enduring and permanent) but that there occur forces (or 'energies', *saṃskāras*) which act as conditions for one another according to certain natural laws, producing sequences of matter and of thoughts (cf. pp. 134f. above).

Prefixed to the 24 books of the *Paṭṭhāna* is a *mātṛkā* listing the 24 kinds of condition recognised in the work, followed by definitions of them. They are as follows.

(1) 'cause' —but the word (*hetu*) is used here in a special restricted sense, not any cause but only the six 'roots' of action, three good and three bad (non-desire, non-aversion or benevolence, non-delusion or understanding, desire, aversion and delusion); 'root' (*mūla*) is a more usual synonym in the *Abhidharma* (cf. p. 224 above).

(2) 'support' (*ālambana*), of consciousness (p. 128 above), any mental object.

(3) 'dominant' (*adhipati*), such are the 'powers' (*ṛddhi*, p. 89 above) of 'will', 'thought', 'energy' and 'investigation' which are capable of strengthening some principle in the sequence of thoughts.

(4) 'immediate' (*anantara*), such is the relation of successive states of consciousness, or thoughts, for example 'mind' (thought) and the 'consciousness of mind' which immediately follows it.

(5) 'quite immediate' (*samanantara*) is a mere synonym for 'immediate' (the word is used in the *Vibhaṅga*, which presumably is why it is listed here only to be reduced to its synonym).

(6) 'simultaneous origin' (*sahajāta*) is the relation between principles which occur together in the same sequence, for example the four groups consciousness, forces, perception and emotion which originate together in a living being, similarly the four 'great existents' (elements), which in this system are no longer the simple old concepts earth, water, etc., though called by the traditional names, but (as the *Dhammasaṃgaṇi* defines them) the properties of hardness, cohesion, heat and agitation which are held to occur in all matter in varying proportions; examples of simultaneous origin are very numerous in the sequences of the system.

(7) 'reciprocal' (*anyonya*), this covers part of the preceding one, since the relation of reciprocal dependence obtains between principles which can occur only together.

(8) 'dependence' (*niśraya*), e.g. of secondary matter on the four great existents, of consciousness of sight on the sense of sight, of mind on the matter on the basis of which it proceeds.

(9) 'immediate dependence' (*upaniśraya*) is similar to 'immediate' but of wider extension, in fact it would seem to

obtain between any member of a sequence and that immediately preceding it.

(10) 'produced before' (**purojāta*) is similar to 'dependence', matter and sense objects for consciousness.

(11) 'produced after' (*paścājjāta*) considers principles which are going to occur later as conditions operating on those which are going to produce them, for example future experience operates on the body (acts as a stimulant, we might say).

(12) 'habit' (*āsevana*, 'practicing')—repetition strengthens mental principles, this is therefore an important condition relating similar principles in the same sequence.

(13) 'action' (*karman*) as condition for its result, i.e. moral action, which is always conjoined with volition.

(14) 'result' (*vipāka*); a result does not produce any direct moral effect, assuming, as appears to be the case, that what is meant here is simple results, morally indeterminate; nevertheless the results attained on the Buddhist way (and perhaps in other connections), which have the nature of effortless calm, are conducive to the attainment of other similar results (such is the commentarial explanation).

(15) 'food' (*āhāra*), the 'four foods' (pp. 117f. above).

(16) 'faculty' (*indriya*), including the senses and the other 'faculties', 'life', etc., as specific conditions.

(17) 'meditation' (*dhyāna*) as condition for the principles occurring in it.

(18) 'the way' (*mārga*) likewise for the principles occurring on it.

(19) 'conjoined with' (*saṃprayukta*) : principles occurring together; hardly distinguishable from 'simultaneous origin', but a much used older *abhidharma* term (cf. pp. 221f. above).

(20) 'disjoined from' (*viprayukta*) is the relation between material and immaterial principles as conditions for each other.

(21) 'existing' (*asti*), i.e. existing at the time, appears to reduce to 'simultaneous origin' or, if wider, to 'dependence'.

(22) 'not existing' (*nāsti*) is the cessation of an 'immediate' condition operating on principles present at the same time.

(23) 'without' (*vigata*, 'free from') is a synonym for 'not existing.'

(24) not without' (*avigata*) is a synonym for 'existing'.

The *Paṭisambhidāmagga* is in content a supplement to the *Vibhaṅga*. Of the thirty discussions (*kathā*) in it about one third appear under various of the eighteen headings of the *Vibhaṅga*. As a rule they do not conform to the *abhidharma* type of analysis of the *Vibhaṅga* : they take up various points from the *Sūtra* and the *Abhidharma* and add miscellaneous discussions on these. The *Paṭisambhidāmagga* might even be regarded as a record of various discussions which had taken place in the Sthaviravāda school, in which agreed doctrine, supplementary to what was found in the *Tripiṭaka* at that time, was noted and handed down.

The overall form of the work, however, as well as the title ('The Way of Comprehension'), suggest that at least the present arrangement of the discussions is not entirely casual, and that the work sets out in systematic order the way to enlightenment. The commentary of Mahānāma affirms that this is the character of the work and attempts to introduce each discussion as following on naturally from the last one, along this 'way'. We would thus have a detailed account of the way originally taught by the Buddha, built up in much the same manner as our own much briefer attempt in Chapter Four, except that we were there of set purpose confined to the earliest phase of doctrine only, whereas the *Paṭisambhidāmagga* adds much that is new.

The central discussion which gives its name to the whole work, that on 'comprehension' (Pali *paṭisambhidā*, but Sanskrit *pratisaṃvid* from a different root is the equivalent which occurs in similar formulae of other schools), would appear to be meant to expound the school's special doctrine that insight does not come gradually but is a sudden flash of enlightenment. The matter is not put in such a clear cut manner, using these terms, but instead is presented as a discussion on what happened when the Buddha first taught the Four Truths and at least one person (Kauṇḍinya) understood them, 'insight (*cakṣus*) into principles (or into nature, *dharma*) occurred', as the *Sūtra* says, — how did it occur, what does this mean? It is the knowledge which occurred in Kauṇḍinya which is called 'comprehension', and it had four aspects: comprehension of principles, of the meaning (*artha*) of what was said, of the language (*nirukti*) and finally of the 'intuition' (*pratibhāna*, 'inspiration' — the same word is used of the genius which enables a poet to improvise verses). The last of these is explained as that kind of 'knowledge' (*jñāna*, or 'knowing') which makes possible the first three aspects of comprehension, a sort of 'meta-knowing' or underlying power which inspires the others. (It should be added that there is so far, probably, no new wording invented by the Sthaviravādins: they have used an old formula known to the other schools but are putting it into a new context in this work and understanding it differently from other schools.)

Leading up to this discussion (which is in the sixteenth *kathā*) the *Paṭisambhidāmagga* begins with a large miscellaneous collection of all kinds of 'knowledges' (or 'knowings') — since, says the commentator, right theory stands at the beginning of the way. This includes some preliminary explanations of the four kinds of comprehension (we may note here that 'knowledge' or 'knowing' as used in these discussions is practically a synonym for the older word 'understanding'). There follows a collection of the wrong theories, the (false) opinions (*dṛṣṭis*), mentioned in the *Sūtra*. Next is an account of the exercise of self-possession with reference to breathing, a favourite exercise among the Buddhists of this period (but having authority in the *Tripiṭaka*). A discussion on the faculties, supplementary to that in the *Vibhaṅga*, follows, stating their purposes and when they should occur on the way. Next we have a collection of the 'freedoms' (*vimokṣas*), where we may note three of significance for future developments: the 'empty' (*śūnyata*), the 'signless' (*animitta*) and the 'uncommitted' (*apraṇihita*, 'not held', 'undirected' — towards any target or aim, as, particularly, with hostile intent) freedoms. Short notes follow on how consciousness is 'reborn', on action as of four kinds according to the timing of the result (perhaps a response to the Sarvāstivāda) and on 'error' (*viparyāsa*), this last briefly stated but of very great significance for the future workings out of the system. There are four 'errors' : perceiving, thinking or having the opinion that there is permanence in the impermanent, happiness in unhappiness, a soul in non-soul, beauty (*śubha*) in the ugly. In effect these 'errors' are the basis of delusion and 'ignorance'.

The ninth discussion, on the way, interrelates the factors of this, as the way to enlightenment, with the 'factors of enlightenment', strengths, faculties, powers, truths, 'calming' (*śamatha*), 'insight' (*vipaśyanā*), the freedoms, 'science', freeing (*vimukti*), knowledge (knowing) and extinction. Thus we have a note (little more) for systematising the way. The next discussion is just a coda to this; then the pair 'calming' and 'insight' are taken up. Discussion twelve expounds the view that all Four Truths are penetrated (comprehended) at once (*ekaprativedha*). The next discussions are on the 'factors of enlightenment', on freeing of thought by benevolence (p. 95 above), and on dispassion (*virāga*) as the way to freeing as the result. This brings us to the central discussion on 'comprehension' already referred to. The one that follows it is a continuation of it, on 'starting the wheel of the doctrine' (i.e. the occasion when someone first understood or comprehended it).

The remaining discussions are more miscellaneous, less easy to see as a regular exposition of the way following what has preceded, yet contributing to its theory. The seven topics of the 'Vaiśālī summary' (Chapter Four) are 'transcendent' (*lokottara*) — which for the Sthaviravāda means leading to extinction, so are the stages on the way and the results of those stages and extinction itself. Discussion nineteen is a useful and necessary addition to the *Vibhaṅga* in that it is devoted to the strengths (*bala*), unaccountably missed out of the *Abhidharma* work. They are in fact mentioned in several other discussions in the *Paṭisambhidāmagga* besides this one, always with the simple function of making unshakable whatever thought is being developed (cf. p. 93 above). Discussion twenty is on the topic 'the universe is empty (*śūnya*)', explained as meaning that it is empty of any 'soul' or 'self' (*ātman*), empty of anything 'belonging to a 'self' (*ātmanīya*, or 'having the nature of a self/soul'). The theme of 'empty' is then developed under twenty four headings (a favourite number in this school), all aspects of the same point : everything is empty of a soul/self (which means empty of anything permanent, eternal). This leads to discussion twenty-one on understanding (*prajñā*), explained as observing impermanence, unhappiness, non-soul and so on. 'Intuition-understanding' (*pratibhāna-prajñā*) is called 'smiling (*hāsa*) understanding', where 'smiling' is explained as 'joyous' : evidently the true happiness of one who understands the universe in its true nature and is freed from the unhappy pursuit of error. The remaining discussions are brief supplements of less importance (22 : power, *ṛddhi*; 23 : 'insight', *abhisamaya*; are worth noting).

Most (but not all) of the ideas in the *Paṭisambhidāmagga* may be found in the *Tripiṭaka*, though a proportion of these may belong only to a slightly later stratum than the texts we studied in Chapter Four. Some of the terms used are practically synonyms for what seem to have been the more original expressions (no doubt the language, the current vocabulary, was changing as fashions in vocabulary change in all languages). What is really new in the Sthaviravāda book is that a considerable step has been taken from the short and apparently simple description of the way given by the Buddha, though repeated in varying manners, with varing aspects and stresses, on countless occasions in the different dialogues and discourses, towards a single all embracing account in which, ideally, everything he was recorded to have said should find its proper place. The Buddha had taught orally and spontaneously; suppose now he had instead retired to some quiet place and written a book, a single book setting out his doctrine fully, then it might be thought he would have produced some such book as this (which the school later ascribed to Śāriputra). To answer the need in an age of highly organised 'monasteries' and 'schools' for a more academic type of text book than the old *Tripiṭaka Sūtra*, works such as the *Paṭisambhidāmagga* were compiled. Later writers of the Sthaviravāda school made several more attempts to produce this 'book of the way', which should include everything and interrelate everything, until the ideal was practically achieved (in the 5th century A.D.). Other schools made similar attempts in accordance with their own views. The date of the *Paṭisambhidāmagga* has not been worked out, even approximately. It could be later than any of the *Abhidharma Piṭaka* of its school, but on the other hand it might represent a somewhat divergent development, from the same beginnings in the *Vibhaṅga* but not taking much account of the studies which produced the *Dhammasaṃgaṇi* and the *Paṭṭhāna*. It is of course practical whereas those works are theoretical.

The *Peṭakopadesa* 'Instruction (Directions) about the (3) Traditions', is a work quite different from anything we have met so far (but cf. p. 278 above, Prajñaptivāda *Abhidharma*). It is not concerned with the doctrine as such but with scholastic methodology. As distinguished from the study of logic, which overlaps with it in part in that it aims to determine what statements can be deduced from, or are compatible with, certain given statements and what are the relationships between given terms in a system, this 'methodology' (Pali *netti*, Sanskrit *netrī* if used in this sense — cf. p. 403 below, chapter ten) is concerned with all aspects of interpretation, including the re-exposition or paraphrasing of doctrine for teaching purposes. It should be compared with parallel developments in the same period in the Brahmanical tradition of Vedic exegesis and of the organisation of knowledge generally : *mīmāṃsā* ('investigation', 'exegesis') with its elaboration of rules of interpretation of Vedic texts; *tantrayukti* ('combination', 'scheme', 'congruence' — *yukti* — of the 'system' — *tantra*), the methodology of constructing a branch of science or a treatise on it, the earliest discussion on which, now extant, appearing to be the appendix to Kauṭalya's *Arthaśāstra*.

The methodology of the *Peṭakopadesa* operates at two levels, with reference to (1) the wording of a statement and (2) the meaning.[1] The *Tripiṭaka* is vast in extent : suppose now one wishes to expound its doctrine, or part of it, how can one proceed in such a way as to restate this (as a commentary on a particular text from it or as an independent exposition) without misrepresentation or falsification (unintentional, of course) ? How can one guard against mistakes and misunderstandings ? By following this method attributed to Mahākātyāyana, which considers the whole *Tripiṭaka* in its aspects as wording and as meaning and shows how the extremely various wordings found reduce to a simple yet all embracing scheme of meanings. Many examples are given, particularly from the poetic texts of the *Kṣudraka*, to show how with all their varied imagery and metaphor every one of them in fact expounds the teaching of the Buddha. If these poetic texts are used in teaching, therefore,

1. See Ñāṇamoli's introduction to his translation of the text, pp. xxiiif.

these fundamental meanings are to be drawn from them and pointed out.

When scrutinising the wording one should look for such points as whether a word (or phrase) states the 'characteristic' (*lakṣaṇa*) of some principle (indicating its class), or its immediate cause, or whether a word is actually a synonym for the standard name of a principle in the system. We may have a 'reversal', that is a statement of the opposed factor (such as 'wrong' contrasted with 'right') which may be converted into its opposite for explanatory purposes. There is of course the 'combination' or 'congruence' (*yukti*) of a statement one wishes to make by way of comment, with the *Sūtra*, by making a citation (*apadeśa*) from the latter. One should determine whether the text is about the Truths, groups, elements, spheres, faculties or conditioned origination, for, it is said, there is no *sūtra* which is not about one of these six (this is done by collating with other *sūtras*). There is also a fourfold purely linguistic analysis investigating the grammar, etc. Altogether there are sixteen investigations of this type which may be applied to the wording in order to clarify it.

On the side of the meaning, according to the *Peṭakopadesa*, the doctrine of the *Tripiṭaka* may be summed up in any of three ways. All the teaching is (1) about either the four 'errors' (see pp. 313f. above) or their four opposites (the right views that there is ugliness in the ugly, unhappiness in unhappiness, impermanence in the impermanent and no soul in non-soul : meaning of course that one having right views will not seek happiness in the unhappiness which is transmigration but will instead seek freedom from this, seeing the unhappiness for what it is and not being attracted by its delusory promises); or (2) about either the three 'roots' of bad action or the three roots of good action (above p. 305); or (3) either about desire (in the bad sense, *tṛṣṇā*) and ignorance (*avidyā*) or about calming (*śamatha*, the basis of concentration and meditation) and insight (*vipaśyanā*, the basis of understanding : these two principles were made prominent in the *Paṭisambhidāmagga*). All the other statements of doctrine may be subsumed under one of these three types (this is set out in some detail in the text), moreover the first (known as the pair of 'tetrads' since it has four bad principles and four good) can be reduced to the second (the pair of 'triads') and this in turn to the third (the pair of 'dyads'). These three (1-3) are known as the three 'schemes' (*naya*) of the meaning.

Having checked the wording according to the sixteen investigations proposed above (having therefore reduced it to the standard terms of the system) there are two 'schemes' (*naya*) to be applied to it in order to fit it into the above standardised meanings: (4) it is to be classified under one of the three schemes of meaning according as it has tetrad, triad or dyad form; (5) it is to be classified as referring to the bad or the good and ranged accordingly under the bad or good member of the 'pair' within that meaning scheme. These two (4-5) are known as the two schemes of the wording.

This in broad outline is the method proposed by 'Mahākātyāyana' (incidentally with some picturesque terminology: of the five 'schemes' the first is called the 'lions' play', the second the 'trefoil' and the fifth the 'elephant hook'). Afterwards it was put to practical use by commentators of the Sthaviravāda school in writing commentaries on all the books of the *Tripiṭaka*. Apart from this method, however, there are a few new doctrinal ideas introduced incidentally (and quite casually) in the course of working the examples used. One or two of these are of major significance for the later history of Buddhism and must not be overlooked.

In a discussion on conditioned origination[1] we find the following distinction noted between 'cause' (*hetu*) and 'condition' (*pratyaya*) : the cause is the 'own-nature' (*svabhāva*) (of a principle); the condition is the 'other-nature' (*parabhāva*). The cause is internal (to the sequence, series, stream of a 'person's' thoughts); the condition is external. The important new concepts here are the 'own-nature' contrasted with the 'other-nature', especially the idea that any principle has an 'own-nature'. In the *Peṭakopadesa* the idea is not further developed and 'own-nature' may mean no more than 'internal' as opposed to external, but afterwards the school (and other schools) put new significance into it and thereby laid

1. p. 104.

themselves open to sweeping denunciation by Nāgārjuna in the 2nd century A.D.

In giving definitions the work uses in one place a threefold scheme : the 'characteristic' (*lakṣaṇa*), the 'appearance' or 'manifestation' (*pratyupasthāna*) and the 'immediate cause' (*padasthāna*).[1]

It appears that the school was not entirely satisfied with the *Peṭakopadesa*, consequently we find in the *Nettippakaraṇa* a complete recomposition of the work, with some omissions and some additions. The method is practically the same, with the introduction of one or two refinements in the investigations of the wording and an inversion in the order of the three meaning schemes. The chapter on the 'schemes' is somewhat enlarged and covers the reduction of a further range of doctrinal statements to the three meaning schemes, making the method more comprehensive or at least showing clearly how it is to be used over a much wider range of texts. On the whole, however, the improved work is considerably shorter and much more compact.

Ceylon

All the Sthaviravāda texts we have considered above may be presumed to have been composed in India, probably in Avanti (there is little tangible evidence : it is a matter of probabilities at present; Avanti with Daśārṇa and perhaps still the original Sthaviravāda centre at Kauśāmbī in Vatsa was the main territory of the school in the period when these texts were composed; the literary activity we find later in Ceylon shows a fresh phase of theorising). As the *Tripiṭaka* was brought to Ceylon in and after the 3rd century B.C. (probably piecemeal as monks who knew the various sections of it settled in the Island and passed on what they knew to their students) these newer texts were gradually brought in with it.

The centre of the Sthaviravāda in Ceylon was the Great Vihāra just outside the capital, Anurādhapura, founded in B.C.

1. pp. 128 f.

256[1] in the reign of King Devānāmpriya Tiṣya. The same king built other *vihāras* and pagodas around his capital and Buddhism became firmly established.[2] Unfortunately it is not possible within the scope of this book to enter into any detail of the history of Ceylon. The next important reign in Ceylon was that of (in Pali) Duṭṭhagāmaṇi (B.C. 118-94), regarded as a national hero on account of his successful wars against the Tamils (who had invaded the Island). These wars, however, are of no significance for Buddhism, for we are told that both sides were good Buddhists. After his victory Duṭṭhagāmaṇi engaged in great building works for Buddhism, including a nine storied Brazen Palace at the Great Vihāra for the purpose of holding the *poṣadha* ceremonies and the vast Great Pagoda (enshrining portions of the ashes of the Buddha which had been obtained by marvellous means). In the middle of the 1st century B.C. Ceylon went through a period of disasters : a rebellion dethroned King Vaṭṭagāmaṇi and at the same time there was a Tamil invasion from South India, years of chaos followed and a severe famine. Many Buddhist monks died of starvation along with many of the lay population: if the people could not feed themselves how could they support monks ? The only recourse was to leave the desolate country, and a good many monks succeeded in travelling to India, where they could stay with communities in more prosperous countries.

After fourteen years Vaṭṭagāmaṇi managed to regain his throne and expel the invaders (B.C. 42). The country was gradually restored and the monks returned from overseas and rejoined the remnant who had survived in remote mountain districts of Ceylon. The king built new *vihāras*, but one of these, the Abhayagiri (founded B.C. 38) at once became the centre of a schism : the king donated it to an individual monk with whom he associated instead of to the community. Reconciliation between the Great Vihāra and this new community established by the king for his favourites proved impossible, the recipient of the Abhayagiri was formally expelled from the Sthaviravāda community and the two *vihāras* became separate schools (and remained so for twelve centuries, after which

1. Year 12 of Aśoka : Eggermont, *Chronology*, 51 ff.
2. *Mahāvaṃsa* XX verses 17 ff.

they were at last united). It was after this final blow of the schism, as a result of which the Sthaviravâda lost the favour of the king, that the monks of the school saw how precarious was even the survival of their tradition and of the *Tripiṭaka* itself. The texts were still handed down only by memory and after the famine it had been discovered that one *Tripiṭaka* text, of the *Kṣudraka* (the *Niddesa*, p. 298 above), was remembered only by a single surviving monk. Students were at once set to learn it from him, but the warning was remembered. No doubt a text lost in Ceylon could have been replaced from India in that period, but in any case the Ceylon community sought to secure their tradition. At the Āloka Vihāra, far from the dissensions of the capital, they set to work (*c.* B. C. 35) with materials provided by local patronage and wrote down all their texts on prepared palm leaves. They wrote their *Tripiṭaka* in Pali and, we are told, the commentaries on it in the language of Ceylon of that period (we shall have to say more of these commentaries later).

Henceforth the Sthaviravāda was sometimes in favour, sometimes out of favour, with the kings of Ceylon, but on the whole they flourished and developed their studies and literary work, which now entered a new phase. The Abhayagirivāsins went their own way, which proved to be less conservative and orthodox, receptive to the ideas of the Mahāyāna and so diverging in doctrine from the Sthaviravāda.

The Commentaries

According to the Sthaviravāda tradition[1] commentaries (Pali *aṭṭhakathā*, literally 'discussions on the meaning') were brought to Ceylon by Mahendra along with the *Tripiṭaka* when Buddhism was first introduced into the Island. Whereas the *Tripiṭaka* itself was kept in the Pali language of India, these commentaries were put into Old Sinhalese to enable the islanders to understand the texts. The history of these commentaries has been carefully studied by Dr. Adikāram[2] in a remarkable pioneering work which has been strangely neglected by students of the history of Buddhism (probably because it was published in Ceylon

1. DA I 1, MA I 1, SA I 1, AA I 1, DhsA I 1.
2. *Early History of Buddhism in Ceylon*, Migoda (Puswella), 1946.

and few people outside the Island have been aware of its existence). To summarise his findings very briefly : (1) none of these Sinhalese commentaries is now extant, for they were eventuallv replaced by the Pali versions of them which we now use (made in the 5th century A.D.); (2) nevertheless these Pali versions reproduce the contents, or part of the contents, of the Sinhalese commentaries, apart from introductory and concluding remarks by the translators, and on rare occasions a comment added by a translator (and stated to be his own) on a point not clarified in his Sinhalese sources: they are not word by word translations of specific texts, for there was a plurality of old commentaries which was reduced to a single Pali version for each *Tripiṭaka* book, selecting what the translator considered necessary, but despite this 'editing' and the exceptions noted above they are in effect translations of material much older than themselves, not, as is widely assumed, new compositions of the 5th century A.D.; (3) the period of composition of the Sinhalese originals ended in the 1st century A.D., practically nothing is known — or likely — to have been added later; (4) despite additions down to the 1st century A.D. in Ceylon the formation of these commentaries reaches back into the older Indian tradition expounding the texts of the school; (5) many Sthaviravāda teachers are mentioned by name for their individual views on interpretation, the majority of these lived in Ceylon in the 1st century B.C. and the 1st century A.D.[1]

Whether or not, then, versions of the commentaries were written down, as the tradition states, in the 1st century B.C., some additional explanations were added during the century that followed, after which this corpus of comment became closed. What interests us now is the new ideas which appear in it, which seem to have developed in the school between the composition of the last *Abhidharma* texts, and of the *Paṭisambhidāmagga*, *Peṭakopadesa* and *Nettippakaraṇa*, and the end of the 1st

1. Dhammadinna, Malayadeva, c. 100 B.C. (time of Duṭṭhagāmaṇi); Buddharakkhita, c. 70 B.C.; Upatissa, Mahāpaduma (probably the most famous *ācārya*-exegete), Mahāsumana, Phussadeva (II), Cūlasiva, Mahāsiva (time of Vaṭṭagāmaṇi and his successor); Cūlanāga, Mahādhammarakkhita, Cūlābhaya, Mahābhaya (fl. c. 20-30 A.D.); are among the more outstanding teachers mentioned. Only two named teachers can be dated later than A.D. 50 (one c. A.D. 60 and one c. A.D. 130).

century A.D. For the most part we are not told who first suggested these new ideas (it is only when there is controversy that names are mentioned). Apparently they were already accepted among the Ceylon monks, perhaps even in Duṭṭhagāmaṇi's time (when some of the monks mentioned by name lived). Some of them were accepted in other schools of Buddhism, in India, in which case they are not likely to have originated in Ceylon as late as the 1st century A.D. For our present purpose, however, it is sufficient to have this general impression of the chronology of ideas.

The most significant new idea in the commentaries is the definition of a 'principle' or 'element' (*dharma*) : *dharmas* are what have (or 'hold', 'maintain', *dhṛ* is the nearest equivalent in the language to the English 'have') their own own-nature (*svabhāva*).[1] It is added that they naturally (*yathāsvabhāvatas*) have this through conditions (*pratyaya*). The idea is that they are distinct, definable, elements in the constitution of the universe. This *Abhidharma* commentary which we have quoted seeks to complete and finalise the statements of the *Dhammasaṃgaṇi* by enumerating and defining (by their respective own-natures) all the principles, elements, which ultimately are real. Where the original text says 'and whatever others occur...' the commentary lists them all. All synonymous terms for principles are identified (and explained as approached from different standpoints) so that the apparently exhaustive list reduces to considerably less than one hundred 'elements' out of which all experience is constructed. The additions are not numerous and are all found in the *Sūtra* (they include 'compassion' and 'attention').

The definitions or descriptions of all these principles are based on the threefold scheme anticipated in the *Peṭakopadesa* of stating the 'characteristic', 'appearance' and 'immediate cause' of each, but a fourth aspect is now added, the 'function' ('essence', *rasa* in a technical sense perhaps peculiar to this school). For example 'earth' has the characteristic of 'hardness', the function of 'supporting', the appearance of 'accepting (a weight)'. 'Water' has the characteristic of 'fluidity', the function of 'making increase (i.e. making swell up)', the appearance of 'cohesion'.

1. In Pali *attano pana sabhāvan dhārentī ti dhammā*. DhsA 39.

'Heat' has the characteristic of 'hotness', the function of 'maturing', the appearance of 'making soft'. 'Air' has the characteristic of 'inflating', the function of 'movement', the appearance of 'making move'.[1] As to the immediate causes of these four 'great existents', they are all the immediate causes of one another (for every molecule of matter contains all of them and they cannot occur independently: this is why they are no longer the old four elements but Buddhistic properties or 'principles' not different in nature from the mental forces, with which they are equally momentary) — cf. the *Paṭṭhāna* condition of 'simultaneous origin'.

To add examples from the forces: 'concentration' has the characteristic of 'leading', also 'non-confusion', the function of 'combining principles which originate simultaneously', the appearance of 'calm', the immediate cause of 'happiness'.[2] 'Compassion' has the characteristic of 'promoting the removal of the unhappiness of others', the function of 'not enduring the unhappiness of others', the appearance of 'harmlessness', the immediate cause of 'seeing the state of helplessness of those overwhelmed by unhappiness.'[3]

In this way descriptions are proposed for all the principles recognised. We may note that in many cases alternative definitions (characteristics, etc.) are suggested: we have in these ancient 'discussions on the meaning' not a dogmatic system but an enquiry carried on by these old teachers of the school into the real nature of things. They build on what has come down to them but they also seek to extend and improve it, and some conclusions they offer as tentative or controversial. That they themselves enquired into natural phenomena in order to extend the system and improve it is shown, for instance, by some observations of physical phenomena which are recorded in the commentaries, as: that sound travels more slowly than light, which is observed when one watches a man cutting down a tree from a distance, seeing his body move before one hears the sound.[4]

The study of psychological phenomena, particularly of perception and cognition, is as we might expect the most

1. DhsA 332.
2. DhsA 118f.
3. DhsA 193.
4. DhsA 313.

detailed. Putting together the various suggestions offered by the *Abhidharma* and then making their own observations, the old teachers worked out the mechanism of the stream of consciousness, the thought-series (*cittavithi*) in which mental principles occur.[1] For example when one is disturbed by some outside event producing a sensory impression, this is followed by a mental 'impulsion' and 'supports', a mental impression, investigation, and delimitation of the object. Then a series of mental events may occur, leading perhaps to the 'identification' of the disturbing object. If the object is of no interest the series will then revert to its neutral state (supposing one had been sleeping and then goes back to sleep), otherwise further mental results my occur, which may be of moral significance also. All these events are known as 'moments' (*kṣaṇa*), the moment being a discrete irreducible atom of the series in time. We thus have here an atomic theory of processes in time, with reference to the thought-series of a living being (only, as the commentary carefully points out, there is no being, only the series). In the minimum case considered of a neutral (sleeping) series disturbed, with identification of the object and, since it proves to be of no interest, immediate reversion to the neutral series, there are reckoned seventeen moments, if the preceding neutral moment at the beginning and the succeeding one at the end are included.

A parallel development in the study of logic can be seen in the commentaries on the *Kathāvatthu* and the *Yamaka*. The interesting distinction is pointed out[2] that it is not the expression (words) which is the measure (standard, authority: *pramāṇa*), but the meaning (if this were not so one could not escape the equivocations which threaten the Sthaviravāda in some of the *Kathāvatthu* controversies, particularly that on the 'person'). The point had been worked out in the study of distribution (the word used in the technical sense of 'term' in logic is in fact *artha* in these texts, which generally means 'meaning' outside this technical usage: the logical term, then, is in this school not the words, for which synonyms could be substituted, but the principle they refer to, the meaning;

1. See particularly DhsA 269 ff.
2. YamA 58.

their logic is a logic of meaning, of principles, not of words, and it is governed by the realities alone recognised in the *Abhidharma*, so that whatever does not refer to such a reality has no meaning in the philosophical sense and is not a term).

The Sthaviravāda commentaries contain much else besides philosophy. Here we may just mention the introductory narrative to the commentary on the *Jātaka*, which contains the school's version of the elaborate legend of the Buddha which by now had overlaid the few simple episodes from his life in the authentic *Tripiṭaka*, and which is perhaps best discussed in connection with the schools which concerned themselves most with this 'buddhology'.

The Caitikas, Āndhra and the Sātavāhana Empire

As the Empire of Magadha declined the Southern part of it broke away under a certain Simuka (into whose controversial origins we need not enter here), who founded the Sātavāhana dynasty, which proved to be one of the longest surviving imperial dynasties in history. The date of its origin is not yet established, but the consensus of conflicting records appears to indicate the time of the revolt of the General Puṣyamitra. The Sātavāhanas generally favoured Buddhism, and also Jainism, and should probably be regarded as the most direct successors to the policies of the Mauryan Emperors, whilst Puṣyamitra abolished these in favour of reestablishing orthodox Brahmanism. No hypothesis is more likely than that the separation of the South from Magadha reflected an ideological division produced by Puṣyamitra and the Brahmanical party when they ended the policy of honouring and supporting all the sects and sought to advance only their own. The party of toleration rallied in the South, which refused to accept the rule of the General, and the Empire was divided.

The Sātavāhana Empire was based on the countries of Āndhra and Mahārāṣṭra. Its strength increased while Puṣyamitra's successors fought a series of wars against the Greeks in Vāhīka and finally lost control of most of the countries which Magadha had conquered (Kośala, Pañcāla, Vatsa, Śūrasena, the Ārjunāyana Republic in Matsya, etc., became independent towards the end of the 2nd century B.C.). At this time the Sātavāhanas conquered Avanti and Daśārṇa and other countries. Eventually in B.C. 30 they conquered Magadha itself. It is not established which Sātavāhana emperor achieved this: the most likely one is Meghasvāti (or -svādi), in whose reign the Caitika school originated, according to K'ouei-ki.[1] By the end of the 1st century A.D. the Sātavāhanas had lost both Avanti and Magadha and a new empire had been established over Northern India, as we shall see later in this chapter.

No Caitika literature is now known to exist, unless in a modified form incorporated in Mahāyāna texts. The *Kathāvatthu Commentary* ascribes a good many grounds refuted in the *Kathāvatthu* to the Āndhra schools generally (which would imply the Caitikas) and some to the Pūrva Śaila, Apara Śaila, Rājagirika and Siddhārthika schools. Many of these are grounds of *abhidharma* and progress on the way, but the most significant are probably those relating to the Buddha. The Āndhra schools are said to have held that the Buddha's discourse (*vyavahāra*) is transcendental,[2] that the power (*ṛddhi*) of the Buddha or his pupils enables them to effect whatever they wish, regardless of the laws of nature[3] and that a (or the) *bodhisattva* (future *buddha*) was (among his numerous previous lives sometimes) reborn in very unhappy circumstances ('ruin', i.e. in purgatory, as an animal, a ghost or a demon) of his own free will (i.e. not as a result of his previous actions).[4] They also held that the special 'strengths' (*bala*,

---

1. Lamotte HBI 310, if Hao-yun wang=Meghasvādi (a liberal patron of Buddhism). The Purāṇic chronology of the Sātavāhanas is doubtful for the earlier period and not completely reliable for the later (see e.g. Gopalachari in the *Comprehensive History of India* II 326f., though we do not follow his theory). If we place Puḷumāyi I 105 years before Gautamīputra according to the *Matsya* and *Vāyu Purāṇas* (which agree on the total period though not on all the details) then the accession of Puḷumāyi I falls in about 1 B.C. (following the usually accepted date for Gautamīputra, not Gopalachari's). If the Purāṇic list between Meghasvāti and Puḷumāyi I is then accepted we get c. 55 B. C. for the accession of Meghasvāti, but the intervening kings are not well attested and one or two of them may be 'duplicates' produced by confusion in comparing sources, which would make Meghasvāti a decade or two later. Gopalachari has suggested that 'Svāti' is simply a repetition of Meghasvāti, which would eliminate 18 years.

2. Kvu 221 ff.

3. Kvu 606 ff.

4. Kvu 623 ff.

but not the usual ones) of the Buddha are all common to his pupils as well.[1] The two Śaila schools are said to have held that the *bodhisattva* was born certain of attaining enlightenment.[2] The Rājagirikas and Siddhārthikas are said to have held that principles are not classifiable under other principles, nor conjoined with other principles, and that 'mental principles' (*caitasikas*, i.e. the 'forces') do not exist.[3] All these grounds suggest that the general drift of the ideas of this group of schools was towards making the Buddha completely transcendent, beyond the laws of nature, and then to project this transcendence back over his previous existence as *bodhisattva*. If the Buddha's strengths were shared with his pupils, this might seem to imply that the pupils were, though not *buddhas* (which no school of Buddhism ever asserted), themselves *bodhisattvas* having this transcendent nature. The non-existence of the mental principles would radically change *abhidharma* theory and abolish large parts of it. Limited to the two latest schools of the group it may not be of such significance as the other grounds, yet it suggests that what seem to be fundamental and early *abhidharma* ideas were likely to be challenged by monks in the Āndhra communities.

As we shall see in the next chapter, the Mahāyāna originated in the South of India and almost certainly in the Āndhra country, among these communities. It is here, therefore, that we have to look for the transition which led to this new kind of schism, if it is correct to call it such, when the Mahāyāna put forward its essential new doctrine of 'Buddhahood' (not mere enlightenment as formerly conceived) as the proper aim of the Buddhist and the way of the *bodhisattva*, the future *buddha*, as therefore the proper course of training to be undertaken. The earlier Mahāsaṃgha schools had opened the way towards this eventual development, and indeed they are claimed as forerunners by the Mahāyāna.[4] The original school had made a sharp distinction between the *arhant* and the Buddha, making it relatively easy to become an *arhant*, whereas a *buddha* is still a rare and possibly superhuman being. The

1. Kvu 228 ff.
2. Kvu 480.
3. Kvu 335 ff.
4. See e.g. Demiéville : 'L' origine des sectes bouddhiques d'après Paramārtha', MCB I 15ff.

Lokottaravāda completed that process of separation by putting forward the view that the Buddha was a transcendent being whose body was not of this world. This naturally led to increased interest in the story of the Buddha's life, and to some extent in his former lives leading up to this consummation. The Bahuśrutīyas held that the Buddha had a 'transcendent' teaching as well as teaching which was 'of the world' (where 'transcendent' is clearly connected with *nirvāṇa*). Probably they rejected the Lokottaravāda view, which would surely not so restrict any attribute of the transcendent Buddha. According to the Sthaviravāda tradition the Caitika school was an offshoot of the Bahuśrutīyas, whilst other versions appear to make it secede from the original Mahāsaṃghika school. In either case they evidently developed the transcendentalist ideas in a new way, perhaps parallel to the Lokottaravāda at first but probably going beyond the positions of the older school. The Buddha's discourse was transcendental (all of it), his enlightenment was already determined when he was born, he could set aside natural laws (and so presumably produce any miraculous effects he wished). In his previous lives as the *bodhisattva* he already enjoyed supreme mastery over the principles of transmigration and was reborn in his successive lives at his own free will, having apparently already passed beyond any further effects of his former actions when he first became a *bodhisattva*. Similarly, perhaps, his present pupils enjoyed this mastery and could set aside natural laws, which would imply that they were now *bodhisattvas* as he had been formerly: that they aimed to be *buddhas* in the remote future, not simply *arhants* attaining final *nirvāṇa* now.

Surely we are here in the presence of the ideas which will form the basis of the Mahāyāna, if we can trust our source (the other sources on the schools are all confused or inadequate on the Caitika doctrines and trace their schism only to a legal dispute on 'entrance' to the community; Ceylon would be in closer touch with Āndhra than writers in Northern India). As to their literary expression, some of the early (short) Mahāyāna *sūtras* long afterwards collected in the 'Great' *Ratnakūṭa* group may have been taken over from the Āndhra schools, for example the *Rāṣṭrapālaparipṛcchā*, though they may have been modified in ways which it would be hard to trace. If attention came to be focussed on the way of the *bodhisattva* it would be natural to give literary form to the theory of his long progress, not simply to celebrate the virtues of the Buddha (as in the Sthaviravāda *Cariyāpiṭaka*, see p. 298 above) but in order to lay down the practical programme to be embarked on by new *bodhisattvas*. The *Bodhisattvapiṭakas* of the Dharmaguptakas, Bahuśrutīyas and probably the Āndhra schools no doubt provided extensive materials for such a reworking.

The Lokottaravāda and Bahuśrutīya: The Legend of the Buddha and Aśvaghoṣa

We left the history of Northern India with the Greek invaders established in Vāhīka in the middle of the 2nd century B.C. and several of its countries independent (under various dynasties) soon afterwards, leaving Magadha itself to be conquered by Āndhra a century later. We noted earlier that some of the Greeks supported Buddhism or 'principle' and assimilated themselves to their new home and a new civilisation in this way. One Greek king deserves particular mention: Menandros (Prakrit Menemdra on his bilingual coins, Sanskrit Milindra, Pali Milinda), who reigned according to the latest authority[1] *c.* B.C. 155-130. The Buddhists of the Sarvāstivāda, Sthaviravāda and other schools preserved a celebrated dialogue between the king and a Buddhist monk Nāgasena (for whom the Sarvāstivādins substituted one of their own school, Dhītika), as a result of which the king became a lay disciple. According to the Sthaviravāda tradition their version of the dialogue was written in India during the early 1st century A.D. and immediately brought to Ceylon (where it is quoted in the commentaries). The known versions in fact differ widely (e.g. the Sthaviravāda made large additions to theirs). In form the dialogue is modelled on that between the Buddha and Ajātaśatru but shows also some affinity to the (extant examples only much later) 'biography' (*ākhyāyikā*) form of Indian secular literature, with stylish descriptions and narrative of the hero (Menandros) attaining some end (in this case entering the way of Buddhism).[2] The coins of Menandros show that he

1. A. K. Narain : *The Indo-Greeks*.
2. cf. IKL II p. 74. Nāgasena seems to be a Kāśyapīya (p. 6).

continued to recognise the Greek gods, as Aśoka supported all sects, as well as Buddhism. He used the Buddhist wheel (*cakra*) symbolising the wheel of the doctrine (and the eightfold way) or the 'wheel gem' of a (Buddhist) universal emperor (probably both).

Greek rule in India was of brief duration. The Greeks did not strengthen their position by dividing into two kingdoms. The Śakas (Scythians), barbarian tribes from the North, conquered Sogdia probably during the time of Menandros and immediately pushed on through Bactria and Aria to the Western part of Arachosia, which came to be called Śakasthāna (Seistan) because they settled there in large numbers. The Greeks in Bactria were forced to pay tribute. After this the Śakas pushed up through Arachosia and Kāpiśa into Gandhāra. Their king Moga ('Maues', probably Chinese Mu-kua, with whom the Chinese fought in central Asia in B.C. 102) conquered Gandhāra at the beginning of the 1st century B.C. The situation becomes confused with the simultaneous expansion of Parthia, which had regained its independence from the Greeks (Seleucids) already in the 3rd century B.C. The Parthians enlarged their realm to the East at the expense of the Śakas, but in the case of some of the kings known to have ruled in Śakasthāna and Gandhāra in the 1st century B.C. the historians do not agree whether they were Śakas or Parthians (both were kindred Iranian peoples, which makes distinction of names difficult). Aja I ruled after Moga in these regions, perhaps overthrowing the mysterious Vanāna in Śakasthāna and finally ending Greek rule in India by conquering Vāhīka. Early in the 1st century A.D., his successors were engaged in a struggle with the Parthian Vindapharna ('Gondophernes') in Gandhāra and Śakasthāna. This Parthian ruler, and the earlier ones, if they were Parthians, was independent of the main dynasty in Parthia itself. Aja (I or II ?) was a patron of Buddhism, which continued to make progress among all these peoples regardless of which was the ruling power.

Meanwhile another power had arisen in Central Asia. The Westward expansion of China in the 3rd and 2nd centuries B.C. led to a Westward movement of the barbarians of Mongolia (Hūṇas, 'Huns') and Sinkiang. Among these the Yüeh-chih (this is the Chinese name, pronounced something like 'Yuerja'), later known as the Kuṣāṇas, about B.C. 160 were driven out of Sinkiang down the Ili valley by other tribes and themselves pressed hard on the Śakas. By about B.C. 100 they had conquered Sogdia and Bactria from the Śakas. More than a century later their five tribes were united under the rule of a single king, Kujula Kathphiśa, who conquered the Eastern Parthian kingdom and Kāpiśa during his long reign (*c.* A.D. 15-65). On his coins he refers to himself (in Gāndhārī Prakrit) as 'established in principle (*dharma*)', as had some of his Greek and Parthian e.g. (Śpalahora) predecessors in these regions. It would seem, then, that the Kuṣāṇa people had during the century before his reign been assimilated to the prevailing Buddhist ideology of Eastern Iran and with it various other elements of Indian civilisation (if Kuṇāla had indeed established Indian colonies using Gāndhārī in Khotan and possibly Bactria, and the intervening Tukhāra, they may already have begun to adopt this Indian language before the conquest of Kāpiśa, cf. p. 285 above). Under the next king, Vima Kathphiśa, they conquered Gandhāra, Vāhīka and possibly countries further East and South (it is uncertain whether Vima Kathphiśa or his successor Kaniṣka I conquered Śūrasena, Kośala, Kāśi and other countries and, apparently, subjected Magadha to vassalage). Kaniṣka I (A.D. 78-102[1]) thus became the emperor of a reunified Northern India embracing on the North West all the old Mauryan domains in Iran, including Bactria, Sogdia and some adjacent parts of Central Asia perhaps never directly ruled by the Mauryas. The Śakas became vassals of the Kuṣāṇas, often serving as governors of provinces of the Empire (which seems to imply they became subordinate allies of the stronger power against common enemies). The empire of India was thus divided between the Kuṣāṇas and the Sātavāhanas, both upholding in general the policies set by Aśoka and diffusing the civilisation of India.

The popularisation of Buddhism was by now based very largely on the legend of the Buddha. The doctrine itself could be presented symbolically through this legend, and however

1. This date has long been controversial, but remains the most probable.

far the wandering teachers of *dharma* (in all the senses of that mightily ambiguous word) went in expounding the Four Truths and the eightfold way, and the ideal society, they evidently found that it was generally easier to make the first impression on their multiracial audiences by means of narratives rather than the dialogues of the *Tripiṭaka*. The greatest of these narratives was the story of the Buddha himself, and the more wonderful it could be made, the more surprising its incidents, the more effective it seems to have been. At first sight one might suppose this to correspond to the spread of Buddhism from the more sophisticated and rationalistic people of India, long accustomed to philosophical and critical thought, among less civilised peoples who loved the irrational and the marvellous. However, this supposition would seem to be decisively set aside by the fact that the experience of the Buddhists appears to have been just the same in China, whose people, though attached to a certain mystery and ritualism in the Confucian tradition and magic and marvels mixed with science in the Taoist, were not unaccustomed to philosophical criticism. The truth is, surely, that all societies contain very varied strata of educated and uneducated people, where also the educated (in our sense) do not usually coincide to any appreciable extent with the wealthy and the powerful. When Buddhism was popularised outside the circles of the philosophers, the *śramaṇas* and those influenced by them, of those inclined to 'leave the world' in search of peace of mind and freedom, then even in India the means of appeal to the uneducated were sought and adopted.

We have already referred to the *Mahāvastu* (p. 276 above) as perhaps the first full scale biography of the Buddha, in which around the scanty record of the original *Vinaya* many new episodes have been gathered. It is in a mixture of prose and verse and the metrical part can be dated at about the end of the 2nd century B.C. on the grounds of the history of metre. This does not tell us whether the prose is later or earlier or contemporaneous, but as generally the two forms paraphrase one another this does not greatly affect us here. In roughly the same period every school of Buddhism seems to have equipped itself with a similar biography of the Buddha. The Sthaviravāda version is, as already mentioned (p. 326

above), in their commentary on the *Jātaka*, where it is called the *Nidānakathā*. That it is purely commentarial suggests a date in the 1st century B.C. or later. The less conservative Lokottaravāda included their *Mahāvastu* in the *Tripiṭaka* itself, in the *Vinaya*. The Kāśyapīya *Buddhajātakanidāna* probably had the same status as the *Nidānakathā*. Whether the *Śākyamunibuddhacarita* or *Abhiniṣkramaṇasūtra* was included in the *Tripiṭaka* of the Dharmaguptakas, to whom it is said[1] to belong, is uncertain. The Mahīśāsaka *Vinayapiṭakamūla* may well have been included in their commentary on the *Vinaya*, an extension of a historical introduction to this commentary similar to that of the Sthaviravāda *Vinaya* commentary. According to the *Śākyamunibuddhacarita* the 'Mahāsaṃghikas' called their biography '*Mahāvastu*', which would seem to mean that not only the Lokottaravāda but the more original Mahāsaṃghika school also had such a text, though it has not survived.[2] The Sarvāstivāda produced a more poetic work than any of these, the *Lalitavistara* (afterwards appropriated by the Mahāyānists and further elaborated, in which form the Sanskrit text has come down to us). Much later still the Mūlasarvāstivādins prepared a biography more complete than any of these and boldly placed it in extenso in their greatly enlarged *Vinaya*. Several other biographies are extant in Chinese translations, but have not yet been assigned to any schools.

All these biographies agree in their main outlines and essential episodes, but differ completely in their actual texts, styles, and innumerable details. Whatever borrowing there was between the schools took place not in the period of formation of their common original *Tripiṭaka*, in which no such biography occurs (as we saw in Chapter Three), but much later, when the Sthaviravādins and probably some others had closed their *Tripiṭakas* against further additions. In a sense the legend of the Buddha belongs not to the schools but to the popular Buddhism of the ordinary laity in which the doctrinal differences which split the schools count for practically nothing —

1. By Demiéville, MCB I 61.
2. An episode from it which is not in the *Mahāvastu* is given (Beal 315ff).

in short to Buddhism as a religion, not to Buddhism as a philosophy. There is among the ordinary lay people a Buddhism of simple 'confidence' in the Buddha, flavoured with a more or less vague knowledge of the virtues he taught and some feeling for the renunciation, compassion and peace he exemplifies, expressed through the quiet devotion of offering flowers at a pagoda or in a shrine house (i.e. a temple) where the Buddha is depicted in painting and sculpture along with scenes from his life. The difference is perhaps not very great even between followers of the ancient Sthaviravāda and of the Mahāyāna. All are unmistakably Buddhists, only the Tibetan followers of the Mantrayāna are more overtly fervent, and vigorous rather than calm in their ritual exercises.

The legend of the Buddha usually begins with an account of the meeting of the future Buddha with a Buddha of an earlier cycle of the universe, many thousands of millions of years ago, called Dīpaṃkara Buddha (as 'our' Buddha is Śākyamuni Buddha). He honoured Dīpaṃkara and thought of becoming a Buddha himself, and the latter 'determined' (in effect predicted) that in the remote future he would become a Buddha. It is to be noted that there is no question of his becoming a follower, certainly not a monk, of Dīpaṃkara or of any of the other earlier Buddhas, some of whom he meets. By definition a Buddha has to discover the doctrine for himself, independently, moreover if he followed the way of an earlier Buddha and attained extinction he could not, obviously, be reborn. His way must be different from the eightfold way. Hence, having become a future Buddha, a *bodhisattva*, by forming the wish and having it approved by Dīpaṃkara, the 'great being' (*mahāsattva*), as he is sometimes called, went his own way, which in fact meant the countless lives some of which are described in the *jātaka* stories. The idea here came to be that through this hard and long way of training he gradually perfected himself, through practice established himself unshakably in all the virtues necessary for a *buddha*.

After the last of these previous lives on earth the *bodhisattva* was reborn among the Tuṣita gods (p. 153 above), where for an inconceivably long time he enjoyed divine bliss, resting and relaxing, as it were, before his final labours. When he felt the time was right he chose a suitable place to be born, and suitable parents, and descended to earth. In the imperial age in which this legend was developed it would not do to have the *bodhisattva* born in anything less than an imperial family. The republican nature of the Śākya state is glossed over. Śuddhodana is now a king, at least equal to his contemporary Bimbisāra of Magadha, and the *bodhisattva* is the heir apparent. Moreover Śuddhodana's family is descended from the first king, the 'Great Elect', via the great emperors who ruled justly, who are described in the *Tripiṭaka*, and the Solar Dynasty of the Purāṇic tradition. The birth is attended by miracles: the conception of the *bodhisattva* is an immaculate one, so is his birth. His mother experiences no pain, only pleasure, and he is born magically through her side without even touching her. Gods and goddesses are standing by to take him up and streams of warm and cool water descend from the heavens to wash him, although there is no impurity and the action is a purely ritual one. The babe takes seven steps in each direction (said to symbolise the seven factors of enlightenment) and announces his greatness and that this is his last birth. Lotuses spring up under his feet as he walks. From now on marvellous signs will accompany the *bodhisattva* throughout his life, the gods will be his constant servants and there will be any number of miracles. His mother cannot live longer as an earthly woman and after seven days dies and is reborn among the Thirty Three gods, where eventually her son will visit her and teach her the doctrine.

The brahmans examine the babe and foretell a great future for him: he will become either a universal emperor or a *buddha*. Here occurs the popular episode of the great seer Asita ('Black'), who predicts that he will definitely become a *buddha* and then weeps because he himself will not live long enough to hear the Buddha teach. This episode existed (separately) before B.C. 200, for a poetic version of it is found in the *Suttanipāta* of the Sthaviravāda *Tripiṭaka*: [1]

'Then to Asita the Śākyas showed the son,
    a boy flaming like gold

1. Sn 679-698 (what then follows is a much older poem).

In a crucible, gladdening the expert smith,
brilliant with good fortune, unequalled in beauty.

Seeing the boy brightening as a flame,
like the pure bull of stars, the sky-goer,
The Sun radiant as in autumn when the clouds have gone,
he rejoiced and was filled with affection...'

This is comparatively restrained and the whole poem is quite short.

When still in early childhood, the *bodhisattva* is taken out to see a ploughing ritual, but sits under a tree and attains the first meditation. Miraculously the tree's shadow remains without moving, protecting him from the Sun as long as he meditates. Śuddhodana, however, is determined that his son shall be an emperor, not a *buddha*, and takes all possible steps to prevent Asita's prediction from coming true. This is primarily the responsibility of the ladies; luxurious palaces are built and the *bodhisattva* is married as soon as possible as well as being provided with innumerable female attendants skilled in all the arts. But knowledge of the true nature of the world and human life cannot be permanently kept from the young man. On drives through the city of Kapilavastu and out to parks he inevitably sees four 'portents' (all predicted by Asita in some versions): a man broken down with age, one suffering from a filthy disease, a corpse at a funeral, one who has 'gone forth' (a wanderer or *śramaṇa*). Greatly distressed by the first three, he is pleased by the last, who advocates non-violence and compassion and symbolises a way other than that of the world. He sees the unhappiness of the worldly life and makes up his mind to renounce this and 'go forth', losing all interest in pleasures.

His escape from the well guarded palace, aided by the gods, is attended by miracles. From this point there were more episodes available from the *Tripiṭaka* (see Chapter Three), such as the Buddha's teachers and the narratives of the enlightenment and starting the wheel of the doctrine. New episodes are inserted, such as the messengers sent by Śuddhodana to persuade the *bodhisattva* to return home, of course without success. The experiments in asceticism as the *bodhi-*

sattva tries out the methods recommended by other wanderers are made much of, but the most celebrated episode in this part of the story is the 'temptation' by Death and by Death's daughters : the final 'battle' leading to the victory of enlightenment.

The majority of these biographies end with the initial teaching episodes of the Buddha's career, his being joined by his most famous followers (Mahākāśyapa, Śāriputra, Maudgalyāyana, etc.) and especially the return to Kapilavastu with its 'human interest' of again meeting his family and the 'going forth' of Rāhula and Nanda. In fact they end where the *Vinaya* introductory narratives ended and are themselves of an introductory character. They add miracles, such as the Buddha's power of flight, and some of them add his visits to the heavens. Many incidental narratives are inserted in some of the versions, especially *jātakas* and stories of former lives of persons other than the Buddha (*avadānas*). The doctrine is not completely forgotten. The whole quest of the *bodhisattva* symbolises it in an easily understandable manner and sometimes philosophical discussions are directly introduced.

One of the richest of these biographies is certainly the *Mahāvastu* of the Lokottaravādins, which improves the supernatural elements of the legend with the 'transcendentalist' doctrine of the school and yet remains more closely within the old *Vinaya* framework than do the others, being regarded as a genuine *Vinaya* text. It also incorporates many incidental narratives and a good deal of poetry from the *Kṣudraka*. Its endless and disorderly riches made it popular even outside the school which produced it.

There is little we can add to the account of the other branches of the Mahāsaṃgha in this period. One of them, however, probably the Bahuśrutīya,[1] produced in the 1st century A.D. the greatest of the Buddhist poets, Aśvaghoṣa, who is one of the half dozen greatest poets of India and, for those who know him, among the first ten poets of the world. Such judgments are largely subjective and are probably as a rule strongly influenced by one's preferences and antipathies in

1. Such is the conclusion of his editor and translator, Johnston; see especially the introduction to his translation of the *Buddhacarita*.

religion. In Aśvaghoṣa's case, at least, his genius is so to say a 'secular' fact independent of his being a Buddhist. His works belong to the secular tradition of Indian literature (*kāvya*), not to the religious tradition (a fact which worried him considerably). Nothing is really known about his life. Legends connect the famous poet with the nearest available famous emperor, Kaniṣka, as is the way of legends, but Johnston more convincingly places the poet half a century earlier. He could hardly have met any of the Kuṣāṇa rulers but his poetry and dramas attained great popularity in the empire they established not long after he had written them. He was born in Ayodhyā (Sāketa) in Kośala and had a thorough Brahmanical education. In poetry and drama he was immensely learned in all the by then highly complex techniques and theories of those arts. He loved the rules of grammar and poetics, finding in them excellent combustible material for his genius to work on. Equally he loved the systems and subtleties of conflicting philosophical doctrines.

Aśvaghoṣa's originality is perhaps best indicated by the equal gusto with which he enters alternately into the spirit of the world and the spirit of renunciation. This is far from the superficial enthusiasm of a versatile writer. For all his display of humour and lightness of touch he cannot conceal his deep earnestness and complete involvement in the ambiguity of life. He claims to use the attractiveness and popularity of the poetic art simply as a vehicle for the doctrine of Buddhism: worldly people will be drawn along by the charm of art, but by imperceptible degrees into the way of renunciation. Consequently he unites in his work joy in the pleasures of the world and their poetic presentation, and joy in the peace and freedom attained by renouncing them. He is most realistic in portraying the pleasures which he afterwards dismisses as ephemeral and unreal. Surely he is writing from poignant experience and his autobiography is hidden behind the tension of his poetry. If he renounced the world it was not through any natural aversion to it but rather the result of deep entanglement in it affecting a sensitive and exceptionally clear mind.

His best known work is his epic poem *Buddhacarita* ('Life of the Buddha'). This is the first known complete biography of the Buddha, from his birth to the *parinirvāṇa*. Its 28 cantos are divided into four equal parts: (1) birth and youth up to the renunciation; (2) wanderings, asceticism, battle with Death (in an epic poem there must be a battle) and enlightenment; (3) teaching, campaign of 'conquest' through many countries in the four directions; (4) the last journey and *parinirvāṇa*, followed by the building of the pagodas and a reference to Aśoka's establishment of eighty thousand of these. This framework thus corresponds to the four main places of pilgrimage: Kapilavastu, Bodh Gayā (Gayanagarī), Vārāṇasī, Kuśinagarī.

The shorter epic *Saundarananda* ('The Handsome Nanda') describes how the extremely worldly Nanda was induced to become a monk by the Buddha. He can be weaned away from the pleasures of love only by the promise of superior pleasures of the same kind, attainable in union with the nymphs of heaven. The way to secure this, however, lies through the ascetic training offered in the community of monks, which Nanda therefore embarks on with the utmost seriousness. When he has made rapid progress on the way and risen sufficiently far above his former entanglement in the world, his colleagues are able to make him feel the absurdity of his position as a monk devoted to the nymphs and redirect him towards true happiness.

Unfortunately only fragments or mere references survive of Aśvaghoṣa's plays: *Śāriputra* (in 9 acts), *Rāṣṭrapāla*, *Somadatta* and an allegorical drama of unknown title in which there were such characters as Glory, Fortitude and Intelligence (nymphs? —*Jātaka* No. 535 has some similarly named nymphs in it). Rāṣṭrapāla had great difficulty in obtaining his parents' consent to become a monk. Even after succeeding through the threat of a fast to death he has to overcome their attempts to lure him back again. *Somadatta*, unlike all the above works (except perhaps the allegorical play), evidently had a story of the poet's own invention, which unfortunately we can now only guess at. Somadatta is the lover of a geisha girl, Magadhavatī. Other characters included a prince, a rogue, a jester (Somadatta's friend), etc., and there were scenes between Magadhavatī and another lover, in a garden, and at a festival. Certainly it was a comedy of worldly entanglements; whether it led any of its characters to renunciation is a mere guess.

We see from this unhappily scanty evidence that there was a flourishing Buddhist theatre in India in the 1st century A.D. From central Asian sources we can infer the existence of further plays on *jātaka* stories by unknown dramatists.

The Sarvāstivāda, proto-Sautrāntika and the Kuṣāṇa Empire

We have seen the Sarvāstivādins spreading from Mathurā (Śūrasena) into Gandhāra and Kaśmīra, whilst keeping a foothold in the East (Śrāvastī, Vārāṇasī). This movement seems to have begun during the 3rd century B.C. Having separated from the Sthaviravāda, this school made its own additions to the *Tripiṭaka*. We noted (p. 297) that where comparisons can be instituted the Sarvāstivāda is the least conservative of the schools in the matter of preserving the *Tripiṭaka* in its more original form, and this applies to the old Sarvāstivāda already, not merely to its later offshoot the Mūlasarvāstivāda with its wholesale revision of the *Vinaya*. A substantial part of their *Tripiṭaka* is now available, in a more or less fragmentary state in Sanskrit or in intact translations in Chinese and more rarely Tibetan. In addition we have some works which may not have been included in their *Tripiṭaka*, some commentaries and some monographs by teachers of the school.

Presumably as part of their Minor Tradition (*Kṣudraka Āgama*), the Sarvāstivāda, like the Sthaviravāda, prepared an *Avadāna*, or rather several *avadānas*, including a *Vimānāvadāna* and a *Pretāvadāna* corresponding to the Sthaviravāda *Vimānapetavatthu*.[1] The divergence between these literatures of these two schools is very great, particularly between the Sthaviravāda *Apadāna* and the Sarvāstivāda *Avadānaśataka* — which is hardly surprising since both works are centuries later in composition than the schism between the schools[2] and probably have not even a common kernel. The Sarvāstivādins seem to have possessed versions of all the more original *Kṣudraka* texts listed above (pp. 203f.) A new addition unknown to the old lists of these texts is the *Anavataptagāthā*, in which the Buddha takes 499 monks on a legendary excursion to Lake

1. Bechert : *Anavataptagāthā*, 14f.
2. Above p. 298, Speyer : *Avadānaśataka*, Preface, p. xv.

Anavatapta in the Himālaya. Each of 36 monks recalls in the verses an action (good or bad) done by him in a previous life and its subsequent result, so that the text is in effect an *avadāna* (which should deal with previous lives, usually of monks or nuns). The Buddha himself then adds a remarkable series of bad actions committed by himself in past lives and their unpleasant results, including illnesses from which he suffered even after becoming the Buddha (backache, dysentery). It seems that at one time the Sthaviravāda accepted this text as canonical, in a Pali version, for their *Nettippakaraṇa* quotes it[1] as a *sūtra* and the final verses of the Buddha himself are included in their *Apadāna*.[2] It is otherwise not now found in their *Tripiṭaka*. In this particular case we have to do with a borrowing, it seems, by one school from another in a comparatively late period, not with a text shared with them before their schism. In the middle of the 1st century A.D. Dharmatrāta (see below) rearranged and probably enlarged the existing *Dharmapada* of the Sarvāstivāda and produced the text called the *Udānavarga* of which he is sometimes supposed to be the actual author.

The Sarvāstivāda *Abhidharma* (fortunately intact in Chinese and Tibetan versions) grew up around the *Saṃgītiparyāya*, *Dharmaskandha*, part of the *Dhātukāya* and perhaps part of the *Vijñānakāya* already mentioned (pp. 219 ff. above), which formed the school's version of the original *Abhidharma*. After the schism which produced their school the Sarvāstivādin monks composed further *abhidharma* texts to consolidate their doctrinal position. Though these were regarded as part of the *Tripiṭaka* and were supposed to contain nothing which had not been promulgated in the *Sūtra* by the Buddha, they have the names of individual monks recorded as their authors (unlike most of the Sthaviravāda *Abhidharma*). First (c. 200 B.C.) Kātyāyanīputra composed the *Jñānaprasthāna*, which came to be regarded as the basic *abhidharma* text of this school. This shows some similarities to the *Dhammasaṃgaṇi* of the rival school, for example the use of some of the same 'triads'

1. *Netti* 141 f., Bechert : *Anavataptagāthā* 81 (metre : *vaṃśasthā*, which is not found in the earlier strata of *Tripiṭaka* poetry).

2. *Apadāna* 299 ff.

of classes, but its rather chaotic arrangement (like a notebook in which points have been jotted down from time to time) has nothing in common with that text. Its eight sections deal with: miscellaneous, the connections (*saṃyojana*), knowledge, action, the great existents, faculties, concentration and opinion (*dṛṣṭi*). It contains a refutation of the doctrine on *arhants* specific to the Mahāsaṃgha. Among its new conceptions is the principle (*dharma*) 'attainment' (*prāpti*), the presence of which is made to explain the fact of the combination of various other principles in the sequence of a living being. Then there are two kinds of cessation (*nirodha*): through understanding or through a natural process of extinction (these two with space make up the three 'unsynthesised elements' of this school). Also perhaps new is the principle 'unmanifest' (*avijñapti*), meaning the unseen aspect of an action, which is the morally potent aspect.[1] The contrasted 'manifest' includes speech and gesture. Now the same gesture, for example, may be made deliberately or accidentally. No difference is manifest, but there is a difference in fact, which is explained as due to the presence of the principle 'unmanifest' in the case of a deliberate gesture. Six kinds of cause (*hetu*) are defined: conjoined with, simultaneously existing, similar (matter continuing 'unchanged'), universal (innate morally significant tendencies), result and instrumental (*kāraṇa*, as a sense object, corresponding to dominant in part in the Sthaviravāda system, but dominant is itself a 'condition' for the Sarvāstivāda).

Devaśarman a little later enlarged, or perhaps entirely composed, the *Vijñānakāya*. This deals in part with the theory of conditions (especially 'cause', see above, and 'support'). Its first section, however, refutes the doctrine of the Sthaviravāda concerning the non-existence of past and future principles, thus upholding the special 'all exist' theory of the school. It is noteworthy that this section actually refers to the opponent as Maudgalyāyana, who must surely be the author of the *Kathāvatthu*, in which, as we saw above, a corresponding refutation of 'all exist' is found. The second section contains a refutation of the Vātsīputrīya doctrine of a 'person', very similar in its arguments to the first controversy in the *Kathāvatthu* and

1. It is found in the *Śāriputrābhidharmaśāstra* but not in the Sthaviravāda *Abhidharma*. Harivarman also has it, so it may be original.

probably inherited from the older school as it was immediately after the personality schism. The proposition refuted is the same and there are common arguments such as those beginning: is the (supposed) person a moral agent, is it perceived, does it transmigrate, is it synthesised or unsynthesised? Basically the method is the same, of setting the proposition in opposition to *sūtra* statements, moreover the logical form in which it is set out is the same conditional (substituting a ponential, etc., in the opponent's thesis and producing a pair of related propositions of which the opponent has affirmed one and denied the other). The detailed formulation of the argument, however, is very much simpler, leaving out what were presumably the formalities of a debate and keeping only the logical essentials. The opponent here is called a *pudgalavādin* and it is of interest that the orthodox protagonist is called a *śūnyatāvādin* ('of the emptiness school'—i.e. that principles are empty of a 'person').

To about the same period belongs the *Prajñaptiśāstra*, in which the cosmological concepts of the *Sūtra* and the school were collected, along with an elaborate study of action (moral, therefore beginning with the question of free will and continuing with 'volition' etc.; distinction between the volition itself and the action which follows it) and a third section on the nature of the Buddha and of universal emperors.

Rather later (probably *c.* B.C. 100[1]) Vasumitra (I, not the commentator) enlarged the *Dhātukāya* with new discussions on the principles (*dharmas*) and their classification and definitions (prefixed to the original work), and composed a new work, the last of the seven *Abhidharma* treatises of the school, the *Prakaraṇapāda*, which consists of miscellaneous supplementary *abhidharma* discussions. Its main contribution is a new scheme of 5 categories of *dharmas*: matter (*rūpa*), thought (*citta*), mental principles (*caitasikas*), those disjoined from thought (*cittaviprayukta*), the unsynthesised (*asaṃskṛta*). The fourth category includes forces independent of the stream of consciousness, such as 'life', 'attainment', 'birth', 'impermanence'.

1. Some time after Dhitika (p. 330 above) according to a tradition preserved in China : Suzuki : *Essays* I 157 f.

Later works on *abhidharma* produced by the Sarvāstivādins were not included in their *Tripiṭaka* but were for example teaching manuals. Such is the first known of these, the *Abhidharmasāra* of Dharmaśrī, who lived in Gandhāra *c.* A.D. 50 or earlier, a concise manual.

Other works were more controversial. A little after A.D. 50 Dharmatrāta (I) drastically revised the list of principles, denying the ultimate reality of most of the mental principles. This was rejected by the school and his work has not been preserved, but his ideas found others to develop them further (first Buddhadeva, probably his junior contemporary, who held that the mental principles were not different from 'thought' itself, as secondary matter was not different from the four great existents). Thus began the trend later usually called Sautrāntika, since it rejects the special theories of the *Abhidharma* and regards only the *Sūtra* as finally authoritative.

The Kuṣāṇa emperor Kaniṣka I (A.D. 78-102) became a patron of Buddhism and of the Sarvāstivāda school in particular. His Empire was centred on Gandhāra with the capital at Puruṣapura in the Kubhā valley and a secondary (winter ?) capital at Mathurā in Śūrasena : both countries were strongholds of the Sarvāstivāda school. Kaniṣka emulated Aśoka in his support for Buddhism and also in his toleration, for his coins display besides the Buddha the gods of Brahmanism, Zoroastrianism and the Greek religion (especially Zoroastrianism, it may be noted, which presumably flourished alongside Buddhism in the Iranian and central Asian provinces of the Empire, as well as in Gandhāra itself, where it had been established in the time of the Persian Empire). His reign inaugurated a period of exceptional prosperity for India, following a long period of invasions and wars. He is notable for his building operations, though nothing now remains standing. In particular he appears to have inaugurated the tall tower type of pagoda as contrasted with the ancient hemispherical type: at least he built one said to be the tallest in India, more than 600 feet in height, at Puruṣapura.[1] Under his patronage the Sarvāstivāda school held a great assembly or 'rehearsal' with the object of stabilising the doctrine, particularly

1. *A Comprehensive History of India* Vol. II p 716.

with reference to the recent *abhidharma* controversies : indeed we may regard this assembly as that which rejected the Sautrāntika revisions, as a result of which the revisionists formed themselves into a new schismatic school.

This assembly was held towards the end of the reign, therefore *c.* A.D. 100, and its chief achievement was, according to tradition, the writing down of commentaries on the *Tripiṭaka*. The most important of these is the *Mahāvibhāṣā* ('Great Commentary') on the *Jñānaprasthāna*, composed by Pārśva and Vasumitra (II, nephew of Dharmatrāta). It is interesting that Pārśva, in setting aside Sautrāntika criticisms that certain *abhidharma* doctrines are without *sūtra* authority, proposes to infer the former existence of *sūtras* now lost which contained them and were available to Kātyāyanīputra and other earlier teachers (following probably the Mīmāṃsaka system of inferring the existence of lost Vedic texts). The *Mahāvibhāṣā* rejects explanations of 'all exist' given by Dharmatrāta and Buddhadeva and upholds that proposed by Vasumitra (II), the theory of 'change of situation' (*avasthāpariṇāma*) : a principle has different designations in different situations, such as past, present and future, though its nature does not change and exists in all three situations. As a parallel he gives the place system in arithmetic : the same symbol is differently designated according to its situation as 'unit', 'ten', 'hundred', etc. This became the orthodox explanation of the school. Vasumitra also contributed important refutations of Brahmanical philosophical doctrines (Sāṃkhya, Vaiśeṣika).

Another contemporary of Kaniṣka and the Emperor's own teacher,[1] therefore a generation or two older than the teachers at the assembly (as is required by a tradition which places him before Dharmatrāta[2]), was Saṃgharakṣa, who wrote a biography of the Buddha and a treatise on meditation (*Yogācārabhūmi*). His biography is a complete one like Aśvaghoṣa's and apparently had the same title (*Buddhacarita* — it is extant only in Chinese), though its form is different, being mixed prose and verse. Presumably it was a Sarvāstivādin counterpart to the other work.

1. Lamotte HBI 726.
2. Lamotte HBI 773.

We may mention finally another younger writer of Kaniṣka's time and after it, Ghoṣaka, whose explanation of 'all exist' is rejected in the *Mahāvibhāṣā* but whose manual *Abhidharmāmṛtarasaśāstra* has been preserved in a Chinese translation. On the basic question of the principles he is orthodox. Henceforth the 'orthodox' Sarvāstivādins are often called the 'Vaibhāṣikas', since their various commentaries were called *vibhāṣās*. These commentaries, it appears, were written in Sanskrit, the learned language of the brahmans, not the vernacular, and probably it was about this time that the Sarvāstivāda *Tripiṭaka* was translated into Sanskrit.

South East Asia

It seems to have been during the period we have now reached that Buddhism was established in various countries of South East Asia, both on the mainland and among the islands of Indonesia. The earliest literary reference to voyages from India to these countries appears to be that in the *Niddesa* (p. 298 above), a late addition to the Sthaviravāda *Tripiṭaka* (c. 100 B.C. ?). In two places[1] this text deplores the bad consequences of desire, and among these the exceedingly dangerous voyages across the ocean in quest of wealth. Long lists are given of the places which are the destinations of such voyages, a number of which are in South East Asia : Takkola (Isthmus of Kra in Siam, across which lay the direct trade route from the Indian Ocean to the China Sea), Java (Java?), Tambaliṅga (the country south of Takkola), Vaṅka (Bangka), Vesuṅga (in N. or W. Borneo ?), Suvaṇṇakūṭa (Malay Peninsula), Suvaṇṇabhūmi (the Mōn country of Lower Burma and Siam), Eḷavaddhana (on Gulf of Siam), Tamali (Mekong Delta ? ?), Gumba (in Tonkin ?) and perhaps others not yet identified.) There is no evidence that Buddhism spread to these countries so early, except for the Sthaviravāda traditions which later say that a Buddhist mission went to the Mōn country (Suvarṇabhūmi) in Aśoka's time. In fact the colonisation and Indianisation of South East Asia seems to have begun only later, though the gradual

1. *Niddesa* (*Mahāniddesa*) pp. 154 f., 414 f. A Chinese source, the *Annals of the Former Han Dynasty*, gives itineraries to and from India relating to the same period.

beginnings of it are lost to history and cannot be dated. Coedès[1] places in the 1st century A.D. the origins of the empire of *Śailarāja (Khmer Kurung Bnam, Chinese Fou-nan) on the Mekong River with its capital at Vyādhapura. This is the earliest known Indianised state in South East Asia, which extended its rule over Cambodia, Champa (South Vietnam), Siam and the Malay Peninsula. The legendary traditions of its origin are strikingly similar to those of the Pallava Dynasty which ruled a large part of South India from Kāñcī. Tamil history[2] finds a king Toṇḍaimān Iḷandiraiyan ruling at Kāñcī at the end of the 2nd century A.D. On the assumption that Tamil *toṇḍai* here=Sanskrit *pallava* he was one of the earlier Pallava rulers: how far back before him the dynasty stretched is unknown. It would appear, then, that the main colonising effort from India was at first from Kāñcī. It was not long, however, before Āndhra and Kaliṅga, and the port of Tāmralipti at the mouth of the Ganges, joined in these enterprises.

The earliest evidence for Buddhism in South East Asia is archaeological: statues of the Buddha found in Sumatra, Java and Celebes which are in the Āndhra style of the 2nd and 3rd centuries A.D.[3] As for the Mōn country which should be (very likely was) the first to be penetrated by Buddhism there is no tangible evidence until *c.* A.D. 500, when we find some gold plates inscribed in Pali.[4]

Art

As the popularisation of Buddhism developed it naturally found expression in painting, sculpture and architecture (three arts which were especially closely interconnected in India and sometimes treated as one:[5] architecture with its subordinate parts) as well as in poetry, story telling and drama. The building of pagodas, placing of commemorative columns with symbolic sculptures and construction of temples has been noted above (pp. 226ff., 254, 267 319f., 345), as well as the use of narrative sculpture (reliefs), which no doubt derived from narrative painting of which fewer examples survive.

1. *Les États Hindouisés d'Indochine et d'Indonésie*, 68 ff.
2. Nilakanta : *A History of South India*, p. 121.
3. Coedès p. 39.
4. Coedès p. 108.
5. See IKL I pp. 31-2.

There are traces of the continuation of the Mauryan style of monumental sculpture at Pāṭaliputra and Mathurā, but the most notable development of the period of the decline of Magadha and rise of Āndhra is the elaboration of the ancient pagoda with its subordinate railings, gateways, terraces, stairs, etc., adorned with narrative and symbolic sculptures (in the round and reliefs). The best preserved of these is the great complex at Sāñcī (Caityagiri near Vidiśā, see p 265 above), that at Bhārahat (South of Kauśāmbī on the road to Vidiśā) has vanished into the Calcutta Museum, fragments of reliefs of the period exist at Bodh Gayā. Besides the symbols (among which the lotus, i.e. non-attachment, is prominent) and a profusion of flowers and creepers, attendant gods and goddesses and animals, the great feature of these sculptures is the *jātaka* narratives, with a few scenes from the life of the Buddha as well (in which it should be noted he is not represented directly but only by symbols: his seat, wheel, footprint, sunshade, tree, pagoda, etc., though the *bodhisattva* is represented in the *jātakas*). In the narrative sculptures successive incidents are depicted in a single 'composition', preferably in long panels which might reproduce rolls of painting on cloth: properly speaking these are not compositions but are essentially dynamic in style; the eye is drawn to look at each main figure in turn and the leading characters are repeated. During the period the number of *jātakas* depicted is sharply reduced in successive phases, concentration on a few of the most popular ones following, whilst the scenes from the last life of the Buddha are multiplied correspondingly. This strikingly confirms the trends we have found in literature: numerous *jātakas* in the *Tripiṭaka* and little record of the Buddha's life; elaborate legendary biographies composed later.

Meanwhile newer schools of architecture and sculpture flourished in the more original Sātavāhana dominions, in both Mahārāṣṭra and Āndhra, showing the same trend. In Mahārāṣṭra, owing to the terrain, large numbers of excavated *vihāras* and temples are found (at Ellora and Ajaṇṭā on the road from Mahārāṣṭra north to Avanti, at Nāsikā and along the coast); in fact this is our main record of the history of architecture in this period, since excavated buildings have survived where structural ones have long ago been swept into oblivion except for their foundations. In Āndhra we find the originally hemispherical pagoda become higher, so that the height of its dome is equal to the diameter at the base (the best known example, however, the Amarāvatī near Dhānyakaṭaka, has been razed to the ground: some of its reliefs are preserved in a small museum on the spot, others in the British Museum, London). A new element in the reliefs is the showing of perspective by varying the degree of relief, deep for the fore-ground figures, shallower successively towards the rear.

The pagodas and sculptures of the period in Ceylon (Duṭṭhagāmaṇi, his successor Saddhātissa, Vaṭṭagāmaṇi and his successors) are very similar to those of Āndhra. The pagodas are much better preserved: the large one at the Mahāvihāra built by Duṭṭhagāmaṇi (and Saddhātissa ?) is 300 feet high and two feet less in diameter (it has been restored but these dimensions seem to be fairly original), that built by Vaṭṭagāmaṇi at the Abhayagiri is 350 feet high and 355 feet in diameter (both were to be surpassed by that built for the schismatic Jetavanīya school c. 300 A.D , which is 400 feet high).

Towards the end of this period the practice began of representing the Buddha in sculpture even in his final life. The date of the earliest known examples of this appears to be near the beginning of the lst century A.D.[1] and the place of origin probably Mathurā or Kauśāmbī. Legend has it, however, that the first such statue was commissioned by the Paurava King Udayana of Vatsa at Kauśāmbī during the life time of the Buddha: the craftsmen worked in sandalwood under the direction of Maudgalyāyana. Of course we know nothing of the work in wood which probably preceded that in stone in all branches of architecture and sculpture (except when the mason copies the constructions of the joiner, as in fact he often did) and which was almost certainly much more plentiful at all times.

Of painting of the period practically nothing survives but the earliest frescoes at Ajaṇṭā, showing the same traditions of

1. For a recent discussion by an art historian see Willetts : *Chinese Art*, London, 1958, Vol. 1 325 ff., also 316 ff.

narrative (*jātakas*, also scenes of pilgrims at pagodas or the enlightenment tree, who have not been identified — Aśoka ?) and of lyric portrayal of flowers and animals.

The *vihāras* consisted essentially of a square courtyard enclosed by the lines of monks' cells, which might be raised in three or more stories. In the centre of the courtyard was a small hall constructed with pillars of wood or stone. Usually a temple (shrine house) was built nearby, enclosing a small pagoda (later sometimes a statue of the Buddha) at one end surrounded by an ambulatory formed of columns; the columns continued from the semicircle of the ambulatory in parallel lines down either side of the temple, which was entered either through a large doorway at the end or through two smaller doors at the sides; a barrel vaulted roof was supported by the columns, whilst on the outside was a verandah or terrace with a row of large columns. The *poṣadha* hall also stood nearby, whilst the kitchen, refectory, bathroom, etc. usually formed part of the same building as the *vihāra* and were grouped behind one of the lines of cells. Often a *vihāra* had its own 'enlightenment tree' enclosed by a railing.

The vigorous culture of Mathurā became still richer under the Kuṣāṇa emperors, in whose time the city became a great metropolis (and notably a centre of the drama) and Buddhist and other art flourished there. Meanwhile in Gandhāra we find a curious hybrid school of sculpture, due apparently to Greek craftsmen who were Buddhists (or working for Buddhists): their themes are Buddhist but their technique has derived in great part from a Hellenistic school. Their work shows the coldness of the Greek tradition when compared with the warmth of Indian sculpture. During the Kuṣāṇa period some interactions have been traced between the schools of Śūrasena and Gandhāra, but gradually the Gandhāra art was assimilated to the main Indian tradition, which spread out through Gandhāra to central Asia and China.

CHAPTER TEN

MAHĀYĀNA AND MADHYAMAKA

Mahāyāna — The Bodhisattva — The Perfection of Understanding — Madhyamaka — Nāgārjuna — Further Development of the Madhyamaka School — New Trends in Mahāyāna — The Ratnagotravibhāga and the Abhisamayālaṅkāra — Developments in the Early Schools after the Rise of the Mahāyāna.

Mahāyāna

The Mahāyāna movement claims to have been founded by the Buddha himself, though at first confined to a select group of hearers. The consensus of the evidence, however, is that it originated in South India in the 1st century A.D. There are references[1] in the Mahāyāna *sūtras* themselves to their being known in the South after the *parinirvāṇa*, after which they will spread to the East[2] and then the North. Several of the leading teachers of the new doctrines were born in South India, studied there and afterwards went to the North to teach: one of the earliest and most important being Nāgārjuna. Other major *sūtras* are circumstantially connected with the South, for example the detailed itinerary there of the *Gaṇḍavyūha* and location of the *bodhisattva* Maitreya there, whilst the *Laṅkāvatāra* is connected with Ceylon (both these *sūtras* are later and show a new phase of Mahāyāna which we shall discuss in the next chapter, but they show that the South was then vigorously creative in producing Mahāyāna *sūtras*, which may well have been a continuation of earlier creativity). The idea that the *sūtras* had been confined to the South would of course have been a convenient way of explaining to Buddhists in the North why it was that they had not heard these texts directly from their own teachers, without admitting that they were recent fabrications. An alternative explanation recorded by Buddhist

1. *Aṣṭasāhasrikāprajñāpāramitā* p. 225. Other references in Lamotte MPPŚ Vol. I 25f.

2. Variant reading : 'West'.

historians[1] was that though the Buddha had taught them they were not in circulation in the world of men at all for many centuries, there being no competent teachers and no intelligent students: the *sūtras* were however preserved in the Dragon World and other non-human circles, and when in the 2nd century A.D. adequate teachers suddenly appeared in India in large numbers the texts were fetched and circulated. This to us is as good as an admission that no such texts existed until the 2nd century A.D. However, it is clear that the historical tradition here recorded belongs to North India and for the most part to Nālandā (in Magadha). The sudden appearance of large numbers of teachers and texts there would seem to require some previous preparation and development, and this we can look for in the South.

When we consider the likely milieu for the development of Mahāyāna ideas, on the other hand, we naturally look among the Mahāsaṃgha schools. These in fact were regarded as predecessors by some Mahāyānists, for example Paramārtha,[2] who sought Mahāyāna doctrines and tradition among them. We have noted certain trends of doctrine in the Mahāsaṃgha schools, and particularly the Caitikas of Āndhra (pp. 328f. above), anticipating Mahāyāna ideas. A further significant piece of evidence is that certain verses taken from the Pūrva Śaila tradition, described either as 'Pūrva Śaila verses' or as 'in the *sūtras* of the *Āgamas*' (therefore as in the *Tripiṭaka* of that school), are quoted as authoritative by the Madhyamaka (Mahāyāna) philosopher Candrakīrti[3] in order to justify the doctrine of his school that principles do not in reality occur (originate) and cease, so that the Buddha expounded origination and cessation only as a provisional teaching conforming to the ideas of the world (otherwise he would not have been understood). It is possible that the Pūrva Śailas intended these verses to refer only to the non-origination and non-cessation of 'beings' and of the 'world' in the sense of

1. Tāranātha, Chapter 13 : many teachers appear, and the greater *Ratnakūṭa*, Mahāyāna *sūtras* are written down and later brought to Nālandā (period after Kaniṣka).

2. Demiéville MCB I 19ff.

3. *Madhyamakāvatāra* 134f., *Prasannapadā* 548. See Lamotte in *Asiatica*, p. 387, on *Prajñāpāramitās* in Prakrit among the Śailas.

the totality of 'beings' or 'persons', whereas Candrakīrti makes them refer to all principles. Nevertheless they were at least ambiguous enough to serve his purpose and stood close to the border line between the doctrine that there is no 'person' and the doctrine that there are no 'principles' (in the sense of ultimately real 'natures'), suggesting that the Pūrva Śailas had arrived almost at the typically Mahāyānist position of making little distinction between 'persons' and 'principles' (for the background to this cf. pp. 134-142 above, but we shall return to the Mahāyāna doctrine in detail later). The conclusion seems indicated that some time after the founding of the Pūrva Śaila school in the 1st century B.C. certain monks felt the need not simply for new interpretations of the original *sūtras* (such as, for example, the new *abhidharma* texts of the schools, or the *Paṭisambhidāmagga* of the Sthaviravāda) but for wholesale restatements of the doctrine.[1] For this purpose they rewrote the *sūtras*, or wrote new *sūtras*, sufficiently similar in content as well as style as to appear authentic, but differently arranged, with different emphases and, on close checking, proving to contain here and there a new phrase slipped into an old formulation, opening up a new avenue of thought. It is a matter of speculation how far there was deliberate deception in this fabrication of new *sūtras*. At all times while there was an oral tradition it would seem possible for new versions of old texts to be produced more or less by accident, and for new episodes to get inserted in older *sūtras*, even perhaps for a commentarial work or a manual composed by a monk to acquire the trappings of a *sūtra* by mere confusion. At some stage, however, if not at the origin of the Mahāyāna, we can protect the good faith of the Mahāyāna monks only by supposing that they believed themselves to have intuitive or inspired knowledge of *sūtras* not handed down in the *Tripiṭaka* known to men, though spoken by the Buddha to a human audience which failed to hand them on or to a divine audience. In short a monk might think himself enlightened in such a way as to have omniscient knowledge of past events, or he might imagine

1. To clinch the evidence for the place of origin of the Mahāyāna *sūtras* the Ceylon tradition ascribes the *Ratnakūṭa* to the Āndhras (EHBC 100).

he was inspired in his meditations by a divine being revealing a *sūtra* preserved by the gods or dragons.

The Mahāyāna, 'Great Vehicle' or 'Great Carriage' (for carrying all beings to *nirvāṇa*), is also, and perhaps more correctly and accurately, known as the Bodhisattvayāna, the *bodhisattva*'s vehicle.

The Bodhisattva

It is the teaching about the *bodhisattva* which is the characteristic feature of the Mahāyāna or Bodhisattvayāna. Thus Candrakīrti in distinguishing the special characteristics of the Mahāyāna (which differentiate it from the earlier teaching, which Mahāyānists refer to rather disparagingly as the Śrāvakayāna, the 'Pupils Vehicle', as if its followers were mere laymen and not true *śramaṇas*, when they are being polite, and as *hīnayāna*, 'inferior vehicle', when they wish to be rude) lists seven points.[1] Six of these relate to the training of the *bodhisattva*, only one to the nature of the universe. In principle, of course, the theory of the *bodhisattva* on his way to Buddhahood was nothing new. The conception is found in the earliest stratum of *Tripiṭaka* texts as referring to the Buddha before his enlightenment, and also to other (earlier) *buddhas* before their enlightenments.[2] In addition *jātakas* relating to his previous lives seem to have been narrated by the Buddha himself and were at any rate extremely popular by the 4th century B.C. among the early schools. What is different is that whereas for the early schools (except, perhaps, the Caitikas) the *jātaka* stories and other accounts of the former lives of *buddhas* may be said to be purely descriptive, intended simply to inspire confidence in the Buddha, for the Mahāyāna the training of *bodhisattvas* is prescriptive: the way of the *bodhisattva* is substituted for, or at least is superior to, the old eightfold way. The monk should not aim at *nirvāṇa* directly, but at first becoming a *buddha*, the highest possible attainment and one for which there is the greatest need in the universe, for the worlds are innumerable and time is endless so that the demand for *buddhas* to start the doctrine in different worlds, or restart it when it has been lost,

1. *Madhyamakāvatāra* 22, the *Ratnāvalī* quoted on p. 23 in this connection mentions only the *bodhisattva* and his training.

2. The *Mahāvadāna Sūtra* in the *Dīrgha*.

can never be fully satisfied. Evidently it is a superior aim to 'delay' one's extinction until one has been a *buddha* and made this supreme contribution to the happiness of living beings.

It goes without saying that the way of the *bodhisattva* is infinitely more difficult than that of the *arhant*, at least from the standpoint of the Mahāyāna doctrines. Only the Sthaviravāda maintained such a high standard for the *arhant* that few among them aspired to attain extinction in their present lives and most looked forward instead to making sufficient progress now to ensure a better chance next time. Meanwhile they would have plenty of time to teach for the sake of others. In the Mahāsaṃgha, on the other hand, becoming an *arhant* could seem easy, given that one could be counted one whilst still subject to some of the weaknesses of human nature. For the Mahāyāna becoming an *arhant* is the easy way out, evading one's responsibilities to future generations and future worlds. The *arhant* is felt to be lacking in compassion. The Mahāsaṃgha separation of the *arhant* from the *buddha* and subsequent raising of the *buddha* to the status of a transcendental being, not merely an enlightened being, was thus the necessary prerequisite for the development of the Mahāyāna.

The earliest Mahāyāna *sūtras* now extant appear to be some of these collected in what came to be called the *Ratnakūṭa*. Sometimes this is spoken of as if it were one great *sūtra* containing 49 chapters (it is about as long as an *āgama*). On the other hand these chapters are independent of one another and each is a complete *sūtra* in itself, moreover one of them by itself bears the name *Ratnakūṭa Sūtra*. Probably the collection as a whole, as it now appears in the Chinese and Tibetan Mahāyāna *Tripiṭakas*, was put together in a comparatively late period and contains *sūtras* of differing ages (some of which had been translated into Chinese separately much earlier). Unfortunately only four of the 49 *sūtras* seem now to be available in the original Sanskrit, which accounts for the neglect of a collection so important for the history of Buddhism and the understanding of the Mahāyāna. Some of these *sūtras* were translated into Chinese as early as the latter part of the 2nd century A.D.

The *Ratnakūṭa Sūtra* in the narrow sense is among these early translations and it is also one of the few available in Sanskrit (the only known manuscript of it, damaged and with some pages missing, was found in Khotan in the 1890s and purchased by the Russian consul at Kashgar; it is more than a thousand years old and must have spent about a thousand years hidden in a cave or vault[1]). It is concerned mostly with the *bodhisattva* and his training, but includes important theoretical discussions on the nature of principles which call for separate consideration (see below). It is important to note that it refers by name to the *Bodhisattvapiṭaka*[2] for the basic doctrine of the six 'perfections' (*pāramitā*). The Bahuśrutīya and other schools had a *piṭaka* so named (pp. 298, 330 above), which presumably included the *Jātaka*. Later Mahāyāna writers such as Asaṅga (*Bodhisattvabhūmi* pp. 9, 68, etc.) use the same name for the Mahāyāna *sūtras* as a whole. It appears that the oldest *sūtras* of the Great *Ratnakūṭa* in their original form were part of the *Bodhisattvapiṭaka* of the early school from which the Mahāyāna arose, probably the Pūrva Śaila (see below). The proto-Mahāyānists changed a description of six perfections of the *bodhisattva*, a variant of the ten perfections of the Sthaviravāda *Cariyāpiṭaka*, to a prescription. According to the Sthaviravādins[3] the *Ratnakūṭa* itself, whether as *sūtra* or as collection is uncertain, was composed in the Āndhra schools (and the '*Raṭṭhapālagajjita*', which may be the *Rāṣṭrapālaparipṛcchā* of the *Ratnakūṭa* collection, by the Pūrva Śailas). Here we may trace the gradual evolution from Caitika to Mahāyāna. The six perfections are: generosity, virtue, toleration (*kṣānti*), energy, meditation and understanding. During his countless lives the *bodhisattva* must perfect all these qualities in himself, mostly by performing astonishing acts of self-sacrifice such as are related in many *jātakas*. The Thesis of the author's student Professor N. Schuster, 1976, discusses the Great *Ratnakūṭa* and shows in detail the evolution of the *Ugraparipṛcchā*, a derivative of an old *sūtra* on the famous lay disciple Ugra (A IV 208ff. =T. 26 No. 38), the hero being now a *bodhisattva*.

In the *Ratnakūṭa* we meet the term 'thought of enlightenment' (*bodhicitta*) used in its Mahāyāna sense. 'Enlightenment' here does not mean simply the understanding of the Four Truths in

1. The *Kāśyapaparivarta* (=*Ratnakūṭa Sūtra*) edited by von Staël-Holstein, Shanghai 1926, pp. vii, xviif.

2. *Ratnakūṭa* (previous note) p. 13.

3. Adikāram EHBC p. 100 (*Nikāyasaṃgraha*).

their true nature, the acquisition of the 'three sciences', which as we have seen constituted the original enlightenment of the Buddha as of the other *arhants* who comprehended and verified his teaching. Now it is assumed that the Buddha was not merely enlightened in the old sense, but literally omniscient, whilst the enlightenment of those of his followers who became *arhants* was no more than that old specific enlightenment which sufficed to produce freedom and extinction. The 'thought of enlightenment' as understood in Mahāyāna *sūtras* is restricted to the thought of becoming a Buddha, with all that that now implied, consequently it is a thought peculiar to the *bodhisattva*: when one has the 'thought of enlightenment' it means one has set out on the long way of the *bodhisattva* towards Buddhahood. The occurrence of this thought, even its first occurrence, is said in the *Ratnakūṭa*[1] to make the *bodhisattva* surpass ('conquer') all the 'pupils' (presumably the *arhants* !) and isolated *buddhas* ('private *buddhas*', *pratyekabuddhas*).

In accordance with this idea the *Sūtra* denounces[2] the pupils as not really 'sons' of the Buddha, i.e. not really Buddhists. Thus an open breach or schism is declared with the earlier schools: the Mahāyāna secedes from the Mahāsaṃgha and starts out on its independent history. Practically every Mahāyāna *sūtra* repeats this denunciation of the 'inferior' (*hina*) way of the pupils in more or less shrill tones and at varying length, contrasting rather unpleasantly with the tolerance and understanding characteristic of most earlier Buddhist texts.

The enumeration of things helpful to or harmful to the development of this thought of enlightenment, however, is generally similar to the older ideas about moral progress, with frequent reference to the 'roots' (causes) of the good (*kuśala-mūla*) as in the *abhidharma* system of the Sthaviravāda. Moreover we find a passage[3] amounting to an elaboration of the theory of the four 'errors' and their antidotes (cf. pp. 313 f. above), with some additions, notably 'attention to reasoning which initiates all imaginations, constructions and imaginings (three practically synonymous terms)', the antidote to which is 'signlessness' (or

1. p. 123.
2. p. 116.
3. p. 137.

'characteristiclessness'), and abandoning of the three kinds of existence, the medicine for which is 'uncommittedness'. In what follows this is related to self-possession and the other topics of the old Vaiśālī summary of the doctrine as antidotes to the various wrong theories (that there is a soul, a person, etc.). Finally we have the transcendent 'knowledge-medicine' of the Buddha, which is knowledge of causes and conditions, of non-soul and so on.

At the end of the *Sūtra* we may note that it is said that the thoughts of 800 monks (not *bodhisattvas*) are freed by hearing it. 500 'meditators' at first go away because they find it too deep for them (i.e. the preceding discussion on the nature of thought, which we shall take up below). Eventually they too are freed when they understand that all principles are 'empty'. Normally to say that their thoughts were freed would mean that they had attained the state of being *arhants*: either the *Sūtra* is confused and we still have the conclusion of an older text not dealing with the way of the *bodhisattva* (which was later inserted into it) or we have to understand that this freedom merely allows them to set out on the way of the *bodhisattva* and does not produce their extinction as yet.

One of the other *sūtras* of the *Ratnakūṭa* collection available in Sanskrit, the *Rāṣṭrapālaparipṛcchā*, deals somewhat more elaborately (though still unsystematically) with the way of the *bodhisattva*, referring for illustration to fifty *jātaka* stories. There is no external evidence for its great antiquity, but its content would harmonise with its being even earlier than the *Ratnakūṭa Sūtra*, before the open breach with the 'pupils' (who are not here denounced), in fact a *sūtra* of the Pūrva Śaila school not remodelled after the breach. The ethical principles do not differ from those of the more original *Tripiṭaka* except for the commendation of the way of the *bodhisattva* and, in connection with this way, the additional stress on self-sacrifice (in fulfilling the perfections).

Very different is another *sūtra* of the collection extant in Sanskrit, the *Amitābhavyūha* (or *Sukhāvatīvyūha*, longer version, or *Amitābhaparivarta*). It was one of those early translated into Chinese, along with the *Ratnakūṭa* itself. In it the Buddha recalls, talking to Ānanda, a large number of former *buddhas* who had successively occurred in the universe. Going on with the story, when he comes to the *buddha* Lokeśvararāja he tells Ānanda how this *buddha* had a monk named Dharmākara. This monk (who is a *bodhisattva*) proceeds to lay down a fantastic set of conditions on which he will become a *buddha*, requiring Lokeśvararāja to endorse them (which would be a guarantee, much as Dīpaṃkara had 'determined' the Buddhahood of Śākyamuni). The basis of this is the idea of the *buddha*-field (*buddhakṣetra*), meaning the particular world (among the thousands or rather millions of worlds in the universe as conceived by the Buddhists) in which a given *bodhisattva* is going to become a *buddha*. Dharmākara was obviously a hedonist, though an enlightened and compassionate one, and he was prepared to accept an appointment as *buddha* only in the finest possible world. First he asked Lokeśvararāja to describe the qualities of the worlds of many other *buddhas*, then he selected the best qualities among all of them and laid down forty six (in some Chinese versions forty eight) conditions which would have to be satisfied in a world if he were to be its *buddha*. When Lokeśvararāja approved the conditions Dharmākara formally made his 'commitment' (*praṇidhāna*) to become a *buddha* in a world satisfying them thousands of millions of years later.

In general this world was to be perfect in every conceivable way and all the beings in it were to be perfectly happy and gifted with insight and understanding. There would be no purgatory in it, nor would anyone be born as an animal or demon there. All the beings there would have 'comprehension' (*pratisaṃvid*) when studying. The world would be full of radiance, jewels, incense, fragrant jewel-flowers, musical clouds, etc. Apart from the general requirement that the beings there, and especially *bodhisattvas* born there, would enjoy happiness and get whatever they wanted, there are some particular stipulations, as that no one should ever have to wash any clothes, all garments becoming clean automatically. Anyone who wished to hear the Buddhist doctrine could do so immediately. No one would have any sense of possessing anything, even his own body.

Ānanda asks what happened afterwards and is told that Dharmākara realised his ambition and is at this very moment the *buddha* Amitābha ('Unmeasured Radiance') in a world called Sukhāvatī which satisfies his conditions. It is billions of worlds away from this one, in the Western direction. Amitābha also enjoys immeasurably long life (during which he will remain with his marvellous world) and therefore has another name, Amitāyus ('Unmeasured Life'). Sukhāvatī is then described by the Buddha in more detail, with for example its enormous jewel-lotuses, its absence of mountains, its fragrant rivers bearing jewel-flowers and making sweet sounds, its heavenly music whose soft and lovely sounds produce happiness by suggesting 'impermanence, calm and non-soul'. The beings there spend their time in pleasurable play and enjoy whatever they wish. If they bathe in the rivers the water seems to each one to be at the exact temperature he wishes ; if any do not wish to hear the music they do not hear it, whilst those who wish to hear it do hear it and hear whatever music they would like to hear, including of course the chanting of the doctrine if they so wish, the doctrine of emptiness, signlessness, uncommittedness, non-synthesising, not being born, non-occurrence, non-existence, cessation, etc. There is no difference between gods and men there.

Now any beings who set their minds on the *buddha* Amitābha, cultivating unmeasured 'roots of good' (*kuśalamūla*) and developing the thought of enlightenment, and commit themselves to rebirth in that world, are reborn there when they die. Even those who have not often set their minds on Amitābha and not cultivated the roots of good very much can be reborn there if they imagine ('create with their intelligence') Amitābha in front of them at the moment of their death. Even a single thought of Amitābha, with yearning for his world, is sufficient: by it one can become a *bodhisattva* in his world. Moreover *bodhisattvas* born in that world can become *buddhas* after only one more birth, if they wish. Among the *bodhisattvas* already in that world is Avalokiteśvara (henceforth one of the most famous *bodhisattvas* in popular Mahāyāna Buddhism). The fact is that as required by Dharmākara anyone born in his world has sufficient intelligence to be able to speak on the doctrine 'charged with omniscience' : it seems all are *bodhisattvas* and practically *buddhas* already.

At this point we have the following remarks about the beings in Amitābha's world, which are more in consonance with earlier Buddhist teaching than the descriptions of the pleasures of this heaven appear to have been. They have no sense of possessing (which was one of the conditions). They have no thought of pleasure or of non-pleasure. They have no thought of "all beings". They have no sense of 'another's' or of 'own' or of 'unequal'. There is no quarrelling, dispute or opposition. Their thoughts are all impartial, benevolent, soft, affectionate, unobstructed, etc. and in accordance with the way of the perfection of understanding.

Ānanda expresses the wish to see this world and Amitābha immediately releases a ray of light from the palm of his hand which lights up the whole universe and enables Ānanda to see him and his world. The Buddha (Śākyamuni) points out its wonders to one of his own *bodhisattvas*, and the beings being reborn there sitting on lotus flowers. Sukhāvatī is indistinguishable from the heaven of the Paranirmitavaśavartin gods. The Buddha adds at the end that discourses of his like this one will not be heard by those who have generated no merit but only by 'heroes' who have accomplished some welfare.

The Perfection of Understanding

The *Amitābhavyūha* may seem puzzling at first sight, when we come to it after the study of earlier Buddhist *sūtras*. What are all these beings going to a heaven world full of the pleasures of the senses, even if tempered with the spice of impermanence, non-soul, emptiness, uncommittedness, non-existence, etc. ? The details are insisted upon and apparently made as vivid as possible. Is this a Buddhist text, or have we arrived at the Brahmanical conception of eternal souls going to heaven ? The answer does not clearly appear in this *Sūtra*, though the reader who has studied Buddhism is likely to recall many repudiations of the idea that any soul or being or person exists. He is likely also to have heard that though the Buddha sometimes spoke of 'beings' and of their being reborn, he was adopting the popular point of view and conventional language : his real, philosophical, doctrine was that of the sequence of conditions with no permanent entity among them (cf. pp. 150ff. above). Is this whole *Sūtra* at the 'concealing' level of knowledge, its meaning requiring to be 'drawn out' ? Unless this text teaches a doctrine totally different from almost all other Buddhist *sūtras* (there are two similar texts, versions of the same *Sūtra*) we must interpret it in this way. The description of Sukhāvatī must be a kind of meditation at the concealing level, contrasting with the sordid experience of human society and in a way encouraging the cultivation of the roots of good and confidence in the doctrine, though empty.

The *Ratnakūṭa Sūtra* is quite unambiguous about emptiness. All principles, it says,[1] are empty. They are not permanent, nor are they impermanent.[2] (That they are not impermanent may be an innovation, but it is probably to be interpreted as meaning that they are not non-existent, just as 'permanent' may mean 'really existent' —such was the trend of Mahāyāna ideas.) The intermediate way, or practice, is being aware of this nature of principles. 'Permanent' (*nitya*) is one extreme, 'impermanent' is the other extreme: the intermediate way lies between them (cf. the *Kātyāyanāvavāda Sūtra*, 129f. above). 'Soul' (*ātman*) is one extreme, 'non-soul' (*nairātmya*) is the other. 'Real (existing, *bhūta*) thought' is one extreme, 'unreal thought' is the other. In short all such dyads as 'good' and 'bad', 'worldly' and 'transcendent', 'synthesised' and 'unsynthesised' and so on are pairs of extremes of the same type. At the end of this passage the *Sūtra* adds the original pair, 'exists' (*asti*) and 'does not exist' (*nāsti*), to which perhaps all the others are to be reduced, and the sequence of conditioned origination according to which principles should be regarded from the intermediate way. Thus we arrive back at the more original formulation after an excursion which seems to go significantly beyond it. The main innovation to note is that 'soul' seems here to be no more (and no less) false a conception than 'non-soul' : the question of the soul or self or person is apparently being placed on the same level as the existence of 'principles' (*dharmas*).

Also significant are the statements that thought has no own nature,[3] because it neither exists nor does not exist and is not produced (*ajāta*), and that it is unsynthesised and is what is called the 'clan' (*gotra*) of the Aryans (excellent ones) because it is

1. p. 94.
2. *Ratnakūṭa Sūtra* pp. 83-92.
3. p. 149.

unsynthesised. This kind of statement led to a variety of speculation later about thought, but here the implication seems to be that thought (and other principles) is not synthesised in the sense of having no own nature, no real existence, and is therefore at the ultimate level of knowledge extinct (in *nirvāṇa*). In this case it would be 'by nature' — if we could apply the expression to it, contrary to the *Sūtra* — extinct and not really involved in transmigration. The so-called 'freeing' of one's thought, attaining extinction, would therefore be not a real freeing (at the ultimate level of statement) but, at the most, a realising that one was already in reality free, one's involvement had been imagination only. As for the 'clan', the conception here is of all 'beings', all sequences of thought, being as it were kindred in their original and ultimate extinction. The 'excellent ones' are distinguished from others only in that they are aware of this kinship. Where this 'clan' is there is not thought, nor a mental principle, not mind, not consciousness, no action nor its result, no happiness or unhappiness, etc., because it is like space.[1]

There is one other Mahāyāna *sūtra* which was translated into Chinese as early as the *Ratnakūṭa Sūtra*, the *Aṣṭasāhasrikā-prajñāpāramitā*, 'Eight Thousand Perfection of Understanding'. This is the first known *sūtra* of a new type, called *vaipulya* ('abundance', 'largeness', 'breadth'), distinguished by their great length relative to all previous *sūtras* : they are roughly ten times the length of the 'long' *Dīrgha sūtras*. The 'Eight Thousand' is one of a class of 'Perfection of Understanding' *sūtras*, comprising a score or more (it depends how many are recognised by a given school as 'canonical') of texts of different dates. There is much overlapping of content between them and several of them (especially the longer ones) may be regarded as different recensions of a single work. They are generally distinguished simply by their various lengths, measured in units of thirty two syllables (originally a metrical unit, but applied equally to prose; the lengths of Indian texts were usually recorded for the purpose of paying scribes). Thus the Eight Thousand contains that number (we are told) of units.

1. p. 151.

There is a Seven Hundred, written later and added to the *Ratnakūṭa* collection (exceptionally: all the others form their own 'collection') and so on. Of those now available the Eight Thousand is apparently the oldest. According to a tradition recorded in Tibet[1] the Pūrva and Apara Śaila schools had a Perfection of Understanding (in 'Prakrit', those extant are more or less in Sanskrit, the older ones probably 'Sanskritised' and the later ones written in Sanskrit; the least Sanskritised is the only one in verse, the *Ratnaguṇasaṃcayagāthā*, which is closely related to the Eight Thousand and may preserve parts of the old Śaila text, though with later additions). We have noted above that the Eight Thousand itself says it will first be spread in the South: it is presumably a Mahāyāna rewriting, probably greatly enlarged, of the prose parts of the Śaila text. A careful comparison of the verse text and the Eight Thousand might enable us to carry the history of the text a little further back.

The unwieldy mass of these *sūtras* can be reduced to a few main points, much of the 'abundance' being repetition and paraphrasing in discursive dialogue, although (as we shall see later) commentators have found entangled in the discussion about the 'emptiness' of principles an elaboration of the way of the *bodhisattva.*

The Eight Thousand begins in a similar way to the old *sūtras*, the Buddha in this case being on Mount Gṛdhrakūṭa (Vulture Peak) near Rājagṛha with a community of monks. The Buddha speaks to the elder (*sthavira*) Subhūti (whom we have not met before, but he is mentioned in the *Ekottara*) and asks him to improvise something on how *bodhisattvas* should 'go out to' (*nir-yā*, or 'be freed in') the perfection of understanding. Subhūti says: "As to this '*bodhisattva*' spoken of by the Master, of which principle (*dharma*) is it a designation (*adhivacana*)? Master, I do not observe (*sam-anu-dṛś*, or 'envisage') such a principle as '*bodhisattva*'. Moreover I do not observe such a principle as 'perfection of understanding.' Not finding, not perceiving (*upa-labh*, active) and not observing either '*bodhisattva*' or 'the principle *bodhisattva*' or the 'perfection of understanding', on which *bodhisattva*, in which perfection

1. Lamotte, 'Sur la formation du Mahāyāna', *Asiatica* (Weller), 387.

of understanding, shall I give admonitions and instructions? However, if a *bodhisattva's* thought is not discouraged, etc., does not despair, if his mind does not become...frightened (etc.) when this is being said ...then he is surely a *bodhisattva*, a 'great being' who can be instructed in the perfection of understanding ...Moreover living in (or proceeding in, *car*) the perfection of understanding, developing the perfection of understanding, a *bodhisattva* should train thus: that he should not flatter himself (*manyeta*) with the thought of enlightenment (i.e., says the commentator Haribhadra, hypostatise his 'self' or 'soul' or 'being' with it). Why? Because that thought is non-thought: the nature of thought is translucent (or 'clear', *prabhāsvara*)."

So far there seems to be nothing which would not be endorsed by the earlier schools (except perhaps the 'person' schools). From the ultimate standpoint there is no 'being' (living being), *bodhisattva* or otherwise, hence strictly speaking one cannot lecture on the *bodhisattva*. 'Understanding' is a principle (*dharma*) recognised by most of the schools in their *Abhidharmas*, but 'perfection of understanding' was probably not found there (though presumably it would 'reduce' to understanding). We shall see, however, that from this point the Eight Thousand begins to go beyond the system of the *Abhidharma*. Already the question of the nature of thought (or specifically of the thought of enlightenment, *bodhicitta*) has been raised. Śāriputra now asks Subhūti whether that thought, which he had called 'non-thought', exists (*asti*). Subhūti replies: 'In that non-thought does existence ('it-is-ness', *astitā*, cf. p. 129 above) or non-existence ('it-is-not-ness', *nāstitā*) occur (*vidyate*), is it perceived (or does it exist — *upa-labh*, passive)?' Śāriputra agrees that this cannot be said, but asks what this 'non-thoughtness' (*acittatā*) is. Subhūti replies that it is 'non-changing' (*avikāra*), 'non-imagining' (*avikalpa*). Evidently there is a problem of interpretation here: it may still be possible to equate this with the position of the *Kātyāyanāvavāda Sūtra* on 'existence' and 'non-existence' as the extreme views which Buddhist doctrine avoids with its intermediate teaching, but we begin to be uncertain just what 'existence' means.

A little later (p. 10) Subhūti takes a more definite stand with reference to the teachings of the schools. He says that matter (*rūpa*, i.e. the first of the five groups) is without (*virahita*, 'separated from') the 'own-nature' (*svabhāva*) of matter; so are the other groups without their 'own-nature', likewise the perfection of understanding and omniscience (*sarvajñatā*) are without their own-natures. This does not necessarily contradict anything in the *Tripiṭaka*, but it certainly contradicts the commentaries of the Sthaviravāda school (see p. 323 above), which define the ultimate principles as those which have own-nature. The commentaries and the Eight Thousand seem to be contemporary in origin and probably developed in deliberate opposition to one another, or at least the writer of the Eight Thousand wished to attack the conceptions of the *abhidharma* commentators (other schools besides the Sthaviravāda held the own-nature theory).

On the next page Subhūti goes much further and says that all principles are 'not produced' (or 'not born', *ajāta*). This sounds as if it contradicts the ancient Second Truth and conditioned origination (Chapter Five), but again it is a question of interpretation.

The point first made, about (living) beings, including *bodhisattvas*, not being observed (ultimately) is repeated a number of times in this and other Perfection of Understanding *sūtras*. The writers seem to have enjoyed the apparent paradox. The Buddha says to Subhūti a little further on in the discussion[1] : "A *bodhisattva*, a great being, thinks: 'Countless (*aprameya*, 'immeasurable') beings should be made extinct (i.e. freed in *nirvāṇa*) by me, innumerable beings should be made extinct by me. And they do not exist (*na santi*), those (*bodhisattvas*) by whom these (beings) should be made extinct.' He makes so many (*tāvatas*) beings extinct. Yet there is no being who has become extinct, or by whom a being has been made extinct. Why? This is the nature (*dharmatā*, or true nature) of principles: that they are based on (*upādāya*) the nature (*dharmatā*) of illusion (*māyā*, a 'trick', 'artifice', as for example a puppet show, clay models, or a sculpture or painting). As a showman (*māyākāra*) or his apprentice may produce (*abhi-nir-mā*) a large crowd of people in the square and then make

1. 8,000, 20f.

them disappear: is anyone, by anyone, killed, dead, destroyed or made to disappear ?[1] ...so no being makes extinct or becomes extinct ...because omniscience (*sarvajñatā*) is not made, not changed, not synthesised (meaning the omniscience of the *bodhisattva* when he becomes a *buddha*)."

That there are no 'beings' is not new and the apparent paradox that a *bodhisattva* or *buddha* causes beings to attain extinction whilst no beings become extinct is merely the conjunction of two statements, the first at the 'concealing' everyday level and the second at the 'ultimate' philosophical level (cf. p. 150 above). In case there should be any doubt about this the commentators[2] explain the statements using these terms. What is entirely new is that 'principles', the elements (*dharma*), are spoken of in exactly the same terms as 'beings'. The old distinction between everyday appearance and philosophical reality has been obliterated and something new is being put in its place. The stream of consciousness, the sequence of conditions, is apparently no more real than the soul or person, or if it is anything (the soul being nothing at all) it is only a puppet show, not the principles mentioned in the *Tripiṭaka* but some more ultimate substance (*kāya*).

Subhūti then takes up the argument :[3] the groups (matter and the others) are not 'bound' (*baddha* — in transmigration) and not 'freed' (*mukta*). Asked by the monk Pūrṇa which matter, etc., he means, which 'thusness' (*tathatā*, or 'truth', actuality, actual nature, cf. p. 135 above) of matter, etc., Subhūti replies : that of a person shown by artifice (*māyāpuruṣa*, i.e. a puppet, etc.), because it does not really exist (*asadbhūtatvāt*), is 'separated' (*viviktatvāt*, i.e. without the own or particular nature it is commonly supposed to have) and does not (actually) occur (*anutpannatvāt*). Later[4] he says that a '*buddha*' also is only a name, like the 'soul' (*ātman*, self). Since all principles are without own-nature, what matter, etc., could it be which does not originate? The

1. cf. 25,000, 186.
2 e.g. Haribhadra AAĀ 38 on the opening paragraphs of the *Sūtra*, also p. 85 on the present passage (and cf. pp. 272, 297, 372, 430, 434).
3. 8,000, 21f.
4. 25ff.

non-origination (*anabhinirvṛtti*) of all principles (means) they are not principles... The non-occurrence and non-cessation of matter, etc., (means) it is not matter, etc. Thus when examining all principles with reference to the perfection of understanding, according to all their features (*sarvākāram* ; Haribhadra explains this as meaning such features as having no own-nature), 'matter', etc., does not apply (*upa-i*), one does not reach matter, etc., one does not observe its occurrence or cessation. The non-occurrence of matter, etc. (means) there is no duality (*dvaya*) in it, no making twofold; the non-cessation of matter, etc., (means) there is no duality in it, no making twofold.

In later chapters of the *Sūtra* there are several variations on the theme of all principles having no own-nature. For example: 'All principles are 'separated' (*vivikta*) from (any) nature (*prakṛti*), and the perfection of understanding is this being separated from (any) nature. This is because all principles are not made... Those principles are by nature nothing (*na kiñ cit*). The nature of all principles is non-nature and their non-nature is their nature. Their one characteristic (*lakṣaṇa*) is having a non-characteristic.'[1]

What is the 'perfection of understanding' ? 'The perfection of understanding is only a name.'[2] 'This perfection of understanding cannot be specified (*nir-diś*) or heard or observed ... according to (*-śas*) the groups, elements (*dhātu*) and spheres. Why ? Because of the separation (*viviktatva*) of all principles ... Also the perfection of understanding cannot be recognised (or understood, *ava-budh*) apart from (*anyatra*) the groups, elements and spheres. Why ? Because it is precisely (*eva*) the groups, elements and spheres which are empty (*śūnya*), separated and calmed (*śānta*). Because of this the perfection of understanding and the groups, elements and spheres are not a duality, not a making twofold... The non-perception (*anupalambha*) of all principles is called the perfection of understanding. When there is no perception (*saṃjñā*), designation (*samajñā*, or 'agreed usage'), concept or convention (*vyavahāra*, or 'usage'), then it is

1. 8,000 p. 192.
2. p. 200.

called the perfection of understanding.'[1] This passage ascribed to the Buddha may be compared with one quoted in Chapter Five above (pp. 110 f.), where some of the same terms appear, in order to see how far the Mahāyāna had moved away from the earliest teaching whilst seeming to speak the same language. On page 203 of the *Sūtra* the gods are made to remark that this is a 'second starting of the wheel of the doctrine.' In other words it is new, or at any rate was unknown to the original followers of the Buddha and the early schools, though certain privileged persons (Subhūti, etc.) and especially some of the gods are supposed to have been allowed to hear it. In this *Sūtra* three 'floors' (*bhūmi*) or vehicles (*yāna*) are distinguished, those of the 'pupils', the isolated (private) *buddhas* and (public) *buddhas*. The Buddha is made to attack the back-sliders from the last and highest one who in future will revert from the way of the *bodhisattvas* to that of the pupils, whose *sūtras* are merely the 'branches, leaves and straw.'[2]

The sixteenth chapter of the Eight Thousand deals with 'thusness' (*tathatā*, 'truth'). Subhūti says the doctrine is taught as the non-perception of all principles. Nothing can obstruct (*prati-han*) it. Its characteristic is non-obstruction, because it is the same as space and because there is no perception of any resting place (*pada*, 'step', 'basis', i.e. object for perception). The gods praise Subhūti for this as the thus-gone's (the Buddha's) younger brother (*anujāta*, literally 'born after'). Subhūti replies that it is because he is not born that he is 'born after'. He is 'born after' the thusness (*tathatā*) of the thus-gone. As the thusness of the thus-gone has not come and has not gone (it is possible to analyse *tathāgata* as either 'thus-come', *tathā-āgata*, or 'thus-gone', *tathā-gata*), so the thusness of Subhūti has not come and has not gone...The thusness of the thus-gone is the thusness of all principles and the thusness of all principles is the thusness of the thus-gone, and also the thusness of Subhūti...This thusness of the thus-gone and of all principles is one(*eka*) thusness, not a duality (*advaya*), not a making twofold (*advaidhikāra*), a non-duality-thusness, a nowhere-thusness, a from-nowhere thusness, the thusness of nothing at all (*na kasya cit*).

1. p. 177.
2. p. 234.

Because it is the thusness of nothing at all this thusness is a non-duality, a not making twofold, a non-duality-thusness. This not made (*akṛta*) thusness is never not thusness, therefore it is a non-duality, etc....As the thusness of the thus-gone is everywhere and in all principles non-imagination, without imagination, so is the thusness of Subhūti ... Finally it is on account of this thusness that the name 'thus-gone' is applied to a *bodhisattva* when he becomes enlightened (a *buddha*).

At the end of the same chapter it is said that a *bodhisattva* wishing to 'go out to' the supreme, perfect enlightenment (*anuttarā samyaksambodhi*) must remain impartial (*sama*, or 'equal') with reference to all beings, his thought impartial, benevolent (*maitra*), beneficient (*hita*), good (*kalyāṇa*), harmless (*avihiṃsa*), and so on, and pursue the six perfections. Among these, 'understanding' is significantly defined as examining conditioned origination.

In the nineteenth chapter Subhūti asks the Buddha about becoming enlightened. Does the *bodhisattva* become enlightened by the first occurrence of the thought (of enlightenment) or by the last occurrence of the thought? The Buddha replies with an analogy: is the wick of a lighted oil lamp burned by the first onset of the flame or the last? Subhūti thinks by neither, yet agrees that it is in fact burned. The Buddha says it is the same with the *bodhisattva* becoming enlightened: it is not by the first or the last occurrence of the thought, nor without depending on (*anāgamya*) the last nor apart from the occurrences of the thought. And he does become enlightened. Subhūti remarks here that conditioned origination is profound. A discussion follows which is reminiscent of a section of the *Yamaka* (p. 302 above) which studies the occurrence and cessation of thought. Does a thought which has ceased occur again? No! Has a thought which has occurred[1] the nature of cessation? Yes. If it has the nature of cessation will it cease? No! Then has a thought which has not occurred the nature of cessation? No! If it has the nature of cessation will it cease? No! If a thought has the nature of not occurring and not ceasing will it cease? No! If a principle has by nature

1. So Haribhadra reads (p. 435 of Tucci's edition).

(*prakṛti*) ceased to have any own-nature will it cease ? No! Will the nature (*dharmatā*, true nature) of principles cease ? No! In that case it will remain as thusness ? Yes. If so, then it will be 'immovable' (*kūṭastha*, 'immovable as a peak', cf. p. 143 above; a synonym for 'eternal') ? No ! Thusness is profound ? Yes! — Is thought in thusness ? No! Is thought thusness ? No! Is thought different from thusness ? No! Do you observe thusness ? No! He who proceeds (*car*) so proceeds in what is profound ? He who proceeds so proceeds nowhere ! . . .As Haribhadra points out in his commentary this discussion evidently begins at the everyday 'concealing' level (a being becomes enlightened). It leads round to the ultimate level by introducing 'thusness' (Haribhadra : the thought is not the same as thusness because one is at the 'concealing' level and the other at the 'ultimate' ; at the same time it is not different from thusness, cannot be independent of it). The position of the *Sūtra* appears to be that thought is impermanent, like all principles according to all schools of Buddhism, but thusness provides the possibility of continuity between momentary thoughts forming a series, so that they can lead to some effect, such as enlightenment. However, thusness also is not something permanent, because it is 'the thusness of nothing at all' (as we read in chapter sixteen).

A few further points from the Eight Thousand : (1) beings transmigrate because of the supposition of an ego, a self, and of possessing; this is their 'defilement', and not having such a supposition, not 'superimposing' it, is their 'purification';[1] (2) principles are completely 'separate' (without own-nature), therefore neither 'it is' nor 'it is not' applies to them;[2] (3) 'immeasurable' (*aprameya*) is a designation of emptiness, of signlessness and of uncommittedness, and all principles are empty and cannot be differentiated;[3] (4) the impermanence of matter, etc., should not be misunderstood as the destruction (*vināśa*) of matter, etc.[4]

---

1. p. 400.
2. p. 439.
3. p. 347.
4. p. 113.

Madhyamaka

The Tibetan historian Tāranātha gives a detailed account of the rise of Mahāyāna Buddhism,[1] which appears to be the only such account now extant. Unfortunately he seems to have found considerable confusion in his sources, and no doubt had great difficulty in fitting his heterogeneous materials together into a consistent whole. Faced with numerous dynastic lists relating to different parts of India he tried to establish synchronisms between them and also with the many Buddhist teachers of whom records survived. Some of his identifications and synchronisms are very wide of the mark, which has tended to discredit his whole work. Nevertheless a compilation of this sort cannot be judged as a whole: the constituent parts must be taken separately and checked with whatever other sources exist for their respective periods.

Tāranātha places the rise of the Mahāyāna after his account of Kaniṣka I and his son (not named, presumably Vāsiṣka known to us from other sources) and some of the Sarvāstivādin teachers (Vasumitra II, Ghoṣaka) contemporary with these Kuṣāṇa emperors. A Buddhist teacher named Aśvagupta is noted as living at Pāṭaliputra in the time of Kaniṣka's son. Then 'in the West lived king Lakṣāśva' who supported Buddhism (this name has not been identified with any known king, and 'West' appears vague, though we find a little later that it included Saurāṣṭra: the reference may be to the successor of 'Kaniṣka's son', using a name — kings often used several names — not recorded elsewhere, in which case it would presumably be to Huviṣka, A.D. 106; an alternative would be one of the Kṣaharāta governors of Aparānta in the broad sense, who seem to have been Śakas appointed by the Kuṣāṇas[2]). At this time an elder named Nanda taught the Mahāyāna in the Aṅga country, then 'suddenly' countless teachers (Avitarka and others) of the Mahāyāna appeared in different places, who had learned this teaching from Avalokiteśvara (a *bodhisattva* in Amitābha's world — see p. 361 above), Maitreya and other *bodhisattvas*. At the same time a number of Mahāyāna *sūtras* appeared, beginning with the

1. Chapter XIII of Schiefner's version.
2. e.g. Nahapāna; but even a Sātavāhana such as Gautamīputra is a possibility.

Ratnakūṭa, most of which had been brought from the Dragon World (under the Earth), some from the worlds of the gods. Lakṣāśva became a keen supporter of the new movement, building *vihāras* for it and encouraging students, and arranged for the new *sūtras* to be written down. These were afterwards brought to Nālandā (where Tāranātha's source for this part was written, it appears), celebrated as the place where Śāriputra lived and later the greatest Buddhist university of India.

Those of us who do not believe in a Dragon World under the Earth and have studied the evidence adduced above will prefer to locate this source of most of the Mahāyāna *sūtras* in Āndhra. We may see further an agreement with that version of the Perfection of Understanding which says that that *sūtra* will be known at first in the South, then in the West, afterwards in the North.

Tāranātha remarks that the followers of the early schools mostly rejected the Mahāyāna as not the words of the Buddha (not in the *Tripiṭaka*) and that the small minority of Mahāyānists were spread thinly among the Buddhist communities. We may add here that the available evidence shows that the majority of Buddhists in India at all times have followed the early schools and the Mahāyāna there was always a minority movement: it is only in certain countries outside India (China and Tibet and the countries which derived their Buddhism from them) that the Mahāyāna completely supplanted the earlier Buddhism.

After this, in the time of king Candanapāla of Aparāntaka (who may perhaps be identified with Kaniṣka II, A.D. 119)[1], Rāhulabhadra[2] learned the Mahāyāna from Avitarka and with other teachers established the philosophical school of Mahāyāna called the Madhyamaka. Still more new *sūtras* appeared. Little is known of these teachers, but after them a far greater philosopher appeared in Nālandā, Nāgārjuna (Bu-ston, II p. 123, makes him a pupil of Rāhulabhadra).

Nāgārjuna

According to Bu-ston[3] Nāgārjuna was born in the Vidarbha

1. On the connection of 'Candana' and 'Kaniṣka' see Lévi, *JA* 1936 75ff.
2. Tāranātha Chapter XIV.
3. II 122ff.

country in Mahārāṣṭra. The same authority says he became a monk at Nālandā and was taught by Rāhulabhadra. The young Nāgārjuna was a very unusual person — expressed in the legend by his contacts with the dragons, who were ready to fetch whatever he needed from their World. Eventually the Dragon King invited him to visit this World himself. Nāgārjuna accepted, but returned to Earth as soon as possible with the Hundred Thousand Perfection of Understanding, the culminating Mahāyāna *sūtra*, which he found in the Dragon World. He taught in many countries, and our sources stress also his building activities, constructing and improving pagodas, *vihāras* and temples. Tāranātha records[1] that towards the end of his life he returned to the Sātavāhana domains, but to Āndhra, not Mahārāṣṭra. Many sources in Indian literature[2] confirm Nāgārjuna's association with the Sātavāhana emperor, who became his pupil, and the tradition seems to be confirmed by archaeology and inscriptions.[3] The particular Sātavāhana in question, whom the traditions identify with the 'Hāla' famous in the history of Indian secular literature as a connoisseur and patron, would appear to be Puḷumāyi II (Vāsiṣṭhīputra), who is recorded in an inscription to have improved the pagoda at Amarāvatī.[4]

It is fairly certain that there were several authors named 'Nāgārjuna' in Indian literature. Among the numerous works ascribed to them it is not easy to settle precisely how many were written by the one we are now concerned with. There is, however, no doubt about the most important of them, the *Mūlamadhyamakakārikā*, which is the foundation of the doctrine of the Madhyamaka school. The other works probably his are: *Vigrahavyāvartanī*, *Śūnyatāsaptati*, *Yuktiṣaṣṭikā*, *Vaidalyasūtra* and *Prakaraṇa*, *Suhṛllekha*, perhaps the *Ratnāvali* and some 'hymns' (*stotra*) in praise of the Buddha. Among these the *Suhṛllekha*, Letter to a Friend, is an epistle to the Sātavāhana emperor, expounding traditional Buddhist morality in no

1. p. 72.
2. The novel *Līlāvaī*, Jaina works such as the *Purātanaprabandhasaṃgraha*, books on alchemy (with which Nāgārjuna was traditionally associated): *Rasaratnākara*, etc.
3. see Lamotte MPPŚ XIIf.
4. *Comprehensive History of India* II 316.

way different from that we have found in the *Tripiṭaka*.[1] This literary genre seems to have been very popular for several centuries, and the Buddhism thus communicated to distinguished laymen by monks of different schools is not unlike that advocated by Aśoka. The *Ratnāvalī* is similarly a 'popular' work and also addressed to a king, traditionally the same Sātavāhana, but it expounds philosophy as well, the Madhyamaka doctrine, in a poetic manner. The *Śūnyatāsaptati* and *Yuktiṣaṣṭikā* are short works summarising the Madhyamaka doctrine, whilst the other two works named above are controversial writings taking up particular points raised by other Buddhists against the Madhyamaka and also criticizing the Brahmanical Nyāya (Vaiśeṣika) school of philosophy. We are left then with one basic work and a few supplementary points added in the two controversial writings.

Tāranātha notes[2] that the 'pupils' (*śrāvakas*, followers of the earlier schools) alleged that Nāgārjuna himself wrote the Hundred Thousand Perfection of Understanding supposed to have been brought by him from the Dragon World. In actual fact there seems to be no reference by Nāgārjuna in the works certainly his (particularly the basic work) to the Mahāyāna or Mahāyāna *sūtras*.[3] His references to *sūtras* are all to the old *Tripiṭaka*, mostly to the *Saṃyukta*. He writes simply as a Buddhist trying to establish the correct interpretation of the *Tripiṭaka* as recognised by all Buddhists. It would hardly be possible to prove even that he knew of the existence of the new *sūtras*, whose doctrines he is supposed to vindicate in his work. The rather intolerant and misrepresenting denunciations of the 'pupils' which frequently appear in Mahāyāna *sūtras* and often enough in the theoretical writings of Mahāyāna teachers, doubtless a high pitched expression of annoyance at the rejection of the new *sūtras* by the established schools as not to be found in the *Tripiṭaka* and contrary to its doctrine, are refreshingly absent from Nāgārjuna's pages. Confident of his doctrine, he seeks to persuade, to argue. He was claimed by the Mahāyānists as their own, but his real position would seem to have

1. See IKL II p. 232. The mention of Avalokiteśvara and Amitābha may derive from a Pūrva Śaila *sūtra*, the original of the *Sukhāvatīvyūha*.
2. p. 71.
3. See 'Is Nāgārjuna a Mahāyānist ?'

been not to take sides in a provocative controversy hardly conducive to progress on the way. He perhaps hoped to reunite the schools, old and new, in a single Buddhist doctrine agreed by all to be the re-establishment of the original teaching of the Buddha himself. The name of the school he effectively founded (even if it existed earlier), the Madhyamaka (the 'Intermediate'), suggests the re-establishment of the original 'intermediate way' in all possible senses of 'intermediate', avoiding extremes of speculative opinion, of conduct and perhaps of the divisions of school and 'vehicle'.

Nāgārjuna's main contention is that it was not the intention of the Buddha to set out a list of 'ultimate' principles or elements which in some metaphysical sense 'exist', still less to define their 'own-natures', by implication immutable. He opposed therefore the general tendency of *abhidharma* discussion to hypostatise certain philosophical concepts, to superimpose metaphysical constructions on the real universe which did not correspond to them, and more particularly the scholastic trend of the commentators of the schools who had introduced the conceptions of the 'own-nature' (borrowed apparently from the Lokāyata) and 'other-nature' of principles along with the exegetical methodology represented by the Sthaviravāda *Peṭakopadesa* (pp. 316 ff. above) and no doubt found in other schools as well. The Buddha taught, essentially, the Four Truths and conditioned origination: the *Mūlamadhyamakakārikā* presents itself as the correct interpretation of these. The doctrine is not speculative but empiricist: the Buddha emphatically rejected all speculative opinions (*dṛṣṭi*) and propounded no such opinion himself, only an empiricist account of conditioned origination and the way to end unhappiness. The basic concepts of philosophy, even 'time', 'space', 'motion', 'causality', and so on, are themselves speculative, and Nāgārjuna shows by rigorous analysis that it is inconceivable how, for example, a 'motion' as understood in philosophy could ever take place.

If Nāgārjuna holds no such speculative opinion himself, as he claims, if no philosophical positions or concepts at all are tenable, then in discussing the opinions of others it is clear that he cannot consistently take up any position himself, any standpoint in philosophy, and argue from that against other positions. So we find, in fact, that given any concept or opinion he proceeds to argue from it, to work from the opponent's own position, in order to show that it is untenable. In the debates of the early schools (e.g. in the *Kathāvatthu*) the method generally followed was to deduce from an opponent's position a conclusion which was clearly contrary to the *Tripiṭaka*. Thus a position held to be erroneous was opposed to a position held to be true. In Nāgārjuna's arguments, on the other hand, the usual method is to deduce from the opponent's position a 'necessary consequence' (*prasaṅga*) which shows the absurdity of that position and the self-contradiction inherent in it. That he holds no position, makes no 'assertion' ('statement' — philosophical — *pratijñā*), is most clearly explained by Nāgārjuna in one of the minor works, the *Vigrahavyāvartanī* (29), written after the main work (which it quotes) as a rejoinder to criticisms made especially by other Buddhists. His doctrine of no own-nature, emptiness (that principles are empty of own nature) is not itself an 'assertion', a speculative opinion, it is only not holding any such opinion. Nāgārjuna could have adduced in support of his doctrine the *sūtra* we referred to above (p. 141) where the Buddha says that the thus-gone does not hold any opinion at all, but instead has seen matter, etc., and their origination and cessation (i.e. the doctrine is empiricist, not speculative), or the *Brahmajāla Sūtra* (p.149 above). The question naturally arises whether Nāgārjuna in any way goes beyond the *Tripiṭaka* doctrine.

Nāgārjuna took over from the *Tripiṭaka* the dialectics of the tetralemma (*catuṣkoṭi*), for example does the thus-gone exist after death, or not exist, or both, or neither (see pp.122 f. above), and the other 'undetermined' questions (p. 139 above). These are explained in Chapter 27 of the *Mūlamadhyamakakārikā*, and Nāgārjuna draws from them the method of the dilemma (a given hypothetical entity, e.g. the 'soul', is either the same as or different from some other entity, e.g. the 'body') as well as of the tetralemma. He explains that anything eternal could not be born and transmigrate, whilst if it were non-eternal (i.e. totally destroyed) the sequence of conditions would not apply to it. The theory of both at once does not escape the difficulty (the entity would be partly eternal and partly non-eternal, which does not help us); that of neither would make sense only if the term denied (eternal and non-eternal) did. He concludes that there is no basis for any of the speculative opinions because all the 'existents' (or natures, *bhāvas*) are empty. The term 'existents' (*bhāvas*) is not synonymous with 'principles' (*dharmas*), but represents the misconception of them as independent 'own-natures' (*svabhāvas*), stressing the idea that they are supposed to 'exist' rather than that they have a specific 'nature'. They are empty in the sense that there is nothing permanent in them, such as a 'soul', about which it could be argued whether it was eternal or not, infinite or not, and so on. There is perhaps a subtle difference here between the doctrine of the *Tripiṭaka* and that of Nāgārjuna: in the *sūtras* it is the supposed life-principle or (living) being or soul or thus-gone (as well as the 'universe') about which the speculative opinions are formed, here the 'existents' are brought into relation with them in that they contain no such entity. Now for the *Tripiṭaka* there are no souls or beings, but there are principles. For Nāgārjuna there are no existents and so the principles seem to be in question too. This will be clarified in his Chapter 24, but first the question of 'existence' must be examined.

We can approach this question via Nāgārjuna's refutation of the commentarial doctrine of the 'own-nature' of principles as contrary to the *Tripiṭaka* (Chapter 15 of his work). If an 'own-nature', he says, were related to causes and conditions it would be artificial (*kṛtaka*, something made). This would contradict the conception of its 'own' nature, which by definition should be independent of anything else (*nirapekṣa*). If there is no 'own-nature' then there can be no 'other-nature' either, since this could be understood only as contrasted with an 'own-nature'. In the absence of either 'own-nature' or 'other-nature' how can there be any 'existent' (nature, *bhāva*) ? If 'existent' (*bhāva*) is (thus) denied, then 'non-existent' (*abhāva*) also cannot be affirmed, for 'non-existent' is only the 'otherwiseness' (*anyathā-bhāva*, or otherness) of 'existent'. Those who see 'own-nature' and 'other-nature', 'existent' (nature) and 'non-existent', do not see the reality (*tattva*) of the doctrine of the Buddha. In the *Kātyāyanāvavāda Sūtra* (see above, pp. 129f.) the Master, explaining (or perhaps just contemplating — *vi-bhū* causative) 'existent' and 'non-existent', has rejected both 'it is' and 'it is not' ... These correspond to eternalism (*śāśvatavāda*) and annihilationism (*ucchedavāda*), eternalism deriving from the idea that what existed by its own-nature could not (ever) be said not to exist and annihilationism deriving from the idea that something exists no more after having formerly existed.

We see from this that Nāgārjuna takes the words 'exist' or 'are' and 'existent' (the verb *as* and the noun *bhāva*) as meaning 'existing eternally' and implying the eternalist opinion. Momentary 'existence' will have to be described in other words. The object of the critique is to show that the eternalist view is untenable and further to show that the 'own-nature' theory adopted by some Buddhists did not really differ, when its implications were strictly worked out, from the eternalist theory of Brahmanism (theory of an eternal 'soul' and other eternal 'substances'). What could an 'own-nature' be but something continuing to exist eternally, independent of causes or conditions? To say that a principle has an *own* nature which was yet produced by something *other* than itself (conditions) is self-contradictory.

Then suppose we call it an 'other-nature'? This also will not do because we have to explain 'other than what' this would be, and could do so only by saying 'other than itself' or 'other than its own', so that we are back where we started. It is an important methodological principle with Nāgārjuna that such pairs of contradictory statements as 'natures exist' and 'natures do not exist', or 'natures have own-nature' and 'natures have other-nature', are interdependent. Though they contradict one another they cannot be understood separately. If we could give an intelligible and rational account (applicable to the real world) of one of them (e.g. of 'existent') then we might be able to do the same for the other (e.g. 'non-existent'). It certainly does not follow that because we reject the idea that natures 'exist' we should accept the contradictory idea that they do 'not exist', and this has important practical implications for Nāgārjuna. He rejects each 'extreme' view, each speculative opinion (eternal, non-eternal, infinite, finite, a soul different from the body, a soul identical with the body, etc.), precisely because he rejects also the opposite extreme. More generally, if '*a*' does not exist, then 'not *a*' does not exist either.

From the above it follows that if the 'synthesised' (*saṃs-kṛta*) natures do not exist then an 'unsynthesised' (*asaṃskṛta*), i.e. extinction (*nirvāṇa*), does not 'exist' either (Nāgārjuna 7.33).

We can now read Nāgārjuna's First Chapter, which deals with the question of the 'conditions' (*pratyaya*) and is intended to refute the interpretations of the doctrine of conditions which had grown up among the early schools (along with their 'own-nature' theory). There are no existents (natures, *bhāvas*) anywhere, Nāgārjuna begins, which occur (*ut-pad*, we may also understand 'originate', usually *sam-ut-pad*) out of themselves (*svatas*), or out of an other (*paratas*), or out of both, or without any cause (*ahetutas*)... There is no 'own-nature' of an existent (nature) in the various kinds of condition proposed in the schools (the 'cause', the 'support', the 'immediate', the 'dominant'). In the absence of any 'own-nature' there can be no 'other-nature' either...Let those things be called 'conditions', conditioned by which things occur, but how can they be 'conditions' before the latter have occurred ? Neither a non-existing object (*artha*) nor an existing one is congruent with (*yujyate*) having a condition: of what non-existing thing can there be a condition ? And what use is a condition for a thing which (already) exists ? ...If existents (natures) have no 'own-nature' then they have no 'existence' (*sattā*, 'existing-ness'). Thus (the formula: p. 113 above) 'this being, that is' has no application (*na upa-pad*). The result does not exist in any of the conditions taken singly, nor in all of them together. How could there be something 'from the conditions' which was not in them? Or, if something which did not exist in them started 'from the conditions', why should the result not start equally well (*api*, 'even') from what were not conditions? ...We conclude that there are no conditions and no non-conditions, since no results of them exist.

Does this mean that Nāgārjuna rejects the doctrine of conditioned origination? No. It is because he accepts it that he rejects the idea that there is anything eternal, that anything 'exists' (in the sense we found above), that anything has an 'own-nature', and the opposites of these speculative theories: What is conditioned by something is not identical with it (*tad eva*) nor different from it. That is why there is nothing which is annihilated or which is eternal (18.10). This means that the result is not the same as its condition (which would mean eternal existence of the condition) nor is it different from it (which would mean that the condition was annihilated, became non-existent). From Nāgārjuna's own day onwards his doctrine was subject to being misunderstood as nihilistic: because he rejected 'existence' of natures and spoke of their 'emptiness' (of own-nature) careless students (and critics who were either not very careful or not very scrupulous) have concluded that he maintained that ultimately the universe was an utter nothingness. In fact his rejection of 'non-existence' is as emphatic as his rejection of 'existence', and must lead us to the conclusion that what he is attacking is these notions as metaphysical concepts imposed on the real universe. Before we read more of what he has to say of such concepts we may look at his 24th Chapter, where he replies to a Buddhist who suggests that he has rejected the Four Truths (and with them conditioned origination) and therefore rejected Buddhism.

The opponent says: If everything ('all this') is empty then there is neither origination nor cessation, from which it necessarily follows that according to you the Four Truths do not exist...(and with them Buddhism as a whole does not exist, there is no good and bad, etc.). Nāgārjuna replies (24.7) that the opponent does not know what emptiness means. The *buddhas* teach the doctrine on the basis of the two levels of truth, the concealing and the ultimate (p. 150 above). Those who do not discern the difference between these two 'truths' (*satya*) do not discern the profound reality (*tattva*) of the doctrine of the Buddha. The ultimate truth cannot be taught without depending on (*anāśritya*) conventional usage (*vyavahāra*); extinction cannot be attained without depending on (*anāgamya*) the ultimate truth. Like a snake grasped in the wrong way or a science wrongly applied, emptiness misunderstood (*durdṛṣṭa*) destroys (*vi-naś* causative) those of weak intelligence...For whom emptiness is 'congruent' (*yujyate*) everything (in the Buddhist doctrine) is congruent; for whom the empty is not congruent everything is not congruent...If because of the (supposed) 'own-nature' you see (envisage) an 'existing (real) existence' (*sadbhāva*), of existents (natures, *bhāvas*), then you must see these existents (natures) as without causes and conditions. You must reject cause and effect (causality); agent, instrument and action; origination and cessation; and any result (of conditions). It is conditioned origination which we call 'emptiness'. It is a 'concept based on' (*upādāya prajñapti*, 'concept attached to') something (else, i.e. not in itself some entity, something 'existing'), and precisely it is the 'intermediate way' (avoiding the extremes of 'it is' and 'it is not').

Since (Nāgārjuna continues) no principle (*dharma*) occurs (*vidyate*) which is not originated by conditions, no principle occurs which is not empty. If everything were not empty (as the opponent would maintain) then there would be neither origination nor cessation, from which it would necessarily follow that according to you (the opponent) the Four Truths would not exist...(these being dependent on conditioned origination). Nothing could originate, nothing cease...No one would be able to do any good or bad actions ...

Thus for Nāgārjuna principles are not 'non-existent' or 'existent': it can be said that they 'occur' (*vidyate*, *ut-pad*), that thay 'originate' and 'cease', provided that this is understood only of 'empty' principles, not of 'existents' (natures, *bhāvas*) such as were being discussed in his First Chapter or of principles defined as having 'own-nature'. Most important of all, this is no speculative doctrine of hypostatised concepts, it is an empiricist one: (even) the best concepts (e.g. 'emptiness') are only 'concepts based on' something. The concepts generally used in philosophy do not apply to the world of conditioned origination.

The question of 'emptiness' is further clarified in Nāgārjuna's Chapter 13, where he supposes another Buddhist to take emptiness itself as a speculative opinion instead of as it should be understood. This opponent is supposed to argue that emptiness itself is the 'own-nature' of existents (natures, *bhāvas*) (13.3). Nāgārjuna gives the answer that if anything which was not empty existed, then an 'empty' could exist; since however there exists nothing not empty, how can an 'empty' exist? The *buddhas* have taught emptiness as liberation (*niḥsaraṇa*) from all speculative opinions (*dṛṣṭis*), but they have declared that he who holds emptiness itself as such an opinion is beyond help (*asādhya*, they cannot accomplish his liberation) (13.7-8).

If everything is empty, then what of extinction (*nirvāṇa*) ? In his Chapter 25 Nāgārjuna argues that it is not an existent (*bhāva*), not a non-existent, not both existent and non-existent, not neither existent nor non-existent (just as the thus-gone after his extinction is none of these). But we seem to have found above that the 'principles' of the universe are equally none of these things, is extinction then the same as they are ? Nāgārjuna says : There is no distinction (*viśeṣaṇa*) at all between extinction and transmigration (*saṃsāra*). There is no distinction at all between transmigration and extinction. The limit of extinction would be the limit of transmigration (but neither has a limit)...The speculative opinions about (the thus-gone) beyond cessation, about finite and infinite, eternal and non-eternal (concerning the universe, transmigration) are of the same kind as those concerning extinction. Since everything is empty what is finite or infinite or both or neither, what is identity or difference (in the speculation about the 'soul' and the body), what is eternality, non-eternality, both, neither? Happiness consists in the calming of these differentiations (*prapañca*) (not in the 'cessation' of 'existents').

It remains to add some brief notes on Nāgārjuna's critiques of the various concepts used in philosophy, showing that none of them are valid as customarily applied. He uses what may be called a 'temporal analysis' to dispose of any concept involving a process in time, as well as of the concept of 'time' itself. In effect it is a trilemma showing that it is impossible to give a coherent explanation of the concepts in relation to 'past', 'present' or 'future' time. In his Second Chapter Nāgārjuna investigates the concept of 'motion'. First he formulates the trilemma as follows: (1) that which is 'gone' (*gata*, i.e. past) is not 'being gone' (*gamyate*, i.e. present as being moved, the 'motion' which we seek to identify, to catch in the act of 'happening' in order to define it); (2) that which is 'not gone' (*agata*, i.e. future) is not 'being gone'; (3) a 'being gone' (*gamyamāna*, i.e. present — here the participle is used, not the present tense, distinguishing the concept as subject of the proposition from the predicate intended to define it) independent of 'gone' (past) and 'not gone' (future) is not 'being gone' (*gamyate*, present tense). In other words we cannot understand the motion as 'being' what has already happened and ceased, or as being what has not yet started. As for a 'being gone' to be understood as happening at present, we could understand 'present' only as being something in between the 'past' and the 'future', not independently of these two; since, however, we have not been able to understand 'being gone' as related to 'gone' or 'not gone', the possibility of understanding a present motion dependent on past and future is not open to us. In the ensuing discussion the opponent is imagined to seek to define a present 'motion' independent of 'being gone', in order to evade the trilemma and understand 'being gone' by reference only to this present 'motion' and independently of 'gone' and 'not gone', to which Nāgārjuna replies that there cannot be a 'being gone' distinct from 'motion', which could be defined by pointing out the relation between them. The attempt to improve the definition merely multiplies the entities for which definitions must be sought: we have two motions (*gamanas*, 2.5) instead of one and are no nearer any solution, rather we would have to look for two agents supposed to perform the two motions. This incidentally brings up the question of an 'agent' who or which moves, the absurdity of which (according to Nāgārjuna) offers another method of exploding the concept of 'motion'. There are various other methods besides these: for example the absurdity of the concept of 'being stationary' is demonstrated, whence it follows that the contradictory of this (being gone, motion), which we would have to understand by contrast as other than stationary, is equally absurd.

The connected, or more basic, critique of 'time' is given in Chapter 19. Suppose we try to conceive a 'present' or a 'future' time in relation to (*apekṣya*) 'past' time (i.e. by contrast with it), this relation cannot occur unless the 'present' or 'future' occurs simultaneously with the 'past', therefore in the past. Occurrence in the past, of course, destroys the concepts of 'present' or 'future', yet there is no way of demonstrating their occurrence independently of a 'past'. Therefore 'time' does not occur (*na vidyate*). Evidently the concept of a 'past' time can be exploded in exactly the same way, but the triple analysis is equally destructive of other triads of concepts, such as 'low', 'intermediate' and 'high'. In principle it can be applied to any pair of contradictories also, such as 'unity' and 'multiplicity', whence we see that it is nothing but an extension of the principle of the interdependence of contradictories which we met above in studying the 'own-nature' and 'other-nature'. The same Chapter shows also the futility of attempting to demonstrate a 'time' conditioned by an existent (nature), and the impossibility of conceiving either a 'time' which was changing or a 'time' which was constant.

The triple method of analysis applies also to the concept of 'occurrence' (*utpāda*) if hypostatised : neither that which 'has occurred', nor that which 'has not occurred', nor that which 'is occurring'; occurs, by what we may call the first 'theorem' of the Second Chapter (7.14). If, further, there were an 'occurrence' of that which 'is occurring', we would then be led to posit the 'occurrence' of that 'occurrence' and so on *ad infinitum* ('occurrence' of the 'occurrence' of the 'occurrence' of the...of the 'occurrence') (7. 18f.) — the infinite regress (*anavasthā*) being another useful weapon in Nāgārjuna's dialectical armoury.

Nāgārjuna's Fifth Chapter is directed against attempts to set up a 'characteristic' (*lakṣaṇa*) of an existent (nature, *bhāva*) which would then be 'characterised' (*lakṣya*) by it. Any alleged existent (nature), e.g. 'space', does not occur before its 'characteristic' (otherwise it would follow that it could occur without it). If, however, we suppose a 'commencement' (*pravṛtti*, 'starting') of the 'characteristic' we introduce an additional concept of which we are unable to give a satisfactory account (the 'characteristic' alone would be sufficient, if present; a 'commencement' is redundant). But then in the absence of the 'commencement' of the 'characteristic', the 'characterised' has no application (whence also the 'characteristic' has no application). Thus the 'characterised' and the 'characteristic' do not occur. It will follow for the opponent that his 'existent (nature)' also does not occur, since by his definition it cannot occur independently of its 'characterised' and 'characteristic'.

In general, Nāgārjuna sums up his method at the end of Chapter 4, if one argues on the basis of emptiness, then whatever argument an opponent uses to evade the consequences (and set up his concepts or his speculative opinions) he is begging the question (*samaṃ sādhyena jāyate*, i.e. the fallacy of *sādhyasama* of Indian logic must occur, the opponent merely assumes his opinion, his concept, without being able to prove it).

Further Development of the Madhyamaka School

Evidently Nāgārjuna did not succeed in reuniting the old schools and the Mahāyāna on the basis of his interpretation of the *Tripiṭaka*, though it is probable that he greatly strengthened the Madhyamaka. The Sthaviravādins and others adhered to their 'own-nature' theory,[1] whilst it is probable that most Mahāyānists followed the tone of the majority of their new *sūtras* in writing off the old *Tripiṭaka* as an inferior teaching which could be discarded by the superior *bodhisattvas*. The exact position of the Madhyamakas in Nāgārjuna's time in this connection is not positively known (on his position as inferred from his writings see above, pp. 376 ff.), but it appears that after his time they moved rapidly towards the extreme Mahāyānist position of an almost complete break with early Buddhism.

Two of Nāgārjuna's pupils first claim our attention. Āryadeva, who came originally from Ceylon, was his closest pupil and stands closest to him in doctrine. Unlike Nāgārjuna, however, he already places the *bodhisattva* in the foreground, presenting Buddhism as the way of the *bodhisattva*. Apart from this major difference in presentation (for Nāgārjuna has nothing about the *bodhisattva* and the aim of Buddhahood, but speaks of extinction and the eightfold way) his works may be regarded (as the School regarded them) as a supplement to Nāgārjuna's. The *Catuḥśataka* deals in its first half with the way of the *bodhisattva*, beginning with chapters on the 'four errors' (pp. 313 f. above), taken over from the early schools, and continuing with the more properly *bodhisattva* practice. Its second half on the other hand is a direct supplement to the *Mūlamadhyamakakārikā*,

1. But modified it to escape the critique, substituting the innocuous expression 'own-characteristic' which does not imply 'existent'.

which deals almost entirely with a selection of the same concepts for criticism (the 'permanent', the 'soul', 'time', speculative opinions, etc.), whilst avoiding the repetition of the same arguments. On the whole his critiques are aimed more at particular doctrines of schools and less at philosophical concepts in general. Besides the views of the earlier Buddhist schools, he criticises the fundamental notions of the two great Brahmanical philosophical schools of the day, the Sāṃkhya and the Vaiśeṣika, who held among other things the interesting 'extreme' opinions, the former that an effect is identical with its cause and the latter that it is different from it (criticised at *Catuḥśataka* 11.15). In another important work, the *Śataśāstra*, Āryadeva carries the attack on the various schools much further, naming his opponents and refuting their doctrines systematically and in detail: this is really a polemical work rather than primarily an exposition of the doctrine of his own school (the schools mostly attacked are the Sāṃkhya, Vaiśeṣika, Jainas, Lokāyata and — significantly for this period — the two theistic schools which now rise to prominence in India from obscure origins, the Vaiṣṇavas and Śaivas: cf. pp. 18 and 24 above). The methods employed are those of Nāgārjuna.

The other prominent pupil of Nāgārjuna has often been confounded with the master himself, having had a very similar name (either simply Nāga or some such compound as Nāgabodhi), easily assimilated to 'Nāgārjuna'. Tāranātha[1] carefully distinguishes him as 'Nāgāhvaya' ('called Nāga', which could be either the whole name or an abbreviation) or more properly 'Tathāgatabhadra' and as the author of commentaries on some of the Mahāyāna *sūtras*. It is in his works that we find for the first time the connection between Madhyamaka and the Mahāyāna *sūtras*, particularly the 'Perfection of Understanding', directly shown. It is presumably this 'Nāga' who was the original author of an enormous commentary on the 'Twenty Five Thousand' or 'Great Perfection of Understanding', which is known only in a Chinese version.[2] The version is not apparently very faithful, since it inserts

1. p. 86. For a Nāgabodhi, pupil of Nāgārjuna, see Bu-ston p. 132 and Tajima, *Étude sur le Mahāvairocana-sūtra*, Paris, 1936, p. 21.

2. '*Mahāprajñāpāramitāśāstra*' translated by Lamotte.

explanations about 'Indian' words,[1] etc., thought necessary for foreign readers. The latter part of it moreover is believed to be abridged. This commentary gives word by word explanations of its text in the tradition of the commentaries of the early schools and not differing very much from these in its merely linguistic explanations. Like Nāgārjuna (I), this Nāga (— arjuna II) quotes texts from the original *Tripiṭaka* and interprets them in the Madhyamaka sense in order to establish the correctness of the views of his school.[2] However, it is the 'Great Perfection of Understanding', which the Buddha is here supposed to have taught, which is at the 'ultimate' level of exposition, whilst the *Tripiṭaka* texts which appear to speak of principles existing are only at the 'concealing' level, according to the exigencies of teaching.[3] Besides other commentaries, the same Nāga is presumably also the author of an independent manual on Madhyamaka, the **Dvādaśadvāraśāstra* extant in Chinese.

Nāgārjuna (I) is credited with a number of poetical works, the 'hymns' (*stotras*) to the Buddha, and his *Ratnāvalī* and 'Letter to a Friend' are also literary rather than purely philosophical. In all periods, in fact, Buddhism has provided itself with artistic expression as well as philosophical treatises, and each new school used the poetic medium and the other arts. The composition of hymns to the Buddha was especially popular in the Mahāyāna movement, in consonance with the conception of a transcendent Buddha inherited from the Mahāsaṃgha schools, a conception which is duly reflected in Nāgārjuna's hymns. Most of the philosophers of the Madhyamaka and other Mahāyāna schools exercised themselves in the composition of hymns, but the most admired in this field is, as might be expected, a writer who was primarily a poet and is not credited with any purely philosophical works.

This poet was Mātṛceṭa. Tradition confirmed by the internal evidence of his writings has it that originally he was not a Buddhist but a worshipper of Śiva.[4] He himself says

1. e.g. Vol. I p. 76 of Lamotte's translation on words meaning 'time'.
2. e.g. Vol. I pp. 39ff. of Lamotte's translation.
3. Vol. I pp. 27ff., 4f. of Lamotte's translation.
4. See Dr. D.R.S. Bailey's Introduction to his edition of the *Śatapañcāśatka*, pp. 2ff.

that he had written non-Buddhist hymns, and one account (in Bu-ston) says without being very specific that he had then done great harm to the Doctrine and won many people over to the sectarian (presumably Śaiva) teaching. Unable to resist these encroachments of his seductive verses, the monks of Nālandā are said to have sent an appeal for help to Nāgārjuna, then resident in Āndhra. Āryadeva volunteered for the mission to the North, and by means of the Doctrine persuaded Mātṛceṭa to become a Buddhist. The poet then made amends for the 'harm' he had done by composing numerous hymns to the Buddha and some other literary works conveying Buddhist teaching. His date may be fixed by the fact that like Nāgārjuna he composed an epistle to a king, the 'Letter to the Great King Kani(ṣ)ka.' According to the chronology we have followed for Nāgārjuna this can be only Kaniṣka III, who succeeded to the Kuṣāṇa Empire in, or a few years after, A.D. 176. Mātṛceṭa himself says in his 'Letter' that he was then old, too old to go in person to visit the king (hence this epistle), who on the other hand was young. In this case it would seem that Mātṛceṭa had become a Buddhist *c.* 160 A.D. or even earlier (to allow time for his various Buddhist works).[1]

The favourite among Mātṛceṭa's hymns has been the 'Hundred and Fifty'[2] (strophes), in sections describing different qualities and actions of the Buddha, including special attention to his former lives as *bodhisattva* engaged in a career of unlimited self-sacrifice for the sake of other living beings. Despite this stress on the *bodhisattva*, however, there is hardly anything specifically Mahāyānist in these hymns, reference to the deeds of the Buddha as *bodhisattva* being perfectly acceptable to the earlier schools. On account of this broad and non-sectarian outlook Mātṛceṭa's poetry became popular among various schools of Buddhists. The hymns of Mātṛceṭa and other poets were chanted at the evening assemblies of the monks, when ceremonies were performed at pagodas and shrines.[3] Since we have reason to believe that monks of various schools lived together in the same *vihāras*, verses which

1. This incidentally would make our date for Nāgārjuna more precise, his floruit being *c.* A.D. 125-160.
2. *Śatapañcāśatka Stotra.*
3. Schlingloff : *Buddhistische Stotras*, p. 8.

would please all Buddhists and offend none would be specially appropriate for such use. The strophes of Mātṛceṭa are apparently of the greatest simplicity and unpretentiousness in construction, but this appearance is deceptive. The vocabulary is large and avoids clichés, the verses abound in poetic figures, though these are handled with a masterly restraint, or rather with the reticence of true humility and detachment. We are as far as possible here from the involvement of Aśvaghoṣa: we are circumambulating the symbol of extinction (a pagoda) in the stillness of the hour of sunset at some *vihāra* raised on a hill, above the endless turmoil of ordinary human life.

The typical Mātṛceṭa strophe opposes the nature of the *bodhisattva* to ordinary human nature: People are not as intent on helping others who return the help, as you are intent on helping even those intent on harm (119). The joy of living beings in regaining their lives after thinking they had lost them is nothing when compared with your joy in abandoning your life for another's sake (17). You have conquered revilers by tolerance, the malicious by securing their safety, the false by truth and the injurious by benevolence (122).

According to Tāranātha Śūra, or Āryaśūra, is the same person as Mātṛceṭa, though the works assigned respectively to these two have been kept quite distinct in the known manuscript and printed versions in Sanskrit, Chinese and Tibetan.[1] Dr. Bailey has shown that there is some tangible substance in the impression one has that the terse, elegant and often highly elliptical (no doubt idiomatic for its period) style, the simple grammatical structure of which is belied by the always unexpected turns of expression (extreme compactness and large and idiomatic vocabulary), is very similar in the verses of the two poets (it carries over into the prose of Śūra, which is as compact and unobvious as his verse). Tāranātha's assertion may be merely a guess, and we have no other evidence for it at present, but at least we can say that Śūra appears to have belonged to the same period as Mātṛceṭa.

Śūra's best known work is the *Jātakamālā*, a selection of 34 favourite *jātaka* stories retold in this carefully wrought and fastidious style, illustrating particular points of moral teaching

1. Bailey, *Śatapañcāśatka* 10ff., discusses this.

(primarily the self-sacrificing virtues of the *bodhisattva*) mentioned to introduce each one. Śūra's narratives here proceed in a mixture of prose and verse (a form afterwards known as *campū*), many different metres being used. His excellent style won him a place among the foremost Sanskrit poets, even in the opinion of Brahmanical critics (Rājaśekhara[1]), and caused many Buddhists to substitute his volume for the more original *jātaka* collections.[2]

The minor works of Mātṛceṭa and Śūra include a number of short texts called *parikathās* (or just *kathās*), which might be described as 'sermons' or 'tracts', on such subjects as the evils of the present age, the deceptiveness of life in the world, and alternatively the good way (*supatha*). The genre was popular for a time and a score or more of examples have been preserved in Tibetan translations, ascribed to a number of otherwise famous authors such as Nāgārjuna and Aśvaghoṣa (and Vasubandhu among later writers), as well as the little known Gopadatta and Rāmendra. A few have survived in Sanskrit but so far none seem to have been published.

New Trends in Mahāyāna

At the beginning of the third century A.D. (a little earlier in the case of the Kuṣāṇas) both the great empires in India in this period went into rapid decline. At first this appears to have been a purely internal process at work in both empires. We find that, by contrast with the Magadhan administration of the preceding period, both the Sātavāhanas and the Kuṣāṇas had introduced some elements of what may in a broad sense be called 'feudalism'. Whereas the Magadhan provincial governors were appointed for limited terms, rotated from province to province and paid salaries like other officials (though they might be princes), thus maintaining a strong centralised control at Pāṭaliputra, methods which could only result in decentralisation replaced these in the newer empires. The Kuṣāṇas maintained a Śaka family as governors of Avanti (and Aparānta) at Ujjayinī, allowing them to govern there for life and hand down their province by hereditary succession. It is likely that this arrangement had arisen as part of a condi-

1. *Kāvyamīmāṃsā* (GOS) p. 55 ('Sūra')
2. On Mātṛceṭa and Śūra see IKL Vol. II pp. 235-58.

tional submission of the Śakas in India to the newer power. In the second century, however, we find the Śaka governors behaving practically as independent rulers, issuing their own coinage and celebrating their victories without reference to their presumed overlords on whose behalf they were supposed to be fighting. The Sātavāhana emperors appear to have had similar arrangements with what we may call 'vassal' kings ruling over parts of the empire. They went further in the direction of feudalism in making grants of land to favoured persons or institutions (including Buddhist communities), giving up the administrative rights of the central government along with at least part of the revenue. The trend thus initiated developed gradually all over India to a system whereby hereditary local rulers administered their 'fiefs' and collected the revenue, sending a part of it to the central overlord but keeping a very substantial income for themselves in lieu of a salary. In return for their enjoyment of practical independence and perhaps of most of the revenue of their lands, these 'vassals' were required to render military service to the overlord.

The reasons for this decisive change in administration are obscure. They must have been very strong to compensate for the obvious and seemingly disastrous disadvantages of so great a degree of decentralisation. A resolute and shrewd vassal might at any time defy a less resolute or insufficiently watchful overlord, or, more cautious, he might reduce his remittance of revenue to the centre or on some pretext fail to render his military service. It would seem natural enough that most vassals would attempt to 'get away with' as little as possible in the way of contributions of either kind. In order to enforce his claims the overlord often had to rely largely on the military services of other vassals despatched against a defaulter, so that the way was open for intrigues and combinations. The heir to an empire of this kind who proved unskilful in handling his vassals would soon lose control over some or all of them.

The Kuṣāṇas thus lost control of much of their empire to their Śaka vassals and to a number of Indian rulers of the Eastern and central parts of Northern India, including a number of ancient republics which had preserved their institutions intact under periods of Magadhan and Kuṣāṇa overlordship. Thus weakened, the Kuṣāṇas were defeated by Sāsānian invaders from the West, to whom they had to surrender their Central Asian domains and the Western parts of their empire, including eventually Gandhāra. Finally they had to accept vassalage under the Persian conquerors. Meanwhile the Sātavāhanas were overthrown and their domains divided between a number of local rulers, notably the Ikṣvākus in Āndhra proper, who there continued the patronage of Buddhism, and, later, the Brahmanical Vākāṭakas in Mahārāṣṭra, who were more successful in rebuilding a large empire.

These changes in the structure of society, not merely in the personnel ruling, were reflected in or even anticipated by the Brahmanical literature of the period, particularly the law books which make provision for grants of land to the revenue collectors.[1] When we find great changes in the philosophical and religious outlook of the times, as we do within the Buddhist tradition, it is natural to think that these may be related to changes in the social outlook. The democratic ideals of early Buddhism (the organisation of its communities, the insistence by the Buddha that he had only discovered and taught a doctrine but accepted no personal responsibility for the community (pp. 73 f. above), so that the monks must rely on themselves 'as islands' and also on the doctrine, not on any person) might survive the rule of 'principle' of Aśoka (who set 'principle' in place of his personal rule much as the Buddha set the doctrine in place of his — and 'principle' and 'doctrine' here both translate *dharma*). They were ill adapted to a society in which individuals looked for protection to strong lords and more and more entered into feudalistic, hierarchical relations with them, comparable sometimes with the practice known in Europe as 'commendation'. In some of the Mahāyāna *sūtra*s, on the other hand, we find the Buddha becoming the supreme overlord of the universe, just as in the same period the theistic religions were with great success exalting Śiva or Viṣṇu as creator and ruler of the universe. Henceforth there was a decline in the influence of the older atheistic Brahmanism of the Mīmāṃsā, the Sāṃkhya and the early Vaiśeṣika, corresponding to the growing

1. On all this see Sharma : *Aspects of Political Ideas and Institutions in Ancient India*, Chapter XIV.

influence of theistic Vedānta, Yoga and Nyāya, which tended to become assimilated to Vaiṣṇavism or Śaivism. In Mahāyāna Buddhism the central ideal of the compassionate *bodhisattvas*, beginning with Avalokiteśvara (p. 361 above), the 'Observing Lord (*īśvara*)' or 'Watching Lord' (where the prefix *ava* adds a suggestion that this lord is looking downwards, with compassion, on unhappy humanity), may not be entirely unrelated to a social ideal of a protecting lord who gives security to helpless individuals in times of difficulty. In either case the chief advantage of the new system would appear to be the ease with which help and protection can be obtained by the humble suppliant. One can be reborn in Sukhāvatī without having very strenuously cultivated the roots of good, even without having cultivated them at all, if one thinks of the Buddha Amitābha with yearning for his world. Passive submission was probably the only indispensable qualification for entering the service of a feudal lord.

The appearance of new Mahāyāna *sūtras* continued and even increased in frequency. The 'Eight Thousand Perfection of Understanding' was followed by several other very long *sūtras*, whilst the production of short *sūtras*, some now in the *Ratnakūṭa* collection, perhaps more outside it, seems endless. Apart from new recensions of the Perfection of Understanding, the large *sūtras* which followed the Eight Thousand are the *Samādhirāja* ('King of Concentration'), *Saddharmapuṇḍarīka* ('White Lotus of the True Doctrine'), *Vimalakīrtinirdeśa* ('Exposition of Vimalakīrti') and *Suvarṇabhāsa* ('Golden Lustre'). The King of Concentration (also called *Candrapradīpa*, 'Lamp of the Moon', or of Prince Candra) is usually reckoned to stand closest to the Perfection of Understanding in doctrine, but expresses this primarily as the knowledge of the 'sameness' or 'equality' (*samatā*) of own-nature of all principles, the realisation of which is the object of the practice of concentration. This 'sameness' is nothing but the emptiness of principles of any own-nature. The *Sūtra* contains long discourses on the conduct of *bodhisattvas* and a mass of narratives bearing on this topic.

The White Lotus contains very little doctrine, its bulk being filled almost entirely with descriptions of *buddhas* and *bodhisattvas* and their worlds, with all kinds of wonders produced by them:

not trivial miracles but universal transformations, illuminations, appearances of *buddhas* from the remote past in all their glory, and so on. There is perhaps a sense in which one can say that this is a truly 'religious' as opposed to a doctrinal or (especially) philosophical text. The doctrine is practically taken for granted (though hidden in the middle of these several hundred pages there is one short paragraph of significance), though constantly alluded to. The function of the text is simply to give it a tremendous 'build-up,' to inspire reverence for it, to dramatise it. The Buddha presides over this universal drama: at the outset he tells his assembled followers that he has not yet taught the real doctrine because it is so difficult to understand it might cause confusion and even harm. He has taught only at the concealing level. Urged to reveal the ultimate truth he still hesitates on the ground of the danger to some of the assembled monks and nuns. Taking the hint, several thousand of these who were satisfied with the concealing teaching withdraw, so that the Buddha can now expound the ultimate doctrine to the 'fearless' ones who have remained.

First he develops at great length the point that he teaches by way of expedients (*upāya*, 'means'), according to the different needs and aptitudes of his hearers. Thus there appears to be more than one 'vehicle' (*yāna*), though in fact there is only one plus the expedients. Living beings are introduced to the teaching by different means, but all of them attain enlightenment eventually. The use of expedients is illustrated by a number of parables. Occasionally the emptiness and sameness of principles is mentioned in passing, but the real doctrine laid down by this *Sūtra* is reserved for its fifteenth chapter. There the Buddha says: It should not be thought (literally 'seen') that the thus-gone Śākyamuni (i.e. himself) attained enlightenment at Gayā. On the contrary, I attained enlightenment millions of ages ago... The thus-gone has seen that the universe in its true nature (*yathābhūtam*) (or perhaps: that in the universe in its true nature one is not...) is not born, does not die, does not pass away, is not reborn, does not transmigrate, does not attain extinction, etc... The thus-gone demonstrates extinction without actually becoming extinct, for educational purposes...I have still twice as long to live as the millions of ages I have already lived, my career as a *bodhisattva* is not yet fulfilled. ...

This text can be understood in the light of the emptiness doctrine, that ultimately transmigration does not take place, nor extinction, whether of a *bodhisattva* or *buddha* or of any living being; there is no distinction between transmigration and extinction. Popularly, however, the White Lotus has satisfied the desire of millions for an eternal and omnipotent Buddha watching over the world. What the philosophers interpret according to the Madhyamaka dialectic the masses are content to make the basis of an unphilosophical religion of the worship of a transcendent being who is yet in the world to save them and take them to heaven. Moreover the Buddha is assisted by the great *bodhisattvas* such as Avalokiteśvara, to whom much of this *Sūtra* is devoted. You have only to remember the name of Avalokiteśvara in any trouble, for example the perils of the sea, and you will be freed from it (chapter 24, generally thought to be a later addition to the *Sūtra*, however).

The Exposition of Vimalakīrti is a popularisation of Mahāyāna (or Madhyamaka) doctrine of a more sophisticated and also humorous kind. The idea for it was probably drawn from the dialogues in the Perfection of Understanding between Subhūti and the Buddha, Subhūti and Śāriputra and others. These seem to have become a sort of intellectual exercise, in which one interlocutor asks questions and another answers, bearing in mind the doctrine of emptiness and so avoiding the affirmation of anything which cannot ultimately be affirmed. Such a conversation may start at the concealing level, but if the correct answers are given it must immediately switch to the ultimate. The hero of the present *Sūtra*, the *bodhisattva* Vimalakīrti, is particularly skilful at this empty conversation (perhaps more originally called 'pure' conversation[1]). He is a Licchavi householder in Vaiśālī in the time of the Buddha, living very much in the world, even to the extent of visiting the geisha girls, taverns and casinos and indulging in all the pleasures of life. However, he is in reality a model *bodhisattva*,

1. Lamotte : *L'Enseignement de Vimalakīrti*, p. 219.

even a *śramaṇa* (ascetic-philosopher), and mixes with worldly people in order to show them the disadvantages of pursuing pleasure. He is universally respected and his conversation is in conformity with the doctrine as well as skilful, so that his activities in the world serve to ripen people's understanding and draw them away from attachment to pleasures.

One day Vimalakīrti gives out that he is ill, though this is only another expedient. According to Indian custom many people go to visit him and enquire whether he is feeling better, to which enquiry he replies with discourses on the impermanence, unhappiness, etc., of the elements of which the body is composed and the diseases to which it is subject. Naturally when the Buddha, who happens to be staying in Vaiśālī at Āmrapāli's park with a large community of monks, knows of Vimalakīrti's illness he wishes to send a monk to visit the sick man (in the section of Chapter Six on the lay disciple we have read of several such visits). In turn he asks Śāriputra, Maudgalyāyana, Subhūti, Ānanda and many others to go. All refuse, on the ground that they are incapable of holding conversation with Vimalakīrti, having been humiliated by him on some previous occasion, when they were each reduced to silence. For example the *bodhisattva* Maitreya had been told by the Buddha that he will be the next *buddha*, after one more birth. Vimalakīrti found him discussing the stage he had reached with the Tuṣita gods and took him up on this question of 'birth': it is only by non-birth that one can reach this stage, Maitreya's thusness is only the thusness of all principles, there is no duality between him and all other living beings, so that when he becomes enlightened all beings will become enlightened; anyway all beings are extinct already, this is their thusness, so Maitreya ought not to deceive the gods with this talk about his going to attain enlightenment. Maitreya could think of nothing to say to this on that occasion and declares himself now incapable of asking Vimalakīrti about his illness.

At last the *bodhisattva* Mañjuśrī agrees to go, though the task is difficult. Many monks, *bodhisattvas* and gods go with him to hear what promises to be a remarkable conversation. They find the house appropriately empty and Vimalakīrti tells Mañjuśrī he is well-come, especially as he has not come (Nāgārjuna on the absurdity of 'motion', pp. 384 f. above).

As to his illness, it will last as long as living beings are ignorant and desire existence. Starting thus, the conversation and the episodes which follow express in narrative and dramatic form the main teachings of the Madhyamaka. Śāriputra plays the part of the clown who asks foolish questions (i.e. at the concealing level), complaining that there are no seats for the visitors, not enough food for them, etc. The house-goddess of Vimalakīrti's house makes game of him with displays of magic. Seeing that she has made such progress on the way Śāriputra is foolish enough to ask her why she does not change her female sex (traditionally regarded as a disadvantage, at least by monks), evidently having the power to do so. The goddess replies that so far she has not been able to discover what this 'female sex' is: like all principles it is only an artifice or illusion (*māyā*), it is not real (is nothing in itself), so there isn't anything to change. However she punishes Śāriputra for his suggestion, making a woman of him by her magic: he finds he has the body of the goddess whilst she appears like the elder Śāriputra and asks him why he does not change his 'female sex'. She restores him after a sufficient lecture, adding that ultimately no changes take place.

After this Vimalakīrti explains to Mañjuśrī how a *bodhisattva* lives in the world without being attached to it, conforming to passion and aversion, though being free from these, and to delusion though he has understanding. He asks Mañjuśrī to tell him what the 'clan of the thus-gone' is — a new concept which we shall find more fully elaborated elsewhere. This 'clan', says Mañjuśrī, is that of ignorance, desire for existence, passion, aversion, delusion, error, the obstacles, etc., in other words of all bad principles which lead to transmigration. Asked what this signifies he explains that the thought of enlightenment can occur only in transmigration (among synthesised principles), as lotuses grow only in the mud.

The Golden Lustre appears to be the latest of this series of *sūtras*. Doctrinally it is basically similar to the Perfection of Understanding (on emptiness) and the White Lotus (the Buddha is eternal), except for a few passages interpolated in some later recensions of its text and containing ideas of a later period of Buddhism. The most notable feature of the Golden Lustre is the appearance of a number of gods and goddesses of the Brahmanical tradition in conversation with the Buddha. Naturally they are all good Buddhists anxious to spread and uphold the doctrine. To the Four Kings (p. 153 above) the Buddha expounds especially the duties of kings on earth, which include the spreading of this particular *Sūtra* in their realms. Most striking is the appearance in separate chapters of the *Sūtra* of three celebrated goddesses successively attending on the Buddha: Sarasvatī (the goddess of learning and literature), Śrī (Fortune) and Dṛḍhā (Earth). It is Sarasvatī's function to aid all those who study this *Sūtra*, improving their intuition and memory. Having said this, however, she goes on to prescribe a curious ritual bath in an infusion of 32 healing herbs, with recitation of magic formulae, for the partisans of this *Sūtra* in case they meet with any trouble on account of unfavourable stars. These ideas — ritual, magic formulae, astrology — seem to be quite new graftings onto the tradition of Buddhism and astrology was perhaps new to India at this time. In the multinational Kuṣāṇa Empire it might be suggested that the leading ideology was gathering to itself various popular practices of diverse origin.[1] Fortune promises to bring those who spread this *Sūtra* practical aid in the form of food, clothing, gold, silver and various precious stones. Earth will honour the *Sūtra* wherever it is found, in cities and villages, forests, mountains, etc. Delighted by hearing the doctrine she will increase the juices of the earth and the whole earth up to the four oceans will become more fruitful and beautiful, so that living beings will have plenty of good food and drink and hence long life, strength, intelligence, lustre and lack nothing in understanding. All activities will flourish. Because of their happiness people everywhere will love and honour this *Sūtra*.

It is among the shorter *sūtras* which appeared in this period that the new speculations are pressed furthest and implications drawn which lead to new schools of thought within the Madhyamaka and sometimes foreshadow a new trend which will break with the Madhyamaka outlook. The *Śrīmālā Sūtra*[2]

1. Nobel has pointed out in his translation of this *Sūtra* (pp. 230 and 248ff.) significant resemblances to ideas in the *Harivaṃśa*, a supplement to the epic *Mahābhārata* composed in about this period.

2. The work is extensively quoted in the *Ratnagotravibhāga*, extant in the original Sanskrit; here we use these quotations.

(included in the *Ratnakūṭa* collection) elaborates a theory of the 'embryo' (*garbha*) of the thus-gone, the essence or potentiality of the Buddha-nature. The *Sūtra* explains[1] that the teaching about the cessation of unhappiness does not imply the destruction of principles but refers to the 'substance of the doctrine' (*dharmakāya*) of the thus-gone (i.e. the Buddha as the embodiment of the doctrine, or the eternal doctrine as the real nature of the Buddha, or of *buddhas*), which is beginningless in time, not made, not produced (or born), has not occurred, is not 'exhausted', is permanent, fixed, safe (*śiva*), eternal, naturally pure, free from all defilements, etc. This 'substance of the doctrine' means the 'embryo' of the thus-gone. Thus the Truth of cessation is to be understood. Evidently we have in this *Sūtra* a working out of the idea of the eternal existence of the Buddha : it is the doctrine which is this eternal aspect, and the potentiality of enlightenment, of being a Buddha. The 'pupils' ' (*śrāvaka*) interpretation of the Truth of cessation, on the other hand, that cessation is like the extinction of a lamp, should not be followed, for theirs is a way involved in the characteristics of what is synthesised (*saṃskṛta*), therefore false, untrue (*asatya*), impermanent and no refuge (*aśaraṇa*).[2]

The *Śrīmālā Sūtra* further explains its position as follows:[3] The idea that the forces (*saṃskāra*) are impermanent may lead to the annihilationist opinion. That extinction (*nirvāṇa*) is permanent may lead to the eternalist opinion. Therefore it is said that ultimately (*paramārthatas*, i.e., the ultimate truth is that) transmigration itself (*eva*, 'only') is extinction (this can also be translated 'extinction is only transmigration', 'extinction is identical with transmigration'), by applying the scheme (*nayamukha*, the application of a scheme — a technical term used in commentaries of the setting out of new matter by applying a previously given scheme of analysis to it) of the 'element of principles' (*dharmadhātu*). We have met this expression, 'element of principles', in the *Tripiṭaka* (p. 135 above), where the meaning is 'the (ultimate) reality of principles', their real nature, which according to the

1. *Ratnagotravibhāga* p. 12.
2. Quoted *Ratnagotravibhāga* p. 19.
3. Ibid. p. 34.

Sthaviravāda commentary is their conditioned nature. With Mahāyāna writers, who often use the expression, the emphasis is on the idea that there is an ultimate reality in (or underlying) principles, an ultimate reality of the universe. Here it seems clear that the point is that the ultimate reality of principles is extinction, that ultimately they are extinct even whilst they appear to be transmigration.

The *Śrīmālā* directly confronts the earlier idea of the four 'errors' (see pp. 313 above, where they are noted from a Sthaviravāda text, the *Paṭisambhidāmagga*, though they seem to have been common ground to all the schools) : the opinions that there is permanence in the impermanent, happiness in unhappiness, a soul in non-soul or beauty in the ugly. Following, perhaps, a hint in the *Ratnakūṭa* (p. 363 above) the *Sūtra*[1] speaks of the perfections (*pāramitā*) of permanence, of happiness, of soul and of beauty. These should not be sought where they are not to be found, on the other hand they should be sought where they really are, which is in the 'substance of the doctrine' (*dharmakāya*) of the thus-gone.

As we saw above, this substance of the doctrine is the 'embryo' of the thus-gone. It is a kind of 'absolute', the ultimate unchanging reality. The *Śrīmālā* says[2] that the 'embryo' is not born, does not grow old or die, pass away or get reborn. It passes by (*vyativṛtta*, transcends) the domain of the characteristics of the synthesised and is permanent, fixed, safe and eternal. Further[3] it is the embryo of the transcendental (*lokottara*) and of the purity of nature (i.e. principles are ultimately pure by nature). It is the resting place (*pratiṣṭhā*) of the unsynthesised principles. Finally[4] it is empty, without defilements, and the knowledge (*jñāna*) of it is the knowledge of emptiness.

Another of these *sūtras* quoted in the *Ratnagotravibhāga*, the *Anūnatvāpūrṇatvanirdeśa*, adds[5] a few points to this doctrine: the substance of the doctrine is safe and has the nature of being without duality (*advaya*) and without imagining (*avikalpa*)

---

1. Quoted *Ratnagotravibhāga* pp. 30f.
2. Ibid. p. 46.
3. Ibid. p. 73.
4. Ibid. p. 76.
5. Ibid. pp. 12 and 40f.

(here 'duality' is explained as action and defilement, imagining as unmethodical attention which is the cause of the origination of action and defilement). The 'element of beings' (*sattvadhātu*, the real nature of beings), which is beginningless transmigration, is identical with the substance of the doctrine — which is hidden by defilements.

Another of these *sūtras*, the *Dhāraṇirāja*, develops the idea of the 'clan' (*gotra*), which we have met in the *Ratnakūṭa* and in the Exposition of Vimalakīrti (pp. 364 and 399 above). This is clarified by the simile of a jewel mine (*maṇigotra*, 'clan of jewels') : as the jewels from it are purified, polished, etc., so the beings in the 'element of beings' are purified, etc., by the doctrine and discipline. The thus-gone purifies beings as the jeweller polishes jewels, making them understand the methodology (*netri*) of the thus-gone by empty, signless and uncommitted discourse and by discourse of the triple purity (that ultimately there is no agent, patient or action).[1] Following the Perfection of Understanding (p. 366 above) this *Sūtra* notes[2] that thought is by nature translucent, and goes on 'so is knowledge (*jñāna*); therefore it is said that perfect enlightenment is enlightened by understanding in a single moment (*ekakṣaṇa*).'

The Ratnagotravibhāga and the Abhisamayālaṅkāra

The *Ratnagotravibhāga* from which we have quoted above, which has the subtitle *Mahāyāna Uttaratantra Śāstra*, was apparently written by one Sthiramati[3] (not to be confused with later writers of that name), sometimes called Sāramati, with a view to systematising the ideas of this new trend in Mahāyāna. His outlook is regarded as Madhyamaka, though it is very different from Nāgārjuna's. From the strict Madhyamaka standpoint of the latter it might be said that the *Ratnagotravibhāga* sets up a metaphysical absolute, which is eternal and has various other characteristics, vulnerable as such to

1. Quoted *Ratnagotravibhāga* pp. 5f.
2. Ibid. p. 22.
3. Johnston, Foreword to his edition, p. xi, Chinese tradition; the (later) Tibetan tradition ascribes the basic text to 'Maitreya' and the commentary (*vyākhyāna*) to Asaṅga : this is unlikely, nevertheless the work may still be composite. The main doctrinal points seem to be covered by the basic text. cf. below p. 407 and n. 1.

the various critiques set out in the *Mūlamadhyamakakārikā*. Of course, Sthiramati found scriptural warrant in the *sūtras* we have just reviewed. Those who accepted his doctrine as well as Nāgārjuna's adopted what might be called a form of mysticism : the ultimate truths about the nature of the universe and of the Buddha could not be known by the ordinary intellect and empirical enquiry, but the insight gained at the end of the *bodhisattva's* progress to buddhahood, at the moment when he attained omniscience, contained an intuitive knowledge of these truths, of the reality underlying the transient principles of the world of transmigration. These truths had been intuited by the Buddha and were now handed down in the *sūtras*, from which source we could know them, disregarding the critiques of Nāgārjuna which applied to all other philosophical positions but not to this absolute and ultimate truth. The critical philosophy of Nāgārjuna now becomes simply a part of the theory of Mahāyāna Buddhism, required as a theoretical preparation for progress on the way (of the *bodhisattva*) but not indicating the way itself. For the latter, the practical aspect of the training, the revelations of the Mahāyāna *sūtras* are to be the guide.

As Sthiramati understands these *sūtras*, they teach that the ultimate reality has several aspects and is described and named from several standpoints, though in each case it is the same reality which is referred to. It is not a duality (*advaya*), thus there is in reality no action (*karman*) and no defilement (*kleśa*). From one standpoint it is the substance of the doctrine (*dharmakāya*). This same reality is the embryo of the thus-gone (*tathāgatagarbha*), which has the nature of thought (*cittaprakṛti*), pure (*pariśuddha*, or 'purity') and translucent (*prabhāsvara*). The *bodhisattvas* see buddhahood through this translucent thought-nature, seeing (at the same time) the no-nature (unreality) of defilements (*Ratnagotravibhāga* I.13). The thought-nature (*cittaprakṛti*) is hidden by the traces (*vāsanā*) of the defilements, which are 'accidental' (*āgantuka*) to it (do not really belong to it, even though they prevent all beings from being *buddhas* all the time). Again, the substance of the doctrine is the same as the 'element of beings' (*sattvadhātu*, I.47, etc., i.e. the real nature of beings), which is nothing but this thought-nature of the embryo of the thus-gone, hidden by the traces of defilements. This element of beings is the 'clan' (*gotra*, I.24, 28, etc., which might also be translated in this context as 'mine' or 'quarry') which contains (all) the beings who have to be purified. The same ultimate reality is called the element of principles (*dharmadhātu*) when considered in its own proper nature. Sthiramati often calls it just 'element' (*dhātu*), having all these aspects in view and regarding this 'element' as the reality which is to be understood in enlightenment (*bodhi* or *anuttarā. samyaksaṃbodhi*). Or he says that the element is itself enlightenment, and calls it further the element of extinction (*nirvāṇa-dhātu*). There are still other terms for the ultimate reality (*paramārtha*): the 'domain of the thus-gone' (*tathāgataviṣaya*), the 'range (*gocara*) of the thus-gone', 'thusness' (*tathatā*). Further, extinction is spoken of and the fact that it is equal to (*samatā*) transmigration (I.38). The list of aspects of the ultimate reality might be extended almost indefinitely.

The thus-gone's knowledge (*jñāna*) has entered into all beings, but they do not understand it. It is their 'unmethodical attention' (*ayoniśas manasikāra*) which is the cause of the origination of action and defilement. The ultimate reality itself is 'without imagining' (*avikalpa*). The defilements, therefore, are 'unreal imagined' things (*abhūtaparikalpita*, *Ratnagotravibhāga* pp. 49-50 — *pari-kḷp* and its derivatives seem practically synonymous with *vi-kḷp* and its, the former indicating rather the completed product of imagination and the latter the constructive act of imagining). On account of the purity of nature of the element of the thus-gone there is nothing to be removed, nothing to be obtained, simply reality must be seen (I.154, p. 76). Here by way of explanation Sthiramati quotes the *Śrīmālā* as saying that the embryo of the thus-gone is empty (it may be noted that otherwise he appears to ignore the doctrine of emptiness, so prominent in the earlier Madhyamaka). There are no defilements to be removed because the defilements are pure imagination. There is no buddhahood to be obtained because this is nothing but the real nature of (or underlying the appearance of) beings themselves. The embryo of it is within them, though hidden, hence they have only to look into their own thoughts (IV.24-6). The Buddha sees that beings are equal to himself (*sattvātmasama*,

IV.12), and this (original moral standard of Buddhism, as we have seen in earlier chapters) is here said to be his reason for teaching as long as existence (*bhava*, i.e. transmigration) continues. But here this old idea of the similarity of all beings has been transformed into absolute identity, and the argument runs from the Buddha seeing himself in all beings to their need to see the Buddha in themselves.

With this doctrine we have crossed the threshold of idealism: the ultimate reality has the nature of thought and everything else is the product of imagination. The two main aspects of reality are its own perfectly pure nature, the 'thusness free from dirt' (*nirmalā tathatā*) of Sthiramati's second chapter, which is the 'element without the influences' (*anāsravadhātu*), buddhahood which is permanent, eternal, is omniscience, and its defiled nature, the 'thusness with dirt' (*samalā tathatā*) of his first chapter, which is the embryo hidden in the world of beings. In reality the element of the thus-gone, the unsynthesised element (p. 54), remains always undefiled by nature, permanent, fixed, safe and eternal, and this is the real or proper substance (*svābhāvika* substance) of the Buddha (I.151, p. 72). It has the perfections of beauty, soul (self), happiness and permanence mentioned in the *Śrīmālā Sūtra* — despite which Sthiramati describes buddhahood as 'the point (limit) of non-soul' (*nairātmyakoṭi* I.13). Perhaps he means here that at this point the non-soul of beings in transmigration, the imaginary beings, vanishes in the eternal reality, or soul, of the thus-gone. Sthiramati notes the theory of the three 'substances' of the Buddha (p. 72) : besides the real substance, considered in its own nature, there are the 'enjoyment' (*sāmbhoga*) substance, which is the Buddha's aspect as 'king of the doctrine', and the 'creation' (*nirmāṇa*) substance, the mere reflection of the real Buddha (which appears in the world).

The 'element' (the ultimate reality) is to be understood through enlightenment. It is beyond deduction (*tarka*, logical deduction), inconceivable (*acintya*, 'unthinkable'), without duality, pure, is not existing (*sant*), nor non-existing, nor both existing and non-existing, nor neither. Such, equally, is the nature of the doctrine, which is said in a *sūtra* quoted by Sthiramati (the *Dṛḍhādhyāśaya Parivarta*) to be incapable of being either uttered or heard. Such is the mysticism of this trend in Buddhism: the doctrine, ultimate reality, cannot be known intellectually but only by intuition.

Sthiramati says that the way to this knowledge, to obtaining the substance of the doctrine, is set out in detail in the 'Perfection of Understanding' (p. 13). This would imply that that *Sūtra*, or rather *Sūtras*, should contain an account of the practical way to enlightenment (buddhahood). On the surface the *Sūtras* appear to be dialogues and discussions about the ultimate truth, but from this time a branch of the Madhyamaka school makes a special study of the 'Perfection of Understanding' on the assumption that they give a systematic account of the way of the *bodhisattva*. This study, or subject, is generally known as Pāramitā ('Perfection'), and it is concerned with 'perfection', with ethics, rather than with understanding or theory (for which it generally follows the old Madhyamaka, with the necessary concessions required by Sthiramati's doctrine and even with a certain eclecticism assimilating ideas from other schools of Buddhism).

At approximately the same period as the *Ratnagotravibhāga* (about the middle of the 3rd century A.D.[1]) a text was composed which purports to be a summary of the 'Perfection of Understanding' from the standpoint that it is an account of the way of the *bodhisattva*. This is the *Abhisamayālaṅkāra*, attributed to 'Maitreya'. By 'Maitreya' is understood (see especially the greatest commentator on this text, Haribhadra[2]) the *bodhisattva* Maitreya, who is to be the next *buddha* in this world. Since the teachers of Buddhism, Asaṅga (c. 290-350 A.D.) and others, were unable to explain the *Sūtras* from this point of view (as an account of the way), Maitreya, residing

1. According to the Tibetan tradition the *Ratnagotravibhāga* is a work of 'Maitreya' and Asaṅga — see below — though admittedly it does not represent the usual viewpoint of Asaṅga's school. Chinese tradition ascribes it to Sthiramati. Doctrinally it is intermediate between the old Madhyamaka and Asaṅga, and this probably corresponds to its historical position. Even if part of the text is later commentary this hardly affects the doctrinal chronology. It has much in common with the *Abhisamayālaṅkāra* in terminology and even in complete phrases, and seems identical in doctrine with that text. Both were studied by Asaṅga's school as well as by the Madhyamakas. cf. now Ruegg, *La Théorie du Tathāgatagarbha*.

2. Tucci's edition, p. 73.

among the Tuṣita gods prior to his final life as a *buddha*, composed the *Abhisamayālaṅkāra*, a brief synopsis in verses (*kārikās*) indicating how the way is described in detail in the 'Perfection of Understanding', and revealed it to Asaṅga. In fact we are presumably in possession of the composition of some earlier teacher (of the Madhyamaka school, not sharing Asaṅga's special views) whose name has been forgotten, perhaps of Sthiramati himself or a contemporary.

The *Abhisamayālaṅkāra* and the *Ratnagotravibhāga* appear to be identical in doctrine, though not in style (the latter being a thoroughly poetic work, expanding its theme in numerous verses in elaborate metres, partly covered by prose elaborations, the former a piece of doggerel, highly condensed — all the more remarkable, therefore, their occasional coincidences of expression). The former work, the 'Ornament of Insight', carries out for us the exposition of the 'Perfection of Understanding' as an account of the way, as required by Sthiramati. Such an exposition is in fact highly artificial. The *Abhisamayālaṅkāra* proceeds to set out the way, following the actual order of the *Sūtras*, as if these were arranged in such a systematic fashion. In spite of all its ingenuity, and its very arbitrary manner of stretching out the supposed implications of the words of the *Sūtras* (thus a series of thirteen distinct topics has to be drawn out of two lines of the Eight Thousand *Sūtra* according to Haribhadra pp. 516f, i.e. out of p. 478, lines 9-10, of the *Sūtra*, which hardly suggests any of them), it had to be admitted by the Pāramitā school that it was impossible to make the way follow exactly the order of the 'Perfection of Understanding.'

According to 'Maitreya' the Perfection of Understanding is expounded through eight subjects of study (called *padārthas*, literally 'meanings of words' but used generally to refer to categories of meaning, classes of objects to which words refer, and often translated 'categories'), namely (1) knowledge of all features (*sarvākārajñatā*), which refers to the special knowledge of a *buddha* (the 'features' are taken in the Tibetan tradition[1] as meaning all the peculiarities of both the universe of transmigration and the ultimate reality); (2) knowledge of the way (*mārgajñatā*); (3) omniscience (*sarvajñatā*), i.e. in the

1. Obermiller, *The Doctrine of Prajñā-pāramitā*, p. 62.

conventional sense of knowledge of all the grounds in the universe of transmigration (also called knowledge of grounds, *vastujñāna*); (4) insight into all features (*sarvākārābhisambodha*), meaning all the features under subjects 1-3; (5) the insight on attaining the highest stage (*mūrdhāprāpta abhisamaya*), i.e. after mastering subject 4; (6) systematic insight (*ānupūrvika abhisamaya*), which is reviewing the whole scope of subject 4 systematically; (7) the single moment (p. 403) of (final) insight (*ekakṣaṇābhisambodha*); (8) the substance of the doctrine (*dharmakāya*). The apparent artificiality of this scheme evidently results from the attempt to follow the order of the *Sūtras* as a systematic exposition of doctrine.

These eight subjects are further subdivided into altogether 70 topics (*arthas*, 'terms'), again following the *Sūtras* yet attempting to cover all the stages and all the principles of the way. The first topic is, reasonably enough, the 'occurrence of the thought' (of enlightenment). Also under the first subject (as topic 4) comes the 'clan' (*gotra*), or mine of beings who have to be purified, here explained as having as its own (ultimate) nature the 'element of principles' (*dharmadhātu*), i.e. the ultimate reality. The clan is the resting place (basis) of the principles required for progress and of the abandoning of those which are undesirable, also (in more detail) of understanding, compassion, acting for the welfare of others, knowledge which operates effortlessly, etc., i.e. the positive principles required. As the 'element of principles' is without distinctions(difference) there is really no distinction in the clan (e.g. of 'pupils' distinguished from *bodhisattvas*), yet such distinctions can be described though the different principles founded on them (it is of course important for the Mahāyāna to discriminate the actions of the way of the *bodhisattva* from those of that of the 'pupil', even if ultimately both lead to the same goal).

The kinds of 'practice' (*pratipatti*) on the way are discussed at length under the same subject, as topics 7-10. Here we find an elaborate account of the moral training to be undergone in the course of progress though the ten successive stages (*bhūmis*, 'floors') of the way of the *bodhisattva* to buddhahood. For example on the first stage disposition (towards good principles), beneficence, sameness of thoughts towards all beings, abandoning (property, etc.), resorting to good friends, seeking support in the doctrine, always having thoughts of renunciation, longing for the 'substance of a *buddha*' (to become a *buddha*), teaching the doctrine and speaking the truth. On the second, virtue (*śīla*, explained by Haribhadra in his commentary as acting for the welfare of others), gratitude (not forgetting others' help), toleration (*kṣānti*), joy *prāmodya*, defined as absence of regret when helping others), great compassion, respect, desire to hear one's teachers and energy in the (six) perfections ('donation' or giving, etc.). On the third, insatiability in learning, teaching without thought of personal advantage, indefatigability in transmigration (of the *bodhisattva* working for others, not aiming at his own rapid liberation) and others. On the fourth, contentment, fewness of desires, austerity, disgust for pleasures, indifference (*nirvid*, towards worldly values) and others. On the fifth, avoiding various worldly connections and values (including the 'four errors', pride, excusing the defilements, etc.). On the sixth, fulfilling the six perfections and avoiding six undesirable things (the attitude of a 'pupil' and others). On the seventh, eliminating twenty faults, namely the various (wrong) opinions, that there is a soul, a (living) 'being', a person, the annihilationist and eternalist opinions, erroneous views about the groups, elements, spheres, etc., and acquiring instead twenty kinds of correct understanding which are contrary to these and also have moral significance. On the eighth, it is the insights connected with enlightenment which predominate and on the ninth the infinite 'commitments' (*praṇidhānas*), 'intuitions' (*pratibhānas*) and other aspects of the immediate preparation for buddhahood. The tenth is the stage of buddhahood itself.

Under the second subject we find such topics as the way of the 'pupils' and the way of the isolated *buddhas*, which the *bodhisattva* is expected to know about, and the twofold division of the way (common to practically all schools and not peculiar to the Mahāyāna) as that of 'seeing' (*darśana*), meaning knowledge of the Truths, and that of 'development' (*bhāvanā*), meaning practical training to overcome the influences or defilements. Another topic here is that of 'ripening' (*pariṇāma*, 'change' in various senses), i.e. of good principles in general into specific factors of enlightenment (in Mahāyāna writings these are often considered to be peculiar to attaining buddhahood and therefore to the way of the *bodhisattva* as contrasted with the 'pupil').

The knowledge of all grounds in transmigration includes an elaborate theory of the Four Truths under the heading 'way of seeing' (topic 30) which has already been touched on above. This third subject includes the finding, through understanding, that there is no 'place' (or situation) in existence (i.e. transmigration) and, through compassion, that there is no 'place' in calm (i.e. extinction). In other words the *bodhisattva* is not at home in the world of transmigration, because he understands all the unhappiness in it, but cannot abandon it for his own extinction, because of his compassion which urges him to continue trying to help other beings.

Under subject four all the 'features' (*ākāra*) of knowledge of the three kinds are listed together (173 of them). These 'features' would be called 'principles' according to the terminology of the early schools. They include many such 'principles' of early lists, not the least significant being all those of the seven topics of the earliest accessible doctrine, which we have reviewed in Chapter Four, the 37 principles on the side of enlightenment (the four bases of self-possession, the four right exertions, etc.). The avoidance of the term 'principle' (*dharma*) by this Mahāyāna writer is no doubt deliberate, since he would wish to distinguish the features of a *buddha's* knowledge from the — for him — discredited ancient theory of principles studied by the 'pupils'. It should be noticed that all these 37 features are here listed under the special knowledge of a *buddha* (the first subject), though it had to be admitted that their study was shared by the 'pupils'. 'Maitreya' under this subject and the next seems to stress the idea that all principles are to be looked upon as in dreaming. The 'equality' (*samatā*) of transmigration and extinction also appears under subject four (as topic 39). The same subject gives some account of the methods of training (under 'undertakings', *prayogas*, topic 32, and some of the following topics).

The fifth subject begins with the dream-like nature of all principles and also discusses briefly the point that both objects (*grāhya*, objects of perception) and subjects (*grāhaka*, 'persons' perceiving) are imaginary, a point noted already at

I. 35-6. The imagining (*vikalpa* or *kalpa*, the latter probably *metri causa*) of objects is described as of two kinds, and alternatively as of 'grounds' (*vastus*, a term which came to be used in the sense of a 'reality', 'real object' in Buddhist philosophical discussions from this period on) and of the 'antidotes' (*pratipakṣas* — i.e. the principles used in purification on the way) to them (I.35) or of objects as commencing (*pravṛtti*, i. e. occurring, originating) and as ceasing (*nivṛtti*) (V.5). The imagining of subjects is also of two kinds, as of a 'substance' (*dravya*) and of a 'concept' (*prajñapti*) (I.36, V.6, 13 and 30). It is the (living) 'being' (*sattva*) or the 'independent soul (self)' (*svatantra ātman*) which is imagined as a substance. As a concept it is imagined as the 'resort' (*āśraya*, 'dependence on') of such principles as the five groups (*skandhas*), i.e. of the directly observable components of living beings. It is under this subject that we find a verse (V.21) practically identical with one in the *Ratnagotravibhāga* (p. 405 above), to the effect that there is nothing to be removed, nothing to be obtained, but simply reality (*bhūta*) has to be seen.

The topics listed under subject six include the six perfections and the absence of any own-nature in principles. (The doctrine of emptiness is more prominent in this text than in the *Ratnagotravibhāga*, but this may merely reflect the emphasis on it in the *Sūtras*.)

Subject seven states that, in the final moment, any one of the principles 'without influences' (*anāsrava*) being known, the totality of all the principles without influences is known simultaneously. This is because reality (*tattva*) has no duality of principles.

The substance of the doctrine has first (topic 67) its proper substance, its own-nature substance (*svābhāvika kāya*), which is permanent, appearing whenever a fit (enlightened) person appears. It is described as being the characteristic of the nature of the various principles without influences, which are enumerated as the (37) principles on the side of enlightenment, the immeasurables, the freedoms (*vimokṣas*) and a long list of other attainments on the way (mostly the old way described in our Chapter Four and worked out in more detail by the early schools, but including some principles attained only by *buddhas* and the 'knowledge of commitment' and great compassion for beings characteristic of the way of the *bodhisattva*). Secondly it has the 'enjoyment substance' (*sāmbhogika kāya*), which possesses the characteristic physical (bodily) marks of *buddhas* (of which there is an elaborate theory) and might therefore be regarded as a personification of enlightenment (cf. the *Ratnagotravibhāga's* 'king of the doctrine', p. 406 above). Thirdly it has the 'creation substance' (*nairmāṇika kāya*), the ordinary human body of a *buddha* (and of all *buddhas* as long as transmigration lasts) which acts for the benefit of the whole world. It appears (from the commentaries) that the substance of the doctrine when regarded as synonymous with 'knowledge of all features' and with the list of 'principles without influences' just mentioned constitutes a separate topic (No. 68). From this some have inferred that this 'knowledge substance' constitutes a distinct substance, so that there will be four instead of three 'substances' (*kāyas*).

The 'Ornament of Insight' became the basic text of a school of philosophers expounding the subject of 'perfection' (*pāramitā*), loosely affiliated to the Madhyamaka but conspicuous later as forming a separate department of study in Buddhist universities. Numerous commentaries were written on this basic text with the object of stabilising its doctrinal position (in the light of later developments in logic and the theory of knowledge as well as in relation to Madhyamaka) and showing its relation to the *Sūtras*.

Developments in the Early Schools after the Rise of the Mahāyāna

We have noted already (p. 374) that most Buddhists in India (and in Ceylon and South East Asia) appear to have continued to follow the early schools: a situation which obtains even today after the violence which has engulfed India during the last eight centuries and left very little of the doctrine of calm and the happiness of all beings. As Tāranātha tells us, most Buddhists rejected the Mahāyāna *sūtras* as not being the words of the Buddha. It was enough for them that these texts were not to be found in the *Tripiṭaka* as it had come down in their schools. Occasionally, however, we do meet with references[1] to the Mahāyāna in the writings of the early schools after its rise, which go a little further than simply rejecting it as an imposture and indicate their views on its teaching. These views are similar, whether expressed by the Sthaviravādins in Ceylon or the Sarvāstivādins in Northern India. The doctrine of the 'great emptiness' (*mahāśūnyatā*) or 'inconsequential', 'wrong emptiness' (*ayogaśūnyatā*) of all phenomena is regarded as sheer nihilism, which leaves nothing of the Four Truths, of morality or any of the other teaching of the Buddha. It is more or less synonymous with Vaitulika, or is a part of the Vaitulika, the doctrine of the 'Magicians' (this is probably the sense attached to this term[2] by those who use it to refer disparagingly to the Mahāyāna, alluding perhaps to the doctrine of illusion, *māyā*, or to the miraculous nature of transcendent *buddhas* with their 'creation' bodies manifested in this world and play-acting the extinction, or to the doctrine that extinction is nothing but transmigration itself), the Vetulyavāda mentioned in the Ceylon histories as corrupting Buddhism. Another term applied to the Mahāyānists is 'nihilists' (*vaināśikas*, literally 'destructionists'), again on the ground that they had carried the emptiness doctrine to the point of abolishing the teaching of the Buddha. In studying Nāgārjuna's works we have seen his reply to criticisms of this kind. We have also seen that Nāgārjuna based his doctrine on *Tripiṭaka* texts accepted by all the schools, so that he seems to have confronted his critics on their own ground. Most Mahāyāna writers have not troubled about the question of authenticity of texts, merely asserting that whichever *sūtras* they favoured were the words of the Buddha. The early schools, wherever they were strongly established, adhered to the textual tradition of their *Tripiṭaka* and denounced the Mahāyāna *sūtras* as fabrications, 'not the words of the Buddha.'

At least one early school, however, produced a kind of reform and rewriting of texts apparently intended to keep up

1. e.g. those noted by Dr. Jaini from the Sarvāstivādin *Abhidharmadīpa* (*BSOAS*, 1958, 48ff.), Sthaviravāda *Dīpavaṃsa* XXII. 43ff., *Kathāvatthu Commentary* p. 167, *Cūlavaṃsa* LXXVIII. 22, etc.

2. cf. *vaitālika*, 'magician' (able to raise the dead, etc.), but perhaps also *vaidālika*, 'destruction' (these words were homonyms in some Prakrit dialects), was in the minds of the critics of Mahāyāna.

to date and abreast of contemporary fashions in language and literature in the period of composition of large 'abundance' (*vaipulya*) *sūtras* in Sanskrit rather than in vernaculars or in the old dialects of the *Tripiṭaka* texts. The Sarvāstivādins translated their recension of the *Tripiṭaka* into Sanskrit, as we noted above (p. 347), standardising the language and terminology of their system in the interests of precision in exegesis. A branch of this school went much further than simple translation with (probably) a minimum of revision. Calling themselves the Mūlasarvāstivāda ('Basic Sarvāstivāda'), as if their branch and its tradition were more original, they produced an elaborate rewriting of their *Tripiṭaka*, probably with the idea of assimilating it to current trends in literature (without, however, changing the doctrine) and so making it more popular. A notable example of their work is their *Vinaya*, a great part of which is extant in Sanskrit (all of it in a Tibetan translation). The original *Vinaya* consisted primarily of rules of discipline, with a certain amount of narrative showing how the community of monks was established and how and why the rules came to be formulated. Some schools, as we have seen (see pp. 333f. and 338f.), extended these narratives in such a way as to produce a more or less full biography of the Buddha. The Mūlasarvāstivāda produced the most complete of these biographies, drawing on whatever *Tripiṭaka* texts offered contributions to such a biography and so incorporating long *sūtras* in their *Vinaya* (e.g. the dialogue with King Ajātaśatru and the *Mahāparinirvāṇa Sūtra* used in our Chapter Three above). The huge, unwieldy text which resulted might be compared in size and in its rambling organisation with the longest Mahāyāna *sūtras*, or on the other hand with the contemporary Brahmanical *Harivaṃśa* (a long 'supplement' to the *Mahābhārata* narrating the life of Kṛṣṇa) or *Purāṇas* (except that these Brahmanical texts are mostly in verse).

It was apparently the Mūlasarvāstivādins who composed the *Saddharmasmṛtyupasthāna Sūtra*, a veritable 'abundance' *sūtra* in extent but which keeps firmly within the older doctrine (as can be seen from our Chapter Four, the subject of 'self-possession', *smṛti*, and its bases covers a great part of the doctrine when set out in detail, besides being fundamental; in this new *sūtra* composed in about the 3rd or 4th century A.D. the fullest advantage is taken of the tendency of this subject).[1] Despite the nature of the subject, being exercises in training for the monks and covering much of the theory of Buddhism, a popular character is given to this great *sūtra* by bringing in detailed descriptions of the various worlds of transmigration and the beings living in them, including gods, demons, ghosts and animals, illustrating the results of (moral and immoral) action. It is noteworthy that this *Sūtra* makes frequent reference to works of art depicting the figures and scenes it describes, and thus moves parallel with the vigorous development of Buddhist painting and sculpture in its period. The drama also is referred to. It can hardly be doubted that such a *sūtra* was produced in direct competition with the Mahāyānists at a time when the ancient *sūtras* had become so much out of fashion, from the literary point of view, as to place those who depended on them at a disadvantage in propagating their teachings. Many *avadānas* or collections of *avadānas* (e.g. the *Avadānaśataka* and *Divyāvadāna* still available in Sanskrit), were produced in this period, evidently with the aim of popularising the teaching through simple narratives.

If the early schools kept abreast of literary developments in this period, they also did not neglect the progress of philosophy, that is its more technical aspects in the field of logic and the theory of knowledge, whilst adhering to the Buddhist teaching handed down to them. In India the main stimulus to the development of logic came from the practice of debating, great public debates in which rival philosophical schools engaged in argument under the chairmanship of an umpire and sought to uphold their doctrines and refute their opponents. In following the history of the early schools through their schisms we have seen them developing the techniques of debate and logic (see pp. 299 ff. and 344 above), as well as the related subject of methodology (pp. 316 ff.). Probably in the 2nd century A.D. one of the early schools produced a manual on debating, which has been preserved in a Chinese translation under the title

1. See Lin Li-kouang, *L'Aide-mémoire de la Vraie Loi*, especially pp. 98 and 115 and 1ff.

Fang pien sin louen,[1] meaning something like the 'essentials of method (in debate)'.

This work first offers a justification of debate as necessary to protect the truth (against an opponent who suggests it promotes anger and other harmful principles). It then sets out the eight main topics of the debate. The first of these is the 'examples' or sense data, data of experience, appealed to by debaters in constructing their arguments. Such an example must be something accepted by everyone. Very important is the seventh topic, 'illusory middle terms', i.e. fallacies, which include begging the question, equivocation, contradicting experience, undistributed middle term, etc. The method of argument, or demonstration, which is followed (and which was more or less standard at this time for all schools of philosophy in India) is one of five steps, as follows:

1. (To prove) S is P, — 'statement'
2. (We assign the middle term) M, — 'middle term'
3. (All) M is P as (for example) M_1, — 'example'
4. (Now) S also is M, — 'application'
5. Therefore it is P. (Q.E.D.) — 'conclusion'

If, of course, the opponent can adduce a counter example, say M_2, which is not P (from experience), then the argument is overthrown, the statement is not established.

It is interesting that as an illustration of an argument based on equivocation this text gives that for the statement that all principles are empty, using the 'example' space. The equivocation here is that 'empty' appears to mean 'non-existent', as in the example. There is the (equivocal) implication that the whole class (or 'universal') 'principles' have the same characteristic as the example space, which is one of them, as if this was the characteristic of the class, leading then to the conclusion that all are empty, all have no own-nature. It may be doubted whether the Mahāyānists used such an argument (as a logical argument), though similar statements may be found in the *Ratnakūṭa* and the Perfection of Understanding about principles being like space. Nevertheless this illustration suggests that the early schools (or one of them, we do not

1. Retranslated into Sanskrit by Tucci in his collection *Pre-Diṅnāga Buddhist Texts on Logic from Chinese Sources* under the conjectural title *Upāyahṛdaya*. The school may be the Bahuśrutīya, whose peculiar doctrine of the *mahābhūtas* as concepts is mentioned on p. 18.

know which) developed a critique of the Mahāyāna *sūtras* and perhaps of the Madhyamaka, by pointing out such equivocations.

The fifth topic is the means of knowledge, given here as four in number: sensation, inference, reliable authority (of a text or a person) and similarity. Of these sensation is the best and the others depend on it. Inference depends on previous sensation (of examples enabling one to establish a middle term, i.e. a universal proposition of the type M is P from which the presence of P can be inferred whenever M is seen, even in cases when P itself cannot be observed). Similarity here is mere similes or analogies (common enough in the *sūtras*) and Buddhist logicians after the 'Essentials of Method' dropped it from the list of means of knowledge, as fallacious.

Three shorter chapters follow the main one on debate, including one dealing with the situations in which a debater is deemed defeated and one on sophistical refutations. The latter are said all to be based on confusions in applying the inductive methods of agreement and difference. Agreement between two principles in one respect is falsely supposed to extend to other respects, leading to a fallacious argument, similarly for difference between two principles.

A little later (c. 200 A.D.) is a somewhat similar text, of which only part has been preserved in a Chinese translation under the title *Jou che louen*, probably from Sanskrit *Tarkaśāstra*, 'Science of Logic'.[1] This is the first known work to formulate a 'canon' of the middle term, the conditions under which it will be valid, thereby marking an important advance towards a more rigorous form of demonstration or proof. The actual proof has the same five steps as in the 'Essentials of Method' and this work appears to have had the same topics as its predecessor, though the sophistical refutations are dealt with in a new way, with discussions showing at some length precisely why each is sophistical and setting out a fivefold method for refuting any of them by exposing it in debate. The canon of the middle term consists of three rules:

1. Retranslated into Sanskrit by Tucci in *Pre-Diṅnāga*... Perhaps a Dharmaguptaka work.

1. The middle term must be an attribute of the minor term (subject),

2. The middle term must be present in the agreeing examples,

3. The middle term must be absent from the different examples.

Rule 1 requires that S is in fact M (step 4 of the demonstration). Rule 2 requires that all the examples adduced for (method of agreement) the relation between M and P, namely M_1, M_2, M_3, etc., are in fact M (step 3). Rule 3 requires that any examples adduced by the method of difference for whatever is not M being not P (the relation between not M and not P) are in fact not M (also step 3, checked by the alternative method). A middle term which satisfies these conditions cannot be refuted. One which fails to satisfy any one of them must be rejected.

It may be noted that in the illustrative arguments used in these two Buddhist texts on logic the opponents usually being refuted are, in the 'Essentials' those who maintain that there is a soul (and seek proofs for it) and in the 'Science of Logic' those who maintain that speech is eternal (meaning the supposed eternal words of the *Veda*). Numerous other schools are mentioned on occasion but the main opponents are evidently the orthodox Vedic (Mīmāṃsaka) brahmans.

Among the schools of the Mahāsaṃgha in this period we have definite evidence at present only about one of them, the Bahuśrutīya. A treatise of the *abhidharma* type, Harivarman's *Tattvasiddhiśāstra* (mentioned p. 278 above), was translated into Chinese early in the 5th century A.D. and became extremely popular there among the Mahāyānists because it appeared to expound something very like their emptiness doctrine, in relation to *abhidharma*. It seems that the Bahuśrutīya school itself was never established in China and the survival of this text thus appears as mere chance based on misunderstanding. Since practically all the texts of the early schools in India itself have been destroyed, however, we have to use such random survivals as this, preserved by Mahāyānists, in an attempt to follow developments in India.

The *Tattvasiddhiśāstra*, 'Treatise on Establishing Reality', appears to have been written in about the 3rd century A.D. Probably it is basically a summary of the doctrines of the

Abhidharma of the Bahuśrutīya school, which otherwise seems to be completely lost, and in a skilful manner it appears to comprehend the whole field, including refutations of the theories of other schools. Harivarman has arranged his work in the form of an exposition of reality as expressed by the Four Truths. He does not set out lists of principles as the Sthaviravāda and other schools do (the 84 of the Jojitsu are not justified, most being mere concepts), nor give definitions of them, though he does set out several *mātṛkās* similar to those of other schools and clarify the nature of various principles and concepts in the course of his discussions. He uses twenty dyads, five triads, also ten tetrads, a pentad, etc., evidently derived from a text similar to the *Saṃgītiparyāya* and showing a kind of *abhidharma*-analysis more archaic than that of the triads and dyads of the Sthaviravāda. By way of introduction, Harivarman takes up ten grounds of controversy among the schools.

Harivarman argues (against the Sarvāstivāda) that past and future principles and actions do not exist. Thought is not by its nature pure (against the Mahāsaṃghika, Kaurukullaka, etc.). The 'person' does not exist (against the Vātsīputrīyas, etc.). His position is very close to those of the Sthaviravāda and the Sautrāntika, but unlike the former he accepts the 'unmanifest' (*avijñapti*) and unlike the latter he rejects the 'intermediate existence' (*antarābhava*) of consciousness between death and birth. The agreement of these three schools on most of the grounds of controversy is of the greatest significance and might be taken as defining the original common philosophy of the Buddhists.

Against the closely related Prajñaptivāda, Harivarman holds that unhappiness is the five groups (thus he explains the first truth, cf. the parent Kaurukullaka school, p. 242 above) and that the groups are principles (*dharmas*; the Prajñaptivāda holds they are mere concepts, but that unhappiness is ultimately real, *paramārtha*). The four conditions are set out here (see pp. 223f above). Harivarman also maintains that matter (*rūpa*) consists of visible object, object of taste, object of smell and the tangible, which four are principles whereas the four elements, the five senses and sound are mere concepts. All emotions are unhappiness. Perception is that which grasps the sign (*nimitta*) of a concept (this is in general agreement with the other schools).

All mentals (*caitasikas*, including the forces such as contact, etc., and perception), which are innumerable, are merely particular kinds of thought. There are no 'conjunctions' because they occur only one at a time. Thought, mind and consciousness are the same principle.

Origination is action and defilement (*kleśa*), the latter causing transmigration. Various *mātṛkās* for these are given.

Cessation is (1) of thoughts of concepts, (2) of thoughts of principles and (3) of the thought of emptiness. Thoughts of concepts cease through the knowledge of conditioned origination. In this connection Harivarman gives a refutation of the Madhyamaka. He also accepts three means of knowledge of what exists, sensation, inference and tradition (Katsura p. 182). Thoughts of principles cease through the knowledge of emptiness after perceiving the five groups as impermanent, etc., and their cessation, which is non-soul and non-own-nature (for this, Harivarman refers, amongst other *sūtras*, to the *Dhātuvibhaṅga*, M No. 140, T 26 No. 162, as implying that only extinction has the principle of non-falsity). The thought of emptiness ceases either in the 'attainment' (*samāpatti*) of cessation or in final extinction.

The way is concentration and knowledge, with the thirty-seven principles on the side of enlightenment and other *mātṛkās* for these. The 'persons' are also set out here.[1]

We may notice finally the definite establishment of the Sautrāntika school in this period by Śrīlāta[2] (probably 2nd century A.D.), who wrote treatises to establish its doctrines (which unfortunately are not extant). It was noted above (p. 345) that this trend arose from a critique of the Sarvāstivāda *Abhidharma*, taking its stand on the *Sūtra* as the authoritative words of the Buddha. In consequence the new school approached the doctrine of the Sthaviravāda, by rejecting the special theories of the Sarvāstivāda, but it also

1. For Harivarman we now generally follow S. Katsura's Thesis *A Study of Harivarman's Tattvasiddhi*, Toronto, 1974.

2. And presumably Kumāralāta with his more popular *Kalpanāmaṇḍitikā* (See Lüders in his edition, pp. 22f.). For the date see Tāranātha (time of Candanapāla, p. 67, cf. p. 374 above) and Schlingloff, *Chandoviciti* p. 10.

rejected the mental forces as separate principles, holding that they were nothing but thought itself. In connection with thought it then proceeded to work out what appears to be a new theory of the stream of consciousness. There is a continuity of consciousness which passes on from life to life in transmigration, though each moment in it is transient. An action having moral significance leaves a 'trace' (*vāsanā*) in this stream, which ultimately produces the appropriate result. There is a continuum of 'subtle thought' (*sūkṣmacitta*) which bears the 'traces' until the time comes for them to produce their results. It may be noted that several schools had investigated the mechanism of the stream of consciousness: that of the Sautrāntika was particularly influential on Mahāyāna writers subsequently. The Sthaviravāda had the theory of the thought-series (see p. 325 above) with the continuing neutral state called 'existence limb' (*bhavāṅga*), mere continuity. The Mahāsaṃgha had a doctrine of 'basic consciousness' (*mūlavijñāna*) and the Mahīśāsakas that of the 'group which continues until the end of transmigration' (*āsaṃsārikaskandha*) (Asaṅga, *Mahāyānasaṃgraha*, Chapter I § 11). Candrakīrti notes the related theories of the 'not being lost' (*avipranāśa*, of the Vātsīputrīyas) and of 'attainment' (*prāpti*, see p. 343 above, of the Sarvāstivāda) (*Madhyamakāvatāra* p. 126).

Chapter Eleven

IDEALISM AND THE THEORY OF KNOWLEDGE

Idealism — Asaṅga — The Theory of Knowledge — Sautrāntika Eptstemology : Vasubandhu II and Diṅnāga

Idealism

Sthiramati in his *Ratnagotravibhāga* appears to put forward an idealist interpretation of the Perfection of Understanding: the ultimate reality has the nature of thought and everything else is the product of imagination. However, to assert positively the existence of such an ultimate reality, an absolute idea (the 'substance of the doctrine'), would seem to be incompatible with the orthodox Madhyamaka standpoint (extinction transcends is, is not, both is and is not and neither is nor is not) as well as with all earlier forms of Buddhism. This newer trend in Madhyamaka reached the threshold of idealism, perhaps without working out the possible consequences. Very soon a new form of Mahāyāna developed which accepted fully the consequences of the current trend. It began with a series of new *sūtras*, like other Mahāyāna trends, and continued with the systematic writings of philosophers.

The main *sūtras* of the idealist trend appear to have been composed in the 3rd century A.D. Although in certain cases additions or revisions were made later, the work of philosophers on them in the fourth century and Chinese translations of parts of them in the third century and of a long major *sūtra* in the fourth century assure our chronology. The Chinese[1] preserve a tradition of there being a kind of canon of *sūtras* of the idealist school, consisting of two main *sūtras*, the *Avataṃsaka* and the *Sandhinirmocana*, and four other *sūtras*, the *Laṅkāvatāra*, *Ghanavyūha* (? if this means the *Gaṇḍavyūha*, the longest *sūtra* in the *Avataṃsaka* which is really a collection), *Jou lai* (Sanskrit original not certain — *Vimalakīrti* ?) and *Abhidharmasūtra*. We may follow the main *sūtras*, with a glance at the *Laṅkāvatāra* and the (*Mahāyāna*) *Abhidharmasūtra*.

There are two main recensions of the *Avataṃsaka*, one in 34 chapters (60 fascicules in the Chinese version) and one in 39

1. Yi-tsing (T 2125).

chapters (80 fasc. in Chinese), besides which many of the chapters, which in fact are separate *sūtras*, have circulated independently. By far the most important of the chapters is the last, the *Gaṇḍavyūha Sūtra* (40 fasc. in Chinese). The *Daśabhūmika Sūtra* (chapter 22 or 26 according to the recension) is an important Mahāyāna text, as setting out in detail the ten stages of the *bodhisattva's* progress, but does not appear to contain anything specifically of the new trend.

The *Gaṇḍavyūha* is a literary masterpiece, the most readable of all the Mahāyāna *sūtras* and almost the only one organised as a balanced work of art on an effective plan. The progressive plan leads the reader on, whilst the formidable prose style is impressively in keeping with the outlook embracing the whole universe and its inconceivable nature. The elaborate descriptions and wealth of similes and figurative language generally mark this as a work of art. In fact it is a highly imaginative religious novel, though it opens in the manner of a *sūtra.* The title *Gaṇḍavyūha* is obscure, being generally interpreted as 'array of flowers', 'bouquet'. It is just possible that the rhetorical device called *gaṇḍa*, a speech having a double meaning (understood differently by two hearers), should be thought of here, since the universe as described in the *sūtra* is simultaneously the everyday universe of transmigration and the transcendent ultimate reality, which are identical though seen differently by *bodhisattvas* and ordinary persons. From the internal evidence of the place names mentioned it appears that this *sūtra*, like the Perfection of Understanding, was written in South India, very likely in Āndhra, in which case the country of origin of the Mahāyāna continued in the lead in the development of new ideas in India.

The main theme of the *Gaṇḍavyūha* is the *bodhisattva's* quest for enlightenment, beginning with the thought of enlightenment. Alternatively (and this gives the story a subtitle) it is the progress from seeing the universe as ordinary people see it, when filled with attachment and petty, selfish desires, to seeing it as the (true) *bodhisattva* sees it. In the former aspect it is known as the 'element of the world' (*lokadhātu*), in the latter as the 'element of principles' (*dharmadhātu*), i.e. the ultimate reality. The subtitle, therefore, is 'Entering the Element of Principles'.

In the preliminary scene the theme is indicated by the

Buddha attaining, by means of his infinite compassion, a certain kind of concentration, through which the pavilion in which he is sitting expands until it embraces the entire universe. The universe is thus transformed for all those present in the Buddha's assembly, taking on its 'element of principles' aspect and becoming beautiful and perfect. The Buddha shows them the entire element of principles as present in a single atomic particle of dust (*paramāṇurajas*). He shows all the *buddhas* of the past and the future in a single pore of his skin. The 'clouds of creation' pervading all the worlds are like an atom containing the entire element of principles, emerging from one pore of the Buddha's skin. Then the entire evolution and involution of the universe is shown in one of the Buddha's pores. After many similar marvels the preliminary scene ends with the departure of the *bodhisattva* Mañjuśrī ('Sweet Fortune') from the Buddha's presence in Śrāvastī (cf. pp. 63 and 398 above) to teach the doctrine in South India, at Dhanyākara (probably the great city of Dhānyakaṭaka in Āndhra, cf. pp. 293, 350 above).

It is here that we meet the hero of the novel, Sudhana, the son of a rich merchant. He hears Mañjuśrī teaching and on account of his favourable disposition, resulting from previous good actions, he is excited and has the thought of enlightenment (said to be a rare thing). Muñjuśrī gives him some individual tuition and launches him on the way of the *bodhisattvas*, advising him that he must be tireless in the quest of 'good friends' who will teach and guide him (cf. pp. 105 above). Mañjuśrī is the first of Sudhana's good friends, and having instructed him he directs him to another friend, a monk. By attending on one friend after another Sudhana will gradually increase his knowledge and understanding and learn to practice various kinds of meditation in which they are proficient. The friends are *bodhisattvas* whether they are monks (few are) or laymen and whatever their professions. Altogether Sudhana attends on 52 good friends, travelling all over India in order to find them, but with a preference for the South. All classes of society are represented among them and a few are gods. One is a slave and most of the others follow a variety of ordinary worldly occupations, the pursuit of some of which is in fact praised in this *sūtra* as a form of well doing. It is noteworthy that 20 out of the 52 friends are women (or goddesses)

In his instruction Mañjuśrī tells Sudhana that great compassion is the first essential for attaining enlightenment, with the aim of liberating all beings. The *bodhisattva* must attain 'all round benevolence' (*samantabhadra*). This quality is personified in the *Sūtra* as the *bodhisattva* Samantabhadra, and said in the preliminary scene to be the basis of all the *bodhisattvas* : the latter go out to the way (*caryā*, conduct) and the commitment (*praṇidhāna*) of Samantabhadra.

The second friend describes to Sudhana the contemplation of the thus-gones in the various directions, in which he is engaged, but being unequal to instructing him in the way of the *bodhisattva* sends him on to a third friend. The latter stresses great compassion, the desire to save all beings and great benevolence (*maitrī*, loving kindness, also translatable as 'friendliness'). This friend lives on the coast of South India, contemplating the vastness of the ocean which is like the inconceivable mind of the thus-gone. He too is unable to teach the way of the *bodhisattva* and sends Sudhana to another friend. Thus he goes on from friend to friend, learning a little from each of them. He learns many 'freedoms' (*vimokṣas*, see pp. 131 f. but here new ones have been added), non-attachment, something about the perfection of understanding, rules of conduct for the *bodhisattva.*

Eventually Sudhana reaches the *bodhisattva* Maitreya, friend No. 51, who as the next *buddha* to appear in this world is presumably the most advanced *bodhisattva* at present. In this *Sūtra* he lives not among the gods but in South India in a country on the coast named Samudrakaccha, in a large pavilion in a park there. This pavilion is called the 'embryo (*garbha*) of the ornament of the arrays of illuminations'. It is very elaborately described. It is the dwelling place of those who delight in emptiness, signlessness and uncommittedness, and in not being separate from the element of principles. It is the dwelling place of those who delight in experiencing that all the ages of the universe interpenetrate: the entrance (*anupraveśa*) of one into all and all into one, that all the worlds are not separate, that all principles do not obstruct one another (*anāvaraṇa*), that all beings are not different from each other, that there is non-duality of all *buddhas*, that all objects enter into a single moment. The inhabitants of the pavilion go everywhere in a single thought, manifest themselves in the homes of all beings, desire the welfare and happiness of all beings. They have plenty of other remarkable qualities, such as non-attachment, non-duality and surprising combinations of qualities which might seem contradictory: they have great equanimity yet they do not abandon the world of beings, they delight in emptiness yet do not hold any opinion, they delight in benevolence yet are not conciliating, they delight in the Four Truths, conditioned origination and the rest of the doctrine but without leaving the world, they delight in thusness yet they do not go to the 'point' (*koṭi*, end, limit) of existence (*bhūta*), i.e. abandon transmigration. In brief they are free but do not use their freedom to enter extinction and remain to help others.

In the course of this description we learn more about the ultimate reality, the element of principles, and the main contribution of the *Gaṇḍavyūha* to philosophy : the conception of the perfect interpenetration of everything in the universe, in which everything is as if reflected in everything else, without any mutual obstruction. The worldly and transcendental universes are identical, with separateness of principles on the surface but perfect harmony and unity within.

As Sudhana approaches he sees Maitreya in the distance, outside the pavilion with a large number of people round him. Maitreya praises Sudhana to his retinue and then welcomes him. Sudhana explains his quest and Maitreya expounds the qualities of this to the audience, how he has been sent by Mañjuśrī to attend on the good friends, his perfections as a *bodhisattva*, his desire to save the whole world. Then he talks to Sudhana. First he praises at great length the thought of enlightenment, which few have, using countless similes. Among these there is a reference to alchemy: there is a marvellous liquid a little of which will turn a vast quantity of bronze into gold, likewise a little of the thought of enlightenment will turn a vast quantity of ignorance into enlightenment. There is a certain gem which produces the images of the Sun and Moon in India (i.e. on Earth), though their discs are 40,000 leagues away (this estimate of the distance is approximately correct for the Moon, not of course for the Sun) ; likewise the thought of enlightenment gem produces the image of the knowledge of the thus-gone, though this is (far away) in the range of the element of principles 'sky'.

Maitreya then opens the pavilion. It is as high as the sky and occupies the whole of space. It is full of beautiful palaces made of precious stones. There is every kind of decoration: trees, birds, flowers, sculptures, paintings, mirrors, lanterns, music and so on. In the pavilion there are countless other pavilions all as beautiful as the original one. There is perfect interpenetration and non-obstruction between them. All are in one, one in all, yet not interfering with each other, harmoniously interpenetrating.

With Maitreya's aid Sudhana concentrates and enjoys a glimpse of enlightenment: all obstructions disappear from his thought. He finds himself in all the pavilions simultaneously, and in each one the *bodhisattva* Maitreya is engaged in good works in one or other of the worlds in the universe. For example he visits the hells (purgatories) in order to relieve the sufferings of those undergoing punishment there. Among the good works praised we find the 'worldly' arts and crafts. The name Maitreya, from *maitrī*, 'benevolence' (or 'friendship') is explained.

Maitreya having enabled Sudhana to see all these 'arrays' by the inconceivable artifice (*māyā*) of his determining knowledge (*adhiṣṭhāna-jñāna*) says to him: 'This is the nature (*dharmatā*) of these principles (*dharmas*). They have the characteristic of the appearance (*pratyupasthāna*, or 'manifestation') of delimitation (*viṣṭhapana*): they are determined (*adhiṣṭhita*) by the knowledge of *bodhisattvas*. Thus they are not perfected (*aparinispanna*) in their own nature (*svabhāva*), they are like illusions (*māyā*, 'artifice'), dreams or images (*pratibhāsas*)' (p. 524).

When he comes out of this concentration Sudhana asks what 'freedom' this is which he has seen with the aid of his good friend. He is told it is the 'embryo of the arrays of self-possession without confusion entering the knowledge having as its support all the three times (past, future and present)'. — Where has this array gone? — Where it came from. — Where did it come from? — From the accomplishment of determining (fixing one's attention on) the knowledge of *bodhisattvas*. It remains in that 'determining', has gone nowhere...does not accumulate, is not immovable (*na kūṭastha*), is not in 'existents' (*na bhāvastha*)...has no place. It is like an array (*jāla*, 'network') of clouds of the dragons...which rains without measure because it is possessed by the volition of the dragons, through the inconceivability of the domain of the dragons. Or it is like the artifice (*māyā*) of a showman which comes from nowhere, etc.

Sudhana asks from how far Maitreya has come and is told that the 'going' of *bodhisattvas* is without coming, without moving or staying, homeless and so on. Yet it is great compassion, great benevolence, etc. Still, Maitreya says he has come from his birthplace, Kūṭagrāmaka in Mālaṭa (in South India). There he has set up or exhorted various people in the doctrine and from there he has come here. On the other hand the birthplace of the *bodhisattvas* is wherever there is the thought of enlightenment. He has been born here in South India to help people and afterwards will go to the Tuṣita Palace, whence he will be reborn to become a *buddha*. Then he will again see Sudhana and Mañjuśrī.

Sudhana is then sent back to Mañjuśrī, who congratulates him on having accepted the good friends and guides him in the way of all round benevolence (*samantabhadra*). Finally Samantabhadra himself appears to Sudhana (he is the last friend, No. 52), who sees his inconceivable 'play' (*vikrīḍita*) consisting of showing the entire universe in his body and other marvels and himself attending on the Buddha Vairocana ('Illumination', the Buddha in his transcendental aspect). Sudhana thereby attains ten perfections of knowledge, such as pervading all the worlds with his body. Samantabhadra touches him on the head and he sees more marvellous 'play' in the worlds of all the *buddhas*. Samantabhadra gives him final instructions on the way of the *bodhisattva* and Sudhana attains all the powers of a *buddha* and becomes the equal of all the *buddhas* and *bodhisattvas*. The *Sūtra* concludes with Samantabhadra reciting verses on the commitment of the *bodhisattva*, to honour the *buddhas*, praise the thus-gones, renounce evil, study and teach the doctrine, etc., and especially to save all beings.

The *Gaṇḍavyūha* is usually assumed to reflect the idealist view, but perhaps makes nothing like a definitive statement of such a position. Since it is a literary and poetic work we should probably not expect to find in it clear philosophical formulations, and indeed the followers of the Madhyamaka school had no difficulty in interpreting it within the framework of their own outlook. It is the other main *sūtra* of the idealist trend, the *Sandhinirmocana*, which seems for the first time to assert clearly that there is an absolute, ideal reality, that everything else is at best only a relative reality dependent on this, otherwise purely imaginary, and that the support of consciousness is nothing but consciousness. Unfortunately the Sanskrit text of the *Sandhinirmocana* is not known to be extant, so we depend on Lamotte's translation from the Tibetan.[1]

Lamotte believes that the *Sandhinirmocana* originated as a number of separate texts independently circulated, which at some stage were collected to form a *sūtra* of moderate length (it is about as long as the old *Mahāparinirvāṇa Sūtra*, hardly 'abundant' though it appears to have been admitted to that class of Mahāyāna *sūtras*). The result has no particular literary plan and is simply a series of independent dialogues making clear the current trend of ideas. The title means 'freeing the *sandhi*', where *sandhi*, 'junction', 'connection', means the intention with which the Buddha spoke, what he had 'in mind' in certain statements. The idea is that in certain statements in earlier *sūtras*, particularly the Perfection of Understanding, what the Buddha really had in mind was not the literal, apparent meaning but a deeper implication. Thus the Buddha taught the Four Truths to those who became the founders of the early schools (the 'pupils') and emptiness to those who were to initiate the Madhyamaka or early Mahāyāna trend. Finally, however, he taught that 'all principles are without own-nature, have not occurred, have not ceased, are calm from the beginning and extinct by nature'. Thus the *Sūtra* tells us (VII. §30) that the Buddha 'started the wheel of the doctrine' three times with these teachings of increasing profundity. Even the last is liable to be misunderstood through being taken too literally (VII. §20), so that some hold the opinion of the non-existence of principles and deny all principles and all characteristics, including the 'imaginary character' (*parikalpitalakṣaṇa*), 'dependent character' (*paratantralakṣaṇa*) and 'perfected character'

1. *Saṃdhinirmocana Sūtra*, Recueil de travaux..2e. Série, 34e. Fascicule, Université de Louvain, 1935.

(*pariniṣpannalakṣaṇa*) of principles. Yet there must be a dependent and a perfected character, otherwise the imaginary character (which we seem to see in the world) could not be discerned The *Sandhinirmocana*, according to its own statement (repeated at the ends of chapters VII to X), is perfectly explicit, 'has its meaning drawn out' (*nītārtha*, cf. p. 150 above) and so claims to make everything clear and definitive. By presenting the correct interpretation of the final (most profound) teaching it avoids the wrong opinion denying all principles and all characteristics, which some (would-be Buddhists) follow and by which others (of the early schools) are repelled from the doctrine (of the Mahāyāna), saying this (Mahāyāna doctrine) is the words of Death (Māra). (It is interesting to note the implication here of controversy about the early Mahāyāna or Madhyamaka, which the new trend now proposes to settle.)

The first part (chapters I to IV) might be regarded as texts of the Perfection of Understanding class (so Lamotte), but they have their meaning drawn out to the extent of giving explanations of statements of the Perfection of Understanding type instead of leaving apparent paradoxes. Moreover they seem to assert from the outset an ultimate reality (*paramārtha*) as the basis of all that we imagine and as in some sense real and existing, though inconceivable and unstatable, a conclusion which the Perfection of Understanding and the Madhyamaka seem carefully to avoid.

The three characteristics (*lakṣaṇa*) of principles already mentioned are probably the most significant contribution of this *Sūtra* to Buddhist thought. Of these the 'perfected' (*pariniṣpanna* — Tibetan *yoṅs su grub pa*) is the ultimate reality, the ultimate absence of own-nature (*paramārthaniḥsvabhāvatā — don dam pa ṅo bo ñid med pa ñid*) of principles (VII. §6) and the thusness (*tathatā — de bzhin ñid*) of principles (VI. §6). The 'dependent' (*paratantra — gzhan gyi dbaṅ gi*) is the conditioned origination of principles (VI. §5), their absence of own-nature in occurrence (*utpatti — skye ba*) (VII. §5) and the range (*gocara — spyod yul*) of imagining (*vikalpa—rnam par rtog pa*) (VII. §25) The 'imaginary' (*parikalpita — kun brtags pa*) is the assigning of the convention of names of principles through 'own-nature' or 'distinction (s)' for the purpose of the conventional (agreed) usage of concepts (VI.§4) and their absence of own-nature as characteristic (VII. §4). It is the assigning of names to the range of imagining (VII. §25).

The three characteristics are thus related to three absences of own-nature in principles. In this context (VII. §6) it is also stated that the ultimate reality is the 'pure support' (*viśuddhālambana — rnam par dag paḥi dmigs pa*), i.e. principles as the support of consciousness (at the ultimate level). It is natural to proceed from this to the discussion (VIII. §7) on the nature of the 'range-disc' (*gocarabimba—spyod yul gzugs brñan*), i.e. the mental image, of insight-concentration. Here it is said that such images are not different from thought and are only makings-of-consciousness (*vijñaptimātra—rnam par rig pa tsam*). This last expression, which might also be interpreted as 'mere products of the act of being conscious', will be the subject of much speculation later. It is further said here that the support of consciousness is only a making-of-consciousness. Consciousness and its 'support' (the support in it, of which it is supposed to be conscious) are not different. This statement is generally taken to mean that the objects we think we are conscious of are nothing but our consciousness itself and as the enunciation of an idealist outlook. For these discussions it is worth noting that *vijñapti* is a causative form, grammatically, implying what is caused or made by the action of being conscious, as contrasted with simple consciousness, *vijñāna*.

In the fifth chapter of this *Sūtra* we meet another major idea of the idealist trend, namely its conception of the mechanism of the stream of consciousness (cf. the end of our Chapter Ten). It is thought 'possessing all the seeds' (*sarvabījaka — sa bon thams cad paḥi*) which, in transmigration, grows through attachment to the material faculties with their 'determinings' (resolutions) and to the traces (*vāsanā — bag chags*) of differentiations (*prapañca — spros pa*) through the conventional usage imagining 'signs' and 'names'. This consciousness (thought) is called 'attachment consciousness' (*ādānavijñāna — len paḥi rnam par çes pa*) and 'home consciousness' (*ālayavijñāna — kun gzhi rnam par çes pa*), the latter because it unites with a body seeking a common security. These are descriptions of consciousness in transmigration, with its 'seeds' (these are taken to be the latent ideas in it, through which it is productive), an elaboration of the old theory of consciousness. We are told here that the conception of an attachment consciousness has not been revealed to 'fools', lest they should take it to be a 'soul'.

In this connection we may notice that the Madhyamakas took a very different view of the question of which texts have their meaning 'drawn out', are definitive, and of what the Buddha had in mind in various *sūtra* discourses. Thus Candrakīrti[1] holds that the discourses on the 'home consciousness' are not 'drawn out' at all: this term is only a name for emptiness, used, provisionally covering what the Buddha ultimately had in mind, for the sake of those of limited understanding, accustomed to other ways of thinking; it may be compared with the term 'person' used in other discourses of the Buddha. For the Madhyamakas it is the Perfection of Understanding texts which are drawn out, those of the 'third starting of the wheel of the doctrine', like those of the first, requiring their meaning 'to be drawn out.'

The *Laṅkāvatāra* carries this doctrine a little further. It is much longer than the *Sandhinirmocana* (whichever of its various recensions be taken) and seems still more chaotic in composition, almost certainly because it grew gradually, collecting discussions on a great variety of topics which interested the idealist movement. The scene is set in Ceylon (Laṅkā), which the Buddha visits at the request of Rāvaṇa, King of the Demons, who has his capital there. However, nothing is heard of Rāvaṇa after the opening of the *Sūtra* and Laṅkā is mentioned only once after the first chapter, as the place where the Buddha is teaching. In actual fact the *Sūtra* is a simple dialogue between the Buddha and a *bodhisattva* named Mahāmati (who is otherwise obscure). The 'interesting' setting was no doubt a later addition, along with some of the last chapters.

The basic conception of the *Laṅkāvatāra* is that of 'thought only' (*cittamātra*): that there is nothing in the universe except thought (pp. 62, 79, 111, 154, 176, 184, 186, 199), existents such as matter and the other groups are only imaginings in

1. *Madhyamakāvatāra* p. 131.

thought. This is a much more categorical statement of idealism than we find in the *Sandhinirmocana*.

Thought may be differentiated into two aspects: (1) home consciousness (*ālayavijñāna*) and (2) mind (*manas*) and the consciousnesses of the six senses (of mind, sight, etc. — for this entire scheme cf. the Sthaviravāda *Abhidharma*, (pp. 305f. above) (pp. 220f.). These eight (principles) are sometimes called the eight consciousnesses (e.g. p. 126). At the same time the home consciousness is more fundamental, less ephemeral, than the others and seems to be practically synonymous with thought itself: the other seven are simply imagined and are to be abandoned in order to attain calm (pp. 221, 44ff.). All experiences, differentiated by the various kinds of consciousness, are simply waves in the 'ocean' of thought, or of the home consciousness. It is the imagining of subject and object, that which is conscious of and that of which it is conscious, which gives rise to the various kinds of consciousness as subjects and objects out of the home consciousness (pp. 37f., 46, 48). This imagining of the various consciousnesses originates through the traces (*vāsanās*) which have accumulated in the home consciousness during beginningless time (p. 38). When this imagining ceases in the home consciousness, that is extinction (*nirvāṇa*) (pp. 61f., 98f., 126f.).

In chapter six the *Laṅkāvatāra* identifies the home consciousness with the 'embryo of the thus-gone' (*tathāgatagarbha*) and, moreover, refers by name to the *Śrīmālā Sūtra* for the Buddha having spoken of this there (cf. our discussion pp. 400ff. above, where we did not find explicit mention of the 'home' consciousness, possibly because we depended on the *Ratnagotravibhāga* but perhaps because it really is not named and the *Laṅkāvatāra* is merely appropriating the account of the 'embryo' and assimilating it to the new theory of the 'home consciousness'). The home consciousness which is the embryo is a kind of medium with potentialities for bad (imagining) or good (calm), the seven other consciousnesses occur in it, leading to other principles, including unhappiness, but when the truth is understood all this ceases and it becomes pure. There is no 'soul' in it. Without it there could be no occurrence of principles. Nevertheless in one place (p. 78) it is said that the embryo is 'emptiness', is extinction—in order to underline its distinction from the Brahmanical 'soul' (probably referring to the theory of the soul being *brahman*, the ultimate being which underlies the entire universe). Here the *Sūtra* seems to draw back from a definitively idealist position towards that of the (early) Madhyamaka and to make it easy for the Madhyamakas to interpret the whole text from their standpoint. The alternative position is apparently maintained later (p. 167), when it is said that the *bodhisattva* should not hold that all principles are empty and without own-nature, but rather that their own-nature is like an artifice (*māyā*, or 'illusion') or like a dream : in one sense they exist, in another they do not. Further on (pp. 198f.) we read that the Buddha's doctrine goes beyond this duality of existing and not existing, and other dualities, all these being only the imaginings of thought.

We are back at the question of 'thought only', as (in its pure nature) beyond existence and non-existence. All multiplicity is imagined by it, merely occurs in it. It is thusness (*tathatā*), emptiness, the element of principles (*dharmadhātu*), the 'substance made of mind' (*manomayakāya*) (p. 154).

The *Abhidharma Sūtra* does not appear to have assumed the importance it might perhaps have claimed as a specifically Mahāyāna *abhidharma*. It enumerated the principles, in relation to the *bodhisattva* and his way, following earlier *abhidharma* traditions with the necessary modifications to suit the latest trend. It evidently belonged to the idealist movement, discussing the home consciousness possessing all the 'seeds', etc., the home of all principles, the element (*dhātu*) in beginningless time which is the support of all principles and also the approach to extinction. In practice this *abhidharma* seems to have been overshadowed by the numerous systematic writings of the Mahāyāna philosophers of the new trend who followed, beginning with Asaṅga, who makes extensive reference to it at the beginning of his *Mahāyānasaṃgraha*, taking his *mātṛkā* from it.

Asaṅga

After the fall of the Kuṣāṇas and Sātavāhanas the feudalistic system developing in India was consolidated under the hegemony of the Gupta dynasty in the North and the Vākāṭakas in the Deccan (Mahārāṣṭra and some of the surrounding countries), these two entering into a matrimonial alliance about the year 400, an alliance which proved enduring and stabilised both empires. Various schools of Buddhism received patronage from both royal families, no doubt following a policy of toleration. However, both were primarily committed to the new Brahmanism of the *Purāṇas* (which appear to have been largely rewritten in the 4th century, incorporating wholesale the mythology and theology of Viṣṇu and Śiva, whose worship became steadily more popular throughout the medieval period). Consequently it is likely that on the whole the Buddhists enjoyed less support than during the preceding period. In the far South the ancient Pallava dynasty strengthened its power, conquering Āndhra in the 4th century and stationing a viceroy at Dhānyakaṭaka. This dynasty too was Brahmanical in religion and is not recorded to have given much support to Buddhism, nevertheless Buddhist institutions flourished in its realm, especially at the capital, Kāñcī.

The Vākāṭaka power was established about the year 250, the Gupta in 320 on the basis of a marriage between Candra Gupta, an obscure local ruler in Magadha, and a daughter of the ancient Licchavi aristocracy of the Vṛji Republic (which, it seems, had been independent again in this period), Kumāradevī. It was not until about 350 that Candra's son, Samudra, established a wide paramountcy over North and East India in a remarkable series of military campaigns, and not until about 395 that his son, Candra II ('Vikramāditya'), overthrew the Śakas of Western India and occupied Ujjayinī, then in many ways the cultural metropolis of India (especially in science and literature, particularly the theatre).

Asaṅga was born about or after the year 290 in Puruṣapura, Kaniṣka's capital in Gandhāra (see p. 345 above), and died about 360[1] (some of the works of his younger brother Vasubandhu were known in China by about the latter date). Consequently he lived in a period of political instability before the new imperial system was completely established, though he may have lived to see the weak remnant of the Kuṣāṇa kingdom invaded by Samudra Gupta and

1. His *Yogācārabhūmiśāstra* was translated into Chinese from 413 onwards.

attached to his empire by a rather tenuous form of vassalage (to be made firmer by his son). Asaṅga founded a philosophical school of the Mahāyāna based on the idealist trend of the latest *sūtras*, which we have just reviewed, called the Yogācāra or alternatively (but probably only later) the Vijñānavāda. The first name refers to the way of the *bodhisattva*, the second, 'Consciousness School', to the idealist outlook (consciousness only). According to the Buddhist traditions preserved in Tibet[1] Asaṅga was born in the time of a king Buddhapakṣa and lived under his successor Gambhīrapakṣa, afterwards travelling east to Ayodhyā, living 12 years at Nālandā and dying at Rājagṛha. The identity of these two kings has not been conclusively established, they may have been Kuṣāṇas.

Asaṅga wrote possibly seven main works (a minor work ascribed to him is a verse summary of the content of one of the short Perfection of Understanding *sūtras*, the Three Hundred or 'Diamond Cutter'; it contains nothing of the new doctrines): a commentary on the *Sandhinirmocana* and six independent books : *Abhidharmasamuccaya*, *Dharmadharmatāvibhaṅga*, *Madhyāntavibhaṅga*, *Mahāyānasaṃgraha*, *Mahāyānasūtrālaṅkāra*[2] and *Yogācārabhūmiśāstra*. There are traditions that some of these were really composed by Maitreya, but these may be held to have originated from the idea that that *bodhisattva* inspired Asaṅga with them (the traditions conflict : in China the last work is supposed to be Maitreya's, in Tibet instead three of the others are). His authorship of the commentary also has been doubted.

Asaṅga is the systematiser of the idealist doctrines of the new trend and wrote comprehensively in such a way as to provide the school he founded with theoretical and practical treatises covering the whole field of Buddhism from the new standpoint. Thus the *Abhidharmasamuccaya* summarises the whole ancient system of the *abhidharma* as modified for the Yogācāra: here we find the list of principles totals 100 items, of which the home consciousness is one, being the same as 'thought' and 'consciousness of mind' and, as in the *Sandhinirmocana*, 'possessing all the seeds' and 'impregnated with the traces.'[3] The

1. Tāranātha pp. 107ff.
2. This may be by some earlier author.
3. *Abhidharmasamuccaya* edited (from an incomplete manuscript supple-

three 'characteristics' or (absences of) own-natures of all principles, of the *Sandhinirmocana*, are also noted and the *bodhisattva* is briefly touched on, including his superiority to the 'pupil'. At the end of the text there are brief notes on debating and logic, giving the five steps of a proof and three means of knowledge (similarity having been dropped). These five plus three items are here collected and called 'eight provings', implying eight parts of a complete proof, including the checks that it is not contradicted by any of the three means of knowledge, sensation, inference and reliable authority.

In the *Mahāyānasūtrālaṅkāra* ('Ornament of the Mahāyāna Sūtras') Asaṅga appears as a strong partisan of the Mahāyāna, defending its *sūtras* against the criticism that they are not the words of the Buddha. Only the Mahāyāna *sūtras* contain the deepest teaching of the Buddha, the way to Buddhahood. This work summarises the practice of the way of the *bodhisattva*, including for example the thought of enlightenment, the perfections and the good friends, but it also covers the theory of the new trend (especially in its sixth, ninth and eleventh chapters). The ultimate reality (*paramārtha*) is neither existing (*sant*) nor not existing. Objects (*artha*) are mere ideas (*jalpa*), thought only : when the *bodhisattva* discerns this he perceives the 'element of principles' and is separated from the characteristic of duality, remaining in the element of principles. Freedom (*mokṣa*) is simply (*-mātra*) the elimination of error (*bhrama*, or 'mistake') (VI). Buddhahood is all principles yet is not a principle. It is thusness (*tathatā*). It is neither existent (*bhāva*) nor non-existent, therefore 'undetermined' (*avyākṛta*). What has no occurrence (*avidyamānatā*, from *vidyate*) (i.e. with its imagined own-nature — Vasubandhu's commentary), ultimately has occurrence (i.e. with its 'perfected' own-nature) (IX). Reality (*tattva*) is that which is always without duality, is the basis of illusion (*bhrānti*, or 'error', 'mistake'), is undifferentiated (*aprapañca*), cannot be expressed ... nothing other than it occurs (*vidyate*) in the universe, though through delusion the world has abandoned the existing (*sant*) and superimposed

mented by retranslations from the Tibetan and Chinese) by Pralhad Pradhan, Santiniketan, 1950, 11f.

(*abhiniviṣṭa*) the non-existing (*asant*). On the one hand its appearance (*ākṛti*) exists (*asti*), on the other hand its existing (*bhāva*) does not occur (*na vidyate*, but here this seems to be used as a synonym for 'does not exist', perhaps under pressure of the metre), therefore 'existence' (*astitva*) and 'non-existence' (*nāstitva*) (of it) is affirmed with reference to illusion (*māyā*), etc. Here the argument leads into the theory of the three characteristics : everything knowable (*jñeya*) is included in (1) the imaginer of the unreal (*abhūtakalpa*), which (itself) is neither real nor unreal, (2) the non-imaginer (*akalpa*) (i.e. thusness, transcendental knowledge, presumably the substance of the doctrine and the ultimate reality), and (3) that which is neither 'imaginer' nor 'non-imaginer' (worldly knowledge, according to the commentary). This verse seems almost deliberately obscure and the commentary of Vasubandhu is curiously unhelpful. The imaginer we know from elsewhere to be the 'dependent' (*paratantra*) character. The non-imaginer is the 'perfected' (*pariniṣpanna*). That which is neither of these should be the 'imaginary' (*parikalpita*), which could be identified with worldly 'knowledge'. However, after this verse Asaṅga works round to somewhat clearer statements about these three characteristics. The imaginary is the 'sign' (*nimitta*, or 'cause') of perception corresponding to the object of an idea, the trace of this (idea — commentary) and the 'knowing' that arises from the trace; also it is knowing an object by its name and a name by its object. The dependent is the imaginer of the unreal, which is subject to various kinds of illusion (*ābhāsa*, false appearance) and has the characteristics of 'subject' (*grāhaka*) and 'object' (*grāhya*) (two classes of the illusions). The perfected is the existence (*bhāvatā*) of the non-existing (*abhāva*), which is the equality (*samānatā*, sameness) of 'existing' and 'non-existing'; it is the calming of what is not calmed and the non-imaginer (XI). The style of these formulations indicates that Asaṅga was fond of a certain mystification, with apparent paradoxes.[1]

It is the *Madhyāntavibhaṅga* (or *-vibhāga*), 'Discrimination of the Mean and the Extremes', which is the most fundamental

1. The difficulties of interpretation may lend support to those who believe this work is not by Asaṅga but by some earlier writer.

philosophical work of Asaṅga and clarifies his position among the schools of Buddhism. Here he gives his own conception of what is meant by avoiding the extremes 'it is' (or 'exists' — *asti*) and 'it is not' : all Buddhists were agreed that these were to be avoided but they disagreed as to precisely which the extremes were : Nāgārjuna gave a different interpretation from the early schools and even among these the Sarvāstivāda differed from the others. Asaṅga now asserts that these earlier Buddhist interpretations are incorrect, so much so that the Madhyamaka doctrine on the one hand and that of the early schools (especially the Sarvāstivāda) on the other are actually themselves the two extreme opinions which the Buddha intended to avoid. He opens with the categorical statement that the imaginer of the unreal (*abhūtaparikalpa*) exists (*asti*). Vasubandhu in his commentary points out that this contradicts the opinion that all principles have no own-nature in the sense of being completely non-existent: here the imaginer at any rate is understood to exist with its own-nature. It also contradicts the opposite opinion that various principles exist, by referring to these as 'unreal'. Asaṅga continues that no duality occurs (*vidyate*, again probably meaning the same as 'exists') in it, but 'emptiness' does occur (exist), whilst the imaginer occurs (exists) in emptiness. The imaginer is consciousness (*vijñāna*). Emptiness is synonymous with thusness, the 'point (limit) of existence' (*bhūtakoṭi*), the signless, ultimate reality, the element of principles. Emptiness can, however, be defiled (not in reality but by the imaginer). If it were not defiled all beings would have been freed (already); if it were pure, exercise (to attain freedom) would be futile.

The *Dharmadharmatāvibhaṅga* (or *-vibhāga*) supplements this philosophical discussion as an account of the 'Discrimination of Principles (*dharma*) and Nature (*dharmatā*)'. 'Nature' here is the ultimate reality, the unsynthesised, extinction. 'Principles' are the synthesised, transmigration, illusion (*bhrānti*). Every principle (here the 'dependent') is on the one hand a mere dependent principle and on the other (when viewed with true understanding, ultimately) it is 'nature', which is thusness. These are the two 'characteristics' of principles of the *Sandhinirmocana*; the third, being 'imaginary', is totally unreal and is not considered here. The correct view of principles thus leads to the knowledge of extinction.

The home consciousness receives full treatment in the *Mahāyānasaṃgraha*, 'Compendium of the Mahāyāna'. It has to be assumed, according to Asaṅga, as a morally indeterminate 'home' containing all the 'seeds' (*bīja*) of future events, despite their contrary characters. Also it is the resort (*āśraya*) of the knowable (*jñeya*), i.e. the basis of the possibility of being conscious. It is also called the 'attachment consciousness' because of its attachment to the senses. The home consciousness is the cause of defilement, receiving the traces and retaining the seeds of this. The seeds are neither identical with nor different from the home consciousness: it is furnished with them but they are not separate from it. They enable it to imagine principles. There is reciprocal conditionality between it and them. The home consciousness is the same as 'consciousness' in general and as 'thought'. 'Mind' (*manas*) on the other hand is distinct (contrary to Sthaviravāda and Sarvāstivāda theory and perhaps to all schools of early Buddhism), being the consciousness of each of the six senses. This is 'starting' (*pravṛtti*, i.e. active). Here again there is reciprocal conditionality between this 'active' consciousness and the home consciousness. There are further descriptions of the seeds, which are momentary but form a continuous series, are morally good or bad, dependent on a complex of conditions and productive of their individual specific results. Actions (moral) leave enduring traces in the home consciousness, which eventually produce their results, though in themselves, as traces, they are morally indeterminate. In another chapter the *Mahāyānasaṃgraha* deals with the 'substance of the doctrine' (*dharmakāya*), i.e. the ultimate reality. The 'clan' (*gotra*) is there described as the seed of this in a living being.

The *Yogācārabhūmiśāstra* is several times longer than all these other works combined. In part it appears as an expansion and reworking of the *Abhidharmasamuccaya*, arranged within the framework of the stages ('floors') of the way of the *bodhisattva*, which, however, is set out in conjunction with the inferior 'floors' of the ways of the pupils and isolated *buddhas* and of Buddhist theory (*abhidharma*) in general (with special reference to the functioning of consciousness and of course modified according to the new doctrines of home consciousness, etc.). The work opens with an account of the consciousnesses of the senses ('first floor'), goes on (at greater length) with the mind ('second floor') and then the processes of meditation, leading up to the way(s). The opening 'floors' constitute a substantial work of *abhidharma* overlapping the scope of the ancient *Tripiṭaka* and the latest Mahāyāna *sūtras*. Asaṅga shows particular interest in the various (wrong) opinions of numerous schools of philosophy, on which he follows basically the *Brahmajāla Sūtra* (see above 141 ff.) but makes various additions to this, bringing it up to date, and in logic and debating. Revising his doctrine of the proof in the *Abhidharmasamuccaya* (if we are right in assuming that to be the earlier work, an assumption for which this logical doctrine is our main evidence) he here gives a proof in eight steps : (1) statement, (2) middle term, (3) example (*udāharaṇa*), (4) agreement (*sārūpya* of examples), (5) difference (*vairūpya*), (6) sensation, (7) inference, (8) reliable authority (*āptāgama*).[1] In this scheme he rather unobtrusively carries out a revolution in the doctrine of proof: he has discarded the old steps four and five, the application and conclusion, evidently as redundant against steps one and two (the conclusion is the original statement; the application is nothing but assigning the middle term to the minor term or subject). Whether Asaṅga himself was the innovator who first did this is not certain: we find that a Vasubandhu (possibly the Vasubandhu who was Asaṅga's brother) in writing on logic makes the same innovation and in fact reduces the proof to three steps only. Possibly the two brothers worked together on logic, with Vasubandhu (as we shall see) going furthest in this field. In place of these redundant steps Asaṅga proposes checking the examples systematically, implying an empirical enquiry, or at least studying the results of empirical enquiries, into the evidence for the relation between the middle term and the major (M and P) by the two inductive methods of agreement and difference.

Coming to the three means of knowledge which he accepts, Asaṅga defines sensation as that which is direct (*aviparokṣa*), not judged (reasoned) or to be judged (*anabhyūhitānabhyūhya*) and without error (without illusion). Inference is knowledge

1. *Śrutamayībhūmi*, p. 356 of T 1579. Sanskrit MS in Patna.

of an object through imagining. It depends on various relations: characteristic, own-nature, action, predicate (*dharmatas*), causation (*hetuphalatas*).[1]

Everything we have noted so far is included in the first of the five books of the *Yogācārabhūmiśāstra*. The remaining four books constitute commentaries of several kinds on this basic one.

The Theory of Knowledge

How do we know anything as true or valid? Why should we accept some statements or doctrines and reject others? What constitutes proof, whether in private study or in a public debate? We have seen that Buddhist philosophers were from time to time—perhaps all the time—concerned with these fundamental questions on which all knowledge and all philosophy must be based. The Buddha himself, as we found in Chapter Five (particularly pp. 132 ff., cf. also Chapter Four, p. 102), derived his knowledge from experience and the investigation of the empirical evidence thus acquired; he had no use for authority and recommended his followers to proceed as he had done, relying on first hand experience and not accepting things merely because even he himself taught them. He allowed that his doctrine should serve as a guide, and no doubt believed it would stand any amount of empirical checking by his followers (that it was 'verifiable'), but this was evidently to provide a short cut to help others (instead of leaving them to learn the 'hard' way by trial and error) and did not affect the fact that each must ascertain the truth for himself individually if he was really to attain enlightenment.

Subsequently the Buddha's followers found themselves in an apparent dilemma: they were to rely ultimately on experience, yet they attributed complete authority to the statements of the Buddha as handed down to them in the *Tripiṭaka*. They had at least two alternative means of knowledge, experience (i.e. sensation) and whatever they might deduce from it and authority (of a reliable person, i.e. the Buddha). Of course there ought to be no possible discrepancy between these two: the Buddha's words proceeded from experience and the laws of nature (he held) do not change, therefore anyone else's experience must

1. Ibid. pp. 357-8. Sanskrit MS in Patna.

lead to the same conclusions. In practice, however, there were certain difficulties. It was agreed that learning the truth from experience was no easy matter—the Buddha himself pointed out that some philosophers had jumped to wrong conclusions on the basis of incomplete investigations—and as time went by the Buddhists became less and less confident of the ability of any but very exceptional persons (i.e. the rare *buddhas*) to make important discoveries independently. This was hardly the view of the Buddha himself, since he speaks quite freely of '*śramaṇas* or brahmans' discovering, for example, the conditions of origination of principles (not of *buddhas* only). Nevertheless it led gradually to the Doctrine of the Buddha (his recorded statements) becoming not merely a guide and the basis for the study of life and experience but rather the almost exclusive subject of study itself. At the same time it was found after the lapse of some centuries that there were possibilities of varying interpretations of the Buddha's statements. It was this latter fact and the schisms it led to among the Buddhists which produced the formal logic of the schools (see pp. 299ff. above) and the *abhidharma* as restatements of the doctrine in strictly formalised language, where every term is defined. These studies established certain techniques of deduction: what propositions were consistent with the accepted statements of the Buddha? All this scholasticism produced reactions at times in favour of going back to the original *sūtras* and making a deeper study of their meaning, and no doubt appealing also to experience and independent study (how otherwise could new *sūtras* have been composed and eventually accepted by some as statements of the Buddha?). The main results of it were a science of logic and debating and (by reaction) the critique of the Madhyamakas (Nāgārjuna).

This science developed in spite of the Madhyamaka critique and gradually became more rigorous. Inevitably the means of knowledge came to be studied as a prerequisite for debating and investigations, since what constitutes acceptable evidence would be a matter of controversy between the schools, especially between Buddhists and non-Buddhists. We have noted these developments in the last Chapter and in the work of Asaṅga. Vasubandhu, it was observed, went further in this particular study.

Vasubandhu (or rather several Vasubandhus) has been the subject of much controversy among modern scholars, concerning the number and chronology of the philosophers of that name. It is agreed that one of them was Asaṅga's brother, but then we have the problem, not yet solved, of which of 'Vasubandhu's' works were written by this one. We can rely only on probabilities. Since (it is agreed) Asaṅga 'converted' his brother to his own views, those works which show a close correspondence of doctrine to Asaṅga's may well be his brother's contributions to the founding of the school (this is not of course conclusive, it is adopted here as a working hypothesis merely). Tradition records affirmatively that the commentary on the *Madhyāntavibhaṅga* is by Asaṅga's brother and it would seem likely that the other commentaries on works of Asaṅga are by this Vasubandhu. There seems to be hardly anything in them which goes outside Asaṅga's doctrine. Two other works like-likewise bring practically nothing new : the *Triṃśikākārikāprakaraṇa* and the *Viṃśikākārikāprakaraṇa*. The first, the 'Treatise of Thirty Verses', is a brief summary of Asaṅga's doctrine which became very popular in the school as a textbook. Its main argument is that the allegedly real 'soul' (*ātman*) or 'principles' (*dharmas*) of other schools of philosophy are nothing but the changes (*pariṇāma*) of consciousness. The 'perfected' and the 'dependent' are neither different nor not different, one cannot be perceived without the other. This ultimate reality is thusness and the fact of (there being) only makings of consciousness (*vijñaptimātratā*). The second, the 'Treatise of Twenty Verses', is a piece of polemic against the views of other schools (fortunately Vasubandhu added a prose commentary to explain the concise verses). He begins by rejecting the doctrine that thought, mind and consciousness are identical and goes on to argue that the makings of consciousness are possible even though there are no real objects for them to derive from, just as in dreams objects are seen without deriving from realities. Although there is nothing but the makings of consciousness the different streams of consciousness do affect one another—one person can influence another.

'Vasubandhu' is known to have written three works on logic, of which unfortunately nothing survives but fragments of two of them, which happen to be quoted by later writers. That these were written by the brother of Asaṅga[1] is made possible by their agreement in reducing the old five steps of proof to three. One might note the logically formulated polemic of the 'Thirty' as evidence of its author's interest in logic. Of one of the three works nothing is known but a bare reference. The others were entitled *Vādavidhāna* and *Vādavidhi*, indicating (as did that of the first also) that the subject was the debate (*vāda*). They were arranged in two sections: proof (*sādhana*) and refutation (*dūṣaṇa*). The means of knowledge were treated under 'proof'. Reducing the proof to three steps, Vasubandhu says that the last two steps of the old proof were redundant (and the first three wrongly defined, so that he must redefine them). On the whole, however, he follows the *Tarkaśāstra* (e.g. the 'canon' of the middle term, the sophistical refutations), with some exclusion of what seemed to him superflous and some clarifications.[2]

There is however one other major innovation in the *Vādavidhi*, though we do not know the position of the *Tarkaśāstra* on this point since it belongs to the missing part of that text. Vasubandhu accepts only two means of knowledge: sensation (*pratyakṣa*) and inference (*anumāna*). Introducing the subject he says that proof is used for instructing or convincing another person; for instructing oneself the means of knowledge are to be used. Thus the latter topic becomes independent of proof and gains in importance. His definitions are: sensation is consciousness (*vijñāna*) on account of an object (*artha*). He clarifies this as that it must arise from the object only and that it must exclude consciousness depending on imagining and on the conventions of language (therefore a sensation cannot include the name of the object, it is a pure sensation). Inference is the cognition (*darśana*) of a necessarily related (*nāntariyaka*) object for someone who knows this (necessary relation). It is explained that an object which does not occur without a certain other object is necessarily related to it, for example smoke is related to fire. Through the relation one can conclude

1. The main alternative is the author of *AK Bhāṣya*. See below.

2. Vasubandhu's logic has been resuscitated by Frauwallner: WZKM Vol. 40, 1933, 281ff. However, the *Vādavidhi* and *Vādavidhāna* may be by different authors, for Diṅnāga criticizes the former, as not by his teacher, but accepts the latter. The *Vādavidhi* may thus be by Asaṅga's brother.

to the presence of an object not actually perceived, by perceiving its characteristic (the middle term)—if one knows the relation. Vasubandhu's reasons for rejecting the third means of knowledge, reliable authority, do not seem to have been preserved. He probably held, as some others did, that it was not an independent, distinct means but, if true, merely the record of some person's sensations in the past and of his inferences. Thus it was no more than these two and added nothing to what was learned from these.

As to the steps of proof, the statement is the expression of what is to be proved (*sādhya*), the middle term is the expression of a predicate (*dharma*: in logic this term is used for qualities or predicates, contrasting with *dharmin*, 'subject', and not in its usual Buddhist sense) universally concomitant (*avinābhāvin*) with what is like that (*tādṛś*; i.e. like what is to be proved, namely the major term, the predicate of the statement, 'P'), the example (*dṛṣṭānta*) is the evidence (*nidarśana*) of the relation (*sambandha*) between these two (i.e. of the universal concomitance, *avinābhāva*, between the middle and major terms, whatever is M is also P and whatever is not M is not P).

Sautrāntika Epistemology : Vasubandhu II and Diṅnāga

A Vasubandhu of the Sautrāntika school, generally dated in the 5th century, wrote a critique of the Sarvāstivāda (Vaibhāṣika) *Abhidharma* in the form of a commentary (*Bhāṣya*) on the *Abhidharmakośa* (it is not clear whether the *kārikās* of the *Kośa* itself are also his or were compiled by an earlier writer). For the date we may tentatively follow Frauwallner (*On the Date... of Vasubandhu*), who distinguishes this Vasubandhu (II) from the brother of Asaṅga (who certainly lived no later than about the middle of the 4th century, see p. 436 above), divides the life of 'Vasubandhu' according to Paramārtha into two lives and deduces from it that Vasubandhu II lived in Ayodhyā and was at 'the climax of his fame' (p. 32) during the reign of the Gupta emperor Skanda Vikramāditya (A.D. 455-67).

By definition the Sautrāntikas reject the *Abhidharma* (of the Sarvāstivāda from which they seceded, see pp. 345, 421 above) and regard only the *Sūtra* as authoritative for the doctrine of the Buddha. Yet evidently they found it necessary to do more than just ignore the *Abhidharma* discussions : they must define their own position on the controversial questions. To this end, Vasubandhu II reviewed the entire system of the *Abhidharma*, including the 'Great Commentary', and criticised it by quoting the *Sūtra*. The subject is presented from the standpoint of the 'discrimination of principles' factor of enlightenment (see pp. 97-9 above) and the definition is accepted that a principle is that which has (maintains) its own-characteristic (*svalakṣaṇa*, cf. p. 323 above) (p. 2). The first chapter being set out under the heading of the eighteen elements (p. 306 above) deals particularly with problems of sensation, perception and the processes of consciousness, all of which bear directly on epistemology, distinguishing for example the sense-object or datum (*viṣaya*), as (instrumental) cause (*kāritra*, cf. p. 343 above), from the support (*ālambana*) perceived by thoughts and by mental principles (p. 19). In discussing whether the characteristics such as impermanence are really principles (*dharmas*), Vasubandhu rejects the suggestion by saying there is no means of knowledge (*pramāṇa*) to establish it, specifying sensation, inference and reliable tradition as the three means (p. 76). He accepts the four conditions (p. 224 above) and finds a *sūtra* (probably apocryphal) to support their enumeration (p. 98).

The same Sautrāntika Vasubandhu seems to be the author of a treatise on (moral) action, the *Karmasiddhiprakaraṇa*, of a critique of the Brahmanical Sāṃkhya system, the *Paramārtha-saptatikā*, and of the *Vyākhyāyukti* on interpretation and teaching.

Diṅnāga (also written Dignāga) according to Buddhist tradition was a pupil of a Vasubandhu. Since he wrote a commentary on the *Abhidharmakośa Bhāṣya*, the *Marmapradīpavṛtti* (extant in Tibetan), it appears he was in fact a pupil of the Sautrāntika teacher. He also wrote a commentary on the *Vādavidhāna* (both text and commentary appear to be lost), implying that the Sautrāntika Vasubandhu was the author of that work on logic and epistemology. In his *Pramāṇasamuccaya*, moreover, Diṅnāga quotes the *Abhidharmakośa Bhāṣya* as an authoritative work and shows that his own doctrines are consistent with it. The statements of Vācaspatimiśra and others that Diṅnāga was a Sautrāntika thus seem correct (on this question the Thesis of the author's student Dr. A. Singh Moriya, 1978, on the philosophical standpoint of Dharmakīrti, deals exhaustively with the evidence and concludes that both Diṅnāga and Dharmakīrti were Sautrāntikas).

Diṅnāga was born in the Pallava country at a place called Siṃhavaktra, near Kāñcī, the capital (according to Tāranātha). Becoming a Buddhist monk, he joined a community who turned out to be of the Vātsīputrīya school. He was puzzled by their doctrine of a 'person' which was neither the same as the groups nor different from them (pp. 241-2 above), not being able to discover any such person. Accordingly he left them and in due course met Vasubandhu and studied with him (in Ayodhyā or before Vasubandhu settled in Ayodhyā?). Diṅnāga lived mostly in Kaliṅga (modern Orissa) in an excavated rock dwelling, but visited Nālandā, by this period the main centre of Buddhist learning and a great university (cf. pp. 353, 374 above). There he found students and established his new doctrines of the theory of knowledge, leaving a tradition of teachers to perpetuate it. Eventually he returned to Kaliṅga, where he is said to have written his final, definitive work, the *Pramāṇasamuccaya*. He afterwards toured again, especially in the South, but ended his days in Kaliṅga, in a remote forest dwelling.

Apparently through studying the Sautrāntika critique of *Abhidharma*, Diṅnāga developed the epistemological ideas of Vasubandhu II into a general critique of knowledge. We cannot make any assured progress in philosophy, or, therefore, in the practice of Buddhism which is founded on knowledge of the truth, unless we first ascertain what sources of knowledge can be accepted. The theory of knowledge therefore becomes the basis of all study and of all practice; it replaces the old *Abhidharma* enquiries, going to the root of all philosophical problems. Even the *sūtras* cannot be accepted without question, as the Buddha himself had indicated (see p. 133 above and A I 189, II 191, T 26 No. 16, *Outline of Indian Philosophy* p. 49). Therefore the means of knowledge (*pramāṇas*) must first be studied, in the light of which claims to truth may be examined. Starting from Vasubandhu's *Vādavidhāna*, therefore, Diṅnāga later reworked his theory in a more consistent manner as basically a theory of knowledge, not primarily of logic or debating. The Buddha himself is assimilated to this conception as simply being the means of knowledge themselves (not as conferring any additional truth on them, not as an additional means). This revolutionary theory was elaborated by later Sautrāntikas such as Dharmakīrti and Dharmottara, but the impression made by it was so great that Buddhists of other schools also took it up and tried to assimilate it to their own doctrines. Sthaviravādins in South India, Ceylon and Burma studied the works of Diṅnāga, Dharmakīrti and others and incorporated a version of the means of knowledge and of what is known into their sub-commentaries on the *Tripiṭaka*. Mahāyānists of both the Madhyamaka and Yogācāra traditions and of the later syncretistic schools wrote commentaries on Dharmakīrti, endeavouring to interpret him consistently with their special doctrines. The non-Buddhist Jainas, Vaiśeṣikas and Śaivas also borrowed wholesale from Diṅnāga and Dharmakīrti.

At least fourteen philosophical works are believed to have been written by Diṅnāga, besides which he seems to be the author of some hymns in praise of the Buddha and of a commentary on some hymns by a fellow student. It is remarkable that not one of these works seems now to be available in the original Sanskrit, so thorough were the Turks in their holocaust of Indian libraries. Six of the philosophical works are available in Tibetan translations, one of these in Chinese also, and three further philosophical works in Chinese translations. Fortunately about thirty later Buddhist works on Diṅnāga's doctrines are extant in Sanskrit (mostly preserved in Tibet), which include numerous quotations from Diṅnāga's works. About forty-five more such works are preserved in Tibetan translations, showing the sustained study of epistemological problems in the Buddhist schools over a period of seven or eight centuries in India, before the great Buddhist universities there were destroyed under the Turkish terror. In Tibet the study was pursued under the auspices of the syncretistic Madhyamaka of Haribhadra down to modern times. The Tibetan *Tripiṭaka* attributes some further, probably apocryphal, works to Diṅnāga, as usually happens with famous teachers (e.g. Nāgārjuna). Two of these are extant in Sanskrit (one with a Chinese translation also). Of these, the very short *Yogāvatāra* on ultimate reality, thusness or the 'perfected' according to the Yogācāra, seems in fact to be by one Dharmendra, named in the Sanskrit colophon of one version, the *Yogāvatāropadeśa*. The *Prajñāpāramitāpiṇḍārthasaṃgraha* is a set of *kārikās* summarising the contents of the Perfection of Understanding according to the Yogācāra standpoint but accepted as authoritative by the syncretistic Madhyamaka philosopher Haribhadra (end of the 8th century), who moreover calls its author 'Diṅnāga'. Haribhadra follows the epistemology of Dharmakīrti, but these *kārikās* have nothing to do with the theory of knowledge or anything else in Diṅnāga's works and seem to be apocryphal or by another author of the same name. Through the work of Kitagawa and Hattori especially, a large number of Sanskrit quotations from Diṅnāga's most important work, the *Pramāṇasamuccaya*, have been replaced in their proper places according to the Tibetan translations, so that we can now study the most essential parts of it in his own words.

Diṅnāga's brief commentary *Marmapradīpa Vṛtti* on the essentials of the *Abhidharmakośa Bhāṣya* is available in Tibetan, but his commentary on his teacher's *Vādavidhāna* seems to be lost. Other lost works known from references include critiques on the three Brahmanical schools, Sāṃkhya, Vaiśeṣika and Nyāya. The very brief *Sāmānyaparīkṣā*, criticising the 'universal' of the Vaiśeṣika doctrine, supposedly a 'reality', is available in Chinese.

The 'Critique of the Three Times' (*Traikālyaparīkṣā*), extant in Tibetan, is a curious piece of polemic against Brahmanism, specifically against the doctrine of the absolute *brahman* as interpreted by the grammarian Bhartṛhari. In his great work on general linguistics, *Vākyapadīya*, Bhartṛhari relates the concept of time to the *brahman*, which for him is the absolute 'speech' (*śabda*), the ultimate reality out of which everything in the universe has evolved. Time is one of the powers causing the appearance of all the 'features' of the universe out of the speech-*brahman*. Diṅnāga took a passage of about 35 verses from the *Vākyapadīya* (III, *Prakīrṇaka*, *Sambandhasamuddeśa* 53ff., etc.) and by altering only about two words converted it into a proof of the unreality of time, as something purely imaginary. Bhartṛhari's discussion here is on the relation of speech to objects and Diṅnāga repeats from it that understanding produced by speech is as if imposed on reality as a condition produced from objects (*arthas*) (53), which is similar to his view in the *Pramāṇasamuccaya* that words do not refer to real objects.

In the same way, such ideas as existence and non-existence are imagined. The idea of a sequence in time is based on those of past and future non-existence and thus is also imaginary (Bhartṛhari had intended here that on the basis of time, which is a real power, existence and non-existence are only imagined). This critique by Diṅnāga resembles those of Nāgārjuna that our concepts do not apply to the real world, or the general Buddhist critique that everyday concepts do not refer to the ultimately real principles.

The 'Trunk and Tail Treatise' (*Hastavālaprakaraṇa*), extant in Chinese and Tibetan translations, considers the nature of the objects supposed to exist in everyday discourse. According to Diṅnāga they are only concepts. What we suppose we perceive is always analysable into something else or into smaller parts. As to the theories of 'atoms' as ultimate, indivisible, real particles, we cannot perceive these, moreover they are inconceivable, because however small they are supposed to be they must still be imagined as having parts, for example an atom must have an East side and a West side. Therefore the universe of everyday discourse is nothing but concepts; he who seeks freedom must know ultimate reality. The curious title of this work is no doubt an illustration: the parts of an elephant (cf. the *Udāna* story, 68-9, of the blind men and the elephant).

The 'Treatise on Concepts Based On' (**Upādāyaprajñapti-prakaraṇa*), extant only in Chinese, distinguishes three kinds of concepts: (1) wholes (in space), (2) series (*santāna*, in time) and (3) situations (*avasthā*, in both). These cannot be said to be the same as or different from their parts. Only real principles (*dharmas*) are the same as or different from one another. The concepts are only makings of consciousness based on the principles, which alone are real.

The 'Critique of the Support' (*Ālambanaparīkṣā*) is extant in Chinese and Tibetan and two or three quotations from it in Sanskrit. Though atoms cause a making of consciousness (*vijñapti*) through a sense-faculty, they are not the datum (sense-object, *viṣaya*) of it, because they do not have the same appearance as it, as for example in the case of the sense of sight (producing consciousness of sight) (1). A whole (aggregate of atoms) also is not the datum, because it is not real (cf. the Treatise on Concepts Based On) and is not (as a whole) the cause. Thus neither the atoms nor the whole is perceived. Nor do we perceive the combination of atoms and a whole, because every object is manifold and we thus perceive only a part of it. If atoms were the data, a jar and a dish would look alike, because their atoms are alike. The shapes are only in the appearance of the objects (*artha*), not in the atoms. When the atoms are removed the consciousness may remain, although there is no object present : The object (*artha*) is a visible datum (*rūpa*) to be known internally, which appears as if external, because it is a visible datum in consciousness and because it is a condition (*pratyaya*, the support, *ālambana*, condition, *Vṛtti*) for this (6). The support condition, which is always internal, appears with consciousness in invariable concomitance and there is the duality that consciousness both appears as if it were the external object (being the support, as condition) and is produced by it. The datum and the sense-faculty function as reciprocal conditions and consciousness occurs depending on them. (What this datum is, is clarified in Diṅnāga's discussion on sensation as a means of knowledge in other works.)

Diṅnāga's main contribution to philosophy is found in three extant works on logic and epistemology. The first of these is the short but momentous 'Drum of the Wheel of Middle Terms' (*Hetucakraḍamaru*), available only in Tibetan. This is a basic contribution to the doctrine of proof: a table (the 'wheel') showing how middle terms in proofs can be either valid or invalid. It makes clear the implications of the 'canon' of rules for the middle term and exposes the true nature of sophistical refutations. The text is accompanied by a diagram (the table) to illustrate the concomitance between the middle and major terms as indicated by examples of the two kinds—by agreement and by difference. In three horizontal columns we have the middle term (1) present in the agreeing examples, (2) absent from the agreeing examples, (3) present in some, but not other, agreeing examples. Three vertical columns intersecting with these are for the middle term (1) present in the different examples, (2) absent from the different examples, (3) present in some, but not other, different examples. This covers all possible cases, and it is clear that of the nine possibilities, for which Diṅnāga inserts concrete illustrations, i.e. present in the agreeing and in the different examples, and so on, only two show the middle term valid: those at the top and bottom of the central vertical column. Those middle terms in the middle of the first and third vertical columns are wholly contradictory. Those at the four corners are uncertain, as they overlap into both kinds of example; that in the centre is also uncertain, since it is not present in any example at all, of either kind. The minor term is assumed constant throughout, the middle and major terms are varied in order to fit the various possibilities. The nine cases are of course equivalent to nine proofs, two of them valid and seven fallacious. A little study with this table (for which we have no space here) will show that the sophistical refutations are mostly attempts to overthrow a valid proof of the type shown at the bottom of the central column: in such a proof any example of M is also an example of P (these are the 'some agreeing' examples) and any example of not P is also an example of not M (these are the different examples), but there are, besides these, examples of P which are not M (these are the 'other' agreeing examples—they 'agree' with P). The proof is valid because whatever is M is P. It is not necessary that whatever is P should be M, so the last kind of example is irrelevant to the argument, though it may be used sophistically to baffle one in debate. The fallacies (uncertain middle terms) at the bottoms of the other two columns are also not always obvious and similarly repay study.

The 'Introduction to Logic' (*Nyāyamukha*), extant in Chinese, which appears to have been written after this work of clarification of the proof, is a comprehensive manual like the *Tarkaśāstra* or the *Vādavidhi*. It follows the same arrangement as these, two sections, one on proof and one on refutation. The means of knowledge are discussed at the end of the section on proof. The content, however, differs from the *Vādavidhi* on almost every detail, with improved definitions and of course the use of the 'wheel'. The proof has three steps, as in the *Vādavidhi* but rearranged: (1) middle term, (2) example, (3) 'thesis' (*pakṣa*, replacing the 'statement' but equivalent to it). There are as in the *Vādavidhi* two means of knowledge, sensation and inference, 'reliable authority' or 'reliable speech' and 'similarity' being held to be included in inference (where true). Diṅnāga's definitions of the two means he accepts are new and show the starting point of his new theory of knowledge.

Sensation is knowledge without imagining. This is explained here as the knowledge (*jñāna*) without imagining (*avikalpaka*), not through the metaphors (*upacāra*, more strictly 'transfer') of dividing (*bheda*) by classification (*viśeṣaṇa*, distinguishing or distinction) or words (*abhidhāyaka*, wording, naming), which happens in each of the senses with reference to objects (*artha*): visible object (*rūpa*), etc.

Inference is knowledge through a middle term. It cognises a subject as belonging to a class, to the class of things having that particular characteristic (the middle term). The subject will belong to other classes also if other characteristics are selected. Whereas inference cognises only characteristics of classes, sensation cognises only the 'characteristic' of the object itself, of the object in itself, not classified (which presupposes imagining). Classes are imagined by the intellect, they do not exist objectively.

Diṅnāga says here that there is nothing else knowable except these two—objects in themselves and classes. Each of the two has its own separate means of being known and these two means of knowledge are thus completely distinct, they cognise two entirely different things. Sensation relates to objective reality but stops short at it because it cannot classify or even name its objects, which would necessitate 'imagining'. Real objects remain unclassifiable particulars. Inference is restricted to imagining (words and classifications) and deals in classes having no objective reality, it cannot reach real objects.

Here we can leave the Introduction to Logic, since Diṅnāga develops these doctrines further in his last great work, which was the definitive statement of his views. In between he is believed to have produced the **Hetumukha*, now lost, in which he studied the problem of meaning, to which he was led by his enquiry into the means of knowledge. What is the relation between words and objects? Having rejected the theories of other schools, that classes existed in objective reality, and the assumption that our concepts, or words, relate directly to real external objects, he requires a new theory of meaning.

Although words do not relate directly to external reality,

Diṅnāga came to admit an indirect relation. Words, which imply classifications, make dichotomies in the totality of knowledge: though they do not relate directly to objects it may be allowed that (at most) they exclude a part of the totality, negate part of it. The meaning of a word, the relation between the word and objects, therefore, may be defined as 'the exclusion of what is other' (*anyāpoha*). Here, by negation, or 'dialectically', it may be possible to bridge the gap, which had appeared absolute, between the two universes of our experience, the real universe of sensation and the unreal universe of our imagining.

In the final work, in which, as Diṅnāga says, he collects and summarises the ideas scattered in earlier writings, the whole theory is presented under the title 'Compendium of the Theory of Knowledge' (*Pramāṇasamuccaya*). Apart from quotations it is now available only in two Tibetan translations. Instead of logic or proof or debating it is now the more fundamental theory of knowledge which is the real subject of investigation, and proof merely an incidental part of the doctrine of inference.

The work opens with a salutation to the Buddha as the personification of the means of knowledge, desiring the welfare of the universe, the teacher who has succeeded in becoming 'well-gone' himself and who saves others. In explaining this, however, Diṅnāga says that the acquisition of what is knowable depends on the means of knowledge. Therefore he must refute the many erroneous views on this subject and demonstrate the true means. In fact it is sensation and inference which alone are to be relied on, the Buddha being—if this salutation is more than poetry—the illustration of these two and his authority, along with the authority of the tradition of what he said, deriving from them.

Diṅnāga then proceeds to the question of the discovery of what is to be known, which depends on what the means of knowledge are. There are only two means (I.2), because of the two characteristics (*lakṣaṇas*), 'own' (particular) and 'universal', of what is to be known and because there is nothing else to be known except these two. The own-characteristic (*svalakṣaṇa*) is known by sensation. The universal-characteristic (*sāmānyalakṣaṇa*) is known by inference. Moreover no third means of knowledge is needed to connect these, nor for recognition or memory, for any attempt at connecting anything is simply inference. To suppose further means to know what is known (in recognition) would lead to an infinite regress. Also the means would become innumerable if special means were defined for every special kind of knowledge.

Sensation is excluding imagining (*kalpanāpoḍha*) (I.3), imagining being here defined as uniting something with a name (word), a class, a quality (*guṇa*), an action or a 'substance' (*dravya*). Here the further category of 'relation' is rejected, there being just distinguishing by the five kinds of predicate mentioned. Where there is any imagining, that is not sensation. Sensation is described according to the senses (*akṣas>pratyakṣa*) (I.4), not to the data (*viṣayas*, sense-objects), since the latter might be common to more than one sense, to both a sense and consciousness and to different 'streams' of consciousness ('persons'). Here the *Abhidharma* (Sarvâstivāda *Vijñānakāya*, T 1539 p. 559b) is quoted for the explanation that in sensation and in consciousness of sensation one is conscious of for example blue, but not of: "It is blue". In the object (*artha*) one has perception (*saṃjñā*) of the object, but in the object one does not have perception of a 'predicate' (*dharma*, here presumably in its logical sense, see p.447 above, but even if it meant 'principle' the same would be true, for to bring it under a principle would be to name it, etc., which is 'imagining'; 'blue' in any case is not a principle, only 'visible object' is).

Apparently referring to Vasubandhu's *Abhidharmakośabhāṣya*, p. 34, that the 'five bodies of consciousness' (of the five senses) 'have an accumulation (*sañcita*) as their support' (individual atoms being invisible), apparently implying something imagined, namely many as one, Diṅnāga explains that there is the range (*gocara*) of the universal here because it is produced by many objects (*arthas*) even with reference to its own-object. But it is the range of the universal only because it is produced by many 'substances' (*dravyas*, many atoms) through the particular sense (own-sense), not because of imagining no difference between different things (there is only one object sensed and imagining is not coming in to compare different objects and say they are the same). In this connection *Abhidharmakośabhāṣya* p. 7 is quoted: "These (five bodies of consciousness) have own-characteristic data according to the own-characteristic of a sense-sphere, not according to the own-characteristic of a substance". (This implies as stated above that what is sensed, and is thus projected into consciousness, is not a plurality of substances, atoms, but a simple datum, an 'own-characteristic' without imagining.)

A 'faculty' (sense organ) does not have comprehensive access to the many aspects (*rūpas*) of a subject (*dharmin*, here the logical term is used, meaning that which possesses predicates: in sensation there is no such subject, which is given only by imagining, by trying to put together several aspects as belonging to a 'subject'). The range of a faculty is an aspect to be experienced on its own and indescribable (*anirdeśya*, because it is without imagining, without words) (I.5).

Besides sensation of the 'five senses' there is mental (*mānasa*) sensation (of the mind, *manas*, as sixth sense), which is 'own-experience' (*svasaṃvitti*, 'own' here in the sense of 'internal') of an object (*artha*) such as desire, without imagining (I.6). Its 'support' (*ālambana*, mental object) is its datum (*viṣaya*, it has its own data unrelated to those of the 'five senses').

The experience of an object (*artha*) by a student (*yogin*, especially the Buddhist student in meditation), when it is not interfered with by the instruction of a teacher, is also sensation (I.6). (If the student is only reflecting on some instruction, it is imagining, not yet sensation in his own experience.)

In itself, imagining (*kalpanā*, as an object) may also be accepted (as a mental sensation, like desire), but not of course in relation to an object of imagining, because that would be the activity of imagining (*vikalpana*) (I.7). Imagining is not sensation when it refers to its object, just as desire is not (sensation, not itself an object when it refers to an object desired).

Illusion (such as a mirage), knowledge at the 'concealing' level of truth (imagined objects superimposed on reality), inference, that which is inferred and remembered desire (etc.) are obscure 'semblances' (*ābhas*) of sensation (false sensations) (I.7-8). (The reference to 'concealing' implies that sensation works at the ultimate level, knows ultimate realities, on which of course imagined objects are often superimposed, whereupon it is no longer pure sensation 'excluding imagining'.) The 'result' of the means of knowledge is the same as the means of knowledge itself, because it is a cognition (*pratīti*) possessing the 'act' (of knowing) (I.8, the act, *vyāpāra*, is not real, since it would imply an agent (person, etc.), whereas in reality there are only the principles). The 'result' simply bears an image of what is known and is understood as including the 'act' of knowing it. But this is only imposed on the means of knowledge, just as an effect has the form of its cause.

Finally, own (internal) experience is a variety of sensation and the 'result' may be considered to be a form of this (I.9). In fact knowledge occurs having two 'semblances' (or 'images', *ābhāsas*). There is the image of knowledge itself (as knowledge) and the image of the datum. (There are two images: knowledge of the datum and knowledge of the knowledge of the datum; the latter is 'own (internal) experience', cf. I.11-2.) The 'result' is then the own (internal) experiencing of this consciousness having both images. This is because the determining (as desirable, etc.) of an object (*artha*) also possesses the aspect (*rūpa*) of the object. When a knowledge with its object is known as object, there is also the corresponding own (internal) experiencing determining that it is desirable or undesirable. (The 'result' is the internal experience of the object as desirable, etc., but the object is simultaneously there just as the object, simply with its 'aspect'.)

When what is to be known is an external (*bāhya*) object (*artha*) only, the means of knowledge is simply there as the feature (*ākāra*, peculiarity) of the datum (I.9). (Presumably when there is no accompanying internal desire, etc.) In this case the own (internal) experience is only there being an image, through which the object is known. For the brighter the feature of the object, the stronger the cognition of the datum as 'aspect' of the object.

The 'image' is what is to be known and is both the means of knowledge and the 'result'. Therefore these three, the means (*grāhaka*, sense function), the feature to be known and the experience = result, are not separate from each other (I.10). This first chapter continues with critiques of the accounts of sensation given by the *Vādavidhi* and by the Nyāya and other schools.

There are two kinds of inference, for oneself and for another (according to Dharmottara, *Nyāyabinduṭīkā*, p. 42, Diṅnāga was the first to introduce this distinction). That for oneself is that which experiences an object (*artha*) through a middle term (or characteristic, *liṅga*) which has three aspects (II.1-2). (That for another is communicating such an inference to another; sensation cannot be so divided because it cannot be communicated.) The 'result' is as before (in the case of sensation, the same as the means of knowledge).

Inference cannot work on the objects of sensation (because it always generalises, universalises). It can refer to the instrumental cause (*kāraṇa*) as the 'seen', etc., but not to the own-characteristic of what is seen. When we say 'It is blue' we are using a universal name and what we express has a different aspect from the (particular) own-characteristic (II.3).

The sentence of a reliable person may be of the nature of inference if it has in common with it not being contradicted (*avisaṃvāda*) (II.5a-b). And if this is so it is because it was based on sensation (did not, therefore, refer to the metaphysical unseen substances of speculative philosophy).

The three aspects are: occurrence in that 'to be inferred' (*anumeya*, i.e. the subject, *dharmin*, which is to be distinguished by the predicate), also in what is like this (predicate), and non-occurrence in what is not (like this predicate) (II.5c-d). We need not observe all instances of what is like this, as long as we have some, because the non-occurrence of what is not like this in any instance whatsoever confirms the same. (We cannot in any case observe a whole class, which would be infinite in number, we have to proceed by the exclusion of what is other, which will be discussed in Chapter V.) Middle terms which fail to satisfy all three aspects are of no use (fallacious arguments are here illustrated). Through the invariability (*avyabhicāra*) of the middle term, which is seen elsewhere with the predicate, there will be implication (of the predicate) in the case of a subject established as connected with it (with the middle term) (II.11).

It is not the case that many predicates are known through one middle term. Those which follow the middle term are known, excluding others (II.13). We can know severally the characteristics of a lotus, first that it has a scent, then an agreeable scent, then a more specific scent not found in non-lotuses (II.14). Otherwise, if there were no exclusion (if inference were simply positive like sensation), either nothing would be known or everything would be known (II.15). (Inference consists in making dichotomies.) This knowledge is based on exclusion, not on the supposed universals (II.16). Only some of the predicates of the middle term are used for the purpose of that which is to be inferred, others are irrelevant (II.17).

Inference for others makes public to another (as in a debate) an object which one has experienced oneself (III.1). (This is not strictly inference but only communicating an inference, however:) we have called it so by transfer, naming the effect after its cause. Again it will be defective if we do not mention the three aspects. The statement of that which is to be inferred is not part of the proof, because it is in itself doubtful and is what has to be proved by the actual proof. If this thesis is already contradicted by an object of sensation, or by an inference, a reliable sentence or common usage we have a 'false thesis' which should be rejected.

The middle term as a predicate of what is to be proved (the subject, i.e. it is *pakṣadharma*) is of nine kinds as in the 'Drum of the Wheel of Middle Terms' (III.9). 'That which is to be proved' (*sādhya*), meaning a combination (of subject and predicate), by transfer and not in this primary sense may refer to a part, namely the subject only or the predicate only, as being 'that which is to be proved' (III.10). Because the debate is to be with a predicate (the middle term) established for both sides, it is unacceptable if for one or both it is contrary or not proved or not established as in the subject (III.11). Only a predicate of a subject can be a proof, and it proves another predicate. The 'wheel' is repeated as in the 'Drum' (III.21-2), but with one example changed. There are only two kinds of fallacious middle terms, the uncertain and the contradictory, again as in the 'Drum'. Refutation is simply pointing out that the opponent's middle term does not have the three aspects.

When a middle term is established as a predicate of the subject, its other two aspects are shown by the example (*dṛṣṭānta*, the 'major premise' step of the proof) (IV.1). The 'example' (major premise) is twofold as agreeing (*sādharmya*) and otherwise (different), being stated as the following of the middle term by the predicate to be proved (whatever is M is P) and, in the absence of the predicate to be proved, its (the middle term's) absence (whatever is not P is not M) (IV.2). The predicate to be proved is shown as present by an agreeing example or as absent by a different example (IV.3). Contraposition in the stating of the different example is essential, otherwise one could not show that the middle term occurs only in the agreeing examples and does not occur in what does not have the predicate to be proved. (Absurd consequences of breaking this rule are illustrated; IV.4, the concept of 'pervasion', *vyāpitva*, of a middle term by a predicate being used: i.e. the middle term need not pervade the predicate, but the predicate must pervade the middle term. This pervasion in fact excludes what is other, which leads us to the subject of the next chapter.) It is desirable to state both kinds of example to avoid uncertainty, although one may simply imply the other. There can be fallacious examples such as so-called agreeing examples where in fact the middle term is absent, or the predicate is absent, and so on.

The verbal (*śābda*) is not another means of knowledge, for it likewise is through inference, as in the case of 'artificiality', etc. (as middle terms), it expresses its own meaning through the exclusion of what is other (V.1). Speech refers to classes (*jātis*), not to particulars (*bhedas*, the members of a class), because these are innumerable and variable (*vyabhicāra*); nor is it an expression of a class plus its union (*yoga*) with the members, because the sound (*śruti*) is not many (*pṛthak*, thus capable of specifying the members separately) (V.2). What is true of classes is also true of 'substances', 'qualities', 'actions' and union with these. These predicates all imply 'existence' as the highest class.

Speech of existence (i.e. of classes, etc.) states that a 'substance' (such as a pot) is subordinate to the own-aspect (*svarūpa*, nature) of a class (such as artificial), not that it is observed (*sākṣāt*). There is no common location, there being no reference to members, because there is no indication (*ākṣepa*) of such a member as a pot included in it (in the class) (*Vṛtti* on V.4).

In expressing the whiteness of jasmine or of oyster shell (for example, speech applies simultaneously to a class and to what possesses it, *Vṛtti*)...(but) without the understanding there may be 'excess' (extending outside the natural class) when referring to a substance because of the 'conferring' (lending) of a quality (V.5). For example in the case of crystal taking the quality red from some nearby lacquer (there would be confusion and 'excess' if the understanding could not discriminate the imposed, unnatural colour).

A sound makes an exclusion of what is other (it does not positively refer to a class), for example referring to a place possessing 'non-white', that is not because of a class, because it is not a class, moreover there is uncertainty in indicating an object (V.11). Also from speech there is not a comprehensive access to what is expressed, which is manifold. It makes a meaning by demarcation, by conforming to its own-relation (simply in possessing that, V.9) (V.12). ... For that is not entirely blue, nor is it entirely a waterlily, because what is expressed is a combination (V.15). (Many words may be used for one object expressed, but they do not exhaust it, their access is not 'comprehensive'.)

A member (particular, part) is not abandoned by its own 'universal', because there is the expectation (in the meaning) of only that (universal). Nor is it received (accepted into the universal), because of the occurrence of doubt. And there is oneness of meaning of both (particular and universal) in respect of their similarity (V.26).

But a member excludes (*apohate*) the meaning of another member, because of there being contradiction (*virodha*) between them. (The members of a class exclude one another,) like the sons of a king in their different domains, or like the species of 'treeness' (V.28).

There is facility (*saukarya*) of relation of a sound (to a meaning), and no variability, because it is not observed in the meaning of other speech (different sounds) and because it is observed in a part of its own meaning (V.34). 'Facility' here means certainty or decisiveness. The knowables (*jñeyas*) 'treeness', 'earthness' (solidity), 'substance' and 'existence', if their order is reversed refer to an uncertainty whether the four are in the three, in the two, in the one, otherwise the sign refers to a certainty (V.35). (It is certain that 'treeness' is pervaded by 'earthness', both by 'substance' and all three by 'existence'; since existence is not pervaded by substance (there are qualities, etc., also), nor substance by earthness (there is also waterness or fluidity, etc.), nor earthness by treeness, there is uncertainty in the latter order. In other words there is a hierarchy of classes through dichotomies or exclusions into substance and non-substance, earthness and non-earthness and so on. In each class the members oppose one another by exclusion and become classes themselves.)

When it is not contradicted by sensation and when there is a pervasion which excludes what is other, so that the meanings different from that other are made non-different among themselves, a predicate of a class (*jāti*) is established (V.36). (i.e. the meanings different from some other meaning are grouped in a class pervaded by the excluding predicate, which makes them non-different among themselves.)

At the end of this presentation of the exclusion of what is other Diṅnāga quotes some verses from Bhartṛhari's *Vākyapadīya*, again showing his profound interest in that great Vedist work on linguistics and his desire to interpret its findings on the basis of Buddhist epistemology.

In analysis (*apoddhāra*), the meaning of a word is discriminated from the sentence: therefore the meaning of a sentence, called 'intuition' (*pratibhā*), is produced at first (V.46, cf. *Vākyapadīya* II.145 ff.). (This 'intuition', 'instinct', 'insight' or 'inspiration', cf. p. 313 above, is for Bhartṛhari the innate, instinctive understanding of the meanings of sentences among native speakers of a language, which resembles the instinctive behaviour of birds and other animals and the intuition of creative genius. Here it seems to be assimilated to the ancient Buddhist theory of 'comprehension' with the 'comprehension of intuition', the 'knowing' which makes other kinds of comprehension possible (these include comprehension of meaning), the knowledge of knowledge, the power of understanding, the flash of enlightenment. According to Bhartṛhari only complete sentences really have meaning, in actual practice, not words, but by analysis one can try to assign parts of the meaning of a sentence to the words in it, though this is an artificial procedure on the part of grammarians and words have no meaning in reality, in real life. People talk sentences, not words, and 'word' is an abstraction artificially analysed out by grammarians.)

An expression referring to 'water', for example, refers both to a drop and to a combination, it functions without regard to number, measure or shape (V.50 = *Vākyapadīya* II.160). The function of speech which is used referring to that which is distinguished by shape, colour or parts is not perceived actually referring to a (particular) part (V.51 = *Vākyapadīya* II.157).

Thus speech approaches parts or particulars by means of exclusions, but it can never actually reach them, never reach the objects of sensation, because its meaning is always a class, however restricted.

'Similarity' (*upamāna*) is not a separate means of knowledge because it consists simply of speech plus inference (*Vṛtti* after V.51).

The sixth and last chapter deals with sophistical refutations, restating the corresponding part of the Introduction to Logic. Thus of the six chapters the first is on sensation and the rest are all on various aspects of inference, which latter appears to reduce to 'exclusion'. To each chapter critiques of other schools are appended.

Sensation and inference are not absolutely separate, as inexpressible sense data and fictitious imaginings. Inference according to Diṅnāga is controllable by reference to sensation, though it can never relate directly to it nor indicate any particular sense datum. Inference is exclusion, sensation is non-exclusion, but that itself is an indirect relation. Though every datum is different from every other datum, Diṅnāga does allow the uncertain classes of inference an approximate truth. The fire in the kitchen has something in common with a forest fire and presumably the generalisations of the Buddha about unhappiness, conditions, etc., have sufficient validity to serve as a practical guide, though always subject to verification through our own sensations.

Chapter Twelve

THE GREAT UNIVERSITIES AND THE MANTRAYĀNA

The Development of the Medieval Schools—Dharmakīrti and Pramāṇa —Abhidharma in and after the 5th century—The Syncretistic Trend of Madhyamaka—Mantrayāna—The Kriyā, Caryā, Yoga and Anuttarayoga Systems—The Spirit of Destruction

The Development of the Medieval Schools

We have followed above the rise of the new schools of the Middle Ages : the Madhyamaka and the Pāramitā, the Vijñānavāda and the Sautrāntika. Each of these produced a succession of teachers who continued to make refinements in the doctrines which they passed on to their students. A major part of their work consisted of criticism of other views, Buddhist and non-Buddhist, since the latest opinions and arguments had always to be met and the students in each school prepared for the public debates which were the life-breath of Indian philosophy.

Almost from its origin Buddhism had been organised in the dwellings of its monks, in monasteries. Under the conditions of an increasingly academic tradition, needing large libraries of non-Buddhist as well as Buddhist texts of every school for reference purposes and systematically training its students as professional philosophers, it was natural enough that some of the greater monasteries should develop into what in modern terms would be called universities. Smaller communities of monks no doubt remained closer to the conditions of early Buddhism, their members concerned more with meditation than with theory, but the magnetism of the great universities tended to draw the ablest scholars and the keenest philosophers to them.

The most famous of all the universities was Nālandā, a few miles north of Rājagṛha, which seems to have owed its foundation to the fact that Śāriputra had lived, taught and died there. Since Śāriputra according to the tradition was largely responsible for the systematic study of the doctrine and was particularly connected with the elaboration of *abhidharma* (see pp. 219 ff. above), this choice of a site for academic work would be appropriate. Whether his students continued his studies and a 'school' existed at Nālandā in the early centuries of the history of Buddhism is uncertain. It is only after the time of Kaniṣka I that it begins to be mentioned as an important centre of learning. The early Madhyamaka teachers and especially Nāgārjuna are supposed to have worked there. Diṅnāga taught his new doctrine there, after which Nālandā remained the main centre for the study of the theory of knowledge. It was endowed by some of the Gupta emperors and attained its maximum size under the patronage of the Pāla emperors who ruled Magadha and North Eastern India from the 8th to the 12th century A.D. Some detailed descriptions of its day to day life have been left us by Chinese visitors and their statements, such as that several thousand monks and students resided there, that there were about a hundred lectures every day and a regular system of admission and registration of students, bear out the impression of high organisation given by the present majestic ruins. The Indian and Tibetan tradition records that its Library occupied three many storied buildings.

In Western India Valabhī had become a centre second only to Nālandā by the 5th century, frequented chiefly by followers of the Saṃmitīya and Vijñānavāda schools. Under the Pāla patronage several other universities flourished in their empire alongside Nālandā: Vikramaśilā, Uddaṇḍapura, Somapurī, Jagaddala, Vajrāsana (at Both Gayā) and Trikaṭuka being the most famous. The foundations at Dharmacakra (Sārnāth) near Vārāṇasī and at Jetavana near Śrāvastī (both receiving Gāhaḍavāla patronage during the 11th and 12th centuries) were less famous, though associated so strongly with the teaching of the Buddha himself. The colleges of Kaśmīra in the vicinity of the cities of Śrīnagarī and Parihāsapura are rarely distinguished by name but produced a succession of scholars of the early (especially Sarvāstivāda) and the Medieval schools. The main centre of the Sthaviravāda was Anurādhapura in Ceylon. The South of India, though it produced so many philosophers and scholars, seems to have been unable to resist the magnetism of the North and none of its centres of learning could rival those in the original homeland of Buddhism, to which its best students migrated. For a time Ratnagiri in Kaliṅga (Orissa) prospered (it could perhaps claim a connection with Diṅnāga) but could not seriously compete with Nālandā.

It was in these great centres of learning that scholars elaborated the study of Abhidharma, Madhyamaka, Pramāṇa and other subjects into a series of academic disciplines. They wrote introductions, commentaries on the difficult treatises of the great philosophers, monographs on special problems and critiques on the concepts and speculations of other schools. Some took up the study of linguistics, astronomy, medicine, music, painting, sculpture and other arts and crafts. Still others contributed to literature and literary criticism, for which they found their libraries made ample provision of secular poetry, drama and fiction. Among the literary critics we may mention Bhāmaha (who applied the logic of Vasubandhu and Diṅnāga, with modifications of his own, to the study of literature), Ratnaśrījñāna and Vidyākara, the last a connoisseur who made a remarkable anthology from the works of 250 poets.

Of the Madhyamaka philosophers we may note Buddhapālita and above all Candrakīrti (end of the 6th century), who produced the definitive working out of the doctrine of Nāgārjuna. 'Emptiness' and the two levels of truth are here treated consistently and rigorously with no concessions to the logicians of Diṅnāga's school or to those who would mix the methods of the Madhyamaka and Pramāṇa disciplines. Principles 'exist' at the concealing level, not at the ultimate level. He has a particularly interesting discussion in his Introduction to the Madhyamaka (*Madhyamakāvatāra*) on the 'false view of the existence of a soul', which according to him is the source of all 'faults' (*doṣas*) (*kārikā* 120 and the discussion connected with it). This rigorous school of Madhyamaka is known as the Prāsaṅgika school to distinguish it from a compromise school which had arisen and which we shall discuss below. The name indicates that the only method used by these philosophers is that of drawing a 'necessary consequence' from an opponent's position (in order to refute the latter).

At the 'concealing' level of Madhyamaka discussion, concerned with the ethics of living in the world, we may note the work of Śāntideva (early 8th century) based on the ethical parts of the *Sūtras* in relation to the way of the *bodhisattva*. Later Madhyamaka writers include Parahita (*c.* 1000) and Prajñākaramati (11th century).

The study of Pāramitā was for a time carried on primarily by the school of Asaṅga rather than by the Madhyamakas. However, Ārya Vimuktasena, a pupil of Vasubandhu I, wrote a commentary on the *Abhisamayālaṅkāra* of 'Maitreya' from the Madhyamaka standpoint (says Haribhadra) and with reference to the Twenty Five Thousand Perfection of Understanding (in effect a commentary on both texts simultaneously, showing their interconnection). A similar double commentary was written by his pupil Bhadanta Vimuktasena, dealing especially with the views of opponents. The later development of the study of Pāramitā, involving a syncretistic trend among the schools, will be taken up below.

After Vasubandhu I the Vijñānavāda tended to take his Treatise of Thirty Verses as their basic text and to write commentaries on that, though not neglecting the works of Asaṅga. There were ten famous commentators on the Thirty, among whom a certain Sthiramati, Paramārtha, Dharmapāla and Asvabhāva were the most prominent. It was their work, synthesised in a translation by Hsūan-tsang, which became the basis of the very influential Vijñānavāda school in China from the 7th century onwards. Sthiramati wrote a series of commentaries and sub-commentaries on the works of Asaṅga. After the 7th century we have practically no information on the history of this school in India, chiefly because it did not become established in Tibet and its tradition has therefore disappeared. Some of their writings on Pramāṇa are noted below.

The most brilliant of these academic disciplines was that of the theory of knowledge. After Diṅnāga, Śaṅkarasvāmin (followed much later by Jitāri) developed the theory at an elementary level, distinguishing more kinds of fallacy in inference, whilst Īśvarasena and especially Jinendrabuddhi, with his great commentary on the *Pramāṇasamuccaya*, carried on the study of the most advanced parts.

Dharmakīrti and Pramāṇa

In the 7th century Dharmakīrti (perhaps a contemporary of

Jinendrabuddhi since they do not appear to refer to one another[1]) took up the doctrine of Diṅnāga and in effect completely reworked it, though his main work is presented in the modest guise of a kind of commentary on, or rather a supplement to, the *Pramāṇasamuccaya.* His object was to meet all the criticisms and difficulties that had arisen in the field since Diṅnāga's pioneering work. He was so successful that his seven treatises, regarded as a kind of 'canon', were afterwards taken as the basis for the study of the theory of knowledge by most Buddhist logicians and Diṅnāga was comparatively neglected. Certainly he is one of the world's greatest philosophers in his own right.

Dharmakīrti's *Pramāṇavārttika,* the great commentary or supplement we have just referred to, is in four chapters and does not follow Diṅnāga directly. Perhaps Jinendrabuddhi had already provided his direct and systematic commentary expounding the actual words of Diṅnāga in a manner accepted as standard, so that Dharmakīrti could reasonably confine himself to new discussion but also restatements and reformulations such as seemed to him desirable. He begins (according to the order in which the chapters are usually taken, a matter which became controversial) with the subject of inference (for oneself), presumably as a prerequisite for all discussion on the theory of knowledge, as an enquiry into the nature of reasoning. All inferences, he finds, are based on either a characteristic of identity ('own nature') or a characteristic of causality ('effect', from which one argues to its cause). Alternatively they may be negative (based on 'non-perception'). In other words, we may perhaps say, all inferences are either analytic (the middle and major terms in fact characterise the same object, or rather an object and a part of it) or synthetic, or they are negations of these. The discussion on identity leads naturally into a discussion of the meanings of words and an exposition of the 'exclusion of what is other': this is the object of intellection as well as of words and the basis of inference.

The purpose of inference is stated to be to enable one to

1. Hattori, however, suggests that Jinendrabuddhi followed Dharmakīrti's doctrine of *pratyakṣābhāsa* (*Miscellanea Indologica Kiotiensia,* 6-7, 1965, p. 124).

act successfully in attaining various objects. Successful action is the aim of the investigation of the theory of knowledge.

The second chapter deals with the theory of knowledge in general, a (valid) means of knowledge being defined as knowing which is not contradicted by experience, its correctness known through practice, and with the Four Truths.

Sensation (the subject of the third chapter) is defined as being without imagining and without illusion. It is an 'effect' of reality. Sensation is established just by itself, by our awareness of sense-experience when we are not thinking at all. We cannot sense the same particular more than once, nor can we sense any relation among our experiences. Sensation is of the own-characteristic (the universal-characteristic is the 'concealing' object of inference). The object of sensation is the extreme particular, the real object, ultimate reality. This is known to be 'real' because it is 'efficient', it produces effects.

Inference for another (discussed in the fourth chapter) is communicating the three characteristics of a valid middle term to another person. It is of three kinds ('own-nature', 'effect', 'non-perception') like inference for oneself and further has two 'figures' according as it is set out by the methods of agreement or difference. This gives six kinds, but Dharmakīrti worked out further sub-varieties of the negative inference, eventually (in another treatise), eleven of them, negation of identity, negation of effect, negation of cause, negation of an 'inclusive term' and combinations of these, with the conditions for their validity.

Dharmakīrti's other works mostly overlap with the *Pramāṇavārttika* or its parts, but the *Santānāntarasiddhi* should be separately mentioned as a monograph on a special philosophical problem: the inference of the existence of other minds than one's own (i.e. against the solipsist position). Observing that our own purposive actions are preceded by intelligence (i.e. mental activity), when we see similar actions on the part of others we may infer that these also are preceded by intelligence, in other words that other minds exist.

Dharmakīrti's doctrine is intrinsically difficult and also fraught with all kinds of possible implications. He himself did not write fully on every point raised or implied but left it to his students to continue the work. Among them, Devendrabuddhi wrote a commentary on Chapters II to IV of the *Pramāṇavārttika*, Dharmakīrti himself having provided one only on the first chapter. Devendrabuddhi's student Śākyabuddhi then wrote a sub-commentary on Dharmakīrti's commentary on the first chapter as well as a new commentary on Chapters II-IV, thus completing the explanation of this great supplement to the *Pramāṇasamuccaya*. At the end of the 8th century Dharmottara wrote excellent commentaries on Dharmakīrti's more independent and more comprehensive works on Pramāṇa, namely the *Pramāṇaviniścaya* and the *Nyāyabindu*, and also five monographs on such topics as the exclusion of what is other. Arcaṭa or Dharmākaradatta, the teacher of Dharmottara, commented on the *Hetubindu* of Dharmakīrti, a study of the middle term which covers part of the ground of the first chapter of the *Pramāṇavārttika*, and wrote two monographs (of which the *Pramāṇadvitvasiddhi* establishing that there are only two means of knowledge appears to be the same as the *Pramāṇāntarbhāva* published anonymously in 1969). Śubhagupta, another teacher of Dharmottara, also wrote five monographs, including one to establish the reality of external objects (against the Vijñānavāda) and two critiques, of Mīmāṃsā and of Nyāya theology. Śaṅkarānanda (9th century), author of a most elaborate, though unfinished, commentary on *Pramāṇavārttika* I, may perhaps be associated with the tradition of these three Sautrāntika philosophers of Kaśmīra. Durvekamiśra (*c.* 1000) wrote very detailed and useful sub-commentaries on the commentaries on the *Nyāyabindu* and *Hetubindu* just mentioned, which, being extant in Sanskrit along with the texts commented on, serve even now as the best introduction to the Buddhist theory of knowledge. Jitāri (10th century?—there seem to be two or three authors of this name), who wrote short introductory manuals and monographs, also appears to be a Sautrāntika. So probably was Vidyākaraśānti (*c.* 1100), whose *Tarkasopāna* is a simplified students' manual based closely on the *Nyāyabindu* and Dharmottara's commentary, but adding further subvarieties of negative inference from Durvekamiśra or his unknown source.

As was noted above when introducing Diṅnāga, the impact of his ideas was such that several other schools borrowed them with suitable adaptations. The Madhyamaka Bhāvaviveka adopted Diṅnāga's logic, as we shall see below, and was followed, with modifications, by several other syncretistic philosophers, among whom Śāntarakṣita wrote a commentary on Dharmakīrti's *Vādanyāya* on 'defeat situations' in debate and Kamalaśīla commented briefly on the *Nyāyabindu*. Subsequently certain philosophers of the combined Madhyamaka-Pāramitā-Mantrayāna trend, such as Ratnākaraśānti (11th century) and Abhayākaragupta (12th century), wrote monographs on Pramāṇa.

After Dharmakīrti had elaborated the doctrine so extensively, other Mahāyānists proceeded to annex his theories and even his works wholesale. First Prajñākaragupta (late 7th century), regarded in Tibetan tradition as a combined Madhyamaka-Yogācāra, wrote a long and digressive commentary or 'ornament' (*alaṅkāra*) on chapters II-IV of the *Pramāṇavārttika*. He uses the Madhyamaka term *dharmanairātmya* (p. 116) and Mahāyānism might be indicated by his addition of *aparinirvāṇadharmatvāt* to the explanation of *tāyin*, unless it means no more than that the Buddha remained in the world long enough to teach. The conjunction of *sarvākārajñatā* and *bodhisattvas* (p. 146) suggests Mahāyāna. However, he cannot disguise the fact that Dharmakīrti took *Pramāṇasamuccaya* I.1 simply as referring to the Buddha and his teaching of the Four Truths, etc. At about the same time, the Mahāyānist Karṇakagomin enlarged Śākyabuddhi's commentary on *Pramāṇavārttika* I. Sub-commentaries were written on Prajñākaragupta's work by his student Ravigupta, by the more polemical Mahāyānist Jinamitra (early 8th century, who insists that the second chapter was in reality intended to be the first, thus beginning the whole *Pramāṇavārttika* with the *bodhisattva* doctrine and the nature of the Mahāyānist Buddha) and by the more moderate Yamāri (9th century, a truly enormous sub-commentary). The Yogācāra Jñānaśrībhadra, teacher of Yamāri, commented on the *Pramāṇaviniścaya*, whilst Vinītadeva (8th century) had already supplied Vijñānavādin commentaries on the remaining five works of Dharmakīrti. Two other Yogācāra philosophers, Jñānaśrīmitra and his student Ratnakīrti (11th century), wrote a large number of monographs to establish what they held to be the real views of Dharmakīrti and Prajñākaragupta, against

Dharmottara and also against the Brahmanical Nyāya. Manorathanandin (12th century?) contributed a relatively simple commentary on the *kārikās* only of the four chapters of the *Pramāṇavārttika*, in Jinamitra's order and aiming to establish the Vijñānavāda doctrine. It is not clear what school Mokṣākaragupta (*c.* 1100) belonged to, though he was probably a Madhyamaka, for in his introductory manual *Tarkabhāṣā* he presents the views of various schools without offering his own comments. This manual is much more elaborate than the *Nyāyabindu* and includes refutations of many non-Buddhist doctrines.

Abhidharma in and after the 5th century

We have already noted that the main centre of the Sthaviravāda by this period was Ceylon and the Great Vihāra there. The school continued to flourish in South India until at least the 14th century and also maintained some establishments in Magadha, besides which it became increasingly strong in various countries of South East Asia. This most conservative school added very little to the inheritance of doctrine which we have already reviewed. But alone among the early schools it has survived intact to the present day. Moreover no other form of Buddhism has preserved its ancient literature intact in the original Indian language, so that all serious research on Buddhism is dependent on the Pali sources. Besides a complete *Tripiṭaka*, we have a complete and ancient set of commentaries[1], sub-commentaries on these from about the 10th century and many other ancillary works for the study of the doctrine and of related subjects such as history and linguistics. The later philosophers of the school aimed at the further systematisation and clarification of the tradition they had received, though they carefully recorded old controversies and were also aware of the newer developments in other schools, from which they occasionally assimilated concepts which seemed useful.

In the 5th century Buddhaghosa, besides translating most of the Old Sinhalese commentaries into Pali for use in India, wrote the final great 'book of the way' (cf. p. 315 above), the *Visuddhimagga*. This covers a great part of the *Abhidhamma* as

1. On the nature of the extant versions of these see pp. 321 f. above.

well as treating elaborately of meditation. According to Buddhaghosa the 'own-nature' of principles is fully understood according to their 'own-characteristic' (*svalakṣaṇa*), this being the 'characteristic' of each as recorded in the commentaries. He also calls it the 'individual characteristic' and the 'synthesised characteristic'. This substituting of 'characteristic' throughout for 'nature' or 'existent' (the *bhāva* of the old commentarial tradition) appears to be a response to Nāgārjuna's critique. The 'universal-characteristic' (*sāmānyalakṣaṇa*) of principles is the three characteristics 'impermanent', 'unhappiness' and 'non-soul' which they all share (see *Visuddhimagga* pp. 107, 499, 501, 520ff., 543). A contemporary, Buddhadatta, also from India, wrote an 'Introduction to the Abhidhamma' (*Abhidhammāvatāra*) in which he groups his material under five headings: thought, mental principles, matter, extinction and finally 'concept' (*prajñapti*), the last being whatever is not ultimately real[1]. Mahānāma in the 6th century, commenting on the *Paṭisambhidāmagga* (p. 312 above), gives an alternative system of categories or 'ways' of the knowable, namely the synthesised (i.e. the principles), 'change' (*vikāra*, occurrence or origination of principles according to the second truth, etc., and their changing or being expended), characteristics (the 'own' and the 'universal'), extinction and concept (PsA pp. 58, 523, 596.)

Ānanda in the 10th century, in his sub-commentary on the *Abhidhamma*, besides further clarifying 'concepts' offers a definition of one of them, 'time' (*kāla*), as 'not occurring' (i.e. there is no reality corresponding to it) but providing or being perceived as a 'receptacle' or 'locus' in relation to the absences before and after of momentary events (*Atthasālinī Ṭ* p. 47 of Colombo edn.). This Ānanda's student Dhammapāla (II) was the greatest author of sub-commentaries (and a sub-sub-commentary on Ānanda's work), rivalling Buddhaghosa in the extent and importance of his works. He also wrote a short manual of Abhidharma as an exposition of the two truths (*Saccasaṅkhepa*), the ultimate, which concerns the principles, and the concealing, which concerns concepts, which are unreal

1. For a review of the work of Sthaviravāda philosophers on this see 'The Concept of a Concept'.

(*avastu*). In his sub-commentaries Dhammapāla II adapts the Pramāṇa theory of Diṅnāga: there are two means of knowledge, sensation, which excludes inference and knows the own-characteristic, and inference, which knows the universal-characteristic (DṬ Vol. I pp. 191-2, *Visuddhimagga Ṭ* Burmese edn. p. 888). Tradition (*āgama*) is included in inference. He argues, following Buddhaghosa, that the Buddha had actual sensation of the past and future because his thought was undisturbed (DṬ Vol. III p. 119, quoting *Vākyapadiya* I.37 in support). The three universal characteristics, impermanent, etc., are not included in the five groups because they are without own-natures, but they are not separate from the groups because they cannot be perceived apart from these, therefore, they are concept (*Visuddhimagga Ṭ* Burmese edn. p. 825). Thus the 'universal-characteristic' known by inference is 'concept' and the distinction between the two means of knowledge, with what is known by them as the two truths, is perfectly maintained. The anonymous *Gaṇṭhipada* on PsA, of about this date, follows the same doctrine on the means of knowledge (p. 34) and states that extinction is attained through the knowledge of the two characteristics, own and universal (55ff.).

Among twelfth century manuals of Abhidharma, the *Paramatthavinicchaya* of Anuruddha II is the most original, carrying to completion the programme of Buddhadatta under the same headings and with an especially elaborate working out of concepts. Discussing the two truths, he states that the ultimate is not contradicted by reality (and perhaps by sensation if we read *sacchika* here with one manuscript), whilst the concealing is not contradicted by agreed usage (1083-4). Kassapa's *Mohavicchedanī* is a very convenient and most comprehensive synopsis of the entire *Abhidhamma* and its commentaries, in the guise of a commentary on the original *Mātṛkā* extracted again from the seven treatises of the school. An extensive literature of commentaries grew up around the numerous Abhidharma manuals of this school, the most noteworthy commentators being Mahābodhi, Sumaṅgala and Vācissara.

In the later Middle Ages the Sthaviravādins of Burma took the lead in Abhidharma. The most outstanding among them are Ariyavaṃsa (15th century), Saddhammālaṅkāra and Mahānāma (16th century) and Tilokaguru (17th century). Their main objects of study are the four treatises *Dhammasaṅgaṇi*, *Dhātukathā*, *Yamaka* and *Paṭṭhāna*, with their commentaries and sub-commentaries, and the aim is to work out completely the implications of the system. This tradition has continued into the present century.

Little is known of the history of the Sarvāstivāda in this period, since the school, and all the other early schools, was totally destroyed by the Turkish invasions of India. The final systematisation of their Abhidharma appears to have been carried out by Skandhila, Saṃghabhadra and Vimalamitra in the 5th and 6th centuries. The latter two criticise the *Abhidharmakośa Bhāṣya* of Vasubandhu II (p. 447 above) in order to reestablish the Abhidharma tradition of the Sarvāstivādin 'Vaibhāṣikas'. Vasubandhu was then defended by Sautrāntika commentators on the *Bhāṣya*, of whom the most important is Yaśomitra (8th century).

Besides these schools just mentioned, the Tibetan historian Tāranātha tells us that the following early schools continued to flourish in the Pāla Empire (i.e. up to the time of the Turkish conquest): Mahāsaṃghika, Lokottaravāda, Kaurukullaka, Prajñaptivāda, Vātsīputrīya and Saṃmitīya. Practically nothing of the history of any of these in this period is now known, only the names of a few of their followers who happened afterwards to join the Mahāyāna. The same historian tells us[1] that the followers of the early schools, the Śrāvakas, still formed the majority of Buddhists in India in the 12th century, though he adds the claim that they acknowledged the greatness of the Mahāyāna and Mantrayāna teacher Abhayākaragupta.

The Syncretistic Trend of Madhyamaka

Some followers of the Madhyamaka school were not satisfied with the purely critical philosophy of Nāgārjuna, at least as interpreted by Buddhapālita, confined to drawing necessary consequences from the positions of opponents, showing that the concepts of philosophy were meaningless and leaving us, apparently, with a purely empirical enquiry. Bhāvaviveka (or Bhavya), under the influence of Diṅnāga and presumably at the end of the 5th century, wrote a series of works from a

1. Chapter XXXVI of Schiefner's version.

modified Madhyamaka point of view and established a new school which at once became very strong. Since Ārya Vimuktasena (p. 469 above) according to Tāranātha was a nephew of Buddhapālita and a pupil of Vasubandhu (Asaṅga's brother), we place him in the latter part of the 4th century. At the end of the 6th century Candrakīrti upheld Buddhapālita by criticising Bhāvaviveka.

Bhāvaviveka adopted the improved methods of logic, apparently from Diṅnāga, and proceeded to set out independent proofs of the Madhyamaka doctrine. His school is consequently known as the Svātantrika, 'Independent', school: independent arguments and proofs could be set up, whereas the Prāsaṅgika school of Buddhapālita depended on the positions and arguments of others. His works include a commentary on Nāgārjuna's *Mūlamadhyamakakārikā*, in which he argues against Buddhapālita that logical proofs must be elaborated in order to realise the full implications of Nāgārjuna's laconic statements. The *Madhyamakahṛdaya* with its commentary *Tarkajvālā* sets out the Madhyamaka doctrine of the ultimate reality, followed by a critique of the opinions of other schools: the Buddhist 'Śrāvakas' and Vijñānavādins and the Brahmanical Sāṁkhya, Vaiśeṣika, Vedānta and Mīmāṃsā. The ultimate reality or 'thusness' is not an existing eternal entity like the *brahman* of the Vedānta and similar 'realities' of other schools, although other philosophers have occasionally had correct intuitions and even given correct formulations of its nature. The fact of occasional agreements with Vedānta and other statements does not imply that the Madhyamaka doctrine is false (as critics of the early schools had suggested, holding that the Mahāyānists had gone over to the Vedists with their conception of an ultimate reality and abandoned the doctrine of the Buddha). The *Karatalaratna* sets out the independent arguments for the Madhyamaka doctrine. Ultimately (at the ultimate level of truth) the synthesised principles are empty (of any own-nature), because of their conditioned origination (middle term), as things illusorily created (example; i.e. works of art, paintings, clay models and the like, which do not in fact have the real nature of the things they represent, women, elephants and so on). At the concealing level, on the other hand, the principles commonly accepted may be admitted. We do not contradict the experience of the world but say that ultimately the principles of this experience are not real. The Vijñānavāda is criticised for its doctrine of the 'dependent' (*paratantra*) as some kind of reality: if this 'dependent' is empty we agree, otherwise the *sūtras* are contradicted and the eternalist theory is implied. Ultimately also the unsynthesised principles are unreal, because they do not occur (middle term), as a flower of the sky (example: flowers do not grow in the sky). Here again the unsynthesised principles are regarded as real at the concealing level, so that at this level it is possible to attain liberation or extinction (*nirvāṇa*) through understanding. Again the Vijñānavāda doctrine of thusness as ultimate reality, empty but nevertheless real (ultimately), is criticised as leading to Brahmanism. Thus the extremes of existence (or 'reality') and non-existence are to be avoided and are refuted by logical argumentation.

The work of Bhāvaviveka was continued especially by Avalokitavrata (probably 8th century) in a vast sub-commentary on his commentary on the *Mūlamadhyamakakārikā*, defending him from the criticisms made by Candrakīrti.

In the 8th century lived two Buddhist philosophers whose work was of decisive importance for the development of the doctrine and also in the more practical field of spreading it, Śāntarakṣita and his pupil Kamalaśīla. They were followers of the Svātantrika-Madhyamaka of Bhāvaviveka but went much further than him in accepting the methods of Pramāṇa discipline, now improved by Dharmakīrti. We have noted above that both of them wrote commentaries on works of Dharmakīrti, Bhāvaviveka on the other hand appears to have been critical of Diṅnāga as a follower of a different school, a Śrāvaka, and to have adopted only such methods of logic as were generally accepted, leaving aside Diṅnāga's special doctrines. Śāntarakṣita is basically a Madhyamaka (he rejects the Vijñānavāda explanation of the nature of the ultimate reality) but he departs from the usual Madhyamaka doctrine that principles can be taken as existing as commonly accepted at the concealing level, substituting the explanation of sensation given by the Pramāṇa writers (the objects perceived are not in fact the phenomena they are imagined to be, are not the direct meanings of our words). From this point of view he wrote a new textbook on Madhyamaka, the *Madhyamakālaṅkāra*. A much more remarkable work is his *Tattvasaṃgraha*, a kind of encyclopaedia of Indian philosophy giving critiques (*parīkṣā*) of 26 'realities' (*tattva*), i.e. ultimate realities, first causes, categories and the like, covering the whole field of Indian philosophical speculation and leaving only the Buddhist doctrine of conditioned origination, as understood by Nāgārjuna, as valid, assimilated to Dharmakīrti's theory of knowledge.

It was Śāntarakṣita who was responsible for the definitive establishment of Buddhism in Tibet and his philosophy has formed the basic theoretical outlook of Buddhists in that country ever since. Buddhism of various schools had spread into Tibet some time earlier than this (we have no space here to embark on a history of Buddhism in Tibet), but it was only after the *bodhisattva* Śāntarakṣita had been invited by the Tibetan government that an effective and lasting school was established in a Tibetan monastery. Leaving this monastery in the hands of properly qualified Tibetan monks he returned to India, but is said to have predicted a schism and left instructions that his pupil Kamalaśīla should be invited to settle the controversy.

Kamalaśīla wrote a very thorough commentary explaining his teacher's *Tattvasaṃgraha* and another on his *Madhyamakālaṅkāra*. In due course he was invited to Tibet, whose Buddhists had become divided, in fact because simultaneously with the missions of Indian Buddhists there the Chinese Buddhists of the Dhyāna (Ch'an, Zen) school were spreading their own version of the Buddhist teaching. Briefly, the position of the Dhyāna ('Meditation') school, an offshoot of the Vijñānavāda founded in China and apparently unknown in India, was that enlightenment did not require a long course of training with tedious study of endless *sūtras* but could be attained 'all at once' (*yugapad*) by a sudden flash of insight in meditation (in this their position was similar to that of the old Sthaviravāda school), or indeed in going about one's ordinary daily round in a suitable frame of mind. The Madhyamakas on the other hand, following their interpretation of the Perfection of Understanding as the way of the *bodhisattva* (as laid down by 'Maitreya' in the *Abhisamayālaṅkāra*), the Pāramitā doctrine, held that enlightenment (buddhahood) must be approached 'gradually' (*kramaśas*) through a long course of training and study. An assembly was held at bSam yas and the question debated. Kamalaśīla and his party were victorious and his views accepted and declared orthodox by the king of Tibet. Afterwards Kamalaśīla wrote three manuals summarising the gradualist Madhyamaka-Pāramitā course of training (under the title *Bhāvanākrama*, 'Course of Development') and criticising the Vijñānavāda generally[1] as well as the 'sudden' school. He quotes widely from the *sūtras* (including the apparently idealist *Laṅkāvatāra*) to show that his views are derived from them. The practice of meditation is prominent in his expositions, with particular reference to 'calming' (*śamatha*) and 'insight' (*vipaśyanā* or *vidarśana*), which have to be united. Despite the Assembly of bSam yas the path of Buddhism was as yet far from smooth in Tibet and Kamalaśīla did not return to India; he was murdered, apparently by followers of the ancient Tibetan religion. He had also written (presumably before going to Tibet) a summary of a work of Śāntideva on the way of the *bodhisattva*.

It was another pupil of Śāntarakṣita, Haribhadra (sometimes known as Siṃhabhadra), who took up the subject of Pāramitā and prepared a series of works on it according to the views of his teacher. The comments of the two Vimuktasenas he found insufficiently full and clear. He also criticises the attempts of Asaṅga and Vasubandhu I to interpret the Perfection of Understanding *sūtras* according to their Vijñānavāda standpoint and without referring to the work of 'Maitreya' (thus omitting the 'way'). In the course of his work he particularly criticises the Vijñānavāda doctrine of the ultimate reality. Such an eternally pure 'element of principles' (*dharmadhātu*) without duality could not be attained. The knowledge of this reality being already pure, there could be no question of getting rid of its defilements and imaginings, otherwise it would not in fact be completely pure (which would contradict the original position).[2] No doubt following his teacher, Haribhadra quotes Dharmakīrti and Prajñākaragupta and freely uses the terminology of the former. In fact the study of the Pāramitā according to Haribhadra presupposes that of Pramāṇa as well as of Madh-

1. I p. 217.
2. *Abhisamayālaṅkārāloka*, p. 77 of Tucci's edition.

yamaka and Abhidharma (the *Abhidharmakośa* is often quoted). In Tibet (no doubt following Indian tradition) Haribhadra is regarded as the principal source for the interpretation of 'Maitreya's' *Abhisamayālaṅkāra*, the basic text on Pāramitā. His fundamental commentary on it, taken as the basis for its exegesis, is the *Sphuṭārthā*, also known as his 'Small Commentary'. His 'Great Commentary' is the *Abhisamayālaṅkārāloka*, which explains the same text, often in the same words, but incorporates also a full commentary on the Eight Thousand Perfection of Understanding. It aims to show how each passage of the *Sūtra* is in fact related to a topic of the way, quoting in conjunction with it the corresponding verse from 'Maitreya' (and without departing from the sequence of the latter's verses). Occasionally the Twenty Five Thousand version of the *Sūtra* is referred to as well. This last version is the subject of another of Haribhadra's works, a summary of the Twenty Five Thousand according to the *Abhisamayālaṅkāra*. He also wrote a commentary on the *Abhisamayālaṅkāra* with reference to the verse Perfection of Understanding, the *Ratnaguṇasaṃcayagāthā*, entitled the *Subodhinī* (cf. p. 365 above), a 'Development of the Perfection of Understanding' and other works.

The basis of the interpretation of the Perfection of Understanding *Sūtras* is the distinction of the two levels of truth, the two levels of statement. In addition the non-perception of principles is stressed, i.e. not perceiving them as separate principles, since in the ultimate reality there is no duality. The training (*yoga*) is at the 'concealing' level,[1] ultimately (*tattvatas*) it is a non-training (*ayoga*). Enlightenment is attained at the concealing level.[2] Good and bad, actions and results, are only at the concealing level, not at the ultimate.[3] All beings are at the ultimate level pure by nature and the thought of the thus-gone is not subject to change, to origination or cessation (cf. the *Ratnagotravibhāga*). The thusness of the thus-gone is no different from that of all principles.[4]

1. Ibid. p. 299.
2. Ibid. p. 434.
3. Ibid. p. 440.
4. Ibid. p. 370.

Contrary to the Vijñānavādins the nature of thought and the so called three characteristics are to be understood as follows: as imaginary (*kalpita*) thoughts are imperceptible, being unreal (*asattva*), because they have no characteristics; as dependent (*paratantra*) they are imperceptible, being unreal, because they have no causes (do not originate, therefore); as perfected (*parinispanna*) they are imperceptible, being unreal, because they are not perfected (*aparinispanna*), since they have no own nature (or own, particular, characteristics, the term used here is *svarūpa*).[1] Elsewhere Haribhadra says that the Vijñānavādins misinterpret the Perfection of Understanding and that their view either will not account for experience or will conflict with non-duality (*advaya*).[2] Fairly often, however, he quotes from Asaṅga's works, particularly the *Mahāyānasūtrālaṅkāra*[3] on the thought of enlightenment, sometimes giving his own interpretations of them. Though he generally follows Dharmakīrti even in details (see for example the discussion on *svabhāva*[4]), Haribhadra utilises three means of knowledge, sensation, inference and tradition (*āgama*), apparently taking the last as an independent means.[5] There is according to Haribhadra only one 'vehicle' (*yāna*), for the Śrāvakas and Isolated Buddhas (generally distinguished as having two separate 'vehicles', that of the *bodhisattvas* being a third) attain their extinction, which in fact is the 'element without the influences' (*anāsravadhātu*) in the worlds of Amitābha and other *buddhas*, where they are awakened by the *buddhas* to the thought of enlightenment and become *bodhisattvas* and *buddhas*.

Haribhadra's work of expounding Pāramitā was continued by his pupil Buddhaśrījñāna (or simply Buddhajñāna), who also wrote a commentary on the *Abhisamayālaṅkāra* and another on the same text with reference to the *Ratnaguṇasaṃcayagāthā*. The same author apparently wrote a *Mahāyānalakṣaṇasamuccaya* on Abhidharma and works on the Mantrayāna, for example on the *Guhyasamāja Tantra*. After this the teachers of the Pāramitā school are with increasing frequency concerned also

1. Ibid. p. 338. cf. p. 494.
2. Ibid. pp. 374ff.
3. But it has been suggested this work is not Asaṅga's (cf. p. 439 above).
4. Ibid. pp. 372ff.
5. Ibid. pp. 168, 258, 463, 494f.

with the Mantrayāna and we may speak of a further development of syncretism. Early in the 9th century Dharmamitra wrote a very important commentary on Haribhadra's basic *Sphuṭārthā*. His contemporary Dharmakīrti (II, or Dharmakīrtiśrī) wrote a commentary on the *Abhisamayālaṅkāra* and one on the *Hevajra Tantra*. Among commentators on the Perfection of Understanding *Sūtras* the most important was probably Daṃṣṭrāsena, a contemporary of these writers, who produced a commentary on the Hundred Thousand (*Śatasāhasrikābṛhaṭṭīkā*), in fact covering the three recensions of the 'Great' Perfection of Understanding (the Hundred, Twenty Five and Eighteen Thousand).

Haribhadra and his school flourished in the time of the Pāla emperors Dharmapāla and Devapāla (c. 765-850), Daṃṣṭrāsena in Kaśmīra. A fresh peak of activity of the syncretistic trend begins in the time of Mahīpāla (c. 990-1040) and continues under his successors. Ānandagarbha (better known as a Mantrayāna teacher) wrote 'Courses of Development' (*Bhāvanākrama*) following Kamalaśīla's example. Ratnakīrti, doubtfully the same as the writer on Pramāṇa, wrote a new commentary on the *Abhisamayālaṅkāra*. His pupil Ratnākaraśānti (or simply 'Śānti') wrote two more such commentaries, the *Sārottamā* with reference to the Eight Thousand Perfection of Understanding and the *Śuddhimati* with reference to the Twenty Five Thousand. The *Sārottamā* contains an important discussion on the classes of text in the *Tripiṭaka*, in which those of the Mantrayāna are included. From Tāranātha it seems there were two Ratnākaraśāntis (the second in the 12th century). However, this may be a confusion and at present it is not clear how the works attributed to this name might be divided. They include besides the two just mentioned a commentary on Śāntarakṣita's *Madhyamakālaṅkāra*, one on Haribhadra's 'Development of the Perfection of Understanding', one on the *Hevajra Tantra* (the *Muktikāvali*), one on the *Guhyasamāja*, four other *tantra* commentaries and treatises on logic and metrics. Prajñākaramati, already mentioned, wrote on the *Abhisamayālaṅkāra* as well as on Śāntideva's ethical study of the way of the *bodhisattva* (on which several other writers of this period worked). Kumāraśrībhadra wrote a summary of the Perfection of Understanding.

In the time of Rāmapāla (c. 1075-1120) lived Abhayākaragupta (died 1125), regarded as one of the greatest teachers of Mahāyāna and Mantrayāna Buddhism and especially revered in Tibet (as an incarnation of Amitābha). Along with Ratnākaraśānti he should perhaps be looked upon as the final systematiser of the Madhyamaka-Mantrayāna synthesis, which appears to have been the last great movement in Indian Buddhism and which has dominated Tibetan Buddhism. His works include a commentary on the *Abhisamayālaṅkāra* with reference to the Eight Thousand Perfection of Understanding (the *Marmakaumudī*), a *Munimatālaṅkāra* summarising the Perfection of Understanding (its last three chapters constitute another commentary on the basic text of 'Maitreya'), in which we find significant agreements with Ratnākaraśānti's *Śuddhimatī*, other works on Madhyamaka, logic and Vinaya and a series of works on the Mantrayāna (the *Vajramālā*, *Sādhanasāgara*, *Niṣpannayogāvalī*, *Abhayamārgakrama* and commentaries on the *Kālacakra*, *Buddhakapāla* and *Sampuṭa Tantras*, the last being the *Āmnāyamañjarī*). The school of Abhayākaragupta flourished in India until its members were murdered or scattered by the Turks early in the 13th century, and afterwards in Tibet.

Mantrayāna

The composition of new *sūtras* continued unabated after those of the idealist trend discussed in Chapter Eleven. The Buddhists continued to respond to the changing outlook of society as the 'Middle Ages' advanced. The gradual and complex changes in Indian society and their reflection in popular ideologies as well as in philosophy cannot be traced here. Much more preliminary research on the sources will have to be done before such a study could be effectively attempted. Here we may note that somewhat similar trends in outlook can be seen in the Brahmanical or 'Hindu' literature of this period and content ourselves with the provisional statement that the movements we are following in Buddhist literature are part of the social history of Medieval India. We are looking at one of the sources for that history and are not yet prepared to 'explain' what we find here by insights from other sources.

Probably in the 4th century, for the most part, should be placed the leading *sūtras* of a group afterwards collected under the title *Mahāsannipāta*. The first *sūtra* in this collection, the *Ratnaketudhāraṇī* (translated into Chinese early in the 5th century), strongly marks a new trend in *sūtras* of this period and in interpolations in older *sūtras* probably made in about this period. This is the use of the *dhāraṇī*, an utterance, usually of a mystical nature, 'preserving' or 'maintaining' the doctrine of Buddhism and aiding its followers. We have met the idea of the use of magic formulae already in the Golden Lustre (p. 400 above). In the *Ratnaketudhāraṇī* Śākyamuni seeks the aid of all the Buddhas, of innumerable worlds, to spread the doctrine in one 'incantation-word' (*mantrapada*), i.e. a *dhāraṇī*, which will maintain the teaching and aid its followers in all ways. The Buddhas assemble (this is the 'Great Assembly', *Mahāsannipāta*, which gives its name to the whole of this collection of *sūtras*) and deliver the *dhāraṇī*. This *dhāraṇī* occupies about two pages of text[1] and is for the most part unintelligible, consisting of repeated syllables (*guru guru*, *muru muru*, *hili hili*, *hala hala*, and so on), generally alliterative, sprinkled with occasional words which might be significant ('great compassion', etc.) though they are not grammatically connected in meaningful sentences. We need not dwell on this incantation or here trouble ourselves with the attempts which have been made to explain the origin of such *dhāraṇīs* from non-Indian languages and alphabets. The *Ratnaketudhāraṇī* is a fairly long *sūtra* of considerable literary merit. It begins with the story of how Śāriputra joined the Buddha and presents this and the events which follow in the dramatic form of a conflict with Death (Māra). It seems possible that it was inspired by and even partly based on Aśvaghoṣa's play on Śāriputra, though our fragmentary knowledge of the latter does not enable us to make a detailed comparison.

A large number of texts of about this time and later are associated with this *dhāraṇī* trend. We may mention those centred on the figure of Bhaiṣajyaguru[2], the Buddha of Healing, who may be compared with Amitābha in some respects, the incantation (*mantra* or *japa*) of the *Ekādaśamukha*[2] and

1. *Mahāsannipāta-Ratnaketudhāraṇīsūtra* edited by N. Dutt and S. N. Sharma in *Gilgit Manuscripts* Vol. IV, Calcutta, 1959, pp. 114-6.

2. The *Bhaiṣajyaguru Sūtra* and other texts edited in *Gilgit Manuscripts* Vol. I, Śrīnagar, 1939.

that of the *Hayagrīvavidyā*[1] (for protection against enemies). Hayagrīva is connected with Avalokiteśvara, who in the *Sarvatathāgatādhiṣṭhānavyūha*[1] is given an abode on Mt. Potalaka in Āndhra.

In the 7th century Dharmakīrti criticised the use of incantations (*mantras*). In the 8th century a new school was introduced into China by Indian monks. Śubhākarasiṃha (born in Kaliṅga, studied at Nālandā) was the first, and translated a text (called a *sūtra*) named *Mahāvairocana*, 'Great Illumination' (an aspect of the Buddha, cf. p. 429 above, sometimes understood as 'Great Sun').[2] He was followed by Vajrabodhi (studied Mantrayāna in the South, went to China at the request of 'Avalokiteśvara of Potalaka'), who translated the *Vajraśikhara*, 'Diamond Pinnacle' (or 'Diamond Point'). The latter's pupil Amoghavajra translated the version of it called *Sarvatathāgatatattvasaṃgraha*. These texts are regarded as containing the utterances of the Buddha as *dharmakāya*, 'substance of the doctrine'. In the 'Great Illumination' the Buddha as Mahāvairocana is attended on by the *bodhisattva* Samantabhadra (cf. the *Gaṇḍavyūha*, which seems to have inspired this text) and other *bodhisattvas* and by the *vajradhara* (one who knows the 'diamond', on which see below) Vajrapāṇi and other *vajradharas*. The whole universe becomes illuminated as by the Sun. All beings are to find enlightenment in their own thoughts, which ultimately are pure (the doctrinal position of this phase of the Mantrayāna is perhaps not too distant from that of the *Gaṇḍavyūha* and the idealist trend). The student of the text is supposed ultimately to 'become' the Buddha Vairocana through his meditation. He identifies his thoughts with a 'diagram' (*maṇḍala*) which is also that of the Buddha: the Buddha (enlightenment) is to be found in his own thought, in his 'thought of enlightenment' (*bodhicitta*). The means for this communion include incantation (*mantra*), diagrams (*maṇḍala*: which includes the whole layout of the site where the ritual is to be performed, much as for a Vedic rite and like that in the open air, there is even a *homa*, 'oblation', though the aim is purely Buddhist: the oblation symbolises the burning up of passions and delusion in

1. The *Bhaiṣajyaguru Sūtra* and other texts edited in *Gilgit Manuscripts* Vol. I, Śrīnagar, 1939.
2. He also translated the *Susiddhikara*, a 'Kriyā' Tantra.

the fire of understanding), symbols (*mudrā*) and *yoga* ('union', 'unification', the rites and meditations by which the 'union' is attained). The first rite to be performed is the 'consecration' (*abhiṣeka*) of the student. The latter must be carefully selected as pure, self-controlled, earnest, devoted to his teacher, etc., and ready to sacrifice his life for the sake of the study of the doctrine. The main rite can then be carried out, with offerings of flowers and so on. However, this tangible rite is stated to be a preliminary or elementary exercise to make the 'diagram' visible to living beings (and so attract them to it). The real or highest rite takes place only in the thoughts of the student, who after the preliminary exercise is to imagine the diagram in his own body and finally in thought only.[1]

These three, or rather two, texts are important items in the collection known as *tantras*, 'systems', on which the Mantrayāna is based, and which appear as a separate group, alongside the *sūtras*, in the Tibetan *Tripiṭaka*. This new 'vehicle' claims to be as ancient and authentic (as taught by the Buddha) as any other, but it evidently grew up gradually in the milieu of the texts we have just discussed and others like them. Increasingly it was ritual, and then special kinds of meditation, which was used to attain the desired end, though incantations form part of most of the 'systems'. The followers of the Mantrayāna contrast it with the Sūtrayāna, 'Vehicle of the Sūtras', or with Pāramitā as the other main branch of the Mahāyāna. An alternative title is Vajrayāna, 'Diamond Vehicle', 'diamond' symbolising the unchangeable, indestructible, non-dual nature of the ultimate reality, identification with which is the aim of the student of each system. Perhaps the earliest of the major *tantras* is the *Guhyasamāja*, 'Secret Assembly'. According to the traditional interpretation of it the means here is meditation only, the visualisation of the Buddha with whom, or through whom, the 'union' is sought. However, the interpretation standardised by later commentators may have been preceded by more tangible conduct of its rituals.

The origins of the Mantrayāna thus seem to be datable to about the 6th century. The Japanese tradition[2] is that the

---

1. For the contents of this text see Tajima : *Étude sur le Mahāvairocana-sūtra*, Paris, 1936. For an early Śaiva tantric rite see IKL Vol. IV, §1665.
2. Tajima, op. cit. pp. 21, 31ff.

Mantrayāna doctrine was deposited in a pagoda in South India (Āndhra ?) by Vajrasattva, on the instructions of the Buddha, until men capable of understanding it should appear. Nāgārjuna eventually opened the pagoda, was 'consecrated' by Vajrasattva and spread this doctrine. Tāranātha holds that the *tantras* began to appear in the world of men at the same time as the Mahāyāna *sūtras* but that the Kriyā and Caryā Tantras (see below) were handed down in great secrecy and so unknown except to those actually engaged in their practice. On the other hand he says that the Anuttarayoga Tantras (see below) were procured by a series of individual teachers and so appeared gradually. The teachers he names (Saraha, Kambala, Padmavajra alias Saroruha, Kukkuri, Kṛṣṇācārya, Lalitavajra, Lūyipāda, Gambhīravajra and Piṭo) all lived between c. 800 and 1040 A.D., which appears to give us the dates of 'publication' of a series of *tantras*. In one case, however, he says elsewhere that the text, or at least the essence of it (an earlier version ?) was known to a teacher earlier than any of these, Ḍombiheruka, along with two very short texts, and that his teacher Virūpa knew a more important *tantra*. Ḍombiheruka was a contemporary of Vilasyavajrā, teacher's teacher of Kambala (or Kampala).[1] His date apparently is in the second half of the 8th century and he was a contemporary of the celebrated Padmasambhava (who is identified with Padmavajra Saroruha by some) of Uḍḍiyāna (the Suvastu valley, an old centre of the Dharmaguptaka school), who was engaged in spreading Buddhism in Tibet at the same time as Śāntarakṣita (according to later tradition in collaboration with him, but this assumes that Śāntarakṣita followed the Mantrayāna, of which there is no hint in his available works).

Allowing that the *Guhyasamāja*, *Mahāvairocana*, *Sarvatathāgatatattvasaṃgraha* and *Vajraśikhara* are earlier than the 8th century we can add first that three other major *tantras*, the *Cakrasaṃvara*, *Vajrabhairava* and *Mañjuśrīmūlakalpa*, may conjecturally be placed in about the 8th century. As to those named in connection with the teachers mentioned above, we have the following: *Raktayamāri* (known to Virūpa c. 750),

1. Snellgrove, *The Hevajra Tantra*, Vol. I, p. 13. cf. IKL Vol. IV, §2510.

Hevajra (which refers to the *Sarvatathāgatatattvasaṃgraha*, second half of 8th century, its 'essence' known to Ḍombiheruka along with the brief *Kurukullīkalpa* and *Ārāli* and its full text known to Kambala and Saroruha), *Buddhakapāla* (c. 800, known to Saraha, a pupil of Haribhadra, though there seem to have been 2 Sarahas: we recall that Haribhadra's other celebrated pupil, Buddhajñāna, is supposed to have written on Mantrayāna, the syncretism of Pāramitā with the latter thus beginning at this date), *Mahāmāyā* (c. 800, known to Kukkuri, a contemporary of Kambala and Saroruha), *Kṛṣṇayamāri* (known to Lalitavajra of Uḍḍiyāna, who appears to have been of the same period as this group of teachers), *Sampuṭa* (*Caturyoginisampuṭa*) and *Tilaka* (*Mahāmudrātilaka*) (early 9th century, both procured by Kṛṣṇācārya or Kṛṣṇapaṇḍita, the first of two or more writers of that name), *Yoginisaṃcaryā* (Lūyipāda, apparently 11th century), *Vajrāmṛta* (Gambhīravajra, beginning of 11th century) and *Kālacakra* (procured by Piṭo c. 1040).

If we compare this series of *tantras* with the collection preserved in the Tibetan *Tripiṭaka* edited by Bu-ston we find that we have an apparently fairly representative selection of the main texts. The whole collection does not appear to have been thoroughly studied by any recent scholars outside Tibet and the probable dates of the other texts remain completely undetermined, so that we should perhaps here attempt at the most a brief survey of the *tantras* named above. Most of them seem to be extant in Sanskrit, though few are so far published. It is worth noting, however, that whereas all Mahāyāna *sūtras* were supposed to be written in Sanskrit the *tantras* were, according to the commentary *Vimalaprabhā* on the *Kālacakra*, written in Sanskrit, Prakrit or Apabhraṃśa, 'etc.', Apabhraṃśa being the spoken language of northern India in the period of composition of the *tantras*. An Apabhraṃśa *tantra* has in fact been published, the *Ḍākārṇava* (Calcutta, 1935, edited by N. N. Chaudhuri). Altogether there are more than fifty *tantras* of some consequence, being more than a few pages in length, and many more than that number of very brief texts.. The *Mañjuśrīmūla* is the longest, being longer than any Mahāyāna *sūtra* except the Great Perfection of Understanding. The *Kālacakra* also is fairly long (about half its length) and the

Sarvatathāgatatattvasaṃgraha (and *Vajraśikhara*) about the same. Most of the others are quite short.

As regards chronology and country of origin we can divide the *tantras* here considered into perhaps four groups. In about the 6th and 7th centuries we may place the composition of the *Guhyasamāja*, *Vajraśikhara*, *Sarvatathāgatatattvasaṃgraha* and *Mahāvairocana*. The place of origin of this group may, since it is connected with Nāgārjuna and Nāgabodhi and the South, have been in Āndhra, that great creative centre of Mahāyāna movements, or Kaliṅga. A little later, perhaps about the early 8th century, we have the *Cakrasaṃvara*, *Vajrabhairava* and *Mañjuśrimūla*, of which the last seems to have been written in the North as we now have it but to have originated much earlier in the South (Āndhra). We seem to be on firmer ground with the next group, the series beginning with the *Raktayamāri* and *Hevajra*. These appeared between 750 and 850 and several of them are clearly represented as originating in Uḍḍiyāna (whose kings were adepts in these *tantras*), which evidently was the major centre of the Mantrayāna in the 8th century. These texts are shown as soon brought to such universities as Nālandā for study, and as taught there by successions of teachers, but it is not necessary to suppose that any of them were composed in the Pāla Empire: though Kṛṣṇācārya procured two of them he need not have done this in the Empire. After this there seems to be a gap of about a century or more before the origin of the *tantras* procured at the beginning of the 11th century. The gap is probably due to the incompleteness of our information, but the most important of the last three *tantras* of our selection, the *Kālacakra*, represents a new phase sometimes even dignified with the title of a new 'vehicle', the Kālacakrayāna. It appears to have originated in Āndhra, since the Buddha is stated to have spoken it at Dhānyakaṭaka.

We have already mentioned some of the leading teachers of Mantrayāna and given their dates. A few more, and also commentaries by those above, may now be noted. Important commentaries on the *tantras* were written by Virūpa (*Raktayamāri*), Saraha (*Buddhakapāla*), Saroruha (*Hevajra*), Kukkuri (*Mahāmāyā*), Kṛṣṇācārya I (*Hevajra*), the latter's pupil Kṛṣṇācārya II (*Cakrasaṃvara*), Dharmakīrti II (*Hevajra*), another Nāgārjuna (9th century, *Guhyasamāja*), a Candrakīrti

(9th century, also on *Guhyasamāja*), Bhavyakīrti (9th century, *Cakrasaṃvara*), Vimalamitra (9th century, *Guhygarbha*), Jayabhadra (10th century, *Cakrasaṃvara*), Śrīdhara (10th century, *Yamāri*), Bhadrapāda (10th century, *Hevajra, Cakrasaṃvara, Vajraḍāka* and *Catuḥpīṭha*), Līlāvajra (10th century, *Yamāri and Guhyagarbha*), Ānandagarbha (*Sarvatathāgatatattvasaṃgraha, Guhyasamāja, Māyājāla, Paramādi* and others), Vajragarbha (11th century ? *Hevajra*), Taṅkadāsa (11th century, *Hevajra*), Mañjuśrīkīrti, (11th century ? *Kālacakra*), Ratnākaraśānti, Abhayākaragupta, Śubhākaragupta (12th century, *Ekavīra*) and Ratnarakṣita (end of 12th century, *Saṃvarodaya*).

Besides the commentaries, of which these are only a selection of perhaps the most important (there are several others, mostly undated at present, on the *Cakrasaṃvara*, several on the *Guhyasamāja*, several on the *Durgatipariśodhana*, others on the *Abhidhānottara, Vajraḍāka, Ḍākārṇava, Ḍākinījāla, Sarvatathāgatatattvasaṃgraha, Mahāvairoçana, Dhyānottarapaṭala*, etc., and a number of sub-commentaries : two major commentators not yet precisely dated are an Āryadeva some time after the Candrakīrti above and Buddhaguhya some time after Ānandagarbha), we find a series of textbooks on Mantrayāna by some of these, and other, writers. Nāgārjuna's *Pañcakrama* is perhaps the most outstanding, many commentaries being written on it (by Bhavyakīrti, Nāgabodhi, Rakṣitapāda), together with his *Caturmudrāniścaya.* His pupil Maitṛpa (or 'Advayavajra') wrote a *Caturmudropadeśa.* Nāḍapāda (11th century) ('Nāropa') wrote a whole series of works. The great teacher Atīśa (982-1055) is best known for his activities in Tibet but he also worked in various ways in India (he acted as peacemaker between the Emperor Nayapāla and the Kalacuri King Karṇa and his writings include an epistle to this emperor, the *Vimalaratnalekha*). Anupamarakṣita wrote a *Ṣaḍaṅgayoga* on the *Kālacakra* system and Vibhūticandra (early 13th century, continued writing as a refugee in Tibet) wrote his *Antarmañjarī* on the same system.

Some of these teachers contributed to anthologies of poetry which present the quest for enlightenment, with very varied imagery, according to the Madhyamaka philosophy and Mantrayāna systems of ritualism (for example the quest is a game of chess). To popularise their ideas they wrote in the Apabhraṃśa vernacular (probably as spoken in Magadha as well as further West). Translations of a selection of these poems will be found in IKL Vols. IV and V, chapters XXXVI (§§2512-9) and XXXVIII (end). Such poetry is attributed to Saraha, Kambala, Kṛṣṇācārya, Tailapāda, Lūyipāda, Bhusuka and others. Though the teaching of these *dohā* and *caryāpada* poems is essentially the same as that of the later Mantrayāna generally, it sometimes seems to be regarded as a new 'vehicle', the Sahajayāna, 'Natural Vehicle', stressing the idea that the new 'systems' are simple and that following them to realise one's identity with the ultimate reality involves nothing but the most 'natural' behaviour.

The Kriyā, Caryā, Yoga and Anuttarayoga Systems

In the Tibetan *Tripiṭaka* the *tantras* are arranged in four groups, of which the last is also subdivided into three (representing later developments) making an eventual total of six. The *tantras* of the earliest period seem to have included the four kinds of system: the *Mahāvairocana* is reckoned as Caryā, the *Vajraśikhara* and *Sarvatathāgatatattvasaṃgraha* as Yoga, the *Guhyasamāja* as Anuttarayoga; as for Kriyā, this 'lowest' system has been comparatively neglected, its texts occupy a subordinate place, but the *Susiddhikara* is of the 8th century or earlier and another early example is the *Dhyānottarapaṭalakrama* of unknown date but before the 9th century.

The distinctive feature of the Mantrayāna is ritual. In this period of Indian history there was a strong trend, affecting all religions, to substitute a tangible and so popular ritual for the earlier abstract meditations. It was even proposed (by the Śaivas) to set aside the ancient Vedic ritual, which, though more elaborately developed in some respects than any other, is 'abstract' in the sense that its equipment is simple and totally undecorative, carried out on temporary, unadorned brick altars in the open air with crude wooden implements (and plenty of incantations). In place of this there should nowadays be a richly decorative cult of the supreme Being (Śiva) represented in sculpture, personified or symbolically, with all the company of heaven, in permanent and magnificent temples, a cult which should make use of all the arts, including painting, music, dancing (especially) and drama. No doubt the Buddhists responded to this trend when they produced new rituals of their own, incorporating some of the popular forms as well as developing their rich and ancient arts. This development was a very different matter from the ancient pilgrimages and reverence offered at pagodas and shrines or the narrative art depicting the legend of the Buddha and other stories. Whatever festival performances took place in connection with the popularising of early Buddhism were means of propaganda intended to induce people to live the Buddhist way, they did not themselves constitute the way. Now, however, ritual itself becomes the way and supersedes the *sūtras*: the doctrine is to be acted out in tangible form, not 'simply' understood mentally (we have to be careful of our expression here: in either case the way is realised or 'lived').

The *Mañjuśrimūla* is vast in extent and clearly not the work of a single period. It includes a substantial history of Buddhism down to the beginning of the Pāla dynasty in the 8th century, so that as we have it it cannot be earlier than that. However, some parts may well be much earlier. As to its system, it would seem to include both Kriyā and Caryā. It supplies us with a great deal of information on ritual (*kriyā*) in its most tangible forms, with symbols and diagrams but also instruction for painting (on cloth, *paṭa*, i.e. silk, etc.), which has to represent the perfections and benevolence as well as all the Buddhas and *bodhisattvas* and other beings (even the Śaiva deities are included). Much of the ritual is designed simply to honour the compassionate *bodhisattvas* and other beings (these include the compassionate Tārā[1], consort of the *bodhisattva* Avalokiteśvara, who is further multiplied into a whole series of Tārās). The student is to observe virtue and meditation as preparation for the ritual, then he is consecrated and taught the incantation by his 'diagram teacher'. Instruction in esoteric symbolism follows. Caryā means generally 'conduct' (including for example the way of the *bodhisattva*) but here it means the actions to be performed in the ritual and the whole conduct of the performer whilst preparing for it and carrying it out. A distinction familiar later would seem to

1. Cf. IKL Vol. IV, § 2528.

make Kriyā ordinary public ritual and Caryā the esoteric or secret ritual performed only by the initiate after consecration.

We noted briefly the content of the *Mahāvairocana* above. As a Caryā we notice that it involves a consecration and postures for meditation as well as the rituals of symbol and diagram, all of which is to lead the student to a realisation of identity with the Buddha (as Vairocana). The *Vajraśikhara* or *Sarvatathāgatatattvasaṃgraha* being a Yoga *tantra* the ritual and 'conduct' are subordinate to meditation, in other words the student is led beyond the outward forms of the ritual (though there is an elaborate description of diagram preparation) to some kind of inner realisation.

As an Anuttarayoga system the *Guhyasamāja* should operate through meditation only, though of a kind quite different from early Buddhist meditation, namely the visualisation of the Buddha (here again as Vairocana) with whom 'union' is to be realised, accompanied by a circle of female *bodhisattvas* (Locanā, Māmakī, Pāṇḍarā and Tārā), a group which constitutes a 'diagram'. The ritualistic diagram is thus only to be imagined, it is transferred from concrete representation into pure meditation. In this text the term 'diamond' (*vajra*) is used to symbolise the ultimate reality in which there is no duality. In stressing the point that there is, ultimately, no duality of any sort the *Tantra* goes on to deny all distinctions whatsoever, of male and female, wife and mother, passion and detachment, proper and improper food, etc., for ultimately everything is identical with the diamond, which is also the Buddha, everything is part of the non-dual reality. This may be regarded as an extension of the doctrine of the Madhyamaka that there is no distinction between extinction (*nirvāṇa*) and transmigration (*saṃsāra*). The statements which have startled some modern readers should in this system be understood as paradoxes analagous to those of the Perfection of Understanding.

The following series of *tantras* all belong to a class known as Yoginī (the feminine of *yogin*, i.e. the female student) or as Anuttarayoga either in the general sense as above or in a restricted sense as a subdivision of that group (the form 'Anuyoga' is also used for this). When the group is divided we have the three subdivisions Mahāyoga (into which the *Guhya-*

samāja then falls), Anuttarayoga in the restricted sense and Atiyoga (which will contain the *Kālacakra*). These Yoginī Anuttarayoga systems include the *Cakrasaṃvara* (or *Mahāsaṃvarodaya*), *Vajrabhairava*, *Hevajra*, *Buddhakapāla*, *Mahāmāyā*, *Kṛṣṇayamāri*, *Caturyoginīsampuṭa* and *Mahāmudrātilaka* (the later *Yoginīsaṃcaryā* also belongs to this subdivision, so do the *Ḍākārṇava* and the important *Abhidhānottara* on incantations).

The student (*yogin*) of the *Cakrasaṃvara* is to use the following meditation or visualisation. When about to go to sleep he should imagine his body to be that of the Buddha as Vajrasattva (Diamond Being, the unchanging ultimate reality; in this text also called Heruka) and then merge into emptiness. When he awakes he should look upon everything around him as constituting the diagram of himself as Vajrasattva. He has already been consecrated. Sitting comfortably facing the South he should take a drop (on the tip of a finger) of *amṛta* (wine, permitted only for ritual purposes), then recite the three 'refuges' (p. 187 above) and the Good Wishes ('May all beings be happy...be free from unhappiness....experience equanimity'). Then he should imagine himself in the state of 'great happiness' (of the Buddha as Heruka) in union with his *yoginī* (who is Heruka's consort Vajravārāhī; sexual union in this system symbolises the highest happiness). Imagining his body to be that of the Buddha he should say 'I am Śrī Heruka' and meditate on these syllables as symbolic of non-duality, etc. Then he should imagine the letter 'a' in the centre of his heart (symbolising the knowledge of the unreality of all principles), on it the disc of the Moon (symbolising knowledge of all objects) and on that the incantation syllable '*hūṃ*' (symbolising thought free from any object; all the parts of the syllable are further symbolic). From this incantation syllable blue, green, red and yellow light radiates and fills the whole universe. Then he should again think of the Good Wishes, adding 'May all beings be free from both desire and aversion...' He then snaps his fingers in the ten directions wishing happiness to all. Then he has to imagine the constituent groups of his body (matter, consciousness, etc.) to be various *buddhas*, Vairocana, Vajrasattva, etc., all the groups becoming thus-gone and the whole constituting Heruka. The sense organs (eyes, etc.) of Heruka are 'diamond-delusion', 'diamond-aversion', 'diamond-passion' and other defilements. The earth, water and other elements are female *bodhisattvas*.

The *yogin* should then honour the various beings with incantations, flowers, incense, lights, music, etc., in his imagination creating and offering everything conceivable. Next he repeats his commitment as a *bodhisattva* and to cultivate virtue and avoid defilements, and repeats various incantations.

Afterwards he should imagine a grand dwelling (*vihāra*) constructed and adorned with everything beautiful: sculptures, bells, flowers, etc. Outside it are eight cemeteries adorned with trees, rivers and clouds and presided over by eight Vedic gods, beautifully dressed, and guarded by goddesses. He should think of himself as the Buddha in the state of great happiness at the centre of a lotus in this dwelling (the lotus in this system symbolises the female organ, the diamond the male: the *yogin* is now the Diamond Being at the centre of his lotus, which is the stage of great happiness). He has four faces (of different colours) and twelve hands (two embracing his *yoginī*, the others holding a thunderbolt, which is the symbol for 'diamond' symbolising emptiness, a bell symbolising compassion, a knife which cuts away defilements, etc.). An immense array of details of his ritual equipment, dress and ornaments is described. He embraces his *yoginī* Vajravarāhī, who clings to him (showing that she is the 'means', *upāya*) and is red in colour (passionate, loving all beings, symbolising compassion). One of her hands, encircling him, symbolises the concealing truth and holds a skull full of blood. The other symbolises ultimate truth and holds a knife (the knowledge which cuts away all 'imagining' and defilements). She is naked, which symbolises her freedom from the obscuring influence of the defilements, but has various ornaments.

The pair are attended by four female *bodhisattvas* or *yoginīs* on the petals of the lotus, naked but holding symbolic objects. In a circle of 'thought' outside these are eight more female *bodhisattvas* or *yoginīs*, beyond these another eight in a circle of 'speech' and beyond these another eight in a circle of 'body' (these are the three kinds of action[1]). The positions of these

1. These plus 'action' are the four signets or symbols (*mudrās*).

yoginis are identified with places in India, and even Sumatra, celebrated as centres of the 'system'; they include Uḍḍiyāna, Lambaka and other places in the North West as well as Āndhra, Sindhu, Kāmarūpa (Assam) and other countries. Some of the outer *yoginis* are united with their male consorts. There are also female guardians of the eight entrances to the dwelling.

All this 'diagram' must be made vivid in the mind of the *yogin*. The 37 *yoginis* are to be thought of as symbolising the 37 principles on the side of enlightenment (as in the earliest Buddhism). After further symbolisations this meditation concludes with the thought that everything is emptiness and 'that is myself'. Other similar meditations follow.

It is the emphasis on the *yoginis* which underlies the grouping of these Anuttarayoga systems separately from the Mahāyoga systems which emphasise the central Buddha. The two groups are also known respectively as 'mother' systems and 'father' systems.

The *Hevajra* opens like a *sūtra*, but without stating where the Buddha is supposed to be plunges abruptly into a dialogue between the Buddha as Vajrasattva and a *bodhisattva* Vajragarbha. First it is said that the Buddha is in a state of sexual union with his 'diamond women'. The Buddha then explains 'diamond' as meaning without difference and 'Hevajra' as the vocative *he* symbolising compassion plus 'diamond' symbolising understanding. This text is the cause of the occurrence and continuance of the *yoginis* and Heruka (the latter is more or less a synonym for Hevajra). A list of incantations is given (some reminiscent of those of the *Atharva Veda*, for producing rain and so on). The practice of the meditation of pervading the directions with benevolence, compassion, sympathetic joy and equanimity (see pp. 95 f. above) is the first requirement of the student here. That on emptiness follows (the Madhyamaka philosophy is assumed as the basis throughout this *Tantra* and occasionally expounded briefly). The student (*yogin*) should then imagine himself as Heruka seated on a corpse (symbolising the element of principles) in an enclosure covered only by a network (of diamonds), the Sun before him and various mystic syllables visualised in space. Then he should imagine these in his heart. He is attended by eight goddesses (*devīs*), Gaurī and others, being embraced by one of them, the passionate Ḍombī.

His own form is that of a 16 year old youth. Alternatively he is said to be embraced by his 'understanding', namely Vajravārāhī. The student is consecrated by the goddesses and other beings, 'diamond songs' being sung by Locanā and other female *bodhisattvas* (an example is given later, in Apabhraṃśa: the words, mostly metaphorical, celebrate eating, drinking, acting and making love, II.iv 6-8) (I.iv).

A section briefly indicating the philosophical position follows: reality (*tattva*) has no visible object or seer (and similarly for the other senses), no thought or thinker (as in Madhyamaka), no developer or development, no incantation or divinity, the last two being 'figured' (*saṃsthita*, set up) only as having non-differentiation as their own-nature. Reality has Vairocana, Akṣobhya (names of *buddhas*) and other names, including 'Brahmā', 'Viṣṇu' and 'Śiva' (syncretism is here seeking to embrace the whole of Vedism and 'Hinduism', however we are told below that the *Veda*, etc., will not bring success) (I.v).

The *yogin*, dressed in a tiger skin and wearing a variety of symbolic ornaments, should meditate at night under a tree, in a cemetery or in a temple of the 'mothers' (goddesses), or rather in any remote, deserted place. After developing some 'warmth' (power from concentration) he should select a suitable (beautiful) 'diamond' girl and perform the 'conduct' (*caryā*), which includes dancing and (optionally) diamond songs, whilst being 'concentrated'. Dancing symbolises development, song symbolises incantation (I.vi.13).

Here it is observed that the student should abandon 'greed' (desire), delusion, fear, anger, shame, give up drowsiness, make no distinctions over food and drink, taking what comes and not imagining anything to be desirable or undesirable. He is freed from training, vows, incantations, meditation, etc. He just wanders about full of compassion, continuing the 'conduct' (presumably of a *bodhisattva*). There are secret signs for identifying initiates (*yogins* and *yoginīs*), i.e. responsive partners for the rites (the *yoginīs* will welcome a suitable *yogin* with garlands after identifying and choosing him). A list of centres of ritual performances is given (it includes Jālandhara, Uḍḍiyāna, Lambaka, Nagara(hāra), Sindhu, Kaliṅga, Sumatra and other countries, with a concentration in the NW), but any cemetery will do (I.vii).

The performance is now described in detail. First the 'diagram' is laid out in an enclosure (as before for the consecration): the *yogin* for this purpose meditates on a female organ in space and develops a wheel (diagram) in it. In the centre of this is a corpse (presumably the element of principles as above). On it sit fifteen *yoginīs* wearing tiger skins round their hips and holding skulls (symbolising the imagining of existent and non-existent) and knives (symbolising cutting out faults such as pride). Then (in union) the female organ, called 'knowledge', is in the 'lotuses' (*yoginīs* ?) and the 'wheel' developed is called happiness. The sexual excitement and experience of each partner (in the symbolism the fluids, so called *śukra*, excited in the bodies of both of them, it being important to note the full mutuality of the experience, sometimes obscured by inaccurate translations of such texts as this; the system is for women to practice as well as men and with complete parallelism, for the *śukra* of the *yoginī* see e.g. I.x.6 and II.viii.7) symbolises the thought of enlightenment (both are *bodhisattvas*). This 'natural' thought of enlightenment experienced by them is explained at the two levels of truth: the fluids are the appearance at the concealing level; the happiness, or joy, is at the ultimate level (extinction, the 'joy of cessation', enlightenment). It is also said here that the woman symbolises understanding (*prajñā*) and the man 'means' or compassion (I.viii.28; in the *Cakrasaṃvara* understanding was symbolised by the diamond; everything is relative and ultimately identical, for in reality there is no duality). One ought to remain continuously in union with reality (*tattvayoga*). A man should think of his *yoginī* at all times (II.ii.2-6), in all his daily actions. The *yoginī* is there understood to be Non-Soul (Nairātmyā), the central one of the fifteen in the diagram and one of the names of Heruka's consort. It is also said that one wishing for success should remain always in union with either Heruka or Nairātmyā.

Of the 'natural' (*sahaja*) joy (enlightenment, knowledge) it is said that it is the life (breath) of living beings, the universe is made of it, existent and non-existent occur because of it and likewise all consciousness, 'man' (*puruṣa*, 'spirit'), 'God' (*Īśvara*), soul, life-principle, being, time, person and the own-nature of all existents. The *bodhisattva* Vajragarbha and the other hearers of the *Tantra* are astonished at this statement by the Buddha (I.x.8-14).

The text goes on to describe the consecration of the *yogin*, in a 'diagram' and with a *yoginī* (here the *yoginī* is knowledge, which is emptiness, the *yogin* the means, which is compassion). This is done by a teacher (*ācārya*, *śāstṛ*). He himself embraces the *yoginī*, consecrating her (exciting her with the 'thought of enlightenment'), then establishes a communion between her and the *yogin* and entrusts her to him after honouring her. Having honoured the teacher the *yogin* embraces the *yoginī*. As he attains the moment of highest joy, free from all differentiation (this is his 'union'), the teacher tells him he should remember this great happiness and work for the welfare of all beings until he attains enlightenment (I.x, II.iii.13-23).

In the course of the description several comments occur. There is no happiness without a body. Transmigration (*bhava*) is purified by transmigration, passion by passion, imagining by counter-imagining (*prati-kḷp*). The consecration is not for enjoyment (*bhoga*) but for contemplating one's thoughts (to see whether the mind is steady or not). The whole universe is 'natural' (*sahaja*), its own-nature is extinction (that *saṃsāra* is *nirvāṇa* is added below). Reality is emptiness: there is no incantation, diagram, etc. (II.ii).

After the consecration the *yogin* is taught his rule of conduct for the future: he should 'take life', 'speak falsely', 'take what was not given' and 'pursue others' women'. This, however, is said to mean (respectively) that he should concentrate his thought (bringing about its translucence), say 'I shall save all people' (ultimately there aren't any, this is the old Perfection of Understanding 'paradox'), take the *śukra* of a woman (which is 'not given', which symbolises knowledge which has to be gained) and pursue the beautiful girl who only seems to be his (Non-Soul, 'others' ' referring to her remoteness). An intelligent person eats and drinks what comes and does not bother about what is 'suitable'. He does not perform any rites or meditations and does not avoid sex: he enjoys all women without fear. He loves and hates no one, friend or enemy. He does not honour the gods made of wood, stone and clay, for he is his own divinity (II.iii.29ff).

Towards the end of the text the *yoga* diagram of Hevajra himself is briefly described to Non-Soul (Nairātmyā), since most of what precedes has been about the *yoginī* diagram (as it should be in a *Yoginī tantra*; but the first meditation above was of the Heruka, i.e. Hevajra variety, the usual distinction being that if the Buddha is at the centre we have a *yoga* system and if Nairātmyā is at the centre we have a *yoginī*). The *Sarvatathāgata-tattvasaṃgraha* is referred to for fuller details (being a Yoga system). Here there are eight goddesses or 'knowledges' (*vidyās*). The *yogin* honours and kisses them and they eat and drink. Then he removes their garments and makes love to them, with dancing and singing. New *yogins* may be brought in (blindfolded at first) and consecrated in this diagram (II.v).

This *Tantra* with its realistic and circumstantial details seems to imply 'real' performances, actual ritual promiscuity, noisy orgies. Though the text itself repeatedly says that all this is imagined, is meditation, and dwells all the time on the aim of enlightenment, describing all its symbols as pointing towards ultimate reality, we still remember the total ambiguity of a universe where transmigration is extinction and where everything in our concealing experience, or at least as we ordinarily think of it, is imagining. What difference is there between a 'live' orgy in imagined transmigration and an imaginary orgy? The only difference possible seems to be that the 'imagined' performance is not an orgy at all but a description of the way to enlightenment (the *Tantra* tells us that beings are simply *buddhas* but are covered with accidental defilements), in metaphorical language. Perhaps the new metaphors are more powerful than the old ones of crossing the ocean of transmigration and the like. Perhaps in a society free from some of the inhibitions of the 'modern' world orgies were commonplace social occasions causing no surprise to anyone and considered natural. Those who aimed at extinction might then use the imagery of the highest happiness recognised in the world of transmigration to symbolise the happiness of extinction. Putting aside such conjectures, however, we should note that the commentators are solidly in favour of the text being metaphorical, though aware that some people practice the rites literally. Thus Vajragarbha says the text is 'having its meaning requiring to be drawn out' (*neyārtha*, see p. 150 above), though Dr. Snellgrove in pointing this out to us[1] suggests Vajragarbha represents a later trend than the *Tantra* itself (since the *Tantra* itself stresses the metaphorical meaning of its statements we cannot accept his opinion of a difference of outlook between it and Vajragarbha).

For Kṛṣṇācārya (early 9th century) this system of *yoga* leads to enlightenment in this present life (and the *Hevajra* is the best account of it, being clearest), it thus excels the Pāramitā scheme, the way of the six perfections, because the *bodhisattva* following the latter takes an immensely long time, countless lives, to complete it.[2] This then is a system for attaining enlightenment and it is better than any other. The *Hevajra* itself outlines a progressive course of Buddhist teaching as follows: beings should first be taught the Vaibhāṣya (i.e. the Sarvāstivāda doctrine, according to Kṛṣṇācārya the *Avadānas* in the first place, in other words edifying stories), then the *Sūtra* (both early and Mahāyāna), then the Yogācāra (*cittamātra* idealism), then the Madhyamaka, then the schemes of the Mantrayāna leading up to the *Hevajra* as the highest. In other words the *Hevajra* system, or any Mantrayāna system, was not open to any student at all but only to those of profound understanding. Perhaps even such statements as that passion is purified by passion are to be understood as applying purely at the level of meditation. However, we may probably conclude that at some earlier period, before the recension of the *Tantra* in its present form, these rituals were literally carried out, in circles not necessarily Buddhist or religious, perhaps as a kind of therapy (which has recommended itself so strongly to some contemporary readers interested in psychology). Some of our Buddhist commentators mention that foolish persons sometimes carried the rites out literally, adding that their actions will bear the usual results in long continuing transmigration. For the Mantrayāna school from at least the 9th century the ancient Buddhist social teaching applies (at the concealing level, in the universe of transmigration, just as for Nāgārjuna) and its special esoteric 'systems' are methods of meditation, enabling very bright students to attain enlightenment in a very short time. The motive was the same as that of the Chinese Dhyāna school, moreover certain parallelisms of technique may

1. *The Hevajra*, p. 17 of the Introduction.
2. pp. 129f.

be discerned. The other and more obvious parallelism is with the later Kṛṣṇa cult of Vaiṣṇavism (inspired chiefly by the *Bhāgavata Purāṇa*), the dances and orgies of the young Kṛṣṇa and his circle of milkmaids, which are taken as a subject for devotion, as a model for the seeking of the human soul for God. A third and more philosophical parallel is the school of Śaivism which developed in Kaśmīra, the Pratyabhijñā or Trika doctrine, its origins in time (c. 800 A.D.) and space being so close to the Mantrayāna of Uḍḍiyāna that mutual knowledge and some interaction must be assumed. The 84 *siddhas* ('accomplished' persons, teachers) were recognised by both schools.

Of all the *tantras* the *Guhyasamāja*, *Cakrasaṃvara* and *Hevajra* seem to have been regarded as the most important, to judge from the numbers of commentaries written on them. Of equal or even greater importance in the view of the school in Tibet there remains only the *Kālacakra*, which has fewer Indian commentaries only because it was current in India for a much shorter period than these. It is supposed to have been procured, as was noted above, as recently as 1040 A.D., and the at least four Indian commentaries on it (by Mañjuśrīkīrti, Dārika, Abhayākaragupta and the anonymous *Vimalaprabhā*) are apparently all to be dated between 1040 and 1200 (apparently there were two Dārikas of importance as Mantrayāna teachers). We have also noted that the *Kālacakra* is an Atiyoga system, the highest of the subdivisions of the Anuttarayoga, and that it was probably composed in Āndhra. In fact it seems to be the only important work available of the Atiyoga. The meditation system proposed here is generally similar to those of the Yoginī systems, the student visualising the whole universe in his body, with the characteristic addition that 'time' (*kāla*) is equally contained in the body in the form of the process of the breath or life (*prāṇa*). The meditation on time, thus conceived, apparently gave its name to the new system. There is greater stress than before on the theory of the nervous system as a basis for *yoga*, though this also is briefly outlined in the *Hevajra*, *Sampuṭikā*[1] and elsewhere. The statement that success and the highest happiness is impossible without the body, is based on bodily success, is also paralleled

1. In which Non-Soul normally resides in the navel but in the *yoga* moves up through the body producing joy.

in the *Hevajra*. The aim now is stated as union with Kālacakra as the all embracing Buddha. Non-duality is stressed here, but this is hardly new. We have, then, a restatement of the same general principles with certain new emphases, especially on physical *yoga* as contrasted with meditation, and bringing into the system of unification the universe of time as well as of space.

Such was the last major text to be added to the Indian *Tripiṭaka*, as authentic words of the Buddha according to the Mantrayāna school. Philosophically it reaffirms the Madhyamaka doctrine which claimed to be the original teaching, the Intermediate way (see pp. 376 ff. above), with some show of reason. Compared with the early doctrine the great difference is that ultimately principles are no more real than 'souls' or 'beings' whilst at the concealing level the latter are apparently as real as the former. If we accept the Madhyamaka as Buddhism we may accept the Atiyoga. Its basic position is the ancient Buddhist non-soul doctrine that there is nothing which is eternal. The presentation has changed, the techniques of the way to enlightenment have changed. The outward appearance of Buddhism is now dominated by ritualism and the array of *buddhas*, *bodhisattvas*, gods and goddesses imagined to exist at the concealing level (who all disappear in emptiness at the ultimate level). In this way some Buddhists sought to adapt Buddhism to medieval India. This was the India of Kharjuravāhaka (Khajuraho) and Bhuvaneśvara; the ruins of the parallel Buddhist art can be seen in the latest phases at Sāñcī and in fragmentary condition further north at Nālandā and Vārāṇasī (Sārnāth), also in the museum at Kharjuravāhaka itself, which once had its quota of Buddhist temples probably harmonising well with their Śaiva neighbours.

About a century after the presumed writing of the *Kālacakra* the Mantrayāna-Madhyamaka doctrine, incorporating the Pāramitā and Pramāṇa, was put in its final form by Abhayākaragupta, as we saw above, receiving a few supplements from later writers of his school: Śubhākaragupta, Raviśrījñāna, Sunayakaśrī, Dharmākaraśānti and others, including Vibhūticandra. Within a century of Abhayākaragupta's time most of Indian Buddhism was reduced to ashes and the monks slaughtered, Vibhūticandra being one of those who escaped to Tibet and worked to preserve the tradition there.

The Spirit of Destruction

'In the middle of the city there was a temple larger and firmer than the rest, which can neither be described nor painted. The Sultan thus wrote respecting it: "If any should wish to construct a building equal to this, he would not be able to do it without expending an hundred thousand red dinars, and it would occupy two hundred years, even though the most experienced and able workmen were employed." ... The Sultan gave orders that all the temples should be burnt with naphtha and fire, and levelled with the ground.'[1] 'Many of the inhabitants of the place fled and were scattered abroad...Many of them thus effected their escape, and those who did not fly were put to death.'[2] 'Islam or death was the alternative that Mahmūd placed before the people.'[3] 'Muhammad Bakhtiyar with great vigour and audacity rushed in at the gate of the fort (sic—the University of Uddaṇḍapura !) and gained possession of the place. Great plunder fell into the hands of the victors. Most of the inhabitants of the place were brahmans with shaven heads (i.e. Buddhist monks). They were put to death. Large numbers of books were found there, and when the Muḥammadans saw them, they called for some persons to explain their contents, but all the men had been killed. It was discovered that the whole 'fort' and city was a place of study. In the Hindi language the word Behar (*vihāra*) means a 'college'.'[4] 'When they reached the place they laid siege to it. . . The town was reduced to extremities and God prevailed over it in the same year. The people were forbidden to worship the Budd (statue of the Buddha), which the Muhammadans burned. Some of the people were burned, the rest were slain.'[5] 'Mahmūd replied: The religion of the faithful

1. Elliot : *The History of India as told by its own Historians*, 2nd edition, Calcutta, 1952, Vol. V, 39f. ('Utbi).
2. Ibid. p. 41.
3. 'Utbi, quoted by Majumdar, *History and Culture of the Indian People*, Vol. V, p. 499.
4. Elliot op. cit., Vol. XVI, 54f. (Minhaju-s Siraj).
5. Ibid. XVII. 102f. (Ibn Asir).

inculcates the following tenet: "That in proportion as the tenets of the Prophet are diffused, and his followers exert themselves in the subversion of idolatry, so shall be their reward in heaven;" that, therefore, it behoved him, with the assistance of God, to root out the worship of idols from the face of all India.'[1] 'This has been the principle of my ancestors from the time of Asadu-lla Ghalib until now : to convert unbelievers to the one God and the Musulman faith. If they adopt our creed, well and good. If not, we put them to the sword.'[2] 'The Muhammadan forces began to "kill and slaughter on the right and on the left unmercifully, throughout the impure land, for the sake of Islam," and blood flowed in torrents. They plundered gold and silver to an extent greater than can be conceived, and an immense number of brilliant precious stones . . . They took captive a great number of handsome and elegant maidens, amounting to 20,000, and children of both sexes, "more than the pen can enumerate" . . . In short the Muhammadan army brought the country to utter ruin, and destroyed the lives of the inhabitants, and plundered the cities, and captured their offspring, so that many temples were deserted and the idols were broken and trodden under foot . . .'[3] 'The nephew of Dahir, his warriors, and the principal officers have been despatched, and the infidels converted to Islam or destroyed. Instead of idol temples, mosques and other places of worship have been built, pulpits have been erected, the Khutba is read, the call to prayers is raised, so that devotions are performed at the stated hours. The takbir and praise to the Almighty God are offered every morning and evening.'[4] '. . . orders proscribing the residence of any person other than Muhammadans in Kashmīr... Many of the Brahmins, rather than abandon their religion or their country, poisoned themselves; some emigrated from their native homes, while a few escaped the evil of banishment by becoming Muhammadans. After the emigration of the Brahmins, Sikandar ordered all the temples in Kashmīr to be thrown down. . . Among other good institutions of Sikandar was the

1. Ibid. XVIII, 30f. (Firishta).
2. Ibid. XVIII, 123 (Chishti).
3. Ibid. XXII, 47f. (Wassaf).
4. Ibid. XXV, 66 (Chach-Náma : Muhammad Kasim's report to Hajjaj after conquering a predominantly Buddhist country).

prohibition of vending wine . . .'[1] '. . .he fell upon the insurgents unawares, and captured them all, to the number of twelve thousand—men, women, and children—whom he put to the sword. All their valleys and strongholds were overrun and cleared, and great booty captured. Thanks be to God for this victory of Islam! '[2] 'The Amir marched out towards Lamghan, which is a city celebrated for its great strength and abounding in wealth. He conquered it and set fire to the places in its vicinity which were inhabited by infidels, and demolishing the idol-temples, he established Islam in them. He marched and captured other cities and killed the polluted wretches, destroying the idolatrous and gratifying the Musulmans. After wounding and killing beyond all measure, his hands and those of his friends became cold in counting the value of the plundered property. On the completion of his conquest he returned and promulgated accounts of the victories obtained for Islam, and every one, great and small, concurred in rejoicing over this result and thanking God.'[3]

These examples from Muslim sources sufficiently illustrate the policy of kings inspired by the new religion which appeared in Arabia in the 7th century. The Buddhist historian Tāranātha explains this 'anti-Buddhism' or Mleccha (Barbarian) religion as being caused by Death (Māra), who misled the kings (especially the Turkish kings). It is hardly necessary to emphasise the thoroughness with which the older religions have been obliterated in practically every country where Muslims have ruled for any length of time.[4] Though India was never completely conquered and large areas remained under Hindu rule, there is hardly any part of it which has not been ravaged at some time by Muslim invaders or raiders, and the temples which still stand in the more remote regions almost all (apart from those recently built) bear the scars inflicted by those who defaced what they lacked the time and the means to destroy. Since the usual Muslim word for what they understand to be an 'idol' (*but* or *budd*) is in fact borrowed from the Sanskrit

---

1. Firishta, quoted by Majumdar, op. cit. Vol. VI p. 379.
2. Elliot op. cit. Vol. XVI p. 141.
3. Ibid. V, 18f.
4. cf. *Kālacakra* I. 26 : *siddhāntānāṃ vināśaḥ*.

(or Prakrit) *buddha*, we can imagine that the '*buddha*-smashers' on their religious campaigns took particular care to seek out and destroy Buddhist institutions.

We have no space to enter into the details of the Muslim campaigns. After the fall of Persia in the 7th century the Arab conquerors linked up with Turkish nomads on the northern borders of the Persian Empire, who readily embraced the teaching of fellow nomads so successful against their common enemy. Most of Central Asia, then predominantly Buddhist but a region of many religions, was overrun by the Arabs and Islamised, whilst in Iran they advanced up to what was then the most westerly conutry ruled by an Indian dynasty, Jāguḍa (modern Kandahar but with the capital at Gajani, founded by the Yādavas), where they were checked about A. D. 650. Early in the 8th century the Arabs attacked Sindhu by land and sea and gradually conquered it. Raiding further into India from this base they destroyed Valabhī with its university later in that century but afterwards were confined to Sindhu by the stiffening resistance of the Hindu 'Rājput' rulers (especially the Pratīhāras). Many Buddhist monks from the west now took refuge in the Pāla Empire. The Turks now became the champions of Islām in Asia. They repeatedly attacked Jāguḍa, which barred the way to the legendary riches of India, and conquered it completely towards the end of the 9th century (the Yādava family retired to Rājasthān, where they were able to establish themselves at Jaisalmir). The old Yādava capital of Gajani (Ghazni) then became the Turkish base for further operations against the empire of Gandhāra. Gandhāra, including Kāpiśa or Kubhā (Kābul), had formerly been ruled by a dynasty of 'Ṣāhis' or 'Kṣatriyas' who appear to have claimed descent from the great Kuṣāṇas, but from the middle of the 9th century it was ruled by another 'Ṣāhi' dynasty of a family of brahmans who had usurped the throne and then built up a large empire. They were able to check the Turks for another century, then a new Turkish dynasty (the Yamīnīs) was established at Gajani and launched a most determined war against Gandhāra. The war was long and for India unprecedentedly bitter: contemporary Indian writers speak of the 'Turkish Wars' as a new kind of war quite different from the traditional chivalrous contests between Indian aristocrats. India was fighting to save her civilisation from total destruction. In a series of campaigns at the end of the 10th century and the beginning of the 11th the Ṣāhis were gradually driven back through the mountain passes of Kāpiśa and Gandhāra. By 1020 they had lost everything and the last survivors of the family took refuge in Kaśmīra or in the Paramāra Rājput kingdom of Mālava. The Turkish leader (the Sultan Mahmūd mentioned above) then attacked the Pratīhāra domains, which luckily for him were in a state of disarray since the feudatories had asserted their independence of the Emperor. Mahmūd raided far and wide in successive years and amassed enormous loot and countless slaves, besides demolishing thousands of temples (which usually yielded much gold, silver and gems). Mathurā was pillaged (as described at the beginning of this section) and after the defeat of the main Pratīhāra army the capital, Kānyakubja, was sacked. 10,000 temples are said to have been destroyed there, with all their sculptures, and any inhabitants who had not fled were put to the sword. Finally Mahmūd was checked by the Candrātreya king Vidyādhara and forced to retire, but he was able to hold all the former Ṣāhi domains, including the Panjāb, and to incorporate Sindhu into his empire. A large Turkish empire was thus established in India. For more than 150 years after this a series of wars between the Turks and various Indian states produced no further change. What is chiefly remarkable is that the Indian states remained numerous and divided : none was able to attain and hold imperial hegemony over the others.

In 1173 a Turkish ruler named Muhammad, from Central Asia, overthrew the Yamīnīs. In 1178 he attacked the kingdom of Gujarat but was heavily defeated and lost most of his army. It seemed that the divided Indians had really nothing to fear from the Turks, if one small kingdom could rout them. A rising Rājput power, the Cāhamānas, concentrated on wars against the Gāhaḍavālas who now tried to exercise imperial hegemony from Kānyakubja, as well as against Gujarat and the Candrātreyas, although they were the neighbours of the Turks. They actually defeated the Turks in 1190-1, annexing part of the Panjāb, and were confident of establishing a great empire, but Muhammad raised a new army at Gajani and made a supreme effort in 1192. The overconfident Cāhamānas were defeated by more careful tactics and driven back to their capital (Ajayameru, Ajmere), leaving the way east across the plain of Northern India open. The following year Muhammad sent one of his generals to attack the Gāhaḍavāla kingdom, which included Vārāṇasī as well as Kānyakubja. He was victorious, Vārāṇasī was looted and a thousand temples are said to have been destroyed and mosques erected in their places. Beyond Vārāṇasī lay the domains formerly ruled by the Pālas, but the Pālas had been overthrown by their feudatories, the Senas, in 1162, after which their empire had distintegrated into many small kingdoms. The Senas failed to establish a strong state. What happened early in the 13th century is obscure, but Tāranātha says that the 'worshippers of Īśvara' (God, either Śiva or Viṣṇu), probably the Senas, did not oppose the Turks, whilst the latter plotted with several minor feudal rulers to extend their hegemony over the east. The Turkish sources seem to confirm this with their accounts of annexing Bihar and Bengal with a small force of cavalry led by an adventurer, the Turkish captain Bakhtyār. Almost incidentally the great universities of the former Pāla Empire were massacred and burned. Uddaṇḍapura was made a Turkish base, and soldiers from there repeatedly raided Nālandā, a few miles away, murdering and burning, though they could not obliterate the immense, thick walled college and temple buildings (they were apparently more successful, or more thorough, with the library buildings). Similar raids were sent to destroy the other universities.[1] With these universities a great segment of the cultural heritage of India, secular as well as Buddhist, perished for ever. Bakhtyār in 1206 pressed on eastwards with a large army for the serious war he planned, to conquer Kāmarūpa (Assam), Tibet and the Turks beyond Tibet. In Kāmarūpa his army was defeated and practically annihilated and he himself was killed in the rout. A Turkish military corridor remained across northern India and many Muslim settlers flooded into it, especially after the Mongol conquests in Central Asia in the 13th century drove them South and East. From this base the Turks attempted

1. For example Vajrāsana (Bodh Gayā), described by a Tibetan eyewitness, Gro-bdud-rtse; see R. Sāṅkṛtyāyana in JBORS XXIII, Part I, p. 18.

gradually to annex all India and in the 14th century reached the far South, opposite Ceylon, but Hindu resistance by 1336 had grown equal to Turkish fanaticism and, with the foundation of the state of Vijayanagara, a unified Hindu Empire was set up in the South, which stabilised the position though it could not expel the Turks from the North.

According to Tāranātha the majority of Buddhist refugees went to South East Asia (through Burma), many to Tibet and some to South India (Kaliṅga, which remained independent until the 16th century, Vijayanagara and elsewhere). A few monks hung on near the ruined universities for a time. For example a Tibetan traveller about 1235 visited Nālandā and found an ancient monk teaching Sanskrit grammar to seventy students among the ruins. Only one or two monks had books (which some must have carried with them when they escaped the Turks who destroyed the library). Even while the traveller was there there was another Turkish raid from Uddaṇḍapura, the object of which was presumably to massacre the monks who obstinately remained and perhaps to ransack the ruins further in the hope of finding buried treasure. The monks were warned by a messenger from Uddaṇḍapura and withdrew to places at a safe distance. Three hundred Turkish soldiers scoured the ruins and then returned to their base, after which some of the monks returned to their burnt out university. The Tibetan pilgrim found none of the books he had hoped to get copies of and wandered elsewhere.[1] Tāranātha reports that even after this a succession of four more teachers followed the ancient Rāhulaśrībhadra referred to above. However, there was no hope of restoring Buddhist learning while the Turks ruled Magadha. The physical heart of Buddhism had been destroyed.

It is a matter more or less of speculation why Buddhism succumbed without much or any resistance to Islamic conquerors when 'Hinduism' after initial setbacks gradually consolidated an effective opposition and recuperated its strength until India could be freed from Muslim rule. Buddhism has always been a philosophy and religion of peace in all senses

1. Paraphrased by S. Dutt, *Buddhist Monks and Monasteries of India*, 347f., from Roerich, *Biography of Dharmasvāmin*.

of that word. When confronted with a religion of 'holy war', offering its enthusiastic followers the reward of rich plunder, not as a crime but as a virtue, the Buddhist countries of Central Asia and North Western India could apparently not find enough good soldiers, enough military spirit, to defend themselves. The teaching of non-violence surely had had some effect.[1] Formerly Buddhism had spread among the barbarian peoples themselves (notably the Kuṣāṇas) and thus defied the forces of militarism and destruction by civilising the people who had practiced them. But the new barbarians were different. They were not open to the ideas of the people they had conquered, for they had their own religion, which admirably served the purpose of conquest by providing ideological justification and incentives for it. The Kuṣāṇas saw in Buddhism a means to consolidate a great empire by promoting the harmony of its peoples. The Turks did not concern themselves with consolidation (until Akbar) but only with expansion and accumulating more plunder and more slaves. Buddhism condemned their whole way of life, Islam encouraged it and glorified it as commanded by God. Here indeed was an 'anti-Buddhism' which appealed to all the powerful passions which Buddhist moral principles opposed (see Chapter Six). Here were violence, plunder, rape and vandalism. The Turks chose the way of violence and took all India with them, destroying her civilisation.

'Hinduism' is more flexible than Buddhism. It is almost everything. In much of India it was stronger than Buddhism at the time of the Turkish conquests, especially in the South, which was precisely where resistance to Islam was most effective. It is often supposed that Brahmanism and especially Vaiṣṇavism and Śaivism had slowly gained ground against Buddhism among the masses of the people of India during the first millennium A.D. As opposed to the Buddhist advocacy of a classless society and

2. E.g. *Abhidharmakośabhāṣya* IV 72 : As in the case of war, hunting and assault, many, united, rush for the purpose of killing others, and one takes life; who is endowed with that (taking life)?—In an army, etc., because of having the same objective all are like agents possessing (the action) (72). . . . for in reality they are inciters of each other. In the case that someone is taken away by force (into the army), he too is endowed (with the action) unless he should go having resolved thus: 'Even to save my life I will not kill a living being'.

democratic institutions, 'Hinduism' harmonised with the feudalistic trend of the middle ages (we cannot take up the question why such a trend should prevail) advocating a social hierarchy. Theism, especially the monotheism of Vaiṣṇavism or of Śaivism, is natural as the ultimate corollary of a hierarchy: men commend themselves to their superiors, their earthly lords, and all men ultimately commend themselves to God. Even in Buddhism a 'theistic' trend may be observed, even if it is in reality only an outward show, a 'concealing' appearance. Evidently, however, Śiva has a clear advantage over the shadowy Hevajra who disappears in emptiness. In large parts of India, then, and particularly in the South, 'Hinduism' in its many forms was by the 12th century a much more 'popular' religion than Buddhism. Buddhism again was to a much greater extent a philosophical and indeed academic tradition in that period. The heart of its tradition was then in the universities rather than among the masses of the people. When these were destroyed the strength of its tradition was broken. The masses are not likely to have understood much of its profound philosophy, probably did not see it as very different from, say, Vaiṣṇavism, and honoured the Buddha and *bodhisattvas* with much the same simple devotion that their neighbours accorded to Kṛṣṇa and the Vaiṣṇava saints. Without the guidance of learned monks the Buddhism of the laity would tend to merge with the manifold and lively local cults of Hinduism. There are indeed some Hindu legends of great Hindu philosophers such as Śaṃkara or Kumārila defeating Buddhist philosophers in debate and so popularising Hinduism. There are counter legends on the Buddhist side of Dharmakīrti defeating Śaṃkara and Kumārila. History would seem in fact to support the Buddhist claim, since Dharmakīrti flourished a little later than the two Hindu philosophers, refuted their views in his works and established a highly successful school to continue his line of philosophical enquiry. But all this could have no effect on the masses of the people. In fact probably neither Dharmakīrti, nor the two Vedic philosophers who specialised respectively in the problem of illusion and in the ancient abstract ritual, had the slightest effect on the people. Hinduism for the people meant Vaiṣṇavism and Śaivism, not Vedism, and the philosophers of Vaiṣṇavism and Śaivism strongly criticised Śaṃkara's non-theistic Vedānta and Vedic ritualism.

The strength of 'Hinduism' manifested itself not in any opposition to Buddhism (the two usually lived side by side in harmony) but in its successful resistance to Islam where Buddhism was swept away. The Hindu warrior was ready to fight and understood this to be his duty and death in battle to be his supreme glory (leading straight to heaven as the reward for doing one's duty). Legends grew round the heroes who had died in the struggle to defend India and maintain her ancient traditions. A heroic and popular literature in the languages of the people upheld the ideal of determined struggle for what was considered right and just, of defence of Indian civilisation against a ruthless barbarism, murderous terror and reckless tyranny. Eventually the spirit of India prevailed. As the ancient intellectual freedom and spirit of toleration were restored a renaissance of Buddhism become possible.

Kaśmīra fell under Muslim rule in the 14th century, leading to the violent persecution (which included a 'burning of the books') by Sikandar (mentioned above) early in the 15th, which Buddhism seems not to have survived except in Ladakh, which remains predominantly Buddhist (but, like all the Himālayan countries where Buddhism survives, under the dominating influence of the vigorous Buddhism of Tibet and having long neglected Sanskrit studies).

Tāranātha reports that some refugees from Magadha went South, mentioning Kaliṅga, Gujarat, Rājasthān, Vijayanagara (Vidyānagara, which was founded only in 1336, however) and other places. Gujarat and central India fell about 1300, Kaliṅga[1] and the city of Vijayanagara (though the latter was razed to the ground, the Muslim army retired again and left the empire of the South only slightly reduced in area, but its central authority weak and power in the hands of a series of provincial governors) in the 16th century. By this time whatever Buddhists remained in the war-torn South seem to have gone to Ceylon.

The Turks did not succeed in completely Islamising even Northern India. India was too large, too populous, too divided

1. According to Tāranātha (256f.) Mukundadeva (the last king of Orissa or Kaliṅga, who was overthrown by Akbar in 1568 or 1570) supported Buddhism by building shrines and spread the Doctrine to some extent.

up geographically and the Turkish domains were always surrounded by independent or only temporarily subdued Indian kingdoms. Above all, the spirit of the 'Hindus' never submitted and even in long conquered areas it was kept alive by the popular literature in the vernaculars (mostly of the Vaiṣṇava movements), much of it composed under the patronage of the independent rulers (of Rājasthān, Kaliṅga, Tīrabhukti, etc.) and then circulated in the Turkish provinces. In the 16th century most Indians were still 'Hindus'. Akbar, having succeeded in extending his empire over most of India, recognised this and developed a new policy, in fact an Indian as opposed to an Islamic policy. He granted religious toleration and so consolidated his empire, gaining Rājput contingents for his army (in order to face the Persian Shah, who claimed overlordship over him). Thereby, however, he outraged the orthodox Muslims at his court. After his death toleration was ended and the old persecutions renewed, with the destruction of Hindu temples and schools and the reimposition of the religious tax for being a Hindu. This led to widespread revolts, in which the Marāṭhas gradually took the lead. In 1674 Śivāji was proclaimed king of the Marāṭhas, his successors extended an empire over most of South India and then set about the liberation of the North. In the first half of the 18th century they brought most of India South of the Ganges under their rule, occupying the Turkish capital (Delhi) from 1750 and forming a protectorate over Akbar's descendants. We need not recount the complexities of the subsequent internal divisions of the Marāṭhas and the establishment of a British instead of a Marāṭha empire in the 19th century. The decisive point for us is that the Turkish power and Muslim rule had collapsed, the Marāṭhas had reestablished religious toleration over most of India and the British continued this Marāṭha policy over a still larger area. It became possible for Buddhists not merely to make clandestine pilgrimages to India but to start restoring Bodh Gayā, Sārnāth and other favourite centres and once more to build dwellings (*vihāras*) for monks there.

CONCLUSION

The effect of the Arab and Turkish conquests was the destruction of most of the early schools of Buddhism, the main centres of which had remained in Magadha and North West India. Only one survived and flourished, the Sthaviravāda, whose main centres were in the South and especially in Ceylon, with strong branches all over South East Asia. In China, and those countries which derived their Buddhism from China, the early schools had been entirely superseded (except for the academic study of certain texts of the *Abhidharma* and the use of the *Vinaya* as the basis of discipline: the Sautrāntika, Sarvāstivāda, Bahuśrutīya and Dharmaguptaka thus survived in a partial and attenuated form) by the Mahāyāna (especially the Vijñānavāda). In Tibet and the countries where Tibetan Buddhism spread the early schools are even more neglected, since they seem never to have been established in Tibet (except again as academic subjects in the case of Sautrāntika and Sarvāstivāda and monastic discipline in the case of the Mūlasarvāstivāda). The Mahāyāna schools were more fortunate, being widely diffused over Eastern Asia, but whereas the Sthaviravāda continued its Indian tradition directly, retaining an Indian language (in which its monks have continued to write), the Mahāyānists almost everywhere adopted either Chinese or Tibetan as their canonical and academic languages and have more and more depended on translations of their original sources. It is only in Nepal that the Indian Mahāyāna, representing on the whole the Madhyamaka-Mantrayāna synthesis of the 12th century and of Tibetan Buddhism, has continued without violent interruption, in a restricted but secluded region, to the present day. Yet the Buddhists of Nepal came more and more to look towards Tibet, the stronghold of Buddhism, for strength and guidance. Gradually they neglected their Indian texts and sent their students to Tibet for training. Here too, as a result, the Indian tradition has not been preserved intact and many texts have been lost for want of recopying, although it is here that our main collections of Sanskrit Buddhist literature survived; the Tibetan versions became standard. The

Buddhism which escaped destruction in the border regions beyond Muslim penetration is thus effectively either Sthaviravāda or Tibetan speaking Madhyamaka-Mantrayāna.

Under Muslim rule some Buddhist traditions survived for a time among the laity, though the communities of monks had been completely rooted out, leaving no competent teachers to guide them. The more popular tradition of the Mantrayāna, often referred to as the 'Naturalist' (Sahajiyā) tradition, continued for a time in Magadha, Bengal and Orissa on the basis of the poetry of Kṛṣṇācārya and others. Gradually it appears to have been assimilated into the generally similar Vaiṣṇava tradition of the Kṛṣṇa cult, which in the later middle ages also developed a 'Naturalist' phase with techniques very similar to those of the later Mantrayāna. Part of the Mantrayāna tradition coalesced with the Śaiva Tantric tradition (particularly the so called Nāth cult) which has appropriated, if only in name, several of the Buddhist *siddhas*. The least assimilated of these Buddhist folk traditions is the so called Dharma cult, primarily in Orissa (where Buddhism with its organised communities survived longer, until the conquest in the 16th century), which has maintained the observance of some Buddhist festivals. The Dharma here is 'empty' but is sometimes identified with the Sun and with Viṣṇu, less often with other gods. 'Diagrams' are used, which might be compared with those of the *Cakrasaṃvara* and other *tantras*. The cult has preserved no old texts, however.

As a result of an assembly held in Pulastinagara (then the capital) in Ceylon in the 12th century the Abhayagirivāsins (Dharmarucis) and Jetavanīyas (Sāgalīyas) were 'conciliated' and reabsorbed into the Sthaviravāda. King Parākramabāhu I was the patron who presided over this assembly, which seems to be the only recorded case of the conciliation of schismatics, and his work is compared with that of the great Aśoka by the historians of the Sthaviravāda school. Similar processes appear to have taken place in South India (Cola) and South East Asia, resulting in the consolidation of the one Sthaviravāda school everywhere (except Vietnam, whose Buddhists followed those of China) and the disappearance of all others (including the Mahāyāna). Such consolidation parallels that of Tibetan Madhyamaka-Mantrayāna in the Himālaya and probably reflects the weakness of Buddhism as a whole as the Turks conquered and obliterated so many of its old centres. The Indian monks of various schools who escaped from India evidently threw in their lot with the established school of Buddhism in whichever country they reached.

The restoration of Buddhism in India began effectively in the 19th century and has gathered momentum in the 20th. The Buddhists of Ceylon (therefore the Sthaviravāda school) have probably played the leading part, especially financially in setting up new *vihāras*, for example at Nālandā (which is once more a college and may again become a university), Sārnāth (Vārāṇasī) and Sāñcī (Caityagiri, an ancient centre of the Sthaviravāda). Those of Siam have not been far behind, whilst the Tibetans, being closer and never having abandoned their pilgrimages to the Indian shrines, have supplied most of the 'pilgrim-power'. The Sinhalese missions claim considerable success in spreading the Doctrine in India once more, but it would be premature as well as beyond the scope of this book to consider Indian Buddhism today. India is now reclaiming its ancient heritage, including its Buddhist heritage, quite apart from any efforts by Buddhists to spread their teaching, or from the partly political question of Buddhism attracting the underprivileged in a society emerging from the long domination of feudal hierarchies. Indian governments (especially that of the State of Bihar, ancient Magadha) are once more giving some support to Buddhist scholarship and the Buddhist academic tradition is again becoming an essential part of the humanism of Indian universities. At the same time this is only a part of the worldwide revival of Buddhist studies.

The teaching of Buddhism, especially its social programme of non-violence and its exploration of the problem of freedom, has always been relevant to humanity. It has not always been practicable. It was swept out of India a few centuries ago because it had no immediate answer to the violence of Islam. 'Death' triumphed over freedom. This, however, was because a number of men in Western and central Asia, sufficiently large to impose their will on their neighbours, chose the way of violence, or war and plunder glorified as a religion. The ideals of Buddhism were, for reasons not entirely clear, not at that time able to command the widening acceptance, reaching out to new peoples, which had defended and spread Indian civilisation particularly at the time of the Kuṣāṇa invasions (although even in this dark period they reached the Mongols). Today we live in a very different world. It is violence, not non-violence, which has at last become impracticable. Reluctantly, its partisans are being brought to see that war, if pursued as formerly, will lead not just to the deaths of a few inconvenient or unimportant people but to the obliteration of mankind, including themselves. Any plunder which might have accrued to a conqueror will be destroyed in the process of trying to seize it. The recognition of the impracticability of violence would be nothing but the recognition of the primary social principle of Buddhism (see pp. 168, 170 above). The study of the problem of freedom naturally depends on human societies enjoying peace and security (as we also saw above, pp. 175 f.) instead of being swept along in the pell mell of militarism and false propaganda. In societies dominated by violence and militarism words like 'freedom', which most people find attractive, are debased to mean their exact opposite and used to rally people to the cause of violence. This is possible only by concealing the truth, by the suppression of the facts and the misuse of words. Truth, non-violence, freedom, toleration and other principles are inseparable. If we lose one, we lose all. The Doctrine we have been reviewing in this book shows the mutual consistency and solidarity of all these aspects of the 'good' very clearly.

Whether Buddhism is the answer to the problem of human unhappiness, it is not the purpose of this book to enquire. Here we have attempted to ascertain what Buddhism is, doctrinally, as defined in its texts, thus to establish the facts about it as a prerequisite to evaluation or application. In particular we have attempted to discover what Buddhism was, in the stricter sense of the teaching of the Buddha c. 500 B.C., and to place other kinds of Indian 'Buddhism' in relation to that. If the reader should feel that this book is most incomplete, even as regards the Doctrine, the author will at least have succeeded in suggesting that Buddhism, still more all the 'Buddhisms', is not simple (cf. p. 108 above). At the same time he hopes to have shown that its principles are not vague or mysterious. He has picked up a handful of points from the earliest *Tripiṭaka* now accessible to us, following the evidence as to what is most essential. These are drops from an ocean, but from an ocean which, we are told, has a single taste—that of freedom.[1]

1. A IV 203, T 125 section 42 No. 4, T 26 No. 35.

BIBLIOGRAPHY

A. The Early *Tripiṭaka*

(1) *Sūtra* :

Dirgha Sth (Pali) ed. T. W. Rhys Davids and J. E. Carpenter in 3 vols. PTS 1890-1911 (reprinted 1947-60); also in the Bangkok ed. of the *Tipiṭaka*, 2nd ed. 1925-7; a Ceylon ed. and the new ed. of the *Tipiṭaka* with its commentaries and sub-commentaries published in Burma, 1956ff, by the Marammaraṭṭhe Buddhasāsana-samiti, 'Chaṭṭhasaṃgīti edition'. Translated by Rhys Davids as *Dialogues of the Buddha* PTS 1899-1921 (since reprinted).

Sa (Sanskrit) fragmentary texts of the following *sūtras* have been published : *Daśottara* ed. Mittal and Schlingloff (Berlin, DAWB, IO, 1957, 1962); *Catuṣpariṣat* ed. Waldschmidt (Abhandlungen DAWB, Kl. f. Spr., Lit. u. Kunst, 1952, 1957, 1962); *Mahāvadāna* ed. Waldschmidt (Abhandlungen DAWB, Kl. f. Spr., Lit. u. Kunst, 1952, 1956); *Mahāparinirvāṇa* ed. Waldschmidt (Abhandlungen DAWB, Phil. hist. Kl. 1950 and Kl. f. Spr., Lit. u. Kunst, 1951, two parts); *Āṭānāṭiya* ed. Hoernle (*Manuscript Remains of Buddhist Literature found in Eastern Turkestan*, Vol. I and only, Oxford 1916, 24ff) and Hoffmann (Leipzig, Brockhaus, 1939); the *Saṃgīti* ed. Mittal and Stache-Rosen (DAWB 1968). See *Turfan* (Waldschmidt in Miscellaneous below) Parts 1, 3 and 4 for fragments of *Śrāmaṇyaphala*, *Ambaṣṭha* and several others.

Sa (Tibetan) — a few *sūtras* are included in the Tibetan *Tripiṭaka* (on which see below), among them the *Brahmajāla* ed. Weller, *Asia Major IX*, 1933, 195 ff. and 381 ff., and *Mahāsamaya or -samāja.*

Dhg ? (Chinese) T 1 in Vol. I of the Taishō *Tripiṭaka* (see below).

There are also separate Chinese translations of various recensions of individual *sūtras* (of schools not yet determined), including the *Mahāparinirvāṇa* (T 5, T 6, T 7), *Mahānidāna* (T 14, T 52), *Mahāgovinda* (T 8), *Mahāsamaya* (T 19), *Brahmajāla* (T 21), *Saṅgīti* (T 12), *Śṛgālāvavāda* (T 16, 17, see *Viśvabhāratī Annals*).

Madhyama Sth (Pali) ed. Trenckner and Chalmers in 3 vols. PTS 1888--99 (reprinted 1948-51); also Bangkok (as above) and the new edition in Burma. Translated by I.B. Horner as *Middle Length Sayings* PTS 1954-9.
Sa (Sanskrit) fragments ed. Hoernle MR (*Upāli*, *Śuka*, etc.) and *Turfan* (*Mahānidāna*, *Rāṣṭrapāla*, etc.).
Sa (Tibetan) — 6 or 7 *sūtras* (corresponding to Sth Nos. 86, 115, 121-2, 133 and 139 and to Sa No. 62 in Chinese).
Sa (Chinese) T 26 in the Taishō.

Saṃyukta Sth (Pali) ed. Feer in 5 vols. PTS 1884-98 (reprinted 1960); also Bangkok, etc. Translated by C.A.F. Rhys Davids and F. L. Woodward as *Kindred Sayings* PTS 1917-30 (since reprinted).
Sa (Sanskrit) fragments of *Nidānasaṃyukta* ed. Tripāṭhī Berlin DAWB, IO, 1962; others in JRAS 1913 (La Vallée Poussin), Hoernle MR, NG 1957 and Waldschmidt *Bruchstücke buddhistischer Sūtras aus dem zentralasiatischen Sanskritkanon*, *Kleinere Sanskrit-Texte* IV, Leipzig 1932; *Bodhyaṅgasaṃyukta* and others in *Turfan*.
Sa (Tibetan) — 6 *sūtras* (*Dharmacakrapravartana*, etc.).
Sa (Chinese) T 99 in Vol. II of the Taishō.
Kā (Chinese) T 100 (incomplete).

Ekottara Sth (Pali, *Aṅguttara*) ed. Morris and Hardy in 5 vols. PTS 1885-1900, since reprinted and second edition of Vol. I by A. K. Warder PTS 1961; also Bangkok, etc. Translated by Woodward and Hare as *Gradual Sayings* PTS 1932-6 (since reprinted).
Sa (Sanskrit) — fragments in *Turfan*, etc.
Sa (Tibetan) — 1 *sūtra* (*Giryānanda*).
Dhg ? (Chinese) T 125 in the Taishō.

Kṣudraka

(a) *Khaḍgaviṣāṇagāthā*, *Munigāthā*, *Śailagāthā*, *Arthavargīyāṇi Sūtrāṇi* and *Pārāyaṇa* : Sth (Pali) versions included in the collection called *Suttanipāta*, ed. Andersen and H. Smith PTS 1913 (reprinted 1948) and translated by Chalmers HOS 1932; fragments of the Sa (Sanskrit) versions of the last two *Turfan* No. 30 (*Pārāyaṇa*) and No. 1072 (*Arthavargiyāṇı*); Dhg ? (Chinese) version of the *Arthavargīyāṇi* T 198 (see P. V. Bapat, *Viśvabhāratī Annals III*, 1950).

(b) *Sthaviragāthā* and *Sthavirigāthā* : Sth (Pali) ed. Oldenberg and Pischel PTS 1883 and translated by C. A. F. Rhys Davids as *Psalms of the Early Buddhists* PTS 1909 and 1913; Sa (Sanskrit) fragments in Bechert, *Bruchstücke buddhistischer Verssammlungen*, part 1, Berlin DAWB, IO, 1961, 260ff.

(c) *Ityukta* : Sth (Pali) ed. Windisch PTS 1889 (reprinted 1948) and translated by Woodward PTS 1935; Sa ? (Chinese) T 765.

(d) *Udāna* : Sth (Pali) ed. Steinthal PTS 1885 (reprinted 1948) and translated by Woodward PTS 1935.

(e) *Dharmapada* : Sth (Pali) ed. Fausbøll, 2nd. ed. London 1900 and translated by C. A. F. Rhys Davids (with a text) PTS 1931; Sa (Sanskrit) in Dharmatrāta's recension entitled *Udānavarga* ed. Bernhard, Abhandlungen A. W. Göttingen, 1965, Index Vol. 1968, its Tibetan translation ed. Beckh Berlin 1911 and translated by Rockhill London 1892; Dhg ? (Gāndhārī, the school is quite uncertain at present) ed. Brough, London 1962.

(f) *Jātaka* : Sth (Pali) ed. Fausbøll in 6 vols. London 1877-96 (recently reprinted by the PTS) and translated (with most of its commentary) by Cowell, Chalmers, Rouse, Francis and Neil, Cambridge 1895-1907 (reprinted PTS 1957).

(g) *Avadāna* : Sth (Pali) has a (*Thera*-and *Therī*-) *Apadāna* ed. Lilley in 2 vols. PTS 1925-7 and a *Vimānavatthu* and *Petavatthu* ed. Hardy PTS 1901 and 1894 and translated by Kennedy and Gehman PTS 1942; Sa (Sanskrit) has an *Avadānaśataka* ed. Speyer, St. Petersburg BB 1902-9 (reprinted in the Indo-Iranian Reprints Series) and translated by Feer, Paris AMG 1891, an *Anavataptagāthā* ed. Bechert in *Bruchstücke buddhistischer Verssammlungen* part 1, Berlin DAWB, IO, 1961, and a *Vimānāvadāna* and *Pretāvadāna* (fragments, see Bechert *Bruchstücke* 1 pp. 2 and 14f.); Sa (Tibetan) has the *Karmaśataka* (see Feer JA 1901), *Avadānaśataka*, *Anavataptagāthā* (ed. from Mū *Vinaya* by Hofinger Louvain Muséon 1954) and other *Avadānas*; Sa (Chinese) has the *Avadānaśataka* (T 200), the *Anavataptagāthā* (incorporated, however, in the Mū *Vinaya* : it is reprinted by Hofinger with the Tibetan version and his own translation), two versions of an *Aśokāvadāna* (T 2042 and T 2043, on which see Przyluski's study *La légende de l'empereur Açoka*, Paris AMG 1923) and other texts; Mū has besides the version of the *Anavataptagāthā* in its *Vinaya* already mentioned a *Divyāvadāna* presumed to belong to that school (ed. Cowell and Neil, Cambridge 1886, and, more complete but without critical apparatus, Vaidya, Darbhaṅgā BST 1959). All the Sth Pali *Kṣudraka* texts are included in the 2nd. Bangkok edition of the *Tripiṭaka* already mentioned and we may also note three Ceylon editions of importance for textual readings : *Therīgāthā* ed. Devarakkhita, Hewavitarne Series, 1918; *Jātaka* ed. Piyatissa, Hewavitarne Series, 1919 and *Apadāna* ed. Buddhadatta, Ambalangoda, 1930.

(2) *Vinaya* : Sth (Pali) ed. Oldenberg in 5 vols. London 1879-83 (recently reprinted by the PTS), also Bangkok, etc., and translated by I. B. Horner in 6 vols. PTS 1938-66.

Sa (Sanskrit, *Daśādhyāya*) fragments ed. Finot (*Prātimokṣa*) JA 1913, Waldschmidt (*Bhikṣuṇīprātimokṣa*) in his *Kleinere Sanskrit-Texte* III, Leipzig 1926, Rosen (*Vinayavibhaṅga*) Berlin DAWB, IO, 1959, Härtel (*Vinayavastu : Karmavācanā*) Berlin DAWB, IO, 1956, Ridding (*Vinayavastu : Bhikṣuṇīkarmavācanā*) in BSOS Vol. I 123ff., also Filliozat and Kuno in JA 1938, 21ff.; Rosen includes in the appendix (No. 2) of her work above some fragments from the *Upāliparipṛcchā* of the *Vinayottaragrantha*.

Sa (Chinese) T 1435, T 1436, T 1437 and T 1441.

Mū (Sanskrit) *Prātimokṣasūtra* ed. Banerjee IHQ 1953; *Vinayavibhaṅga* ed. (a few fragments) Rosen in the appendix (No. 1) of her Sa *Vinayavibhaṅga* (see above); *Vinayavastu* partly ed. Dutt (*Gilgit Manuscripts* III, parts 1-4, Srinagar and Calcutta 1942-50) and a further part (from the same manuscript, which was divided) ed. Gnoli and Venkatacharya in 2 vols., SOR 1977-8, and Gnoli 1 more vol. SOR 1978; Dutt's text is being reprinted in BST, 1967 in progress.

Mū (Tibetan, complete) extracts translated by Rockhill in his *The Life of the Buddha*, London 1884.

Mū (Chinese) T 1442-51 and 1454-5 (incomplete).

Dhg (Sanskrit) a few fragments (noted by Hirakawa in his *Ritsuzo no Kenkyū* mentioned below), *Turfan* 656.

Dhg (Chinese) T 1428-31 (complete).

Mś (Chinese) T 1421-4.

Kā ('Haimavata', Chinese, a *Vinayamātṛkā* only) T 1463.

Ms (Chinese) T 1425-7; *Śāriputraparipṛcchā* T 1465.

Lo (Sanskrit) *Prātimokṣasūtra* ed. Pa-chow and Mishra, Allahabad, 1956; *Mahāvastu* ed. Senart, Paris, 1882-97, trs. Jones PTS 1949-56; *Bhikṣuṇī* — ed. G. Roth TSWS 1970.

(3) *Abhidharma* : For the *Mātṛkā* see A. K. Warder in *Mohavicchedanī* (below under Works of the Schools, Sth) xix-xxvii.

The earliest *Abhidharma* now accessible and more or less common to the schools may be studied through the following texts of the schools :

Sth (Pali) *Vibhaṅga* ed. C. A. F. Rhys Davids PTS 1904, Bangkok etc.; translated by Thittila PTS 1969; *Dhātukathā* ed. Goonaratne PTS 1892 (recently there has been a corrected 2nd. edn.), Bangkok and Rangoon; translated by Narada, PTS 1962; *Paṭṭhāna* 2nd. Bangkok ed. and two Burmese editions (the PTS has published only excerpts, which moreover are not reliable : C. A. F. Rhys Davids 1906 and 1921-3).

Sa (Chinese) *Dharmaskandha* T 1537; *Dhātukāya* T 1540; *Vijñānakāya* T 1539; *Saṅgītiparyāya* T 1536 ; Sa (Sanskrit) fragments *Turfan* No. 15 of *Dharmaskandha*; *Saṅgītiparyāya* with *Sūtra* see above.

Dhg ? (Chinese) *Śāriputrābhidharmaśāstra* T 1548.

B. Works of the Schools

(Histories are grouped separately below; grammars and

other primarily linguistic works are generally omitted, as are works on law and medicine; works in Sinhalese and other modern languages are also omitted.)

(1) Sthaviravāda :

Additions to the *Sūtra* (all in their *Kṣudraka*) :

Khuddakapāṭha ed. H. Smith PTS 1915, translated by Ñāṇamoli as *The Minor Readings*, PTS 1960.

Niddesa ed. La Vallée Poussin, E. J. Thomas and W. Stede in 3 vols. PTS 1916-8.

Paṭisambhidāmagga ed. Taylor in 2 vols. PTS 1905-7, translated by Ñāṇamoli PTS in the press.

Buddhavaṃsa ed. Morris PTS 1882, translated B. C. Law PTS 1938.

Cariyāpiṭaka ed. Morris PTS 1882, translated B. C. Law PTS 1938.

Additions to the *Abhidharma* :

Dhammasaṅgaṇi ed. Müller PTS 1885 and Bangkok and Burmese editions, translated C. A. F. Rhys Davids as *A Buddhist Manual of Psychological Ethics*, London, Royal Asiatic Society, 2nd. edn. 1923 (recently reprinted by the PTS).

Puggalapaññatti ed. Morris PTS 1883, translated Law PTS 1924.

Kathāvatthu ed. Taylor in 2 vols. PTS 1894-7, also Bangkok, translated S. Z. Aung and C. A. F. Rhys Davids as *Points of Controversy* PTS 1915 (since reprinted).

Yamaka ed. C. A. F. Rhys Davids in 2 vols. PTS 1911-3.

Works in some places included in the *Sūtra* (as in Burma) :

Milindapañha ed. Trenckner, 2nd. edn. London, Royal Asiatic Society, 1928 (recently reprinted by the PTS), translated I. B. Horner PTS 1963 (2 vols.).

Peṭakopadesa ed. Rangoon 1917 and 1956 (the latter as part of the new edition of the *Tipiṭaka*) and A. Barua PTS 1949, translated by Ñāṇamoli as the *Piṭaka-Disclosure* PTS 1964.

Nettippakaraṇa ed. Hardy PTS 1902 (recently reprinted), translated by Ñāṇamoli as *The Guide* PTS 1962.

Commentaries (*Aṭṭhakathā*) and sub-commentaries (*Ṭīkā*) on the *Tripiṭaka* (in the order of the texts as given above), including the additions of the School :

DA *Sumaṅgalavilāsinī* by Buddhaghosa ed. T. W. Rhys Davids, Carpenter and Stede PTS 1886-1932.

DṬ *Līnatthappakāsinī* by Dhammapāla II ed. Rangoon in 3 vols. 1924, ed. de Silva in 3 vols. PTS 1970.

DṬ (Nava) *Sādhuvilāsinī* by Ñāṇābhivaṃsa ed. Rangoon in 2 vols. 1913-23 and new edn. 1961 (on D vol. I).

MA *Papañcasūdanī* by Buddhaghosa ed. Woods, Kosambi and Horner PTS 1922-38.

MṬ *Līnatthappakāsinī* by Dhammapāla II ed. Buddhasāsanasamiti in 2 vols. 1961.

SA *Sāratthappakāsinī* by Buddhaghosa ed. Woodward PTS 1929-37 and Piyatissa, Hewavitarne Series, Colombo 1924-7.

SṬ *Līnatthappakāsinī* by Dhammapāla II ed. Buddhasāsanasamiti in 2 vols. 1961.

AA *Manorathapūraṇī* by Buddhaghosa ed. Walleser and Kopp PTS 1924-56 (2nd. ed. of Vol. IV — almost all the 1st. having been destroyed by bombing in 1940 along with most of the then PTS stock — by Kopp in 1964).

AṬ *Sāratthamañjūsā* by Sāriputta ed. Rangoon in 2 vols. 1910, there is also a Ceylon edn. Colombo 1907.

Paramatthajotikā (A on Kh and Sn) by Buddhaghosa ed. H. Smith PTS 1915-8, first part translated by Ñāṇamoli as *The Illustrator of Ultimate Meaning* PTS 1960.

KhṬ *Paramatthasūdanī* by Ādiccavaṃsa unpublished.

Suttanipātaṭīkā unpublished.

Dhammapadaṭṭhakathā ed. H. C. Norman PTS 1906-14, translated by Burlingame HOS 1921.

DhṬ *Dhammapadatthadīpanī* and DṬ (Nava) both unpublished.

Paramatthadīpanī (A on Ud, It, Vv, Pv, Th and Cp) by Dhammapāla I ed. Müller, Hardy, Woodward, D. L. Barua and Bose PTS 1893-4, 1901, 1926, 1934-6, 1939-40, 1952, 1959, but for the *Therīgāthā* part Devarakkhita's edn., Hewavitarne Series, Colombo 1918 is much better.

The *ṭīkās* on Ud, It, Vv, Pv, Th and Cp do not appear to have been published.

JA ed. Fausbøll in his edition of the text (see above) and separately in Bangkok, translated by Cowell, etc. (see above).

JṬ *Linatthappakāsini* by Dhammapāla II unpublished (MSS in Rangoon, Copenhagen, etc.).

JṬ *Asammohavilāsini* unpublished.

JṬ *JA-Gaṇṭhipadatthavaṇṇanā* ed. Sumaṅgala, Colombo 1911 (on Vols. I and II, Fausbøll, only).

NdA *Saddhammapajjotika* by Upasena ed. A. P. Buddhadatta PTS 1931-40 (3 vols).

Mahāniddesaṭikā unpublished.

PsA *Saddhammappakāsini* by Mahānāma ed. Joshi PTS 1933-47 (3 vols.).

Ps Gaṇṭhipada (anon) ed. Ariyavaṃsa, Colombo, Semage, 1967.

ApA *Visuddhajanavilāsini* ed. Godakumbura PTS 1954.

Therāpadānaṭikā unpublished.

BvA *Madhuratthavilāsini* by Buddhadatta ed. Horner PTS 1946.

Buddhavaṃsaṭikā by Dhammapāla unpublished.

VinA *Samantapāsādikā* by Buddhaghosa ed. Takakusu, Nagai and Mizuno in 7 vols. PTS 1924-47, introductory (historical) part translated by Jayawickrama as *Inception of Discipline* PTS 1962.

VinṬ (Porāṇa) by Vajirabuddhi ed. Rangoon in 2 vols. 1919-21; new edn. Rangoon, 1960, Chaṭṭhasaṅgīti.

VinṬ *Sāratthadipani* by Sāriputta ed. in 4 vols. Rangoon 1902-24 and 3 vols. 1960, Devarakkhita and Medhaṅkara (unfinished), Colombo, 1914, 1933.

VinṬ *Vimativinodani* by Kassapa ed. Rangoon in 2 vols. 1913 and by Dhammādhāra Tissa in 1 vol. Colombo 1935, ed. Buddhasāsanasamiti in 2 vols. 1960.

VinṬ (Nava) *Atthayojanā* by Ñāṇakitti ed. Bangkok in 2 vols. 1927-8.

Kaṅkhāvitaraṇi (separate commentary on the *Prātimokṣa* section of Vin) by Buddhaghosa ed. Maskell PTS 1956.

Vinayatthamañjūsā (*ṭikā* on preceding) by Buddhanāga ed. Ekanāyaka, Colombo 1912.

DhsA *Atthasālini* by Buddhaghosa ed. Müller PTS 1897,

also Bangkok and Rangoon, translated by P. M. Tin as *The Expositor*, 2 vols., PTS 1920-1 (since reprinted).

DhsṬ *Atthasālinī Mūlaṭīkā* (or *Līnatthapadavaṇṇanā* or *Abhidhamma Mūlaṭīkā* part I) by Ānanda I ed. Paññāsāra and Vimaladhamma, Vidyodaya Ṭīkā Series, Colombo, 1938, also in Burma (see below).

Anuṭīkā (sub-sub-commentary to Dhs) by Dhammapāla II (see below).

Maṇidīpa by Ariyavaṃsa unpublished (there are also several other DhsṬs, unpublished).

VbhA *Sammohavinodanī* by Buddhaghosa ed. A. P. Buddhadatta PTS 1923.

VbhṬs see below.

Pañcappakaraṇaṭṭhakathā (A on the other five Abhidharma works of the School) by Buddhaghosa : part I ed. with *Dhātukathā* text (see above); part II ed. in JPTS 1913-14 by Landsberg and C. A. F. Rhys Davids; part III ed. in JPTS 1889 by Minayev; part IV ed. in JPTS 1910-2 by C. A. F. Rhys Davids; part V ed. with PTS edn. of *Paṭṭhāna* excerpts (1921-3, see above). Part III has been translated by B.C. Law, PTS 1940, as *The Debates Commentary* (it is also summarised in the *Kathāvatthu* translation *Points of Controversy*, see above).

Abhidhamma Mūlaṭīkā (Ṭ on all seven Abhidharma books) by Ānanda I, two complete Burmese editions, 1924-6 (3 vols.) and 1960, Buddhasāsanasamiti.

Anuṭīkā (sub-sub-commentary on preceding) by Dhammapāla II, Burmese edition with the *Mūlaṭīkā* 1960.

(There are several other Abhidharma sub-commentaries not yet published; the published *Mohavicchedanī* by Kassapa, listed below under 'Manuals', is in effect also a sub-commentary on the whole Abhidharma, as the same author's VinṬ is on the Vinaya).

Milindaṭīkā by Cūlābhaya (who, since he calls his commentary a *ṭīkā*, does not recognise the *Milindapañha* as canonical : any non-canonical work is at best a 'commentary' already in the view of the School) ed. Jaini PTS 1961.

Peṭakopadesa Aṭṭhakathā by Nārada ('Jetavana Sayadaw') ed. Mandalay 1926.

Nettippakaraṇassa Atthasaṃvaṇṇanā by Dhammapāla I ed.
Piyatissa, Colombo, Hewavitarne Series, 1921.

Netti Ṭ (Porāṇa) by Dhammapāla II ed. U Hpye,
Rangoon, Pyi Gyi Mundyne Piṭaka Press, 1909.

Nettivibhāvanī by Saddhammapāla ed. Rangoon with
preceding, Buddhasāsanasamiti, 1961.

Netti Mahāṭīkā (Nava) by Ñāṇābhivaṃsa unpublished.

Manuals :

(a) General or Sūtra :

Vimuttimagga by Upatissa (the Pali text was long believed lost, having been superseded by the next; it is
reported rediscovered in Ceylon and an edition
planned); there is a Chinese version published in the
Chinese *Tripiṭaka* as T 1648, this has been translated
into English by Ehara, Soma and Kheminda as *The
Path of Freedom*, Colombo, Weerasuria, 1961.

Visuddhimagga by Buddhaghosa ed. Warren and Kosambi
HOS 1950, translated by Ñāṇamoli as *The Path of
Purification*, Colombo, Semage, 1956, 2nd. edn. 1964.

Paramatthamañjūsā (*ṭīkā* on preceding) by Dhammapāla
II ed. Dhammānanda, Colombo (various publishers),
3 vols., 1928, 1930, 1949 (incomplete), Bangkok
(3 vols. 1925-7 complete) and Rangoon (2 vols. 1909-
10 complete and 2 vols. 1960 complete).

(There are also other *ṭīkās* on the *Visuddhimagga*.)

(b) Vinaya :

Khuddasikkhā by Dhammasiri ed. Müller JPTS 1883.

Porāṇa Ṭ on preceding by Revata unpublished.

Nava Ṭ by Saṅgharakkhita unpublished.

Sumaṅgalappasādanī by Vācissara unpublished.

Mūlasikkhā by Dhammasiri ed. Müller JPTS 1883.

Porāṇa Ṭ on preceding by Vimalasāra unpublished.

Abhinava Ṭ by Vācissara unpublished.

(There are still other *ṭīkās* on Dhammasiri's two
manuals).

Vinayavinicchaya by Buddhadatta ed. A. P. Buddhadatta
PTS 1928.

Uttaravinicchaya by Buddhadatta ed. A. P. Buddhadatta
PTS 1928.

Porāṇa Ṭs by Upatissa on these two unpublished.

Ṭs on Buddhadatta's two manuals by Revata and Vācissara unpublished.

Pāḷimuttakavinayavinicchayasaṅgaha (or *Vinayasaṅgaha*) by Sāriputta, ed. Buddhasāsanasamiti, 1970, as *Vinayasaṅgahaṭṭhakathā*.

At least two *ṭikās* on the preceding are extant.

Vinayasamuṭṭhānadīpanī by Saddhammajotipāla unpublished.

Pātimokkhavisodhanī by Saddhammajotipāla and other works on Vinaya by this writer unpublished.

(There are several other Vinaya manuals).

(c) Abhidharma :

Abhidhammāvatāra by Buddhadatta ed. A. P. Buddhadatta PTS 1915.

Porāṇa Ṭ on preceding by Vācissara unpublished.

Abhidhammatthavikāsinī by Sumaṅgala ed. A. P. Buddhadatta, Ambalangoḍa, 1961.

Rūpārūpavibhāga by Buddhadatta ed. A. P. Buddhadatta PTS 1915.

Ṭ on preceding unpublished.

Saccasaṅkhepa by Dhammapāla II ed. Dhammārāma JPTS 1917-9.

Porāṇa Ṭ on preceding by Mahābodhi unpublished.

Atthadīpanā by Vācissara unpublished.

Nava Ṭ Sāratthasālinī by Sumaṅgala unpublished.

Nāmarūpasamāsa by Khema ed. Dhammārāma JPTS 1916.

Khemappakaraṇaṭīkā by Vācissara ed. Dhammapāla, Ceylon, 1908.

Abhidhammatthasaṅgaha by Anuruddha of Ceylon ed. Rhys Davids JPTS 1884, translated by C. A. F. Rhys Davids as the *Compendium of Philosophy* PTS 1910 (reprinted 1957).

Porāṇa Ṭ on preceding by Vimalabuddhi unpublished.

Abhidhammatthavibhāvanī by Sumaṅgala (ed. Paññāsāra and Wimaladhamma, Colombo, 1933, the PTS plans an edition).

Maṇisāramañjūsā by Ariyavaṃsa unpublished.

Saṅkhepavaṇṇanā by Saddhammajotipāla unpublished.

(There are several other *ṭikās* on the *Abhidhammattha-saṅgaha*).

Paramatthavinicchaya by Anuruddha of Kāñcī ed. A.P. Buddhadatta PTS in the press.

Porāṇa Ṭ on preceding by Mahābodhi and a *Nava Ṭ* unpublished.

Nāmarūpaparicchеda by Anuruddha of Ceylon ed. A. P. Buddhadatta JPTS 1914.

Porāṇa Ṭ on preceding by Vācissara and one by Sumaṅgala unpublished.

Mohavicchedani by Kassapa ed. A. P. Buddhadatta and A. K. Warder PTS 1961.

Nāmācāradipaka by Saddhammajotipāla unpublished (edition planned by PTS).

Paṭṭhānagaṇanānaya by Saddhammajotipāla unpublished.

Paccayasaṅgaha by Vācissara unpublished.

(d) For the laity :

Upāsakajanālaṅkāra by Ānanda III (Araññaratana) ed. Saddhātissa PTS 1965.

(An earlier manual which this superseded, the anonymous *Paṭipattisaṅgaha,* is also extant in MS in Ceylon.)

(2) Abhayagirivāsin (Dharmaruci) :

Saddhammopāyana (Pali) by Ānanda II (among Pali writers) ed. Morris JPTS 1887.

Saddhammopāyanaviggaha (anon. commentary on preceding) ed. Ratanasāra, Colombo 1911.

(3) Sarvāstivāda :

Additions to the *Abhidharma* :—

Jñānaprasthāna by Kātyāyanīputra (Chinese T 1543-4; there are some Sanskrit fragments; the first part has been retranslated from Chinese into Sanskrit by Śānti Bhikṣu, Santiniketan 1955).

(*Vijñānakāya* additions by Devaśarman).

Prajñaptiśāstra (Chinese T 1538 and 1644; Tibetan, which is more complete or more authentic, in the Tibetan *Tripiṭaka*). (T 1538 of a different school?)

Prakaraṇapāda by Vasumitra I (Chinese T 1541-2).

Commentaries on the *Tripiṭaka* (including the additons) :

Udānavarga Vivaraṇa by Prajñāvarman (Tibetan).

Vinayavibhāṣā (Chinese T 1440).

Prātimokṣasūtra Ṭīkā (*Vinayasamuccaya*) by Vimalamitra (lost ?).

Mahāvibhāṣā (on *Jñānaprasthāna*) by Pārśva and Vasumitra II (Chinese T 1545-7).

Vibhāṣā on *Prakaraṇapāda* fragments *Turfan* 19, 20 and others ed. Imanishi, NG 1969.

Manuals :

Yogācārabhūmi by Saṃgharakṣa (Chinese T 606), translated by Demiéville BEFEO 1954.

Abhidharmasāra by Dharmaśrī (Chinese T 1550).

Saṃyuktābhidharmasāra (on preceding) by Dharmatrāta II (Chinese T 1552).

Another commentary on the *Abhidharmasāra* by Upaśānta (Chinese T 1551).

Abhidharmāmṛtarasaśāstra by Ghoṣaka (Chinese T 1553), retranslated into Sanskrit by Śānti Bhikṣu, Santiniketan 1953.

Abhidharmāvatāra by Skandhila (Chinese T 1554; Tibetan).

Sārasamuccaya (anon. *ṭikā* on preceding) (Tibetan).

Nyāyānusāra by Saṃghabhadra (Chinese T 1562).

Samayapradīpikā by Saṃghabhadra (Chinese T 1563).

Abhidharmadīpa and *Vibhāṣāprabhāvṛtti* by Vimalamitra (?) ed. from an incomplete Sanskrit MS by Jaini TSWS 1959.

(4) Mūlasarvāstivāda :

Addition to the *Sūtra* :

Saddharmasmṛtyupasthānasūtra (Chinese T 721; Tibetan : *Āryasaddharmānusmṛtyupasthāna*; also an abridged Chinese version T 722; see the study of this *sūtra* by Lin Li-kouang, *L'Aide-mémoire de la Vraie Loi*, Paris, Musée Guimet, 1949).

Dharmasamuccaya (a compendium by Avalokitasiṃha of the verses only from the preceding; Chinese T 728) Sanskrit MS in Paris, first five chapters ed. Lin Li-kouang, Paris, Musée Guimet, 1946, with the corresponding Chinese versions, the Tibetan and a French translation, chapters 6 — end (36), revised by Demiéville and others, in 2 further vols., 1969 and 1973.

Commentaries :

There are several commentaries on the *Prātimokṣasūtra* and one on the *Bhikṣuṇīprātimokṣa*, all anonymous, in Tibetan versions.

Vinayavibhaṅgapadavyākhyāna by Vinītadeva (Tibetan).

Vinayavastuṭīkā by Kalyāṇamitra (Tibetan).

There are a number of other commentaries or manuals of Vinaya available in Tibetan, such as the *Vinayasaṃgraha* by Viśeṣamitra, the *Śrāmaṇerakārikā* (or *Triśatakārikā*) and *Vṛtti* (*Prabhāvati*) by Śākyaprabha.

It has not been ascertained whether the *Puṣpamālā* (*Kārikā*) by Viśākhadeva (Tibetan, also a fragmentary Sanskrit MS in Sa-skya) belongs to this school.

(5) Sautrāntika :

Addition to the *Sūtra* :

Arthaviniścayasūtra (Tibetan, Chinese T 762) Sanskrit ed. N. H. Samtani TSWS 1971.

Commentary :

Nibandhana on *Arthaviniścayasūtra* by Vīryaśrīdatta (Tibetan) Sanskrit ed. Samtani with the *Sūtra* TSWS 1971.

Manuals :

The early works of this school, by Śrīlāta, etc., appear to have been lost, except for Kumāralāta's *Kalpanāmaṇḍitikā* (see under Belles-lettres below) and fragments of his commentary on Śarvavarman's grammar *Kātantra* (Lüders : 'Kātantra und Kaumāralāta', *Sitzungsberichte der Bayerischen Akademie der Wissenschaften*, XXV, 1930, pp. 483-538; as a rule grammars have been ignored in the present Bibliography).

Abhidharmakośa and *Bhāṣya* by Vasubandhu (Tibetan, Chinese T 1558-60) Sanskrit ed. Pradhan TSWS 1967; translated by La Vallée Poussin in 6 vols., Louvain/Paris (Istas/ Geuthner) 1923-31.

Marmapradīpa Vṛtti on AK by Diṅnāga (Tibetan).

Sūtrānurūpa Vṛtti on AK by Vinītabhadra (Tibetan).

Lakṣaṇānusāra on AK by Guṇamati (fragment in Chinese T 1641).

Sphuṭārthā Vyākhyā on AK by Yaśomitra (Tibetan) Sanskrit ed. Wogihara, Tokyo (Publishing Association of Abhidharmakośavyākhyā), 1932-6.

Lakṣaṇānusāriṇī Ṭīkā on AK by Pūrṇavardhana (Tibetan,) also called *Bṛhaṭṭikā.*

Upāyikā Ṭikā on AK by Śamathadeva (Tibetan).

Tattvārthā Bhāṣyaṭikā on AK by Sthiramati (Tibetan).

Karmasiddhiprakaraṇa by Vasubandhu (Tibetan); translated by Lamotte MCB IV 1936.

Karmasiddhiṭīkā by Sumatiśīla (Tibetan).

Vyākhyāyukti by Vasubandhu (Tibetan. See Yaśomitra, p. 6, Bu-ston translated by Obermiller, etc.).

Pramāṇa :

(The works of Diṅnāga, Dharmakīrti and others who were probably Sautrāntikas are listed here; Mahāyānist commentators and authors of manuals are listed below under Vijñānavāda, etc., according to their apparent affiliations. For the beginnings of the study of logic and the theory of knowledge among the Buddhists of various schools, mainly Sthaviravāda, see the paper 'The Earliest Indian Logic' and for a sketch of its subsequent development see the article 'The Date of Bhāmaha', also the *Outline of Indian Philosophy* (all under Warder in Miscellaneous below). On the development before Diṅnāga see also Tucci : 'Buddhist Logic before Diṅnāga', JRAS 1929, pp. 431ff. and his *Pre-Diṅnāga Buddhist Texts on Logic from Chinese Sources,* GOS 1929, which includes two treatises on logic retranslated from Chinese into Sanskrit : **Upāyahṛdaya/Fang pien sin louen* T 1632 and **Tarkaśāstra/Jou che louen* T 1633. On these see *Outline* pp. 138ff. and 160ff. The first appears to belong to the Bahuśrutīya School, the second perhaps to the Dharmaguptaka.)

Vasubandhu : *Vādavidhāna* (lost ? See Frauwallner WZKM 40, 1933, pp. 281ff.; it now appears that the *Vādavidhi* was by the earlier, Vijñānavādin Vasubandhu, see below).

Diṅnāga : Commentary on Vasubandhu's *Vādavidhāna* (apparently lost : see Frauwallner WZKSO 1959, pp. 103f.).

Marmapradīpa (listed above).

Traikālyaparīkṣā (Tibetan), the Tibetan ed. with the corresponding Sanskrit passages from Bhartṛhari (*Vākyapadīya* III.3.53ff., etc.) by Frauwallner WZKSO 1959, pp. 145ff.

Hastavālaprakaraṇa (Tibetan, T 1620-1) Tibetan ed. Frauwallner WZKSO 1959, pp. 152ff.; Sanskrit reconstructed and translated by F. W. Thomas and H. Ui, JRAS 1918.

**Upādāyaprajñaptiprakaraṇa* (T 1622) see Frauwallner WZKSO 1959, pp. 121ff., and Kitagawa (under *Pramāṇasamuccaya* below) pp. 430-9, *Ch'ü-yin-chia-she-lun*, who misunderstands the argument that concepts (only) are makings of consciousness.

Ālambanaparīkṣā (Tibetan, T 1619 and 1624) Tibetan ed. and translated by Frauwallner WZKM Vol. 37, 1930, pp. 174ff. and again WZKSO 1959, pp. 157ff.; also Tibetan and Chinese and translation by Yamaguchi, JA 1929 and a summary by Stcherbatsky in *Buddhist Logic* I (see below under Miscellaneous) pp. 518ff.

Sāmānyalakṣaṇaparīkṣā (Chinese T 1623 *Kuan-tsung-hsiang-lun-sung*) see Kitagawa pp. 430-1.

Hetucakraḍamaru (Tibetan) Tibetan ed. Frauwallner WZKSO 1959, pp. 161ff.; Sanskrit reconstructed and translated by D. Chatterji IHQ 1933.

Nyāyamukha (T 1628-9) translated from the Chinese by Tucci MKB 1930 (Vibhūticandra mentions a *ṭikā* on this, apparently pre-Dharmakīrti and now lost, see his notes on *Pramāṇavārttika Vṛtti* of Manorathanandin, IV. 27 and 122).

Pramāṇasamuccaya (Tibetan, two translations) translated from the Tibetan, and giving the available Sanskrit fragments, by M. Hattori (Chapter 1 in *Dignāga on Perception* HOS 1968) and H. Kitagawa (Chapters 2-4 and 6 into Japanese in *A Study of Indian Classical Logic — Dignāga's System = Indo-Koten-Ronrigaku no Kenkyū*, Tokyo 1965); Hattori has also made a collection of

Sanskrit fragments in the *Journal of Indian and Buddhist Studies*, Vol. VII, 1958, and has promised a translation of the remaining chapter (5).

**Hetumukha* (lost, see Frauwallner WZKSO 1959, pp. 103f).

The critiques of Sāṃkhya, Vaiśeṣika and Nyāya appear to be lost, except in so far as they are reproduced in the *Pramāṇasamuccaya*.

Śaṅkarasvāmin : *Nyāyapraveśa* (Tibetan, T 1630, often wrongly attributed to Diṅnāga, following the Tibetan which apparently took it for the *Nyāyamukha*) ed. in Tibetan and Sanskrit by Dhruva in 2 vols. GOS 1927-30.

Jinendrabuddhi: *Viśālāmalavatī Pramāṇasamuccayaṭīkā* (Tibetan).

Dharmakīrti : *Pramāṇavārttika* and *Vṛtti* on its first chapter (Tibetan) Sanskrit : first chapter and *Vṛtti* ed. Mālavaṇiyā, Vārāṇasī, Hindu Vishvavidyalaya Nepal Rajya Sanskrit Series Vol. II, 1959, and by Gnoli SOR 1960; the other chapters (II-IV) ed. Sāṅkṛtyāyana, TSWS 1953, Index 1959; the *kārikās* of all four chapters ed. Sāṅkṛtyāyana with Manorathanandin's *Vṛtti* (see below under Vijñānavāda); part of the first chapter translated by Frauwallner WZKM Vols. 37, 39 and 40, 1930-3, from the Tibetan; the first part of the first chapter translated by S. Mookerjee and H. Nagasaki from the Sanskrit, Nalanda, Navanālandā Mahāvihāra, 1964.

Pramāṇaviniścaya (Tibetan), first chapter ed. and translated from the Tibetan, with the Sanskrit fragments, by T. Vetter, *Sitzungsberichte der Österreichischen Akademie der Wissenchaften*, Wien, 1966; second chapter ed. and translated by E. Steinkellner, ibid., 1973.

Nyāyabindu (Tibetan) Sanskrit ed. Stcherbatsky, Petrograd BB 1918 and translated by him in *Buddhist Logic* Vol. II BB 1930 (reprinted I-IR 1958); also ed. Mālavaṇiyā TSWS 1955.

Hetubindu (Tibetan) ed. in Tibetan and reconstructed in Sanskrit (from commentaries on it) by E. Steinkellner, *Sitzungsberichte der Österreichischen Akademie der Wissenschaften*, Wien, 1967.

Sambandhaparīkṣā (Tibetan) the available Sanskrit *kārikās* are given by Sāṅkṛtyāyana in the Introduction to his edition of chapters II-IV of the *Pramāṇavārttika* (above); Tibetan including the *Vṛtti* ed. and translated by Frauwallner WZKM Vol. 41, 1934, pp. 261ff.

Vādanyāya (Tibetan) Sanskrit ed. Sāṅkṛtyāyana JBORS Appendix to Vols. XXI and XXII, 1935-6.

Santānāntarasiddhi (Tibetan) Tibetan ed. Stcherbatsky BB Vol. XIX, 1916, and translated by him as *Obosnovanie chuzhoi oduschevlennosti*, Pamyaniki Indiiskoi Filosofii I, St. Petersburg, 1922, summary in *Buddhist Logic* I, pp. 521ff., English translation from the Russian translation by H. C. Gupta, Soviet Indology Series No. 2, Indian Studies Past and Present, Calcutta, 1969, pp. 71-121.

Devendrabuddhi : *Pramāṇavārttikapañjikā* (Tibetan), on Devendrabuddhi see Frauwallner WZKSO IV 1960.

Śākyabuddhi : *Pramāṇavārttikaṭīkā* (Tibetan).

Arcaṭa : *Hetubinduṭīkā* (Tibetan) Sanskrit ed. Sanghavi and Jinavijaya GOS 1949.

Pramāṇāntarbhāva (? seems to be identical with his work referred to as *Pramāṇadvitvasiddhi*) Sanskrit ed. S. C. Nyayacharya BI 1969.

Kṣaṇabhaṅgasiddhi (lost ?).

Śubhagupta : *Śrutiparīkṣā*, *Anyāpohavicāra*, *Sarvajñasiddhi*, *Bāhyārthasiddhi* and *Īśvarabhaṅga* (all in Tibetan).

Pramāṇavārttika commentary (? lost).

Dharmottara : *Pramāṇaviniścayaṭīkā* (Tibetan).

Nyāyabinduṭīkā (Tibetan) Sanskrit ed. and translated by Stcherbatsky with the text (above) and ed. by Mālavaṇiyā with the text (above).

Pramāṇaparīkṣā (two texts in Tibetan share this title, presumably using alternative methods of examination).

Paralokasiddhi (Tibetan) translated by G. Roerich in *Indian Culture* Vol. 15, 1948-9.

(*Anya-*) *Apohaprakaraṇa* (Tibetan) Tibetan ed. and translated by Frauwallner WZKM Vol. 44, 1936, pp. 233ff.

Kṣaṇabhaṅgasiddhi (Tibetan) Tibetan ed. and translated by Frauwallner WZKM Vol. 42, 1935, pp. 217ff.

Śaṅkarānanda : *Pramāṇavārttikaṭīkā* on first chapter, unfinished (Tibetan).
Anusārā Sambandhaparīkṣāṭīkā (Tibetan).
Apohasiddhi (Tibetan).
Pratibandhasiddhi (Tibetan).
Sarvajñasiddhisaṃkṣepa Sanskrit MS in Ngor and copy in Patna.

Jitāri : *Hetutattvopadeśa* (Tibetan) Sanskrit ed. Tucci SOR 1956.
Dharmadharmiviniścaya (Tibetan).
Bālāvatāratarka (Tibetan).
Sahopalambhaprakaraṇa Sanskrit MS in Ngor and copy in Patna (Bihar Research Society).
Nairātmyasiddhi Sanskrit MS in Ngor and copy in Patna.
Jātinirākaraṇa Sanskrit ed. Tucci in *Annals of the Bhandarkar Oriental Research Institute* Vol. XI, 1930.
Vādasthāna Sanskrit ed. H. R. R. Aiyangar, Mysore, 1944.

Durvekamiśra : *Pradīpa* on Dharmottara's *Nyāyabinduṭīkā*, Sanskrit ed. Mālavaṇiyā TSWS 1955.
Āloka on Arcaṭa's *Hetubinduṭīkā*, Sanskrit ed. Sanghavi and Jinavijaya GOS 1949.
Viśeṣākhyāna, *Svayūthyavicāra*, *Catuḥśatī* and *Kṣaṇabhaṅgasiddhi* (all apparently lost).

Aśoka : *Avayavinirākaraṇa* and *Sāmānyadūṣaṇadikprasāritā* Sanskrit ed. Haraprasād BI 1910 (MSS of both in Ṣalu).

Muktākalaśa : Commentary on Dharmottara's *Kṣaṇabhaṅgasiddhi* (Tibetan).

Vidyākaraśānti : *Tarkasopāna* Sanskrit ed. Tucci SOR 1956.

(6) Saṃmitīya :

**Āśrayaprajñaptiśāstra* (Chinese T 1649) translated from the Chinese by K. Venkataramanan in *Viśvabhāratī Annals* V, 1953.

(7) Dharmaguptaka :

Abhiniṣkramaṇasūtra (addition to the *Sūtra*? Chinese T 190. Sometimes called *Śākyamunibuddhacarita*) translated from the Chinese ('abbreviated translation') as *The Romantic Legend of Śākya Buddha* by Beal, London, Trübner, 1875.

**Tarkaśāstra* (see above under Sautrāntika, Pramāṇa; the school is conjectural: Chinese legend connects the text with a monk named Dharmagupta arriving in China from Central Asia).

(8) Mahāsaṃghika :

Sphuṭārthā Śrīghanācārasaṃgrahaṭīkā by Jayarakṣita (commentary on a compendium extracted from the *Vinaya* on the conduct of novices) ed. Sanghasena TSWS 1968.

(9) Bahuśrutīya :

**Upāyahṛdaya* (see above under Sautrāntika, Pramāṇa).
**Tattvasiddhiśāstra* by Harivarman (Chinese T 1646) see S. Katsura : *A Study of Harivarman's Tattvasiddhi*, University of Toronto thesis, 1974.

C. Buddhist Histories

(A few other narrative works which are relevant are included, and certain works on literature; Pali histories of South East Asia are omitted as well as most works in modern languages; much scattered historical information is to be found in the commentaries of the schools listed above : here we note only a few which have continuous historical sections. The early *Tripiṭaka* is itself in a sense a historical record.)

Buddhaghosa : *Samantapāsādikā*, Introduction (VinA of Sth, see above, where Jayawickrama's translation of this Introduction is also listed).

Sāriputta : *Sāratthadīpanī* (Vin Ṭ on preceding, see above).

anon. : *Nidānakathā* (Introduction to JA of Sth, see above); translated by T. W. Rhys Davids as *Buddhist Birth-Stories* (intended originally as the first part of a complete translation of the *Jātaka* itself with its commentary), London, Routledge, new edition (no date — about 1925; original edition 1880 with some of the *Jātaka*, Trübner).

Buddhaghosa : *Kathāvatthuppakaraṇa Aṭṭhakathā* (Part III of *Pañcappakaraṇaṭṭhakathā* of Sth, see above); its historical information has been translated in the translation of the *Kathāvatthu* text, *Points of Controversy*, see above.

anon. : *Dīpavaṃsa*, ed. and translated by Oldenberg, London, Williams and Norgate, 1879.

Mahānāma : *Mahāvaṃsa*, ed. Geiger, PTS 1908 (reprinted 1958), translated by Geiger, Colombo, Government of Ceylon, 1912 (reprinted 1950).

Dhammakitti and others : *Cūlavaṃsa*, ed. Geiger in 2 vols., PTS 1925-7, translated by Geiger, Colombo, Government of Ceylon, reprint 1953.

anon. : *Vaṃsatthappakāsinī* (*ṭīkā* on *Mahāvaṃsa*), ed. Malalasekera in 2 vols., PTS 1935.

Upatissa : *Mahābodhivaṃsa*, ed. Strong, PTS 1891.

Dhammakitti : *Dāṭhāvaṃsa*, ed. Sīlālaṅkāra, Alutgama, 1914 and T. W. Rhys Davids and Morris JPTS 1884.

Vācissara (II) : *Thūpavaṃsa*, ed. Law, PTS 1935, translated by Law as *The Legend of the Topes*, Calcutta (BI) 1945.

Dhammanandin : *Sīhalavatthuppakaraṇa*, ed. Buddhadatta, Colombo, 1959.

Raṭṭhapāla : *Sahassavatthuppakaraṇa*, ed. Buddhadatta and Somadāsa, Ambalaṅgoda, 1959.

Vedeha : *Rasavāhinī*, ed. Saraṇatissa, Colombo, 1939, 1948 (2 parts).

Buddhaputta : *Pūjāvaliya*, ed. Colombo, 1924, and by Saddhātissa, Kalutara, 1930.

anon. : *Rājāvaliya*, ed. B. Gunaṣekera, Colombo, 1926.

Devarakṣita (Dharmakīrti) : *Nikāyasaṃgraha*, ed. de Silva, A. Gunasekera and Gunawardhana, Ceylon Government Press, 1907; translated by Fernando, Ceylon Govt. Press, Colombo, 1908.

anon. : *Buddhaghosuppatti*, ed. and translated by Gray, London, Luzac, 1892.

Dhammakitti (III) : *Saddhammasaṅgaha* (this work is not very reliable), ed. Saddhānanda, JPTS 1890; translated by Law as a *A Manual of Buddhist Historical Traditions*, University of Calcutta, 1941.

Paññāsāmin : *Sāsanavaṃsa*, ed. Bode, PTS 1897, and Upāsak, Nālandā 1961, translated by Law, PTS 1952.

Nandapañña : *Gandhavaṃsa* (a history of Pali literature), ed. Minayeff, JPTS 1886.

anon. : *Piṭakatthamain* (a catalogue of Pali literature), ed. Rangoon, Sudhammavatī Press, 1905.

Vasumitra : *Samayabhedoparacanacakra* (Tibetan), translated by Bareau, JA 1954, 235ff. (Chinese T 2031).

(For the Sarvāstivādin *Avadānas* see above, Early *Tripiṭaka*).

Saṅgharakṣa : **Buddhacarita* (Chinese T 194).

anon. : *Lalitavistara*, ed. Lefmann, Halle 1902-8 (reprinted by Vaidya, BST, Darbhaṅgā 1958), translated by Foucaux in 2 vols., Paris AMG 1884-92.

Śākyaprabha : *Prabhāvatī* (Tibetan, see above under Mū commentaries).

Bhāvaviveka : *Nikāyabhedavibhaṅgavyākhyāna* (Tibetan), translated by Bareau, JA 1956, 167ff.

Bhāvaviveka : *Madhyamakahṛdaya* and *Tarkajvālā* (Tibetan), see Gokhale in IIJ II, 165ff. and V, 271ff.

Paramārtha : see Demiéville in MCB I, 1931-2, 15ff., 'L'origine des sectes bouddhiques d'après Paramārtha'.

Vinītadeva : *Samayabhedoparacanacakre Nikāyabhedopadarśanasaṃgraha* (Tibetan), translated by Bareau, JA 1956, 192ff.

Padmākaraghoṣa : *Bhikṣuvarṣāgrapṛcchā* (Tibetan: Narthang Mdo XC, 2—used by the Tibetan historians).

(Bhaṭaghaṭī's History of the Ācāryas, Indradatta's *Buddhapurāṇa*, Kṣemendrabhadra's history, etc., seem to be lost : see Tāranātha, Schiefner, p. 281.)

Mañjuśrimūlakalpa, *Rājavyākaraṇaparivarta*, ed. by R. Sāṅkṛtyāyana and translated by Jayaswal in *An Imperial History of India*, Lahore (Motilál Banarsidass) 1934.

Dharmasvāmin (see under Roerich in Miscellaneous).

anon: *Svayambhūpurāṇa* ed. Haraprasād BI 1894-1900.

Bu-ston : *Chos-ḥbyung* (Tibetan) translated by Obermiller, MKB 18 and 19, 1931-2.

Tāranātha : *Geschichte des Buddhismus in Indien* (translated by Schiefner, St. Petersburg, 1869); *Edelsteinmine* (translated by Grünwedel, Petrograd, BB 1914); *Die vierundachtzig Zauberer* (translated by Grünwedel in *Baessler Archiv* Vol. 5, 1916).

(Many traditions preserved in China will be found through Lin Li-kouang's study of the *Saddharmasmṛtyupasthānasūtra* listed above, some through *Suzuki's Essays in Zen Buddhism*, Vol. I, London, 1927).

D. The Mahāyāna *Tripiṭaka*

(The new *sūtras* are here arranged approximately chronologically; the two main collections extant, Chinese and Tibetan, in their various recensions, appear to include all commentaries, manuals and other works of Buddhist teachers of any period as '*Tripiṭaka*', whilst the old division into three has become obscured : in fact there is no Mahāyāna *Vinaya*, the Mahāyānists having contented themselves with those of one or other of the early schools, particularly of the Mūlasarvāstivāda and the Dharmaguptaka, in India also the Lokottaravāda and others, and with the so called *Vinayasūtra* written by Guṇaprabha, a pupil of a Vasubandhu; the *Mahāyānābhidharmasūtra* does not appear to have survived in any form and is known to us only from a very few quotations, so that for *Abhidharma* the Mahāyāna schools studied to some extent the works of the Sarvāstivāda but more especially the Sautrāntika criticism of them, using the *Abhidharmakośa* as their standard textbook, whilst for their own systematic doctrine substituting the works of their teachers such as Nāgārjuna, Asaṅga—whose *Abhidharmasamuccaya* and *Yogācārabhūmiśāstra* are written very much in the old *abhidharma* style — and others, all such *śāstras* being taken as equivalent to *Abhidharma* texts; the tendency is thus towards the twofold grouping into *Sūtra* (words of the Buddha) and *Śāstra* (commentaries, manuals, etc., works of later teachers) as in the Tibetan editions of 'Kanjur' and 'Tanjur'.) The Sanskrit texts are scattered and far from complete, the various editions of those that survive will be specified below in detail. For the Chinese we refer to the comprehensive edition (for our present purposes we omit to notice the extant texts and manuscripts not included in it) by Takakusu and Watanabe : *Taishō Issaikyō, Canon Bouddhique de l'ère Taishō*, Tōkyō, 1924 ff. Although there are indexes, it is useful to refer to the texts of this collection by number as 'T' (Taishō) Nos. according to the Index published in *Hōbōgirin*, Fascicule Annexe, ed. by Demiéville, Tokyo, Maison Franco-Japonaise, 1931.

For the Tibetan we refer to the only edition at present generally available, printed originally in Peking (between 1763 and 1795) and reprinted by the Otani University, Kyōto, ed. by Suzuki, 1957. 'Tibetan' below without further qualification refers to the texts in this edition : since it is well indexed (with the Sanskrit titles) it seems unnecessary to give details. There have been several other editions of the Tibetan *Tripiṭaka* (besides Mongolian translations mainly, but not exclusively, dependent on them) and there are numerous copies, especially in manuscript, of individual texts : these increase the total collection appreciably (exactly how much is very far from having been ascertained, there being vast unexplored collections of such books and manuscripts at present). For our present purposes these have been disregarded (except as used in a few separate editions by modern scholars noted below), but it is well to be aware that our bibliography is very far from aiming at completeness. The best known Tibetan *Tripiṭaka* edition other than that mentioned above is that of Snar-thaṅ (Nar-thang), printed in 1742 (there are copies in the possession of the Academy of Sciences of the U.S.S.R., the Bibliothèque Nationale and Musée Guimet in Paris, the Newberry Library in Chicago and other institutions).

The Early Mahāyāna :

The 'Great' *Ratnakūṭa*, as a collection, now contains 49 *sūtras* of very varying periods (Tibetan and Chinese T 310-56, both complete, 4 *sūtras* known to be extant in Sanskrit), among these, four which are early may be mentioned here separately :

Ugraparipṛcchā (T 322) trs. Schuster University of Toronto thesis 1976.

Ratnakūṭa (or *Kāśyapaparivarta*), Sanskrit, Chinese and Tibetan ed. by von Staël Holstein, Shanghai, 1926 (Vorobyov-Desyatovsky has since published more fragments of the Sanskrit).

Rāṣṭrapālaparipṛcchā (Tibetan, T 312) Sanskrit ed. Finot BB 1901 (reprinted I-IR 1957 and by Vaidya without the apparatus in *Mahāyānasūtrasaṃgraha* I, BST 1961); translated by Ensink, Zwolle, 1952.

Amitābhavyūha (or *Amitābhaparivarta* or *Sukhāvatīvyūha*), longer version (Tibetan, T 360-7) Sanskrit ed. Müller, Oxford, 1883 (reprinted in *Mahāyānasūtrasaṃgraha* I above), and Wogihara, Tokyo, 1931.

(8,000) *Aṣṭasāhasrikāprajñāpāramitā* (Tibetan, T 224-8) Sanskrit ed. R. Mitra Calcutta BI 1888 and by Wogihara in his edition of Haribhadra's *Āloka* commentary, see below under Pāramitā. Both ed. BST 1960.

Ratnaguṇasaṃcayagāthā (Tibetan, T 229) Sanskrit ed. Obermiller BB Leningrad 1937 (reprinted I-IR 1960) and Vaidya (using an additional MS) in *Mahāyānasūtrasaṃgraha* above (1961).

The Later Versions of the *Prajñāpāramitā* :

100,000 (Tibetan, T 220) Sanskrit ed. R. Ghoṣa BI Calcutta 1902-14 (unfinished).

25,000 (there are two main recensions of this text, the later one having been adapted to agree better with the *Abhisamayālaṅkāra*; Tibetan has both, Chinese only the earlier : T 221-3) Sanskrit (the later version) ed. N. Dutt, Calcutta Oriental Series 1934 (unfinished).

18,000 (Tibetan) Sanskrit incomplete text ed. Conze SOR 1962, 1974.

10,000 (Tibetan) two chapters retranslated into Sanskrit by Konow, Oslo (Avhandlinger utgitt av Det Norske Videnskaps-Akademi, Hist.-Filos. Klasse) 1941.

2,500 (or *Suvikrāntavikrāmiparipṛcchā*) (Tibetan, Chinese part of T 220) Sanskrit ed. Hikata, Fukuoka, 1958 (reprinted in *Mahāyānasūtrasaṃgraha* above).

700 (Tibetan, Chinese in T 220, also T 232; this *sūtra* also appears in the *Ratnakūṭa* collection above) Sanskrit ed. Tucci, *Memorie d. R. Accademia dei Lincei*, 1923, Masuda, Tokyo (*Journal of the Taisho University*) 1930 (reprinted in *Mahāyānasūtrasaṃgraha* above).

500 (Tibetan, T 260).

300 (or *Vajracchedikā*) (Tibetan, T 235-9, also in T 220) Sanskrit ed. Müller, Oxford 1881 (reprinted in *Mahāyānasūtrasaṃgraha* above), translated by Müller SBE 1894 (since reprinted).

150 (or *Naya*) (Tibetan : in *Tantra* section No. 121 of the Peking/Kyōto edition, also No. 119 of that edition as *Paramādya* (a *Yoga Tantra*); Chinese in T 220, also T 240-1 and 243-4) Sanskrit fragments mixed with Khotanese translation ed. Leumann in *Zur nordarische Sprache*, Strassburg, 1912, the Sanskrit part reprinted in *Mahāyānasūtrasaṃgraha* above.

Devarājapravaraparipṛcchā (Chinese only, in T 220 and as T 231).

Nāgaśrī (Chinese only, in T 220).

Svalpākṣarā (Tibetan in *Tantra* section, T 258) Sanskrit ed. Conze in *Sino-Indian Studies* (reprinted in *Mahāyānasūtrasaṃgraha* above).

Kauśika (Tibetan in *Tantra*, T 249) Sanskrit ed. Conze in *Sino-Indian Studies* (reprinted in *Mahāyānasūtrasaṃgraha* above).

Hṛdaya (Tibetan in the *Tantra*, T 250-7) Sanskrit ed. Müller and Nanjio (two recensions) Oxford 1884, translated by Müller SBE 1894 (since reprinted).

50 (Tibetan, T 248).

Pañcaviṃśatikāprajñāpāramitāmukha (Tibetan in *Tantra*).

Ekākṣarī (Tibetan in *Tantra*).

4,000 (Chinese only, in T 220 : a shorter and perhaps more archaic version of the 8,000).

Pañcapāramitānirdeśa (with particular reference to the other five *pāramitās*, related to the 2,500; Tibetan, Chinese in T 220).

(There are still other short texts, mostly in Tibetan only; those above noted as in the Tibetan *Tantra* do not properly belong here but rather with the Mantrayāna texts below, they contain incantations. Chinese has an 800 in T 230.)

The Later Mahāyāna :

Samādhirāja (or *Candrapradīpa*) (Tibetan, T 639) Sanskrit ed. Vaidya BST 1961.

Saddharmapuṇḍarīka (Tibetan, T 262-5) Sanskrit ed. Kern and Nanjio St. Petersburg BB 1908-12, N. Dutt Calcutta BI 1953; translated by Kern SBE 1909 (since reprinted).

Vimalakīrtinirdeśa (Tibetan, T 474-6), translated (incorporating Sanskrit fragments) by Lamotte, Louvain, Muséon, 1962.

Suvarṇa(pra)bhāsa Sanskrit ed. Nobel, Leipzig, 1937; ed. BST 1967; translated by Emmerick, PTS 1970; translated (from the Chinese) by Nobel, Leiden, 1958.

Śrīmālā (included in *Ratnakūṭa* collection above; Tibetan, Chinese in T 310 and also T 353).

Avataṃsaka (Tibetan, T 278-9 : the two recensions).

Gaṇḍavyūha (T 293-5) Sanskrit ed. Suzuki and Idzumi, Kyoto, 1934-6, Vaidya BST 1960.

Daśabhūmika (T 285) Sanskrit ed. Rahder, Louvain, 1926.

Sandhinirmocana (Tibetan, T 675-9) Tibetan ed. and translated by Lamotte, Université de Louvain, Recueil de travaux...2e série, 34e fascicule, 1935.

Laṅkāvatāra (Tibetan, T 670-2) Sanskrit ed. Nanjio, Kyoto, 1923, translated by Suzuki, London, Routledge, 1932, ed. Vaidya BST 1963.

(There are countless other Mahāyāna *sūtras* in the Chinese and Tibetan *Tripiṭakas*, most of them short; the above are generally recognised as the most important in all the main traditions of Mahāyāna; among the others the Mahāyāna version of the *Mahāparinirvāṇa* has been influential in China, the *Mahāmegha* and *Ratnamegha* are quite often referred to as authoritative by the Indian teachers of the schools, whilst the *Kāraṇḍavyūha* and *Karuṇāpuṇḍarika* though seemingly less well known have at least been preserved in Sanskrit and published in Calcutta, ed. by Samasrami 1873 and Das and S. C. Sastri 1898 respectively, the latter re-edited by I. Yamada London SOAS 1968. The *Mahāparinirvāṇa* is translated by Yamamoto, Ube, Karinbunko, 1973-5.)

E. The Mahāyāna Schools

(1) Madhyamaka :

Nāgārjuna : *Mūlamadhyamakakārikā* ed. La Vallée Poussin St. Petersburg BB 1903-13, translated by Stcherbatsky (chapters 1 and 25) Leningrad, Academy of Sciences, 1927 (in his *Conception of Buddhist Nirvāṇa*), May (2-4, 6-9, 11, 23-4 and 26-7) Paris, Maisonneuve (Collection Jean Przyluski Vol. II), 1959, Schayer (5, 12-6) in *Ausgewählte Kapitel aus der Prasannapadā*, Krakow, Polska Akademja Umiejetności, 1931, (10) in RO 1931, 26ff., Lamotte (17) in MCB Vol. 4, 1936 and de Jong (18-22) in *Cinq chapitres de la Prasannapadā*, Paris, Geuthner (Buddhica), 1949; (Tibetan, T 1564).

Vigrahavyāvartani and *Vṛtti* ed. Johnston and Kunst MCB IX, 1951 (Tibetan, T 1631); the Chinese translated by Tucci in *Pre-Diṅnāga*.

Śūnyatāsaptati and *Vṛtti* (Tibetan).

Yuktiṣaṣṭikā (Tibetan, T 1575) translated from the Chinese by Schaeffer MKB 1923.

Vaidalyasūtra and *Prakaraṇa* (Tibetan, ed. Kajiyama in *Miscellanea Indologica Kiotiensia*, Kyoto University 1965; Kajiyama promises a translation also).

Suhṛllekha (Tibetan, T 1673) translated from the Tibetan by Wenzel JPTS 1886.

Ratnāvali (Tibetan) Sanskrit partly ed. by Tucci JRAS 1934 and 1936, with translations.

(The *stotras* and other *parikathās* are omitted here.)

Āryadeva : *Catuḥśataka* (Tibetan, T 1570) Sanskrit fragments have been edited by Haraprasād (Calcutta 1914), Vaidya (Paris 1923, attempted reconstruction and translation of chapters VIII-XVI, not very successful) and V. Bhattāchārya (VII Allahabad, Fourth Oriental Conference, 1926; VIII-XVI in Tibetan and Sanskrit, Viśvabhāratī, Calcutta, 1931); the Chinese (which contains only IX-XVI) has been translated by Tucci, *Rivista degli Studi Orientali* Vol. X.

Śataśāstra (Chinese, first half of text only : T 1569) translated by Tucci in *Pre-Diṅnāga*.

Nāgabodhi (? or Nāgārjuna II or Nāga) :

Mahāprajñāpāramitāśāstra (T 1509) translated by Lamotte, Louvain, Muséon, 3 vols. 1944, 1949 , 1970.

**Dvādaśadvāraśāstra* (T 1568).

Sthiramati I (or Sāramati) :

Ratnagotravibhāga Mahāyāna-Uttaratantra-Śāstra (Tibetan, T 1611) Sanskrit ed. Johnston, Patna, Bihar Research Society, 1950; translated from the Tibetan by Obermiller as 'The Sublime Science...' in Acta O, Vol. IX, 1931.

(An *Upadeśa* on this by Satyajñāna or Sajjanapāda is extant in Sanskrit but unpublished, it is promised in the SOR.)

'Maitreya' : *Abhisamayālaṅkāra* (Tibetan) Sanskrit (and Tibetan) ed. Stcherbatsky and Obermiller BB 1929; translated by Conze SOR 1954; most helpful for the understanding of this text are Obermiller's *Doctrine of Prajñāpāramitā as exposed in the Abhisamayālaṅkāra* (see below) and his *Analysis of the Abhisamayālaṅkāra* (Calcutta Oriental Series, 1933-43, 3 parts, incomplete, representing about three fifths of the whole work).

(The commentaries on this are listed below under Pāramitā).

Buddhapālita : *Mūlamadhyamakavṛtti* (Tibetan, part edited by Walleser BB 1913-4.)

Candrakīrti : *Madhyamakāvatāra* (Tibetan ed. by La Vallée Poussin BB 1907-12) translated partly by La Vallée Poussin in *Le Muséon*, Louvain, 1907, 1910, 1911 and completely by K. Fujimoto (unpublished).

Prasannapadā Madhyamakavṛtti (Tibetan) Sanskrit ed. La Vallée Poussin BB 1903-13; translated by Stcherbatsky and others along with Nāgārjuna's *Kārikās* (see above).

Catuḥśatakavṛtti (Tibetan) Sanskrit fragments partly edited and text reconstructed by Haraprasād and Bhattāchārya (see above under Āryadeva).

Commentaries on *Śūnyatāsaptati* and *Yuktiṣaṣṭikā* (Tibetan).

Pañcaskandhaprakaraṇa and *Madhyamakaprajñāvatāra* (Tibetan).

Śāntideva : *Śikṣāsamuccaya* (Tibetan) Sanskrit ed. Bendall BB, 1897 (reprinted I-IR 1957), translated by Bendall and Rouse, London, Indian Texts Series (Murray), 1922.

Bodhicaryāvatāra (Tibetan) Sanskrit ed. La Vallée Poussin BI 1902-14, Vaidya BST 1960, translated by La Vallée Poussin, Paris, 1912.

Jayānanda : *Madhyamakāvatāraṭikā* (Tibetan).

Parahita : Sub-commentary on Candrakīrti's *Śūnyatāsaptativṛtti* (Tibetan).

Prajñākaramati : *Bodhicaryāvatārapañjikā* (Tibetan) Sanskrit ed. with Śāntideva's text above.

(2) Vijñānavāda (or Yogācāra) :

Asaṅga : *Abhidharmasamuccaya* (Tibetan, T 1605) Sanskrit ed. and retranslated from an incomplete MS and the Tibetan and Chinese by Pradhan, Santiniketan, 1950; translated by W. Rahula, Paris ÉFEO, 1971.

Madhyāntavibhaṅga (or *-bhāga*) (Tibetan, T 1601) Sanskrit ed. Yamaguchi in 2 vols., Nagoya, 1934, first part translated by Stcherbatsky BB Moscow/Leningrad 1936; ed. with Vasubandhu's Commentary (below).

Dharmadharmatāvibhaṅga (Tibetan) Sanskrit unpublished, MS in Spos-khang (JBORS XXIV, 4, p. 163).

Mahāyānasaṃgraha (Tibetan, T 1592-4) Tibetan ed. Lamotte with a reprint of T 1594 and a translation (based on the Tibetan), Louvain, Muséon, 1938-9 (4 parts); synoptic ed. of the four Chinese versions (T 1592-4) by Sasaki and Yamaguchi, 1930.

300 *Kārikāsaptati* Sanskrit, etc. ed. Tucci SOR 1956.

Mahāyānasūtrālaṅkāra (Tibetan, T 1604) Sanskrit ed. and translated by S. Lévi, Paris (Champion), Bibliothèque de l'école des hautes études, fascc. 159 (1907) and 190 (1911).

Yogācārabhūmiśāstra (Tibetan, T 1579) Sanskrit *Bhūmivastu* 1-5 ed. Bhattacharya, University of Calcutta, 1957; 13 ed. Shukla TSWS 1973; 15 ed. Wogihara Tokyo 1930-6 and Dutt TSWS 1966; MS of rest in Patna; of the 4 *Saṅgrahaṇīs* only fragments are known (see Schmidthausen Wien AW 1969).

Sandhinirmocanabhāṣya (Tibetan).

Vasubandhu : *Viṃśatikā* (*Viṃśikākārikāprakaraṇa*) and *Vṛtti* and *Triṃśikā* (*Triṃśikākārikāprakaraṇa*) (Tibetan, T 1586=*Triṃśikā*) Sanskrit ed. and translated by S. Lévi, Paris, Bibl. éc. hautes études, fascc. 245 (1925) and 260 (1932).

Commentary (*bhāṣya* or *vṛtti*) on *Madhyāntavibhaṅga* (Tibetan, T 1599-1600) Sanskrit ed. Nagao, Tokyo, 1964, and Tatia and Thakur TSWS 1967.

Dharmadharmatāvibhaṅgavṛtti (Tibetan).

Mahāyānasaṃgrahabhāṣya (Tibetan, T 1595-7).

Sūtrālaṅkārabhāṣya (Tibetan).

Vādavidhi (?see Frauwallner WZKM 40, 1933, 281ff. and WZKSO 1, 1957).

Sthiramati : Commentary on *Triṃśikā* (Tibetan) Sanskrit ed. S. Lévi with the text (above) and translated by him (above) and by Jacobi (Stuttgart, Kohlhammer, 1932).

Abhidharmasamuccayavyākhyā (Tibetan, T 1606), Sanskrit MS in Ngor and photocopy in Patna.

Sub-commentary on *Sūtrālaṅkāra* (Tibetan).

Madhyāntavibhaṅgaṭikā ed. Yamaguchi, Nagoya, 1934; I translated by Friedman, Utrecht (Utr. Typ. Ass.), 1937.

Asvabhāva : *Mahāyānasaṃgrahopanibandhana* (Tibetan, T 1598). Sub-commentary on *Sūtrālaṅkāra* (Tibetan).

Dharmapāla, Citrabhānu, Nanda, Bandhuśrī, Guṇamati and other commentators on the *Triṃśikā* are known to us through a synthetic Chinese commentary (T 1585), translated by La Vallée Poussin as *Vijñaptimātratāsiddhi* : *La Siddhi de Hiuan-tsang*, Paris, Geuthner (Buddhica), 1928-9, 1948 (2 vols. and index vol.).

Diṅnāga (II) : *Prajñāpāramitāpiṇḍārtha* (Tibetan, T 1518) Sanskrit ed. and translated by Tucci JRAS 1947.

Vinītadeva : *Triṃśikāṭikā* and *Viṃśikāṭikā* (Tibetan).

Commentaries on Diṅnāga's *Ālambanaparīkṣā* and Dharmakīrti's *Nyāyabindu*, *Hetubindu*, *Vādanyāya*, *Sambandhaparīkṣā* and *Santānāntarasiddhi* (Tibetan), the last ed. and translated by Stcherbatsky with the text (see under Sautrāntika above).

Jinaputra : Commentary on *Abhidharmasamuccaya* (Tibetan).

Guṇaprabha and Sāgaramegha : Commentaries on parts of the *Yogācārabhūmiśāstra* (Tibetan).

Dharmendra : *Yogāvatāra* (Tibetan) Sanskrit ed. Frauwallner WZKSO 1959, 144f.

Jñānaśrībhadra : *Pramāṇaviniścayaṭikā* (Tibetan).

Yamāri : *Supariśuddhā Ṭikā* on *Pramāṇavārttikabhāṣya* (Tibetan).

Jñānaśrīmitra : *Kāryakāraṇabhāvasiddhi* (Tibetan), *Kṣaṇabhaṅgādhyāya*, *Vyāpticarcā*, *Bhedābhedaparīkṣā*, *Anupalabdhirahasya*, *Sarvaśabdābhāvacarcā*, *Apohaprakaraṇa*, *Īśvaravāda*, *Yoginirṇayaprakaraṇa*, *Advaitabinduprakaraṇa*, *Sākārasid-*

dhiśāstra and *Sākārasaṃgrahasūtra* all ed. in Sanskrit by A. Thakur TSWS 1959.

Ratnakīrti : *Sarvajñasiddhi*, *Īśvarasādhanadūṣaṇa*, *Apohasiddhi*, *Kṣaṇabhaṅgasiddhi* *Anvaya* and *Vyatireka*, *Pramāṇāntarbhāvaprakaraṇa*, *Vyāptinirṇaya*, *Sthirasiddhidūṣaṇa*, *Citrādvaitaprakāśavāda* and *Santānāntaradūṣaṇa* all ed. in Sanskrit by A. Thakur TSWS 1957.

Kalyāṇakāṇḍaprakaraṇa and *Dharmaviniścayaprakaraṇa* (Tibetan).

Kīrtikalā commentary on *Abhisamayālaṅkāra* (Tibetan).

Ratnākaraśānti : *Antarvyāptisamarthana* (Tibetan) Sanskrit ed. Haraprasād BI 1910.

Vijñaptimātratāsiddhi (Tibetan).

Sārottamā 8,000/*Abhisamayālaṅkārapañjikā* (Tibetan) Sanskrit MSS in Sa-skya and copies in Patna, edition promised in TSWS.

Śuddhamatī 25,000/*Abhisamayālaṅkāravṛtti* (Tibetan).

Manorathanandin : *Vṛtti* on *Kārikās* of *Pramāṇavārttika* Sanskrit ed. Sāṅkṛtyāyana JBORS Appendices to Vols. XXIV-VI 1938-40.

(3) Svātantrika Madhyamaka :

Bhāvaviveka (Bhavya) : *Prajñāpradīpa* (Tibetan, T 1566) Tibetan ed. Walleser BI 1914; partly translated by Kajiyama WZKSO VII-VIII 1963-4.

Madhyamakahṛdaya and *Tarkajvālā* (Tibetan) see Gokhale in I-IJ Vols. II and V; Sanskrit MS in Sa-skya.

Karatalaratna (Tibetan, T 1578); translated by La Vallée Poussin MCB II, 1933, and by Aiyasvami *Viśvabhāratī Studies* 9, 1949.

Avalokitavrata : *Prajñāpradīpaṭīkā* (Tibetan).

Karṇakagomin : *Ṭīkā* on Dharmakīrti's *Vṛtti* to *Pramāṇavārttika* I, Sanskrit ed. Sāṅkṛtyāyana, Ilāhābād 1943.

Prajñākaragupta : *Pramāṇavārttikabhāṣya* or *Alaṅkāra* (Tibetan) Sanskrit ed. Sāṅkṛtyāyana with *Pramāṇavārttika* II-IV (above).

Sahāvalambanirṇayasiddhi (Tibetan).

Ravigupta : *Ṭīkā* on *Pramāṇavārttikabhāṣya* III (Tibetan).

Pramāṇavārttikavṛtti (Tibetan).

Jinamitra : *Pramāṇavārttikālaṅkāraṭīkā* (Tibetan).

Jñānagarbha : *Satyadvayavibhaṅga* (see *Buddhist Logic* II 315).
Śāntarakṣita : *Madhyamakālaṅkāra* and *Vṛtti* (Tibetan).
Abhisamayamañjarī Sanskrit MS in Kathmandu (Kaiser No. 117).
Vipañcitārthā *Ṭikā* on *Vādanyāya* (Tibetan) Sanskrit ed. Sāṅkṛtyāyana with the text (above).
Tattvasaṃgraha (Tibetan) Sanskrit ed. E. Kṛṣṇamācārya in 2 vols. GOS 1926; ed. Dvārikādāsa, Bauddhabhāratī, Vārāṇasī, 1968; translated by G. Jha in 2 vols. GOS 1937-9.
Kamalaśīla : *Madhyamakālaṅkārapañjikā* (Tibetan).
Madhyamakāloka (Tibetan).
Nyāyabindupūrvapakṣasaṃkṣipti (Tibetan).
Tattvasaṃgrahapañjikā (Tibetan) Sanskrit ed. and translated with the text (above).
Bhāvanākrama I-III (Tibetan, T 1664), I Sanskrit ed. Tucci SOR 1958, III Sanskrit ed. Tucci SOR 1971.
Mokṣākaragupta : *Tarkabhāṣā* (Tibetan) Sanskrit ed. E. Kṛṣṇamācārya GOS 1942, translated by Y. Kajiyama, Kyōto University 1966.
(4) Madhyamaka-Pāramitā :
Ārya Vimuktisena : 25,000/*Abhisamayālaṅkāravṛtti* (Tibetan) Sanskrit ed. Pensa SOR 1967 in progress.
Bhadanta Vimuktisena : 25,000/*Abhisamayālaṅkāravārttika* (Tibetan).
Haribhadra : 8,000/*Abhisamayālaṅkārāloka* (Tibetan) Sanskrit ed. Tucci GOS 1932 and Wogihara Tokyo 1932-5.
Sphuṭārthā (Tibetan) Sanskrit MS in Rome.
Subodhinī Saṃcayagāthāpañjikā (Tibetan) Sanskrit MS in Ṣalu.
25,000/*Abhisamayālaṅkāra* Commentary (Tibetan in the Snar-thaṅ edition of the Tanjur, MDO. III-V).
Buddhaśrījñāna : *Prajñāpradīpāvalī* *Abhisamayālaṅkāravṛtti* (Tibetan).
Saṃcayagāthāpañjikā (Tibetan).
Mahāyānalakṣaṇasamuccaya (Tibetan).
Dharmamitra : *Prasphuṭapadā Sphuṭārthā* Commentary (Tibetan).
Dharmakīrtiśrī : *Durbodhāloka* (Tibetan).
Daṃṣṭrāsena : 100,000 *Bṛhaṭṭīkā* (Tibetan).
Prajñākaramati : *Abhisamayālaṅkāravṛttipiṇḍārtha* (Tibetan).
Kumāraśrībhadra : *Prajñāpāramitāpiṇḍārtha* (Tibetan).

Jagaddalanivāsin : *Āmnāyānusāriṇī* 8,000/*Abhisamayālaṅkāra-vyākhyāna* (Tibetan).

Abhayākaragupta: *Marmakaumudī* 8,000/*Abhisamayālaṅkāra* Commentary (Tibetan).

Munimatālaṅkāra (Tibetan).

(5) Vinaya (for Mahāyāna) :

Guṇaprabha : *Vinayasūtra* and *Vṛtti* (Tibetan) Sanskrit MSS in Sa-skya and Ṣalu, copies in Patna.

Ekottarakarmaśataka (Tibetan).

Dharmamitra : *Vinayasūtraṭīkā* (Tibetan).

Prajñākara : *Vinayasūtravyākhyāna* (Tibetan).

(6) Commentaries on Mahāyāna *sūtras* (several have been noted above : the series on recensions of the *Prajñāpāramitā* by the Pāramitā school, Nāgabodhi's *Mahāprajñāpāramitāśāstra* and Asaṅga's commentary on the *Sandhinirmocana*; here we add a few others of importance):

Kāśyapaparivarta Ṭīkā (Sthiramati I) Tibetan, T 1523, ed. in Tibetan and Chinese by von Staël-Holstein, Peking, 1933.

Akṣayamatinirdeśa Ṭīkā (a Tibetan version under this title anonymous, but Tāranātha notes such a commentary by Vasubandhu, possibly this actual text; there appears to have been an early 'Vasubandhu' or 'Vasu' in the Madhyamaka school, if not Asaṅga's brother, who may be the author of all the commentaries about to be noted under that name; Tibetan tradition, reported by Obermiller, 'Sublime Science' p. 92, sometimes regards the *Akṣayamatinirdeśa*, one of the *Ratnakūṭa* Collection, as the foundation of Madhyamaka).

Amitābhavyūha commentary (Vasubandhu) T 1524.

700 *Prajñāpāramitā* commentaries (Vimalamitra, Kamalaśīla) Tibetan.

300 *Prajñāpāramitā* commentaries (Kamalaśīla, Tibetan and Vasubandhu, T 1511 see Tucci SOR IX. I p. 8).

Samādhirāja Ṭīkā (Mañjuśrīkīrti) Tibetan.

Saddharmapuṇḍarīka Vṛtti (Vasubandhu) T 1519-20 (the Tibetan translated from the Chinese may be this).

Daśabhūmi Vyākhyāna (Vasubandhu) Tibetan, T 1522.

Laṅkāvatāra Vṛtti (Jñānaśrībhadra) Tibetan.
Laṅkāvatāra Vṛtti Tathāgatahṛdayālaṅkāra (Jñānavajra) Tibetan.
Nirvāṇaśāstra (Vasubandhu) T 1527.

F. The Mantrayāna

Mahāsannipāta (Tibetan, T 397, etc.), including next.
Ratnaketudhāraṇī (Tibetan—No. 806, T 397 and 402) Sanskrit ed. Dutt and Sharma *Gilgit MSS* Vol. IV, Calcutta, 1959.
Bhaiṣajyaguru (Tibetan, T 449) Sanskrit ed. in *Gilgit MSS* I, Śrīnagar, 1939.
Ekādaśamukha, *Hayagrīvavidyā* and *Sarvatathāgatādhiṣṭhānavyūha* all ed. in Sanskrit in *Gilgit MSS* I.
Mañjuśrīmūla (Tibetan, T 1191) Sanskrit ed. Gaṇapati TSS 1920-5 (3 vols.), see also under 'Buddhist Histories' above. Reprinted BST 1964.
Guhyagarbha (Tibetan, T 884).
Dhyānottarapaṭala (Tibetan).
Ekavīra (Tibetan) Sanskrit MS in Sa-skya.
Susiddhikara (Tibetan, T 893).
Mahāmayūrī (Tibetan, T 982-8) Sanskrit MS in Ngor.
Mahāpratisarā (Tibetan, T 1153-4) Sanskrit MS in Ngor.
Amoghapāśa (Tibetan, T 1002 and 1092-5) Sanskrit MS in Sa-skya.
Krodhavijaya (Tibetan, T 1217).
Mahāvairocana (Tibetan, T 848-9) partial translation by Tajima in *Étude sur le Mahāvairocana-sūtra*, Paris, Maisonneuve, 1936.
Sarvatathāgatatattvasaṃgraha (Tibetan, T 865 and 882) Sanskrit MS in Nepal.
Vajraśikhara (a version of the preceding, Tibetan, T cf. 866-7 and 1665). Read *-śekhara* ?
Guhyasamāja (Tibetan, T 885) Sanskrit ed. Bhattacharya GOS 1931.
Māyājāla (Tibetan, T 890).
Advayasamatā (Tibetan, T 887) Sanskrit MS in Ṣalu.
Durgatipariśodhana (Tibetan, T 967-71, 974a, 978 and possibly 1398) Sanskrit MSS in Kathmandu and Paris.

Vajrabhairava (Tibetan, T 1242) Sanskrit MS in Sa-skya.

Kṛṣṇayamāri (Tibetan).

Raktayamāri (Tibetan) Sanskrit MS in Ṣalu.

Cakrasaṃvara (or *Saṃvara*, Tibetan; also referred to as *Ḍākinijāla*, but there is some obscurity about the various Tibetan recensions of this text) one Tibetan version has been partially edited, and part of it translated, by Kazi Dawa-samdup as *Shrīchakrasambhāra Tantra*, London and Calcutta 1919 in the series Tantrik Texts; this, however, appears to belong to an elaboration of the basic text incorporating some later supplements and commentaries, perhaps arranged by some school in Tibet.

Hevajra (Tibetan, T 892) Sanskrit ed. and translated by Snellgrove in 2 vols., London 1959.

Mahāmudrātilaka (Tibetan).

Abhidhānottara (Tibetan) Sanskrit MS in Nepal.

Vajraḍāka (Tibetan).

Ḍākārṇava (Tibetan) Apabhraṃśa ed. N. N. Chaudhuri, Calcutta 1935.

Caturyoginīsaṃpuṭa (Tibetan) Sanskrit MS in Ṣalu.

Buddhakapāla (Tibetan).

Mahāmāyā (Tibetan) Sanskrit MSS in Ṣalu and Sa-skya.

Ārāli (Tibetan).

Yoginīsaṃcaryā (Tibetan).

Catuḥpīṭha (Tibetan).

Caṇḍamahāroṣaṇa (Tibetan) Sanskrit MS in Ngor.

Vajrāmṛta (Tibetan) Sanskrit MS in Ṣalu.

Mahākāla (Tibetan) Sanskrit MS in Ngor.

Kālacakra (Tibetan) Sanskrit ed. Raghu Vira, Śatapiṭaka, Delhi, 1966 (the *Sekoddeśa* is part of the *Kālacakra*).

Mañjuśrīnāmasaṃgīti (Tibetan, T 1188-90, T 1187?) Sanskrit ed. Minayeff, St. Petersburg, 1885 (formerly a *Yoga Tantra*, later attached to the *Kālacakra*).

(*Prajñāpāramitā sūtras* of the Mantrayāna have been noted above, including the *Paramādya* or *Paramādi*.)

Sādhanamālā (a collection of very short Mantrayāna texts, probably mostly to be found in Tibetan) Sanskrit ed. Bhattacharya (2 vols.) GOS 1925-8.

G. Mantrayāna Commentaries and Manuals

Nearly all the works mentioned in Chapter Twelve are preserved in Tibetan, along with many other Mantrayāna commentaries and handbooks to the ritual, etc. Only the early commentaries of Virūpa, Saraha, Kukkuri and some others mentioned by the historians seem to be missing (some may be included under other names). There is little point in detailing the Tibetan versions here. In Chinese we should note that Śubhākarasiṃha appears to have taken only an oral tradition of interpretation of the *Mahāvairocana* to China with him : as a record of this we have T 1796 and T 1797 written down by his students. Below we list some works known to be extant in Sanskrit.

Saroruha (or Padmavajra) : *Padminī* (*Hevajra* commentary) MS in Ngor.

Kṛṣṇācārya I : *Yogaratnamālā* (*Hevajra*) ed. Snellgrove with the text (see above).

Nāgārjuna (III) : *Pañcakrama* ed. La Vallée Poussin, Gand, 1896.

Candrakīrti II : *Pradīpoddyotana* (*Guhyasamāja* commentary) MS in Ngor and photocopy in Patna.

Āryadeva II : Commentary on *Ḍākinījāla* (i.e. *Saṃvara* ?) MS in Ngor.

Bhadrapāda : Commentary on *Saṃvara*, MS in Sa-skya.

anon : *Vimalaprabhā* (on *Kālacakra*) MSS in Ngor, Sa-skya, etc.

Nāḍapāda : *Sekoddeśaṭīkā* ed. Carelli GOS 1941.

Abhayākaragupta : *Niṣpannayogāvalī* ed. Bhattacharya GOS 1949.

Advayavajra (Maitṛpa) ? : *Advayavajrasaṅgraha* (20 short works ascribed to Advayavajra by the editor, but the ascriptions have been contested) ed. Haraprasād GOS 1927.

In Sa-skya there are MSS of commentaries on the *Guhyasamāja* by 'Nāgabuddhi', on the *Kṛṣṇayamāri* by Dharmadāsa and on the *Vajrabhairava* by Kumāracandra, and elsewhere various other works are extant in Sanskrit MSS; Bhattacharya has edited in the GOS, 1929 (Vol. 44), a *Jñānasiddhi* by Indrabhūti and a *Prajñopāyaviniścayasiddhi* by Anaṅgavajra.

H. Belles-lettres (Histories are given above)

Aśvaghoṣa : *Buddhacarita* ed. and translated by Johnston,

Sanskrit text of I.8 to XIV.31 Panjab University Oriental Publications, Calcutta 1935, translation of I to XIV (from Sanskrit and Tibetan) ibid. 1936, translation of XV to XXVIII Acta O 1937 (from Tibetan and Chinese, T 192); *Zwei Zentralasiatische Fragmente des Buddhacarita* (Sanskrit) ed. Weller, *Abhandlungen der Sächsischen Akademie der Wissenschaften zu Leipzig*, Phil. -hist. Kl., 1953.

Saundarananda ed. and translated by Johnston, Panjab University Oriental Publications, 1928, 1932.

Plays—*Bruchstücke buddhistischer Dramen* ed. Lüders in *Kleinere Sanskrit-Texte* I, Berlin 1911; *Sitz. d. Kön. Preuss. AW*, Berlin 1911, 388 ff.

Mātṛceṭa : *Śatapañcāśatka* (Tibetan, T 1680) Sanskrit ed. D. R. S. Bailey, Cambridge University, 1951, with the Tibetan and Chinese and a translation.

Varṇārhavarṇa Stotra (Tibetan) Sanskrit ed. D. R. S. Bailey BSOAS 1950.

Mahārājakani(ṣ)kalekha Tibetan ed. and translated by F. W. Thomas in the *Indian Antiquary* 1903.

Kaliyugaparikathā (Tibetan).

(Various other works in Tibetan).

Śūra (Āryaśūra) : *Jātakamālā* (Tibetan, T 160) Sanskrit ed. Kern HOS 1891 and translated by Speyer PTS 1895.

(Various *parikathās* in Tibetan.) See also IKL I p. 252.

(*Stotras* by Nāgārjuna are found in Tibetan—not all authentic—including the *Catuḥstava=Lokātita, Niraupamya, Acintya* and *Paramārtha*, of which Tucci has edited in Sanskrit and translated the second and fourth in JRAS 1932; see also Amṛtākara's commentary ed. Tucci SOR 1956. Some *stotras* apparently contemporary with Mātṛceṭa and representing the period between him and the fourth century have been found in very fragmentary Sanskrit MSS and ed. by Schlingloff in *Buddhistische Stotras* DAWB, IO, 1955. In Tibetan we find numerous *stotras* of later periods, also a series of *parikathās* and *lekhas* which need not be detailed here; some are extant in Sanskrit but few published).

Kumāralāta : *Kalpanāmaṇḍitikā—Bruchstücke der* ed. Lüders in *Kleinere Sanskrit-Texte* II, Leipzig 1926.

Candragomin : *Lokānanda* (Tibetan) ed. and translated by M. Hahn, Wiesbaden (Harrassowitz), 1974.

Śiṣyalekha (Tibetan) Sanskrit ed. Minayeff, Imperial Russian Archaeological Society, Oriental Section, *Zapiski*, IV, 1889, 29ff.

Deśanāstava (Tibetan).

Udānakathā (Tibetan).

Triratnadāsa : *Guṇāparyantastotra* (Tibetan) Sanskrit fragment ed. La Vallée Poussin JRAS 1911, edn. promised by Schlingloff.

Bhāmaha : *Kāvyālaṅkāra* Sanskrit ed. Baṭukanāthaśarman and Baladevopādhyāya, Vārāṇasī 1928 (Kashi Sanskrit series No. 61) fragments with a commentary (Udbhaṭa ?) ed. Gnoli SOR 1962.

Śāttan : *Maṇimēkhalai* (Tamil) see Aiyangar, *Maṇimēkhalai in its Historical Setting*, London (Luzac) 1928.

Harṣa : *Nāgānanda* (Tibetan) Sanskrit ed. and translated by Karandikar, Bombay 1953, ed. Gaṇapati TSS 1917.

Suprabhātastotra (Tibetan) Sanskrit ed. with the Tibetan and translated by F. W. Thomas JRAS 1903.

Jñānayaśas : *Jātakastava* Sanskrit ed. and translted by D. R. S. Bailey in *Asiatica* (Weller Festschrift), Leipzig 1954, 22ff.

Sarvajñamitra : *Āryātārāsragdharāstotra* ed. in Sanskrit and Tibetan by Vidyabhusan BI 1908; ed. and translated by de Blonay, Paris, Bibl. éc. hantes ét. fasc. 107, 1895.

Vajradatta : *Lokeśvaraśataka* Sanskrit ed. Karpelès JA 1919.

Caryāgītikoṣa (Apabhraṃśa lyrics of Kṛṣṇācārya or Kāṇha, Tailapāda, Saraha and others) ed. Bagchi and Śānti Bhikṣu, Santiniketan 1956.

Sarahapāda : *Dohākoṣa* and Kāṇhapāda : *Dohākoṣa* ed. Haraprasād in *Bauddha Gāna o Dohā*, Calcutta 1916.

Dohākoṣa ed. (Apabhraṃśa) by Bagchi, Calcutta Sanskrit Series 1938.

Telakaṭāhagāthā (anon.) Pali ed. Goonaratne JPTS 1884.

Śivasvāmin : *Kapphiṇābhyudaya* Sanskrit ed. Gauri Shankar, Panjab University Oriental Publications, Lahore 1937.

Padmaśrī : *Nāgarasarvasva* Sanskrit, Bombay (Gujarathi Printing Press), 1921, also Calcutta (Śrīveṅkaṭeśvara Pustak Agency), 1929.

Ratnaśrījñāna : *Ratnaśrī* Sanskrit ed. A. Thakur and Upendra Jha, Darbhaṅgā (Prācīnācāryagranthāvalī of the Mithilā Institute) 1957.

Buddhaghoṣa : *Padyacūḍāmaṇi* Sanskrit ed. Kuppusvāmin, Madras, 1921.

Kṣemendra : *Bodhisattvāvadānakalpalatā* Sanskrit ed. BI 1888-1918 and reprinted by Vaidya in BST 1958.

Ratnākaraśānti : *Chandoratnākara* Sanskrit MS in Ngor.

Vidyākara : *Subhāṣitaratnakoṣa* Sanskrit ed. Kosambi and Gokhale, HOS 1957; translated by Ingalls HOS 1965 (apart from its own interest as an exercise in literary appreciation this anthology preserves poetry from a number of Buddhist writers otherwise practically lost to us, such as Vallaṇa, Vasukalpa, Aparājita who seems to be the author of the lost novel *Mṛgāṅkalekhā*, c. 900 A.D., and Acala; on Dharmakīrti see IKL IV).

Vairocana : *Rasiapaāsaṇa* (Prakrit anthology) MS in Waltair.

Anuruddha : *Śataka* Sanskrit ed. Colombo, 1866, 23rd print 1972.

Saṅgharakkhita : *Subodhālaṅkāra* Pali ed. Ebraham and Vijayaratna, Colombo (Vidyāprabodha) 1932.

Buddharakkhita : *Jinālaṅkāra* Pali ed. and translated by Gray, London, Luzac, 1894.

Vedeha : *Samantakūṭavaṇṇanā* Pali ed. Godakumbura PTS 1958.

Buddhappiya : *Pajjamadhu* Pali ed. Goonaratne JPTS 1887.

Anomadassin : *Hatthavanavihāravaṃsa* Pali ed. Godakumbura PTS 1956.

Rāmacandra Kavibhāratī : *Bhaktiśataka* Sanskrit ed. and translated by Haraprasād, Journal of the Buddhist Text Society, Calcutta, 1893.

Medhaṅkara : *Jinacarita* Pali ed. Rouse JPTS 1905.

Sīlavaṃsa : *Buddhālaṅkāra* Pali unpublished (MSS in Burma).

(There are several other poetic works in Pali).

I. Miscellaneous (in alphabetical order).

(Works of reference, secondary sources of importance for methodology, Brahmanical texts, modern historical studies, etc.)

Adikāram : *Early History of Buddhism in Ceylon*, Migoda (Puswella), 1946.

Akanuma : *The Comparative Catalogue of Chinese Āgamas and Pāli Nikāyas*, Nagoya (Hazinkaku), 1929.

Bukkyō-kyotenshiron, Nagoya (Hajinkaku), 1939.

Bāṇa : *Harṣacarita* ed. Parab, 1946 and the TSS edition, ed. Pillai, 1958; translated by Cowell and Thomas, London (RAS) 1897.

Bareau : 'La date du Nirvāṇa' JA 1953, 27ff.

Les premiers conciles bouddhiques, Paris 1955.

Basham : *History and Doctrines of the Ājivikas, London* (Luzac) 1951.

Bhartṛhari : *Vākyapadīya, kāṇḍa* I ed. Cārudeva Śāstrī, Lahore (Ramlal Kapur Trust Soc.) 1934 and Raghunātha Sharma, Varanasi (Sarasvatī Bhavana Granthamālā) 1963, II ed. Gaṅgādhara Śāstrī, Benares (Sanskrit Series) 1887, III ed. (1-7) Subramania Iyer, Poona (Deccan College Monograph Series) 1963, and (8-14) ed. Sāmbaśiva Śāstrī and Ravi Varma, TSS 1935, 1942 (2 vols.); I and II trs. Pillai, Delhi 1971.

Bhāsa : *Bhāsanāṭakacakra—Plays Ascribed to Bhāsa* ed. Devadhar, Poona (Oriental Series) 1951, translated by Woolner and Sarup, Panjab University Oriental Publications, London, 1930-1 (2 vols.).

Bibliographie Bouddhique, Paris, Geuthner, later Maisonneuve, in the series Buddhica, 1930 in progress (annual bibliographies beginning with 1928).

Bloch : *Les inscriptions d'Aśoka*, Paris, Institut de Civilisation Indienne (Collection Émile Senart) 1950.

Brāhmaṇas : *Śatapatha* translated by Eggeling SBE (5 vols.), reprint Delhi (Motilal Banarsidass) 1963.

Coedès : *Les États Hindouisés d'Indochine et d'Indonésie*, Paris, Boccard (Histoire du Monde VIII.2) 1948.

Cordier and Lalou : *Catalogue du Fonds Tibétain de la Bibliothèque Nationale*, Paris 1909-31.

Dasgupta : *Obscure Religious Cults*, Calcutta, Mukhopadhyaya, 2nd. ed. 1962.

Edgerton : *Buddhist Hybrid Sanskrit Dictionary*, New Haven, Yale University Press 1953.

Eggermont : *The Chronology of the reign of Asoka Moriya*, Leiden (Brill) 1956.

Eliot : *Hinduism and Buddhism*, London, Edward Arnold, 1921 (3 vols.) reprinted 1954 (Routledge and Kegan Paul).

Elliot : *The History of India as told by its own Historians*, 2nd. ed. Calcutta 1952ff.

Frauwallner : *On the Date...of...Vasubandhu*, SOR 1951.

Gaurinath Sastri : *The Philosophy of Word and Meaning*, Calcutta (Sanskrit College Research Series) 1959.

Guérinot : *La religion Djaïna*, Paris, Geuthner, 1926.

Hemacandra : *Pariśiṣṭaparvan* in *Triṣaṣṭiśalākāpuruṣacarita*, ed. Jacobi BI 1883-91, 2nd. ed. 1932; extracts translated by Hertel, Leipzig 1908.

Hirakawa : *Ritsuzo no Kenkyū*, Tokyo (Sankibō Busshorin) 1960 (A Study of the Vinaya-Piṭaka).

Hōbōgirin, Fascicule Annexe, 'Tables du Taishō Issaikyō', ed. Demiéville, Tokyo, Maison Franco-Japonaise, 1931 (Index to Taishō ed. of Chinese *Tripiṭaka*).

Jaimini : *Mīmāṃsā Sūtra*, Kolhāpūra, Śrīmajjagadguruśaṅkarācāryakaravīrapīṭha, Dhārmikagranthāvali No. 10, 1951.

Kalhaṇa : *Rājataraṅgiṇī* ed. Stein 1892 (reprinted Delhi, Munshi Ram Manohar Lal, 1960) and translated by him in 2 vols., Westminster 1900 (reprinted Delhi, Motilal Banarsidass, 1961).

Kant : *Critique of Pure Reason*, English translation by Meiklejohn, London, Bell, 1890.

Kauṭalya : *Arthaśāstra* ed. Gaṇapati TSS 1924-5 (3 vols.) and Kangle, University of Bombay, 1960, translated by Kangle, University of Bombay, 1963.

Koūhala : *Līlāvaī* ed. Upadhye, Bombay, Singhi Jain Series, 1949.

Kunst : *Kamalaśīla's Commentary on Śāntarakṣita's Anumānaparīkṣā* ...MCB 1947 (Introduction on the bibliography of Tibetan).

Lalou : *Rĕpertoire du Tanjur d'après le Catalogue de P. Cordier*, Paris 1933.

Lamotte : *Histoire du Bouddhisme Indien*, Vol. I, Louvain, Muséon, 1958.

Lin Li-kouang : *L'Aide-mĕmoire de la Vraie Loi*, Paris, AMG 1949.

Mahābhārata ed. Sukthankar and others, Poona, Bhandarkar Oriental Research Institute, 1933-66; translated by P. C. Roy, Calcutta 1884.

Mahāvyutpatti ed. Minaev and Mironov BB 1911; Ogiwara, Tokyo 1915; Sakaki, Kyoto 1916-25.

Majumdar, R. C. : *The Classical Accounts of India*, Calcutta, Mukhopadhyay, 1960.

(editor of) *The History and Culture of the Indian People*, Bombay, Bhāratīya Vidyā Bhavan, 1951-77.

Malalasekera : *Dictionary of Pāli Proper Names*, London, Murray, Indian Texts Series, 1937-8 (2 vols.), since reprinted by the PTS.

Pāli Literature of Ceylon, London, RAS 1928.

Matsumoto : *Butten no Kenkyū*, Tokyo (Heigo Shuppansha) 1914.

E. Mayeda : *A History of the Formation of Original Buddhist Texts*, Tokyo (Sankibō Busshorin) 1964.

Nanjio : *A Catalogue of the Buddhist Tripiṭaka* (Chinese), Oxford, 1883.

Narain : *The Indo-Greeks*, Oxford, 1957.

Nilakanta : *A History of South India*, London, Oxford University Press, 2nd, ed. 1958.

(editor of) *A Comprehensive History of India*, Calcutta, Orient Longmans, 1957 in progress.

Nyanatiloka : *Guide through the Abhidhamma-Piṭaka*, Colombo 1938 (since reprinted).

Nyāyasūtra of Akṣapāda ed. and translated by Nanda Lal Sinha, Allahabad, Sacred Books of the Hindus, 1930.

Obermiller : *The Doctrine of Prajñā-pāramitā*, Acta O, 1932-3.

Pa-chow : *A Comparative Study of the Prātimokṣa*, Santiniketan, Sino-Indian Cultural Society, 1955.

Pargiter : *Ancient Indian Historical Tradition*, reprinted by Motilal Banarsidass, Delhi 1962.

The Purāṇa Texts of the Dynasties of the Kali Age, Oxford, 1913.

Purāṇa : *Viṣṇu* ed. Vāsudevācārya, Bombay, Gopāla Nārāyaṇa, 1902; translated by H. H. Wilson, London, 1840, reprinted Calcutta, Punthi Pustak, 1961.

Vāyu ed. R. Mitra BI 1888.

Matsya, Ānandāśrama ed., Poona, 1907 (see also Ramacandra Dikshitar, *The Matsya Purāṇa, a Study*, Madras, 1925).

Mārkaṇḍeya ed. Banerjea BI 1862, translated by Pargiter BI 1904.

'*Yugapurāṇa*' (from *Gārgīsaṃhitā*) ed. Mankad, Vallabh-vidyanagar (Charutar Prakashan) 1951.

Purātanaprabandhasaṃgraha ed. Jina Vijaya Muni, Singhi Jain Series, Calcutta, 1936.

Przyluski : *La légende de l'empereur Açoka*, Paris AMG 1923.

Le concile de Rājagṛha, Paris (Geuthner) 1926.

Rāhula : *History of Buddhism in Ceylon*, Colombo (Gunasena) 1956.

Rājaśekhara : *Kāvyamimāṃsā* ed. Dalal and R. A. Sastry GOS 3rd ed. 1934.

Ray : *History of Chemistry in Ancient and Medieval India*, Calcutta 1956 (includes text of *Rasaratnākara*).

N. Ray : *Theravāda Buddhism in Burma*, Calcutta (University) 1946.

Ṛgvedasaṃhitā ed. Aufrecht, Bonn, 2nd ed. 1877 (2 vols., recently reprinted), also ed. Max Müller, London, W. H. Allen, 1849-74 (6 vols.) with Sāyaṇa's commentary and Rajwade, Poona, Tilak University, 1933-51 (5 vols.); translated by Griffith, Benaras 1889-92 (4 vols.), reprinted in 2 vols. Chowkhamba Sanskrit Studies, 1963 (this appears to be the most accurate translation, surpassing Geldner's more recent version).

Roerich : *Biography of Dharmasvāmin*, Patna, Jayaswal Research Institute Historical Research Series, 1959.

Rosenberg : *Die Probleme der buddhistischen Philosophie MKB* 1924 (translated from the Russian ed. of 1918, Petrograd).

An Introduction to the study of Buddhism from Chinese and Japanese Sources, Tokyo, 1917.

Śabara : *Bhāṣya* on *Mīmāṃsā Sūtra*, BI 1873 ff., translated by Ganganatha Jha GOS 1933-6 (3 vols.).

Sāṅkṛtyāyana : 'Sanskrit Palm-Leaf MSS. in Tibet' JBORS Vol. XXI, 1935.

'Second Search of Sanskrit Palm-Leaf MSS. in Tibet' JBORS Vol. XXIII, 1937.

'Search for Sanskrit MSS. in Tibet' JBORS Vol. XXIV, 1938.

Sarvadarśanasaṃgraha (Mādhava) ed. Īśvaracandra BI 1858, translated by Cowell and Gough, London, Trübner, 4th. ed. 1904 (repr. 1914).

Schubring : *Die Lehre der Jainas*, Berlin and Leipzig, 1935; English version, *The Doctrine of the Jainas*, Delhi, Motilal Banarsidass, 1962.

R. S. Sharma : *Aspects of Political Ideas and Institutions in Ancient India*, Delhi, Motilal Banarsidass, 1959.

Indian Feudalism, Calcutta (University) 1965.

Soothill and Hodous : *Dictionary of Chinese Buddhist Terms*, London, Kegan Paul, 1937.

Stcherbatsky : *The Central Conception of Buddhism*, London RAS 1923.

Conception of Buddhist Nirvāṇa, Leningrad, Academy of Sciences of the U.S.S.R., 1927.

Buddhist Logic (2 vols.) BB Vol. I, 1932, Vol. II, 1930, reprinted I-IR 1958.

'Die drei Richtungen in der Philosophie des Buddhismus' RO, 1934.

'Erkenntnistheorie und Logik nach der späteren Buddhisten' *Zeitschrift für Buddhismus* (München-Neubiberg) 1922ff. (translated from *Teoriya poznaniya i logika...*, St. Petersburg, 1909, by O. Strauss; there is also a French version, Paris, Geuthner, 1926, AMG; the versions all differ slightly).

Sūryasiddhānta translated by Burgess, reprinted with additions, Calcutta (University) 1935.

Takakusu : *The Essentials of Buddhist Philosophy*, 3rd ed. Honolulu, 1956.

'The Sarvāstivādin Abhidharma Books' JPTS 1905.

Tatsuyama : *Indo Bukkyō-shi*, 8th. impression, revised, 1961.

Upaniṣads : *Chāndogya* ed. Kāśīnātha, Ānandāśrama Series, Puṇya, 1890.

The Principal Upaniṣads ed. and translated by Radhakrishnan, London, Allen and Unwin, 1953.

Die Philosophen der Upanishaden, Ruben, Bern, Francke, 1947.

Vācaspatimiśra : *Nyāyavārttikatātparyaṭīkā* ed. Rājeśvara,

Benares, Chowkhamba (Kāśīsaṃskṛtasīrij = Haridāsasaṃskṛtagranthamālā) 1925-6.

Vālmīki : *Rāmāyaṇa* ed Mudholkara, Gujarati Printing Press, Bombay, 1912-20 (7 vols.).

Waldschmidt, Claviter and Sander-Holzmann : *Sanskrithandschriften aus den Turfanfunden*, Wiesbaden (Steiner) 1965 in progress.

Warder, A. K. : *Introduction to Pali* PTS 2nd. edn. 1974.

Pali Metre PTS 1967.

Outline of Indian Philosophy Delhi (Motilal Banarsidass) 1971.

An Introduction to Indian Historiography, Bombay/New York (Popular Prakashan/Humanities Press) 1972.

Indian Kāvya Literature Delhi (Motilal Banarsidass) Vol. I, 1972, Vol. II, 1974, Vol. III, 1977, Vol. IV in press, other volumes in preparation.

'On the Relationships between Early Buddhism and other Contemporary Systems' BSOAS 1956.

'The Date of Bhāmaha', *Journal of Oriental Research*, Madras 1958.

'Desiderata in Indian Historiography', *Journal of the Economic and Social History of the Orient*, Leiden 1959.

'The Mātikā', in *Mohavicchedanī* PTS 1961.

'The Pali Canon and its Commentaries as a Historical Record', in *Historians of India, Pakistan and Ceylon* (ed. Philips), London (Oxford University Press) 1961.

'The Earliest Indian Logic', in *Trudi Dvadsat Pyatogo Mejdunarodnogo Kongressa Vostokovedov*, Moscow (Izdatelstvo Vostochnoi Literaturi) 1963, Vol. IV.

'The Possible Dates of Pārśva, Vasumitra (II), Caraka and Mātṛceṭa', in *The Date of Kaniṣka* (ed. A. L. Basham), Leiden (Brill) 1968.

'The Concept of a Concept', *Journal of Indian Philosophy*, Dordrecht (Reidel) 1971.

'Dharmas and Data', *Journal of Indian Philosophy*, Dordrecht (Reidel) 1971.

'Is Nāgārjuna a Mahāyānist ?', in *Two Truths in Buddhism and Vedānta* (ed. Sprung), Dordrecht (Reidel) 1973.

'Feudalism and Mahāyāna Buddhism', in *Indian Society* :

Historical Probings (ed. R. S. Sharma), New Delhi (People's Publishing House) 1974.
'Objects', *Journal of Indian Philosophy*, Dordrecht 1975.
'The Ghosts of Nirvāṇa', *Buddhist Studies* Vol. VIII, Hamamatsu (International Buddhist Association), 1979.
Willetts, William: *Chinese Art*, London (Penguin Books), 2 vols., 1958 (the new edition as *Foundations of Chinese Art* is inferior, being abridged and eliminating much of the discussions most important for art history, though it is more richly illustrated, Thames and Hudson 1965).
Woodward and others (ed. Hare, Norman and Warder): *Pāḷi Tipiṭaka Concordance* PTS 1952 in progress.
Zaehner : *Hinduism*, London (Oxford University Press) 1962.
Zürcher : *The Buddhist Conquest of China*, Leiden (Brill), 2 vols., 1959.

ABBREVIATIONS

A	*Aṭṭhakathā* (Commentary, in Pali).
A	*Aṅguttara* (the ambiguity of A is a 'consecrated' one among Pali scholars but causes them no confusion since the references are clear from the contexts, thus AA means *Aṅguttara-Aṭṭhakathā*); see B under *Sūtra* : *Ekottara*.
AAĀ	*Abhisamayālaṅkārāloka* (Haribhadra); see B Pāramitā (references are to Tucci's edition).
Acta O	*Acta Orientalia*, 1923ff., Brill, later Munksgaard, Copenhagen.
ADAWB	*Abhandlungen der Deutschen Akademie der Wissenschaften zu Berlin.*
AK	*Abhidharmakośa*; see B Sautrāntika.
AMG	*Annales du Musée Guimet.*
Ap	*Apadāna*; see B *Sūtra* : *Kṣudraka*, (g).
B	Bibliography (above).
BB	Bibliotheca Buddhica (of the U. S. S. R. Academy of Sciences and its predecessors).
BD	Book of the Discipline = *Vinaya* Sth translated by Horner.
BEFEO	*Bulletin de l'École française d'Extrême-Orient.*
BI	Bibliotheca Indica (of the Asiatic Society of Bengal, Calcutta).
Bv	*Buddhavaṃsa*; see B Sthaviravāda, additions to the *Sūtra*.
Bś	Bahuśrutīya.
BSO(A)S	*Bulletin of the School of Oriental (and African) Studies*, London.
BST	Buddhist Sanskrit Texts, Mithilā Institute, Darbhaṅgā.
CC	*The Central Conception of Buddhism*, Stcherbatsky; see B Miscellaneous.
Cp	*Cariyāpiṭaka*; see B Sthaviravāda, additions to the *Sūtra*.
D	*Dīgha* (Pali recension of *Dīrgha*); see B *Sūtra*.
DAWB	Deutsche Akademie der Wissenschaften zu Berlin.

Dh	*Dhammapada*; see B *Sūtra* : *Kṣudraka*, (e).
Dhg	Dharmaguptaka.
Dhs	*Dhammasaṅgaṇi*; see B Sthaviravāda, additions to the *Abhidharma*.
Divy	*Divyāvadāna*; see B *Sūtra* : *Kṣudraka*, (g).
DJ	*The Doctrine of the Jainas* (Schubring); see B Miscellaneous.
DPPN	*Dictionary of Pali Proper Names*, Malalasekera; see B Miscellaneous.
EHBC	*Early History of Buddhism in Ceylon*, Adikāram; see B Miscellaneous.
GOS	Gaekwad's Oriental Series (University of Baroda).
HBI	*Histoire du Bouddhisme Indien*, Lamotte; see B Miscellaneous.
HDA	*History and Doctrines of the Ājīvikas*, Basham; see B Miscellaneous.
HOS	Harvard Oriental Series, Harvard University Press.
IHQ	*Indian Historical Quarterly*, Calcutta.
I-IJ	*Indo-Iranian Journal*, The Hague, Mouton.
I-IR	*Indo-Iranian Reprints*, The Hague, Mouton.
IKL	*Indian Kāvya Literature*; see B Misc. : Warder.
IO	Institut für Orientforschung (of DAWB).
It	*Itivuttaka*; see B *Sūtra* : *Kṣudraka*, (c) (Pali).
J	*Jātaka*; see B *Sūtra* : *Kṣudraka*, (f).
JA	*Journal Asiatique*, Paris, Société Asiatique.
JBORS	*Journal of the Bihar and Orissa Research Society*, Patna.
JPTS	*Journal of the Pali Text Society*, London.
JRAS	*Journal of the Royal Asiatic Society*, London.
Kā	Kāśyapīya.
Kh	*Khuddakapāṭha*; see B Sthaviravāda, additions to the *Sūtra*.
Kvu	*Kathāvatthu*; see B Sthaviravāda, additions to the *Abhidharma*.
Lal	*Lalitavistara* (ed. Lefmann); see B Buddhist Histories.
Lo	Lokottaravādin.

M	*Majjhima* (Pali recension of *Madhyama*); see B *Sūtra*.
MCB	Mélanges Chinois et Bouddhiques, 1931ff., Louvain and elsewhere.
MK	*Mūlamadhyamakakārikā*; see B Madhyamaka : Nāgārjuna.
MKB	Materialien zur Kunde des Buddhismus, ed. Walleser, Leipzig and Heidelberg, 1923-32.
MPPŚ	*Mahāprajñāpāramitāśāstra*; see B Madhyamaka : Nāgabodhi.
MPS	*Mahāparinirvāṇasūtra* (Waldschmidt); see B *Sūtra* : *Dīrgha*.
MR	*Manuscript Remains of Buddhist Literature found in Eastern Turkestan* (Hoernle); see B *Sūtra* : *Dīrgha*.
Ms	Mahāsaṃghika.
MS(S)	Manuscript(s).
MŚ	Mahīśāsaka.
MSV	*Mūlasarvāstivādavinaya*; see B *Vinaya* (Gilgit MSS ed. or SOR).
Mū	Mūlasarvāstivādin.
Nd	*Niddesa*; see B Sthaviravāda, additions to the *Sūtra*.
NG	*Nachrichten der Akademie der Wissenschaften in Göttingen*.
OIP	*Outline of Indian Philosophy*; B Misc. Warder.
Pre-Diṅnāga	*Pre-Diṅnāga Buddhist Texts on Logic from Chinese Sources* (Tucci); see B Sautrāntika : Pramāṇa.
Ps	*Paṭisambhidāmagga*; see B Sthaviravāda, additions to the *Sūtra*. -Gp = *Ganṭhipada*.
PTC	*Pāli Tipiṭakaṁ Concordance*, Woodward; see B Miscellaneous.
PTS	Pali Text Society, London.
Pv	*Petavatthu*; see B *Sūtra* : *Kṣudraka*, (g).
RAS	Royal Asiatic Society, London.
REBCS	'On the Relationships between Early Buddhism and other Contemporary Systems', Warder; see B Miscellaneous.
RO	*Rocznik Orjentalistyczny*, Lwów—Krakow—Warzawa, 1914ff.

RVS	*Ṛgvedasaṃhitā*; see B Miscellaneous.
S	*Saṃyutta* (Pali recension of *Saṃyukta*); see B *Sūtra*.
Sa	Sarvāstivādin.
Sau	Sautrāntika.
SBE	Sacred Books of the East, Oxford (reprinted Delhi, Motilal Banarsidass, 1962ff.).
ŚBr	*Śatapathabrāhmaṇa*; see B Miscellaneous, *Brāhmaṇas*.
SDS	*Sarvadarśanasaṃgraha*; see B Miscellaneous.
Sm	Saṃmitīya.
Sn	*Suttanipāta*; see B *Sūtra* : *Kṣudraka*, (a).
SOR	Serie Orientale Roma, Rome, Istituto Italiano per il Medio ed Estremo Oriente.
Sth	Sthaviravādin.
T	Taishō (followed by index No. according to *Hōbōgirin*, Fascicule Annexe; see B Miscellaneous) edition; see B Mahāyāna *Tripiṭaka* (the edition includes the Chinese recension of the Early *Tripiṭaka*).
Ṭ	*Ṭikā* (Sub-commentary).
Th	*Theratherīgāthā*; see B *Sūtra* : *Kṣudraka*, (b) (Pali recension).
Thag	*Theragāthā* section of Th.
Thīg	*Therīgāthā* section of Th.
TSS	Trivandrum Sanskrit Series, Government of Travancore, later University of Kerala, Trivandrum (Anantaśayana).
TSWS	Tibetan Sanskrit Works Series, Jayaswal Research Institute, Patna.
Turfan	See B. Misc. Waldschmidt, etc.
Ud	*Udāna*; see B *Sūtra* : *Kṣudraka*, (d).
Vbh	*Vibhaṅga*; see B *Abhidharma*.
Vin	*Vinaya* (Pali recension).
Vv	*Vimānavatthu*; see B *Sūtra* : *Kṣudraka*, (g.)
WZKM	*Wiener Zeitschrift für die Kunde des Morgenlandes*, Vienna, Hölder, 1887ff.

WZKSO *Wiener Zeitschrift für die Kunde Süd—und Ostasien*, Vienna, Österreichische Akademie der Wissenschaften and Indologische Institut der Universität Wien, 1957ff.

Yam *Yamaka*; see Sthaviravāda, additions to the *Abhidharma*.

* Before a Sanskrit term denotes a conjectural restoration from a translation.

INDEX

SIBI